Replacing Truth

Replacing Truth

Kevin Scharp

OXFORD
UNIVERSITY PRESS

OXFORD
UNIVERSITY PRESS

Great Clarendon Street, Oxford, OX2 6DP,
United Kingdom

Oxford University Press is a department of the University of Oxford.
It furthers the University's objective of excellence in research, scholarship,
and education by publishing worldwide. Oxford is a registered trade mark of
Oxford University Press in the UK and in certain other countries

First Edition published in 2013

Impression: 1

British Library Cataloguing in Publication Data
Data available

ISBN 978–0–19–965385–0

Printed and bound in Great Britain by
CPI Group (UK) Ltd, Croydon, CR0 4YY

Contents

List of Figures ix
List of Tables ix
Acknowledgments xi
Conventions xiii

Introduction 1
0.1 Methodology 2
0.1.1 The two camps in the analytic tradition 2
0.1.2 Concepts and philosophy 3
0.1.3 Six philosophical methods 4
0.1.4 Metrological naturalism 7
0.2 Scope and organization 8

1. The Market 11
1.1 Theories of the nature of truth 13
1.2 Philosophical approaches 16
1.3 Logical approaches 23
1.4 Combinations of philosophical and logical approaches 25
1.5 Unified theories of truth 30

2. Inconsistent Concepts 35
2.1 Concepts 35
2.2 Inconsistent concepts 36
2.3 Possessors and principles 43
2.4 Pragmatics and constitutive principles 49
2.5 Competence and constitutive principles 53

3. The Obvious Argument 57
3.1 Monsters 57
3.2 In and out 62
3.2.1 Truth's expressive role 63
3.2.2 Kripke's objections to the orthodox approach 64
3.2.3 Content determination 66
3.2.4 Aletheic contextualism 71
3.2.5 Semantic blindness 73
3.2.6 Field on truth and determinate truth 75
3.3 Logic 78

4. Revenge 84
4.1 Revenge paradoxes 84
4.2 Revenge objections 88
4.2.1 Too easy? 89
4.2.2 Expressibility delimiters 94
4.2.3 A diagnosis 99
4.3 The revenge argument 100
4.3.1 Self-refutation 102
4.3.2 The burden of proof 104
4.3.3 Unintelligible? 106
4.3.4 Importing revenge 110
4.3.5 Language-specific truth predicates 112
4.4 The abductive argument 116
4.5 The meaning argument 121

5. Replacement 126
5.1 Inconsistency views 126
5.1.1 Dialetheism 126
5.1.2 Patterson 128
5.1.3 Ludwig 129
5.1.4 Eklund 134
5.1.5 Yablo 135
5.1.6 Burgess 136
5.2 Replacement arguments 137
5.3 Paradox and persons 139
5.4 Conditions of adequacy 142
5.5 Two theories 143
5.6 The parable of Mindy 144

6. The Prescriptive Theory 146
6.1 The replacements: ascending truth and descending truth 146
6.2 Montague's theorem 149
6.3 Safety 152
6.4 A formal theory: ADT 153
6.5 Other replacements 155
6.6 Semantics for ADT 157
6.6.1 Normal modal logic and relational semantics 157
6.6.2 Problems with using relational semantics for ADT 159
6.6.3 Classical modal logic and neighborhood semantics 160
6.6.4 Yet another problem 161
6.6.5 Xeno semantics 161
6.6.6 First-order modal logic 166
6.6.7 Revision sequences and modal logic 167
6.6.8 Summary of problems and solutions 169

6.7 Features of ADT 169
6.7.1 Interpreting ADT 169
6.7.2 Principles of ascending and descending truth 170
6.7.3 Non-principles 172
6.7.4 The aletheic paradoxes 173
6.7.5 The expressive role 174
6.7.6 Contingent unsafety 175
6.7.7 Revenge 175
Appendix: A fixed-point theorem 178
7. Metrological Naturalism and ADT 188
7.1 Davidson's theory of truth 188
7.2 Measurement theory 192
7.3 Davidson and measurement theory 196
7.4 The nature of ascending and descending truth 200
8. Minimal Mutilation 204
8.1 Proof 205
8.2 Inquiry 205
8.3 Objectivity 206
8.4 Belief 207
8.5 Meaning 207
8.6 Assertion 215
8.7 Knowledge 216
8.8 Validity 217
8.9 Predication 218
8.10 Reference 221
9. The Descriptive Theory 225
9.1 Theories of inconsistent concepts 225
9.1.1 Conditions of adequacy 225
9.1.2 Theories 228
9.2 Confusion and relative truth 230
9.3 Relative truth and formal semantics 232
9.4 An assessment-sensitivity theory of truth 236
9.5 Other options 241
9.6 An example 247
9.6.1 Syntax for L 247
9.6.2 Semantics for L 247
9.6.3 Presemantics and postsemantics for L 250
9.7 Resolving the paradoxes 253
9.7.1 Validity 254
9.7.2 The liar 255
9.7.3 Other paradoxes 255
9.7.4 Truth-tellers 255

9.8 Problems for semantic relativism 256
9.9 Pragmatics and 'true' 263
9.10 The nature of truth 266
9.11 A unified theory of truth: CAM 268
9.12 Expressive role 269
9.13 Revenge 271

10. The Aletheic Revolution 274
10.1 Post-revolutionary practice 275
10.2 Objections and replies 278
10.2.1 Guide to objections 278
10.2.2 My uses of 'true' 279
10.2.3 Indispensability 279
10.2.4 Primary aletheic principles 279
10.2.5 Endorsement 280
10.2.6 Deflationism 281
10.2.7 Retention 282
10.2.8 Retraction 285
10.2.9 Generalization 286
10.2.10 The principle of uniform solution 287

Conclusion 289

Bibliography 291
Index 317

List of Figures

1. Measurement Theory 8
2. Philosophical and Logical Approaches 28
3. Unified Theories of Truth 32
4. Eleven Unified Theories of Truth 34
5. Aletheic Principles from Friedman and Sheard 148
6. Three Kinds of Possible-Worlds Semantics 163
7. Problems and Solutions for Semantics for ADT 169
8. Measurement System for Length 194
9. Presemantic, Semantic, and Postsemantic Theories 211
10. Intensional Semantics 212
11. Presemantic, Semantic, and Postsemantic Phenomena 237
12. CAM Theory 270

List of Tables

1. Revenge Reasoning 85
2. Ascending and Descending Liars 174

Acknowledgments

I started thinking about truth and paradoxes in 1994 at about the time I realized I wanted to go to graduate school in philosophy. I have talked about the ideas presented here with numerous people between then and now. This book is also based on my dissertation, completed at the University of Pittsburgh in 2005. Bob Brandom was the director, and he, more than anyone else, has had an impact on the shape of it. His ideas moved me before I even arrived at Pittsburgh, and his encouragement, constructive criticism, and sound advice will stay with me long into the future. The other members of my committee, John McDowell, Anil Gupta, and Hartry Field, are also owed a huge debt of gratitude. I have learned so much from each of them.

Other people along the way who have had a positive effect on the ideas here and whom I thank include (in roughly chronological order), William Kerr, Bradford Cokelet, Rena Samole, Joel Anderson, Pauline Kleingeld, Todd Reisinger, Geoff Lampsa, Ben Henwood, Heather Matula, Fred Heller, John Koethe, Bob Schwartz, Seth Ard, Peter Guildenhuys, Sebastian Rand, Jason Leddington, Josh Andresen, Daniel Nolan, Ron Loeffler, Arthur Fine, Cristina Lafont, Michael Williams, Jürgen Habermas, Graham Hubbs, Jamsheed Siyar, Hamutal Dotan, Alp Aker, Sam Floyd, Lionel Shapiro, John Morrison, Joe Camp, Cian Dorr, Nuel Belnap, Mark Wilson, Susanna Schellenberg, Steve Leeds, Bryan Weaver, Volker Halbach, Steve Yablo, Michael Miller, Owen King, Eric Carter, Kevin Connor, Sal Florio, Stewart Shapiro, Neil Tennant, Robert Kraut, Ben Caplan, David Sanson, Craige Roberts, Declan Smithies, Abe Roth, Richard Samuels, Gabriel Uzquiano, Judith Tonhauser, Jc Beall, Stephen Schiffer, Matti Eklund, Michael Kremer, Mark Lance, John MacFarlane, Dan Scharp, Dana Scott, Brandon Fitelson, Kenny Easwaren, Crispin Wright, Marcus Rossberg, Philip Ebert, Ole Hjortland, Graham Priest, Kit Fine, John Hawthorne, Roy Cook, Ori Belkind, Doug Patterson, Huw Price, Patrick Greenough, Harvey Friedman, Joe Shipman, Solomon Feferman, Albert Visser, Jeff King, Keith Simmons, Dorit Bar-On, David Ripley, Berit Brogaard, Michael Lynch, David Chalmers, Greg Restall, Henry Jackman, Pat Suppes, Hannes Leitgeb, Gabriel Lakeman, Zachary Hamm, James Shaw, Aaron Cotnoir, Øystein Linnebo, Jeff Ketland, Julien Murzi, Florian Steinberger, and anyone I have overlooked.

Special thanks to Stewart Shapiro, Neil Tennant, and David Ripley, who provided valuable feedback on the entire book, and to Jc Beall, Matti Eklund, Raleigh Miller, and Timmy Fuller who gave comments on portions of the text. My appreciation goes as well to several anonymous referees.

I taught a graduate seminar on this material at the Ohio State University in Spring 2009; the participants provided essential feedback on many of the ideas, arguments, and theories in this book.

Some of this work has been given as talks at the University of Pittsburgh, the University of Georgia, the State University of New York at New Paltz, Wayne State University, the University of Munich, the University of Melbourne, the University of North Carolina Chapel Hill, the University of California at Berkeley, the Ohio State University, the University of Tilburg, the University of Virginia, the University of St Andrews, the University of Aberdeen, the Australasian Association of Philosophy Meeting in Melbourne, the Pacific American Philosophical Association Meeting in San Francisco, and the Munich Center for Mathematical Philosophy.

Parts of "Aletheic Vengeance" made it into Chapter 4; thank you to Oxford University Press for permission to reprint it. Parts of "Truth, Revenge, and Internalizability" also made it into Chapter 4; thank you to *Erkenntnis* for permission to include it. Parts of "Replacing Truth" made it into Chapters 2 and 5; thank you to *Inquiry* for permission to include it. Parts of "Brandom on Communication" made it into Chapter 8; thank you to Peter Lang Publishing for permission to include it. Parts of "Truth, the Liar, and Relativism" constitute Chapter 9; thank you to *The Philosophical Review* for permission to include it.

Finally, I want to express my appreciation to the members of my family for their love and for their help along the way. Thank you to Alison Duncan Kerr for her presence, her passion, her insight, and her unwavering support; my life would be unrecognizable without her.

Conventions

Single quotes are used to form the names of linguistic expressions; e.g., 'Kevin' is the name of Kevin.

Individual constants are in the same font as regular text; e.g., p is a sentence.

Corner quotes are used in conjunction with individual constants for complex sentences; e.g., '⌜~p⌝' is a name of the negation of p.

Lowercase Greek letters are used for sentential variables (both schematic and bindable); e.g., the law of excluded middle is: $\phi \vee \sim\phi$.

Angle brackets are used to form names with sentential variables; e.g., $\langle\phi\rangle$ is true iff ϕ.

Italics are used to specify meanings of linguistic expressions; e.g., 'beer' means *beer*.

The greatest enemy of any one of our truths may be the rest of our truths.

William James, *Pragmatism*

Introduction

Although the concept of truth has a venerable history, it also has a dark side that has been known for millennia: it gives rise to nasty paradoxes, the most famous of which is the liar paradox.[1] Despite the fact that these paradoxes do not surface much in everyday conversations, they pose a serious threat to us. We have discovered that they inhibit our ability to explain our own rational behavior, and the problem is so acute that researchers who study language, reasoning, and thought avoid truth like the plague. The simple fact that we possess this concept has become an impediment to our attempts to understand ourselves. In this work, I argue that these paradoxes are symptoms of an intrinsic defect in the concept of truth; for this reason we should replace truth for certain purposes.

Truth has had its detractors over the years. From Protagoras to Richard Rorty, thinkers have tried to downplay its importance or eliminate it altogether.[2] My views and the reasons for them are wholly distinct from theirs. The case against truth contained in these pages has nothing to do with subjectivism or postmodernism.[3] Rather, it is because of truth's utility, value, and importance that it needs to be replaced. If it were just an antiquated ideal that enlightened agents should discard, then there would be no point in replacing it. It is an unfortunate fact that its utility, value, and importance come at a high price.

The problems caused by truth are severe, but they are *not* unprecedented. Once we understand that the source of the paradoxes is a conceptual defect, we can do what

[1] For example, if we use the name 'Sentence (1)' for the sentence 'Sentence (1) is false', then that very sentence says of itself that it is false. We can reason intuitively that if it is true, then what it says is true, namely that it is false. So it is true that it is false, or, more directly, it is false. On the other hand, if it is false, then what it says is false, namely that it is false. So it is false that it is false, or, more directly, it is true. Thus, we derive that it is false from the assumption that it is true, and we derive that it is true from the assumption that it is false. It takes just a couple of steps from here to the claim that Sentence (1) is both true and false. In what follows we will go through all the steps in this reasoning and the other paradoxes associated with truth in detail.

[2] See Blackburn (2005) for a discussion of this tradition.

[3] Although I end up suggesting that truth has certain features that bear a superficial similarity to those claimed by relativists, my view has none of the radically subjectivist consequences, and my arguments for replacing truth do not depend on such claims.

we have always done in these situations—replace the offender with one or more concepts, at least for certain purposes, that are free of defects. I offer a team of concepts that, together, can do truth's job without the cost of paradoxes. In addition, they can be used in an explanation of our defective concept of truth itself, thus freeing us from our predicament.

I want it to be clear, right from the start, that I do not advocate *eliminating* truth from our conceptual repertoire. I am not trying to persuade people to stop using the word 'true'. There is no need for flyers or public service announcements. For most purposes, the risk posed by our concept of truth is negligible; so it is reasonable to use truth, despite its defect, in most situations. Only those engaged in trying to explain our thought or language will so much as notice the change. Although this revolution will be relatively quiet, it should have a significant impact on the way we think about ourselves at the most fundamental level.

0.1 Methodology

0.1.1 The two camps in the analytic tradition

Several factors make a comprehensive and accessible presentation of work on truth difficult. The first is that the literature on truth in the analytic tradition of Western philosophy is split into two camps, and there is very little interaction between them. One camp tries to understand the nature of truth; i.e., what it is we are saying of something when we call it true. The other tries to figure out what to do about the liar and related paradoxes affecting truth—I call these the *aletheic paradoxes* in what follows. Often what counts as common sense in one camp is regarded as highly contentious in the other.[4] Although there have been some efforts in the past decade to bring the two together, they represent a small fraction of the massive amount of work in each camp.[5]

During the twentieth century, logic, as an independent area of inquiry, blossomed. Its techniques are used throughout philosophy, but especially in response to the aletheic paradoxes. It slowly dawned on us that it is unbelievably difficult to say anything at all about the aletheic paradoxes without contradicting oneself. I do not know of any other area of philosophy where simply saying something *consistent* is such an accomplishment. So it seems that the precision offered by logic was a natural match for investigating the liar. This trend can easily be traced back to Alfred Tarski's work on truth in the early 1930s.[6] The orthodox view for several decades was based on his work until doubts began to grow in the late 1960s. A lecture of Saul Kripke's that was published in 1975 shook the confidence that many had in the orthodox view, and unleashed a flood of

[4] For example, the use of language-specific truth predicates (e.g., 'true-in-English'); these expressions are a topic of Ch. 4.

[5] For example, see Soames (1999), Beall and Glanzberg (2008), Horsten (2011), and the papers in Beall and Armour-Garb (2005).

[6] Tarski (1933).

highly technical, mathematically sophisticated approaches to the liar that continues to this day.[7] Almost all this work is done using artificial languages and advanced logical techniques, including proof theory and model theory. Although it happens occasionally, there is not much emphasis on natural languages or language users. This tradition is very young (in philosophical terms), highly technical, and for the most part divorced from standard issues and topics that arise in philosophy of language and metaphysics.

On the other hand, the literature focusing on the nature of truth in the twentieth century is continuous with that which preceded it. The emphasis is almost always on finding a good analysis of truth—saying exactly what truth consists in or finding a philosophically illuminating definition of 'true'. These theorists often frame their projects by inquiring into what we mean when we call something true. This tradition has also produced a staggering amount of work in the last sixty years, but it too is highly insulated. The received view in this tradition is that, whatever the right solution to the aletheic paradoxes turns out to be, it will not have a significant impact on how to understand the nature of truth.

Besides the complication of two massive and insulated traditions of work on truth, the fact that most of the literature on the liar paradox is highly technical makes it a daunting task to sift through it all. Mastery of this work requires knowledge of set theory and other branches of mathematical logic that most philosophers just do not have. However, to understand the challenge of providing a cohesive unified theory of truth (i.e., one that includes both a view on the nature of truth and an approach to the paradoxes), it is essential to have at least a rudimentary grasp of the pros and cons of the various approaches to the paradoxes.

Finally, the case I present against truth is complex and subtle. It draws from insights that belong to both camps (and seemingly unrelated areas of philosophy and linguistics), and it has implications for both camps as well. As a result, the project requires not just a summary of each of the two traditions, but their unification into a single study of truth. My hope is that once it is clear just how deeply the insights of each tradition affect the other, it will no longer be acceptable for those working in one to ignore the other.

0.1.2 Concepts and philosophy

My view is that philosophy is, for the most part, the study of inconsistent concepts (although I do not argue for that here). Once enough progress has been made to arrive at a set of relatively consistent concepts for some subject matter, it gets outsourced as a science. For the past five-hundred years, since the Scientific Revolution, philosophy has been giving birth to sciences in this way. Of course, these are huge generalizations, but it should give the reader at least some inkling of how I see this academic endeavor.[8]

[7] Kripke (1975).

[8] This view of the philosophical enterprise seems to dovetail with those voiced in Schiffer (2003), Pettit (2004), and Brandom (2009: Chs. 4 and 5); see also Johnston (1993).

These views on philosophy and inconsistent concepts fit well with a dynamic philosophical method, which some have called *conceptual engineering*.[9] A precursor to this kind of philosophical project goes by the name of *explication*, and was popularized by Rudolph Carnap; it involves taking a more or less fuzzy intuitive concept and providing a more precise replacement for it.[10] Like Carnap, instead of sitting back and analyzing our concepts, as many analytic philosophers still do, I prefer to engage in the hard work of improving them. However, there are many other kinds of conceptual engineering besides explication. One can identify a conceptual confusion, where someone assumes that one coherent concept can do a certain job, but it actually requires two or more (e.g., the concept of mass as it occurs in Newtonian mechanics, which I discuss in Chapter 2, is confused). Conversely, there can be cases where we assume that two distinct concepts can do two distinct jobs, but it turns out that these jobs are interrelated in an unforeseen way, which requires a single coherent concept; there is no name for this phenomenon, but we might call it conceptual *confission* (e.g., the concepts of space and time as they occur in Newtonian mechanics get replaced by a single concept, spacetime). And there are others as well.

The very idea that our concepts might need improving is hard for some to accept. Nevertheless, I think a good case can be made that we encounter inconsistent concepts pretty frequently and we alter our conceptual scheme in response to them. The result is a conceptual revolution and a new conceptual scheme that can then be used and developed and pushed until some other part shows itself to be in need of improvement.[11] The philosophical method of conceptual engineering and the idea that philosophy is the study of inconsistent concepts go hand in hand. This work is an illustration of how to do philosophy in this way.

0.1.3 Six philosophical methods

Analytic philosophy goes through stages of being obsessed with its own methodology; it is currently in the midst of one of these stages. Although defending a particular philosophical method is well beyond the scope of this book, a brief look ought to help orient the reader. It seems that there are at least the following six major kinds of philosophical methods being practiced at present.[12]

1. *Conceptual analysis* is specifying illuminating a priori or analytic connections between some concept and other concepts. Often it is seen as doing even more: specifying the conceptual constituents of some complex concept. For example, a conceptual analysis

[9] Robert Brandom (2001) and Simon Blackburn (2001) each use this term.

[10] Carnap (1950).

[11] This talk of conceptual schemes should be taken with requisite care given the work on the scheme/content dualism by Davidson (1974a); see also Child (1994), McDowell (1999), and Davidson (1999b).

[12] This classification is very rough—the list is not exhaustive and the descriptions are in no way definitive; see the cited works for more detailed treatments.

of the concept of bachelor might be that bachelors are unmarried adult human males. In this case, it seems as though the concept analyzed is more complex than the concepts used in the analysis. However, one need not adhere to this basic/complex view of analysis. Conceptual analysis came in for some blistering attacks in the mid-twentieth century,[13] but despite that, it is still dominant in analytic philosophy, which is so-named because of this methodology.[14]

2. *Reductive explanation* is explaining some phenomenon by appeal to a different and usually better-understood kind of phenomena. In reductive explanation, the explanandum (i.e., the item to be explained) is wholly subsumed under the explanans (i.e., the items in terms of which it is explained). For example, reductive naturalism is a particularly popular kind of reductive explanation according to which every genuine phenomenon can be reduced to the phenomena studied by the hard sciences (and often to fundamental physics). Reductive naturalists hold that all genuine phenomena are, at root, physical phenomena. This includes consciousness, moral properties, mental states, and so on. There are versions of reductive explanation that are not naturalistic; for example, reductive phenomenalism reduces all genuine phenomena to experience.[15] The reduction of all genuine phenomena to the explanans class can be accomplished by *translation* (e.g., a reductive naturalist might say that all claims about legitimate phenomena can be translated into the vocabulary of particle physics), but it need not; a laxer reductive explanation appeals to *a priori entailment* instead of translation (e.g., a reductive naturalist of this stripe might claim that all true claims about legitimate phenomena are entailed a priori by true claims about the nature and behavior of fundamental particles).[16] The former is closely connected to conceptual analysis, while the latter is less demanding.[17]

3. *Quietism* is a method that avoids proposing and defending philosophical theories, and instead sees philosophical problems as the result of confusions that are often caused by misunderstanding language. The quietist attempts to rephrase or reformulate common-sense ideas (or perhaps just remind us of things we already knew) in a way that exposes the mistake and allows those taken in by the problem to see it as a pseudo-problem. There are probably two strands of quietism. The first consists of the ordinary language philosophers, like Gilbert Ryle, P. F. Strawson, and J. L. Austin; Charles Travis is

[13] see Quine (1951, 1960), Putnam (1962, 1971, 1975), and Kripke (1972) for examples.

[14] The most influential contemporary defense of conceptual analysis is certainly Jackson (1997); see also Lewis (1994), Jackson (2001a, 2001b), Balog (2001), Stich and Weinberg (2001), Stalnaker (2001), Williamson (2001, 2008), and McGinn (2011).

[15] see Carnap (1928), Quine (1951), and Sellars (1963) for more on phenomenalism.

[16] Even weaker reductions are familiar as well; e.g., the technical relation of supervenience is sometimes used.

[17] See the papers in Hohwy and Kallestrup (2008) on reductive explanation; see Chalmers (2012) for more on the "apriori entailment" version of reductive explanation. See also Block and Stalnaker (1999), Chalmers and Jackson (2001), and Gertler (2002) on conceptual analysis and reductive explanation. See the papers in de Caro and Macarthur (2004) for criticism of reductive naturalism.

a contemporary philosopher pursuing something like this project.[18] The other strand is heavily influenced by the later work of Ludwig Wittgenstein; John McDowell is probably the best-known contemporary practitioner.[19]

4. *Experimental philosophy* is new on the scene; although it has historical precursors,[20] in its current form it is just a decade or so old. Experimental philosophy eschews the kind of armchair reflection and appeals to intuitions that other philosophical methods, especially conceptual analysis, take to be essential to doing philosophy. Instead, experimental philosophy advocates conducting surveys of non-philosophers' intuitions on issues of current interest in philosophy (e.g., influential thought experiments). From these results an experimental philosopher constructs a psychological theory about the source of those intuitions, and that theory is then used to support or attack various philosophical views that depend on those intuitions. Attitudes toward this new methodology run the gamut from adoration to disdain.[21]

5. *Analytic pragmatism*, like experimental philosophy, is a reaction against conceptual analysis and reductive explanation, but it seeks a synthesis of the latter two methods with the insights of Wittgenstein, Wilfrid Sellars, and the classical pragmatists. Instead of emphasizing the relations between sets of concepts on which conceptual analysis or reductive explanation focuses, analytic pragmatism looks to relations between how words are used and the concepts those words express. The goal of an analytic pragmatist project is to specify relations between the concepts used to describe how some words are used and the concepts those words express. Although there are plenty of precursors, analytic pragmatism as a philosophical methodology is new, and its primary expositor and defender is Robert Brandom.[22]

6. *Methodological naturalism*, as a philosophical method, is dramatically different from reductive naturalism, which is a kind of reductive explanation.[23] Methodological naturalists emphasize the similarity or continuity between science and philosophy; they suggest that philosophical problems should be approached by using the methods of the sciences and that philosophical theories should, like scientific theories, not only offer

[18] See Ryle (1931, 1949), Strawson (1950, 1959), Austin (1959), and Travis (2008); see also Chalmers (2011) and Baz (2012).

[19] See Wittgenstein (1953), Malcolm (1959), and McDowell (1994, 2009). See also Zangwell (1992), Wright (1992: Ch. 6, 1998), Pettit (2004), Rorty (2007), and Kuusela (2008) for discussion of quietism. Note that the term 'quietism' has come to have a negative connotation in the hands of philosophers like Blackburn (see his 1998); for this reason, one might prefer the term 'therapeutic'. However, I intend no such implication.

[20] Naess (1938) for example, which bears particular relevance to the topic of this book.

[21] See the papers in Knobe and Nichols (2008) for more on experimental philosophy; see also Cappelen (2012) and Alexander (2012).

[22] See Brandom (2008, 2011) for the presentation of analytic pragmatism. I take the projects in Kripke (1982), Davidson (2001), Stanley (2005), Kukla and Lance (2009), and Cappelen and Hawthorne (2009) to be instances of analytic pragmatism.

[23] The qualifier 'as a philosophical method' is meant to distinguish it from the view in philosophy of science, which sometimes goes under the same name, that one of the criteria for science is that it rejects supernatural explanations.

explanations, but be empirically testable. Beyond that, there is very little agreement on how to pursue methodological naturalism.[24]

0.1.4 Metrological naturalism

The positive view of truth I offer is not an instance of conceptual analysis, reductive explanation, quietism, or experimental philosophy. One can think of it as a work of analytic pragmatism in the sense that I look to our use of 'true' and general features of linguistic practice, focusing especially on what linguists say about communication as a condition of adequacy on a theory of truth. However, that still leaves us short of a theory of truth in any ordinary sense. One might say that once the use has been described, that is all there is to do, but I reject that conclusion entirely.

It is most accurate to say that the methodology in this book is a specific type of methodological naturalism—in particular, it is *metrological naturalism*.[25] I take it that this is Donald Davidson's methodology, despite the fact that he never explicitly defends it or even articulates it as such.[26] This version of methodological naturalism is informed by measurement theory, which is the study of how formal and mathematical structures apply to the physical world. I like to think of measurement theory as somewhat analogous to set theory, but for science—it serves as an all-purpose background theory for science in the way that set theory serves as an all-purpose background theory for mathematics.[27] What I call a *measurement system* is composed of three structures and the links between them: a physical structure, which includes the phenomenon to be explained; a relational structure, which is an idealized theory of the phenomena in question; and a mathematical structure. The links between the physical structure and the relational structure on the one hand and the links between the relational structure and the mathematical structure on the other allow one to apply the mathematical structure to the physical phenomena (see Figure 1). According to metrological naturalism, a philosophical theory of X should be cast as a measurement system for X. That is exactly what I do for truth.[28]

This kind of methodological naturalism fits well with conceptual engineering and a view of philosophy as the study of inconsistent concepts. Trying to arrive at a measurement system for truth shows us that truth is an inconsistent concept, and, moreover, it points the way toward its replacements. The theory of the replacements is cast as a measurement

[24] See Papineau (2007) for an overview of methodological naturalism. See Wilson (2006) and Maddy (2007) for examples. See also Price (2010) for what he calls subject naturalism, which I take to be very similar. See the papers in Braddon-Mitchell and Nola (2009) for a discussion of the relation between conceptual analysis and naturalism.

[25] 'Metrological' means *pertaining to measurement*.

[26] For some of Davidson's remarks about measurement theory, see Davidson (1970: 220–1; 1997a: 130–2; 1997b: 75; 1999a: 253). For background on measurement theory, see Suppes et al. (1971, 1989, 1990), Narens (2002, 2007), and Ch. 7.

[27] The claim about set theory as a foundation for mathematics is controversial; nothing of substance turns on this analogy.

[28] I present the details in Ch. 7 that are relevant to understanding the view of truth I propose, but a full-scale development and defense of metrological naturalism will have to wait for another occasion.

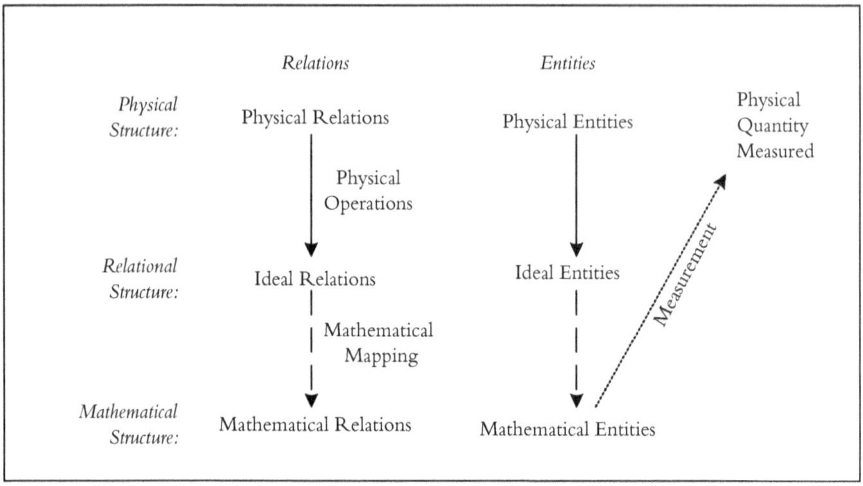

Figure 1 Measurement Theory

theory for those concepts. Then those concepts are employed by the measurement theory for truth. So metrological naturalism and conceptual engineering go hand in hand. I do not think this should come as a surprise, any more than the fact that physics and mechanical engineering are a natural fit.

0.2 Scope and organization

Chapter 1 is a brief survey of work on truth in the analytic tradition. The goal is to present a novel way of thinking about the literature rather than an introduction to the particular views out there, so it presupposes some familiarity with the contemporary discussion. I distinguish between theories of the nature of truth, philosophical approaches to the aletheic paradoxes, and logical approaches to the aletheic paradoxes. Logical approaches offer a mathematical model for our language and truth predicate, while philosophical approaches provide an empirical interpretation of the mathematical model. The distinction is new but without it one is likely to be confused about which theories are genuine rivals. Once these three types of theories are on the table, I consider combinations of philosophical approaches and logical approaches; then the focus turns to what I call *unified theories of truth*, which include a view on the nature of truth, a philosophical approach, and a logical approach as components.

In my view, truth is an inconsistent concept. Saying what that means is the job of Chapter 2, which explains the basics of inconsistent concepts. Chapters 3 and 4 include several arguments for the claim that truth is an inconsistent concept. The first, which I call *the obvious argument*, is the most intuitive and accessible. The other three arguments depend on considerations that arise in conjunction with revenge paradoxes, which are ubiquitous and affect approaches to the aletheic paradoxes. In Chapter 5, I present some of the views that fall in the inconsistency tradition and argue that each one is unacceptable. The main point of this chapter is that an inconsistency approach to the aletheic paradoxes should offer replacements for truth.

We need to replace our inconsistent concept of truth with two concepts, which I call *ascending truth* and *descending truth*. Not only do the replacement concepts perform the explanatory work we ask of truth, they avoid the paradoxes caused by truth as well. Moreover, one can use them as the basis for a theory of our inconsistent concept of truth itself. Thus, there are really two essential parts to the view I recommend. First, there is the prescriptive theory, which explains the replacement concepts. It says how we should expand our conceptual repertoire and provides reasons to think that this expansion will not just result in the same old problems we find with truth. Second, there is the descriptive theory, which explains our defective concept of truth—what principles it obeys and why it gives rise to paradoxes. One of the fundamental commitments of the entire project is that the descriptive theory should *not* appeal to the concept of truth; instead, it uses the replacement concepts. Accordingly, Chapter 6 contains the prescriptive theory and explains how the replacement concepts work. This prescriptive theory amounts to a logical approach and a philosophical approach to the aletheic paradoxes. Chapter 7 presents a view on the nature of truth that is based on metrological naturalism. It introduces some measurement theory and shows how to understand Davidson's theory of truth in light of this material. Finally, it contains a metrological theory of ascending and descending truth. Chapter 8 covers many of the issues that arise when one tries to replace a concept like truth that is so central to our way of thinking about ourselves, the world, and the relationship between them. In particular, it gives an overview of the relations among the concepts of ascending truth and descending truth and many of the concepts that are closely tied to truth, including validity, meaning, assertion, knowledge, predication, and reference.

The central claim of the *prescriptive* theory is that, for certain purposes, we ought to use two new concepts, ascending truth and descending truth, instead of truth. *Ascending truth* is like truth in that the inference from a declarative sentence p to 'p is ascending true' is valid. It differs from truth in that the inference 'p is ascending true' to p is not always valid (although it is valid for the vast majority of sentences). *Descending truth* is like truth in that the inference from 'p is descending true' to p is valid for any declarative sentence. However, it differs from truth in that the inference from p to 'p is descending true' is not always valid (although, again, it is valid for the vast majority of sentences). Together, ascending truth and descending truth can do the work we require of truth without giving rise to paradoxes of any kind. Moreover, the theory of ascending truth and descending truth is compatible with classical logic, and it imposes no expressive restrictions on the languages that contain ascending truth predicates and descending truth predicates.

Chapter 9 introduces the *descriptive* theory, on which a truth predicate of a natural language is assessment-sensitive, which means that it has the same content in every context of utterance, but its extension (i.e., the set of things that are true) depends on a context of assessment. Contexts of assessment model situations in which a person interprets someone's utterance. From different contexts of assessment, the truth predicate has different extensions. The descriptive theory employs the concepts of ascending truth and descending truth, and they determine how the extension of the truth predicate varies across contexts of assessment. This assessment-sensitive theory of truth solves the aletheic paradoxes, it is compatible with classical logic and all the expressive resources we have in natural language, and it does not give rise to any new paradoxes. Chapter 10 considers issues that arise for a language that has a truth predicate, an ascending truth predicate, and a descending truth predicate. It also contains some objections and replies to the unified theory of truth whose components are the prescriptive theory (consisting of the philosophical approach, logical approach, and metrological naturalism for ascending and descending truth from Chapters 6, 7, and 8) and the descriptive theory (consisting of the philosophical approach, logical approach, and metrological naturalism for truth from Chapter 9). A brief *Conclusion* follows Chapter 10.

1

The Market

The literature on truth is vast and it is impossible to summarize in any kind of detail. Instead, in this chapter, and the rest of the book, I assume that the reader is familiar with the broad outlines of work on truth in the analytic tradition.[1] The goal of this chapter is to provide a novel structure for understanding this literature. It should also serve as a refresher for readers who might not remember some of these views and as an update for those who have not kept up. There are many good summaries of various parts of this material; however, there is no systematic overview of theories of the nature of truth together with approaches to the aletheic paradoxes.

Why bother rehashing the literature in this first chapter? The following quote from Simon Blackburn sums up my motivation well:

> I would prefer to introduce myself as doing conceptual engineering. For just as the engineer studies the structure of material things, so the philosopher studies the structure of thought. Understanding the structure involves seeing how parts function and how they interconnect. It means knowing what would happen for better or worse if changes were made. This is what we aim at when we investigate the structures that shape our view of the world. Our concepts or ideas form the mental housing in which we live. We may end up proud of the structures we have built. Or we may believe that they need dismantling and starting afresh. But first, we have to know what they are.[2]

This book engages in some heavy-duty conceptual engineering, but for it to be successful, it is crucial to have a good grip on our current ways of thinking about truth. The reasons for the theory I propose and the way that theory is broken into parts depend on the classification scheme given in this chapter. If this way of looking at the literature on truth already existed elsewhere, then I would have simply pointed the reader in its direction; alas, it does not.

[1] For overviews of work on the nature of truth, see Kirkham (1995), Walker (1997), Künne (2003), Candlish and Damnjanovic (2007), and Glanzberg (forthcoming b). For summaries of approaches to the aletheic paradoxes, see Sheard (1994), Visser (2001), Beall (2006), Leitgeb (2007), Field (2008a), Cantini (2009), Halbach (2011), and Glanzberg (forthcoming b).

[2] Blackburn (2001: 1–2).

Throughout this book, we will focus on the English adjective, 'true', its synonyms, and the expressions of other languages that have roughly the same meaning. However, like most words, 'true' is ambiguous or polysemous and we care about only one of its meanings: cases like 'what Herschel said is true' or 'Albert's theory is true'. 'True' can also be used to mean something like *genuine* (e.g., in 'Milhouse is a true friend') or something like *straight* (e.g., in 'the arrow's flight was true'). It can also be used as a verb meaning *to level* or *to straighten*, as in 'the mechanic trued the bicycle wheel'). And it has other meanings as well. Here we focus on 'true' as it is applied to items with propositional content, like sentences, beliefs, and utterances. I call these words with this understood meaning *truth predicates*.

We apply truth predicates to a dizzying array of objects: sentences, beliefs, propositions, utterances, theories, stories, songs, and probably many other things as well. This motley assortment poses a problem for philosophers and logicians because when one specifies how a truth predicate functions, one has to make certain assumptions about the things that are true or false. The standard way to handle this problem is to specify primary truth-bearers and explain what it is for that kind of thing to be true; one then explains the truth of other kinds of things in terms of the truth of primary truth-bearers. It seems to me deciding on primary truth-bearers is not a pressing issue—very little hangs on this decision. Or, rather, this is the kind of decision to make after one has figured out what to say about more important issues. Throughout the book I focus mostly on sentences and propositions, but I do not say much more about this topic.

Before presenting specific theories of truth, I would like to say a bit about terminology. In particular, it is important to distinguish between a concept (i.e., truth), the associated predicate (i.e., 'is true') and singular term (i.e., 'truth'), the associated property (i.e., being true), and the associated extension (i.e., the set of true things). A person *possesses* the *concept* of truth, she *understands* the *predicate* 'is true' and the *singular term* 'truth', and she is a *competent user* of both these terms. Moreover, the concept of truth is *expressed by* the predicate 'is true', which *applies to* the things in its *extension* and *signifies* the *property* of being true; in addition, the singular term, 'truth', *designates* the property of being true. Throughout the book, I use the preceding italicized words as technical terms.

This chapter is split into five sections. The first three cover distinct types of theories of truth: theories of the nature of truth, philosophical approaches to the aletheic paradoxes, and logical approaches to the aletheic paradoxes. The distinction between the last two categories is a novel aspect of this presentation. *Philosophical approaches* to the aletheic paradoxes do two things: they tell us something about the truth predicate of natural language that is relevant to solving the aletheic paradoxes and they tell us something about the paradoxical truth-bearers and the paradoxical reasoning. Logical *approaches* specify principles truth predicates obey and logics that are compatible with these principles. The theories of truth offered by logical approaches apply to certain artificial languages and these theorists use techniques from mathematical logic to investigate the properties of these theories and to prove things about them (e.g., consistency relative to a background mathematical theory). Although some philosophical approaches are designed to be paired with certain logical approaches, and vice versa, surprising combinations are possible, and without adhering to this distinction, one is apt to make mistakes about which approaches are genuine rivals. The fourth section covers combinations of philosophical and logical approaches to the aletheic paradoxes. The fifth section outlines what I call unified theories of truth. A unified theory of truth contains a theory of the nature of truth, a philosophical approach to the paradoxes, and a logical approach to the paradoxes. It is my view that an adequate account of truth requires a unified theory of truth.

1.1 Theories of the nature of truth

Most of the theories of the nature of truth offer analyses of the concept of truth. That is, they try to provide a definition of the word 'true'. The following analyses have been the most influential over the past century or so:

1. *Correspondence*: a bearer is true iff it corresponds to reality. The correspondence might be singular (e.g., a sentence corresponds to a fact) or piecemeal (e.g., words of a sentence correspond to objects and properties). Correspondence theories continue to be popular and influential.[3]
2. *Coherence*: a bearer is true iff it coheres with other bearers. Coherence is usually taken to entail at least consistency, but stronger notions involving explanation or justification have been used. Although somewhat popular in the nineteenth century, this view of truth has disappeared almost completely.[4]
3. *Pragmatic*: a bearer is true iff it is prudent to have the belief associated with that truth-bearer. Prudence should be thought of as utility-based—it is prudent to have a belief just in case acting on that belief tends to satisfy the agent's desires. William James proposed a version of this theory in the early twentieth century, but it has few if any contemporary defenders.[5]
4. *Epistemic*: a bearer is true iff it would be justified for an ideal rational agent in ideal epistemic circumstances. The key to an epistemic theory is giving an account of an ideal rational agent and ideal epistemic circumstances; also different epistemic theories result from different views on the nature of justification. Epistemic theories were popular with early pragmatists and are currently advocated by many anti-realists.[6]

[3] See Moore (1899), Russell (1910), Wittgenstein (1923), Austin (1950), Davidson (1969), Field (1972, 1973, 1974, 1986), Armstrong (1973, 1997, 2004), Devitt (1984), Millikan (1986), David (1994), Fumerton (2002), Newman (2002), Kitcher (2002), Vision (2004), Englebretson (2006), and Marino (2006, 2008, 2010). Identity theories of truth probably fit best in this category; see Cartwright (1987), McDowell (1994, 2009), Dodd (1995, 1996, 1999, 2000, 2008), and Hornsby (1997, 2005).

[4] See Jocahim (1906), Bradley (1914), Blanshard (1939), Dauer (1974), Young (1995, 2001), da Costa, Bueno, and French (2005), Dorsey (2006), and Thagard (2007).

[5] See James (1907, 1909). Other pragmatists (e.g., Peirce, Dewey, Putnam, Rorty, and Brandom) endorse views of truth that are better classified as epistemic theories or deflationist theories.

[6] See Peirce (1877, 1878), Dummett (1959, 1978, 1999, 2002), Habermas (1973, 2003), Rosenberg (1974), Putnam (1981), Tennant (1997), Misak (2004), and Almeder (2010).

In addition to these analyses of truth, there are the following theories whose proponents deny that truth can be defined but still offer what they take to be illuminating things to say about truth:

5. *Deflationary*: truth is not a substantial notion and has no analysis. Instead, truth predicates play an important expressive role in our linguistic practice. Most deflationists also think that a principle, known as Schema T, is central to a philosophical explanation of truth: b is true iff ϕ. In this schema, 'b' is a name or description of a truth-bearer, and 'ϕ' is a schematic sentential variable—it serves as a placeholder for a sentence that translates the content of b into the language used to formulate Schema T. In addition, deflationists often deny that truth should play any explanatory role whatsoever. There are five main versions of deflationism: *aletheic expressivism* (prima facie truth attributions are not assertions and do not purport to represent the world—instead they express commitments of the speaker), *prosententialism* (sentences containing 'true' inherit their content anaphorically from sentences that do not contain 'true'), *disquotationalism* (sentences are primary truth-bearers and the sentential T-sentences for a language characterize that language's truth predicate), *minimalism* (propositions are primary truth-bearers and the propositional T-sentences characterize the concept of truth), and *inferentialism* (instead of Schema T, the truth predicate is governed by the inference rule that p follows from 'p is true' and vice versa). Deflationism is currently a very popular research program.[7]
6. *Modest*: $\forall$x (x is true iff $\exists\phi$ (x = $\langle\phi\rangle$ and ϕ)). In this formulation 'ϕ' is a bindable sentential variable and '$\langle\phi\rangle$' is a name for whatever sentence takes the place of 'ϕ'.[8] Modest theories do not offer analyses of truth, but they are stronger than deflationist theories. This is a minority position that has yet to be developed in much detail or attract much secondary literature.[9]
7. *Pluralist*: the concept of truth is characterized by a group of platitudes, but the property of being true might differ from discourse to discourse. Aletheic pluralism is relatively new on the scene, and it seems to have two primary defenders: Crispin Wright (who claims that truth predicates signify different properties in different discourses) and Michael Lynch (who claims that there is only one

[7] For aletheic expressivism, see Ayer (1936), Strawson (1950), Kraut (1993), Price (2003), Richard (2008), and Schroeder (2010). For prosententialist theories, see C. Williams (1969), Grover, Camp, and Belnap (1975), Brandom (1994), and Lance (1997). For disquotational theories, see Quine (1970), Leeds (1978), M. Williams (1986), McGee (1993), Field (1994a), Halbach (2002), and Beall (2009). For minimalist theories, see Ramsey (1926), Horwich (1998, 1999, 2001), Soames (1999), and Hill (2002). For an inferential theory, see Horsten (2009, 2011). Other deflationists that are not as easy to classify include Burgess (1997), Blackburn (1998), McGrath (2000), Woodbridge (2006), Kölbel (2008), and Ebbs (2009).

[8] Bindable sentential variables and schematic sentential variables are different, but I use lowercase Greek letters for both and let the reader disambiguate.

[9] See Carnap (1942: 187), Kneale (1972), Mackie (1973), Alston (1996), and Künne (2003). It seems to me that the theory presented in Gupta and Belnap (1993) should be classified as a modest theory as well.

property of being true, but it can be instantiated by different underlying properties).[10]

8. *Davidsonian*: the concept of truth is characterized by an axiomatic theory (Davidson prefers a Tarskian axiomatic theory) and that theory is given empirical interpretation as part of an overall theory of a rational agent's beliefs, desires, and meanings. Davidson's views on the relation between truth and meaning have been very influential, but defenders of his views on what constitutes an acceptable theory of truth are hard to find.[11] This book endorses something like a Davidsonian view on the nature of truth in Chapters 7 and 9.

There are, of course, views about the nature of truth that do not fit nicely into this rough classification, so these eight categories should not be taken to be exhaustive.[12] In addition, some philosophers endorse theories that straddle two of these categories, so they should not be taken to be exclusive either.[13] Nevertheless, they seem to me to do a good job of carving the literature at its joints.

One thing to note about those theories seeking to analyze truth is that they can be cast in less controversial terms. For example, one might deny that truth claims can be analyzed (i.e., translated) into claims about justification by ideally rational agents, but accept that truth can be reductively explained in terms of justification by ideally rational agents. After all, reductive explanations are supposed to be considerably weaker than analyses. Wolfgang Künne's analytical framework helps illuminate the options on this front. Theories in the first four categories offer something like the following universally quantified biconditional:

For all x, x is true iff x is F.

Künne suggests the following five options for interpreting this claim:

(i) 'is F' expresses a concept *coextensive* with the concept of truth (same extension).

(ii) 'is F' expresses a concept *necessarily coextensive* with the concept of truth (same intension).

(iii) 'is F' expresses a concept that *can be known a priori to be coextensive* with the concept of truth (same intension).

(iv) 'is F' expresses a concept that *is self-evidently coextensive* with the concept of truth (same intension).[14]

(v) 'is F' expresses a concept that *is identical* to the concept of truth (same sense).

[10] See Wright (1992, 2003), Lynch (2009), and the papers in Pederson and Wright (forthcoming).

[11] See Davidson (1990) for what is probably the most comprehensive presentation of his theory of truth. See also M. Williams (1999), Lepore and Ludwig (2005), and Patterson (2010).

[12] For example, Frege's views are hard to classify in any of these categories. See Frege (1918).

[13] For example, M. Williams (1999) endorses a combination of deflationism and a Davidsonian theory.

[14] Two predicates express self-evidently coextensive concepts iff nobody who fully understands them can believe that one of them applies to (does not apply to) a certain entity x without believing that the other one applies to (does not apply to) x.

Satisfying condition n is necessary but not sufficient for satisfying condition n+1.[15] Option (v), the strongest reading, is the one on which a theory of truth offers an analysis of the concept of truth. The other four are less demanding and, thus, can be thought of as alternative readings of theories of truth. Option (i) is hardly demanding at all, requiring only a concept that happens to apply to all and only true truth-bearers. Options (ii), (iii), and (iv) are more strict and demand a predicate with the same extension as truth in all possible worlds. Options (iii) and (iv) impose additional epistemic constraints as well.

1.2 Philosophical approaches

This section surveys philosophical views of how truth predicates of natural language work in light of the aletheic paradoxes, while the next summarizes the logico-mathematical technical apparatuses that are used to model natural-language truth predicates and the principles governing them. Let us begin with a quick overview of the aletheic paradoxes. A *paradox* is some reasoning that begins with intuitively acceptable assumptions and proceeds via intuitively acceptable steps, but arrives at an intuitively unacceptable conclusion. A crucial component in understanding the aletheic paradoxes is appreciating precisely which principles are at work. The most common are the following (I refer to these throughout the book as the *primary aletheic principles*):

(T-In) If ϕ then $\langle\phi\rangle$ is true.

(T-Out) If $\langle\phi\rangle$ is true, then ϕ.

(Sub) If $\langle\phi\rangle = \langle\psi\rangle$, then $\langle\phi\rangle$ is true iff $\langle\psi\rangle$ is true.

In the formulation of these principles, 'ϕ' and 'ψ' are being used as schematic sentential variables.

(T-In) and (T-Out) are intuitively acceptable simply because it would be very strange to assert some sentence and also assert that it is not true; likewise, it would be rather odd to assert that some sentence is true, but deny that sentence itself. (Sub) is just a principle that seems to hold of any genuine predicate—to deny it would be to say that a single bearer could be true when called by one name and false when called by another.

Of the aletheic paradoxes, the liar paradox is certainly the oldest and most familiar. It has been known in one form or another for millennia. Epimenides is thought to have come up with one version around 600 BCE, but the most common formulation is probably due to Eubulides (around 300 BCE). One instance concerns the following sentence:

(1) (1) is not true.

Using some logic and the primary aletheic principles, we can derive that (1) is true and (1) is not true:[16]

[15] Künne (2003: 25–7).

[16] For perspicuity, I have suppressed some steps (e.g., step 3 comes by *modus ponens* from an instance of (T-Out) and step 2).

1. (1) is true	[assumption for *reductio*]
2. '(1) is not true' is true	[(Sub) from 1]
3. (1) is not true	[(T-Out) from 2]
4. $\perp$	[conjunction introduction from 1, 3]
5. (1) is not true	[*reductio* from 1–4]
6. '(1) is not true' is true	[(T-In) from 5]
7. (1) is true	[(Sub) from 6]
8. $\perp$	[conjunction introduction from 5, 7]

There are many sentences that can be used in place of (1) (e.g., '(1) is false', 'the negation of (1) is true', etc.), and many ways of reasoning to the unacceptable conclusion.[17]

Curry's paradox focuses on conditional sentences. Consider the sentence:

(2) If (2) is true, then 0 = 1.

Using some logic and the primary aletheic principles, we can derive '0 = 1' as follows:

1. (2) is true	[assumption for conditional proof]
2. 'if (2) is true, then 0 = 1' is true	[(Sub) from 1]
3. If (2) is true, then 0 = 1	[(T-Out) from 2]
4. 0 = 1	[*modus ponens* from 1, 3]
5. If (2) is true, then 0 = 1	[conditional proof from 1–4]
6. 'if (2) is true, then 0 = 1' is true	[(T-In) from 5]
7. (2) is true	[(Sub) from 6]
8. 0 = 1	[*modus ponens* from 5, 7]

One could replace '0 = 1' with any absurd claim; the point is that using the truth principles above and logic, one can derive anything by reflecting on sentences like (2).[18]

Yablo's paradox concerns a sequence of sentences instead of just a single sentence. Consider the sequence of sentences:

(3.0) For k>0 (3.k) is not true.

(3.1) For k>1 (3.k) is not true.

(3.2) For k>2 (3.k) is not true.

...

Each one of the sentences in this sequence says that all the ones that come after it are not true. Using some logic and the truth principles, we can derive a contradiction as follows:

[17] Although some version of each of the three aletheic principles is needed, the logical principles involved can be varied considerably (there are intuitionistic versions, relevant versions, etc.). These issues are treated below.

[18] See Curry (1942); see Beall (1999), Field (2008a), Restall (2008), and Beall and Murzi (forthcoming) for discussion.

1. ∃k≥0, (3.k) is true	[assumption for *reductio*]
2. (3.n) is true	[existential instantiation from 1; 'n' is a name]
3. '∀k>n, (3.k) is not true' is true	[(Sub) from 2]
4. ∀k>n, (3.k) is not true	[(T-Out) from 3]
5. (3.n+1) is not true	[universal instantiation from 4]
6. ∀k>n+1, (3.k) is not true	[arithmetic from 4]
7. '∀k>n+1, (3.k) is not true' is true	[(T-In) from 6]
8. (3.n+1) is true	[(Sub) from 7]
9. ⊥	[conjunction introduction from 5, 8]
10. ∀k≥0, (3.k) is not true.	[*reductio* from 1–9]
11. (3.0) is not true	[universal instantiation from 10]
12. ∀k>0, (3.k) is not true	[arithmetic from 10]
13. '∀k>0, (3.k) is not true' is true	[(T-In) from 12]
14. (3.0) is true	[(Sub) from 13]
15. ⊥	[conjunction introduction from 11, 14]

Notice that none of the sentences in the sequence is self-referential—they refer only to later sentences in the sequence.[19] There is some disagreement about whether Yablo's paradox *really* involves self-reference or not; I do not take this to be a significant issue.[20, 21]

For the purposes of assessing work on the paradoxes, I find it quite helpful to get straight on the multiple problems they pose and the variety of projects that one can undertake in addressing them. The first problem, which I will call *the derivation problem*, concerns the fact that one can derive contradictions from seemingly impeccable assumptions via seemingly unimpeachable inference rules. It seems obvious that the primary aletheic principles are true, that contradictions are not true, and that valid inference rules preserve truth; thus, it seems that there must be some fault in the derivations associated with the paradoxes. However, the problem, if there is one, has been exceedingly difficult to find. A solution to the derivation problem would be an account of what is wrong with the derivations associated with the aletheic paradoxes.

The aletheic paradoxes pose a major problem for anyone engaged in interpretation, which is the practice of determining what something or someone means or thinks. The problem is that the principles involved in the derivation of the aletheic paradoxes are part of any plausible theory of a language containing a truth predicate and part of any plausible theory of mental states for someone possessing the concept of truth. Therefore, an interpreter who attempts to characterize a language that contains a truth predicate by specifying

[19] Yablo (1993c, 2004). See also Ketland (2005c) for a consistent but ω-inconsistent version.

[20] See Priest (1997), Sorenson (1998), Beall (2001a), Leitgeb (2002), Cook (2006, 2009) and Schlenker (2007).

[21] There are many other paradoxes associated with truth not fortunate enough to have names. I mention some in Ch. 6.

the meanings of its sentences ends up accepting contradictions. Consequently, any plausible theory of language or thought turns out to be inconsistent when paradoxical items are present. The problem is exacerbated by the fact that many theories of language and thought appeal to the concept of truth; indeed, one of the most important and influential of these theories implies that the meaning of a sentence or the content of a belief determines its truth conditions (i.e., the conditions under which it is true). It is disturbing that many theories of language and thought attempt to characterize a paradoxical subject matter using the same concept that generates the paradoxes. Further, this problem occurs *even for theories that do not appeal to truth at all*—as long as paradoxical truth-bearers are in their domain, there is a serious problem. I call this the *interpretation problem.*

Finally, the paradoxes pose a problem for the coherence of our conceptual scheme. Many agree that truth is one of the most important and fundamental concepts we have. Moreover, the primary aletheic principles that lead to paradox are absolutely basic to the concept of truth; they are principles we rely on in the paradigmatic cases where we use the concept. Further, the logical principles involved in the paradoxes are basic to the way we reason, and we rely on them in not just everyday reasoning, but in scientific and mathematical reasoning as well. Thus, there does not seem to be an easy way (or even a radically complex way) to solve either of the previous two problems without drastically altering our linguistic and conceptual practice. Perhaps the root of the derivation problem and the interpretation problem lies with inherent flaws in our beliefs, our practice, or perhaps our concept of truth. I call this *the conceptual problem.* A solution to it would be to either adopt the least damaging way to alter our practice so that paradoxical items are rendered benign or explain how we could rationally go on participating in problematic practices, employing incoherent concepts, or adopting inconsistent beliefs.

To sum up, there are at least three problems posed by the aletheic paradoxes:

(i) *The derivation problem*: how can one derive a contradiction from what seem to be logical and conceptual truths?

(ii) *The interpretation problem*: how can a language or a system of propositional attitudes that contains all the ingredients for the aletheic paradoxes have intuitive semantic or pragmatic features?

(iii) *The conceptual problem*: how can our conceptual scheme be coherent given that it contains all the ingredients for the aletheic paradoxes?

There are so many facets to the aletheic paradoxes and such a wide range of writings on them, that philosophers have spent some time reflecting on the kinds of things one might be doing when writing about them. One obvious goal is to explain why they occur, which often takes the form of pointing an accusatory finger at one of the principles used to derive them; we can call this the *diagnostic project.*[22] It offers a solution to the derivation problem.

[22] This term comes from Chihara (1979).

Another worthwhile project is to explain the semantic and pragmatic features of languages containing truth predicates and the semantic features of thoughts involving the concept of truth; this is often called the *descriptive project*, and it targets the interpretation problem.[23] The descriptive project has several sub-projects. First, one might want a theory that specifies the semantic properties of truth predicates and sentences containing them that accords, as well as possible, with the intuitions of native speakers; call this the *semantic project*. Second, one might want to explain how native speakers arrive at their intuitions about the semantic features of sentences containing truth predicates; call this the *psychological project*.[24] Also, it turns out that approaches to the aletheic paradoxes have a great deal of trouble specifying, in the languages under consideration, the semantic features of sentences of those languages; it is very tempting to say "well, we just can't say anything about that" when dealing with some aspect of the aletheic paradoxes. So, an important part of the descriptive project is showing how we can use the natural language under consideration to characterize the semantic features of the sentences belonging to that very language. Call this the *exhaustive characterization project*.[25] Finally, since natural languages seem to obey the logical principles involved in the paradoxes, and they have paradoxical sentences and truth predicates that seem to obey all the aletheic principles involved in the paradoxes, it is not at all clear how they avoid being trivial. A trivial language is one that has a trivial consequence relation (i.e., every sentence follows from every set of sentences). Nevertheless, few things are as abhorrent as the idea that our natural language is trivial; so why is it not trivial? Answering this question is pursuing the *non-triviality project*.[26] So there are at least four parts to the descriptive project (i.e., solving the interpretive problem).

Since the paradoxes are caused by principles that almost anyone would accept (before realizing that they lead to contradiction), some philosophers advocate changing some aspect of our linguistic and cognitive practice in light of them. Some think we should change our logic; others say we should give up some deeply-held principle about truth; still others say we should replace our concept of truth with some other concept(s). These theorists are pursuing the *prescriptive project*, which specifies the changes we should make in our conceptual scheme.[27] The prescriptive project should ideally be paired with at least a rudimentary account of our linguistic and cognitive practice *as it is now*, before the proposed change, but that does not always happen. A prescriptive project would offer a solution to the conceptual problem posed by the paradoxes.[28]

To sum up, there are at least three main projects one might pursue in offering an approach to the aletheic paradoxes:

[23] This term comes from Gupta (1982) and Yablo (1985).

[24] This term comes from Yablo (1985).

[25] This term comes from Beall (2006).

[26] This term comes from Beall (2006).

[27] Gupta (1982) calls this the *normative project* and Chihara (1979) calls it the *treatment project*.

[28] Another goal is to find the most efficient and elegant ways of blocking aletheic paradoxes in artificial languages studied by mathematicians and logicians; this is the *preventative project* (the term comes from Chihara (1979)). Since my main focus is natural language, I do not discuss this project.

(i) *The diagnostic project*: specify where the reasoning goes wrong in the aletheic paradoxes and explain why we have been fooled by the culprit for so long.

(ii) *The descriptive project*: explain the content and use of truth-bearers that involve the concept of truth; it has several subprojects:

 (a) *The semantic project*: explain how to provide a semantics for a natural language that has all the ingredients for the aletheic paradoxes.

 (b) *The psychological project*: explain how users of a natural language attribute semantic properties to it.

 (c) *The exhaustive characterization project*: explain how to assign semantic properties to all the elements of a natural language by using that language.

 (d) *The nontriviality project*: explain why natural languages are not trivial.

(iii) *The prescriptive project*: explain what changes we should make to our natural language and conceptual schemes in light of the aletheic paradoxes.

I use these terms (and those for the problems posed by the paradoxes) repeatedly throughout the rest of the book, and I use the generic term 'approach' for any attempt to pursue one of these projects.

Let us turn to the *philosophical* approaches to the aletheic paradoxes, which include:

1. *Monster-barring*: it is illegitimate to use the sentences in the reasoning involved in aletheic paradoxes.[29] These approaches seek to find something wrong with the paradoxical sentences themselves. There are several versions of this approach: *syntactic* (paradoxical sentences are not syntactically well-formed), *semantic* (paradoxical sentences are meaningless), *pragmatic* (paradoxical sentences cannot be asserted), and *inferential* (paradoxical sentences cannot be supposed in hypothetical reasoning).[30]
2. *Intensional*: substitution of co-referring terms fails for truth predicates. That is, p and q are truth-bearers such that p = q, but p is true and q is not true.[31]
3. *Epistemicist*: one or more of the aletheic principles fail in each aletheic paradox, but we do not know which ones. This view is most closely associated with Paul Horwich but its most precise formulations are due to others on Horwich's behalf.[32]

[29] The term 'monster-barring' was first used in Lakatos (1976), and Crispin Wright suggested it for these approaches (in conversation).

[30] See Jorgensen (1953, 1955) and Kattsoff (1955) for syntactic versions. See Mackie and Smart (1953, 1954), Ushenko (1955, 1957), Skinner (1959), Ziff (1960), Ross (1969), Grover (1977), Goldstein and Goddard (1980), Keene (1983), Brandom (1994), Armour-Garb (2001), Sorensen (2001, 2005), Englebretsen (2006), and Armour-Garb and Woodbridge (forthcoming) for semantic versions. See Prior (1958, 1961), Richards (1967), Martinich (1983), Goldstein (1985, 1986a, 1986b, 1992, 1999, 2001, 2009), and Kearns (2007) for pragmatic versions. See Greenough (2001) for an inferential version.

[31] Skyrms (1970a, 1970b, 1984). See also Woods (2002) for a similar view.

[32] See Horwich (1999, 2011), Armour-Garb and Beall (2005), and Restall (2005). See Horwich (2005) on the ways his version of epistemicism differs from more familiar ones—e.g., Williamson (1994).

4. *Ambiguity*: truth predicates are ambiguous (i.e., they have different meanings on different occasions of use), and the paradoxical reasoning is invalid by equivocation.[33]
5. *Contextual*: truth predicates (or sentences that contain them) are context-dependent (i.e., they express different contents on different occasions of use), and the paradoxical reasoning is invalid because it violates the logic of indexicals.[34]
6. *Circularity*: truth predicates express circularly defined concepts, where a definition is circular if its definiens occurs in its *definiendum*. The paradoxical reasoning is invalid because it violates the logic of circularly defined concepts.[35]
7. *Indeterminacy*: truth predicates exhibit indeterminacy, and the paradoxical reasoning is unsound because it violates the logic appropriate for indeterminacy.[36]
8. *Inconsistency*: truth predicates express inconsistent concepts (or render languages of which they are constituents inconsistent). Often these views take truth's constitutive principles to entail contradictions. There are two main varieties: *dialetheic* (the paradoxical reasoning is sound and paradoxical sentences are both true and not true), and *non-dialetheic* (the paradoxical reasoning is unsound because one of the principles involved is constitutive but not true).[37] This book offers a non-dialetheic inconsistency approach.

Again, this classification is not exhaustive, but it seems to me that the bulk of the work that falls under philosophical approaches to the paradoxes fits into one of these eight categories.[38] Also, one should be aware that since Tarski, the vast majority of philosophical approaches focus exclusively on language-specific truth predicates (which I call *LS truth predicates* from here on), like 'true-in-English'. An LS truth predicate applies only to sentences of a particular language, with the assumption that sentences are individuated coarsely. We will see that LS truth predicates play a crucial role in the standard response to revenge paradoxes (in Chapter 4). Anyone who offers a theory of truth that takes LS truth predicates as its primary explanandum owes us a story about how they relate to natural-language truth predicates. I argue in Chapter 4 that the stories offered so far are inadequate.

[33] Kripke (1975) calls this the orthodox approach when paired with a Tarskian hierarchy as the logical approach. He attributes it to Parsons (1974). See also Williamson (2000b).

[34] See Parsons (1974), Thomason (1976), Burge (1979), Barwise and Etchemendy (1987), Gaifman (1992), Simmons (1993), Glanzberg (2004), Berk (2004), Gauker (2006), and L. Shapiro (2006).

[35] See Gupta and Belnap (1993).

[36] See van Fraassen (1968), Kripke (1975), McGee (1991), Weir (1996, 2005), Soames (1999), Maudlin (2004), Field (2008a), Feferman (2008), Horsten (2009, 2011), Roeper (2010), and Tennant (MS2). It seems to me that Cook (2008) and Schlenker (2011), which emphasize indefinite extensibility, fit best in this category as well.

[37] For dialetheic examples, see Asenjo (1966), Priest (1979, 2006a), and Beall (2009); for the others, see Chihara (1979), Yablo (1993a, 1993b), Ludwig (2001), Eklund (2002a, 2002b, 2005, 2007, 2008a, 2008b), Ray (2002), Patterson (2006), A. Burgess (2006), Badici and Ludwig (2007), and Scharp (2007, 2008).

[38] For example, Hofweber (2008, 2010) is hard to classify, as is Greenough (2011a).

1.3 Logical approaches

We classify logical approaches to the aletheic paradoxes by particular combinations of aletheic principles and logical principles.[39] The aletheic principles are:

(T-In) If ϕ, then $\langle\phi\rangle$ is true.

(T-Out) If $\langle\phi\rangle$ is true, then ϕ.

(T-Intro) $\phi \vdash \langle\phi\rangle$ is true.[40]

(T-Elim) $\langle\phi\rangle$ is true $\vdash \phi$.

The difference between these principles is crucial. The *conditional* principles, (T-In) and (T-Out), are stronger than the *inferential* principles, (T-Intro) and (T-Elim), although they are equivalent in logical systems for which one can prove a deduction theorem (e.g., those that allow conditional proof and *modus ponens*, like classical logic).[41]

The logics are harder to describe, but there are five main options:

(i) *Classical logic*, which has all the standard introduction and elimination rules for each connective plus the meta-rules and the structural rules for derivability.[42, 43]

[39] This classification scheme is found in Field (2008a) except for the categories of classical symmetric and substructural.

[40] '$\vdash$' is a derivability connective. '$\phi \vdash \psi$' says that ψ is derivable from ϕ.

[41] I have found that there is considerable confusion over (T-Intro) and (T-Elim). In a natural deduction system, these are inference rules, and can be used in categorical or hypothetical settings (i.e., reasoning under assumptions). There are two similar rules:

(T-Enter) If $\vdash \phi$, then $\vdash \langle\phi\rangle$ is true.
(T-Exit) If $\vdash \langle\phi\rangle$ is true, then $\vdash \phi$.

These are derivability rules. One cannot use (T-Enter) to derive that p is true from p in hypothetical settings. These rules may be used only in categorical settings (i.e., reasoning from proven claims). Unfortunately, Friedman and Sheard (1987) use the terms '(T-Intro)' and '(T-Elim)' for these derivability rules. However, it makes much more sense to use these terms for the unrestricted introduction and elimination rules (analogous to the introduction and elimination rules for the logical connectives). In sum, the conditional statements, (T-In) and (T-Out) are the strongest, the inference rules, (T-Intro) and (T-Elim) are weaker (in some non-classical logics), and the derivability rules, (T-Enter) and (T-Exit), are the weakest.

[42] The usual meta-rules are:

(~-Intro)
$$\frac{\phi \vdash \psi \wedge {\sim}\psi}{\vdash {\sim}\phi}$$

(∨-Intro)
$$\frac{\phi \vdash \tau \qquad \psi \vdash \tau}{\phi \vee \psi \vdash \tau}$$

(→-Intro)
$$\frac{\phi \vdash \psi}{\vdash \phi \rightarrow \psi}$$

[43] The following are the standard structural rules (where Γ and Γ' are sets of sentences and ϕ and ψ are sentences):

(Reflexivity) If $\phi \in \Gamma$, then $\Gamma \vdash \phi$
(Weakening) If $\Gamma \vdash \phi$, then $\Gamma \cup \Gamma' \vdash \phi$
(Transitivity) If $\Gamma \vdash \phi$ and $\Gamma, \phi \vdash \psi$, then $\Gamma \vdash \psi$.

(ii) *Weakly classical logic*, which has all the inference rules of classical logic and the structural rules, but none of the usual meta-rules.

(iii) *Paracomplete logic*, on which the law of excluded middle and some other inference rules and meta-rules are invalid (it has the structural rules though).[44]

(iv) *Paraconsistent logic*, on which the rule *ex falso quod libet* and some other inference rules and meta-rules are invalid.[45]

(v) *Substructural logic*, on which some of the structural rules governing derivability are invalid.[46]

When we map out the compatible combinations of aletheic principles and logics, we get the following seven options for *logical* approaches to the aletheic paradoxes:

1. *Classical glut*: classical logic and (T-In) (examples: none).[47]
2. *Classical gap*: classical logic and (T-Out) (examples: Tarskian theories, KF, VF, and outer inductive theories).[48]
3. *Classical symmetric*: classical logic, neither (T-Intro) nor (T-Elim) (examples: FS and McGee's theory;[49] this book offers a classical symmetric approach).
4. *Weakly classical*: weakly classical logic, (T-Intro), and (T-Elim) (examples: inner inductive supervaluation theories and outer revision theories).[50]
5. *Paracomplete*: paracomplete logic, (T-In), and (T-Out) (examples: inner inductive Strong Kleene theories and Field's theory).[51]
6. *Paraconsistent*: paraconsistent logic, (T-In), and (T-Out) (examples: Priest's theory, Beall's theory, and Brady's theory).[52]

[44] Paracomplete logics (e.g., K_3) validate *ex falso* and double negation elimination, but not conditional proof, reductio, or contraction.

[45] Paraconsistent logics (e.g., LP) validate excluded middle and double negation elimination, but not disjunctive syllogism, *ex falso*, or contraction. Some paraconsistent logics fail to have all the structural rules; see Brady (2006) for an example.

[46] See Restall (1994, 2000) and Beall and Ripley (forthcoming) for background on substructural logics.

[47] I am unaware of any classical glut theorists; see Field (2008a) for discussion.

[48] Tarskian theories are based on work in Tarski (1933) and are discussed in Kripke (1975). KF is an axiomatic theory proposed in Feferman (1982) and discussed in Halbach (2011). VF is an axiomatic theory proposed in Cantini (1990). Outer inductive theories are based on Kripke's inductive definitions of truth. The 'outer' means that the theory takes the set of sentences defined by Kripke's construction to be the extension of the truth predicate defined. *Inner* theories take the set of sentences defined by a construction to be the theory of truth. See Maudlin (2004) who endorses an outer inductive theory. See also Cook (2008) and Schlenker (2011).

[49] FS is an axiomatic theory proposed in Friedman and Sheard (1987) and discussed in Halbach (2011). See McGee (1991) for his theory. See also Roeper (2010).

[50] Field (2008a) discusses inner inductive supervaluation theories first proposed by van Fraassen (1970a, 1970b). Gupta and Belnap (1993), Yablo (1993a, 1993b), Yaqūb (1993), Kremer (2002), and Shapiro (2006) defend outer revision theories.

[51] See Kripke (1975), Soames (1999), and Horsten (2009, 2011) for examples of inner inductive Strong Kleene theories and Field (2008a) for his theory.

[52] See Priest (2006a, 2006b), Brady (2006), and Beall (2009).

7. *Substructural*: substructural logic, (T-In) and (T-Out) (examples, Weir's theory, Tennant's theory, and Ripley's theory).[53]

Notice that the first two options permit only one (primary) aletheic principle, the third has no (primary) aletheic principles,[54] and the other four have two principles—the weakly classical approaches have the moderate, inferential aletheic principles, and the paracomplete, paraconsistent, and substructural approaches have the strong, conditional aletheic principles. Thus, as one might expect, the strength of the logic and the strength of the aletheic principles vary inversely.

1.4 Combinations of philosophical and logical approaches

Significant features of the presentation in this work include the distinction between descriptive and prescriptive projects and the distinction between philosophical and logical approaches to the paradoxes. These are often ignored, which makes the space of alternatives confusing and muddled. I organize the presentation around philosophical and logical approaches because I think this distinction is blurred more often and to worse effect. One downside to this choice is that it masks important connections between certain philosophical approaches and certain logical approaches that are designed to work together. As part of the remedy, I want to offer a view on the relation between these kinds of approaches and mention some of the portions of logical space that have been spoken for.

Philosophical approaches to the aletheic paradoxes do two things: they tell us something about the truth predicate that is relevant to solving the aletheic paradoxes (i.e., to pursuing one or more of the projects and solving one or more of the problems) and they tell us something about the paradoxical truth-bearers and the paradoxical reasoning.

Logical approaches specify the principles that truth predicates obey and logics that are compatible with these principles. The theories of truth offered by logical approaches apply to certain artificial languages and these theorists use techniques from mathematical logic to investigate the properties of these theories and to prove things about them (e.g., consistency relative to a background mathematical theory).

The connection between them is the relation between a mathematical theory and its empirical interpretation, which is at the heart of the scientific enterprise. The following passage from Patrick Suppes expresses a commonly held view:

> The traditional sketch of scientific theories—and I emphasize the word 'sketch'—runs something like the following. A scientific theory consists of two parts. One part is an abstract logical calculus, which includes the vocabulary of logic and the primitive symbols of the theory. The logical structure of the theory is fixed by stating the axioms or postulates of the theory in terms

[53] See Tennant (1982, 1995, 1997, forthcoming), Weir (2005, 2010), Zardini (2011), and Ripley (2012, forthcoming); see also Beall and Murzi (forthcoming).

[54] However, some classical symmetric theorists accept weak aletheic principles like (T-Enter) and (T-Exit) from n. 41 in this chapter. See McGee (1991) for an example.

of its primitive symbols.... The second part of the theory is a set of rules that assign an empirical content to the logical calculus by providing what are usually called 'coordinating definitions' or 'empirical interpretations' for at least some of the primitive and defined symbols of the calculus.[55]

Suppes goes on to say that this view of scientific theories is roughly correct, but too simplistic. In particular, it needs to be supplemented with the idea of a model—the first part of a theory often characterizes a class of models and the second part often involves models of experimental results. He ends up emphasizing the role of measurement theory in making sense of these two aspects of a scientific theory and the complex constellation of issues associated with linking mathematical formalism and its empirical interpretation by the results of scientific experiments.[56]

Emphasizing the difference between mathematical models and their application to natural phenomena has a place in work on language in particular. For example, Stewart Shapiro and Roy Cook (independently) argue that disputes about the proper treatment of vagueness can be adjudicated by taking care to separate mathematical models from their implications for natural language.[57] My view on the relation between logical approaches and philosophical approaches is similar. I think that the artificial languages, axiomatic theories, and classes of models studied by those who offer logical approaches to the aletheic paradoxes should be thought of as the *first* part of a scientific theory—as a scientific model of our natural language. The claims made about our natural language and its truth predicate by those offering philosophical approaches should be thought of as the *second* part of a scientific theory—as conditions on the application of a mathematical theory to natural language or as conditions on what counts as a good scientific model of natural language. There is much more to be said about this relationship and I prefer to use measurement theory as a way of making sense of it (e.g., logical approaches function like the link between relational structures and mathematical structures in measurement systems, while philosophical approaches function like links between physical structures and relational structures in measurement systems), but it will have to wait until Chapter 7.

Take Hartry Field's combination approach as an example. He begins with the inner Strong Kleene *inductive* theory, but sets out to define a well-behaved conditional for it. He uses a *revision* construction to define an adequate conditional for his logic. So his theory combines elements of Kripke's inductive constructions and Gupta and Belnap's revision constructions. The resulting theory of truth is just a set of T-sentences, but the biconditional occurring in them is based on Field's new conditional. Field's conditional acts just like a material conditional when the law of excluded middle is assumed. Moreover, it allows him to define a determinateness operator, which can be used to classify the liar sentences in the object language as not determinately true and not determi-

[55] Suppes (2002: 3).

[56] See Wilson (2006) for many examples of just how messy the relationship between the two parts of a scientific theory can be.

[57] Shapiro (2002a: Ch. 2) and Cook (2002). See also Dresner (2004).

nately false.[58] Furthermore, the determinateness operator iterates non-trivially so it can even be used to classify liar-type sentences that contain occurrences of the determinateness operator. For example, a sentence Q that is provably equivalent to 'Q is not determinately true' is not determinately determinately true. Indeed, by iterating the determinateness operator, one can generate a transfinite hierarchy of determinateness operators. It is a delicate issue just how far this hierarchy extends since the language in question also contains a truth predicate, which can be used to generalize over the determinateness operators. Field argues that the hierarchy eventually breaks down, but in the interesting cases, the point of breakdown is indeterminate.[59] Thus, according to Field, the determinateness operator serves the purpose of classifying liar-type sentences without giving rise to pesky revenge paradoxes that plague other solutions (I discuss this issue in Chapter 4). For Field, the mistake in the reasoning that leads to the liar paradox is assuming that the law of excluded middle holds of truth claims in general.

He specifies a class of artificial languages that contain their own truth predicates and obey the *intersubstitutability principle* (which says that substituting p for 'p is true' or vice versa in extensional contexts preserves truth value), but the theory of the logical terms of this language is paracomplete—not all instances of the law of excluded middle are valid. However, many familiar logical principles are valid (e.g., double negation elimination, *modus ponens*, etc.). Field uses mathematical techniques to prove certain results (e.g., conservativeness) about his artificial languages, the logical principles governing them, and the principles his truth predicates obey.[60] He claims that natural-language truth predicates display indeterminacy in the sense that one ought not to accept or assert all the instances of excluded middle involving truth predicates. In particular, excluded middle fails for ungrounded sentences of natural languages. However, all the T-sentences for sentences of natural language are true (at least when 'if...then...' constructions are treated as expressing Field's conditional). Paradoxical sentences are indeterminate, which means, for Field, that they are neither determinately true nor determinately not true. Indeed, Field explains 'determinately' in these natural-language sentences by appeal to the determinateness operator defined for his artificial languages. The artificial language models our natural language and helps us explain many of its important features (e.g., what semantic features truth predicates have, what is wrong with the reasoning in the aletheic paradoxes, what status paradoxical sentences have). As a team, Field's philosophical and logical approaches to the paradoxes specify (or at least suggest) a complex mathematical formalism and its intended empirical interpretation. Anyone else who defends a combination approach can be interpreted in the same way.

[58] 'Dp' is defined as '$p \wedge \sim(p \rightarrow \sim p)$'; Field (2008a: 236).

[59] Field (2008a: Chs. 15, 17, and 22).

[60] Field (2008a: 259–66). If Field had offered a proof theory for his logic (he only gives a model theory), then he could have proven several theorems about how deduction in the artificial language and validity relate: a soundness theorem shows that anything provable in the theory of truth and logic is valid in the mathematical structure, and a completeness theorem shows that anything valid in the mathematical structure is provable in the theory of truth and logic.

Describing the other combinations would be tedious and not add much to this chapter. Instead, I have depicted them in Figure 2, which contains a diagram showing philosophical approaches on one side and logical approaches on the other, with important connections between them and the theorists who work on them. The broken line indicates my view.[61]

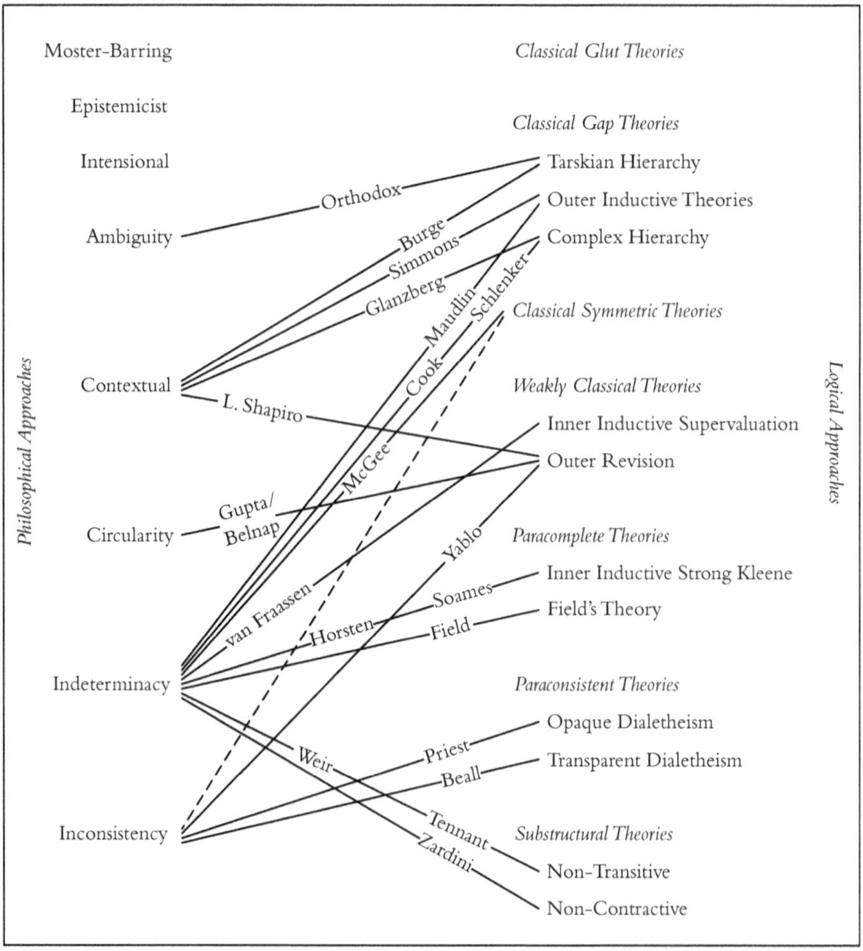

Figure 2 Philosophical and Logical Approaches

[61] In Fig. 2, I have a more precise classification of logical approaches than in the text. The Tarskian Hierarchy is a class of non-partial truth predicates that results from applying Tarski's truth definition to a base language without a truth predicate, then again to the metalanguage, and again to its metalanguage, and so on. An Outer Inductive Theory results from taking one of Kripke's inductive constructions to define the extension of a non-partial truth predicate. A Complex Hierarchy is also a class of non-partial truth predicates,

There are several trends to notice. First, most of the first few philosophical approaches have no connections to the logical approaches—that is because the first few try to find some problem with paradoxical truth-bearers, whether it is that they are syntactically defective, semantically defective, or pragmatically defective. Approaches like these do not need logical approaches to handle paradoxical sentences because they imply that there is no problem to be handled.

Second, a single philosophical approach might be paired with distinct logical approaches. For example, Field, Tim Maudlin, Vann McGee, and Alan Weir champion the indeterminacy approach. Field pairs it with a paracomplete approach, McGee with a classical symmetric approach, Maudlin with a classical gap approach, and Weir with a substructural approach.[62] In each of these combinations, the notion of indeterminacy is interpreted differently. The same point holds of contextual views as well.

Third, a single logical approach might be paired with distinct philosophical approaches. For example, the orthodox approach pairs a Tarskian hierarchy (a classical gap approach) with an ambiguity approach—it interprets 'true' as ambiguous so that it can have the meaning of any one of the predicates in the Tarskian hierarchy. Tyler Burge uses the same logical approach (i.e., the Tarskian hierarchy), but he pairs it with a contextual philosophical view.[63] He claims that 'true' is an indexical, which has an invariant meaning (i.e., character) and variable content; in any given context, 'true' can have the content of any of the predicates in the Tarskian hierarchy. These are very different interpretations (i.e., ambiguity and indexicality) of the same formal structure (i.e., the Tarskian hierarchy). Another example is the revision theory, which is a weakly classical approach and was initially designed by Gupta and Belnap to be paired with a circularity approach (a philosophical approach).[64] However, Lionel Shapiro suggests that the contextual approach is a better fit for revision theories, while Stephen Yablo combines a revision theory with an inconsistency view.[65] Again we have several distinct philosophical interpretations of the same mathematical structure. Someone who is not careful about the distinction between philosophical and logical approaches might think that, for example, revision theories and contextual theories are rivals, but actually, they are

but it results from some more advanced technique of definition (e.g., one of Kripke's inductive methods). Inner Inductive Theories result from taking one of Kripke's inductive constructions to define the theorems of a theory of truth. An Outer Revision Theory results from taking a revision construction to define a truth predicate. Transparent Dialetheism respects the intersubstitutability of p and 'p is true', while Opaque Dialetheism does not. Non-Transitive Substructural Theories reject transitivity, and Non-Contractive ones reject contraction. I have based the combinations listed on the following (from top to bottom): Burge (1979), Simmons (1993), Glanzberg (2004), Maudlin (2004), Schlenker (2011), Cook (2008), L. Shapiro (2006), Feferman (2008), McGee (1991), Gupta and Belnap (1993), Yablo (1993a), van Fraassen (1970a), Soames (1999), Horsten (2011), Field (2008a), Weir (2005), Priest (2006a), Beall (2009), Tennant (1982), and Zardini (2011).

[62] McGee (1991), Maudlin (2004), Weir (2005), and Field (2008a).

[63] Burge (1979, 1982a, 1982b).

[64] Gupta and Belnap (1993).

[65] L. Shapiro (2006) and Yablo (1993a, 1993b).

two different kinds of theories and can be combined so that the mathematics of a revision theory is given empirical interpretation by a context-dependent truth predicate.

Fourth, there is a trade off between thinking of natural-language truth predicates as univocal and invariant (having a single content across uses) and accepting classical logic. Philosophical approaches that posit multiple contents for truth predicates because of ambiguity or context dependence tend to go with classical or weakly classical logical approaches; these theorists retain something close to classical logic by *fragmenting* the concept of truth. On the other hand, indeterminacy approaches and inconsistency approaches tend to get paired with weakly classical or non-classical logical approaches; these theorists prize the unity of truth, but pay for it by losing cherished logical principles.

Fifth, even if we ignore the variations internal to each kind of logical approach (so we have seven logical approaches) and we set aside the three "dismissive" philosophical approaches at the top of the diagram (so we have five philosophical approaches), that gives us thirty-five possible combinations, of which less than a third are spoken for. At least with respect to combinations of approaches to the paradoxes, we have a sparsely populated logical space; or, to accentuate the positive: there are many opportunities for new work in this area.

1.5 Unified theories of truth

We can classify many theories of the nature of truth along two dimensions, first by that in terms of which they explain truth, and second by the strength of the explanation. The options are Correspondence, Coherence, Pragmatic, Epistemic, and Modest. Each of these offers a central universally quantified biconditional:

For all x, x is true iff F(x).

Künne gave us five strengths of the central biconditional offered by a theory of truth:

1) same sense—analytic biconditional
2) same intension and self-evident—self-evident biconditional
3) same intension and a priori—a priori biconditional
4) same intension—necessary biconditional
5) same extension—true biconditional

Deflationism offers a central biconditional for each truth-bearer instead of a general one, and pluralism offers as many biconditionals as there are truth properties. Correspondence, Coherence, Pragmatic, and Epistemic theories all offer analytic biconditionals. Modest theories and deflationist theories offer at least necessary biconditionals—it does not seem that one of these theorists could accept that there is a possible world where some truth-bearer p is true but the claim that p is true is false (or vice versa). Deflationists typically suggest that the T-sentences have status (i), (ii), or (iii). Pluralism certainly does not offer self-evident biconditionals, and it seems to me that they are probably not even a priori—one could find out, from empirical evidence, that a certain discourse has a certain truth property. Anyone who accepts the T-biconditionals accepts that the central biconditional for each truth-bearer is at least true.

As I mentioned, there are several projects one might engage in when addressing the liar paradox, which include the descriptive project (describing our current aletheic practice) and the prescriptive project (describing how our aletheic practice should be). There is also a philosophical aspect and a logical aspect to any project. I also claimed in the last section that a combined philosophical and logical approach offers a formal theory and an empirical interpretation of it. One might need two of these—one for the descriptive project and one for the prescriptive project.

The descriptive/prescriptive distinction is going to affect one's views on the nature of truth—it is entirely possible to pair a descriptive approach to the paradoxes with a certain view on the nature of truth (as it is currently used) and pair a prescriptive approach to the paradoxes with a different view on the nature of truth (as it should be used). Each view on the nature of truth can be thought of as a combination of a central biconditional(s) plus its status.

When we put all these pieces together, we arrive at the following idea. Let us call a *unified theory of truth* a combination of a view on the nature of truth together with a combined approach to the paradoxes. That could involve: (i) a descriptive central biconditional(s) (or an alternative to them), (ii) the reading of the descriptive central biconditional(s) (or alternative), (iii) a philosophical approach to the descriptive project, (iv) a logical approach to the descriptive project, (v) a prescriptive central biconditional(s) (or alternative to them), (vi) the reading of the prescriptive central biconditional(s) (or alternative), (vii) a philosophical approach to the prescriptive project, and (viii) a logical approach to the prescriptive project. It might be that a unified theory of truth says that we need not change our practice in any way, in which case it will not have items (v)–(viii).

Instead of focusing on the central biconditional, one could adopt Davidson's view of truth and combine it with a philosophical approach to the paradoxes and a logical approach to the paradoxes. Davidson presents his view as an empirical interpretation of an axiomatic theory of truth (more on this in Chapter 7). I characterized the philosophical/logical distinction between approaches to the paradoxes in terms of mathematical theories and their empirical interpretation as well. It should not come as a surprise that these two components fit well together. The result would take a philosophical and logical approach to the paradoxes, and embed it in a broader Davidsonian theory of rationality. The overall theory would combine Davidson's view on the nature of truth with a philosophical and a logical approach to the paradoxes. No one has yet attempted such a thing, but this is exactly what I do in Chapters 6 and 7 as a prescriptive theory and again in Chapter 9 as a descriptive theory.

We have seen combinations of philosophical and logical approaches to the paradoxes and been reminded of the views on the nature of truth. Figure 3 displays the connections

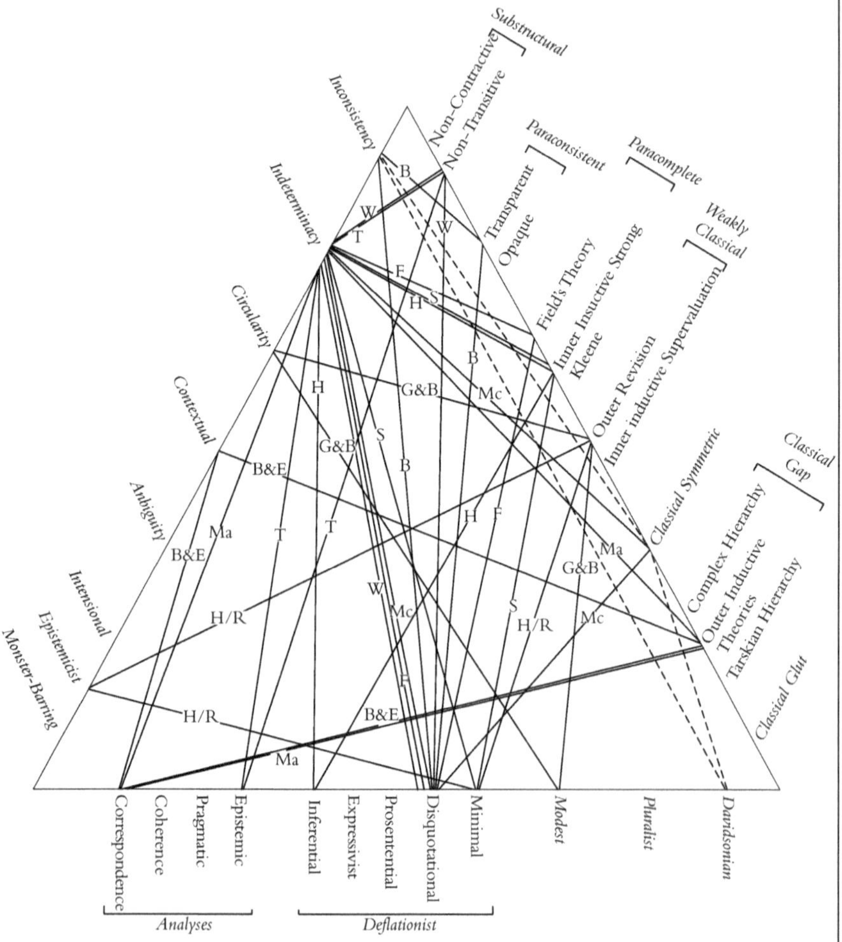

B&E	Barwise & Etchemendy	Ma	Maudlin
B	Beall	Mc	McGee
F	Field	S	Soames
G&B	Gupta & Belnap	T	Tennant
H	Horsten	W	Weir
H/R	Horwich / Restall		

Figure 3 Unified Theories of Truth

between the philosophical approaches to the paradoxes (left), the logical approaches to the paradoxes (right), and the theories of the nature of truth (bottom). Only unified theories of truth are represented; i.e., those that offer a combination of views on the nature of truth, a philosophical approach to the paradoxes, and a logical approach to the paradoxes. These unified theories show up as triangles in this figure.[66] The broken line represents the descriptive part of the unified theory of truth I offer in Chapter 9. One thing that jumps immediately off the page is that deflationists are the primary bridge builders between work on the nature of truth and work on the paradoxes. This is probably owing to two things: deflationism has long been thought to have significantly more trouble with the paradoxes than other views on the nature of truth so deflationists have been especially eager to dispel this myth,[67] and deflationism is more focused on the principles truth predicates obey than are other views on the nature of truth. Another feature of this diagram is that most unified theories of truth incorporate indeterminacy approaches. That fact probably owes more to the popularity of indeterminacy approaches rather than some reason for indeterminacy theorists to be interested in unified theories of truth. Figure 4 lists the individual components of each unified theory.[68]

As an example of a unified theory, focus again on Field, who began his career defending a version of correspondence, but ended up abandoning it for disquotationalism in the early 1990s.[69] After a brief flirtation with paraconsistent dialetheism,[70] he developed a paracomplete logical approach to the paradoxes that is paired with an indeterminacy approach. The result is probably the most thoroughly cohesive unified theory where each component is formulated in detail, vigorously defended, and supports the other two. He is probably the most prominent defender of each component.

Field's approach to the aletheic paradoxes is part of a much larger project that focuses on partially defined expressions. From this account of partially defined expressions he derives a theory of truth and indeterminacy, a theory of vagueness, and a theory of properties.[71] To accompany his account, he presents a new formulation of disquotationalism (within the paracomplete framework), a new paracomplete logic, and a non-standard probability calculus that allows him to explain degrees of belief in propositions that display indeterminacy.[72]

[66] Note that 'B&E' and 'G&B' stand for 'Barwise and Etchemendy' and 'Gupta and Belnap', respectively. These pairs of authors worked together on their respective unified theories of truth. 'H/R' stands for 'Horwich / Restall'; these two authors worked independently on the theory of truth in question.

[67] One can find this view in Dummett (1959) and Simmons (1999); see also Gupta (2005).

[68] These are listed in roughly chronological order.

[69] Field (1972, 1986, 1994a, 1994b, 2001c, 2001d, 2001e, 2001f, 2005c, 2005d, 2006a, 2006b).

[70] Field (2001h).

[71] See Field (2002, 2003a, 2003b, 2003c, 2004, 2005a, 2005b, 2008a, 2008c, 2010a, 2010b) for the theory of truth and indeterminacy, Field (2003b, 2003c) for the theory of vagueness, and Field (2003c, 2004) for the theory of properties. Associated with this project is the work in Field's John Locke Lectures, which focus on the rational revisability of logic; Field (2008b).

[72] See Field (1998, 2000, 2001b, 2001g, 2001h, 2003b, forthcoming) for the non-standard probability calculus. One should be aware that Field presents two non-standard probability calculi, one that is classical and the other non-classical. He now endorses only the non-classical version; see Field (2003c: 462).

(i)	Correspondance	Contextual	Classical Gap	(Barwise and Etchemendy)
(ii)	Modest	Circularity	Weakly Classical	(Gupta and Belnap)
(iii)	Minimal	Epistemicist	Classical	(Horwich / Restall)
(iv)	Disquotational	Indeterminacy	Classical Symmetric	(McGee)
(v)	Minimal	Indeterminacy	Paracomplete	(Soames)
(vi)	Correspondance	Indeterminacy	Classical Gap	(Maudlin)
(vii)	Disquotational	Indeterminacy	Paracomplete	(Field)
(viii)	Disquotational	Indeterminacy	Substructural	(Weir)
(ix)	Disquotational	Inconsistency	Paraconsistent	(Beall)
(x)	Inferential	Indeterminacy	Paracomplete	(Horsten)
(xi)	Epistemic	Indeterminacy	Substructural	(Tennant)

Figure 4 Eleven Unified Theories of Truth

He adds a new conditional to the internal theory of Kripke's Strong Kleene minimal fixed point, and he uses it to define a determinacy operator, which can be used to classify all the paradoxical sentences of the language in question (even those that contain the determinacy operator). He uses this conditional to define a paracomplete biconditional that features in the formulation of the T-sentences for his disquotational theory.[73] In sum, he offers a disquotational/indeterminacy/paracomplete unified theory.

[73] See Yablo (2003), Priest (2005, 2008, 2010), Leitgeb (2008), Rayo and Welch (2008), Scharp (2008, 2009a), McGee (2010), Restall (2010), Shapiro (2010), Caie (2012), Burgis (forthcoming), and Bacon (forthcoming a, forthcoming b) for discussion.

2

Inconsistent Concepts

A central claim of this book is that truth is an inconsistent concept. However, the term 'inconsistent concept' is not found in common usage or in contemporary analytic philosophy discussions; so the first step is to provide an adequate explanation. This chapter introduces the idea, provides several examples, and offers a theory of concepts' constitutive principles.

2.1 Concepts

Before discussing inconsistent concepts, I should say a bit about concepts in general.[1] There are three main views on the nature of concepts:

(i) *Mental representations*: concepts are mental particulars that are the constituents of beliefs and other propositional attitudes. As such, concepts are internal symbols with representational properties.[2]

(ii) *Abstract entities*: concepts are abstract (i.e., non-spatio-temporal) entities that are the constituents of propositions (e.g., Fregean senses).[3]

(iii) *Abilities*: concepts are cognitive abilities or capacities—e.g., the ability to draw certain inferences, classify objects based on perceptions, or react to stimuli in various ways.[4]

The debate about the nature of concepts is rough terrain, and I do not intend to take a stand on this issue.[5] Rather, I do not think that anything I say about inconsistent concepts commits me to one of these views on the ontological nature of concepts. A related issue on which I shall commit myself is concept possession; i.e., a view on what it is to possess a concept, but that needs to wait until we get some examples of inconsistent concepts.

[1] My presentation is based on Margolis and Lawrence (1999).

[2] Advocates include Fodor (1975, 1987, 1998, 2004) and Carruthers (1996, 2000).

[3] Advocates include Peacocke (1992), Zalta (2001), and Chalmers (2011).

[4] Advocates include Evans (1982), Dummett (1993), Brandom (1994), and Millikan (2000).

[5] For background, see the papers in Margolis and Lawrence (1999); for the contemporary debate, see Fodor (1998), Prinz (2002), Murphy (2002), Machery (2009), and Carey (2009).

2.2 Inconsistent concepts

Intuitively, a concept is *inconsistent* iff its constitutive principles are inconsistent. For example, consider the following definition:

(1a) 'rable' applies to x if x is a table.
(1b) 'rable' disapplies to x if x is a red thing.[6]

These rules are *constitutive* for rable in the sense that they determine (in part) the meaning of 'rable' and the identity of the concept expressed by it. There are several ways of explaining the relationship between agents and constitutive principles, but a prima facie plausible explanation is that anyone who possesses a certain concept accepts that concept's constitutive principles. According to this view, if someone uses 'rable' but does not believe (1a) and (1b), then that person's word 'rable' does not mean *rable*. However, for reasons I discuss below, a more subtle account of the relation is required.

The definition of 'inconsistent concept' might cause some confusion since the constitutive principles for 'rable' are not *logically* inconsistent. The problem with 'rable' is instead that its constitutive principles have false consequences (e.g., there are no red tables). We could stipulate that an inconsistent concept has constitutive principles that are incompatible with the empirical facts, or we could say that an inconsistent concept has some false constitutive principles, or we could define a concept's being inconsistent relative to some set of claims.[7] I do not see any practical difference between these amendments.

A person who employs the concept rable might believe and assert that a red shirt is not a rable and that a brown table is a rable. However, such a person will run into trouble when confronted with a red table because the constitutive principles for 'rable' imply that it both applies and disapplies to red tables. For example, let R be a red table. R is a table; hence, R is a rable. R is red; hence, it is not the case that R is a rable. Thus, R is a rable and it is not case that R is a rable. We have arrived at a contradiction via intuitively plausible steps from intuitively plausible assumptions. Consider another example. Assume for *reductio* that some red tables exist. Let R be a red table. The reasoning above shows that R is a rable and R is not a rable. Contradiction. Therefore, no red tables exist. We have proven an obviously false empirical sentence using only logic and the constitutive principles for 'rable'. If one accepts some basic logical principles and treats 'rable' as univocal and invariant, then it will be difficult to avoid these unacceptable conclusions. Since most people do not believe that any contradictions are true (even ones involving odd concepts like rable) and they believe in the existence of red tables, it seems that adding rable to one's conceptual repertoire corrupts it in a certain way.

[6] I use 'disapplies' as an antonym for 'applies'.

[7] Notice that this formulation implies that familiar examples like 'Boche' and 'tonk' (as usually understood) express inconsistent concepts (e.g., the constitutive principles for 'Boche' imply that all Germans are cruel and prone to barbarism). See Dummett (1973) on 'Boche' and Prior (1960) on 'tonk'. See also Williamson (2003).

I can imagine a reader who has been protesting: there is no such thing as an inconsistent concept! The attempted stipulation above failed to define any term at all because the definition is illegitimate. Therefore, 'rable' does not mean anything, and no conceptual harm has been done.[8]

Consider an actual case of conceptual revolution and an excellent example of an inconsistent concept: mass as it occurs in Newtonian mechanics.[9] In Newtonian mechanics, physical objects have a single physical quantity: mass. According to this theory, mass obeys two laws (which are considered equally fundamental): (i) mass = momentum/velocity, and (ii) the mass of an object is the same in all reference frames. We can think of these as constitutive principles for mass. In relativistic mechanics, physical objects have two different "kinds" of mass: proper mass and relativistic mass. An object's *proper mass* is its total energy divided by the square of the speed of light, while an object's *relativistic mass* is its non-kinetic energy divided by the square of the speed of light. Although relativistic mass = momentum/velocity, the relativistic mass of an object is not the same in all reference frames. On the other hand, proper mass ≠ momentum/velocity, but the proper mass of an object is the same in all reference frames. Thus, relativistic mass obeys one of the principles for mass and proper mass obeys the other. Since we live in a relativistic universe (i.e., one where momentum over velocity is not the same in all reference frames), mass is an inconsistent concept. That is, before the twentieth century, we used a concept whose constitutive principles are inconsistent with what would come to be well-confirmed claims about the world (i.e., momentum/velocity is not the same in all reference frames).[10]

Although the objection in question (i.e., that there are no inconsistent concepts) might seem convincing for 'rable', it is not plausible to claim that there is no concept of mass and that 'mass' is meaningless. The word 'mass' has an established use, sentences containing it participate in inferential relations, people use these sentences to express propositional attitudes, etc. To say that such an expression is meaningless severs the concept of meaning from most of the things for which we use it. In addition, if the objection were correct, then when we discovered that the constitutive principles for mass are incompatible, we would have also discovered that our word 'mass' is meaningless. However, it does not seem that an entire community of people can be wrong about whether a word is meaningful. It does not even seem possible to discover that a word one has a history of using is meaningless. Perhaps that is why there are no examples of this sort of thing actually happening.

The objection might seem plausible at first because it also seems plausible that if a concept is inconsistent, then anyone who possesses the concept is in a position to know that it is inconsistent. However, the 'mass' example should dispel this impression. The rules for the employment of a concept often incorporate features of the environment in

8 See Wright (1975) and Patterson (2008).

9 The example is from Field (1973), but Field does not say that 'mass' expresses an inconsistent concept.

10 For more information on this example, see Jammer (2000) and Petkov (2009).

which it is used; if the employers of a concept are ignorant or mistaken about some features of their environment, then the concept in question can be inconsistent without their knowledge. No amount of "reflection on their concepts" will inform them that their concept is inconsistent; they have to go out into the world and discover empirical facts to discover the conceptual inconsistency.

Another worry is voiced by John Earman and Arthur Fine, who claim that 'mass' just means *proper mass*, and that we simply had the false belief that mass is momentum/velocity.[11] Fine gives evidence that Einstein himself held this opinion, while Earman provides an argument for it. It is hard to see why anyone should be persuaded by Fine's appeal to authority; after all, Einstein was no linguist. However, Earman's argument is that when Newtonian mechanics and special relativity are written in four-dimensional intrinsic form, mass and proper mass satisfy three fundamental principles that have the same form, whereas relativistic mass does not. Since this formulation of the two theories is so important, we should think that mass just is proper mass and not relativistic mass. Moreover, in contemporary physics, proper mass is considered to be much more fundamental than relativistic mass because the latter is relative to a reference frame while the former is not. Thus, Earman agrees that 'mass' is meaningful, but argues that it expresses a consistent concept. The general objection would be that whenever it seems like the constitutive principles for a concept are incompatible it must be that some of those principles are not really constitutive.

It seems to me that these are not good reasons to think that there are no inconsistent concepts. Consider a person living in 1850 who denies that mass is momentum/velocity. Probably no one at the time would say that that person's term 'mass' expressed *mass*. Most everyone treated the claim that mass is momentum/velocity as a constitutive principle for mass. In fact, it is often used as a definition of the term. It is hard to find a better example of what people at the time would have called an analytic claim. So if Earman is correct, then we could all be wrong about what the constitutive principles for our concepts are. There would be no evidence we could give that some principle is constitutive for some concept. That might be plausible on some accounts of constitutive principles, but on the one developed below, constitutive principles play their primary role in interpretation. As such, it does not make sense to say that everyone thinks that some proposition is a constitutive principle for some concept, but it turns out that it really is not constitutive. I think it is an empirical fact about our linguistic practice that we use constitutive principles to guide interpretation. Somehow I go from normal (or transparent) interpretation where I am not attending explicitly to the meanings of a speaker's words to a mode of interpretation where I explicitly consider whether the speaker means the same thing I do by a word. The speaker triggers this change by explicitly or implicitly rejecting something I take to be constitutive of the concept in question. Moreover,

[11] Earman and Fine (1977). They focus on Field's claim that the designation of 'mass' is indeterminate and argue that the designation of 'mass' is the property of proper mass. I am interested in how one might use the points they make to object to the existence of inconsistent concepts.

unless we are right about some of these principles, it hardly makes sense to say that we are using the concept in question. For example, if I do not think that grass is green or that it is a plant or that it is growing in my back yard or any of the other familiar claims about grass, then it does not make sense to interpret my word 'grass' as meaning *grass*.

In addition, Earman's point can be handled in stride. It is not surprising that mass satisfies some constitutive principle satisfied by proper mass but not by relativistic mass. We should expect that once we have the conceptual resources to distinguish between the two notions of mass (and all the concomitant mathematical and physical innovations), we can formulate principles like the ones to which Earman appeals. It also is not surprising that proper mass seems like a more important or fundamental notion than relativistic mass. Once we replace an inconsistent concept, one of its replacements might come to be more useful than the other. Indeed, that might happen in the case of truth; but it would not cast doubt on the claim that truth is inconsistent.

I want to make several points about inconsistent concepts. First, it is essential to distinguish between inconsistent concepts and unsatisfiable concepts. An *unsatisfiable concept* is one that is consistent but which cannot apply to anything. An unsatisfiable concept places incompatible demands on the objects for which it is defined, while an inconsistent concept places incompatible demands on its employers. For example:

(2) x is a *squircle* iff x is a square and x is a circle.

Squircle is an unsatisfiable concept, but it is not inconsistent. Someone who possesses squircle has no problem employing it. It should be disapplied to everything.[12]

Second, attempting to place the definition of an inconsistent concept in the standard form often results in a conjunctive or disjunctive definition of a consistent concept. Notice the difference in definitions (1) and (2). Definition (2) prescribes both the application conditions and the disapplication conditions for 'squircle' at once, while definition (1) has two separate clauses for 'rable'. When considering a definition like (2), it is common to assume that if something is not both a square and a circle, then it is not a squircle. This assumption fits well with consistent concepts because the things to which they apply and the things to which they disapply are disjoint. However, the application conditions and disapplication conditions for inconsistent concepts result in an overlap. That makes it impossible to introduce them with definitions that are in the form of (2). Consider another definition:

(3) x is a *non-red-table* iff x is a table and x is not red.

There is a big difference between 'non-red-table' and 'rable'. 'Non-red-table' is consistent and applies to things that are both tables and not red; it disapplies to everything else.

[12] I mention the distinction between inconsistent and unsatisfiable concepts because it is a common mistake to assume that inconsistent concepts are merely unsatisfiable. Even some theorists in the inconsistency tradition still make this basic mistake; for example, see Patterson (2010: 16). See Stenius (1972), Chihara (1979), and Yablo (1993b) for discussions of the distinction and the mistake.

Third, inconsistent concepts characteristically give rise to paradoxes, as evidenced by the arguments above where we derived a contradiction using a red table on one hand, and showed that no red tables exist on the other. It is obvious that something has gone wrong in these arguments, but what? I take it as a condition on any account of inconsistent concepts that it must explain the fallacy in them. It should not be surprising that arguments like these feature prominently in criticisms of theories that posit inconsistent concepts.

The next point is that there is an affinity between inconsistent concepts and partial concepts. A *partial concept* is one that has a limited range of applicability. Some concepts are partial by definition. Here is Scott Soames's example of a partial concept:

(4a) 'smidget' applies to x if x is greater than four feet tall.
(4b) 'smidget' disapplies to x if x is less than two feet tall.[13]

Smidget is a partial concept because it is undefined for entities that are between two and four feet tall. I want to introduce several terms that are helpful in discussing partial concepts and inconsistent concepts. When discussing any partial concept, I assume that there is a set of all the objects that exist; I call it the *domain*. This assumption brings with it several obvious and difficult set-theoretic problems that I will not go into; they do not matter for my purposes. I say that the *range of applicability* of a concept is the subset of the domain to which it either applies or disapplies. The *range of inapplicability* is the complement of the range of applicability. I say that a concept is *inapplicable to an object* if that object falls within its range of inapplicability. Smidget's range of applicability is the set of objects that are either greater than four feet tall or less than two feet tall. Rable's range of applicability is the set of objects that are either tables or non-red things. I call the set of things to which a concept applies its *application set* and the set of things to which a concept disapplies its *disapplication set*. The application sets of consistent concepts are their extensions and the disapplication sets of consistent concepts are their anti-extensions. A concept's *overdetermined set* is the intersection of its application set and its disapplication set.[14] One must be especially careful dealing with negation and partial concepts. The sentence 'b is not a smidget' can mean *smidget disapplies to b* or it can mean *smidget either disapplies to b or it is inapplicable to b*. We can take the former to read 'not' as choice negation and the latter to read not as exclusion negation.

Up to this point I have discussed only inconsistent concepts whose application sets and disapplication sets are not disjoint. However, if a concept's range of applicability and its range of inapplicability are not disjoint, then it is inconsistent as well. For example:

(5a) 'mammamonkey' applies to x if x is a mammal.
(5b) 'mammamonkey' disapplies to x if x is an animal and x is not a mammal.
(5c) 'mammamonkey' is inapplicable to x if x is either a monkey or x is not an animal.

[13] Soames (1999). See Glanzberg (2003) for criticism.

[14] One might think that if a concept's overdetermined set is nonempty, then it is the entire domain. After all, we argued above that a certain red table is a rable and it is not a rable. By *ex falso*, everything is a rable and not a rable. I address this issue on p. 43.

Although the application set and disapplication set for 'mammamonkey' are disjoint, it is an inconsistent concept because its range of applicability and range of inapplicability overlap. A concept can exhibit both types of inconsistency as well. I mark this distinction by saying that an *application-inconsistent* concept (e.g., rable) is one whose application set and disapplication set are not disjoint; a *range-inconsistent* concept (e.g., mammamonkey) is one whose range of applicability and range of inapplicability are not disjoint. I focus primarily on application-inconsistent concepts in the remainder of this chapter, but most of my comments and results hold for range-inconsistent ones as well.

I want to emphasize that in most cases, the inconsistency arises by virtue of the environment in which it is used—reading 'environment' in a wide sense. The following example illustrates this point and is based on a discussion of Anil Gupta's.[15] Consider a community of people who speak a language that is similar to English except that in their language, the rules for using the expression 'x is up above y' (where 'x' and 'y' are replaced by singular terms) are different. I call the members of this community *Higherians*. Two equally important features of the Higherian's 'up above' talk are that they can perceptually distinguish situations in which one object is up above another (these situations are similar to the ones in which an English speaker would say that one object is up above another), and that they can determine when the ray connecting two objects is parallel to a particular ray that is designated as 'Standard Up' (where Standard Up is orthogonal to a tangent plane for the surface of the object on which the Higherians live). 'Up above' applies to an ordered pair <A, B> if either (i) both A and B are constituents of one of the perceptually distinguishable situations (call this the *perceptual criterion*), or (ii) the ray connecting A and B is parallel to Standard Up and A is farther from the surface than B (call this the *conceptual criterion*). 'Up above' disapplies to an ordered pair <A, B> if either (i) A and B are not in the proper perceptually distinguishable relation to one another, or (ii) it is not the case that both the ray connecting A and B is parallel to Standard Up and A is further from the surface than B.

Assume that 'up above' is defined only for perceptible objects and only for objects within the national borders of the Higherian's country. When a Higherian can perceive two objects at the same time then that person can perceive whether they are in the right perceptually distinguishable relation to one another. In addition, every Higherian can determine the ray that connects any two perceivable objects and can determine whether any two rays are parallel. Thus, if a Higherian can perceive object A and he can perceive object B (not necessarily simultaneously), then he can determine whether the ray that connects them is parallel to Standard Up. Assume that the Higherians do not know that their concept is inconsistent because when they can perceive two objects at the same time, they employ the perceptual criterion and when they cannot, they employ the conceptual criterion.

[15] Gupta (1999); see also Weiner (2009).

If the Higherians live on the surface of a spherical planet, and their nation consists of more than just a single point, then 'up above' is inconsistent. If A and B are two objects that are located some distance from where Standard Up intersects the surface of their sphere and are in the right perceptually distinguishable relation then 'up above' both applies to <A, B> and disapplies to <A, B> because they are in the right perceptually distinguishable relation, but the ray connecting them is not parallel to Standard Up. However, if the Higherians' country is confined to one flat surface of a rectangular solid, then 'up above' is consistent because it is defined only within their national borders. Hence, up above is an empirically inconsistent concept in the case where the Higherians live on the surface of a sphere.

The rules for the employment of a concept often incorporate features of the environment in which it is used in this way; if the employers of a concept are ignorant or mistaken about some features of their environment, then the concept in question might be inconsistent without their knowledge. Again, no amount of "reflection on their concepts" will inform them that their concept is inconsistent; they have to go out into the world and learn empirical facts to discover the conceptual inconsistency. The Higherians might not realize that the concept they possess and use presupposes anything about the shape of the object they live on. Consider the history of human inquiry—we (humans) discover false empirical beliefs alarmingly often. Given the degree of our ignorance and error, there is a good chance that many, perhaps most, of our concepts are empirically inconsistent. That sobering thought should lend urgency to the task of constructing an adequate theory of inconsistent concepts.

Here is another worry I hear often:

> There are no inconsistent concepts because it is impossible that a term obeys incompatible rules of employment. One reason for thinking this is that interpretation requires one to use the logic one endorses when interpreting another. Thus, it is inappropriate to ever attribute an inconsistent concept to someone, since the interpreter would have to attribute something that defies the logic she endorses.[16] Moreover, even if one could introduce a term that obeys incompatible rules, it would be overdetermined for every item, so it would be unemployable.[17]

First, the claim that we interpret others as if they endorse our logical standards is simply false. If it were true then there would be no distinction between criticizing someone for failing to follow an inference rule she endorses and criticizing someone for endorsing the wrong inference rule. It is obvious that there is such a distinction and it plays an important role in philosophical discussions (e.g., debates about classical vs. intuitionistic vs. relevance logic).

Second, charity can cut both ways. One might simply introduce an inconsistent concept, begin using it, and describe it as inconsistent (I did this with the concept rable). It seems to me that it would be quite difficult to go on interpreting someone who does this as if they had misunderstood their own stipulative definition and their claims about

[16] One can find a similar objection in Stebbins (1992).

[17] See Gupta and Belnap (1993: 13–15) for this objection; see also Chihara (1984) for discussion.

it. Indeed, one might give an account of all the relevant factors in charitable interpretation and present two situations, one in which the weighted sum of all the factors is higher than that of the second, while in the first one attributes an inconsistent concept, but in the second one does not. The point here is that attributing an inconsistent concept is sometimes the most charitable thing to do. No matter what constraints one imposes on charitable interpretation (except of course, a conceptual consistency constraint), there will be situations in which it is more charitable to attribute an inconsistent concept. It would be exceedingly uncharitable to treat the Higherians, for example, as if they do not really mean what they think they mean by 'up above'. The right way to deal with situations like this is to accept that what they think are constitutive principles are constitutive principles and what they think they mean is what they mean. Then the burden is on the theorist to make sense of it.

I agree that a major problem for a theory of inconsistent concepts is showing that a concept can be both inconsistent and employable (i.e., not overdetermined for every item). I take up this task in Chapter 9.

2.3 Possessors and principles

One problem raised by inconsistent concepts is how they could be possessed. By far the most popular theory of concept possession is *concept pragmatism*, which Jerry Fodor characterizes in the following way:

> *The* characteristic doctrine of 20th Century philosophy of mind/language... was that *concept possession is some sort of dispositional, epistemic condition*. Maybe it's some sort of "knowing that"; or maybe it's some sort of "knowing how"; or maybe it's a bit of both. In any case, "knowing", "believing" and the like must come into the story somewhere, and what you have to know in order to have a concept ipso facto constitutes the concept's content.[18]

The central claim of concept pragmatism is that if an agent s possesses a concept c, then s knows something, or knows how to do something or believes something and this feature of s constitutes s's possession of c. Let whatever epistemic or cognitive capacities s must have in order to possess c be c's *possession conditions*.

As Fodor mentioned in the passage above, one very popular view on possession conditions is that they involve belief. Let us explore this idea. Assume that, for any concept c there is some proposition that ϕ, such that believing that ϕ is a necessary condition for possessing c. This account is clearly inadequate since there are many concept/principle pairs that fail this condition. As discussed above, the concept of mass (as defined in Newtonian mechanics) has the following constitutive principles:

(6a) An object's mass = its momentum/its velocity.
(6b) An object's mass is the same in all reference frames.

[18] Fodor (2004: 29); note that Fodor rejects concept pragmatism.

Of course, it follows from these two principles that momentum/velocity is the same in all reference frames. But we all know that this is not correct—special and general relativity imply that momentum/velocity is relative to a reference frame and the latter is one of our most well-confirmed scientific theories. So, despite the fact that I possess the concept of mass, I do not accept or believe both (6a) and (6b). Paul Boghossian summarizes the point in the following passages:

> The concept itself should not be designed in such a way that, only those who believe a certain creed are allowed to possess it.
>
> You don't ever want the *possession conditions* for a concept to foreclose on the possible falsity of some particular set of claims about the world, if you can possibly avoid it. You want the possessor of the concept to be able coherently to ask whether there is anything that falls under it, and you want people to be able to disagree about whether there is.[19]

There are several options for dealing with this problem.

Boghossian suggests that we pursue an idea proposed by Frank Ramsey of thinking of constitutive principles as conditionalized—following this suggestion we arrive at these constitutive principles for mass:

(7a) If objects have mass, then an object's mass = its momentum/its velocity.
(7b) If objects have mass, then an object's mass is the same in all reference frames.

If we say that (7a) and (7b) are the constitutive principles for mass, then one can believe them (and thereby possess the concept of mass on some views) without believing their consequents. So a person who thinks that mass is defective can still believe these two conditionals (since, presumably, the person rejects their antecedents and their consequents).[20] However, I still use 'mass'. What are the principles according to which I should use it? Well, presumably, they are (7a) and (7b) (plus possibly others). But I do not really use it according to them since I deny their antecedents. I use it, in certain circumstances, according to the consequents of these principles. So the constitutive principles of mass on Boghossian's view do not really say anything about how I use it. Moreover, if there is no such thing as mass (i.e., the property signified by the term 'mass' that obeys the two principles of Newtonian mechanics described above), then (7a) and (7b) are each true. But appeals to inconsistent constitutive principles were supposed to flesh out what we mean by an inconsistent concept. Thus, the conditionalization approach does not work well for useful yet defective concepts like mass.[21]

Matti Eklund also explains concept possession conditions in terms of constitutive principles, but he suggests that $\langle \phi \rangle$ is a constitutive principle for a concept c iff being disposed to believe that ϕ is a necessary condition for possessing c.[22] There are several

[19] Boghossian (2003a: 245) and Boghossian (2003a: 246); see also Williamson (2003, 2006) for a similar point.
[20] Boghossian (2003a); see also Ramsey (1929) and Lewis (1970).
[21] To be clear, I think (7a) and (7b) are constitutive of 'mass', but I am arguing against the view that (6a) and (6b) are not constitutive of 'mass'. See Williamson (2003) for discussion of the conditionalization approach.
[22] Eklund (2002a, 2007).

problems with this view. Let us consider a person, Otto, who has come to possess the concept of rable and realizes that it is an inconsistent concept. Assume also that Otto does not like the idea of accepting contradictions because he thinks that rational agents should avoid doing such things if at all possible. What can Otto do? If Eklund is right, then Otto needs to get rid of his disposition to accept the constitutive principles for 'rable'. Let us assume that he does rid himself of the offending dispositions. Now that he is no longer disposed to accept its constitutive principles, in what sense does he still possess the concept? If Eklund is right that *being disposed to accept* is the relation between concept possessors and constitutive principles, then Otto no longer possesses the concept once he has eliminated those dispositions. But that cannot be right. Even after eliminating the dispositions, it seems like he would still understand the word. Perhaps Eklund would amend his view so that Otto still possesses the concept because he *used to have* the dispositions. If that is correct, then it does not seem like anyone could ever lose possession of a concept.

Another option is to invoke a subpersonal attitude. One can say that we cognize the principles, which means that we feel primitively compelled to accept them even if we do not in fact accept them.[23] The analogy is with visual illusions—it still seems that the lines in the Müller-Lyer figure are different lengths even though one does not believe it. The problem with this suggestion is that the principles governing mass do not seem true—there is no sense in which I am primitively compelled to accept them. Rather, I think that they are approximately true in certain circumstances. That is a big difference, and it suggests that the subpersonal view is inadequate.

Instead of dispositions to accept or subpersonal attitudes, one might appeal to rules of language. Alexis Burgess claims that this approach is better than its rivals. In particular, Burgess claims that, in the spirit of inferential role semantics, the inference rules (T-Intro) and (T-Elim) (mentioned in Chapter 1), which allow one to infer a sentence from its truth attribution and vice versa, govern the use of truth predicates. He thinks that using a truth predicate in sincere assertions commits one to these rules and that semantic competence with a truth predicate is constituted by knowledge of the rules governing its use.[24] The problem I have with this suggestion is that it is incompatible with reasonable uses of inconsistent concepts. That is, for Burgess, one cannot use an inconsistent concept without committing oneself to contradictions. Dialetheism aside, it is irrational to commit oneself to contradictions. Thus, on Burgess's proposal, it would be irrational to employ even very useful inconsistent concepts like mass. What we need is a consistent theory of inconsistent concepts that is compatible with the claim that we can possess *and employ* them without committing ourselves to contradictions.[25]

[23] See Patterson (2007).

[24] A. Burgess (2006: 12–14).

[25] Mackie (1973: 251) compares speaking using a word that expresses an inconsistent concept to driving a car that would fall to pieces at ninety miles per hour but can be safely driven at more modest speeds.

I suggest that instead of using cognitive relations like belief to explain the relation between concept possessors and constitutive principles, we should consider epistemic relations. Of course, knowledge is too strong since it implies belief. However, the notion of *entitlement*, which is introduced by Tyler Burge and taken up by Boghossian and Crispin Wright, is perfect for the job.[26,27] Burge claims that justification and entitlement are kinds of warrant, and he offers the following characterization:

> The distinction between justification and entitlement is this: Although both have positive force in rationally supporting a propositional attitude or cognitive practice, and in constituting an epistemic right to it, entitlements are epistemic rights or warrants that need not be understood by or even accessible to the subject.[28]

Entitlement is defeasible—if an agent finds some reason to doubt the proposition in question, then the warrant is lost. Entitlement is also non-evidential; as Wright puts it: "there is a distinction between being rationally entitled to proceed on certain suppositions and the having of evidence that those suppositions are actually true."[29] Being entitled to some proposition does not require having evidence for it.[30]

Someone who possesses a certain concept is *entitled* to the constitutive principles of that concept. That is, the person is warranted in believing the constitutive principles provided he or she has no reason to doubt them. However, one can be entitled to a principle without believing it, and entitlement is defeasible. Thus, if a person has evidence to the contrary, then he or she is not warranted in believing the principle. In most cases, concept possessors will not only be entitled to the constitutive principles in question, they will also accept them, since they will not have any reason to doubt them. If one knows that a concept is inconsistent, one will reject one or more of the concept's constitutive principles. Instead of accepting the concept's constitutive principles, a person in this situation will probably accept similar principles that permit exceptions. For example, one might accept that *in non-relativistic situations* (i.e., those where the difference between proper mass and relativistic mass is negligible) the mass of an object is the same in all reference frames.[31]

Since entitlements are defeasible, we need to make a choice about how to use 'entitlement'. Let us say that a person is initially entitled to $\langle \phi \rangle$ but then discovers some reason

[26] See Burge (1993), Wright (2004a, 2004b), and Boghossian (1996, 1997, 2003b). There are subtle differences between the ways these theorists use 'entitlement' (Wright discusses three different varieties—the "cognitive project" variety seems most relevant to my discussion), but they do not matter for my purposes.

[27] Two other theorists come close to suggesting entitlement as the relation between possessors and principles: see Eklund (2005: 50), which discusses default acceptability, and Ray (2002: 166–7), which invokes subtle conceptual warrant.

[28] Burge (1993: 458).

[29] Wright (2004b: 167).

[30] To accept entitlement as the relation between concept possessors and constitutive principles does not commit one to accepting the doctrines Burge, Boghossian, or Wright defend. Indeed, it seems to me that accepting entitlement as the possessor-principle link runs counter to some of these projects.

[31] Thinking of the relation between an agent and constitutive principles as one of entitlement represents a change from the account given in Scharp (2008) in which I distinguish between concept possession and concept employment, and I argue that someone who *employs* a concept is *committed* to its constitutive principles. This older view I now reject is incompatible with the claim that it is reasonable to employ some inconsistent concepts.

to doubt that ϕ. That person is no longer entitled to believe that ϕ.[32] So we need a term that is short for 'would be entitled provided one had no countervailing evidence'. Call this *quasi-entitled*. Now, we can say:

(8) A subject s possesses concept c iff s is quasi-entitled to the constitutive principles for c.

Even if speakers disagree on the constitutive principles for a given concept, this definition will work as long as they think there is a fact of the matter as to what the constitutive principles are. If they do not think there is a fact of the matter, then the definition will need to be relativized to speakers, hearers, or linguistic communities. I say a bit more about this option below.

This view of constitutive principles is somewhat different from the received view. First, constitutive principles need not be true. That is a welcome result since inconsistent concepts have constitutive principles that could not all be true. It follows that constitutive principles in my sense are not cut out to explain analyticity, apriority, or necessity since all these notions are factive (if coherent). Second, one need not believe a concept's constitutive principles to possess that concept. A person who possesses a concept and has no reason to think it is defective will probably believe its constitutive principles, but another person who possesses the concept in question and suspects that it is defective will probably not believe all its constitutive principles and might even believe the negation of one or more of them. Third, constitutive principles on this reading still serve as a guide to interpretation. If p is a constitutive principle for concept c then p contains a word w that typically expresses c. If a person denies p then that is good evidence that that person's word w does not express c. However, it is not conclusive evidence since the person might think that the concept in question is defective, or might deny that p is constitutive for c. Fourth, whether a principle is constitutive for a concept is a status the principle can have or lack and it is a status that reasonable people can disagree about. Fifth, constitutivity is vague so there will be borderline cases.

A genuine problem remains: what is the source of the entitlement that is the link between possessors and principles? It seems to me that these entitlements stem from the epistemic nature of the concept's possession conditions. Recall that the received view on possession conditions is that they involve an agent's knowledge, beliefs, or abilities. Consider, for example, Christopher Peacocke's influential discussion of possession conditions as they apply to the concept square:

For a thinker to possess the concept square (C):

(S1) he must be willing to believe the thought Cm_1 where m_1 is a perceptual demonstrative, when he is taking his experience at face value, the object of the demonstrative m_1 is presented in an apparently square region of his environment, and he experiences that region as having equal sides and as symmetrical about the bisectors of its sides...

[32] Thanks to Michael Miller on this point.

(S2) for an object thought about under some other mode of presentation m_2, he must be willing to accept the content Cm_2 when and only when he accepts that the object presented by m_2 has the same shape as perceptual experiences of the kind (S1) represents objects as having.[33]

This example is merely meant to illustrate what possession conditions might be like; although Peacocke's account seems right in this case, nothing hinges on this. The main point is that an agent comes to possess a concept by acquiring certain practical abilities when it comes to thinking, judging, perceiving, and interpreting. Acquiring these practical abilities is a cognitive achievement.

For what it is worth, I prefer an interpretive approach to possession conditions, which is based on Donald Davidson's hypothetical radical interpreter (described more in Chapter 7).[34] On such a view, an agent s possesses a concept c iff a theory of s's beliefs and desires and the meanings of the sentences in s's language entails that some of s's beliefs or desires have c as a constituent. Of course, the justification for this particular theory of s comes in the form of s's interaction with items in the world shared by s and the radical interpreter.

I want to emphasize that nothing turns on accepting the interpretive view of possession conditions. Instead, the important point is that, acquiring a concept takes *effort* on the part of the agent. No matter whether one accepts Peacocke's theory or Davidson's or some other theory of possession conditions, as long as possession conditions involve some kind of cognitive achievement on the part of the agent in question, this is enough to ground the agent's entitlement to the constitutive principles of the concepts thereby possessed. The agent's process in acquiring the abilities that leads up to the agent's possession of some concept institute the agent's entitlement to that concept's constitutive principles. That is the heart of a concept-pragmatist theory of concept possession, and it remains intact even when one admits that some concepts are inconsistent.

Of course, particular views on concept possession might not be compatible with an acceptable theory of how one might possess an inconsistent concept. Peacocke's theory, for example, requires agents to believe certain things to count as possessing a certain concept. That view runs in to the kind of problems mentioned above. The interpretivist view, on the other hand, is more holistic and capable of handling the sorts of cases that arise in connection with inconsistent concepts.

Timothy Williamson has recently objected to the claim that there is a relation between understanding a sentence and assenting to it. His objections are similar in spirit to the ones I posed above. However, he also objects to the claim that there is a relation between understanding a sentence and being prima facie justified (non-factively) in assenting to it. Here is his objection:

Consider someone who is introduced to a long list of mutually inconsistent theories of combustion, including phlogiston theory. Their content is explained without any assurance that there was ever any serious evidence for any of them. Irrationally, this person plumps for phlogiston

[33] Peacocke (1992: 108).

[34] Davidson (1973). See Peacocke (1992: Ch. 1) for discussion.

theory and assents to its principles (unbeknownst to him, he is being influenced by happy associations from early childhood of the sound of the word 'phlogiston'). By ordinary standards, he is linguistically competent with the sentences of phlogiston theory and grasps the corresponding thoughts, but he is not even prima facie justified in assenting to them, since he has no evidence, even by testimony, of their truth.[35]

The idea is that even for a sentence that is a seemingly perfect candidate for being a constitutive principle, a person might understand the sentence and have no reason to doubt it without having any justification whatsoever for assenting to it. If that is right, then it would conflict with my claim that concept possessors are quasi-entitled to their concepts' constitutive principles. There are several problems with Williamson's objection, however. The first is that being entitled to something is not a matter of having evidence for it. In fact, that's the whole point of introducing the notion of entitlement. Thus, the person in Williamson's example (call him Leopold) might be entitled to the constitutive principles for 'phlogiston' even though he has no evidence for them. Indeed, one might be entitled to a principle one does not understand. The second problem is that, presumably, when the content of each theory is explained to Leopold, the explanation proceeds by using constitutive principles for any expressions he does not understand. Simply by going through the cognitive effort to acquire the concept of phlogiston, Leopold becomes quasi-entitled to its constitutive principles. Even if the one providing the explanation does not give Leopold any evidence for its constitutive principles, simply by using them to get across the meaning of 'phlogiston', the one providing the explanation quasi-entitles Leopold to those principles. For example, if Leopold later heard someone else reject one of these principles, then he would probably take this to be evidence that that person means something else by 'phlogiston'. Therefore, I do not see that Williamson's example casts any doubt on the account of constitutivity presented here.

2.4 Pragmatics and constitutive principles

We can understand what it is to treat a principle as constitutive for a certain concept by the role this status has in interpretation. Imagine an interlocutor (call her Iris in what follows) in a conversation with strangers who Iris takes to be speakers of a certain language. She takes all parties to be quasi-entitled to all the constitutive principles of all the concepts expressible by words of the language in question.[36] Focus on a particular concept c expressed by a word w. If Iris does not take c to be inconsistent, then she attributes commitments and entitlements to all c's constitutive principles to all parties. If Iris knows that one of her interlocutors takes c to be inconsistent but she does not, then she attributes entitlements to c's constitutive principles to this person, but not the associated commitments.[37] If Iris takes c to be inconsistent, but does not

[35] Williamson (2008: 81).

[36] One might think of this as what Davidson calls a *prior theory*; see Davidson (1986).

[37] This might happen as well if she knows that an interlocutor explicitly rejects that some claim is a constitutive principle for c.

have any reason to believe that her fellow interlocutors realize this, then she attributes commitments to c's constitutive principles to everyone, but not the associated entitlements. Finally, if she thinks c is inconsistent and knows her interlocutors agree with her, then she will attribute neither commitments nor entitlements to c's constitutive principles.

Let us look at the consequences of rejecting a constitutive principle from a pragmatic perspective. When a speaker denies a principle that the hearer takes to be constitutive of a concept that the hearer takes the speaker to be using, this is an interpretive "red flag." After all, the hearer will take the speaker's denial of what the hearer takes to be a constitutive principle as evidence that the hearer is misinterpreting the speaker. So, when a speaker denies one of these, the hearer has to either take the principle off the conversational record or change the interpretation of the word in question. Either way, when a speaker denies a constitutive principle, the hearer is not just engaging in business as usual—adding something to the record.

To be more precise about exactly how this notion of constitutive principle fits with prevailing pragmatic theories, consider David Lewis's scorekeeping model and Craige Roberts's development of it. Lewis begins with an analogy between the score in a baseball game and the score in a conversation. One can model the score in a baseball game as a septuple with entries for visiting team runs, home team runs, half of the inning, inning, strikes, balls, and outs.[38] Rules of baseball then come in four kinds:

(i) *Specifications of the kinematics of score*: these are rules that specify how the score changes over time in response to the behavior of players (e.g., a home-team runner crossing home plate without being tagged out as the result of a hit or steal increases the home team runs by one).

(ii) *Specifications of correct play*: these are rules that specify what is permissible and obligatory behavior for the players as determined by the score (e.g., if in the top half of an inning, the outs reaches three, then the home team players leave the field, while the visiting team players take the field).

(iii) *Directive requiring correct play*: all players ought to obey the specifications of correct play at all times.

(iv) *Directives concerning score*: players try to make the score change in certain ways (e.g., visiting team players try to increase the visiting team runs, visiting team players try to prevent home team runs from increasing, and in the bottom half of innings, visiting team members try to increase the outs).[39]

Lewis suggests that conversations can be usefully modeled along the same lines. The conversational score consists of a mathematical structure that includes "sets of presup-

[38] Notice that Lewis's formulation is incomplete since it does not account for runners, batting order, pinch hitters, etc., all of which might affect specifications of correct play and directives concerning score.

[39] Lewis (1979: 236).

posed propositions, boundaries between permissible and impermissible courses of action, and the like."[40] The four types of rules carry over:

(i) Conversational score changes in a rule-governed way in response to the behavior of participants (e.g., when an assertion is accepted by everyone, the proposition asserted gets added to the common ground).

(ii) Acceptable behavior for the participants at any stage in the conversation is determined by the score (e.g., it is unacceptable to assert something that has already been accepted by everyone).

(iii) Participants are expected to cooperate by following the rules for acceptable behavior.

(iv) Participants try to change the score in certain ways (e.g., a speaker attempts to get others to accept what she believes by making assertions in the hopes that they are accepted and added to the common ground).

The beauty of Lewis's model is that it is not restricted to assertions—it is able to handle commands, questions, suppositions, challenges, promises, and a wide range of other discourse actions; it also allows information to come off the record through retraction or accommodation. It has been used to explain a variety of pragmatic phenomena.[41]

Roberts expands Lewis's model and fills in many of the details for dealing with non-assertoric utterances. According to Roberts, the conversational score consists of the following structures (these should be thought of as relativized to a time t):

(i) I: a set of *interlocutors* at time t

(ii) G: a function from pairs of individuals in I and times t to sets of *goals* in effect at t such that for each $i \in I$ and each t, there is a set, $G(<i, t>)$, which is i's set of goals at t

(iii) G_{com}: the set of *common goals* at t; i.e., $\{g \mid \text{for all } i \in I, g \in G(<i, t>)\}$

[40] Lewis (1979: 238).

[41] Robert Brandom offers a novel variant of Lewis's model, which takes as primitives the notions of *deontic status* and *deontic attitude*. Statuses come in two flavors: *commitments* and *entitlements*. The former are similar to responsibilities and the latter are similar to permissions. There are three types of attitudes: *attributing*, *undertaking*, and *acknowledging*. One may attribute, undertake, and acknowledge various commitments and entitlements. There are several different kinds of commitments that correspond to aspects of discursive practice. *Doxastic commitments* correspond to assertions and beliefs, *inferential commitments* correspond to reasons, and *practical commitments* correspond to intentions. The members of a discursive practice keep track of each other's commitments and entitlements. At a given moment in a conversation, the score is just the set of commitments and entitlements associated with each participant. Each member of the conversation keeps score on all the participants (including herself). Every time one of the participants undertakes (implicitly adopts), acknowledges (explicitly adopts), or attributes (takes another as if he adopts) a commitment or entitlement, it changes the score. Moreover, each participant keeps two sets of books on the other participants—one for the commitments and entitlements of that participant according to what that participant accepts, and one for the commitments and entitlements of that participant according to what the scorekeeper accepts. See Brandom (1994, 2001) for details; see also Lance and Kremer (1994, 1996), Lance (1998, 2001), Lance and Kukla (2009), Restall (2008, 2009), and John MacFarlane's program GOGAR (Game of Giving and Asking for Reasons) at <http://johnmacfarlane.net:9094/>.

(iv) M: the set of *moves* made by interlocutors up to t with the following distinguished subsets—A, the set of assertions; Q, the set of questions; R, the set of requests; and Acc, the set of accepted moves

(v) $<$: a total order on M that reflects the chronological order of moves

(vi) CG: the *common ground*; i.e., the set of shared presupposed propositions at t

(vii) DR: the set of *discourse referents*; i.e., the ontological commitments of the claims in CG[42]

(viii) QUD: the set of *questions under discussion* at t; i.e., a subset of $Q \cap Acc$ such that for all $q \in QUD$, CG does not entail an answer to q and the goal of answering q is a common goal.

On Roberts's model, the conversational score is updated in the following ways:

(i) Assertion: if an assertion is accepted by all the interlocutors, then the proposition asserted is added to CG.

(ii) Question: if a question is accepted by all the interlocutors, then the set of propositions associated with the question is added to QUD. A question is removed from QUD iff either its answer is entailed by CG or it is determined to be unanswerable.

(iii) Request: if a request is accepted by an interlocutor, i, then the goal associated with the request is added to G_i, and the proposition that i intends to comply with the request is added to CG.

One nice aspect of Roberts's model is that it relates the conversational score back to Grice's original insight that participating in a conversation is a rational enterprise—each participant has certain beliefs and desires, and each participant engages in the conversation to rationally further her ends. The common goals of the conversation and the question under discussion are meant to help explain why the participants are engaging in a conversation at all, and why they pursue their own particular strategies in the conversation. These structures also allow Roberts's model to explain the pragmatic significance of questions and commands. Roberts's model is relatively new, but she uses it to explain recalcitrant data pertaining to demonstratives, anaphora, definite descriptions, ellipsis, and prosody.[43]

To illustrate, assume that Moe takes a principle p to be constitutive of some concept c expressed by a word w. How can we explain this in scorekeeping terms? I think the best way to do that is to say that Moe has adopted a scorekeeping commitment—that is, he has committed himself to keeping score on other rational entities that use w in a certain way. This is a practical commitment—a commitment to follow certain courses of action in certain circumstances. In particular, Moe is committed to using acceptance of p as a test for whether he and his interlocutor mean the same thing by w. As Moe keeps score in a conversation, he uses his scorekeeping commitment in several different ways. First, he

[42] This element plays a role in modeling anaphora.

[43] See Roberts (1996, 1998, 2002, 2003, 2004, 2005, 2010).

will initially refuse to accept an assertion if he perceives it to conflict with the acceptance of p. That is, he will not add a proposition to the common ground if it is inconsistent with p. Second, he will initially refuse to accept a question if he perceives it to conflict with the acceptance of p. That is, he will not add a question to the questions under discussion if that question presupposes the negation of p. Third, he will initially refuse to accept a request if he perceives it to conflict with the acceptance of p. That is, he will not add a goal to the common goals if the request for that goal presupposes the negation of p. Moe's refusal to engage in these scorekeeping activities can be overridden if the interlocutor in question makes a good case for rejecting p. Here, the strength of Moe's commitment will probably play a role. That is, scorekeeping commitments, like other kinds of commitments, are held to different degrees. If Moe strongly holds that p is constitutive of w, then it will take more convincing to get him to play along and keep score in accordance with the interlocutor's moves. A weakly held constitutive principle might be given up without any convincing or even any protest by Moe. Of course, how strongly Moe holds a constitutivity claim will depend on his interests, which are represented as his goals in the conversation. If he really wants to achieve some goal that is at stake in the conversation, he might be more willing to acquiesce to an interlocutor who uses w but denies p. Below, I flesh out this talk of how strongly or weakly a constitutive principle is held.

The key idea is that when Moe participates in a conversation, he keeps score *transparently*—without consciously thinking about the meanings of the words used by himself or his interlocutors. If he perceives a violation of a constitutive principle, then his transparent scorekeeping is interrupted and he thinks explicitly about what his interlocutor(s) mean by a certain word. That is what I mean by saying that violating a constitutive principle is an "interpretative red flag." He might ask the person in question about the word and what the person means by it. They might even engage in a debate about what the word means or consult a dictionary as long as both of them are willing to defer to this sort of authority.

2.5 Competence and constitutive principles

In this last section, we need to be a bit more careful about the distinction between a *proposition* constitutive for a *concept* and a *sentence* being constitutive for a *word*. So far I have used the neutral term 'principle' to cover both cases.[44] However, there is a significant difference between possessing a concept and being competent with a word. As such, we can reformulate (8) from above as two claims:

(9a) A subject s possesses concept c iff s is quasi-entitled to the constitutive propositions for c.

(9b) A subject s is competent with a word w iff s is quasi-entitled to the constitutive sentences for w.

[44] I do not want to rule out constitutive inferences or constitutive abilities, but I do not focus on them in what follows.

I am thinking of concepts as constituents of propositions and words as constituents of sentences. There is, of course, a tight connection between them:

(10a) If a proposition p is constitutive of a concept c, and a sentence s expresses p and a word w (which is a constituent of s) expresses w, then s is constitutive for w.

(10b) If a sentence s is constitutive of a word w, and s expresses a proposition p and w expresses a concept c, then p is constitutive for c.

Here we encounter a problem. (9a) and (9b) are not very helpful for deciding whether a person possesses a concept or is competent with a word. For the most part, we reason in the left-to-right direction of these biconditionals. How, then do we decide whether a person possesses a concept or is competent with a word?

Two features of the account emphasized so far exacerbate the problem. First, there is no particular proposition one must believe in order to possess a certain concept, and there is no particular sentence one must hold true in order to be competent with a certain word. It seems to me that for any concept (word) and any proposition (sentence), one can always come up with examples where a person obviously possesses the concept (is competent with the word) even though that person rejects the proposition (does not hold true the sentence). Williamson in particular has argued (persuasively in my view) that "No given argument or statement is immune from rejection by a linguistically competent speaker."[45] The account of constitutivity I endorse is compatible with this point.

When a speaker rejects what a hearer takes to be a constitutive principle, the hearer need not conclude that the speaker is not competent with the word in question. A hearer will consider: (i) the speaker's recognition that the principle is taken to be constitutive for the concept in question by other members of the community, (ii) the speaker's reasons for either saying that the principle is not constitutive for that concept or saying that the concept is legitimate, (iii) the speaker's recognition that the concept is taken to be legitimate by other members of the community, and (iv) the speaker's recognition that the word in question is taken to express the concept in question by other members of the community. If any of these fail, chances are that the hearer will conclude that the speaker is not competent with the word in question or the concept in question or both.

Second, in my reply to Fine and Earman above, I argued that if one is competent with a word (possesses a concept) then there are some constitutive sentences containing that word (propositions with that concept as a constituent) that one holds true (accepts). I think this principle holds in general even for defective concepts like truth and mass. For example, (other things being equal) someone competent with 'mass' should hold true the sentence 'if Newtonian mechanics were true, then mass would be identical to momentum over velocity'. This point follows from concept pragmatism—if an agent possesses a concept (is competent with a word), then there is something the agent accepts or knows how to do that is somehow associated with that concept. Whatever these turn

[45] Williamson (2008: 97); see the examples of Peter and Stephen in Williamson (2008: 85–98).

out to be, some of them will be constitutive. We certainly make judgments that a particular person is not competent with a word (does not possess a concept) and we do it based solely on evidence from conversations with the person in question. My claim is that whatever such a person fails to do can be construed as not accepting enough constitutive principles for the concept (word) in question.

Putting these two points together, someone who possesses a given concept (is competent with a given word) accepts some of its constitutive propositions (sentences), but need not accept any particular one of its constitutive propositions (sentences). It would be helpful to be able to model these messy features of our discursive practice so that we could have a more substantive answer to the question of when a person possesses a concept (is competent with a word) that invokes acceptance of constitutive principles.

Let us return to Moe. I suggest that for each word Moe understands (concept he possesses), there is a set of sentences (propositions) he takes to be constitutive for that word (concept) and, for each principle in that set, Moe holds that it is constitutive of the word (concept) in question to a certain degree that we might represent as a subjective probability. Call this the *constitutivity credence*. This is not the subjective probability Moe attaches to a principle, but rather the subjective probability he attaches to the claim that that principle is constitutive of the word (concept) in question. Of course, Moe might not have any credences for such claims; in that case, we would have to work out his constitutive credences by considering how he keeps score on others in conversation. In addition, for each word (concept), there is a certain *constitutivity threshold*. For a given word, w, if the sum of the constitutivity credences for sentences taken to be constitutive for w by Moe that are rejected by one of his interlocutors is greater than the constitutivity threshold for w, then Moe takes the interlocutor's word to mean something else or nothing at all (the same holds for concepts). An interlocutor rejecting any principle Moe takes to be constitutive of some word (concept) jumps Moe from the transparent mode of scorekeeping into what we might call the semantic mode, where he tries to determine whether the interlocutor means the same thing as he does by the word in question. Depending on his interests, he might: (i) initiate a conversation to investigate the matter, (ii) keep quiet and gather more evidence by continuing the conversation, or (iii) let it pass without comment if he does not care enough to figure it out. The fact that an interlocutor uses a given word at all is some evidence that he or she is competent with that word and possesses the concept conventionally associated with it. I take it that Moe, like most of us, treats his interlocutors as competent with the words they use until countervailing evidence overturns his assumption.

Different subjects might assign different values to principles for concept/word pairs. Of course, getting with the herd on this matter facilitates communication and so is pragmatically beneficial. The same goes for thresholds. Speakers might disagree about which principles are constitutive for which words/concepts. In fact, it seems to me that many philosophical disagreements take this form. One might think that it is unrealistic to think that speakers keep track of constitutivity credences and thresholds, but I think it is not too hard to come up with examples. If Karl knows that Maude takes 'marriage is between a man and a woman' to be constitutive for 'marriage', then Karl can predict that she will balk when John says that his friend who is a woman got married to another woman.

There is, of course, much more that could be said about this account of constitutive principles, but this should do for my purposes. This model is intended to be descriptive—we behave as if we use constitutivity credences and constitutivity thresholds. The point of the theory in this context is to serve as background for a theory of inconsistent concepts in general and for an inconsistency approach to the aletheic paradoxes in particular.

To illustrate the efficacy of this theory of constitutivity, consider an objection to the epistemic view of the relation between concept possessors and constitutive principles from Alexis Burgess:

> The main problem with this suggestion, it seems to me, is that it fails to capture the sense in which the T schema commands our assent. In particular, it fails to accommodate the fact that we often continue to be vexed by the liar paradox even after we've agreed that some offending instance of the T schema can't be true. . . . Even after we've agreed that some offending instance of the T schema can't be true, the "pull" of the paradox may persist unabated. We may still feel committed to the offending instance in virtue of our semantic competence with the truth predicate.[46]

With the above account of constitutivity, we have the resources to reply to this objection. If one found oneself thinking that truth is an inconsistent concept, that the instances of T-schema for paradoxical sentences are constitutive but false, and one still felt compelled to accept them by virtue of one's competence with the truth predicate, then my diagnosis would be that one's constitutivity credence for the T-schema (or the offending instances of it) is set too high given one's threshold for 'true'. As a person in this situation interprets herself, she takes all the instances of the T-schema to be constitutive for 'true', but she rejects some of them, and the sum of the constitutivity credences she assigns to the rejected instances surpasses the constitutivity threshold she has adopted for 'true'. As a result she feels compelled to either accept the instances of the T-schema or treat herself as incompetent with 'true'. What has happened is that she has found a problem with her scorekeeping commitments. The solution is to either lower her constitutivity credence for the instances of the T-schema in question or raise her constitutivity threshold for 'true'. Because scorekeeping commitments are just practical commitments, this is a practical dilemma where she has committed herself to incompatible courses of action. The solution is to stop doing that, or to behave in such a way as to minimize the likelihood of that happening. I am not assuming that these kinds of changes are easy to institute or that they take effect immediately, but with some practice one can get the hang of changing one's scorekeeping habits.

[46] A. Burgess (2006: 7–8).

3

The Obvious Argument

In the previous chapter, I introduced inconsistent concepts. In this one, I argue that truth is an inconsistent concept. This chapter contains one argument, which I dub the *obvious argument* because it is the standard type of reasoning one gives for the claim that a concept is inconsistent—for example, it is analogous to the arguments found in the last chapter concerning 'rable' and the like. The next chapter contains several other arguments that depend on the revenge paradox phenomenon.

One might expect to find in these chapters a straightforward argument to the effect that an inconsistency view is better than all its rivals. However, it is rather difficult to make explicit the standards for what counts as a better view. Moreover, *any* approach to the aletheic paradoxes is going to be *bad* in the sense that it requires that we give up some of our well-entrenched beliefs. An honest thinker will echo Winston Churchill by admitting that his or her favored approach is the worst approach to the aletheic paradoxes, except for all the others that have been tried from time to time. So the best one could do is give a straightforward argument that the inconsistency approach is the least bad of the alternatives, and that is probably not going to be very convincing at all. Instead, I prefer less literature-driven arguments, to which I now turn.

The most intuitive argument for the claim that truth is an inconsistent concept is that (T-In) and (T-Out) are constitutive of truth, and the liar paradox shows them to be inconsistent as long as we can reason classically and formulate liar sentences (which requires only arithmetic). That is exactly the kind of argument used to show that 'rable', 'mass', and 'up above' are inconsistent. Of course, every approach to the liar paradox except those in the inconsistency category is designed to avoid this very argument. So, let us consider how plausible these moves are.

3.1 Monsters

First, one might attempt a monster-barring strategy. Let us look at a couple of examples.

Laurence Goldstein has long endorsed a monster-barring approach. In a recent paper on this topic, Goldstein (2009), he insists that statements are the only truth-bearers, and that sentences can be used to make statements, but sentences are not the right kind of thing to be true or false. He provides no evidence for this view, and rests his case entirely on an appeal to Strawson's authority.[1] However, people frequently attribute truth to sentences regardless of how those sentences are used. For example, many linguists and philosophers of language care about the semantic features of *sentences* belonging to a particular language and not just the ones that happen to be used. Instead, they are after a compositional theory of meaning (e.g., truth conditions in one of the most familiar and widely used theories) for all the syntactically well-formed sentences of a language. That theory might require specifying the kinds of information from a context of utterance that would be relevant to determining a proposition expressed on an occasion of use (which is what Goldstein means by 'statement'). But there is no sense in which semanticists only care about sentences that actually happen to get used. Indeed, one of the dominant traditions in semantics presupposes that sentences of particular languages have truth conditions—conditions under which they are true or false. Thus, if we take the science of linguistics seriously (and in the Chapter 4, I argue that we should), then we should admit that sentences can be true or false.

Still, let us see Goldstein's view. The basic idea is that paradoxical sentences cannot be used to make statements, and so are neither true nor false. He writes:

> Trying to reveal, by giving truth conditions, the identity of a statement made by the use of [(TT), which is '(TT) is true'] results only in the unrevealing '(TT) is true iff (TT) is true'. Similarly, the attempt to identify what statement is made by the use of (L´) [i.e., '(L´) is false'] by specifying its truth conditions results only in '(L´) is true iff ~(L´) is true'. Both of these biconditionals are uninformative, so no statements are identified by them and it remains in doubt whether there are any statements made by the use of (TT) or (L´).[2]

It is hard imagine that Goldstein really advocates something like this because informativeness is clearly relative to an agent. What is informative to one person might not be informative to another. For example, someone who understands English and is competent with all the relevant English expressions will find the T-sentence ''snow is white' is true iff snow is white' uninformative. Should we conclude that an utterance of 'snow is white' fails to make a statement? Of course not.

We do get some additional discussion of this issue when Goldstein considers whether a paradoxical statement results if we let 'S' be the name of the statement that S is not true. Goldstein writes,

> *That S is not true* has a truth-value different from that of S. Hence 'S' cannot be the name of the statement that S is not true. So the stipulation was unsuccessful. Since the choice of the name 'S' was arbitrary—any letter could have been used—the conclusion, stated in full generality, is that there can be no statement that says of itself that it is not true.[3]

[1] Goldstein (2009: 382).
[2] Goldstein (2009: 383).
[3] Goldstein (2009: 385).

The problem is in the first sentence. To conclude that S and the statement that S is not true have different truth values, one must appeal to the biconditional 'S is true iff S is not true'. But this biconditional is a classical contradiction—from it we can conclude anything, even that S and the statement that S is not true have the same truth value. No one should rely on what can be derived from an obviously inconsistent claim.

A consequence of Goldstein's approach is that contradictions cannot make statements and so are neither true nor false. His reason is that since nothing can satisfy inconsistent conditions, contradictions are not about anything. Thus, they cannot make statements. For example, the sentence 'grass is green and grass is not green' is, despite appearances, not about grass because nothing could be both green and not green.[4] The obvious objection is that given the meanings of the expressions in these sentences and standard principles of compositionality, these sentences are false. Goldstein's reply: "But just consider how we should judge someone who persists in uttering 'Grass is green and grass is not green' and other such contradictions. His problem is far graver than perceptual error. He has completely lost the plot. He takes away with one hand what he gives with the other and so neither gives nor takes anything."[5] It is hard to know how to respond to these considerations, which are a good example of the kind of reasoning that one finds throughout Goldstein's writings about the aletheic paradoxes. I will say that I do not find them the least bit convincing (and I hope the reader does not either), especially since they purport to refute one of the most successful programs in the scientific study of natural language (i.e., truth-conditional semantics). For this reason and those given above, I do not see any hope for a view like Goldstein's.

Another recent monster-barring approach, by Bradley Armour-Garb and James Woodbridge, takes paradoxical sentences to be meaningless.[6] Armour-Garb and Woodbridge distinguish between two different kinds of understanding to forestall the objection that we clearly understand many paradoxical sentences. For example, the predicate 'is a complete sentence in section 3.1 of Scharp's *Replacing Truth* whose first letter is an 'E' ', can be used to construct a version of the liar paradox.

(E) Every complete sentence in section 3.1 of Scharp's *Replacing Truth* whose first letter is an 'E' is false.

The fact that the previous sentence is the only complete sentence in this section to begin with an 'E' is a contingent fact about that sentence. If I had chosen to place it in a different section or if I had included some other sentences in this section, then it might not have uniquely satisfied that empirical predicate and, thus, it would not have been paradoxical. Nevertheless, it does not seem like one would have to know the first letter

[4] Goldstein (2001: 120).

[5] Goldstein (2001: 120).

[6] Armour-Garb and Woodbridge (forthcoming). Their view is meant to dovetail with their particular version of deflationism, but they are clear that it could be accepted by anyone who shares their views on meaning.

of every complete sentence in this section before one could know the syntactic, semantic, pragmatic, and inferential properties of an utterance of (E).[7]

Armour-Garb and Woodbridge claim that we understand (E) in one sense but in another sense we do not understand it. They liken this distinction to the character/content distinction in semantics.[8] The *character* of a sentence containing an indexical expression like 'I am an atheist' is invariant, but its *content* varies depending who utters the sentence. If someone just reads or hears the sentence without knowing who produced it, then that person understands the sentence in the sense of knowing its character but not its content. However, someone who knows that Kevin Scharp produced it understands the sentence in the stronger sense of knowing its content. Armour-Garb and Woodbridge are careful to say that the case of indexicals is simply meant to illustrate that there are different kinds of understanding—they do not claim that these two kinds of understanding are the ones relevant to their approach to the aletheic paradoxes. Instead they claim, "There is an important sense of content that a sentence can have that involves the sentence specifying conditions that can obtain or not. We call such conditions, M-conditions."[9] They are clear that M-conditions are not truth conditions, but instead are more basic than truth conditions. If a person knows the logical form of a sentence and the meanings of all its constituent expressions, then that person understands it in the weak sense (understanding$_2$). A person understands a sentence in the strong sense (i.e., understanding$_1$) if that person knows its M-conditions. Associated with the two kinds of understanding are two kinds of meaningfulness as well.

The central claim of their view is, "it turns out that any M-conditions specified by an instance of truth-talk must be a function of conditions specified by the supposed content-vehicle that is putatively denoted in that instance of truth-talk."[10] The idea is that any sentence containing 'true' acquires its content (or M-conditions) from the contents of the sentences referred to or quantified over by expressions in that sentence. For example, ' 'grass is green' is true' inherits its M-conditions from those of 'grass is green'. For Armour-Garb and Woodbridge, when we try to figure out the M-conditions for a liar sentence, we end up being led right back to that very sentence. Thus, "the process repeats and repeats without ever grounding out."[11] Although they do not quite put it this way, they are endorsing the claim that only grounded[12] sentences can be understood$_1$ (and thus are meaningful$_1$), whereas ungrounded sentences can be merely understood$_2$ (and

[7] Did you look at every sentence in this section to confirm? If so then you now have a great example of knowing the syntactic, semantic, pragmatic, and inferential features of a sentence without knowing whether it is paradoxical. Think for a moment how bizarre it would be to say that while you were perusing the other sentences of this section looking for 'E's, you were learning about that sentence's syntactic, semantic, pragmatic, or inferential properties.

[8] See Kaplan (1989) and Ch. 8.

[9] Armour-Garb and Woodbridge (forthcoming: §1).

[10] Armour-Garb and Woodbridge (forthcoming: §1).

[11] Armour-Garb and Woodbridge (forthcoming: §1).

[12] Following Kripke (1975), by 'grounded' I mean the sentences whose truth values are determined by the truth values of the sentences not containing occurrences of the truth predicate (i.e., those that have a truth value in the minimal fixed point).

are merely meaningful$_2$). This view is not new,[13] but Armour-Garb and Woodbridge give it a different twist with the distinction between kinds of understanding and meaning.

The major problem with their view is the distinction between two kinds of meaning and two kinds of understanding. These are just made up by Armour-Garb and Woodbridge and have no basis in any theory of meaning or understanding.[14] It also has no empirical support whatsoever. Imagine putting sentence (E) in a different section. According to them it would go from merely having meaning$_2$ to having meaning$_1$. But there would be no discernible difference in our understanding of it. Moreover, standard theories of meaning advocated and applied by linguists and philosophers of language admit of no such distinction.[15] In addition, there is no reason to think that truth predicates are subject to the restrictions Armour-Garb and Woodbridge advocate. There are many ungrounded but non-paradoxical sentences (e.g., 'no sentence is both true and false'). If Armour-Garb and Woodbridge were right, then these would have no meaning$_1$. It follows from their view that "they do not have anything, by way of content, that one can accept or affirm."[16] If they were right, then the entire debate over bivalence, dialetheism, and many other views in philosophical logic and the philosophy of language would be illusory—there would be nothing for the participants in these debates to accept, reject, defend, or attack. Finally, because participants in conversations often do not have access to what Armour-Garb and Woodbridge call the M-conditions of sentences containing 'true', all the action is with meaning$_2$. That is what participants in conversations grasp and use to update the conversational score and the common ground. That is what they use to identify entailments, presuppositions, and implicatures of sentences uttered. That is what people accept or reject, believe or disbelieve. Accordingly, meaning$_2$ is what semantic theories and pragmatic theories target. Thus, even if we set aside the fact that the distinction Armour-Garb and Woodbridge draw is totally unmotivated and empirically unsupported, it would not do the kind of work they want it to do.

In sum, monster-barring approaches have an undeniable appeal—if one were successful, then it would easily put an end to all the complex and difficult work involved in specifying a logic and a semantics for natural-language truth predicates. However, a successful monster-barring strategy cannot be just a made-up condition on meaningfulness or expressing a proposition or making a statement (or whatever) that paradoxical sentences fail to meet. One has to motivate it—show that sentences that meet it are intuitively meaningful (or whatever) and sentences that do not meet it (other than the paradoxical ones) are intuitively meaningless.[17] Moreover, simply saying that paradoxical sentences lead to paradoxes is not a legitimate justification—the fact that they have been thought to be paradoxical is actually evidence that they *are* grammatical, contentful, assertible, and supposable. Otherwise, no one would think they pose any kind of problem.

[13] Grover (1976, 1977) and Brandom (1994) advocate this view; see Scharp (2009b) and Brandom (2009b) for discussion.

[14] I am talking about the distinction between knowing a sentence's M-conditions (understanding$_1$) and knowing the logical form and meanings of its constituents (understanding$_2$), *not* about the distinction between character and content.

[15] See Chierchia and McConnell-Ginet (2000) for a survey.

[16] Armour-Garb and Woodbridge (forthcoming: §6).

[17] Weir (2000) makes this point well.

Unfortunately, there is no such condition. There are, of course, plenty of theories of grammar, meaning, assertion, and inference, but I am not unaware of any that justify a monster-barring approach. One would need, for example, an independently motivated theory of meaning that entails that some sentences are rendered meaningless by seemingly inconsequential empirical facts, like the placement of sentence (E) in this book. Because this claim is so implausible, I doubt that any such theory could be empirically motivated. In addition, any successful monster-barring strategy would need to give an account of something like the syntax, semantics, pragmatics, and inferential role for the things that *fail* to meet the condition, given that they are bandied about in a way that calls for theories of these features. That is, people treat these sentences as if they are grammatical, meaningful, assertible, and supposable. The claim that they are meaningful, for example, explains many things about how humans interact with them. We certainly utter these sorts of sentences and take them to have contents, express propositions, and so on. We take them to have inferential roles. We take one another to have propositional attitudes with these contents. We figure out what we take to be their meanings by considering the meanings of their constituents, and we figure out what we take to be the meanings of compounds containing them by considering what we take to be their meanings. A proponent of a monster-barring approach would need to find some way of explaining all these things that is just as good (if not better) than our current explanations.[18] So far, nothing like this has emerged. I take these reasons to be conclusive against these approaches, and I do not consider them again.

3.2 In and out

The second way of avoiding the obvious argument is to deny that (T-In) and (T-Out) are constitutive of truth predicates. But think how odd it would be to participate in a conversation where an interlocutor asserts that some declarative sentence is true but also asserts the negation of that sentence (or asserts a sentence and that it is not true). It would be hard to know how to interpret such an utterance. Indeed, one might wonder whether one had heard the person properly. At a bare minimum, experiencing something like this should make one question whether the interlocutor means what we mean by 'true'. And that is exactly what it takes for a principle to count as constitutive on the account given in Chapter 2.

One might protest: many philosophers (e.g., expressivists) are willing to assert sentences like 'murder is wrong' together with ''murder is wrong' is not true', but surely they count as competent users of the word 'true' with its standard meaning. Fair enough, I am not claiming that denying one of truth's constitutive principles is tantamount to using 'true' with a non-standard meaning. However, I am saying that this would be prima facie evidence of a non-standard meaning. In the case of the moral expressivist, one's concerns about mutual understanding would be put to rest after a conversation about the truth aptness of sentences containing moral terms. Remember, I do not think that accepting all

[18] See Field (2008a: 12–13) for similar considerations.

truth's constitutive principles is a necessary condition for possessing the concept of truth or for being a competent user of a truth predicate. So the fact that moral expressivists reject one of truth's constitutive principles (i.e., (T-In)) does not show that (T-In) is not constitutive of 'true'. Moreover, expressivism is limited to non-factualist discourses—those that are taken by expressivists to be non-representational. In order to avoid the claim that (T-In) is constitutive of truth over the class of sentences that includes the liar, one would have to be a non-factualist about truth itself (or logical notions I suppose). To be sure, some philosophers embrace non-factualism about truth claims, but these are deflationist theories, which are characterized by acceptance of the T-schema (see section 1.1 for discussion). Aletheic non-factualists do not reject (T-In) or (T-Out). Indeed, they make these two principles the centerpiece of their theories of truth. Therefore, although some brands of expressivism reject (T-In) for certain discourses, there is no reason to think that expressivism will serve as part of an approach to the aletheic paradoxes that rejects (T-In) or (T-Out). Moreover, there is no reason to think that expressivism undermines the claim that (T-In) is constitutive of truth over a certain class of sentences that includes the paradoxical ones.

3.2.1 Truth's expressive role

In addition to the fact that denying (T-In) or (T-Out) is an interpretive red flag, there is another reason to think that they are constitutive of truth; namely, that truth predicates play several important roles in our linguistic practices and these roles depend on truth predicates obeying (T-In) and (T-Out). It is widely accepted that we use 'true' to endorse propositions that we cannot assert directly; for example, Ralph can assert 'the Riemann hypothesis is true' and thereby endorse the Riemann hypothesis even though he does not remember or has never learned which sentence expresses it, or he can assert 'all the axioms of ZFC are true' and thereby endorse all the axioms of ZFC even though there are too many for him to assert one by one. We can capture this role by saying that a truth predicate functions as *a device of endorsement*. The flip side of this role is *a device of rejection*; Ralph can say 'the continuum hypothesis is not true' and thereby reject the continuum hypothesis. In order to serve as a device of endorsement, (for a certain class of sentences) the truth predicate must obey (T-Out) (over those sentences), and in order to serve as a device of rejection (for a class of sentences), the truth predicate must obey (T-In) (over those sentences).

Everyone in the debate about the nature of truth agrees that we use truth as a device of endorsement and as a device of rejection. Deflationists think that these exhaust the role truth plays in our linguistic practice, while inflationists think that there is something more substantial to say about truth that explains why it plays these roles. However, no one I know of denies that we use truth predicates for these purposes. Even someone like Mark Richard, who thinks that we should not use truth in these ways for certain claims does not deny that we currently use it like this. Richard writes: "I agree that we typically use the idiom of truth when we blindly agree or disagree. That's the way we talk."[19] He even acknowledges that "linguistic competence requires only that I be aware of the fact

[19] Richard (2008: 6).

that people expect one another to be disposed to use the truth predicate as if it were such a device."[20] Thus, even Richard admits that not only do we use truth as a device of endorsement and rejection, but also that our very competence with the truth predicate requires that we acknowledge that it is used in such a way. That is an admission that (T-In) and (T-Out) are constitutive (in my sense).

3.2.2 Kripke's objections to the orthodox approach

The fact that truth serves as a device of endorsement and rejection is more difficult to accommodate than one might imagine, especially when paired with contingent paradoxicality (i.e., that some sentences are paradoxical in virtue of unrelated contingent facts). Kripke demonstrates the power of these considerations in a couple of highly influential objections to the orthodox approach to the aletheic paradoxes. The orthodox approach specifies a hierarchy of type-restricted truth predicates defined using Tarski's methods and it implies that natural-language truth predicates are ambiguous—they can be synonymous with any of the predicates in the hierarchy. According to the orthodox approach, when a speaker utters a sentence containing a natural-language truth predicate, the speaker must determine which concept of truth from the hierarchy is to be expressed. In the following passage, Kripke describes how each truth predicate in the hierarchy is associated with sentences of a particular level:

> The notion of differing truth predicates, each with its own level, seems to correspond to the following intuitive idea... First, we make various utterances, such as 'snow is white', which do not involve the notion of truth. We then attribute truth values to these, using a predicate 'true_1'. ('True_1' means—roughly—"is a true statement not itself involving truth or allied notions.") We can then form a predicate 'true_2' applying to sentences involving 'true_1', and so on.[21]

Since it is customary to distinguish the predicates in the hierarchy offered by the orthodox approach by using subscripts (e.g., 'true_1'), Kripke sometimes talks about speakers *attaching* subscripts to natural-language truth predicates—all that this means is that the speaker intends the truth predicate for natural language to express a particular one of the concepts in the hierarchy.

The following is a portion of Kripke's remarks on the orthodox approach:

> If someone makes such an utterance as (1), he does *not* attach a subscript, explicit or implicit, to his utterance of 'false', which determines the "level of language" on which he speaks. An implicit subscript would cause no trouble if we were sure of the "level" of *Nixon's* utterances; we could then cover them all, in the utterance of (1) or even of the stronger
>
> (4) All of Nixon's utterances about Watergate are false.
>
> simply by choosing a subscript higher than the levels of any involved in Nixon's Watergate-related utterances. Ordinarily, however, a speaker *has no way of knowing the "levels" of Nixon's*

[20] Richard (2008: 5).

[21] Kripke (1975: 695). Presumably, if a sentence in class C is false, then 'all sentences in class C are true' has level n where n-1 is the highest level of a false sentence in C.

relevant utterances. Thus Nixon may have said, "Dean is a liar," or "Haldeman told the truth when he said that Dean lied," etc., and the "levels" of these may yet depend on the levels of Dean's utterances, and so on. If the speaker is forced to assign a "level" to (4) in advance [or to the word 'false' in (4)], he may be unsure how high a level to choose; if, in ignorance of the "level" of Nixon's utterances, he chooses too low, his utterance of (4) will fail of its purpose. The idea that a statement such as (4) should, in its normal uses, have a "level" is intuitively convincing. It is, however, equally intuitively obvious that the "level" of (4) should not depend on the form of (4) alone (as would be the case if 'false'—or, perhaps, 'utterances'—were assigned explicit subscripts), nor should it be assigned in advance by the speaker, but rather its level should depend on the empirical facts about what Nixon has uttered.[22]

This is Kripke's first objection and it contributed substantially to the decline in popularity of the orthodox approach to the liar. However, the criticism is not exactly clear; I present my preferred reading of it below. Here is the second objection:

Another situation is even harder to accommodate within the confines of the orthodox approach. Suppose Dean asserts (4), while Nixon in turn asserts

(5) Everything Dean says about Watergate is false.

Dean, in asserting the sweeping (4), wishes to include Nixon's assertion (5) within its scope (as one of the Nixonian assertions about Watergate which is said to be false); and Nixon, in asserting (5), wishes to do the same with Dean's (4). Now on any theory that assigns intrinsic "levels" to such statements, so that a statement of a given level can speak only of the truth or falsity of statements of lower levels, it is plainly impossible for both to succeed: if the two statements are on the same level, neither can talk about the truth or falsity of the other, while otherwise the higher can talk about the lower, but not conversely. Yet intuitively, we can often assign unambiguous truth values to (4) and (5). Suppose Dean has made at least one true statement about Watergate [other than (4)]. Then, independently of any assessment of (4), we can decide that Nixon's (5) is false. If all Nixon's other assertions about Watergate are false as well, Dean's (4) is true; if one of them is true, (4) is false. Note that in the latter case, we could have judged (4) to be false without assessing (5), but in the former case the assessment of (4) as true depended on a *prior* assessment of (5) as false. Under a different set of empirical assumptions about the veracity of Nixon and Dean, (5) would be true [and its assessment as true would depend on a prior assessment of (4) as false]. It seems difficult to accommodate these intuitions within the confines of the orthodox approach.[23]

There are several other objections in Kripke's paper as well, but they do not pertain to contingent paradoxicality.

The second objection is the easier of the two to interpret. To do so, one needs an account of falsity by default. A sentence that attributes truth_i or falsity_i to a sentence whose level is greater than or equal to i is *false by default*. It is possible that neither (4) nor (5) is false by default (indeed, Kripke describes situations in which this occurs). However, on the orthodox approach, one of them is false by default. If, for some i, (4) is true_i, then (4) attributes falsity_{i-1} to its targets. (5) is among (4)'s targets. Thus, (5) must have

[22] Kripke (1975: 695–6); bracketed text is in the original.
[23] Kripke (1975: 696–7).

level j where j < i. Of course, (4) is among the targets of (5). So, (5) is a level j sentence that attributes falsity$_{j-1}$ to a sentence whose level is greater than j. Therefore (5) is false by default. Similar reasoning holds for the other direction. Therefore, the orthodox approach implies that either (4) and (5) is false by default, but there are situations in which neither one is false by default.

Notice that this point does not seem to have anything to do with the speaker having to pick a particular concept from the hierarchy in advance. Indeed, we could augment the orthodox approach by saying that the level of a truth predicate contained in a truth attribution is determined not by the intentions of the speaker, but rather by the levels of its targets, so that, if the highest level of a target of a truth attribution is i, then the truth predicate in that attribution has level i+1. This change would not avoid the second objection.

Kripke's first objection is subtler. The problem here is no mere technical glitch. Instead, Kripke points out that we frequently attribute truth to truth-bearers without knowing the levels of those truth-bearers, and although it is perfectly legitimate for speakers to use truth predicates in this way, this fact is incompatible with the orthodox approach. The reason we frequently do not know the levels of the targets when making truth attributions is that the level of a target cannot always be determined by its syntactic or semantic properties, and even these are often unknown when truth is used in its expressive role. The point Kripke makes in this first objection is a combination of truth's expressive role and the phenomenon at the root of contingent paradoxicality. That is, contingent paradoxicality is a special case of a more general phenomenon: the level of a sentence can depend on just about any fact, and so is often not determined by the sentence's syntactic or semantic features. We might call this phenomenon *contingent level-determination*. In many circumstances, speakers have no idea about the levels of the sentences to which they are attributing truth, so they cannot be expected to pick a concept from the hierarchy offered by the orthodox approach. There are plenty of cases where it is permissible for a speaker to assert a truth attribution even though she does not know the levels of its targets. Thus, if the orthodox approach were correct, then it would prohibit these uses of the truth predicate and, consequently, seriously limit truth's expressive role.

One might attempt to rescue the orthodox approach by stipulating that the subscript of the natural-language truth predicate on an occasion of use is determined not by the intentions of the speaker (since the speaker often does not know which subscript to choose), but instead by the levels of the targets in question. That is, when a speaker asserts a truth attribution, the truth predicate automatically gets a subscript that is one greater than the highest level of its targets. Why does Kripke assume that this is impossible? Something is missing in his objection.

3.2.3 Content determination

The missing element in Kripke's first objection is a condition on how content is determined for ambiguous expressions (it applies to indexicals as well). I pause here to formulate the condition. Note that these considerations play a significant role not just in this chapter, but also in the rest of the book.

Recall the discussion of Lewis and Roberts on scorekeeping from Chapter 2. They each use the idea of a common ground of a conversation, which is due to Robert Stalnaker. The main idea is that when a speaker makes an assertion in a conversation, the content of the sentence asserted furthers the conversation in a certain way. In particular, the content rules out ways the world might be that were previously live options in the conversation. If the content asserted is accepted by everyone in the conversation, then the potential ways the world might be have been narrowed, and that is one of the central goals of conversation.[24]

To model this idea, assume that we have a conversation consisting of several people. Each person has many beliefs. Stalnaker defines a participant's *presupposition* as a purportedly shared belief in the conversation. It requires that the participant believes it, the participant believes that everyone else believes it, the participant believes that everyone else believes that everyone else believes it, and so on. Since beliefs are often taken to be attitudes toward propositions, and propositions are often taken to determine a set of possible worlds in which they are true, we can simplify matters by talking about propositions. A participant's presupposition will divide the class of possible worlds into two—those in which the presupposed proposition is true, and the rest. If a participant's presupposition is also a presupposition of all the other participants, then it is a *shared presupposition*. The set of shared presuppositions is called the *common ground*—it is what everyone in the conversation agrees on, agrees they agree on, and so on. The crucial notion for Stalnaker's view is the set of possible worlds in which all the propositions in the common ground are true; call this the *context set*. As the conversation develops, the common ground expands and the context set shrinks. When a participant in the conversation makes an assertion, the proposition asserted should not be entailed by the common ground; that is, it should be false in some worlds in the context set prior to the assertion.[25] That way, if everyone in the conversation accepts the assertion, it narrows the context set. Stalnaker's model of conversation has been extremely influential, and offers a powerful explanation for a variety of pragmatic phenomena.

In the following passage, Stalnaker appeals to his views on conversational contexts to formulate a condition on content determination:

> It is a substantive claim that the information relevant to determining the content of context-dependent speech acts is presumed to be available to the participants of a conversation—that it is included in the presuppositions of the context—but it is a claim that is motivated by natural assumptions about the kind of action one performs in speaking. It is not unreasonable to suppose that speakers, in speaking, are normally aiming to communicate—at least to have the addressees understand what is being said. Succeeding in this aim requires that the information relevant to determining content be available to the addressee.[26]

[24] See Stalnaker (1970, 1973, 1974, 1978, 1998, 2002, 2004, 2009).

[25] Obviously, this feature of Stalnaker's model is an idealization since it would rule out asserting necessary propositions (e.g., in mathematical conversations).

[26] Stalnaker (1999: 6).

Here Stalnaker claims that the information needed to determine the content of an expression (together with the character assigned to it) is part of the common ground. I agree with this condition, at least insofar as natural-language expressions go (one could always make up an expression that violates it, but it is hard to see how such an expression would end up being used by people in actual conversations). However, we can be more liberal on the basis for determining the content of expressions—we can say that the information needed to determine content is either part of the common ground or could easily be added to the common ground by, say, querying the participants in the conversation. Since speakers are capable of uttering whatever they want, we should think of this condition as applying only to *felicitous* utterances—i.e., those that are in accord with the norms of communication.

Stalnaker is not alone in holding this principle; here is Roberts's formulation of a very similar point:

> (Retrievability) In order for an utterance to be rationally cooperative in a discourse interaction D, it must be reasonable for the speaker to expect that the addressee can grasp the speaker's intended meaning in so-uttering in D.[27]

Notice that she applies it to content determination more generally, whereas Stalnaker focuses on context-dependence. Although I agree with Roberts, for our purposes we need it only for context-dependent expressions and ambiguous expressions. I refer to it as the *Content Determination Condition* (CDC).[28]

Why does it hold? If an expression violates the CDC, then certain uses of it will violate the overarching condition of Gricean pragmatics, which is: cooperate! If one utters a sentence and one's audience cannot figure out its content, at least to the extent that they can figure out how it should affect the conversational score (e.g., questions under discussion, common ground, common goals), then one is being uncooperative.

For illustration, consider some potential counterexamples. Assume that, in a conversation with Ned, Lenny utters 'Carl is at the bank', but Ned is unable to disambiguate 'bank' to determine whether Lenny is saying that Carl is at the $\text{bank}_{\text{financial}}$ or the $\text{bank}_{\text{river}}$. I am not saying that that could not happen—just that if it did happen, then Carl would not be using 'bank' felicitously. When language is used properly, competent audience members can understand it.

Consider another potential counterexample: 'here' can have its content determined automatically by the location in which a given sentence is uttered. However, if features unavailable to the conversational participants determine the content of a sentence containing 'here', then it violates the cooperation principle to utter that sentence in that

[27] Roberts (2010). For discussion of what it is to grasp a content, see Chomsky (1986, 1995), Pettit (2002, 2005), Gross (2005, 2006), Devitt (2006a, 2006b, 2009, 2010), Longworth (2008a, 2008b, 2009), and the papers in Barber (2003).

[28] The CDC also fits well with Jeffrey King's coordination theory of how semantic values are assigned to context-dependent expressions; see King (forthcoming).

conversational context. Imagine Apu is hiking when he loses his way and becomes lost. He does not know how to get back or how to find the trail. None of the geographical features are familiar. He does, however, have cell-phone service. So, he calls his partner, Manjula, in the hope that she will know how to advise him. He tells her that he is lost, and she asks him to explain. Then he asserts 'oh, wait, I've figured out where I am', followed by asserting 'I am here'.

The sentence Apu asserted, 'I am here', is syntactically well-formed and it has a meaning (character). The context in which he asserts it determines the proposition it expresses. Moreover, the sentence is true, he believes the proposition it expresses, and he has good reason to believe it. However, his assertion is infelicitous in the sense that in asserting it, he violates conversational rules—he has not conveyed any information to Manjula. She would, of course, respond with "that isn't helpful," or "why are you telling me that?" or "at least you haven't lost your sense of humor," or some other utterance that indicates his assertion is not accepted as legitimate.

Apu could, however, say 'It's cold here'. So it cannot be that it is always wrong to use a context-dependent term in this way. Neither of them knows where Apu is, so it might seem that neither of them knows the content of that claim. Is this a counterexample to the CDC? Not necessarily. In asserting this sentence, Apu most likely intends to convey via conversational implicature that *he* is cold. And Manjula should have no problem retrieving this information from his utterance. If that was in fact his goal, then his utterance is felicitous despite the fact that Manjula cannot determine the content of 'here' any more precisely than *Apu's current location*. Still, that is enough for her to add the proposition that Apu is cold to the common ground. However, if it turns out that Apu is on Mt. Useful, then the content of the sentence has the same truth conditions as 'It is cold on Mt. Useful'. If Apu intended to convey *this* information to Manjula, then, again, his assertion would be improper. This example points up an important lesson: the CDC must be applied in light of the conversational goals of the speaker and the audience.

Now back to Kripke's objection. We were considering whether the proponent of the orthodox approach could stipulate that the natural-language truth predicate, which the orthodox approach treats as ambiguous, takes on a particular content in virtue of the levels of the sentences being called true, regardless of whether the speaker intends it to have this content. The problem with this suggestion is that it violates the CDC. This suggestion would imply that, in many cases, neither the speaker nor the audience has the information to determine what the speaker's sentence means. According to the suggested version of the orthodox approach, 'true' in an utterance of 'Everything Nixon says about Watergate is true' takes the content of a Tarskian truth predicate that is high enough in the hierarchy that all the sentences quantified over have levels lower than it. But since neither the audience nor the speaker know those levels, the content of 'true' in the sentence uttered would not be determined by information that is retrievable by the audience (or the speaker). Therefore, this suggestion violates the CDC. Moreover, there is no way to avoid the problem by appeal to some pragmatic mechanism as in the case of Apu and 'it's cold here'. The speaker intends to convey information about features of

Nixon's utterances. There is no retrievable content implicated by the utterance in question that meets this goal. Although Kripke never formulates or defends the CDC, something like it must be in the background of his objection.

In sum, the combination of truth's expressive role, contingent level-determination, and the CDC sinks the orthodox approach to the aletheic paradoxes. This is how to read Kripke's first objection.

Kripke attacked the orthodox approach, but it should be clear from the above discussion that Kripke's criticism generalizes to other philosophical approaches that appeal to ambiguity. The three characteristics of the orthodox approach that render it susceptible to Kripke's attack are: (i) a natural-language truth predicate is interpreted as having multiple independent contents, (ii) the appropriate content of the truth predicate on an occasion of use depends on features (i.e., the levels) of the sentences to which truth (of some kind or other) is being attributed, and (iii) the features of the sentences to which truth is being attributed might be unknown to a speaker felicitously uttering a truth attribution. Ambiguity approaches are almost always used in conjunction with a hierarchy of some sort (e.g., a hierarchy of truth predicates, determinacy operators, negations, conditionals, truth values). In each case, it is tempting to treat the natural-language term in question as if it is ambiguous, but the considerations offered in this chapter should prove decisive. In each case, the approach in question would satisfy the above three criteria and, thus, it would run afoul of contingent level determination, truth's expressive role, or the CDC.

These points against ambiguity approaches fit well with more general considerations against philosophical appeals to ambiguity. Paul Grice introduces what he calls Modified Occam's Razor: senses are not to be multiplied beyond necessity.[29] He uses this principle in a variety of objections to those philosophers who posit hitherto unrecognized ambiguities to solve philosophical problems.[30] Kripke too rails against many philosophical uses of ambiguity in this oft-quoted passage:

> [I]t is very much the lazy man's approach in philosophy to posit ambiguities when in trouble. If we face a putative counterexample to our favorite philosophical thesis, it is always open to us to protest that some key term is being used in a special sense, different from its use in the thesis. We may be right, but the ease of the move should counsel a policy of caution: Do not posit an ambiguity unless you are really forced to, unless there are really compelling theoretical or intuitive grounds to suppose that an ambiguity is really present.[31]

Elizabeth Anscombe expresses a similar sentiment in the following passage: "where we are tempted to speak of 'different senses' of a word which is clearly not equivocal, we may infer that we are pretty much in the dark about the concept it represents."[32] The lesson for us is that those philosophers who appeal to ambiguity as part of an approach to the aletheic paradoxes are "pretty much in the dark" about the concept of truth.

[29] Grice (1989: 47).
[30] See Neale (1992) for discussion.
[31] Kripke (1977: 19).
[32] Anscombe (1957: 1). See also Atlas (1989).

3.2.4 Aletheic contextualism

Consider another application of the combination of truth's expressive role, contingent paradoxes, and CDC: contextual approaches.

A contextual philosophical approach to the paradoxes claims that sentences containing natural-language truth predicates are context-dependent. However, there has been a tremendous amount of work recently on different kinds of context dependence. We can call the most common view *aletheic contextualism*, which holds that sentences containing 'true' express different propositions in different contexts of use. We can treat 'true' as having an invariant character (or meaning), which can be modeled as a function from contexts to contents, and a variable content, which can be modeled as a function from points of evaluation to truth values.

Tyler Burge proposes a kind of aletheic contextualism. He suggests that the content of 'true' in a context of use is the content of one of the truth predicates in the Tarskian hierarchy. That is, instead of ambiguity as the interface between natural-language truth predicates and the Tarskian hierarchy (as the orthodox approach holds), Burge claims that indexicality is the interface.[33] Other aletheic contextualists disagree with Burge, but they all agree that: (i) there is a set of restricted concepts of truth, (ii) sentences containing natural-language truth predicates have contents that differ from context to context, and (iii) the content of the natural-language truth predicate in a context of use is identical to the content of one of the restricted concepts of truth. If we use the term 'aletheic standards' to mark the information in the context of use that determines which restricted concept of truth is relevant for the utterance in question, then aletheic contextualists hold that the aletheic standard for a given sentence uttered is determined by the context of the utterance in question.[34]

That problem, as you must have guessed, is that when speakers use truth predicates in their expressive roles, it is often the case that neither the speaker nor the audience knows the levels or paradoxicality status of the targets of the truth attribution. Moreover, it is these features of the targets that would determine the content of the truth predicate in a context of use according to aletheic contextualists. Thus, aletheic contextualism confronts a serious violation of the CDC in situations where truth plays its expressive role.

[33] Burge (1979, 1982a, 1982b).

[34] Note that some philosophers have proposed tests for context dependence. For example, Cappelen and Lepore (2005) suggest the Intercontextual Disquotation Test (IDT), which states that e is a context-dependent expression iff one can truly assert that, for some sentence ⟨ϕ⟩ containing e, there are false utterances of ⟨ϕ⟩ even though ϕ. Obviously, in the case of truth, the IDT tests whether (T-In) is truth-preserving. Thus, passing the IDT would prevent truth from playing its expressive role as described earlier. Another example is the disagreement test from Cappelen and Hawthorne (2009). The disagreement test states that if e is a context-dependent expression, then there will be cases where a person A asserts that ϕ (where ⟨ϕ⟩ contains e) in one context, a person B asserts ⟨~ϕ⟩ in a different context, yet they cannot correctly be said to disagree by someone in a third context. Again, it seems as if 'true' fails this test as well. That is bad news for the aletheic contextualist, but I do not put much stock in these kinds of tests since their outcomes are so susceptible to one's antecedent theoretical commitments.

Consider the problem in a bit more detail. Assume Nixon asserts 'All of what Dean says about Watergate is true'. What is happening according to the pragmatic theories outlined so far? Nixon is part of a conversation, and (following Stalnaker, Lewis, and Roberts) that conversation has a common ground, common goals, questions under discussion, etc. These elements of the conversation are the context of Jones's utterance. The aletheic contextualist holds that 'true' in the sentence Nixon asserts is an indexical.[35] According to a Kaplanian treatment of indexicality, the truth conditions of Nixon's utterance are determined by the function from points of evaluation to truth values. The character of the sentence uttered and the context of utterance determine this function. The problem comes when specifying information from the context of Nixon's utterance. What is the aletheic standard in this case? If Nixon's utterance is felicitous, then the aletheic standard will have to be able to encompass all of Dean's claims about Watergate. If we are using the Tarskian hierarchy as our example for the set of restricted truth predicates, then the aletheic standard will have to be higher than the highest level of the sentences Dean uttered about Watergate. The problem is that there is no reason to think that this information will be part of the common ground in Nixon's conversation. Thus, the aletheic contextualist holds that the aletheic standard is to be filled in by consulting the context, but when one looks to the context, at least in the vast majority of cases where truth is being used in its expressive role, that information is nowhere to be found.[36]

All that is needed for Nixon's utterance to be felicitous is that he is following the rules of the conversation—that is, he is cooperating, and so on. Given the description of the context, his utterance is felicitous. However, if the aletheic contextualist is right, then even though his utterance is felicitous, it cannot be assigned truth conditions since the context in which it was made does not determine an aletheic standard. On the other hand, the aletheic contextualist might deny that Nixon's utterance is felicitous for these very reasons. If so, then this move would be tantamount to demanding that sentences containing truth predicates are felicitously uttered only when the context contains enough information to determine an aletheic standard. This view is obviously empirically false—we often use truth predicates in contexts insufficient to determine an aletheic standard, and competent natural-language users correctly regard these utterances as felicitous.

Instead, the aletheic contextualist might claim that the aletheic standard is specified in some other way that goes beyond the information available in the context. If so, then the content of the sentence that Nixon utters is not available to anyone in the conversation. Thus, although Nixon's utterance would be felicitous, it would violate the CDC.

[35] There are aletheic contextualists (e.g., Glanzberg (2004)) that think the context dependence should be traced to a quantifier domain rather than to the truth predicate. The objection carries over easily to these views.

[36] Simmons (2008) contains a discussion of Stalnaker's pragmatic theory in conjunction with Simmons' version of aletheic contextualism, but he mistakenly assumes that if a sentence is paradoxical, then conversational participants would have no problem adding this information to the common ground; see Simmons (2008: 353).

Finally, there is no pragmatic solution to the problem akin to Apu's use of 'it's cold here' to convey via conversational implicature that *he* is cold. One might think that when Nixon asserts 'all of what Dean says about Watergate is true', he is trying to convey something that is retrievable from the conversational context via conversational implicature. However, for this move to save the aletheic contextualist from the objection at hand, it would have to be plausible to assume that every use of 'true' in situations where the information needed to determine its content is not retrievable is an attempt to convey via conversational implicature something that is retrievable. And that is radically implausible. Moreover, the contextualist is barred from saying that when Nixon performs his assertion all he is trying to convey is that everything Dean says about Watergate is true *at some level or other*. The whole point of a contextualist view is to explain facts about our natural-language truth predicate without contradiction by appeal to a batch of restricted truth predicates. If one allows quantification over the restricted truth predicates in question, it is easy to see that the contradiction returns.[37]

To sum up: aletheic contextualism is a popular philosophical approach to the aletheic paradoxes but, when examined a bit more closely, it encounters what I take to be an insuperable difficulty; namely, it is incompatible with the combination of truth's expressive role, contingent paradoxicality, and the CDC.

3.2.5 Semantic blindness

It is important to understand the seriousness of the problem for aletheic contextualists. Compare it to another well-known worry for contextualists: the *semantic blindness objection*, which has been leveled at epistemological contextualists. The objection is that the claim that 'knows' is context-dependent is highly counterintuitive since speakers, even upon reflection, take it to be invariant. Stephen Schiffer was one of the first to push this objection:

> For the speaker would not only have to be confounding the proposition she's saying; she'd also have to be totally ignorant of the sort of thing she's saying. One who implicitly says that it's raining in London in uttering "It's raining" knows full well what proposition she is asserting; if articulate, she can tell you that what she meant and was implicitly stating was that it was raining in London. But no ordinary person who utters "I know that p", however articulate, would dream of telling you that what he meant and was implicitly stating was that he knew that p relative to such-and-such standard.[38]

For Schiffer, the problem with epistemological contextualism is that speakers do not know which propositions they are asserting when they assert knowledge claims. Thomas Hofweber disagrees:

> According to the contextualist, it is not so that when one speaker utters "A knows that p" and another speaker utters the same sentence then the content of the two utterances will be the

[37] See Juhl (1997) for a similar point.
[38] Schiffer (1996: 326).

same. And it is not so that if one speaker utters "A knows that p" and another speaker utters "A does not know that p" then the contents of these two utterances are incompatible. Furthermore, according to contextualism, the speakers won't be aware of these facts about difference and compatibility of contents. This follows from the fact that ordinary speakers are not aware of the semantic context sensitivity of their knowledge ascriptions, and from the claim that lots of details of the context are relevant for what the content of a knowledge ascription is.... A contextualist will thus not only hold that speakers have no access (in the strong sense spelled out above) to the content of their utterances, but also no access to sameness, difference and incompatibility of the contents of their utterances.... I think that *it*, not hidden relativity per se, is the really problematic aspect of the philosophy of language part of a contextualist theory about knowledge ascriptions. It is one thing to deny that speakers have access to the content of their utterances in the strong sense spelled out above.... It is quite another thing to deny that sameness, difference and incompatibility of contents of utterances is inaccessible to ordinary speakers.[39]

According to Hofweber, that speakers do not know exactly which propositions they are asserting when they assert knowledge claims is not a problem; rather, it is the fact that they would be unable to determine when knowledge claims express the same or different or incompatible propositions that poses the real problem. John Hawthorne presents a more general version of this worry:

Suppose that Joe says 'I know that p', and at the time of utterance he expresses the same relation as you do by 'know'. You accept what he says. The sentence 'Joe knows that p (plus a date index)' goes into your belief box. But now suppose that your standards for knowledge rise. Your belief about Joe's knowledge will now come out false—as will, presumably, hundreds of other once true beliefs—unless you somehow update the sentences in your belief box. Moreover, you will no longer have a cognitive hold on those true propositions that your belief box once truly expressed and that, as a result, you once truly believed. Similarly, if the standards for knowledge fall, many beliefs that deny knowledge will now come out false and much true information will be lost, unless updating occurs. Suppose further that we are semantically blind in the way suggested: the semantic content of 'knows' shifts, but our language organ does not supply us with a standards index—analogous to a dating method—with which to enrich knowledge ascriptions that are tokened in the belief box. Then shifting semantic values for 'know' would spell disaster—in the ways just outlined—for our belief set.[40]

Hawthorne takes the problem to be that if we were semantically blind in the way that epistemological contextualists suggest, then we would be unable to keep track of our own and others beliefs dynamically in the way that is a minimal requirement for participating in a conversation.

The semantic blindness objection has come to be one of the major issues in the debate over epistemological contextualism and contextualist views in philosophy more generally. The contextualists' responses to it have mostly been of the "learn to live with

[39] Hofweber (1999: 101).
[40] Hawthorne (2004: 110).

it" and "it is not that counterintuitive" variety.[41] I am not going to evaluate these replies, but I do want to draw some comparisons to aletheic contextualism.

Notice that as long as speakers and audience members are able to determine the epistemic standards that are relevant to a given knowledge attribution, epistemological contextualism is *compatible* with the CDC, which requires that information for determining the contents of properly used context-dependent expressions be available to participants in a conversation.[42] Thus, the semantic blindness objection (or objections, since they seem to differ slightly from one another) appeal to a condition on language use that is *more* demanding than the CDC. The objection I just pressed against the aletheic contextualist is more serious than the semantic blindness objection. At least the information needed to determine the content of 'knows' according to the epistemological contextualist is retrievable from the context of utterance; the aletheic contextualist, on the other hand, has to say either that the interlocutors in the conversation do not know the contents of many claims involving truth or that many obviously felicitous uses of 'true' are impermissible.[43]

3.2.6 *Field on truth and determinate truth*

The previous two subsections on ambiguity and context-dependence point out problems for approaches to the aletheic paradoxes that posit a group of more or less restricted truth predicates and attempt to link them to a natural-language truth predicate via some hitherto unrecognized semantic feature. Earlier I called these *fragmentary theories of truth* since they try to explain a seemingly unitary notion like truth in terms of a group of more restricted notions (e.g., those in the Tarskian hierarchy). It should be pretty clear that any fragmentary theory of truth that appeals to something like ambiguity or context-dependence to relate natural-language truth predicates to the group of restricted truth predicates is going to confront a semantic blindness objection. Moreover, it is going to fall prey to the much more serious objection I have presented in this chapter based on Kripke's criticism of the orthodox approach; namely, it cannot accept the combination of the CDC, the fact that truth predicates have expressive uses, and the fact that there are contingently paradoxical sentences.

What might not be so obvious is that these same problems can crop up even for someone who does not endorse a fragmentary theory of truth. In this subsection, I consider Hartry Field's combination of indeterminacy philosophical approach and paracomplete

[41] See DeRose (2006) and Montminy (2009a). See Cappelen (2008), Brogaard (2008), and Weiner (2009) for discussion.

[42] Of course, if speakers do not know that 'knows' is context-dependent, then they will probably not utilize this information, even though it would be available to them.

[43] Zoltan Szabo's comment seems apt: "appeals to context sensitivity have become 'cheap'—the twenty-first century version of ordinary language philosophy's rampant postulations of ambiguity. Not only is this 'the lazy man's approach to philosophy,' it undermines systematic theorizing about language. The more we believe context can influence semantic content, the more we will find ourselves at a loss when it comes to explaining how ordinary communication (let alone the transmission of knowledge through written texts) is possible" (Szabo (2006: 31)).

logical approach to the aletheic paradoxes. Recall that Field offers an artificial language that has a paracomplete logic (K_3), but with a new conditional (I will call it a *paracomplete conditional*) that is defined via a revision sequence (he also gives a neighborhood semantics for it and an algebraic semantics for it, but we will not be concerned with those details). Using the paracomplete conditional, Field defines a determinateness operator, D. The language Field considers also has its own truth predicate and it can express Field's preferred theory of truth, which is just the set of T-sentences for the sentences of the language, except that the T-sentences contain Field's paracomplete biconditional. The determinateness operator can be paired with the truth predicate to express determinate truth, and there is a crucial difference between saying that a sentence is true and saying that a sentence is determinately true.

Of course, Field's language has liar sentences (e.g., L = 'L is not true'), and his theory of truth contains T-sentences for all of them. However, the paracomplete biconditional and the background paracomplete logic are weak enough to prevent a proof of contradiction from them. As for their truth value, Field's theory neither implies that they are true nor that they are not true (remember, it is a paracomplete logic, so it does not validate the law of excluded middle); moreover, it does not imply that they are neither true nor not true—it is silent about their truth value. However, one can use the determinateness operator to say something about them: liar sentences are not determinately true and not determinately not true; that is implied by the theory. So the determinateness operator comes in handy for classifying paradoxical sentences. Since it is in the language, though, one can formulate revenge liar sentences with it (e.g., R = 'R is not determinately true'). Here, the theory does not imply that they are true or that they are not true, and it does not imply that they are neither true nor not true; in addition, it does not imply that they are not determinately true and not determinately not true either. However, it does imply that they are not determinately determinately true and not determinately determinately not true. That is, the determinateness operator iterates non-trivially so that iterations of it can be used to classify revenge liars. Indeed, Field shows how to define a hierarchy of determinateness operators that stretches into the recursive ordinals. However, his view does not allow for a general notion of determinateness that encompasses all those in the hierarchy.[44]

One might complain that instead of fragmenting truth, Field has fragmented determinateness. His reply? Guilty as charged, but fragmenting determinateness is much less problematic:

> On the views considered here, we do have a unified notion of truth (and of satisfaction too). It is the notions of truth and satisfaction, not determinate truth, that we need to use as devices of generalization.... [T]he ability to use truth as a device of generalization isn't affected at all in the paracomplete theories now under discussion, since the truth predicate isn't even quasi-stratified.[45]

[44] All of this is spelled out in Field (2008a); I also discussed it in Chapter 1.
[45] Field (2008a: 349).

Field's point is that it makes much more sense to fragment determinateness than truth given the expressive role that truth plays. Let us see if he is right.

Consider three examples:

(i) Moe asserts 'The Riemann hypothesis is not true'.

(ii) Carl asserts 'The sentence on the blackboard is not true', where the sentence in question is contingently paradoxical.

(iii) Lenny asserts 'The sentence on the whiteboard is not true', where the sentence in question is a contingently paradoxical revenge liar (e.g., 'Most of Jones's statements about Watergate are not determinately true').

These are all expressive uses of the truth predicate of English and these utterances are all felicitous (given normal conversational circumstances). Our job is to see how Field's theory handles them.

In (i), it is pretty easy; 'true' in Moe's sentence means *True* (which is the concept of truth expressed by the truth predicate in Field's artificial language). It might seem that we want to say the same thing about (ii), but there is a catch. Since the sentence on the blackboard is indeterminate (i.e., not determinately true and not determinately not true), this reading implies that Carl's sentence is indeterminate as well. Moreover, Field claims that it is inappropriate to say of an indeterminate sentence that it is true or that it is not true, and this seems like a good norm to use when assessing assertions of sentences that could turn out to be indeterminate.[46] Thus, if 'true' in Carl's sentence expresses the concept of truth, then his assertion is illegitimate. That move would seriously impact the expressive role of the truth predicate. Instead, we can read 'true' in Carl's sentence as meaning *determinately True*. If we do this, then his assertion is legitimate. Therefore, either Carl's sentence is indeterminate (and so his assertion is unwarranted), or 'true' in his sentence means *DTrue*.

The same problem arises for Lenny's sentence but at a level higher. That is, since the target of Lenny's attribution is not determinately determinately true and not determinately determinately not true, treating 'true' in his sentence as expressing either truth or determinate truth results in his sentence being indeterminate. Again, that would render his assertion infelicitous and this choice would negatively impact the expressive power accorded to the truth predicate. Instead, we should read 'true' in Lenny's sentence as meaning *determinately determinately True*. On this reading, his assertion is fine. Therefore, either Lenny's sentence is indeterminate (and so his assertion is unwarranted), or 'true' in his sentence means D^2*True*.

As I see it, Field takes some of the work traditionally given to the truth predicate and outsources it to his determinateness operators. The problem for Field's view comes when we think about how to interpret an ordinary speaker of English who has never heard of Field's solution or even the liar paradox itself; we are forced to make a hard choice as to how we should interpret some of that person's uses of 'true' as a device of rejection. We

[46] See Field (2008a: 350–3). See Maudlin (2004) for an alternative view.

have to conclude that either 'true' is not univocal and invariant or that some sentences containing the truth predicate that are legitimately used to express rejection are indeterminate. It seems to me that either Field's theory is seriously revisionist not just about our logic, but about our use of 'true', which even in the best-case scenario would leave us without a theory of truth *as we use it*, or he is forced to treat truth predicates as ambiguous or context-dependent. Each of these alternatives has major costs associated with it; the first makes it seem as though Field's points about how we use truth predicates are just cherry-picked to support his theory. However, in light of the criticism of ambiguity and contextual approaches to the aletheic paradoxes given in the last few subsections, we can see that the second option is equally bad. It should be obvious that the features determining which meaning 'true' should have in these three cases are often unavailable to the participants in the conversations in question. Thus, the claim that 'true' is context-dependent in this way violates the CDC, in just the same way we saw before; again, going with ambiguity over context-dependence would not help. I find it remarkable and surprising that even a theory of truth designed around truth's expressive role could encounter this kind of trouble when it is applied to a natural language.

The lesson here is that facts about truth's expressive role, facts about contingent paradoxicality, and the CDC make for an extremely powerful combination. Even theories of truth that do not seem to require interpreting truth predicates of natural language as ambiguous or context-dependent might inadvertently have these consequences, and the considerations in this chapter bring that out.

In sum, if truth is used as a device of endorsement and rejection, then people use it as if it obeys (T-In) and (T-Out). Thus, an approach to the aletheic paradoxes that denies one of these principles to avoid the obvious objection is not going to be an adequate descriptive theory of our linguistic practice as it is now.[47] Of course, if it turns out that truth is an inconsistent concept and (T-In) and (T-Out) are constitutive aletheic principles, then it would make sense to reject one or both of them. Indeed, that is the position I end up defending in Chapter 9.

3.3 Logic

The third way of avoiding the obvious argument is to reject classical logic in favor of a logic that does not validate the reasoning in any of the aletheic paradoxes; a non-classical logic like this would be one in which (T-Intro) and (T-Elim) are consistent, or at least non-trivial. What is wrong with avoiding the obvious argument in this way? One problem is that this sort of approach to the aletheic paradoxes cripples our ability to reason. Or, to be more precise, we behave, talk, write, and think in such a way as to treat as good inferences ones that any non-classical approach to the aletheic paradoxes has to label as invalid. Moreover, it should be clear that these inferences invalidated by the non-classical approaches are constitutive of the logical terms they govern. I argue for these claims in

[47] Field (2008a) does a good job of making this point.

what follows. But first, let us be clear about these two points. I am not saying that classical logic is sacrosanct. I am not saying that we obviously use classical logic in our reasoning. I am not saying that it is easy to read off the correct logic from our reasoning practices. I am not saying that everyone uses the same logic. I am not even saying that there is a single correct logic. There are plenty of disputes about the correct logic or logics. The major alternatives to classical logic in the literature are intuitionistic logic (I) and stronger relevance logics (like E or R). The debates about which of these logics is correct are complicated and fortunately need not concern us here. The reason the details of these debates are irrelevant is that none of these logics allows (T-Intro) and (T-Elim) non-trivially. The non-classical logics that permit (T-Intro) and (T-Elim) are much weaker than I or E or R. The motivation for the logics used by non-classical approaches to the aletheic paradoxes often has nothing to do with reasoning—it is usually of the "well, that's what you have to do to have a truth predicate that obeys (T-Intro) and (T-Elim)" variety.

What, exactly, gets left out of these logics? Nearly everyone takes the inference rule *modus ponens*:

(MP) $A, A \rightarrow B \vdash B$

to be constitutive of the conditional.[48] In fact, those who reject *modus ponens* (e.g., McGee) are now used as stock examples of someone who rejects a constitutive principle and still possesses the concept in question.[49] In addition, the meta-rule, conditional proof:

(CP) If $A \vdash B$, then $\vdash A \rightarrow B$

is also constitutive of the conditional. It just says that if B is derivable from A, then the conditional '$A \rightarrow B$' is derivable. Someone who rejects conditional proof might argue from some claim A to another claim B but reject the conditional whose antecedent is A and consequent is B. That is just as bad as accepting a conditional and its antecedent but rejecting its consequent. So it seems that any acceptable approach to the aletheic paradoxes is compatible with a logic that includes both (MP) and (CP).[50]

Consider the problem as it appears for paracomplete and paraconsistent approaches, which accept both (T-In) and (T-Out) and revise classical logic to avoid triviality. The trick to weakening the background logic is to have a conditional that does not contract because Curry's paradox shows us that there is no way to have both truth principles and a conditional that obeys contraction in these systems. Contraction is the odd-looking axiom:

(Contraction) $\vdash (A \rightarrow (A \rightarrow B)) \rightarrow (A \rightarrow B)$

[48] However, see McGee (1985a) for a potential counterexample.

[49] See Williamson (2006).

[50] (CP) and (MP) are the standard introduction and elimination rules (respectively) for the conditional. There is a long history of taking introduction and elimination rules for logical connectives to be constitutive; see Peregrin (2008) for an overview.

It turns out that one can also formulate a Curry paradox using both truth principles and an axiom that is sometimes called material *modus ponens*:

(MMP) $\vdash A \wedge (A \rightarrow B) \rightarrow B$

However, in a system with conditional proof (CP), *modus ponens* (MP) and material *modus ponens* (MMP) are equivalent—any such system includes either both or neither. Thus, neither paracomplete nor paraconsistent approaches allow conditional proof and *modus ponens*. Thus, they are incompatible with the constitutive principles of a conditional.

One can keep all the classical inference rules including the meta-rules and have (T-In) and (T-Out) if one is willing to restrict the structural rules that govern the derivability operator ($\vdash$). Some of these substructural approaches reject the transitivity structural rule, which says, roughly, that two bits of reasoning can be chained together.[51] By the transitivity structural rule, if I deduce A from some set of premises G and I deduce B from some set of premises that consists of A and everything in G, then I can deduce B from G alone. However, on Tennant's substructural view, one can deduce that a liar sentence is true and that one can deduce that the same sentence is not true, but one cannot combine these two deductions to get a deduction that the sentence is both true and not true (even though he accepts the inference rule of conjunction introduction). Imagine someone who says "I accept that special relativity entails that nothing travels faster than the speed of light, and I accept that special relativity plus the claim that nothing travels faster than the speed of light entail neutrinos do not travel faster than the speed of light, but I do not accept that special relativity entails that neutrinos do not travel faster than the speed of light." I think that this sort of claim would strike the audience as baffling. Thus, I do not see that denying transitivity is any better than denying *modus ponens* or conditional proof. That is, this structural rule is constitutive of the derivability operator.

Other substructural approaches reject the contraction rule, which says, roughly, that a premise can be used any number of times in a deduction. By the contraction structural rule, if I deduce A from some set of premises G, then it does not matter whether I use a member of G (call it B) once, twice, or any other number of times in my deduction.[52] However, on the substructural view Beall and Murzi consider, a liar sentence is derivable from any particular sentence, and from any particular sentence a liar sentence is derivable, but one cannot derive any particular sentence from any other particular sentence because such a move requires contraction. Imagine someone who says "I accept that the standard model of particle physics, the claim that leptons do not travel faster than the speed of light, and the claim that leptons do not travel faster than the speed of light together entail that neutrinos do not travel faster than the speed of light; however, I do not accept that the standard model of particle physics and the claim that leptons do not travel faster than the speed of light entail that neutrinos do not travel faster than the speed of light." It is

[51] See Tennant (1997, MS2), Weir (2005), and Ripley (2012, forthcoming).
[52] Zardini (2011); see also Beall and Murzi (forthcoming).

hard to know how to even interpret such a claim. In fact, I will bet that many readers had to read back over it several times to make sure it says what it seems to say. The very idea that one token of a sentence has certain entailments, but two tokens of the same sentence have different entailments is profoundly antithetical to the way we think and reason.[53] Again, we find that a structural rule is constitutive of the derivability operator.

To summarize, the following are incompatible, where L is any logic (assuming the relevant syntactic resources):

(i) L accepts *modus ponens* and conditional proof.
(ii) L accepts the standard structural rules for derivability.
(iii) The theory consisting of (T-In) and (T-Out) is non-trivial in L.

The upshot is that (T-In) and (T-Out) are incompatible with the intuitive theory of the conditional (i.e., the theory that that conditionals obey *modus ponens* and conditional proof) no matter what the logic as long as it obeys the standard structural rules for derivability. Non-classical solutions to the aletheic paradoxes are forced to say either that there is no such thing as an intuitive conditional or that it is inconsistent or, I suppose, that intuitive derivability either does not exist or is inconsistent. Either way, the non-classical logics used to solve the aletheic paradoxes are incompatible with what are perhaps the most basic and important elements of deductive reasoning—an intuitive conditional that can be used in intuitive derivations. Solomon Feferman once wrote of certain paracomplete logics that, "nothing like sustained ordinary reasoning can be carried on" in them.[54] This oft-quoted quip could be said about any logic that is weak enough to have (T-In) and (T-Out) without triviality.

Again, classical logic is not sacrosanct—perhaps it is wrong. However, the case for adopting a non-classical logic should be made by considering . . . logic! It should not be made by trying to accommodate the constitutive principles of some other concept that is classically inconsistent. I think this point can be made against any attempt to alter our logic in the face of paradoxes. Sure, we could do so, but this move is a "language-wide" change, which means that arguments having nothing to do with the concept in question (truth in our case) that were previously considered valid, will turn out to be invalid. For example, imagine a conversation between Martin and Ralph:

RALPH: I was thinking about it, and I'll bet that there's a greatest prime number.
MARTIN: Actually, there are infinitely many prime numbers.
RALPH: Why do you believe that?
MARTIN: Suppose that there are only finitely many primes. Let p be one more than the product of all the primes. Since p is greater than all the primes, it cannot be prime, so let q be a prime dividing p. However, q cannot be any of the primes whose product is p-1; otherwise q would divide the difference

[53] Non-contractive logics like linear logic have many important applications, but modeling the reasoning practices of everyday people does not seem to be one of them. See the papers in Girard et al. (1995).
[54] Feferman (1982: 95).

between p and the product of the primes, which is 1. But that is impossible. Therefore, there are infinitely many primes.

RALPH: That argument is invalid.

MARTIN: What!? Why?

RALPH: Because of the liar paradox.

MARTIN: What are you talking about? Prime numbers have nothing to do with the liar paradox.

RALPH: *Reductio* arguments are invalid because otherwise the set of all T-sentences for expressively rich languages would be inconsistent. Your argument is missing a premise—either there are infinitely many primes or there are not.

MARTIN: This argument has been taken to be valid for thousands of years by the greatest minds in history—it is the paradigm of a valid argument!

RALPH: Sorry, but my solution to the liar paradox implies that is invalid.

This sort of "collateral damage" is often overlooked when thinking about approaches to a paradox. My attitude is that altering our standards of reasoning is always open to us, but the reasons for doing so should be that there is some independent reason to think that there is something wrong with them (e.g., the paradoxes of implication—for relevance logic—or global anti-realism—for intuitionism).

I can imagine a paraconsistent logician protesting: people do not just infer any old claim from a contradiction, so whatever the correct logic turns out to be, it will not validate the *ex falso* rule. Moreover, people do not reason in accord with many of the inference rules of classical logic. So my claim that paraconsistent logic has nothing to recommend it except for non-triviality in the face of a truth predicate that obeys (T-In) and (T-Out) is unfair to paraconsistent logic.

My reply: attempting to read off a logic from the kinds of inferences people are likely to make is the wrong strategy, and we have known this for decades. In fact, Gilbert Harman made this point in the 1980s.[55] He distinguished between *inference*, a psychological process, and *implication*, a relation between propositions or contents. His point is that one cannot conclude from the fact that a person does not perform some inference that the person does not accept the related implication. For example, a person might find himself accepting a claim p and the conditional with p as antecedent and q as consequent, but he does not infer q (in the sense of coming to believe it) from these two beliefs. Nevertheless, he accepts *modus ponens*. How could this happen? He already believes q's negation, and he believes that more strongly than he believes either p or the conditional. So, instead of thinking of *modus ponens* as some kind of law of thought that governs inference, Harman argues that it is an implication that holds between propositions or contents. That is, q follows from p and $p \rightarrow q$, but it is not the case that anyone who believes p and $p \rightarrow q$ ought to or is even permitted to believe q. Anyone who has digested Harman's obvious point should be immediately suspicious of claims like that made in the objection.

[55] Harman (1986); see also Field (2009) and Harman (2009). Thanks to Alison Duncan Kerr on this point—see Kerr (MS).

I imagine someone sympathetic to the objection would want a positive account of the relation between our reasoning practice and the correct logic. I agree with Greg Restall, who emphasizes the connection between combinations of propositions accepted or rejected and the correct logic. In particular, Restall suggests that if G ⊢ p, then it is a mistake to knowingly accept all the members of G and reject p.[56] Taking the contrapositive: if it is not a mistake to accept all members of G and reject p, then p is not derivable from G in the correct logic. What we have is a *sufficient* condition for *exclusion* of an inference rule from the correct logic and a *necessary* condition for *inclusion* of an inference rule in the correct logic. Certainly anyone who is not a dialetheist thinks it is a mistake to knowingly accept a contradiction and reject anything whatsoever, simply because it is a mistake to knowingly accept a contradiction. That does *not* show that *ex falso* should be *included* in the correct logic; rather, the Restall test *fails* to show that *ex falso* should be *excluded*. And the Restall test is one that does not presuppose the conflation Harman takes pains to uncover. Moreover, the test suggested in the objection obviously runs afoul of the Harman point. This is not the place for a full treatment of this topic, but at least I have said enough to indicate where my sympathies lie.[57]

So much for the obvious argument. The presentation of it is far more detailed and careful than that of the arguments given in Chapter 2 concerning 'rable', 'mass', and 'up above', which, I hope, were conclusive. Still, it has the same basic form as those arguments, and I think it constitutes a good reason to accept that truth is an inconsistent concept.

[56] Restall (2009: 2).

[57] One other major attempt to give independent justification for a logic that can accommodate a truth predicate obeying (T-In) and (T-Out) nontrivially is Ross Brady's logic DJ^d. Brady argues that this weak relevance logic is the proper logic to describe meaning containment. However, Brady does not argue that DJ^d does the best job of modeling our rational activities or that our rational activities have anything to do with meaning containment, and the points made above about the conditional and derivability apply to it as well. See Brady (1996, 2006) for details.

4

Revenge

There are three arguments for an inconsistency approach to the aletheic paradoxes in this chapter, and all three turn on the revenge paradox phenomenon: (i) the revenge argument (on the prospects for revenge-free consistency views), (ii) the abductive argument (on the best explanation for the aletheic paradoxes and the revenge paradoxes), and (iii) the meaning argument (on the negative consequences of consistency views for formal semantics).

4.1 Revenge paradoxes

Because the rest of the arguments for the inconsistency approach given in this chapter turn on various features of revenge paradoxes, I pause in this section to introduce them. Revenge paradoxes have been known for decades, but they used to be called 'strengthened liars'.[1] Sometime in the late 1990s the term 'revenge paradox' caught hold and now seems to be the accepted locution. Just as there are many kinds of aletheic paradoxes, there are many kinds of revenge paradoxes. For example, the following sentence is a liar sentence:

(1) (1) is false.

Assume for a moment that we accept the inner theory of Kripke's Strong Kleene minimal fixed point. According to this approach, (1) is not in the extension of 'true' and not in the anti-extension of 'true'. We could introduce the term 'gappy' into the language in question, and characterize (1) by saying that it is gappy. However, by doing so, we also accept that the language has the following sentence:

(2) (2) is either false or gappy.

This sentence gives rise to a revenge paradox for the approach under consideration. Recall that the liar paradox is generated using principles of logic and the following aletheic principles:

[1] See van Fraassen (1968).

(T-In) If ϕ, then $\langle\phi\rangle$ is true.
(T-Out) If $\langle\phi\rangle$ is true, then p.
(Sub) If $\langle\phi\rangle = \langle\psi\rangle$, then $\langle\phi\rangle$ is true $\leftrightarrow$ $\langle\psi\rangle$ is true.

Now, let us compare the liar reasoning with the reasoning concerning our revenge paradox. See Table 1.

Table 1 Revenge Reasoning

	Liar Reasoning	Revenge Reasoning	Rule
1	(1) is true.	(2) is true.	[assumption]
2	'(1) is false' is true.	'(2) is either false or gappy' is true.	[(Sub)]
3	(1) is false.	(2) is either false or gappy.	[(T-Out)]
4	If (1) is true, then (1) is false.	If (2) is true, then (2) is either false or gappy.	[→ Intro]
5	(1) is false.	(2) is either false or gappy.	[assumption]
6	'(1) is false' is true.	'(2) is either false or gappy' is true.	[(T-In)]
7	(1) is true.	(2) is true.	[(Sub)]
8	If (1) is false, then (1) is true.	If (2) is either false or gappy, then (2) is true.	[→ Intro]
9	(1) is true iff (1) is false.	(2) is true iff (2) is either false or gappy.	[↔ Intro]

From step 9 in the *liar* reasoning, together with the claim that (1) is either true or false, it follows that (1) is both true and false; the contradiction follows from this result and the claim that nothing is both true and false. From step 9 of the *revenge* reasoning, together with the claim that (2) is true or either false or gappy, it follows that (2) is both true and either false or gappy; the contradiction follows from this result and the claim that nothing is both true and either false or gappy. Using the exact same reasoning from the liar paradox, we get a contradiction by reasoning about (2). The approach in question says that (1) is gappy, and this blocks the liar reasoning after step 9 by denying that (1) is either true or false. However, the same move does not block the reasoning after step 9 in the revenge case. It is consistent to say that (1) is gappy but, from the claim that (2) is gappy, it follows that (2) is true since it says of itself that it is either false or gappy.

Notice that the revenge paradox generated by (2) is paradoxical only if we accept the above approach to the liar paradox. That is an important feature of revenge paradoxes: whether a sentence generates a revenge paradox is relative to a particular approach to the liar. (2) is a revenge paradox for the inner theory of Kripke's Strong Kleene minimal fixed point. It is not a revenge paradox for other approaches.

Other examples[2] of sentences that generate revenge paradoxes are:

[2] These examples barely scratch the surface of the revenge paradox literature, which is largely scattered and disorganized. I have focused on common revenge paradoxes for the most prominent approaches to the aletheic paradoxes. Notice that the distinction between philosophical approaches and logical approaches that I took pains to draw in Chapter 1 gets blurred when it comes to revenge paradoxes. Some revenge paradoxes feature terms specific to philosophical approaches (e.g., 'true in a context'), while others involve terms from logical approaches (e.g., 'unstable').

(3)	(3) is either false or unstable	(for revision approaches)[3]
(4)	(4) is not true in any context	(for contextual approaches)[4]
(5)	(5) is either false or indeterminate	(for paracomplete approaches)[5]
(6)	(6) is just false	(for paraconsistent approaches)[6]
(7)	(7) is Bnot true[7]	(for paracomplete and paraconsistent approaches)

Revision theories say that (1) is unstable since its truth value never stabilizes in a revision sequence. The truth value of (3) never stabilizes in a revision sequence either, but if (3) is unstable then (3) is true since it says of itself that it is either false or unstable. So (3) is a revenge liar for approaches that appeal to revision sequences to define truth.

Contextual approaches say that (1) is true in some contexts and false in others. That approach blocks the aletheic paradoxes since it stipulates that the context shifts in the midst of the reasoning. However, (4) poses a serious problem for contextual views because the claim that it is true in one context seems to imply that it is not true in any context.

Paracomplete approaches typically say that (1) is indeterminate and they reject certain principles of classical logic involved in the liar reasoning. However, if the paracomplete approach calls (5) indeterminate, then that claim implies that (5) is true since (5) says of itself that it is indeterminate. Because sentences are not both indeterminate and true, (5) poses a problem for these approaches.

Paraconsistent views say that (1) is both true and false and they offer a non-classical logic on which some contradictions are true (though they hold that not all contradictions are true). Paraconsistentists hold that (1) says of itself that it is false, and it is false, so it is true as well; (1) is both true and false. However, there is a problem with saying that (6) is both true and false since (6) says of itself that it is false only. The paraconsistent view on (1) does not work for (6) since the claim that (6) is both true and false should be incompatible with what (6) says of itself—i.e., that it is only false. So the standard paraconsistent treatment of the liar seems to get the wrong answer for (6).

Sentence (7) contains an unusual term for negation. The 'Bnot' in (7) expresses Boolean negation. In multi-valued logics like paracomplete logic, Boolean negation takes indeterminacy to truth. So a theory that implies that (7) is indeterminate also implies that (7) is true. Thus, the revenge paradox generated by (7) is a variant of the revenge paradox generated by (5). In paraconsistent logics, Boolean negation takes gluts to truths, so a theory that implies that (7) is glutty also implies that (7) is just

[3] See Gupta (1982) and Gupta and Belnap (1993) for revision theories.

[4] See Burge (1979), Simmons (1993), and Glanzberg (2004) for contextual theories. See Juhl (1997) for revenge considerations.

[5] See Kripke (1975), Soames (1999), and Field (2008a) for paracomplete theories. See Ketland (2003), Priest (2005, 2008), Rayo and Welch (2008), and Leitgeb (2008) for revenge considerations.

[6] See Priest (2006a, 2006b) and Beall (2009) for paraconsistent theories. See Thomason (1986), S. Shapiro (2004), and Field (2008a) for revenge considerations.

[7] 'Bnot' expresses Boolean negation.

true. Hence, the revenge paradox generated by (7) is a variant of the revenge paradox generated by (6).

Consider how Graham Priest has long characterized the revenge paradox phenomenon:

There is, in fact, a uniform method for constructing the revenge paradox—or extended paradox, as it is called sometimes. All semantic accounts have a bunch of Good Guys (the true, the stably true, the ultimately true, or whatever). These are the ones that we target when we assert. Then there's the Rest. The extended liar is a sentence, produced by some diagonalizing construction, which says of itself just that it's in the Rest. The diagonal construction, because of its ability to tear through any consistent boundary, may then play havoc. This shows, incidentally, that the extended paradox is not really a different paradox. The pristine liar is the result of the construction when the theoretical framework is the standard one (all sentences are true or false, not both, and not neither). 'Extended paradoxes' are simply the results of applying the construction in different theoretical frameworks.[8]

Priest's diagnosis is a good start. One can see the examples above fit well into the schema he provides. I am not one to care much about how to individuate aletheic paradoxes, and I do not think it matters whether revenge paradoxes are distinct from the liar or whether they are at root the same paradox. What matters is that they affect the concept of truth and that any adequate approach to the aletheic paradoxes has to incorporate some adequate approach to revenge paradoxes. However, it will pay to be a bit subtler about revenge paradoxes, and that is exactly what Jc Beall's analysis delivers.

Beall emphasizes that when one gives a formal theory of truth, one specifies an artificial language, L, that contains its own truth predicate 'true-in-L'. The theorist then shows that 'true-in-L' obeys various principles of the formal theory of truth, and the theorist can use L to show that the formal theory of truth is relatively consistent (often using classical logic and set theory in a metalanguage M). Finally, the theorist claims that natural languages are like L in relevant respects, so the theory of 'true-in-L' also applies to truth. Beall lays out three distinct revenge recipes for this sort of project:

1. Find some semantic notion X that is *used in M to classify sentences of L.*
   Show in M that X is not expressible in L unless L is inconsistent or trivial.
   Conclude that L is explanatorily inadequate since it does not explain how natural language, which contains X, is consistent.
2. Find some semantic notion X that is *expressible in M.*
   Show in M that X is not expressible in L unless L is inconsistent or trivial.
   Conclude that L is explanatorily inadequate since it does not explain how natural language, which contains X, is consistent.
3. Find some semantic notion X that is *expressible in natural language.*
   Argue that X is not expressible in L unless L is inconsistent or trivial.
   Conclude that L is explanatorily inadequate since it does not explain how natural language, which contains X, is consistent.[9]

[8] Priest (2008: 226). [9] Beall (2008b: 11–12).

The italics indicate the contrasts between the three recipes. In the first case, the concept X is used by the theory of truth to classify paradoxical sentences, whereas in the second case, the concept X is just expressible in the language of the theory—it need not be explicitly used by the theory. In the third case, the concept X is expressible in natural language and need not even be expressible in the language of the theory. In each case, the problem is that the theory in question does not apply to natural languages, so it does not really solve the problems posed by the aletheic paradoxes.

4.2 Revenge objections

By using revenge paradoxes like those surveyed above, one can formulate objections to the approaches in question. Namely, the artificial language used to model natural language has an expressive limitation—i.e., it does not contain terms that feature in revenge paradoxes. Thus, the approach in question solves the problems posed by the aletheic paradoxes only for expressively impoverished languages. That is, it does not solve these problems in general. In particular, it does not solve the problems posed by the aletheic paradoxes as they occur in natural languages.

For example, Field's paracomplete approach classifies liar sentences as indeterminate (i.e., not determinately true and not determinately false) and the object languages for his theory can have their own determinateness operators—of course, they will also have sentences like (5) in them as well. However, Field shows that there is no way to construct a revenge paradox using the resources in his object languages and, moreover, his object languages have the resources to classify every sentence in them as true, false, determinately true, determinately determinately true, etc. Thus, his theory is expressible in some of its object languages.[10] Nevertheless, as I argue, it faces revenge paradoxes. The same goes for Priest's theory, McGee's theory, and Beall's theory.[11] Each one is ingeniously constructed so that the theory does not rely on anything that might give rise to a revenge paradox. Each of these authors rightfully emphasizes that theories with this feature are to be preferred (other things being equal) over theories that do not (e.g., Gupta and Belnap's revision theory).

Why doesn't Field's theory have a problem with sentences like (5)? He interprets the 'indeterminate' in (5) as 'not determinately true and not determinately false', and his determinateness operator iterates non-trivially, so he can say that (5) is not determinately determinately true without thereby implying that (5) is not determinately true. If we use 'D' as a determinateness operator and superscripts for iterations, he can say that (5) is not D^2True, but he cannot say that (5) is not DTrue. But what if we want to say that a given sentence is not determinately true in any way—it is not DTrue, and it is not D^2True, and it is not D^3True, . . . ? That, presumably, is what one would think of 'indeterminate' in (5) in the first place without knowing anything about Field's approach. It

[10] Field (2008a).

[11] See Priest (1979, 2006a, 2006b), McGee (1991), and Beall (2009).

is impossible to say something like this in Field's object language. If it contained an idempotent determinacy operator ('idempotent' means that it iterates trivially), which we can use 'ID' to express, then Field's theory would entail that a sentence that says of itself that it is either false or neither IDTrue nor IDFalse is both IDTrue and not IDTrue. So, if it is non-trivial, Field's theory cannot apply to languages with idempotent determinacy operators. Field denies that this is a genuine problem, but we will have to come back to this issue in a moment.

The significance of the revenge paradox phenomenon is most fundamentally that we seem to be unable to say something non-trivial and satisfying about the aletheic paradoxes. Something satisfying would be an account of what goes wrong in the reasoning and a way of defining truth and any other notions one would want to classify sentences of languages capable of formulating these paradoxes that applies to any language that has a truth predicate regardless of the other notions expressible in it. So far, we do not know how to do this (or, rather, most theorists have yet to be convinced that it can be done—but in Chapters 6–10, I argue that it can). We can formulate satisfying accounts for a wide range of artificial languages, but in each case, there is always an Achilles' heel—some notion that, if it were expressible in a language to which the theory applies, the theory would be trivial: 'true in a context' for the contextualist, 'stable' for the revision theorist, 'idempotent-determinately' for the paracomplete theorist, 'just true' for the paraconsistent theorist, and the list goes on. In each case, even if the theory can be formulated in some of its object languages, and so does not officially use its Achilles' heel notion, it always seems odd to think that there is not and could never be such a notion—which is the position most often taken by proponents of these views—or that the expression in question is meaningless or unintelligible.

4.2.1 Too easy?

An advocate of a non-classical approach might respond to the points I have made by pressing the "too easy revenge" worry voiced by Jc Beall (and to some extent echoed by Lionel Shapiro). Beall offers a warning about the efficacy of these objections (I have changed the individual constants—L is the artificial language and E is the natural language being modeled):

> The weight of Rv1 or Rv2 depends on the sort of X at issue.... [I]f X is a classical, model-dependent notion constructed in a proper fragment of [E], then the charge of inadequacy is not easy to substantiate, even if the inexpressibility of X in [L] is easy to substantiate. In particular, if classical logic extends that of [L], then there is a clear sense in which you may 'properly' rely on a classical metalanguage in constructing [L] and, in particular, truth-in-[L]. In familiar non-classical proposals, for example, you endorse that [E], the real, target language, is non-classical but enjoys classical logic as a (proper) extension, in which case, notwithstanding particular details, there is nothing prima-facie suspect about relying on an entirely classical fragment of [E] to construct your model language and, in particular, classical model-dependent Xs. But, then, in such a context, it is hardly surprising that X, being an

entirely classical notion, would bring about inconsistency or, worse, triviality, in the (classically constructed) non-classical [L].[12]

Beall claims that if L (in the above revenge recipes) is a non-classical language and X is a classical, model-dependent notion, then recipes 1 and 2 are not very convincing since the theorist is simply using a classical metalanguage to construct a non-classical artificial language in an effort to argue that natural languages are non-classical:

A would-be revenger, involved in too easy revenge, would have it easy but too easy. What is (generally) easy is showing that some classically constructed notion is inexpressible—or, at least, not consistently expressible—in a (classically constructed) non-classical 'model language'. What is too easy is the thought that showing as much is sufficient to undermine the adequacy of the given model language. The hard part is clearly establishing the relevance of such inexpressibility results, that is, clearly substantiating the alleged inadequacy.[13]

Beall calls these sorts of cases "too easy revenge," and dismisses objections based on them unless they are accompanied by additional considerations (e.g., the semantics for L are intended to model the semantics for E).

There are a couple of wrinkles in Beall's presentation that, when straightened out, cast doubt on his main point. First, it is not obvious what is meant by "classical model-dependent notion." I take it that a model-dependent concept is a mathematical concept that is defined in terms of a particular model or class of models (using 'model' in the mathematical sense of model theory). Although it is problematic in general, for our purposes, we can safely assume that any mathematical concept is expressible in a language that can express set theory (ZFC).

It is less clear what Beall means by classical concept. It seems like a classical concept would be one that is expressible only in a language whose connectives obey classical logic (say, for definiteness, a classical first-order predicate calculus with identity), but this definition applies only to logical connectives. For example, classical negation obeys the inference rules and theorems for negation in a classical language (e.g., double negation elimination, classical *reductio*, excluded middle, and *ex falso*) and classical disjunction obeys the inference rules and theorems for disjunction in a classical language (e.g., or-introduction, reasoning by cases, disjunctive syllogism, and excluded middle). For non-logical concepts, one might think that a classical concept expressed by a one-place predicate is one whose constitutive principles include all the classical theorems and inference rules pertaining to one-place predicates. For example, a classical concept of redness would have 'everything is either red or not red', 'nothing is both red and not red', and all the rest as constitutive principles, provided that the logical terms occurring in these principles are classical (in the sense specific to logical terms). Notice that a classical concept on this definition *is* expressible in a non-classical language without triviality.

[12] Beall (2008b: 12); see also L. Shapiro (2011: 311–12) for a similar point made in defense of Field (2008a) from the objection in Rayo and Welch (2008).

[13] Beall (2008b: 11).

Imagine a first-order language with the usual syntax and Strong Kleene connectives. There is nothing incoherent about this language containing a predicate expressing classical redness without triviality. In a non-classical logic, there are *fewer* rules or theorems than one finds in classical logic. Thus, if one cannot prove triviality for a classical language that expresses a certain concept, then one cannot prove triviality for a non-classical language that expresses that concept, as long as the two languages have all the same non-logical expressions. The inverse does not hold, however. For example, smooth infinitesimal analysis is a theory of infinitesimals (i.e., infinitely small non-zero quantities) that is consistent in intuitionistic logic but inconsistent in classical logic.[14] Assume that the theory of smooth infinitesimal analysis implicitly defines the concept of an infinitesimal; then the concept of an infinitesimal is a non-classical concept in the sense that the theory that implicitly defines it is trivial in classical logic.

Beall's claim that "it is hardly surprising that X, being an entirely classical notion, would bring about inconsistency or, worse, triviality, in the (classically constructed) non-classical [language]," does not make sense given these considerations. Other things being equal, classical notions in this sense are expressible in non-classical logics without inconsistency or triviality. It is *non-classical* notions that bring about inconsistency in *classical* logics. Either there is some hidden assumption in Beall's reasoning—he means something else by 'classical notion'—or he has mistaken the direction of the above conditional.

Instead, Beall might have in mind concepts expressed by terms that force sentences in which they occur to have classical truth values. For example, in a first-order language with usual syntax and Strong Kleene connectives, the negation operator is called *choice negation* ('~'). If a sentence p is a truth-value gap, then ⌜~p⌝ is a gap as well. We can define in such a language another connective called *exclusion negation* (¬). If a sentence p is a truth value gap, then ⌜~p⌝ is true. In fact, any sentence whose major operator is exclusion negation is either true or false. Thus, exclusion negation obeys excluded middle: $p \vee \neg p$. But exclusion negation is not classical negation since it is defined only for non-classical languages that have truth value gaps. Perhaps when Beall talks of classical concepts, he means something like exclusion negation. However, this reading does not make his claim ("it is hardly surprising that X, being an entirely classical notion, would bring about inconsistency or, worse, triviality, in the (classically constructed) non-classical [language]") any more sensible. For exclusion negation *is* expressible in certain Strong Kleene languages without triviality; in fact, it is *defined* above for such a language. For example, a Strong Kleene language with just the usual logical expressions, exclusion negation, and the basic arithmetic expressions used for Peano Arithmetic is not trivial. Again, I do not understand what Beall means by 'classical notion'—at least, if his "too easy" reply is to make sense.

Let us try to interpret Beall's talk of "an entirely classical fragment" of a non-classical language to get a better idea of what he might mean. Let C be the set of all the logical

[14] See Bell (2008) for the theory and Hellman (2006) for some philosophical issues it raises.

consequences among declarative sentences of the natural language E. C is a set whose members are ordered pairs of sets and sentences—for each pair, the sentence is the second entry, and it follows from the set of sentences that is the first entry. Since E is non-classical, only arguments that are valid in the non-classical logic in question are listed in C. Now consider the classical fragment of E. What is the set of logical consequences for this fragment? It is obviously a proper subset of C; otherwise, the fragment would not be a fragment of E. It is clearly the set of pairs where the first entry (the set) contains only sentences from the classical fragment and the second entry is a sentence from the classical fragment. Are there any pairs in this set where the second entry follows classically from the set that is the first entry, but not according to the non-classical logic in question? No. So something has gone wrong here.

I will take one more crack at it. We have the language E and the set of logical consequences C as above, but now we deny that validity is closed under uniform substitution. It is possible that, for some particular sentence p and some particular set of sentences G, p is a logical consequence of G, but substituting uniformly for the sentences of G to get G′ and for p to get p′, p′ is not a consequence of G′. In Beall's preferred approach, which is paraconsistent, he denies the validity of *ex falso* (i.e., q is a consequence of ⌜p∧~p⌝). However, if he denies that validity is closed under uniform substitution, then he could accept that *for some particular sentences p and q*, q is a consequence of ⌜p∧~p⌝. With this idea in place, we can define a subset F of the sentences of our language E such that, for any classically valid argument with set G of premises and p as conclusion, any instance of that argument using only sentences of F is valid (according to the consequence relation C of E). Let the largest such F be the classical fragment of E.[15]

Given this definition of a classical fragment, one could use the classical fragment of a non-classical natural language to construct a non-classical artificial language to serve as a model for that natural language, which is exactly what Beall says. That does vindicate one point Beall makes in his "too easy" reply. However, the revenge objector does not take issue with the way the non-classical theorist constructs the artificial language in question. The problem is that this artificial language is not a good model for what goes wrong with the reasoning in the aletheic paradoxes in natural language because this artificial language (however it gets constructed) is devoid of some crucial, relevant linguistic expression. Thus, even if this is the right way to understand what Beall means by 'classical fragment', it still does not make sense of what a classical concept is, and so does not address the central point of revenge objections. However, a major problem even with this reading of 'classical fragment' is that it depends on the claim that validity is not closed under uniform substitution. That assumption abandons the idea that logically valid arguments are those that are valid by virtue of their logical form. Indeed, it gives up on the idea that logical form has anything to do with logical consequence. Perhaps there is some *independent* reason to make this move, but if there is, Beall has not given us one. Moreover, this reading of Beall's "too easy" reply works only for non-classical approaches that have the

[15] Thanks to Dave Ripley for this suggestion.

feature (or bug) of uniform substitution failure. It is not in any way a general response to revenge worries. So, I do not see that this reading of Beall's reply is very helpful.

In sum, stating the relevance of revenge paradoxes for non-classical approaches is fairly straightforward. The theorist has constructed a theory of truth-in-L. Is that theory consistent or at least non-trivial? One would hope so. How does it avoid the reasoning in liar paradoxes? It tosses out as illegitimate some of the logical principles used in that reasoning. How does it avoid the reasoning in revenge paradoxes? It does not apply to sentences that have those expressive resources, for they are not in the model language. What if we extend the model language by adding these resources? Triviality. So the theory enjoys non-triviality only because it does not apply to languages that have certain linguistic expressions that figure in revenge paradoxes. It makes no difference whether this result is surprising or whether the linguistic expression in question is classical (whatever that means).

But wait! Beall denies that one can simply add these linguistic resources to the model language because some linguistic expressions are incoherent with respect to certain languages; e.g., an exhaustive and exclusive operator (i.e., one for which excluded middle and *ex falso* are constitutive) cannot be added to a paracomplete or paraconsistent language without triviality (call this an EE operator).[16]

Beall defines 'trivial language' in the following way: "a trivial language (or theory) is one according to which everything is true. A non-trivial language is one that isn't trivial."[17] Unfortunately, this definition has a certain difficulty—languages do not make pronouncements about what is true. Perhaps, if one thinks of the expressions of a language as governed by certain constitutive principles, then one might think of a trivial language as having expressions with constitutive principles from which every sentence of the language follows. Still, one might deny that those sentences are true. Instead, a trivial language might be one whose truth predicate has an extension that contains every sentence of the language. That is probably what Beall has in mind here. However, that is still not a very good definition since, according to Beall's claim about EE operators, triviality is a feature of the consequence relation of a language, not its truth predicate. Granted, if one can prove any sentence of a language from the empty set and that language contains its own truth predicate and that truth predicate obeys (T-In) (i.e., if ϕ then $\langle\phi\rangle$ is true), then the truth predicate's extension contains every sentence of the language. I prefer to keep triviality tied directly to a language's consequence relation by defining it in the following way: a language is *trivial* iff for every sentence p of the language and every set G of sentences of the language, p is a consequence of G. This definition says nothing about whether the language has a truth predicate or how that truth predicate might behave. It also avoids the awkward claim that some things are true *according to a language*. Moreover, it fits well with Beall's point about EE operators above. That is, if we add an EE operator to a paracomplete language or paraconsistent language that contains its own truth predicate (which obeys Schema T) and has the means to represent its own syntax, then the extended language is trivial (in my sense).

[16] Beall (2008b). [17] Beall (2006: 330, n. 5).

Now that that matter is settled, we can continue with the objection, which might go in one of a couple of directions from here. One might argue that there are no trivial languages, so it is impossible to add an EE operator to one of the languages in question. I do not find this line plausible. One can construct an artificial language that is trivial and reason about it. It seems ad hoc in the extreme to claim that such a thing is not a language even though it is similar in all relevant respects to a language.

Instead, one might argue that sentences of a trivial language are not translatable with sentences of any non-trivial language. If the inferential role of a sentence determines at least in part its content, then one would think that no sentence with a trivial inferential role would be intertranslatable with a sentence that does not have a trivial inferential role.[18] That seems like a genuine worry.

As a reply, imagine we have a language as Beall describes it as a model for a natural language. It is a good model by any account. Then the natural language changes—the people in that linguistic practice start using a new expression. Let us say they use it just as Beall describes an EE operator. What should we say about the new language? We might say that the new expression is really meaningless or that it has some other meaning—it does not mean what everyone thinks it means. I find this option rather implausible. Part of our job as linguists, philosophers of language, or philosophical logicians is to explain what we find in natural languages—look at how people use certain words and consider their judgments of synonymy, entailment, contradiction, etc. to construct and defend the best theories of natural languages we can. Pretending as if an expression with an established use is meaningless or has a meaning it clearly does not is tantamount to a dereliction of duty.[19]

What should we say in a situation like this? I think the best thing to do is to say is that the word in question means exactly what the participants in the linguistic practice think it means—that is, it has exactly the constitutive principles they think it has. We can, of course, specify artificial languages in whatever way suits our interests, but to say that a language like the one Beall describes cannot be extended to include an EE operator is not a good strategy. Instead, we do better to say that it can, and that operator will mean what people think it means in that it will have what they take to be its constitutive principles. Of course, those constitutive principles might be inconsistent given the other resources in the language. If that is the case, then one will need to appeal to a plausible theory of inconsistent concepts to figure out the semantic values of the expressions and sentences of the language.

4.2.2 Expressibility delimiters

Another sort of criticism of the points I have made could come from someone who endorses Lionel Shapiro's recent reply to revenge paradox objections. Shapiro's formulation involves three characters: the Puzzler, the Solver, and the Avenger. His claim is that the

[18] Given the emphasis linguists and linguistically oriented philosophers put on entailments, the antecedent seems plausible.

[19] See Dowty, Wall, and Peters (1981: 1–3) for a classic statement of this methodology.

Avenger's arguments are based on a fundamental equivocation, and they are either sound but not paradoxical or unsound. Here is the setup.

The Puzzler offers two legitimate puzzles:

> Puzzle 1: There is a language L and a notion n such that without making reference to any features of L's syntax or semantics that distinguish L from English, we can prove that L does not express n, yet English appears to express n.
>
> Puzzle 2: There is a function n(x) from languages to notions such that we can prove that for any L satisfying certain conditions, L fails to express n(L), yet English, which satisfies these conditions, appears to express n(English).[20]

The Solver offers some solution to Puzzles 1 and 2. That solution probably involves a theory of truth, but according to Shapiro, it need not. The Avenger says that even if the Solver is right, there is some other notion that the language in question cannot express on pain of contradiction by liar reasoning.[21]

Shapiro's objections to the Avenger turn on his analysis of the Puzzler's arguments, the Solver's claims, and the Avenger's arguments, each of which depend on the notion of a *classical expressibility delimiter* (CED):

> The notion of being G is a CED for language L iff we have all instances (for H) of the following conditional:
>
> If a formula f(x) in L expresses the notion of being H, then for any name c in L, f(c) is G iff the referent of c is H, and ~f(c) is G iff the referent of c is not H.

It is easy to show that, if the notion of G is a CED for L, then L does not express the notion of being G, which Shapiro dubs the *Inexpressibility Schema*. The argument depends on some classical moves and a standard diagonalization strategy.

With the definition of a CED in hand, we get the reconstructed argument of the Puzzler:

(P1) The notion of being a true sentence of L is a CED for L.
(C1) L does not express the notion of being a true sentence of L (by the Inexpressibility Schema).

Because the Puzzler's argument makes no mention of the syntax or semantics of L, we get Puzzle 1, and because English seems to express the notion of truth, we get Puzzle 2.

Shapiro also considers how the Puzzler might defend the premise (P1), and he "see[s] no other justification"[22] than the following:

[20] L. Shapiro (2011: 299). There is a third puzzle as well, but he thinks it is not legitimate:

> Puzzle 3: For every language L, we can express (in some suitable metalanguage) a notion that is useful in semantic theorizing about L, but is not itself expressed by L.

Shapiro claims (2011: 312–13) that most work on the aletheic paradoxes does not address this puzzle.

[21] There is a second revenge-type worry that Shapiro mentions, but does not address, that is based on what Beall calls the exhaustive characterization project; see L. Shapiro (2011: 298, n. 2).

[22] L. Shapiro (2011: 304).

(T) Our grasp of the notions of a true sentence of a language and of a language's expressing a notion reveals that the notion of being a true sentence of language L counts as a CED for L.

The Solver responds by denying (P1) and, with it, (T). One class of Solvers denies that truth is expressible in a classical metalanguage, and another accepts that it is expressible in a classical metalanguage but denies that it is a CED.[23]

For Shapiro all revenge strategies follow one of two forms, both of which press the Solver for some other CED. The First Avenger's argument is:

(P2) The notion of being a Good sentence of L is a CED for L.
(C2) L does not express the notion of being a Good sentence of L (by the Inexpressibility Schema).

Again, for Shapiro, the First Avenger "must" appeal to the following to justify (P2):

(G) Our grasp of the notions of a Good sentence of a language and of a language's expressing a notion reveals that the notion of being a Good sentence of L counts as a CED for L.

Because the First Avenger does not appeal to the semantics or syntax of L, we get Puzzle 1 back, and because English seems to express the concept of Goodness, we get Puzzle 2 back. However, Shapiro claims that the Solver can simply reject (P2) and with it (G), thus thwarting the First Avenger's strategy.[24]

The Second Avenger's argument pertains to any interpreted first-order language L_M, such that its domain of discourse is a set, it contains its own (language-specific) truth predicate, and its predicates (except the truth predicate) can be translated into a classical fragment of our metalanguage. One can construct a classical model M for the truth-free fragment of L_M. Call the sentences of the truth-free fragment of the language that are designated in M, the *Solver-designated*$_M$ sentences.[25]

(P4) The notion of being Solver-designated$_M$ sentence of L_M is a CED for L_M.
(C4) L_M does not express the notion of being a Solver-designated$_M$ sentence of L_M (by the Inexpressibility Schema).

The Avenger justifies (P4) by appeal to facts about the model M that provides the semantics for L_M. Because the Second Avenger actually proves (P4), the Solver cannot reject it. However, by Shapiro's analysis, the Second Avenger fails to establish Puzzle 1, since the argument for (P4) depends on the semantics of the language in question. Moreover, Shapiro contends, "once we understand how the proposed proof of (C4) works, that should dispel any appearance that English expresses a notion that plays, with respect to

[23] Field (2008a) is an example of the former type of Solver and Maudlin (2004) is an example of the latter.

[24] L. Shapiro (2011: 305–6).

[25] Shapiro actually formulates the Second Avenger's argument for specific notions of designatedness (e.g., Kripke-designatedness). My formulation is meant to cover all the specific instances he mentions. See L. Shapiro (2011: 309–11).

English, the very role we exploited in proving that L_M does not express Solver-designatedness$_M$."[26] Thus, the Second Avenger fails to establish Puzzle 2 as well.

I disagree with just about everything in Shapiro's analysis, and as such I do not think that it does much to defend against revenge objections. Here are some its major problems.

First, Shapiro's two puzzles fail to capture the most obvious problem posed by the aletheic paradoxes, which is that we can derive an intuitively unacceptable conclusion from intuitively acceptable premises via intuitively acceptable inferences. In fact, it seems to many people, myself included, that accepting the premises, accepting the inferences, and rejecting the conclusion are not just intuitive, but *constitutive* of the concepts involved. This is the central problem posed by the aletheic paradoxes and the central problem that just about anyone who offers an approach to them is trying to solve. Shapiro's puzzles are side issues. His entire way of framing the debate suffers from this defect. Revenge objections are not aimed at reinstating those puzzles—they are aimed at showing the approach in question is not an acceptable solution to the main problem.

Second, the fact that Shapiro sees no other justification for the Puzzler's premise (P1) is disturbing. I agree that if (T) is the best the Puzzler can do, then the puzzle is not very threatening. However, a much better case for (P1) comes from considerations about the way we use truth predicates. We treat 'true' as if it obeys the T-schema for a wide range of sentences including liar sentences. Thus, we accept all instances of the following conditional:

> If f(x) in L expresses the notion of being H then for any name c in L, f(c) is true iff the referent of c is H and ~f(c) is true iff the referent of c is not H.

That is just how we use the word 'true' in English. Therefore, we treat it as if it is a CED. That is how we arrive at a justification for (P1) of the Puzzler's argument. It has nothing to do with conceptual analysis, or at least it need not. Of course, any Solver or theorist can deny that we treat 'true' in this way, but all that does is render his or her solution or theory irrelevant. So instead of showing the futility of revenge objections, Shapiro's analysis exposes a flaw in all the traditional approaches to the aletheic paradoxes that deny (P1), namely, that they deny that truth is a CED, but we treat truth as if it is a CED. Thus, Shapiro's attempts to discredit the use of CEDs in revenge arguments never get past the first stage.

Third, just as I do not think that Puzzle 1 or Puzzle 2 captures the central problem posed by the aletheic paradoxes, I do not think that the central aim of revenge objections is to somehow reinstate these puzzles. Instead, the proper way of formulating the dispute is, as I indicated above, as a dispute about the acceptability of the Solver's explanation for what goes wrong in the paradoxical reasoning. As Jc Beall indicates, the Solver responds to the Puzzler by doing three things: (i) proposing an artificial language that contains its own (language specific) truth predicate, (ii) showing that the paradoxical reasoning as represented in that language is unsound (or, at least, does not lead to triviality), and (iii) suggesting that the artificial language is a good model for natural languages. The Solver concludes that the aletheic paradoxes (as they pertain to natural languages) are unsound, and, moreover, indicates exactly what goes wrong in that reasoning.

[26] L. Shapiro (2011: 311).

The Avenger points out that the artificial language avoids triviality only because it is expressively impoverished—it lacks some notion that is either already in the natural language or could easily be added to it. If this notion were added to the artificial language proposed by the Solver, it would be trivial. Thus, the Avenger concludes that the artificial language proposed by the Solver is not a good model for our natural language (as it is or as it could easily be), and so the Solver's conclusion is implausible. Shapiro's analysis misses just about all of the central aspects of the debate.

Fourth, Shapiro's objection to the Avenger's first argument is just as unconvincing as his reconstruction of the Puzzler's argument. Shapiro thinks the Solver can just reject (P2) and (G) along with it, and thereby avoid reinstating the new puzzles. Again, his focus on the two puzzles he thinks are the main problems posed by the aletheic paradoxes allows him to mischaracterize revenge arguments. Frequently, the notion of Goodness that the Avenger uses to point out the expressive limitation is found in the Solver's own theory! When it is not, it is a notion that is either found elsewhere in the logical literature or one that can easily be constructed out of such notions (e.g., exclusion negation, Boolean negation, just true, idempotent determinacy, etc.). The fact that Shapiro cannot conceive of any other justification besides (G) for (P2) does not mean there is not one. There is no reason, other than the Solver's own claims, to think that these notions cannot be used in the way the Avenger suggests. Shapiro's major point here, "Once we allow the Solver to reject the claim that truth in L is a CED for L, it looks like dogmatism to insist without argument that some other notion must qualify as a CED,"[27] is strange. The Avenger does not insist without argument that some notion is a CED. Instead, the Avenger appeals to common usage. If the only reason that can be given for rejecting (P2) is that otherwise the Solver's theory is useless as a model for natural language and so the Solver's proposed approach to the aletheic paradoxes is unacceptable, then it is hard to see why anyone other than the Solver might find this convincing. Instead, to avoid making these sorts of ad hoc moves, the Solver would need to find *independent* evidence for rejecting (P2).

Fifth, Shapiro's criticism of the Avenger's second argument suffers from most of these problems. He points out that once one sees how to prove (C4), that should remove any puzzlement we had at the fact that English cannot have a notion that plays the role of designatedness. But, again, that does not address the main problem, which is that the Solver's solution only works because the Solver's language does not contain the crucial notion of designatedness. If it did, then the language would be trivial. Since English either does have such a notion or it could easily be extended to include one, the Avenger's point stands—the artificial language used by the Solver is a bad model. It makes no difference whether we can understand *why* the bad model cannot contain the notion of designatedness in question. Understanding that does nothing to quell the Avenger's worries. The Avenger says that, say, the Strong Kleene minimal fixed point is a bad model for English because the Strong Kleene minimal fixed point does not contain Kripke-designatedness on pain of triviality, but English clearly does. After all, Shapiro's paper is written in English—or, perhaps an extension of ordinary English. Either way, the Avenger

[27] L. Shapiro (2011: 306).

continues, the problem with the Solver's proposal is that it works only because it is specifically excludes something that would prevent it from working. The Solver says that the paradoxical reasoning formulated in English is unsound because English is like the artificial language, and the reasoning is unsound there. The Avenger says that English contains the notion of designatedness or can easily be extended to include it (after all, Shapiro coins the term in his own paper, thereby extending English to include it), so it is not like the artificial language in one crucial respect. Thus, there is no reason to think that the Solver has hit on what is wrong with the reasoning in English.

Sixth, Shapiro's entire discussion, as he admits, takes classical logic for granted. I do not see that anyone who offers a non-classical approach to the aletheic paradoxes can find any solace in his criticisms of revenge objections. The non-classical theorist might think that one can use classical logic in various situations—those in which there is no threat of paradox. However, reasoning about classical expressibility delimiters is certainly not one of them. Thus, if one thinks that the problem with the aletheic paradoxical reasoning is that it depends on certain classical inferences, then one will find the same problems with Shapiro's argument for his Inexpressibility Schema, and thus, with his entire characterization of the debate in terms of CEDs.

Finally, the whole notion of an expressibility delimiter is the wrong kind of tool for adjudicating these debates. It works fine for artificial languages, but for natural languages, we have no independent access to the semantic features of our expressions. We cannot inspect a truth predicate to see what its extension or intension might be; we cannot simply reflect on our logical concepts to determine whether they are classical or non-classical. Instead, we need to consider usage and that is a messy and complicated business. It is also one Shapiro neglects.

4.2.3 A diagnosis

It is difficult to come up with a single account of revenge paradoxes that works for all the different kinds of approaches to the aletheic paradoxes. Here is my best shot. Any combined approach to the aletheic paradoxes will have a philosophical component and a logical component. In Chapter 1, I classified the logical approaches (following Hartry Field) by the aletheic principles accepted and the logic that is compatible with the approach. Of the two aletheic principles that seem to be constitutive of truth, the most uncontroversial and most widely accepted is (T-Out): $\langle\phi\rangle$ is true $\rightarrow \phi$. Consider again a standard liar sentence:

(8) (8) is not true.

Notice that the instance of (T-Out) for (8) is '(8) is true → (8) is not true'. This instance of (T-Out) is equivalent to (8) itself.[28] That is, given the definition of (8), *an instance of (T-Out) is equivalent to a liar sentence.*

[28] '(8) is not true' is classically equivalent to '(8) is not true or (8) is not true', which is classically equivalent to 'if (8) is true then (8) is not true'.

Whatever status a theory of truth that includes (T-Out) assigns to (8), it assigns to '(8) is true → (8) is not true'. Moreover, every approach to the liar paradox treats (8) as problematic in some way that entails it is not simply true—either it is false, or a truth-value gap, or a glut, or indeterminate, or unstable, or whatever. Thus, theories of truth face a fundamental difficulty:

(i) deny (T-Out),
(ii) weaken the logic to the point that it breaks the equivalence between the instance of (T-Out) and (8), or
(iii) accept (T-Out) and accept that (T-Out) is not true.

Item (i) is not plausible since almost everyone takes (T-Out) to be constitutive of the concept of truth. In addition, denying (T-Out) is incompatible with treating 'true' as a device of endorsement, which is one of its most important functions (I discussed this in the previous chapter). Item (ii) causes problems when applied to natural languages since languages like English have linguistic resources that force classical reasoning, like exclusion negation. When a theory that denies the equivalence is applied to sentences with these linguistic resources, the theory delivers inconsistent results. Call this the *inconsistency problem*. Item (iii) requires accepting that one's theory of truth is not true. Call this the *self-refutation problem*.

In sum, there is immense pressure for a theory of truth to accept (T-Out), but any theory that does so faces either the inconsistency problem or the self-refutation problem because instances of (T-Out) are classically equivalent to paradoxical sentences. That, as far as I can tell, is the source of the revenge paradox phenomenon.

4.3 The revenge argument

With this diagnosis in place, we can turn to our second argument for the claim that truth is an inconsistent concept (the first being the obvious argument from the previous chapter). Let T be a theory of truth that validates the primary aletheic principles and implies that liar sentences have status Δ, where a sentence is Δ only if it is Bnot true. Let 'r' be our revenge liar:

(r) (r) is either false or Δ.

There are three options for T:

(i) T implies that (r), '(r) is either false or Δ', is true.
(ii) T implies that (r) is false.
(iii) T implies that (r) is Δ.

On any of these options, T implies '(r) is true iff (r) is false or Δ'. If T classifies this sentence as true, then T is inconsistent. If T classifies it as false, then T is self-refuting. If T classifies it as Δ, then T is self-refuting. Therefore, T is either inconsistent or self-refuting, unless T is restricted so as to avoid applying to languages that contain sentences like (r). Consequently, any theory of truth that validates the primary aletheic principles (and implies that liar sentences have status Δ, where a sentence is Δ only if it is Bnot true) is either inconsistent, self-refuting, or restricted. Given that any theory of truth that is inconsistent (trivial), self-refuting, or restricted is unacceptable, any theory of truth that implies both that the primary aletheic principles are true and that liar sentences have status Δ is unacceptable.

I have argued that we should accept that the primary aletheic principles are constitutive of truth. Thus, on my view: (i) if a theory of truth is acceptable, then it entails that the primary aletheic principles are constitutive for truth, and (ii) if a theory of truth entails the primary aletheic principles, then it is unacceptable. There seems to be very little wiggle room here. However, there is an additional assumption that connects the two conditionals: if a theory of truth entails that the primary aletheic principles are constitutive of truth, then it entails the primary aletheic principles. I reject this claim. One of the key aspects of the account of inconsistent concepts I endorse is that one or more of the constitutive principles governing the concept are invalid or not true. Thus, I accept that the primary aletheic principles are constitutive of truth, but it is not the case that they are all true; the theory of truth presented in Chapter 9 has this result as a consequence. This result allows anyone with a suitable account of inconsistent concepts to avoid the revenge argument.

The following is a summary of the revenge argument for treating truth as an inconsistent concept:

(i) If a theory of truth is acceptable, then it implies that the primary aletheic principles are constitutive of truth.

(ii) If a theory of truth implies that truth is a consistent concept and it implies that the primary aletheic principles are constitutive of truth, then it implies that the primary aletheic principles are true (valid).

(iii) If a theory of truth implies that the primary aletheic principles are true (valid), then it is inconsistent, self-refuting, or restricted.

(iv) If a theory of truth is inconsistent, self-refuting, or restricted, then it is unacceptable.

∴ (v) If a theory of truth is acceptable, then it does not imply that truth is a consistent concept.

Only an inconsistency theory of truth, on which principles (like the primary aletheic principles) that are constitutive for a concept need not be valid, has a chance of being an acceptable theory of truth. That is the conclusion of the revenge argument for an inconsistency approach.

The obvious objections to the revenge argument focus on (iii) and (iv). Many theorists deny that their theories are restricted at all or claim that they are restricted only in not applying to words that express inconsistent concepts. Others claim that self-refutation is not a problem for a theory of truth. The subsections that follow pursue these theorists as they flee for safety.

4.3.1 *Self-refutation*

At least one theorist, Tim Maudlin, has taken the heroic stance of endorsing a classical gap approach to the aletheic paradoxes and accepting that it implies that it is untrue. That is, Maudlin accepts (T-Out), rejects (T-In), and accepts classical logic. Since the liar sentence is equivalent to its instance of (T-Out), his approach implies that not all instances of (T-Out) are true. Thus, Maudlin's theory is self-refuting in the sense that it implies that it is not true.[29]

More specifically, Maudlin's approach allows three exclusive statuses: true, false, and ungrounded. By 'ungrounded' he means just what Kripke means; namely, that the sentence is not determined to be either true or false by virtue of the truth or falsity of non-aletheic sentences (i.e., those not containing occurrences of the truth predicate). All paradoxical sentences are ungrounded, but there are many non-paradoxical sentences that are ungrounded as well. Some of the principles of the theory turn out to be non-paradoxical, but ungrounded. Thus, the theory implies that some of its principles (e.g., instances of (T-Out)) are ungrounded.

One might wonder: how can Maudlin coherently assert his own theory when it implies that it is untrue? His answer is: truth is not a necessary condition for assertibility. He stipulates that it is permissible to assert some ungrounded sentences, including those that compose his theory of truth. However, all false sentences are not assertible and all true sentences are assertible. He is clear on this point:

> If one accepts the theory and the standard of permissibility, then one is permitted to assert the theory and also to assert that the theory is not true. This would only be self-contradictory if one also claimed that only true sentences should be asserted, but this is something we deny.[30]

Thus, once one rejects the received view that truth is a necessary condition for assertibility, one can both assert Maudlin's theory and assert that it is not true.

However, this move brings with it two additional problems. The first is that once one adds the predicate 'permissible' to the language to which the theory applies, one can generate new paradoxes with sentences like:

(9) (9) is not permissible.

If (9) is permissible, then (9) is false and permissible, but if (9) is not permissible, then (9) is true and impermissible. Either way one is forced to accept that either some permissible sentences are false or some true sentences are impermissible, which is incompatible with Maudlin's permissibility standard. Note that this is a different kind of revenge paradox—an inconsistency problem. In his attempt to lessen the blow of one kind of revenge paradox (i.e., the self-refutation problem), Maudlin stumbles into the other kind of revenge paradox (i.e., the inconsistency problem). This is not a coincidence—as

[29] Maudlin (2004). Maudlin sometimes speaks as if he endorses a non-classical theory of truth, but he uses 'non-classical' in a non-standard way. See Field (2006c) and Maudlin (2006a, 2006b, 2008) for discussion.

[30] Maudlin (2004: 178).

I have mentioned, there is an oscillation between these revenge paradoxes so that, when a theorist turns his attention to fighting one, the other strikes. Then, when he turns his attention to the other, the first returns.

In response to this permissibility version of the inconsistency problem, Maudlin bites the bullet and accepts that every set of rules for permissibility is inconsistent (i.e., in the parlance of this book, that permissibility is an inconsistent concept). "Indeed, the practical advice one is likely to offer with respect to rules of permissibility is this: simply try to avoid conversational contexts which lead into problematic areas (e.g., the discussion of sentences like [(9)]."[31] Maudlin seems to think that this is "a problem we must learn to live with."[32] But notice the evidence he marshals to convince us that permissibility is an inconsistent concept—that it gives rise to paradoxes structurally identical to the liar. For some reason Maudlin is convinced by the "obvious argument" for the inconsistency of permissibility, but resists the obvious argument for the inconsistency of truth. I am at a loss to explain why.

The second problem with revising the received view of permissible assertion is that it is incompatible with truth's expressive role. Although Maudlin fails to consider this problem, it follows easily from his unorthodox views on permissibility. Maudlin writes:

> If a sentence is ungrounded, then it is not appropriate to assert that the sentence is true or that the sentence is false. The claim that an ungrounded sentence is either true or false, such as [the liar is true or the liar is false], is, we shall say, impermissible.

Imagine a situation in which Ned wants to assert some sentence, say, the schematic rule for the biconditional (i.e., a biconditional is true iff both components have the same truth value), but he cannot remember exactly how it is formulated. All he needs to do is use 'true' as a device of endorsement—he should assert 'the biconditional rule is true'. Of course, Ned's utterance is impermissible since the biconditional rule is ungrounded and according to Maudlin, it is impermissible to assert that ungrounded sentences are true. Thus, Maudlin's view gives us the wrong predictions with respect to truth's expressive role. Therefore, it is not a good descriptive theory of our aletheic practice. The problem has nothing to do with Maudlin's claim that any system of principles for permissibility is inconsistent. No matter what one says about how to explain permissibility, Ned's utterance is permissible. It is a datum to be explained.

Notice also that this objection is far more vulgar than the one Kripke poses for the orthodox approach (explained in Chapter 3). In Kripke's objection, the speaker does not know the level of the sentence she wants to endorse, but if she did, then she would be able to use the truth predicate as a device of endorsement. At least the orthodox approach gets the latter situations right. For Maudlin, no matter how much the speaker knows about the ungrounded target, it is still impermissible to assert that it is true. And remember, Kripke's objection to the orthodox approach convinced an entire generation

[31] Maudlin (2004: 175). [32] Maudlin (2004: 177).

of theorists to seek new philosophical and logical approaches to the aletheic paradoxes; it is the meter bar of objections. Maudlin's failure to take any of this seriously should serve as a red flag: avoid tangling with the self-refutation problem.

4.3.2 The burden of proof

Because the standard response to a revenge paradox is to deny the intelligibility of one or more concepts expressed by words composing the revenge paradoxical sentence in question, there is an issue of whether these terms are meaningful, whether they are coherent, and who has the burden of proof in these debates. Take, for example, Priest on Boolean negation. It is easy to show that if the artificial language Priest proposes as a model for our natural language contains Boolean negation, then it is trivial. It would contain a sentence that says of itself that it is Bnot true (again, 'Bnot' expresses Boolean negation) and one could then derive any sentence of the language via revenge-type reasoning.

In response to this objection, Priest denies that there is such a thing as Boolean negation. He responds to any attempt to show that Boolean negation exists or is coherent by claiming that the argument in question begs the question against paraconsistent dialetheism.[33] That is, any attempt to show that Boolean negation exists or is coherent must appeal to Boolean negation, or at least, must presuppose that paraconsistent dialetheism is unacceptable. For Priest, the burden of proof is on the person pushing the revenge objection, while the theorist can sit back and play defense.

However, when criticizing others, Priest is all too happy to assume that the burden of proof is on the theorist. He writes when arguing the same kind of objection to Field: "There are notions which, for all the world, appear to us to be intelligible; these cannot, on pain of contradiction, be expressed in the object language. If we declare them meaningless, this is for no reason, in the last resort, other than that they lead to contradiction. As far as solutions to the paradoxes go, the result is, to put it mildly, disappointing."[34] It seems like Priest would not be satisfied if his target complains that any attempt to prove that the notions in question are meaningful or coherent begs the question against the target's favored theory. Instead, the target has the burden of proof to show that they are indeed meaningless or incoherent, and presumably this sort of argument would have to be *independent* of the favored theory in question. That is, one cannot just trot out the revenge paradoxes as evidence that the notions are meaningless or incoherent. Moreover, we would also need an explanation of why they seemed meaningful or coherent in the first place. Of course, Boolean negation appears for all the world to be intelligible, so Priest's objection to Field seems unfair given Priest's defense of his own view.

Priest's double standard for revenge objections is obviously unreasonable, but it would be good to have a position on who really has the burden of proof in these cases. Beall writes on this topic:

[33] See Priest (1990: 204–9; 2006b: Ch. 5). [34] Priest (2005: 46).

The difficulty in successfully launching Rv3 might be put, in short, as follows. Theorist advances L_m as a model of (relevant features of) L, our real language. Rv3 Revenger alleges that **X** exists in L, and shows that, on pain of triviality, **X** is inexpressible in L_m. The difficulty in adjudicating the matter is that... Theorist may reasonably conclude that **X** is incoherent (given the features of our language that Theorist advances). Of course, if Revenger could establish that we need to recognize **X**, perhaps for some theoretical work or otherwise, then the debate might be settled; however, such arguments are not easy to come by.

The burden, of course, lies not only on the Rv3 Revenger; it also lies with the given theorist. For example, typical paracomplete and paraconsistent theorists must reject the intelligibility of any EE device in our language. Inasmuch as such a notion is independently plausible—or, at least, independently intelligible—such theorists carry the burden of explaining why such a notion appears to be intelligible, despite its ultimate unintelligibility. Along these lines, the theorist might argue that we are making a common, reasonable, but ultimately fallacious generalization from 'normal cases' to all cases, or some such mistake. (E.g., some connective, if restricted to a proper fragment of our language, behaves in the EE way.) Alternatively, such theorists might argue that, contrary to initial appearances, the allegedly intelligible notion only appears to be a clear notion but, in fact, is rather unclear; once clarified, the alleged EE device (or whatever) is clearly not such a device. (E.g., one might argue that the alleged notion is a conflation of various notions, each one of which is intelligible but not one of which behaves in the alleged, problematic way.) Whatever the response, theorists do owe something to Rv3 revengers: an explanation as to why the given (and otherwise problematic) notion is unintelligible.[35]

I agree with Beall on this matter. Any theorist responding to revenge objections should be able to give *independent* evidence that the notions in question are meaningless or unintelligible and explain why they were taken to be intelligible in the first place. Moreover, anyone pushing a revenge objection should be able to provide evidence that the notions in question are meaningful and coherent, or why it does not matter whether they are coherent. I take the latter strategy to be fairly easy to accomplish, as I argue in just a moment.

In particular, I do not see that Priest's response to revenge objections concerning Boolean negation are successful. There is a long-standing problem in philosophy of logic about how one might justify one's basic logical notions and inference rules. For example, if one wants to justify the legitimacy of *modus ponens*, then one will have a hard time not using *modus ponens* in one's justification. The same goes for justifying the legitimacy of the classical conditional or classical negation.[36] Despite the fact that attempts to justify our basic logical rules and logical concepts are bound to be circular, we do not thereby conclude that they are illegitimate or that the linguistic expressions that purport to express them can be dismissed out of hand as unintelligible or meaningless. Instead, one would have to dig into this vexed issue and show somehow that Boolean negation is

[35] Beall (2008b: 13–14).

[36] See Dummett (1978), Boghossian (2000, 2001, 2003a), S. Shapiro (2000), Williamson (2003), Wright (2004a, 2004b), Tennant (2005), Dogramaci (2010), and Kroedel (2012) for discussion.

in an especially bad position—worse than the standard circularity problem. Thus, Priest's strategy for replying to revenge objections should be rejected.

Here is what I take to be the upshot of these considerations on burden of proof. It is hopeless for a theorist to claim that the crucial linguistic expressions that figure in revenge paradoxes are meaningless. To say that is to abandon any reasonable stance in linguistics, which treats established usage as definitive of meaningfulness. Adopting an approach to the aletheic paradoxes that rejects out of hand a foundational assumption of the science of linguistics is just as ridiculous as being a young Earth creationist. I do not see how any self-respecting philosopher could advocate something like that.

Given that the expressions in question are meaningful, the question then becomes: are they intelligible? I think that the best way to understand this question is as asking whether they express consistent concepts. Consider the EE operator example again. An EE operator is one that is stipulated to obey excluded middle and *ex falso*. That is, these are its constitutive principles. I do not take the question of whether there really is such a concept seriously. We can stipulate that our words have certain meanings (in the form of constitutive principles) without any worry that they might not really have these meanings (i.e., constitutive principles). They might not have the extensional, intensional, or metaphysical features that we think they do, but there is no worry about their constitutive principles. As such, there is no worry about whether these concepts exist.

Thus, the best thing for a consistency theorist to say in response to a revenge objection is that the concepts that figure in the revenge paradoxes are inconsistent. As such, there is no reason that the theory of truth being defended should be expected to apply to sentences with words that express them. The theorist can simply dismiss these sentences out of hand, even if they do show up in English or could easily be added to it.

4.3.3 Unintelligible?

As an example of a theorist who admits that the revenge-generating expressions are meaningful, but denies that they express consistent concepts, consider again Hartry Field. Recall that it is impossible to define a completely defined indeterminacy predicate in the language he constructs. Thus, he never has to deal with a real revenge paradox, like:

(5) (5) is either false or indeterminate

where 'indeterminate' is completely defined (i.e., every sentence is either indeterminate or not indeterminate). Field's theory clearly cannot handle sentences like (5). What does he say about them?

Field argues (convincingly in my view) that one need not use any such linguistic expression to formulate his theory (his semantic theory uses a completely defined notion of semantic value, but it is relative to a model and so cannot be used to construct a revenge paradox). In addition, he argues against the claim that the artificial language he constructs avoids revenge paradoxes only because it has expressive limitations. Instead, he claims that sentences like (5) are unintelligible. Indeed, Field argues, any linguistic expression that is not in his artificial language and seems to give rise to a revenge paradox (e.g., 'indeterminate') is unintelligible; however, by 'unintelligible' he does not mean *meaningless*:

I don't want to deny that we have these notions; but not every notion we have is ultimately intelligible when examined closely. A large part of the response to the counterintuitiveness qualm will be an argument, in Part Four, that the notion of "the" hierarchy of iterations of D has a kind of inherent vagueness that casts doubt on there being a well-behaved notion of "$D\alpha$-true for every α"; and without that there is no reason to suppose that there is a well-behaved notion of "determinately true in every reasonable sense of that term". The apparent clarity of such notions is an illusion.[37]

Field then argues that there is no way to extrapolate from the hierarchy of determinateness predicates to define a well-behaved (i.e., intelligible) notion of hyper-determinateness (i.e., a notion of determinateness that obeys excluded middle).[38]

I am willing to admit that if we have only the resources provided by Field's artificial language, then we will be unable to define a well-behaved notion of hyper-determinateness. However, it seems to me that this point does little to quell the revenge worries. The problem is *not*: how can we use the resources Field gives us to generate a paradox his theory cannot handle? The problem is: we have a notion of determinateness that obeys excluded middle (i.e., what Field calls hyper-determinateness) and one cannot express this notion in Field's artificial language. Thus, Field avoids revenge only by an expressive limitation on his language.

If one is not convinced that we either have or can stipulate a notion of determinateness that has LEM as a constitutive principle, then consider negation, about which more can be said. Instead of a truth-table definition, we can define exclusion negation by the following rules:

(LEM) $\vdash p \vee \neg p$
(EFQ) $p, \neg p \vdash \bot$

However, it is easy to show that exclusion negation is not definable in the languages Field considers (and it cannot be added without trivializing the language).

So what? One might wonder why this matters. There are several reasons. First, we seem to have something like exclusion negation in English. Here is a quotation from Kripke:

Liar sentences are *not true* in the object language, in the sense that the inductive process never makes them true, but we are precluded from saying this in the object language by our interpretation of negation and the truth predicate. If we think of the minimal fixed point, say under the Kleene valuation, as giving a model of natural language, then the sense in which we can say, in natural language, that a Liar sentence is not true must be thought of as associated with some later

[37] Field (2008c: 119).

[38] Field also discusses what he calls "model-theoretic revenge," but it is distinct from the sort of worry that I have pressed in this book; see Field (2008c: 106–9).

stage in the development of natural language, one in which speakers reflect on the generation process leading to the minimal fixed point.[39]

The fourth word of the quotation is 'not', but it does not make sense to think that it is choice negation since that reading would make Kripke's own sentence indeterminate. Instead, it makes the most sense to say that it expresses exclusion negation or that he is using classical negation.

Field is well aware that this is a pressing worry and he claims that exclusion negation too is "unintelligible" (he has to say the same about classical negation). He is careful to point out that he thinks that exclusion negation is meaningful; it is just an inconsistent concept.[40] Field defends this response in several ways. First, there is no way to define exclusion negation in the languages he considers. Second, he claims that there is no good argument for the legitimacy of exclusion negation—any purported argument is circular (i.e., it uses exclusion negation). Third, he suggests a way of interpreting someone who mistakenly uses exclusion negation.

I take it that the first point is just that nothing in Field's approach to the aletheic paradoxes requires exclusion negation; nor does it require anything that could be used to define exclusion negation. In terms of Beall's three recipes for revenge, it seems that Field is denying that either recipe 1 or recipe 2 will be successful. I agree with him on this—the presence of exclusion negation, or anything in terms of which it could be defined, would make Field's language trivial, and he has proven that it is not trivial.

The second point is the same argument we saw from Priest. We know that we cannot argue for the coherence of our basic logical concepts without begging the question, so Field's reasoning here is not convincing. The important thing to recognize is that if speakers of natural language use these expressions and have good reason to use them (and I think it is very plausible that they do), then Field's solution will carry serious hidden costs.

That brings us to his third point. Field writes:

I've heard it argued that even if no *good* theory posits a Boolean negation, we haven't solved the paradoxes until we've given an account of how to apply the term 'true' to the sentences of someone who has a *bad* theory according to which the word 'not' obeys all of Boole's assumptions (or at least, to the sentences of someone for whom this bad theory plays such a central role in his linguistic practices that it determines what 'not' means for him.) But I don't think that this raises an interesting challenge. There is bound to be a certain arbitrariness in how we attribute truth-values to sentences that contain concepts we find defective (e.g., 'tonk' (Prior 1960) or 'Boche' (Dummett 1973: 454)). We can't, for instance, regard both 'All Germans are Boche' and 'All Boche are prone to cruelty' as true, unless we share the racist beliefs of those who possess the concept; but a decision as to which (if either) should count as true, in the language of the racist for whom both beliefs enter into his practices in a "meaning-constituting" way, seems both pointless and unlikely to have a principled answer. Similarly for the use of 'not' by someone with a defective theory. Probably the simplest course is to translate his 'not' with our 'not', in which

[39] Kripke (1975: 714). [40] Field (2008a).

case his claims to the validity of excluded middle will come out false even though they were "meaning-constitutive"; but there's no reason to take a stand on this translation, or to think that there's a determinate fact of the matter as to whether it's correct.[41]

There is a lot going on in this passage. The mention of 'tonk' and 'Boche' is a reference to previous work on defective concepts. 'Boche' is an old French derogatory term for Germans, which has the connotation that Germans are barbaric. Michael Dummett popularized it in a discussion of inferential role semantics. It seems inappropriate to use 'Boche' since it seems that any use is an implicit endorsement of the claim that all Germans are barbaric (the same point holds for other pejoratives).[42] When Field writes about 'not' obeying all Boole's assumptions, he is talking about exclusion negation (at least in the context of a paracomplete approach). He describes those who use exclusion negation as having a bad theory of negation. By this, he means that someone who uses 'not' to express exclusion negation has false beliefs about negation. Finally, Field accepts Quine's criticism of analyticity and his argument for the indeterminacy of translation, which are controversial and immensely influential theses in the philosophy of language. The former attempts to undermine the idea that any sentences are true by virtue of their meanings alone, while the latter purports to show that meaning and translation are largely indeterminate.[43] Putting all this together: someone who uses 'not' to express exclusion negation has a bad theory of negation and we should attribute truth values to his or her sentences by simply translating them into Field's paracomplete language since there is no fact of the matter as to what they "really" mean. The effect is that Field advocates treating everyone who uses 'not' as meaning exactly what Field means when he uses 'not'.

Why is this a problem? Most people do not have theories of negation—they utter sentences that contain 'not' in certain circumstances and they interpret others who utter sentences that contain 'not' in certain circumstances. The question for a philosopher of language or a linguist who works on semantics or pragmatics is: what is the best way to make sense of how English users behave? If it turns out that a theory on which 'not' expresses exclusion negation on some occasions provides the best explanation of how English users use 'not', then Field's approach has a major cost—namely, it cannot be applied to English.

Is there any reason to think that people use 'not' in this way? Yes. The intuitive evidence is the following. If I say that p is not true, and I mean to be saying that p is something other than true (which includes falsity, indeterminacy, or whatever), then I take myself to be saying something true, no matter how indeterminate p might be. But Field cannot accommodate this intuition. If Field is correct, then no matter how much I try, if p is indeterminate enough, my sentence will be indeterminate as well. To be a bit more careful about this point: Field will translate my claim that p is not true as 'p is not D^{σ}true'

[41] Field (2008a: 309–10, n. 1).

[42] See Dummett (1973: 454), Brandom (1994b: 125–32; 2009: 124), Williamson (2003, 2006), and Horn (2008).

[43] See Quine (1951, 1960).

for some σ, but no matter how large σ is, if p's level of indeterminacy is higher, 'p is not D^{σ}true' is indeterminate (at some level or other). Moreover, according to Field, it is incoherent for me to say or believe that p is not true, where this claim or belief is true no matter what level of indeterminacy p has.[44]

In addition, linguists claim that 'not' in English (at least sometimes) is properly interpreted as exclusion negation, and linguists use exclusion negation in their theories. Here are two examples.

Jay Atlas in *Philosophy without Ambiguity* (1989) argues that 'not' has a general sense and on particular occasions of use it can express either choice negation or exclusion negation. There is linguistic evidence that 'not' is univocal and invariant because it fails ambiguity tests and context-dependence tests; thus, it is neither ambiguous nor context-dependent. Nevertheless, on many occasions, it makes the most sense to interpret English speakers as meaning exclusion negation when they use 'not'.[45] A second example is that Laurence Horn in *A Natural History of Negation* (2001) surveys views on negation from Aristotle to present, the evidence for choice negation readings of 'not' vs. exclusion negation readings of 'not', and how these readings interact with other linguistic phenomena (presupposition, conversational implicature, scope, etc.). He too argues that 'not' is not ambiguous or context-dependent. Rather, exclusion negation provides the semantics for natural language descriptive (non-metalinguistic) negation or predicate denial (in Aristotle's sense), and what seems like choice negation is an artifact of pragmatic tendencies like that of reading topical/definite subjects as taking wide scope with respect to ordinary predicate denial.[46]

On the other hand, there is no evidence that English contains a transfinite hierarchy of determinate truth predicates. No scientists studying English have ever found any data to support such a view. The only support Field can offer is "well, that's just a consequence of the best way I can think of to solve the liar paradox." Perhaps this kind of armchair justification would be compelling if its consequences were obscure enough to have avoided any scientific inquiry, but that is not the case—linguists have plenty of data that suggest we often use 'not' to express exclusion negation. Blanket dismissal of these results is on par with being a Creationist or a flat-Earther.

I suppose Field could say that the evidence cited by Atlas and by Horn is compatible with English having some kind of expression that behaves like exclusion negation in their examples, but which fails to obey excluded middle in paradoxical settings. Of course, to be convincing, he would have to find some kind of independent evidence to support this claim. However, instead of developing this line of thought, it might be better to just stop banging on a square peg and recognize that the hole is round.

4.3.4 Importing revenge

Even if one restricts one's theory of truth to languages that do not have the resources for explicit revenge paradoxes, seemingly innocent languages can harbor revenge paradoxes

[44] Field (2008a). [45] Atlas (1989: Ch. 3). [46] Horn (2001).

because they have the ability to refer indirectly to languages with explicit revenge paradoxes. That is, using the resources of the seemingly innocent language, one can import a revenge paradox from the restricted language.

Let T be a theory of truth that accepts both (T-In) and (T-Out) and assume that 'pathological' is the status T assigns to paradoxical sentences (I am taking it for granted that if a sentence is pathological, then it is Bnot true, and that excluded middle holds for 'pathological'). Let p be a sentence that gives rise to a revenge paradox for T; for example p might be 'p is either false or pathological'. The standard response to this kind of problem is to say that T is restricted so that it does not apply to languages containing anything like p. Let p be a sentence of language M. Assume that L is a language that does not contain p or any translation of it, L contains an unrestricted truth predicate (i.e., one that is not language-specific), and L contains a singular term that refers to p (we might as well use 'p'). So, L does not seem to contain anything that would give rise to a revenge paradox for T since it does not contain p itself. However, L does contain the sentence 'p is true'; call this q. If p were in the scope of T, then T would imply that p is both true and either false or pathological; that, again, is the conclusion of the argument with which this section began, and it is the reason why T is restricted to avoid p. Nevertheless, q *is* in the scope of T, and an argument with the same form shows that T implies that q is both true and either false or pathological. The upshot is that if p generates a revenge paradox for T, then q generates a revenge paradox for T. Thus, to avoid revenge paradoxes, T should be restricted so that it does not apply to q either. Moreover, it must be restricted so that it does not apply to sentences that attribute truth to q, and those that attribute truth to those that attribute truth to q, and so on. Call this an *importation problem.*[47]

One way to avoid this problem is to formulate a theory of language-specific truth (e.g., 'true-in-English'), and to claim that truth predicates of natural language can be explained in terms of language-specific truth predicates. If L contains 'true-in-L' instead of 'true', then q would be 'p is true-in-L', which is false since p is not a sentence of L. Thus, for approaches to the aletheic paradoxes that give rise to revenge paradoxes, language-specific truth predicates play an absolutely essential role.

Matti Eklund presents a different kind of importation argument in his recent discussion of revenge paradoxes. Eklund argues that even if a language L cannot *directly* formulate revenge paradoxes, it might *indirectly* express the concepts sufficient to formulate revenge paradoxes. Here is his definition of indirect expressibility:

> A property ϕ is *indirectly expressible* in a language L iff there is a predicate F of L such that for some context c, an utterance of F by a speaker of L is such that for all x, 'F(x)' and 'x has ϕ' have the same truth-value.[48]

[47] Importation problems can also take the form of liar pairs. If L contains an unrestricted truth predicate but no pathologicality predicate, and L′ contains a falsity predicate and a pathologicality predicate, but no truth predicate, then L contains a sentence b = 'a is true' where a = 'b is false or pathological' and a is a sentence of L′. T seems to apply unproblematically to both L and L′, but that is not the case; although neither language, by itself, has the resources to construct a revenge paradox, together they have a revenge pair (a and b).

[48] Eklund (2008a: 61).

For example, L might have the predicate 'falls under Frink's favorite predicate', where Frink's favorite predicate belongs to some other language sufficient to formulate revenge paradoxes. (Note that 'falls under' is a satisfaction predicate.) Imagine that Frink's favorite predicate is 'pathological' as used by theory T. Then L would have a sentence r, which is 'r is either false or r falls under Frink's favorite predicate'. It should be obvious that roughly the same argument as above shows that T implies that r is true iff it is either false or pathological. So, indirect expressibility poses serious problems for approaches to the aletheic paradoxes that give rise to revenge paradoxes.

It seems to me that the proponent of an approach that faces this kind of importation problem should follow the same strategy as above. That is, she should stipulate that only language-specific satisfaction predicates are legitimate. For example, if L contains only 'falls-under-in-L' instead of 'falls under', then Eklund's importation argument is thwarted. Presumably, one would want to stick with the same policy for all semantic predicates of L.

Given the crucial role language-specific (LS) truth predicates play in revenge avoidance strategies, it would be a major blow to all consistency views if natural-language truth predicates could not be explained in terms of LS truth predicates. That is exactly what I argue in the next subsection, which should be thought of as supporting the importation considerations above.

4.3.5 Language-specific truth predicates

Just to be clear about the purpose of this section, let us review: the main argument (section 4.3) has as a premise that theories of truth that are restricted to avoid revenge paradoxes are unacceptable. Because of importation problems, any theory of truth that is restricted to avoid revenge paradoxes has to be a theory of a LS truth predicate. Here I complete the case for that premise of the revenge argument by showing that natural-language truth predicates cannot be explained in terms of LS truth predicates.

Let a theory of truth that takes its primary explanandum to be LS truth predicates be an *LS theory*.[49] The first problem for LS theories is that speakers of natural languages routinely apply their truth predicates to foreign sentences. For example, one can attribute truth to a German sentence by using the truth predicate of English (e.g., ''Schnee ist weiss' is true' is a true sentence of English). However, ''Schnee ist weiss' is true-in-English' is not a true sentence of English. Thus, the simple LS theory on which 'true' just means *true-in-English* has false consequences.

A more complex LS theory avoids this problem. For example, an LS theory on which 'true' is ambiguous and can have the meaning of any of the LS truth predicates is

[49] For deflationist theories of this sort (i.e., disquotational theories), see Leeds (1978, 1995, 2007), Field (1986) (in which they are discussed but not endorsed), M. Williams (1986, 1999, 2002), Resnik (1990), Quine (1992), McGee (1993), Field (1994a, 1994b), Weir (1996), Halbach (1999, 2000, 2002), and J. Burgess (2002). For examples of LS theories among approaches to the aletheic paradoxes, see van Fraassen (1968), Parsons (1974, 1983), Kripke (1975), Priest (1979, 2006a), Burge (1979), Feferman (1982), Herzberger (1982), Skyrms (1984), Yablo (1985), Reinhardt (1986), McGee (1991), Gaifman (1992), Gupta and Belnap (1993), Simmons (1993), McDonald (2000), Field (2002, 2003a, 2003b, 2008a), and Maudlin (2004).

untouched by this objection. On this view, in the sentence ''snow is white' is true', 'true' means *true-in-English*. In the sentence ''Schnee ist weiss' is true', 'true' means *true-in-German*. Call this the *ambiguity LS theory*.

There is a substantial body of literature in linguistics on tests one can perform to determine whether a linguistic expression is ambiguous.[50] For example, one cannot express the claim that Carl went to the financial institution and Lenny went to the edge of a river by asserting 'Carl and Lenny each went to the bank' because 'bank' is ambiguous; in addition, sentences like 'Carl went to the bank, but he did not go to the bank' have non-contradictory readings because 'bank' is ambiguous. However, one can express the claim that 'Schnee ist weiss' is true and 'snow is white' is true by asserting ''Schnee ist weiss' and 'snow is white' are true'; in addition, the sentence ''Schnee ist weiss' is true, but 'Schnee ist weiss' is not true' is a contradiction. Thus, 'true' fails the standard ambiguity tests.[51]

In addition, the ambiguity LS theory faces another problem. Consider the following example. Ned and Maude are at a bar, having a conversation in English. Maude is a distinguished expert on ring-tailed lemurs, and Ned is aware of this fact. Maude tells Ned that on Monday she was at a talk given by Helen, another expert on ring-tailed lemurs. Maude informs Ned that Helen argued for a certain thesis, but Maude does not tell Ned what the thesis is because the complexities do not matter for her purposes in the conversation. Maude simply refers to it as *Helen's thesis*. Maude remarks that Helen's thesis implies that a theory Maude recently published is false, and she tells Ned that she now agrees with Helen. Assume that Maude is right about the truth of Helen's thesis and its consequence. Later that morning, Ned bumps into Tim at the library. Tim is writing a paper on ring-tailed lemurs, and he informs Ned that he is planning to rely on Maude's recently published theory. Ned tells Tim that Maude's theory is false. Tim knows that Ned is usually sincere and trustworthy, but that Ned does not know much about the literature on ring-tailed lemurs; accordingly, Tim challenges Ned on his assertion. Ned responds by asserting 'if Helen's thesis is true, then Maude's theory is false' and 'Helen's thesis is true'. Ned, of course, explains to Tim that Maude informed him of these facts. After hearing this, Tim scurries off to the bar to find Maude so that he can find out what Helen's thesis is.

Ned's assertion of 'Helen's thesis is true' is an expressive use of a truth predicate since Ned is using it to endorse Helen's thesis even though he is unable to assert Helen's thesis directly (i.e., it is a blind use). Moreover, it is felicitous. What, according to the ambiguity LS view, is the meaning of 'true' in Ned's sentence? If it meant *true-in-English* and Helen's thesis is a sentence of some other language, then Ned's sentence would be false. The problem is, Ned does not know which language Helen was speaking, so he does not

[50] See Zwicky and Sadock (1975), Cruse (1986), Atlas (1989), Gillon (2004), and Kennedy (2010) for discussion.

[51] It seems to me that these results cast considerable doubt on Kölbel's claim that 'true' is ambiguous; see Kölbel (2008a).

know which meaning to pick. Thus, the ambiguity LS theory requires too much of speakers using 'true' in situations like this. It implies (given the Content Determination Condition (CDC)) that Ned should know what language Helen was speaking in order for his utterance to be felicitous.

An ambiguity LS theorist might claim that 'true' just gets whatever meaning is appropriate independently of what Ned intends. This idea flies in the face of evidence from linguistics about ambiguous terms, but so be it. Assume Helen was speaking French. Now, according to the LS-ambiguity theory, the truth predicate in Ned's sentence means *true-in-French*, and his sentence means that Helen's thesis is true-in-French. However, now the problem is that the meaning of Ned's sentence is not available to anyone in his conversation with Tim. Neither Ned nor Tim knows what Ned's sentence means and there is no way for them to recover its meaning from what has been said or the context of utterance. Thus, the ambiguity LS theorist who follows this path runs afoul of the CDC.

Instead of defending the ambiguity LS theory, some deflationists who advocate LS theories suggest that natural-language truth predicates are synonymous with 'translatable into a sentence of L that is true-in-L'. Call this a *translational LS theory*.[52] For example, on this view the English sentence ''Schnee ist weiss' is true' means that 'Schnee ist weiss' is translatable into an English sentence that is true-in-English.

There are at least two options for how a translational LS theory interprets an English sentence like ''Schnee ist weiss' is true': the *quantificational version*, which treats this sentence as '(∃x)(x is a sentence of English and x is a translation of 'Schnee ist weiss' and x is true-in-English)', and the *constant version*, which treats it as 'p is a sentence of English and p is a translation of 'Schnee ist weiss' and p is true-in-English', where 'p' is a constant. When interpreting multiple-target truth attributions (e.g., 'all the sentences Carl asserted yesterday are true'), the quantificational version of the translational LS theory is the only acceptable option.[53] Thus, one might as well endorse it in general.

Although the translational LS approach seems to explain the English word 'true' with only a single LS truth predicate ('true-in-English'), this is an illusion. Consider

[52] The move is familiar in the face of other criticisms leveled against LS approaches; for such criticisms, see Blackburn (1984), David (1989, 1994), Richard (1997), Soames (1997), Brendel (2000), Horwich (2001), Künne (2002), and S. Shapiro (2002, 2003). These philosophers all address deflationists who advocate the LS approach. Some philosophers who work on the logic of truth have criticized Tarski's commitment to the LS approach; see Field (1972), Dummett (1978: Introduction), and Putnam (1985). See also Davidson (1990, 2005) for a discussion of this issue.

[53] The quantificational version can render this claim as: 'for all x, if x is a sentence Carl asserted yesterday, then for some y, y is a sentence of English and y is a translation of x and y is true-in-English'. How should the constant version treat this sentence? Perhaps 'for all x, if x is a sentence Carl asserted yesterday, then p is a sentence of English and p is a translation of x and p is true-in-English'? This cannot be right because it implies that p is a translation of all the sentences Carl asserted. Another option might be: 'for all x, if x is a sentence Carl asserted yesterday, then p and q are sentences of English, and either p or q is a translation of x, and p and q are true-in-English'. This suggestion works only if Carl asserted at most two sentences on the day in question. A supporter of the constant version might suggest that the logical form of the truth attribution depends on the number of its targets, but this hardly seems plausible. Moreover, it abandons the view that 'true' means 'translatable into a sentence of English that is true-in-English'.

the sentence "'Schnee ist weiss' ist wahr' is true'. This should come out as a true sentence of English. However, according to the translational LS theory, it means "Schnee ist weiss' ist wahr' is translatable into a sentence of English that is true-in-English. What sentence could this be? Perhaps "Schnee ist weiss' is true-in-English'? No, this sentence will not work since it is not true-in-English. The only option for an LS theorist is to use "Schnee ist weiss' is true-in-German' as the translation into English. But, of course, that would require English to have 'true-in-German' as well as 'true-in-English'. Thus, the translational LS theory cannot get away with using a single language-specific truth predicate. It needs just as many as the ambiguity LS theory.

The translational LS approach is plausible only for accounts of language and accounts of translation on which all languages are intertranslatable. Otherwise, it faces an obvious criticism. Pick a true sentence p of a language L that is not translatable into English. The sentence 'p is true' is a true sentence of English, but the translational LS approach implies that it is false (on this view, 'p is true' means that for some x, x is a sentence of English and x is a translation of p and x is true-in-English—but, by stipulation, there is no such sentence of English). Thus, I assume that, given the notions of language and translation employed by the translational LS theorist, all languages are intertranslatable.

This concession does not save the translational LS approach.[54] Consider again the example story with Ned, Maude, Helen, and Tim. Maude tells Ned about Helen's thesis, but she does not tell him which language Helen was speaking when Helen asserted it. We can alter the example so that Maude tells Ned that Helen's thesis cannot be translated into English because it involves technical jargon that currently belongs only to the language Helen was speaking when she asserted it.

Again, Ned is using 'true' to endorse a proposition that he cannot assert directly. Furthermore, Ned believes that Helen's thesis is not translatable into English; consequently, Ned believes that there is no sentence of English that is both a translation of Helen's thesis and true-in-English. However, according to the translational LS theory, Ned's sentence means that there is a sentence of English that is both true-in-English and a translation of Helen's thesis. So, again, this theory imposes too strict a requirement on speakers using 'true' in situations like this. It implies (again, given the CDC) that Ned should know that Helen's thesis is translatable into English in order for his utterance to be felicitous.

In sum, I have argued that the basic LS theory, the ambiguity LS theory, and the translational LS theory all conflict with the combination of truth's expressive role and the CDC. The right conclusion to draw is that truth predicates are not language-specific in any way.[55]

[54] However, it does save the translational LS approach from other criticisms; for example, S. Shapiro (2003) argues that if it is not the case that all languages are intertranslatable, then the translational LS theorist has to accept a notion of logical consequence that is not acceptable to a deflationist. See Field (2001e) and S. Shapiro (2005) for comment.

[55] Gary Ebbs tries to deal with the problem by offering a new account of words. However, if successful, it would work only for attributions of truth (in English) to sentences that contain only words that have the same extensions as English words. Sentences like "Nelson fühlt Schadenfreude' is true-in-English' still pose a problem for Ebbs (as he admits) since there is no English equivalent of 'Schadenfreude'. See Ebbs (2009: 141).

Let us reflect on the relevance of these considerations for the importation results in the previous subsection and the revenge argument in general. Many theorists facing revenge paradoxes deny that the linguistic expressions involved are meaningful or coherent. I argued against these moves in section 4.2.2. Instead, a theorist might restrict his or her approach so that it applies only to languages without the resources to construct revenge paradoxes. The importation arguments in section 4.2.3 together with the results of this subsection show that restricting one's theory in this way only guarantees that it has nothing to say about our natural-language truth predicate or the paradoxes it engenders—for the restriction strategy to avoid importation problems, one has to focus exclusively on LS truth predicates and there is no sense in which the truth predicate of our natural language can be explained in terms of LS truth predicates.

4.4 The abductive argument

The third argument for an inconsistency view is that if one decides to treat truth as an inconsistent concept, then one has available a satisfying explanation of the current situation in truth studies. That is, one has a satisfying explanation of why the aletheic paradoxes occur, why we are taken in by their reasoning, and why other theories of truth face revenge paradoxes, both inconsistency problems and self-refutation problems.

Explaining why the aletheic paradoxes arise and why we have been taken in by them is something other inconsistency theorists have emphasized, especially Matti Eklund.[56] The paradoxes occur because we reason using truth's constitutive principles and some minimal logical principles that are constitutive of the logical connectives involved, but because truth's constitutive principles are inconsistent, they allow us to reason to a contradiction. Those who treat truth as a consistent concept think that anyone taken in by the reasoning is making some kind of mistake—believing in a monster, accepting (T-In) and (T-Out), or using an intuitive conditional and an intuitive notion of derivability. The inconsistency theorist, on the other hand, thinks that our mistake is trusting our concept of truth. The very idea that our concepts might lead us astray is, although not unprecedented in the history of philosophy, certainly a minority view.[57] It was not until analytic philosophers brought the considerable logical resources made possible by the revolution in mathematics at the end of the nineteenth century to bear on the problem that it became evident that the problems with consistency views are systemic. There is no reason to think that prior to the development of these tools, possessors of the concept of truth would have been able to clearly pin the blame on our concept of truth.

The explanation for why theories of truth that imply truth is a consistent concept face revenge paradoxes is straightforward. Our concept of truth is inconsistent in the

[56] Eklund (2002a, 2002b, 2007, 2008a).

[57] See Mates (1981: 55–7; 1989: 67) for an interpretation of Leibniz on which he thinks some concepts are inconsistent.

sense that its constitutive principles are incompatible. That is, there are objects that these rules classify as both true and not true. (In Chapter 2, I called the set of such objects the *overdetermination set* for truth.) All the paradoxical sentences considered so far are members of the overdetermination set for truth.[58] Any theory of truth that implies that truth is a consistent concept and that includes these principles is inconsistent and can be rendered consistent only by restricting it. If a theory of truth implies that some of the sentences in the overdetermined set for truth are gaps, then the theory's fate depends on which of these sentences it classifies as gaps. Recall that many of the members of the overdetermination set for truth are truth attributions, and no matter what truth status (e.g., true, false, gappy, etc.) one assigns them, they are consequences of the assignment. No matter whether one's theory of truth classifies these paradoxical sentences as true, false, or gappy, some of these paradoxical sentences are consequences of the theory. Thus, if a theory of truth implies that all the sentences in the overdetermined set for truth are gaps, then the theory implies that some of its consequences are gaps. On the other hand, if a theory of truth does not classify some of these sentences as gaps, then the primary aletheic principles imply that they are both true and not true. On the first option, the theory is self-refuting, while on the second, it faces an inconsistency problem. Structurally similar accounts explain revenge paradoxes for other types of theories. Therefore, both types of revenge paradoxes can be explained if we assume that truth is an inconsistent concept.

There are at least two well-developed explanations of the revenge paradox phenomenon, one from Hartry Field and one from Michael Glanzberg. Why is the explanation I offer superior to the ones they offer?

I begin with Glanzberg, who offers a contextual approach to the aletheic paradoxes. However, instead of claiming that truth predicates are explicitly context-dependent, Glanzberg argues that sentences that contain truth predicates display an implicit context dependence that is due to the presence of quantification. Glanzberg offers a theory of background domains of propositions for the quantifiers involved, which includes an infinite hierarchy of domains and no "biggest" domain.[59]

If one accepts Glanzberg's theory, then one has to admit that there is no unrestricted quantification. Indeed, one has to accept that we can express the notion of truth-in-a-context and we can even quantify over contexts to a limited degree, but we cannot express an unrestricted notion of truth. "One way or another, hierarchical theories all require that speakers cannot in any one instance express the entirety of a unified concept of truth."[60] He argues that the sort of fragmentation we see in our concept of truth is familiar to us (i.e., it occurs in the concept of mathematical proof as well) and that it occurs because truth fails to be closed under reflection.

[58] It seems to me that truth-tellers (e.g., sentence τ, 'τ is true', is a truth-teller) are in the *under*determination set for truth, but these sentences are not paradoxical and none of my claims or arguments hang on this opinion.

[59] Glanzberg (2001, 2004, 2005). See also Cook (2008) and Schlenker (2011) for similar views.

[60] Glanzberg (2004: 289).

Glanzberg's defense of this feature is based on the idea that any characterization of truth permits one to reflect on the truth of the characterization, and this reflection both shows that the initial characterization is inadequate and points the way toward a stronger one. This process of reflection is unending; hence the infinite hierarchy of contexts.[61] The motivation for this view comes from what has been called the strong liar reasoning. Consider again a liar sentence:

(8) (8) is not true.

The indeterminacy approach to the liar implies that (8) is indeterminate. We know that if a sentence is indeterminate, then it is not true. Thus, the indeterminacy approach implies that (8) is not true. Hence, the indeterminacy approach implies that '(8) is not true' is true; therefore, it implies that (8) is true.[62] It is by reflection on the way the approach classifies (8) that drives us to conclude that (8) is true after all. The claim, 'if the indeterminacy approach implies that ϕ, then $\langle\phi\rangle$ is true', is similar to what is called a *reflection principle*. It states something about a formal theory that cannot be captured by the formal theory on pain of contradiction.[63]

Glanzberg argues that one can begin with a basic formal theory of truth, formulate a reflection principle for that theory, which illustrates the theory's inadequacy, and arrive at a new formalization of the theory that effectively incorporates the reflection principle. We can continue this process to arrive at a transfinite hierarchy of formal theories of truth, which is analogous to the hierarchy of contexts for truth attributions. He claims that truth is a *Kreiselian concept* in this sense: any formal theory of truth points the way to a stronger formal theory, and the process of theory construction is unending.[64]

Glanzberg's point is that what seem to be revenge paradoxes are really just the effects of the Kreiselian aspect of truth. A theory of truth should not be expected to treat as true the claim that its consequences are true. Nor should a theory of truth be found lacking if the result of conjoining a reflection principle to it results in an inconsistent theory. These phenomena are just consequences of the fact that truth is a Kreiselian concept.

There are several places at which I disagree with Glanzberg's analysis. The first is that I do not find the strong liar reasoning compelling. Because the strong liar reasoning involves a move from 'p is indeterminate' to 'p is not true', (8) should be read as:

(8′) is Xnot true.[65]

[61] This view about the relation between reflection and revenge seems to stem from some of Kripke's remarks: "Such semantical notions as 'grounded,' 'paradoxical,' etc. belong to the metalanguage. This situation seems to me to be intuitively acceptable; in contrast to the notion of truth, none of these notions is to be found in natural language in its pristine purity, before philosophers reflect on its semantics (in particular, the semantic paradoxes). If we give up the goal of a universal language, models of the type presented in this paper are plausible as models of natural language at a stage before we reflect on the generation process associated with the concept of truth, the stage which continues in the daily life of nonphilosophical speakers" (Kripke 1975: 714).

[62] See Burge (1979a) for discussion of the strong liar reasoning.

[63] See Feferman (1991) for an overview of reflection principles.

[64] Glanzberg (2005).

[65] 'Xnot' expresses exclusion negation.

We already know that indeterminacy approaches have trouble handling sentences like this, but the trouble has nothing to do with reflection on how the theory of truth in question classifies (8′). In fact, most indeterminacy approaches to the liar are based on fixed-point constructions and so have no consequences for sentences like (8′) at all. Thus, there is no reason to think that one derives a contradiction only by assuming that the theory implies that (8′) is indeterminate. Therefore, the view that reflection on the dictates of a theory of truth has any special role to play in reasoning about the status of paradoxical sentences seems to be a mistake.

A second issue is that there is no reason to think that the concepts described by each of the formal theories Glanzberg identifies have anything in common. In particular, I see no reason to think that they are all "more or less" theories of truth. However, Glanzberg claims that each of the formal theories provides a rough characterization of the unified concept of truth. The problem with this view is that on Glanzberg's own account, it is impossible to express the unrestricted notion of truth that each of these theories is supposed to describe. Thus, we have this concept of truth, but we can never actually give an account of it. That sounds fairly counterintuitive. Moreover, if Glanzberg is right, then it is impossible to arrive at a theory of truth that correctly and completely describes our concept of truth. The best we can achieve is stronger and stronger theories that are always lacking. Although the distinction is a bit slippery, this seems more like relabeling a problem than explaining it.

Hartry Field is another theorist who offers an explanation for revenge paradoxes. Field thinks the problem of revenge paradoxes that I keep pressing is a problem that arises only when truth, which is intelligible, is combined with other resources (e.g., exclusion negation, other non-monotonic sentential operators, hyper-determinateness operators, etc.), which are not intelligible. Thus, it is not that truth is responsible for these revenge paradoxes; rather, truth has been keeping company with some other notions, which are responsible for the trouble.[66]

What is wrong with Field's explanation? Maybe nothing, provided that he could make the case that these concepts are indeed inconsistent. However, his arguments all assume that truth is consistent. So, at best, we can conclude that either truth is inconsistent or these concepts that feature in revenge paradoxes are inconsistent. Notice what has happened here. Both sides in the debate about how best to approach the aletheic paradoxes agree that inconsistent concepts are at fault. The inconsistency theorists think that the inconsistency of truth explains why the aletheic paradoxes and revenge paradoxes occur, while the consistency theorists think that the inconsistency of these other concepts explains why revenge paradoxes occur. So, either way, an adequate approach to the aletheic paradoxes is going to have to say something about inconsistent concepts. Thus, no matter which approach to the aletheic paradoxes one prefers, an essential component of it will be a theory of inconsistent concepts. No matter what one thinks is the source of the aletheic paradoxes, inconsistent concepts are somehow to blame for our inability to solve them.

[66] Field (2008a).

There are several issues to consider when deciding which linguistic items should be blamed for the paradoxes. One issue involves the sort of explanation we get. Field suggests that we should blame classical negation, and blame exclusion negation, and blame the classical conditional, and blame the intuitionistic conditional, and blame completely defined gaphood predicates, and blame idempotent determinacy operators, and blame quantification over partially defined gaphood predicates, and blame paradoxicality predicates, and blame groundedness predicates, and blame truth predicates that are not language-specific, and on and on and on.

I suggest that we should blame truth. That is it. Thus, my explanation is much simpler. It is also much more plausible. We can construct artificial languages that contain the outlaw linguistic expressions, and they are perfectly well-behaved as long as they do not contain truth predicates (or related semantic terms). Of course, we can also construct artificial languages with truth predicates that are perfectly well-behaved as long as they do not contain the outlaw linguistic expressions. However, the difference is that there are many different ways to construct revenge paradoxes; one involves *truth* and exclusion negation, one involves *truth* and another non-monotonic sentential operator, one involves *truth* and the conditional, one involves *truth* and an idempotent determinacy operator, etc. Exclusion negation is not involved in each case, nor are any of the other outlaw linguistic expressions. However, *truth* is involved every time. Truth is the only suspect that has no alibi—it is present at every crime scene; none of the others are. It does not take a Holmes or a Columbo to identify the perpetrator; even a Wiggum could get this one right.

If one looks at the arguments here, the consistency theorist has nothing new to offer—the reason for thinking that these concepts are inconsistent is that one can derive a contradiction from their constitutive principles, which is just an instance of the obvious argument; of course, that is, taking it for granted that truth is consistent. Notice, however, that it is much simpler to treat truth as an inconsistent concept—it avoids having to find inconsistent concepts all over a wide terrain. Moreover, it is more modest to say that truth is an inconsistent concept since all the revenge-prone concepts only give rise to paradoxes in conjunction with truth. It seems almost like willful ignorance to blame all these other concepts for the faults of truth. Finally, as I argued in this chapter, as long as one has a general truth predicate that obeys the primary aletheic principles and some minimal resources (e.g., common descriptions), one can "import" a revenge paradox into the language by way of inter-linguistic truth attributions. Hence, the "blame everything but truth" strategy is not effective. Not only is my strategy simpler and more plausible, it is the only one that works.

I have argued that there are two kinds of revenge paradoxes: self-refutation problems and inconsistency problems. Glanzberg addresses self-refutation problems, which confront theories of truth that imply that they are not true. He argues that this kind of revenge paradox has its source in the fact that truth is a Kreiselian concept (i.e., it is not closed under reflection). However, Glanzberg does not explain or even address inconsistency problems, and there are good reasons to doubt his explanation of the self-refutation problem. On the other hand, Field addresses inconsistency problems and argues that these sorts of revenge paradoxes arise when what are ultimately unintelligible—read that as inconsistent or not well-defined—concepts are combined with truth. However, Field does not explain or even address self-refutation problems, and there are good reasons to doubt his explanation of the inconsistency problem. In contrast to both Glanzberg and Field, I offer an explanation of both types of revenge paradoxes, and my explanation of each type is superior to the one offered by Glanzberg and by Field, respectively.

The following is a summary of the third argument for treating truth as an inconsistent concept:

(i) If we assume that truth is an inconsistent concept, then we can explain the presence of the aletheic paradoxes and the presence of revenge paradoxes.

(ii) The inconsistency explanation of the aletheic paradoxes and the revenge paradoxes is better than any of the others.

∴ (iii) Probably, truth is an inconsistent concept.

Only by admitting that truth is an inconsistent concept can we satisfactorily explain the most significant feature of our long battle with the aletheic paradoxes.

4.5 The meaning argument

In this section, we consider one of the negative consequences of treating truth as a consistent concept: we have to give up truth-conditional semantics as an all-purpose device for explaining facts about natural language. It can still be used piecemeal for certain swaths of natural language, but unless truth is treated as an inconsistent concept, we have no hope for a truth-conditional semantics for a natural language, which is, arguably, one of the main goals of contemporary formal semantics.

The problem comes in specifying truth conditions for sentences containing truth predicates. Since paradoxical sentences are meaningful, any truth-conditional theory of meaning ought to be able to specify truth conditions for them. The truth conditions for a liar sentence like (8) would be: (8) is true iff (8) is not true. But that is a contradiction. To avoid inconsistency, the truth-conditional theory of meaning ought to incorporate some approach to the paradoxes. Most approaches to the paradoxes face revenge paradoxes and respond to them by restricting the class of languages to which they apply so that it does not include those containing revenge-paradoxical sentences. It is this sort of restriction that causes problems for truth-conditional semantics.

Call the languages to which a theory applies its *target languages*. There are at least four kinds of these restrictions:

(i) No target language L can express its own truth predicate ('true-in-L'). Example: Tarski's theory.

(ii) A target language L can express its own truth predicate ('true-in-L'), but it cannot express the theory of truth-in-L. Examples: Kripke's theory (inner Strong Kleene) and Gupta and Belnap's theory (outer revision).

(iii) A target language L can express its own truth predicate ('true-in-L') and the theory of truth-in-L, but it cannot express other linguistic resources associated with revenge paradoxes (e.g., exclusion negation). Examples: McGee's theory (classical symmetric), Maudlin's theory (outer Strong Kleene), Field's theory (paracomplete), and Beall's theory (transparent paraconsistent).[67]

(iv) No expressive restrictions on target languages. Examples: none (yet).

For example, Davidson, the prototypical truth-conditional theorist, accepts a type (i) theory (Tarski's). However, there is good reason to think that this is unacceptable.[68]

Assume Sherri and Terri are interpreting one another and Sherri speaks language S, while Terri speaks language T. Sherri uses S to construct a truth-conditional theory of meaning for T (in the form of a Tarskian definition of truth-in-T or a Tarskian axiomatic theory of truth-in-T), while Terri uses T to construct a truth-conditional theory of meaning for S (in the form of a Tarskian definition of truth-in-S or a Tarskian axiomatic theory of truth-in-S). Obviously, if S and T are natural languages, then they are going to contain truth predicates. However, a Tarskian theory of truth is not acceptable for such a language. Hence, neither Sherri nor Terri can succeed.

A truth-conditional meaning theorist might respond to this objection in the following way. Let S★ be the sublanguage of S that does not express truth-in-S and let T★ be the sublanguage of T that does not express truth-in-T. Now Sherri can construct in S a definition of truth-in-T★ and Terri can construct in T a definition of truth-in-S★. These theories will allow Sherri and Terri to specify the truth conditions for all the sentences of each other's languages that do not contain truth predicates.

Fair enough, but the sentences of S and the sentences of T that contain truth predicates are meaningful, and meaning is supposed to be explained in terms of truth conditions. These sentences have truth conditions. What are they? A theory of meaning that cannot be used on obviously meaningful sentences is not worth calling a theory of *meaning*.

This argument pushes a truth-conditional meaning theorist from accepting a type (i) theory of truth to a type (ii) theory of truth. However, one can run the same argument in terms of *theories of truth* to push the truth-conditional meaning theorist from accepting a type (ii) theory of truth to accepting a type (iii) theory of truth. That is, the sentences left out of the target languages are meaningful, so a truth-conditional theory of meaning ought to be able to specify their meanings. One can then turn the crank again, this time by appealing to the other linguistic resources (e.g., exclusion

[67] Note that there are additional constraints these theories would have to meet. For example, Field's theory and Beall's theory are disquotational, and disquotationalists typically deny that truth can be used to explain anything, much less meaning.

[68] See Chihara (1976) and Lycan (2012) for discussion of this point.

negation) to push a truth-conditional meaning theorist from accepting a type (iii) theory of truth to accepting a type (iv) theory of truth. However, there are no type (iv) theories of truth.

The problem is that anyone who accepts a truth-conditional theory of meaning is committed to giving truth conditions for all meaningful sentences of a language, but virtually all approaches to the aletheic paradoxes are restricted to avoid revenge paradoxes. When a truth-conditional theory of meaning is applied to a language that contains paradoxical sentences, it has to be paired with an approach to the aletheic paradoxes, otherwise it would be straightforwardly inconsistent. However, owing to the restrictions on approaches to the aletheic paradoxes, there will be meaningful sentences that cannot be given truth conditions. The upshot is that since any view on which truth is a consistent concept is bound to be restricted to avoid revenge paradoxes, accepting that truth is a consistent concept is incompatible with accepting a truth-conditional theory of meaning. The problem affects most of formal semantics (dynamic semantics[69] and game-theoretic semantics[70] aside) insofar as it purports to explain meaningful discourse in general.

One way to avoid the meaning argument would be to follow Kirk Ludwig in denying that commitment to a truth-conditional meaning theory requires commitment to a theory of truth.[71] In the next chapter, I discuss Ludwig's views and argue that his view on the relation between meaning theories and theories of truth is a non-starter.

Instead, one might reject the meaning argument because one thinks that truth-conditional semantics is not worth saving—that it is not a big deal if an approach to the aletheic paradoxes is incompatible with truth-conditional semantics. I disagree; indeed, this way of resisting the argument seems to me to be the most desperate because truth-conditional semantics is an important tool of linguistics, one of the sciences. If one's favored view of truth or approach to the aletheic paradoxes conflicts with the sciences, then it is the philosophical view that should go. Thomas Hofweber, who has recently explored this relationship between philosophy and the sciences, writes:

> The *modest attitude* towards the relationship between the sciences and philosophy (modest from the point of view of philosophy) holds that the sciences don't need philosophy for their final vindication, nor does philosophy have the authority to overrule the results of the sciences. They are just fine without us. Collectively, that is. Individual philosophers can of course fruitfully join in on the scientific enterprise, and help out in ways that their philosophical training has especially prepared them for. What is at issue is not that, but how the results of philosophy and metaphysics, the disciplines, relate to those of the sciences. To have the modest attitude is not to have science worship. One can have the modest attitude and be critical of various sciences. One might hold that a particular science overstates its claims, or hasn't gathered enough evidence to be accepted as true, or the like. But what one can't do, with the modest attitude, is to hold that

[69] See van Eijck and Visser (2010) for an overview.

[70] See Hodges (2009) for an overview.

[71] Ludwig (2001); see also Lepore and Ludwig (2005) and Badici and Ludwig (2007). See Patterson (2009) for discussion.

there is an open philosophical question whether p is the case even though one of the acceptable sciences has shown something that immediately implies p.[72]

I think this is exactly right. To endorse a philosophical theory of truth that conflicts with the science of linguistics is just as condemnable as being a creationist or a flat-Earther or a proponent of any other non-empirical superstition. We philosophers should be past this by now.[73]

I imagine that some readers want to protest that the modest attitude makes philosophy impotent to overturn findings in the sciences. This objection is off the mark. If a philosophical position implies that an empirically supported tenet of a science is false, then there are several courses of action a proponent might take. Imagine that Prof. Frink gives a philosophy talk in which he presents a new theory of mereological composition and it comes out that a consequence of his theory is that there are no gauge bosons (e.g., photons and gluons). Of course, if there are no gauge bosons, then the standard model of particle physics is false.[74] In this case, it seems perfectly legitimate to reject his theory of composition out of hand. However, if Frink presents an alternative to the standard model of particle physics that is both compatible with his theory of composition and as empirically verified as the standard model, then he is back on firm ground. The modest attitude implies that if a philosophical theory is incompatible with a tenet of one of the sciences, then empirical confirmation should be the deciding factor.

Hold on! If truth is an inconsistent concept, then how can it be legitimate to use it in a truth-conditional theory of meaning? The central theme of this whole book is that truth ought to be replaced for certain purposes, and it sure seems like giving truth-conditions for paradoxical sentences has to be one of those purposes. So it does not seem like one can accept that truth is an inconsistent concept and accept truth-conditional semantics. Moreover, if that is right, then it seems as if I have violated my own modest attitude in using philosophical considerations to reject an established tenet of the sciences.

Let us revisit a passage from Hofweber on the modest attitude: "To have the modest attitude is not to have science worship. One can have the modest attitude and be critical of various sciences."[75] I am *not* saying that truth-conditional theories of meaning are unacceptable because they are incompatible with my favorite theory of truth (that would be like Hartry Field's view—he thinks that truth-conditional theories of meaning are unacceptable, but he only thinks this because of his philosophical commitments, specifically, his disquotationalism).[76]

[72] Hofweber (2009: 263).

[73] For discussion of linguistics and scientific methodology, see Devitt (2006a, 2006b, 2009, 2010), Culbertson and Gross (2009), Textor (2009), Fitzgerald (2009), Ludlow (2011), Scholz, Pelletier, and Pullum (2011), and the papers in Katz (1985), Everaert et al. (2010), and Kempson et al. (2012).

[74] I am ignoring issues associated with anti-realist interpretations of scientific theories.

[75] Hofweber (2009: 263).

[76] See Field (1994a).

The truth-conditional theory of meaning has tremendous explanatory power, but explanatory power does not trump empirical inadequacy, at least when there is an alternative on the table (consider Newtonian mechanics and the procession of the perihelion of Mercury). "Fine," the objector might say, "but in order for this line of argument to work, the replacement theory would have to have as much explanatory power as truth-conditional semantics." I agree; the meaning argument only works for prescriptive theories that have this feature. And mine does. Ascending and Descending Semantics (presented in Chapter 8) reduces to truth-conditional semantics when the distinction between ascending and descending truth is negligible, just as relativistic mechanics reduces to Newtonian mechanics when the distinction between relativistic mass and proper mass is negligible. So it has as much explanatory power as truth-conditional semantics. Therefore, far from violating my modest attitude toward the sciences, my inconsistency theory of truth embraces the legitimacy of truth-conditional semantics—it is worth saving. However, it cannot be saved if truth is a consistent concept. Obviously it cannot be saved in its current form if truth is an inconsistent concept either. But it can be preserved in the new theory in the way that Newtonian mechanics is preserved in relativistic mechanics—that is, if one accepts the prescriptive theory in Chapters 6, 7, and 8.

The following is a summary of the fourth argument for treating truth as an inconsistent concept:

(i) If truth is a consistent concept, then there are meaningful sentences that cannot be treated by truth-conditional semantics.

(ii) If there are meaningful sentences that cannot be treated by truth-conditional semantics, then truth-conditional semantics is unacceptable.

(iii) Truth-conditional semantics is acceptable.

∴ (iv) Truth is an inconsistent concept.

The force of the argument rests on an assumption that is seemingly independent of truth—premise (iii). The acceptability of truth-conditional semantics comes from linguistics, where it is firmly entrenched and has many explanatory and predictive successes, and the modest attitude toward the relation between philosophy and the sciences.

5

Replacement

In the last two chapters, I argued that truth is an inconsistent concept. In this chapter, I consider several inconsistency theories of truth and explain my reasons for being unsatisfied with them. Then I argue that anyone who endorses an inconsistency approach should offer replacements for truth.

5.1 Inconsistency views

The feature of the inconsistency view that I propose that sets it apart from most of the others is that I think truth should be replaced because it is an inconsistent concept that is useful for certain purposes, but its inconsistency causes problems for some of these (e.g., doing semantics for natural language). We need new concepts to do at least some of the work that truth was supposed to do. In order to get a feel for just how different this view is from the rest, let us take a moment to consider several alternatives.

5.1.1 Dialetheism

Dialetheism is most often treated as a theory of inconsistent concepts.[1] According to dialetheists, the argument in the liar paradox is sound—that is, it is valid and all its premises are true, which makes its conclusion true. The conclusion is a contradiction, namely that the liar sentence is both true and not true. Usually the dialetheist argues that the premises of the argument are constitutive of the concepts involved, and so they must be true; however, the argument is obviously valid, so the conclusion must be true as well. Since the conclusion is a contradiction, some contradictions must be true. Of course, the dialetheist does not think that everything is true, so accepting dialetheism goes hand in hand with adopting a paraconsistent logic (i.e., a logic on which it is not the case that everything follows from a contradiction).[2]

I have said several times that I reject dialetheism, and since it is probably the view that pops into most philosophers' heads when hearing the term 'inconsistent concept', a word or two is in order about why I reject it. First, as should be clear from the revenge

[1] See Priest (2006a, 2006b) and Beall (2009) for discussion.

[2] Some of the classical ways of deriving a contradiction are invalid in paraconsistent logic (e.g., the examples in section 1.2), but others are valid.

argument in the previous chapter, dialetheism faces revenge paradoxes and has to be restricted so as to avoid them. Of course, as I argued, the restrictions do not really work, as evidenced by importation arguments. So, as a theory of truth, dialetheism fails just as badly as Field's theory or any other theory that generates revenge paradoxes.

However, since it is a kind of inconsistency theory, it might be helpful to see exactly which parts of dialetheism I reject. I agree with dialetheists that truth has inconsistent constitutive principles—that is a point on which all inconsistency theorists (as I have defined them) can agree. However, the view that constitutive principles are true is highly suspect, and that is the major point of contention. As I emphasized in Chapter 2, constitutive principles as I understand them are not analytic; they need not be true. Nevertheless, they play an important role in our practice of interpretation. The meanings of our words and the contents of our concepts incorporate some elements of the world—they take a stand on the way the world is. Constitutive principles often turn out to be true, but when they do it is because the world is as they take it to be. Simply stipulating that a certain word has a certain meaning is enough to establish that it does indeed have that meaning, but it does not ensure that the constitutive principles in question are true. If the concept expressed by that word is consistent, then its constitutive principles are true; whether it is consistent often depends on what the world is like. Notice that the dialetheist is more willing to accept contradictions than accept that constitutive principles might not be true; that seems to me like a serious mistake.

The other major problem I want to mention is that the dialetheist's hands are tied when it comes to responding to revenge paradoxes, and here it does worse than paracomplete approaches. Paraconsistent approaches to the aletheic paradoxes face standard revenge paradoxes (e.g., pertaining to 'just true' as mentioned in Chapter 4). Paracomplete approaches face revenge paradoxes as well; however, the paracomplete theorist can say that the concepts involved in the revenge paradoxes are inconsistent. At that point, the debate between someone like me and someone like Field turns on which concepts are inconsistent; I think I win that argument, but that is not the point. Rather, the paraconsistent theorist cannot follow this strategy—claiming that the concepts in question are inconsistent does not justify eliminating them from the scope of the paraconsistent approach. After all, the central claim of paraconsistent dialetheism is that truth is an inconsistent concept. Instead, the dialetheist has to make the radically implausible move of saying that the offending concepts do not exist and that the words that feature in revenge paradoxes for paraconsistent approaches are simply meaningless. As I have stressed, this move flies in the face of contemporary linguistics and so violates the modest attitude toward the relation between philosophy and the sciences. To reject it without any empirical evidence simply because it conflicts with one's favorite theory of truth is as preposterous as rejecting contemporary evolutionary theory without any empirical evidence simply because it conflicts with one's favorite theology.

In Chapter 1, I placed dialetheism in the inconsistency category of philosophical approaches, but from here on, by 'inconsistency approach', I mean *non-dialetheic inconsistency approach*.

5.1.2 *Patterson*

Douglas Patterson is an inconsistency theorist who starts with the idea that an agent who understands a language bears some more or less cognitive relation (knowing, believing, etc.) to a semantic theory for that language. If the language contains a word that expresses an inconsistent concept, then the semantic theory for that language is inconsistent.[3] Thus, linguistic competence is being cognitively related to a semantic theory, and competence with an inconsistent concept is being cognitively related to an inconsistent semantic theory. Patterson argues that because the semantic theory for an inconsistent language is inconsistent, the expressions of that language are meaningless. He claims that even though the sentences of an inconsistent language are meaningless, communication is still possible as long as the participants bear the same cognitive relation to an inconsistent semantic theory. Furthermore, we can translate from an inconsistent language into a consistent one if the need arises (where translation is preservation of perceived meaning).[4]

I can imagine someone thinking: the traditional approaches to the liar paradox have to be better than saying that all the sentences of English are meaningless. I agree. I would much rather accept a traditional approach than say that English is meaningless. I cannot imagine an argument for this claim whose premises I trust more than the negation of the conclusion. Of course, Patterson downplays the radically implausible consequences of his approach by arguing that it does not matter that all natural languages are meaningless. All that matters is that we take them to be meaningful. As long as we treat a language as meaningful, we can get along without any problems. Moreover, most of us never notice that our language is meaningless, because we do not bother to follow out the consequences of our beliefs.

These moves do not make much difference to the overall plausibility of his view because if they were correct, then having meaningful expressions would not be a very important feature of a language. However, most philosophers think that meaningfulness is such an important characteristic that it does not even make sense to say that a natural language is meaningless. In fact, on every theory of language of which I am aware, being meaningful is a defining feature of a language, since languages are individuated in part by the meanings of the words they contain. Thus, if Patterson is right, then English does not even count as a language—it is just a bunch of grunts and marks.

In Chapter 2, I argued that we cannot discover that a word with an established usage is meaningless. Now try to imagine reading in the newspaper that scientists have discovered that the entire French language is meaningless. I, for one, cannot do it (unless I have mistakenly picked up a copy of *The Onion* or some other satirical paper). The reason is

[3] He does not actually discuss inconsistent concepts; instead he focuses on inconsistent languages. However, I assume that a language is inconsistent iff it contains a word that expresses an inconsistent concept.

[4] See Patterson (2006, 2007, 2008, 2009).

that it is inconceivable for us to discover that an entire natural language is meaningless, much less *every* natural language.

Even if we ignore all the empirical evidence, there is an additional problem. Patterson thinks that our language is inconsistent *because* it contains a truth predicate (although there might be other troublesome words as well). If the problem has to do with truth, why should it spill over into meaning? In other words, why does he think that a suitable approach to the liar should have consequences for the meanings of sentences that have nothing to do with truth? It seems to me that Patterson adopts his view because of a commitment to truth-conditional semantics. He reasons that no truth-conditional semantic theory for a natural language can respect the principles that everyone takes the truth predicate to have unless it is inconsistent; thus, if natural languages are meaningful, then they have inconsistent semantics. Patterson then performs a *modus tollens*. The problem, of course, is that he seems to be more confident that meaning should be explained in terms of truth conditions than he is that English is meaningful. That is, he is so sure that meaning should be explained in terms of truth conditions that it has convinced him that there is no such thing as meaning (at least as it is commonly understood); he retains the *explanans* at the expense of the *explanandum*. That is hardly a promising explanatory story; it is more like throwing out the baby *instead of* the bathwater.

5.1.3 Ludwig

Kirk Ludwig's inconsistency approach (part of which appears in work with Amil Badici) has two parts: (i) a characterization of the truth predicate of a natural language and (ii) a meaning theory for languages that contain their own truth predicates.[5] The first part consists of the claim that truth predicates of natural languages do not express the concept of truth; indeed, they do not express any concept whatsoever. Natural-language speakers are under the impression that their truth predicates do express the concept of truth, but they are mistaken. That is not to say, however, that there is no concept of truth. Indeed, Ludwig and Badici claim that there is a concept of truth, but it cannot be expressed by a predicate of a language to which it applies.[6] They set out to show how an attempt to introduce the concept of truth into a language to which it is intended to apply runs into difficulty.

They model the difficulty by considering a language L and a metalanguage M. M contains the predicate 'true-in-L', translations of all the sentences of L, and the means to give structural descriptions of the sentences of L. With these resources, M contains a true T-sentence for each sentence of L. Consider now an attempt to extend L by adding a

[5] Ludwig (2001) and Badici and Ludwig (2007). The first part of the approach appears in the latter paper; the second part appears in the former paper in detail and is mentioned in the latter.

[6] Badici and Ludwig (2007: 623). This should seem like an odd claim; I think the best way to understand it is that they think that there are only language-specific concepts of truth, but no language can express its own language-specific concept of truth.

predicate, 'T(x)', to it, which is supposed to express the concept of truth for the extended language, L^+. They then appeal to what is essentially Tarski's theorem on the indefinability of truth to show that 'T(x)' does not express the concept of truth-in-L^+ on pain of contradiction. Their conclusion: 'T(x)' "expresses no concept, and, hence, fails to have a meaning."[7]

Badici and Ludwig consider the objection that the fact that a contradiction follows from the T-sentence for a liar sentence of L shows that the concept expressed by the predicate 'true-in-L' of M is an inconsistent concept. Their reply:

> We can show that this thought is incorrect. Suppose one adds two truth-predicates, '$T_1(x)$' and '$T_2(x)$' to an extension of L, L^{2+}, with the intention that they express the concept of truth, and suppose that λ_1 and λ_2 refer respectively to '$\sim T_1(\lambda_1)$' and '$\sim T_2(\lambda_2)$', and λ_3 and λ_4 refer respectively to '$\sim T_2(\lambda_1)$' and '$\sim T_1(\lambda_2)$'. The two predicates should have the same meaning, because they are intended to capture the same conceptual content, and on the view in question the two corresponding T-schemas, (T1) and (T2), determine the same meaning.
>
> (T1) $T_1(s)$ iff ϕ
>
> (T2) $T_2(s)$ iff ϕ
>
> Nevertheless, they do not. For λ_1 and λ_2, given (T1) and (T2), lead directly to contradictions and so are pathological, while the result of replacing each truth predicate in these sentences by the other, λ_3 and λ_4, do not, but rather seem to say the right thing about the pathological sentences λ_1 and λ_2. T_1 and T_2 do not have the same meaning then, and it follows that one or the other fails to express the concept of truth with respect to the language. Since there is perfect symmetry between them, the proper conclusion is that neither does.[8]

Their argument depends on the claim that λ_1 (i.e., '$\sim T_1\lambda_1$') is pathological, while λ_3 (i.e., '$\sim T_2(\lambda_1)$'"seems like the right thing to say" (along with the analogous claims about λ_2 and λ_4). However, λ_3 and λ_4 are just as pathological as λ_1 and λ_2. Here is the argument for λ_3:

1. $\sim T_2(\lambda_1)$	(assume)
2. $\sim T_2$('$\sim T_1\lambda_1$')	(definition of λ_1)
3. $\sim\sim T_1(\lambda_1)$	(T2)
4. $T_1(\lambda_1)$	(double negation elimination)
5. T_1('$\sim T_1\lambda_1$')	(definition of λ_1)
6. $\sim T_1(\lambda_1)$	(T1)
7. $\perp$	

1. $T_2(\lambda_1)$	(assume)
2. T_2('$\sim T_1\lambda_1$')	(definition of λ_1)
3. $\sim T_1(\lambda_1)$	(T2)
4. T_1('$\sim T_1\lambda_1$')	(T1)
6. $T_1(\lambda_1)$	(definition of λ_1)
7. $\perp$	

7 Badici and Ludwig (2007: 628).

8 Badici and Ludwig (2007: 629–30).

The argument for λ_4 is analogous. I conclude that Badici and Ludwig's attempt to show that truth predicates do not express the concept of truth fails. So much for the first part of their project.

The second part of this approach consists of Ludwig's suggestion for using an inconsistent theory of truth as a meaning theory for a language. Let L be the target language and let T_t be an *interpretive* truth theory for L, which means that the expressions contained in the axioms of T_t (which is formulated in a metalanguage M for L) are synonymous with the associated expressions of L. For example, an axiom of T_t might be 'for any sentences p and q of L, ⌜p ∧ q⌝ is true iff p is true and q is true'; the expression 'and' of M is used in giving the truth conditions for the expression '∧' of L, and these two expressions are synonymous. A meaning theory, T_m, for L consists of the following components:

(i) T_t is an interpretive truth theory for L
(ii) The axioms of T_t are $A_1,\ldots,A_n,\ldots$
(iii) A_1 means in L that...; A_2 means in L that...;...
(iv) CP is a canonical proof procedure for T_t
(v) For any sentence s of L, if s is the last line of a canonical proof in T_t, then the corresponding M-sentence is true in M.

Ludwig does not say much about canonical proof procedures other than they result in "proofs that draw solely on the content of the axioms" of T_t.[9] I consider several ways of understanding them below.

The key to Ludwig's suggestion is that even if L contains its own truth predicate (i.e., 'true-in-L'), which results in T_t being inconsistent, T_m (the meaning theory for L) need not be inconsistent. From the canonical T-sentences (i.e., those having canonical proofs), one can infer the corresponding M-sentence:

s in L means that ϕ

where s is a structural description of a sentence of L and $\langle\phi\rangle$ is its translation into M. For example, if L contains its own truth predicate and the means to refer to its own sentences, then it also contains a liar sentence like:

(1) (1) is not true-in-L.

Via a canonical proof, we get a T-sentence for (1): '(1) is true-in-L iff (1) is not true-in-L'; from it, the corresponding M-sentence, ' '(1) is not true-in-L' means that (1) is not true-in-L' follows. Thus, even though T_t is inconsistent, we can use it to generate a consistent meaning theory for L. If this strategy works, then there is no reason to pair a truth-conditional theory of meaning with an approach to the aletheic paradoxes because the aletheic paradoxes do not infect the theory of meaning.

9 Ludwig (2001: 149).

It should be clear that everything turns on Ludwig's account of canonical proof. Remember, in the cases we care about, the truth theory is inconsistent and the background logic is classical, so the truth theory is the whole language. That is, every sentence of L is a theorem of T_t. Thus, every sentence of the form 's is true-in-L iff ϕ' (where s is a structural description of a sentence of L and ⟨ϕ⟩ is a sentence of M) is a theorem of the theory. Ludwig tries to pick out the canonical T-sentences (i.e., those whose right-hand side is a *translation* of the sentence described on the left-hand side) by appeal to the notion of canonical proof. For Ludwig, a canonical proof is "a proof meeting certain constraints that ensure that only the content of the axioms is drawn on in proving it. This can be accomplished by restricting the rules we can appeal to in proofs and what we can apply them to. We can call proofs that satisfy the constraints *canonical proofs*."[10] So, which rules are we allowed to use in a canonical proof? Ludwig writes: "For any given theory and logic, it would be straightforward, if somewhat tedious, to write out what restrictions were required. Once we had a characterization of the restrictions required in some logical system, we could in fact weaken the system so that it consisted of only the moves so allowed. In this case every T-theorem of the theory would also be a T-sentence."[11] Ludwig does offer a sample canonical proof procedure, which consists of the following rules:

(UQI) For all sentences σ, all variables υ, and all singular terms τ, Inst(σ, υ, τ) may be inferred from UQuant (σ, υ).

(RPL) For all sentences σ_1, σ_2, S(σ_2) may be inferred from Eq(σ_1, σ_2) and S(σ_1).

(SUB) For all singular terms τ_1, τ_2, S(τ_2) may be inferred from S(τ_1) and Ident(σ_1, σ_2).

In these rules, the following terms are used: 'UQuant(σ, υ)' means *the universal quantification of σ with respect to υ*; 'Inst(σ, υ, τ)' means *the result of replacing all instances of the free variable υ in σ with the singular term τ*; 'Eq(σ_1, σ_2) means *the biconditional linking σ_1 with σ_2 (in that order)*; 'Ident(τ_1, τ_2)' means *the identity sentence linking σ_1 with σ_2 (in that order)*; 'S(x)' stands for a sentence containing the grammatical unit x, which may be a word, phrase, or sentence.[12]

As an example, Ludwig gives us the following canonical proof:

1. 'Fa ∧ Ra' is true-in-L iff 'Fa' is true-in-L and 'Ra' is true-in-L. (by UQI from the axiom defining conjunction).
2. 'Fa' is true-in-L iff the referent of 'a' is red. (by UQI from the axiom defining the predicate 'F').
3. 'Ra' is true-in-L iff the referent of 'a' is round. (by UQI from the axiom defining the predicate 'R').
4. 'Fa' is true-in-L iff Alfred is red (by SUB from 2 and the axiom defining 'a').
5. 'Ra' is true-in-L iff Alfred is round (by SUB from 3 and the axiom defining 'a').
6. 'Fa ∧ Ra' is true-in-L iff Alfred is red and Alfred is round (by RPL—twice—from 1, 4, 5).

[10] Ludwig (2001: 148). [11] Ludwig (2001: 148).
[12] Ludwig (2001: 157–8). All formulations are due to Ludwig.

The last step, line 6, contains the T-sentence for 'Fa ∧ Ra'. Since the above is a canonical proof of this T-sentence, we can infer that 'Fa ∧ Ra' in L means that Alfred is red and Alfred is round.

It should be clear that Ludwig's proposal is not workable. The most obvious problem is that line 1 contains a T-sentence that is arrived at by canonical proof, so we should be able to infer that 'Fa ∧ Ra' in L means that 'Fa' is true-in-L and 'Ra' is true-in-L. So we have two M-sentences that are clearly not equivalent for a single sentence of L.[13] Another problem is that we can derive multiple incompatible M-sentences for liar sentences of L. Let 'T' be the truth predicate in L, and let 'b' be a singular term of L that refers to the sentence '~Tb', which is also a sentence of L. We have the following canonical derivation for '~Tb':

1. '~Tb' is true-in-L iff it is not the case that ('Tb' is true-in-L) (by UQI from the axiom defining negation).
2. 'Tb' is true-in-L iff the referent of 'b' is true-in-L (by UQI from the axiom defining the predicate 'T').
3. 'Tb' is true-in-L iff '~Tb' is true-in-L (by SUB from 2 and the axiom defining the singular term 'b').
4. '~Tb' is true-in-L iff it is not the case that ('~Tb' is true-in-L) (by RPL from 1 and 3).

So far so good—we have a canonical proof of a T-sentence for '~Tb'. However, we can continue:

5. '~Tb' is true-in-L iff it is not the case that (it is not the case that ('~Tb' is true-in-L)) (by RPL from 3 and 4).

Now we have a problem since we now have a canonical proof of a different T-sentence for '~Tb'. Following Ludwig's strategy, we can derive the following M-sentences:

(M1) '~Tb' in L means that it is not the case that ('~Tb' is true-in-L).

(M2) '~Tb' in L means that it is not the case that (it is not the case that ('~Tb' is true-in-L)).

So, we end up with two M-sentences that attribute incompatible (indeed contradictory) meanings to a single sentence of L. I conclude that Ludwig has not given us a workable account of canonical proof. Thus, Ludwig's suggestion for how to use an inconsistent truth theory to arrive at a consistent meaning theory fails. That result dispatches the second part of this inconsistency approach.

[13] Ludwig stipulates that the T-sentences in this example contain no semantic terms, but for languages that contain their own truth predicates, this stipulation would prevent one from deriving canonical T-sentences for sentences containing the truth predicate.

5.1.4 Eklund

Matti Eklund focuses on the constitutive principles for the concepts expressed by the words of an inconsistent language. For Eklund, a language is inconsistent iff its constitutive principles (i.e., the constitutive principles for the concepts expressed by the words the language contains) are inconsistent. Eklund explains linguistic competence in terms of dispositions to accept the language's constitutive principles. He rejects dialetheism (i.e., the view that some contradictions are true), but he accepts that some of a language's constitutive principles might be false. As for the semantic theory for an inconsistent language, Eklund argues that the words and sentences of an inconsistent language have semantic values that come as close as possible to making the language's constitutive principles true. He admits that some constitutive principles might be more important than others, so that would have to be taken into account when deciding on a semantic theory. Also, there will probably be multiple equally good candidate semantic theories for an inconsistent language; thus, the semantic values of the words and sentences of an inconsistent language are indeterminate to that extent.[14]

Although Eklund's view is far superior to the others surveyed so far, it still has several problems. First, it has an unacceptable account of the relation between concept possession and constitutive principles (discussed in Chapter 2). Furthermore, Eklund's theory is intended to provide an approach to the liar paradox. His view is that truth is an inconsistent concept (or that any language with a truth predicate is an inconsistent language). But his theory appeals to the very concept it deems inconsistent. That is, his approach to the liar paradox gives truth, which he takes to be an inconsistent concept, a crucial explanatory role. However, the fact that truth is an inconsistent concept should cast doubt on its ability to perform such a role. Consider again the analogy to mass: once we discovered that mass is inconsistent, we stopped using it for serious theorizing. Why is the case of truth any different?

Consider this problem in a little more detail. Let L be an inconsistent language and M be the language in which Eklund's theory is formulated (L and M might be the same language since, unlike many traditional approaches to the liar, Eklund's theory does not require an expressively richer metalanguage). Both L and M contain truth predicates, but it is the truth predicate of M that is used by Eklund's theory (call it τ). We know that since τ is a truth predicate, it has certain constitutive principles. We also know that because τ expresses an inconsistent concept, not all of its constitutive principles are true (or valid). Eklund does not tell us which of truth's constitutive principles fail, but we know that some do. The question is: how can τ function properly in Eklund's theory, which is supposed to provide a semantics for L, if some of its constitutive principles fail? Mono-aletheism (i.e., no sentence is both true and false) is an essential principle for a non-dialetheic semantics, and I do not see how a semantic theory could assign the right truth conditions to the sentences of L unless the truth predicate it employs obeys the

[14] Eklund (2002a, 2002b, 2005, 2007, 2008a, 2008b).

ascending and descending aletheic principles (i.e., ⟨ϕ⟩ follows from ⟨⟨ϕ⟩ is true⟩, and ⟨⟨ϕ⟩ is true⟩ follows from ⟨ϕ⟩). However, these are the very principles that give rise to the liar paradox. Thus, some of them have to fail; otherwise, Eklund's theory would be inconsistent. In sum, Eklund's theory casts truth in a crucial explanatory role, and it implies that some of truth's constitutive principles are untrue. It seems, however, that if some of truth's constitutive principles fail, then it is unsuited to play this explanatory role. At the very least, Eklund owes us an explanation of how truth can function properly in his semantic theory even though it is an inconsistent concept (and consequently, some of its constitutive principles fail). Specifying a logical approach to be paired with his inconsistency approach would go a long way toward satisfying this demand. I argue in Chapter 10 that the obvious choice of logical approach (classical gap) results in a semantic theory that is empirically inadequate.

5.1.5 Yablo

Stephen Yablo suggested an inconsistency approach in the early 1990s that did not garner much attention, but it was a significant step for inconsistency views because it paired an inconsistency approach (philosophical) with an outer revision theory, which is a logical approach. As far as I know, he was the first person to do so.[15]

Yablo's idea is to use the revision theory as a theory of inconsistent definitions. It was originally designed for what Gupta and Belnap call circular definitions, which they take care to distinguish from inconsistent definitions.[16] According to Yablo, the definition of 'true' is inconsistent because the rules for assigning an extension to it never terminate. Gupta and Belnap agree with this point but they interpret it differently. They think that circularly defined concepts do not have well-defined extensions and anti-extensions. Instead, they suggest three sorts of semantic categories for these terms—things the term categorically applies to, things the term categorically does not apply to, and the uncategorical things. Yablo, on the other hand, sticks with extension and anti-extension, but then has to say that some things constantly switch back and forth from the extension to the anti-extension (e.g., paradoxical sentences). He interprets this behavior as a result of an inconsistency in the semantic rules governing the use of 'true'. According to Yablo, any attempt to follow the semantic rules when dealing with inconsistent definitions is impossible. He draws an analogy with incompatible moral obligations; the difference is that, with inconsistent definitions, an attempt to comply with one obligation creates another that one must defy. One way to think about his use of the revision theory is that he takes successive stages in the revision sequence to model attempts to follow the semantic rules for 'true'. Each attempt fails and brings in its wake a new attempt, and every new attempt shifts paradoxical sentences from the extension to the anti-extension of 'true' or vice versa.

[15] Yablo (1993a, 1993b); see also Yablo (1985).

[16] Gupta and Belnap (1993).

One problem with Yablo's view is that he does not give much credit to those competent with 'true' since he thinks that when we contemplate the truth conditions for paradoxical sentences we keep trying to satisfy the semantic rules for 'true' even though they lead us in a circle. It is as if he thinks anyone contemplating the liar paradox would get stuck in an infinite loop: the liar is true, no, wait, it's false, no, it's true,... That is not very realistic, but I do not see another way of making sense of his view. Also, he underestimates the incompatibility in 'true's rules for use. It is not that trying to follow one rule leads one to accept another incompatible rule. Rather, we simultaneously try to follow incompatible rules for using 'true'. That is an aspect of our engagement with the aletheic paradoxes that Yablo's view cannot capture. However, the major problem I have with Yablo's view is that his logical approach is weakly classical. That is, it is incompatible with (T-In) and (T-Out), but it is compatible with their inferential versions, (T-Intro) and (T-Elim); also, it is not compatible with meta-rules like reasoning by cases because these rules are not validated by the revision theory. My goal is a *classically* consistent theory of our inconsistent concept of truth, and Yablo does not deliver that.

5.1.6 Burgess

Alexis Burgess offers an inconsistency approach that treats talk about truth as akin to fictional discourse.[17] Fictionalism is a view that one finds put to philosophical use in a wide variety of areas, mostly where one wants to avoid ontological commitment to entities of a certain kind (e.g., mathematical entities).[18] According to Burgess's view, truth attributions should be read as 'according to the fiction of the naïve theory of truth'. He suggests that there might be a way to avoid the syntactically awkward results of his view, but I will not dwell on these details.

The most important feature of Burgess's view for my purposes is that he offers the fictionalist theory as a *prescriptive* theory; so the fictionalist truth predicate is supposed to be a replacement for our truth predicate that expresses the inconsistent concept of truth. Thus, Burgess is the only other inconsistency theorist surveyed here to endorse a replacement strategy. Moreover, he takes great pains to make sure that his fictionalist truth predicate does not in any way get explained in terms of our inconsistent concept of truth; so he accepts the most important condition I place on replacing truth. Still, this leaves us without a descriptive theory of 'true'. In addition, I do not see much hope for using his fictionalist truth predicate in an explanatory role. To be sure, he does discuss the connection between it and the concept of assertion, but he does not consider my main focus in this book—meaning. Given that the naïve theory of truth is inconsistent, he would probably have to use something like Ludwig's strategy to get a meaning theory

[17] A. Burgess (2006); for discussion see Burgess and Burgess (2011).

[18] See Yablo (2001), Eklund (2011), and the papers in Kalderon (2005a, 2005b) for background on fictionalism. For discussion of fictionalism about truth in particular, see Price (2003), Woodbridge (2005), and Armour-Garb and Woodbridge (2010).

from it, and we saw how that turned out. Despite the fact that Burgess's view is obviously the closest to my own in the literature, I am confident that the replacements I introduce in the next chapter are superior to his fictionalist truth predicate, and the descriptive theory coming up in Chapter 9 would be impossible if we adopted Burgess's approach.[19]

5.2 Replacement arguments

The major problem with all the inconsistency views in the previous section (with the exception of Burgess's) is that the descriptive theories they offer all suffer from the fact that the theories appeal to the notion of truth. From my perspective, the key to a descriptively accurate inconsistency approach to the aletheic paradoxes is replacing truth for these explanatory purposes. This section is dedicated to clarifying what I take to be the most important aspect of my particular approach to the aletheic paradoxes: an inconsistency approach should be part of a larger account of conceptual change, and in particular conceptual change with respect to truth. The following is a rough account of the stages of conceptual change:

1. *Pre-revolution*: people possess and use concept X and theory T in which X serves an explanatory role (e.g., mass and Newtonian mechanics).
2. *Early revolution*: people discover that X is an inconsistent concept; they have some idea of which situations cause problems for those who use X; because of these problems, doubt is cast on the explanatory force of X and the acceptability of T as fundamental theory; however, without an alternative, people still use T and X.
3. *Late revolution*: new concepts (say $Y_1,\ldots,Y_n$) are proposed and a new theory (say U) is proposed in which the Y_is serve an explanatory role (e.g., relativistic mass and proper mass in relativistic mechanics); U reduces to T in familiar cases, and the Y_is agree with X on familiar cases; U is used to determine the cases in which it is acceptable to use T; at this point the conceptual repertoire and language have been extended.
4. *Post-revolution*: U has replaced T as the accepted fundamental theory, and the Y_is have replaced X as the accepted fundamental concepts; people might or might not still use T (and thus X) in certain cases (e.g., phlogiston theory has been totally superseded, but Newtonian mechanics is still indispensable for everyday situations).[20]

[19] Others that have expressed sympathy with the inconsistency approach, but do not offer detailed theories include Tarski (1933, 1944), Popper (1954), Kattsoff (1955), van Benthem (1978), Chihara (1973, 1979, 1984), Mates (1981), Goddard and Johnston (1983), McGee (1991), Tappenden (1993, 1994), Hill (2002), Ray (2002), Heck (2005), Burgess and Burgess (2011), and Båve (2012). Schiffer (2003) deserves a mention here as well—although he does not endorse an inconsistency view of truth, he does claim that many philosophical problems admit only what he calls *unhappy face solutions*, which entail that one or more of the concepts in question are inconsistent.

[20] For more on conceptual revolutions, see Kuhn (1962), Thagard (1992, 2012), Anderson, Barker, and Chen (2006), and Nersessian (2008).

The fundamental problem with the other inconsistency theorists (other than Burgess) is that although they attempt to give an account of our concepts and language at stage 1, and some of them (e.g., Patterson, Ludwig, Yablo, and Eklund) consider stage 2, they completely ignore stages 3 and 4. An inconsistency approach to the liar that does justice to stages 3 and 4 would propose replacement concepts for truth, and replacement theories for the theories we currently have that appeal to truth. Truth is a very popular concept—it is used in theories of meaning, knowledge, assertion, belief, validity, objectivity, rationality, etc.; thus, replacing it is a big job. Obviously, one wants replacements for truth that can be used to construct new theories to replace the old ones (that is a task of Chapter 8).

In an attempt to understand our language at stages 1 and 2, some inconsistency theorists (e.g., Eklund) have presented traditional semantic theories for inconsistent concepts/languages. Given the role of truth in understanding language, their actions are understandable. However, once we remind ourselves of the stages of conceptual change, we can see that they have jumped the gun—their semantic theories appeal to the concept of truth. Before we can explain our stage 1 and 2 language, we need to find replacements for our concept of truth. Then we can use the replacements to formulate a new semantic theory. Once we have that, we can use it to explain the languages we speak at each of the stages.

Notice that the case of mass is much less complicated than the case of truth because truth is a linguistic concept. We do not use mass to try to explain discourse involving 'mass'. However, we do use truth to explain discourse involving 'true'. If we had used mass in this way, then once we reached stage 2, we would have been tempted to use it to explain our stage 1 and 2 language. When discussing inconsistency approaches to the aletheic paradoxes, it is essential that one maintain one's bearings by keeping the stages of conceptual change firmly in mind.

It is a necessary condition on an acceptable account of inconsistent concepts (and thus, on an inconsistency approach to the liar) that it does justice to all the stages of conceptual change. If we accept a theory that appeals to truth (e.g., Eklund's theory), then we will not be able to progress to stages 3 and 4 without giving up the theory—we will be stuck in stage 2. Of course, as a provisional account of stages 1 and 2, it is fine to use the concept of truth, provided one keeps in mind that one is using an inconsistent concept to describe discourse involving that inconsistent concept and that the provisional theory should be superseded by a more fundamental one once we have acceptable replacement concepts (that is the way I think of Eklund's theory). Thus, I am suggesting that the other inconsistency theorists suffer from a lack of vision—they do not see the larger enterprise in which they are engaged. The moral is that if one endorses an inconsistency approach to the aletheic paradoxes, one should be in the business of replacing truth.

Another reason for replacing truth has more to do with inconsistent concepts in general. Consider the case of mass. Once we discovered that momentum/velocity varies with reference frames, we discovered that the concept of mass is inconsistent.[21] At that point, we knew that using it in certain situations would lead us astray—it would deliver incorrect predictions or even outright contradictions. Nevertheless, we also knew that in many situations, it is perfectly legitimate to use it, just as we had been for hundreds of years. What marks the difference between the two kinds of situations? Only once we had relativistic mechanics, with its two concepts of mass, could we answer this question. The answer is, of course, that when the difference between relativistic mass and proper mass is negligible given one's interests in a given situation, one may use mass; otherwise, one should use the replacement concepts. But this sort of answer is not possible until one has suitable replacement concepts. This example points up a general lesson: a useful inconsistent concept should be replaced since it is only by using the replacements that one can determine in which situations it may legitimately be used. Truth is incontestably useful. Thus, any inconsistency approach to the aletheic paradoxes should offer replacements for truth.

One can find this attitude toward conceptual replacement nicely summarized in the following quote from Albert Einstein:

> Concepts that have proven useful in ordering things easily achieve such an authority over us that we forget their earthly origins and accept them as unalterable givens. Thus they come to be stamped as "necessities of thought," "a priori givens," etc. The path of scientific advance is often made impassable for a long time through such errors. For that reason, it is by no means an idle game if we become practiced in analyzing the long commonplace concepts and exhibiting those circumstances upon which their justification and usefulness depend, how they have grown up, individually, out of the givens of experience. By this means, their all-too-great authority will be broken. They will be removed if they cannot be properly legitimated, corrected if their correlation with given things be far too superfluous, replaced by others if a new system can be established that we prefer for whatever reason.[22]

I suggest that there is not only good reason to break truth's authority over us, but also to prefer a new system of concepts for certain purposes.

5.3 Paradox and persons

Although I have yet to see it in print, I often hear an objection to the replacement strategy that begins with an observation like this one (from Thomas Hofweber):

> No damage has ever been done by [the aletheic paradoxes] outside of a philosophy department. No planes fell out of the sky because of them, no money was ever lost, no one was confused into

[21] Obviously, this is a gross oversimplification of the empirical and theoretical situation that led us to reject Newtonian mechanics and accept special relativity; however, the additional technical details would distract from the philosophical point without any offsetting benefit. See Jammer (2000), Petkov (2009), and the papers in Capria (2005).

[22] Einstein (1916: 102).

believing that Santa exists because of them. But why not? . . . We reason in accordance with rules which allow us to conclude that Santa exists, that planes should take off at 2 mph, and that you should bet everything on that limping horse. But no one is moved by any of the arguments, even though in general we are very moved by arguments we establish using just these rules. We are usually very moved when we establish using classical logic that planes need to go faster than 2 mph to take off. Why is it that the paradoxes are simply insignificant?[23]

The objection then continues: since the paradoxes are simply insignificant, there is no reason for us to bother with the trouble of replacing our concept of truth.

I disagree with Hofweber on this point. In fact, in the opening paragraph of the book, I said that the aletheic paradoxes pose a serious threat to us. That probably sounded like hyperbole at the time, but now I would like to justify it.

Consider what David Lewis calls our "general theory of persons" in the following passages:

Imagine that we have undertaken the task of coming to know Karl as a person. We would like to know what he believes, what he desires, what he means, and anything else about him that can be explained in terms of these things. We see a two-fold interpretation: of Karl's language, and of Karl himself. And we want to know his beliefs and desires in two different ways. We want to know their content as Karl could express it in his own language, and also as we could express it in our language. Imagine also that we must start from scratch. At the outset we know nothing about Karl's beliefs, desires, and meanings. Whatever we may know about persons in general, our knowledge of Karl in particular is limited to our knowledge of him as a physical system.

Both **Ao** and **Ak** are to be specifications of Karl's propositional attitudes—in particular, of Karl's system of beliefs and desires. **Ao** specifies Karl's beliefs and desires as expressed in our language; **Ak** specifies them as expressed in Karl's language; until we find out what the sentences of Karl's language mean, the two sorts of information are different.

M, the third component of our desired interpretation of Karl, is to be a specification, in our language, of the meanings of expressions of Karl's language.

What are the constraints by which the problem of radical interpretation is to be solved? Roughly speaking, they are the fundamental principles of our general theory of persons. They tell us how beliefs and desires and meanings are normally related to one another, to behavioral output, and to sensory input. The general theory of persons serves as a schema for particular theories of particular persons. A particular theory of Karl, for instance, may be constructed by ascribing particular beliefs, desires, and meanings to him. That is, by filling in **Ao**, **Ak**, and **M**.[24]

Lewis goes on to suggest a way of filling in **Ao**, **Ak**, and **M** given only physical facts about Karl. The main point of this passage, for my purposes, is that specifying the meanings of a person's words is an integral part of characterizing that person *as a person*, rather than as a merely physical system. Moreover, specifying the meanings of a person's words goes hand in hand with specifying their propositional attitudes.

[23] Hofweber (2010: 9–10).
[24] Lewis (1974: 108–11).

If Karl is like any person you have ever met, then Karl possesses the concept of truth and Karl's language contains a truth predicate. One's specification of the meaning of Karl's truth predicate and one's specification of the content of Karl's propositional attitudes involving truth ought to respect the fact that (T-In) and (T-Out) are constitutive of truth. That is, for any proposition p, if Karl accepts p (as specified by either **Ao** or **Ak**), then Karl accepts that p is true; likewise, if Karl accepts that p is true, then Karl accepts p. Moreover, Karl's language and thought have the capacity to represent the sentences of Karl's language and the propositions he entertains, and Karl possesses basic logical concepts like negation, conjunction, disjunction, and the conditional (and his language has the associated expressions).

Here is the problem. There is no way to fill in **Ao**, **Ak**, and **M** for Karl. As we have seen, it is impossible to: (i) specify the meaning of Karl's truth predicate or the content of Karl's concept of truth so that (T-In) and (T-Out) are true, while (ii) specifying the contents of Karl's logical terms and concepts accurately (e.g., so that the conditional obeys *modus ponens* and conditional proof), and (iii) respecting the fact that Karl's language contains liar sentences and there are liar propositions that he might entertain.[25] Of course, we might be able to fill in **Ao**, **Ak**, and **M** piecemeal, but that is a far cry from a general theory of Karl, the person, that Lewis envisions. The fact that Karl possesses the concept of truth and his language has a truth predicate seems to render it impossible to treat Karl as a person. Far from being harmless puzzles, the aletheic paradoxes threaten the very idea that we are people, at least if people conform to the general theory of persons articulated above. Moreover, the damage caused by the paradoxes is not confined to philosophy departments; they do damage in linguistics departments, in psychology departments, in cognitive science departments, in sociology departments—or at least they will when the members of these departments who are working on their respective aspects of a general theory of persons get around to thinking hard about what to say about utterances and attitudes associated with truth.

Hofweber has a more specific objection—he argues that my particular replacement strategy is impossible to pull off. Here is a passage from a recent paper:

> Scharp proposes that we replace our inconsistent concept of truth with a better one. But if our concept of truth indeed allows us to infer anything then such a replacement can't be rational. The reasons available to us then wouldn't favor replacement since I can deduce deductively that I should replace, and that I shouldn't replace, leading to a rational dead end.[26]

The worry voiced here is that one can use the reasoning in say, Curry's paradox to infer anything at all (or one could use any of the aletheic paradoxes to arrive at a contradiction and then infer anything one wants from it); in particular, one could infer that truth should not be replaced. The problem with this objection is in the term 'allows'. Our

[25] Notice that this problem does *not* presuppose that we are specifying the meanings of Karl's sentences by giving their truth conditions. It is a problem for everyone, no matter what one's preferred theory of meaning.

[26] Hofweber (2010: 16, n. 10).

concept of truth *does* allow us to infer anything in the sense that if we use its constitutive principles, we can arrive at any conclusion we please. However, it is no part of my view that it is rational to reason according to truth's constitutive principles across the board. Indeed, once we discover that they are classically inconsistent given the resources to construct paradoxical sentences, we should no longer accept these principles. Notice also that my case for replacement does not rely on reasoning in accord with truth's constitutive principles. Rather, I argue that because truth is a useful inconsistent concept, we should introduce some new concepts that should be used instead of truth in certain situations.

5.4 Conditions of adequacy

On the basis of the discussion so far in Chapters 2, 3, and 4, we can formulate conditions for an acceptable unified theory of truth (T):

(1) T implies that (T-In) and (T-Out) are constitutive of truth.
(2) T is compatible with classical logic.
(3) T is a theory of a general truth predicate.
(4) T implies that natural-language truth predicates are univocal and invariant.
(5) T does not give rise to revenge paradoxes (of either kind).
(6) T enjoys generic theoretical virtues (e.g., consistency, simplicity, modesty, power, and depth).

A few comments on these conditions are in order.

Condition (1) stems from truth's expressive role and the intuition that anyone who asserts p together with 'p is not true' or ⌜~p⌝ together with 'p is true' seems to be misusing the word 'true'. Yes, there are theoretical reasons for the former (e.g., p is not in the business of stating facts), but the point here is that liar sentences do not seem to be in this category, so anyone who asserts either of these combinations where p is a sentence in the same category as liar sentences seems to misunderstand the word 'true'. Notice that (1) does not require that T implies that (T-In) and (T-Out) are *true*; rather, T must imply that they are constitutive.

Condition (2) is based on the considerations throughout Chapters 3 and 4; in particular, it seems that we use logical devices (e.g., Boolean negation) in natural language. Nonclassical approaches to the aletheic paradoxes and the unified theories of truth that incorporate them are incapable of applying to languages with these features. Again, there might be good reason to give up classical logic, but any such reason will have to be based on the norms of correct reasoning, not on trying to solve paradoxes that pertain to a specific concept.

Condition (3) stipulates that truth predicates are not language-specific. As argued in Chapter 4, there is no way to explain natural-language truth predicates in terms of language-specific truth predicates. The only alternative is to admit that 'true' applies equally to sentences of English and sentences of other languages.

Condition (4) is justified by the considerations in Chapter 3 on contingent paradoxes; since (i) truth plays an expressive role in our linguistic practice, (ii) the Content Determination Condition (CDC) governs our communicative practices, and (iii) there are contingent paradoxes, it does not make sense to think that truth predicates (or the sentences in which they occur) are ambiguous or context-dependent in a way that would obviate the aletheic paradoxes. This issue will come up again in Chapter 9, where I suggest that 'true' is assessment-sensitive in virtue of expressing an inconsistent concept.

Condition (5) should be obvious at this point; the revenge paradoxes studied in Chapter 4 are as debilitating as they are ubiquitous. Theories of truth that give rise to revenge paradoxes are non-starters—they do not apply to natural languages, they require language-specific truth predicates, and they do not solve the paradoxes.

Condition (6) has nothing to do with truth in particular, but rather with philosophical theories in general. They should be *consistent* (inconsistent theories are unacceptable, and switching from classical to paraconsistent logic does not make them any less so). They should, other things being equal, be *simple*; this is a widely accepted condition on theories. They should, other things being equal, be *modest* in the sense that accepting them should not require giving up other, independent views (this is one major problem with non-classical theories of truth—they go hand in hand with rejecting accepted ways of reasoning even when those have nothing to do with truth). They should be *powerful*, which means that they explain a wide range of issues associated with truth, not just 'true' as it is used in certain specialized circumstances. Finally, they should be *deep*, in the sense that they give us some insight into a diverse set of phenomena that had previously been not as well understood.

5.5 Two theories

The discussion so far illustrates a deep divide between my approach and those of other contemporary inconsistency theorists with the exception of Burgess: I take a *dynamic* attitude toward the aletheic paradoxes, while theirs is *static*. That is, my approach focuses on what we can do and what we should do about the paradoxes. Their approaches are only about how to describe one aspect of the current mess we are in—they focus on how to understand languages that contain words that express inconsistent concepts. They care about where we are; I care about both where we are and where we want to be. Of course, it is important to understand our language as it is; without such an understanding, we would not know what problem needs to be fixed. In fact, we inconsistency theorists all agree that the biggest mistake made by those who propose traditional approaches to the aletheic paradoxes is that they misdiagnose the problem. *We* think that truth is an inconsistent concept (or that a language containing a truth predicate is an inconsistent language), while *they* think that everyone taken in by the reasoning involved in the paradoxes is making some more or less mundane mistake. We think that competence with the concepts involved in the paradox predisposes those who employ them to accept all the assumptions and inferences involved in the paradoxical reasoning. Although we all agree on this matter, we disagree about how to characterize inconsistent concepts and languages.

From my point of view, the biggest mistake made by the other inconsistency theorists is that they do not consider what can be done to change our language and our conceptual repertoire in order to eliminate the liar paradox and its vengeful brethren. Only by understanding the process by which we change our concepts and our language can we really understand both our inconsistent language and what we should do to fix it.

Accordingly, my approach to the liar paradox has two parts: (i) a descriptive theory, which explains our inconsistent language and our inconsistent concept of truth, and (ii) a prescriptive theory, which explains how we should change our language and which introduces new concepts to take the place of our inconsistent concept of truth. It is essential that *the descriptive theory depend on the prescriptive theory*. That is, the theory that explains our inconsistent concept of truth does not appeal to our inconsistent concept of truth. Instead, the descriptive theory appeals to the replacement concepts introduced by the prescriptive theory. Otherwise, one could not accept the explanation of our inconsistent concept of truth without giving our inconsistent concept of truth a crucial explanatory role.

5.6 The parable of Mindy

One might have the following worry about my replacement strategy: we need to understand our current linguistic practice *before* we can figure out how to fix it; otherwise, we have no reason to think that the fix will be successful; that is, we need to know where we are *before* we figure out where we should go. Thus, a descriptive theory should not be based on the prescriptive theory.

My reply is that we need a good enough understanding of our current linguistic practice to figure out what to do. However, we have good reason to think that, although many of our tools for understanding our linguistic practice rely on truth (e.g., truth-conditional semantics), truth is a defective concept. Thus, we simultaneously think that truth is a key to understanding our language and that it is defective. That puts us in the position of being able to understand *well enough* what our current practice is like. We understand what is wrong well enough to see that, using our current concepts, we cannot be completely successful at describing what is going on. Moreover, we understand what is wrong well enough to place some conditions on potential conceptual revolutions.

I would like to use an analogy based on Hasok Chang's recent work on the development of the concept of temperature to illustrate my point (I have changed the story a bit).[27] Imagine that a very nearsighted person, Mindy, has been using a monocle, but

[27] Chang (2004).

now finds that it does not work very well; in particular, there is a major distortion in her field of view. She takes off the monocle and looks at it but cannot see any defects owing to her inability to see much at all without it. She gets an idea and puts on the monocle and looks in a mirror—she can see well enough with the monocle to notice a very large and deep scratch across the lens. Of course, the scratch prevents her from seeing the reflection of the monocle in the mirror perfectly. Nevertheless, she sees it well enough to diagnose the problem—the scratch on the lens—and well enough to figure out what needs to be done—replace the lens. So, it would be impossible for Mindy to see her monocle perfectly given that the tool she is using—that very monocle—is defective. Nevertheless, it works well enough for her to diagnose the problem and arrive at a course of action to fix it. Let us say Mindy calls her optometrist and there is no replacement lens in stock, so she decides to buy a pair of glasses instead. With her new pair of glasses, she can see the scratch on the monocle far better than she could while using the monocle and a mirror—after all, she is not looking through a defective lens anymore. So her monocle was able (with some help from the mirror) to give her enough information about her predicament to allow her to determine what the problem was even though she did not have a perfect understanding of it since the scratch on the lens distorted her view of the scratch on the lens. It also gave her enough information to figure out what to do about it, even though it did not give her perfect understanding of it since the scratch on the lens distorted her view of the scratch on the lens.

The monocle is our concept of truth, the scratch on the lens is truth's conceptual defectiveness, and the new pair of glasses is the team of replacements for truth. Even though we cannot use truth to get a perfect understanding of our linguistic practice and our truth predicate, our tools (which involve the notion of truth) give us enough information to figure out that truth is a defective concept and they give us enough information to figure out what to do about it.

We get a better understanding of our linguistic practice by using the replacement concepts rather than our concept of truth, just as Mindy gets a better view of her monocle using the glasses. That is not to say that the monocle did no work—it allowed her to figure out what was wrong even if it did not give her a perfect view of what was wrong. The same point holds in the case of truth—using it, we have figured out that it is defective. Using it, we have figured out what its replacements should be like. It is a mistake to think that defective tools, whether they are physical or conceptual, are good for nothing.

6

The Prescriptive Theory

This chapter presents one of the two major theories of this book. It outlines the replacement concepts: ascending truth and descending truth. The theory presented here is prescriptive in the sense that it offers a suggestion for changing our conceptual scheme. One of the central tenets of the unified theory of truth I offer is that the descriptive theory of truth should depend on the prescriptive theory of truth—the replacements, not truth, should serve in explanatory roles for the descriptive theory, which is the subject of Chapter 9.

6.1 The replacements: ascending truth and descending truth

I am hardly the first philosopher to suggest replacements for truth. I think Tarski can be read as suggesting a sanitized replacement.[1] More recently, Vann McGee suggested that we replace truth with two concepts—a vague concept of truth and a concept of definite truth.[2] And Alexis Burgess has recently suggested a fictionalist truth predicate as a replacement.[3] Indeed, since most approaches to the aletheic paradoxes require giving up something that seems integral to the everyday concept of truth, most of them can be read as offering a replacement concept.

An inconsistency theorist who thinks we should replace our concept of truth (at least for certain purposes) has a choice to make: what should the replacement(s) be? It is tempting to opt for a single replacement concept, but there are good reasons to reject this strategy.

First, it is widely accepted that we use 'true' as a device of endorsement and as a device of rejection. In order to serve as a device of endorsement, the truth predicate must obey (T-Out), and in order to serve as a device of rejection, the truth predicate must obey

[1] Tarski (1933).
[2] McGee (1991).
[3] A. Burgess (2006).

(T-In). These are necessary (but not sufficient) conditions. Of course, we already know that in a classical setting no single concept obeys these two principles; thus, no concept can serve as both a device of endorsement and rejection given classical logic and the expressive resources to construct liar sentences. However, as I shall show, if we replace truth with two concepts, we can split the workload, allowing one to serve as a device of endorsement and the other to serve as a device of rejection.

The huge variety of aletheic paradoxes hidden in the principles truth seems to obey constitutes a second reason to use a team of replacements. Here is a sample of the many principles truth seems to obey:

Disquotational Principles

(T-Out)	$T(\langle\phi\rangle) \rightarrow \phi$
(T-In)	$\phi \rightarrow T(\langle\phi\rangle)$
(T-Elim)	$T(\langle\phi\rangle) \vdash \phi$
(T-Intro)	$\phi \vdash T(\langle\phi\rangle)$
(~T-Elim)	$\sim T(\langle\phi\rangle) \vdash \sim\phi$
(~T-Intro)	$\sim\phi \vdash \sim T(\langle\phi\rangle)$
(Cat)	$\vdash \phi \rightarrow \vdash T(\langle\phi\rangle)$
(Co-Cat)	$\vdash T(\langle\phi\rangle) \rightarrow \vdash \phi$

Truth-functional Principles

(~-Imb)[4]	$\sim T(\langle\phi\rangle) \rightarrow T(\langle\sim\phi\rangle)$
(~-Exc)[5]	$T(\langle\sim\phi\rangle) \rightarrow \sim T(\langle\phi\rangle)$
(∧-Imb)	$T(\langle\phi\rangle) \wedge T(\langle\psi\rangle) \rightarrow T(\langle\phi\wedge\psi\rangle)$
(∧-Exc)	$T(\langle\phi\wedge\psi\rangle) \rightarrow T(\langle\phi\rangle) \wedge T(\langle\psi\rangle)$
(∨-Imb)	$T(\langle\phi\rangle) \vee T(\langle\psi\rangle) \rightarrow T(\langle\phi\vee\psi\rangle)$
(∨-Exc)	$T(\langle\phi\vee\psi\rangle) \rightarrow T(\langle\phi\rangle) \vee T(\langle\psi\rangle)$
(→-Imb)	$(T(\langle\phi\rangle) \rightarrow T(\langle\psi\rangle)) \rightarrow T(\langle\phi \rightarrow \psi\rangle)$
(→-Exc)	$T(\langle\phi \rightarrow \psi\rangle) \rightarrow (T(\langle\phi\rangle) \rightarrow T(\langle\psi\rangle))$

Misc. Principles

(Taut)	$T(\langle\phi\rangle)$ for ϕ a tautology
Contra)	$\sim T(\langle\phi\rangle)$ for ϕ a contradiction
(T-Del)	$T(\langle T(\langle\phi\rangle)\rangle) \rightarrow T(\langle\phi\rangle)$
(T-Rep)	$T(\langle\phi\rangle) \rightarrow T(\langle T(\langle\phi\rangle)\rangle)$
(TT)	$T(\langle T(\langle\phi\rangle) \rightarrow \phi\rangle)$

Implication Principles

(MPC)	$(\phi_1 \wedge \ldots \wedge \phi_n \rightarrow \psi) \rightarrow (T(\langle\phi_1\rangle) \wedge \ldots \wedge T(\langle\phi_n\rangle) \rightarrow T(\langle\psi\rangle))$
(SPC)	$(\phi \rightarrow \psi) \rightarrow (T(\langle\phi\rangle) \rightarrow T(\langle\psi\rangle))$

[4] 'Imb' is short for 'imbibe'.

[5] 'Exc' is short for 'excrete'.

$$
\begin{array}{ll}
\text{(Sub-In)} & \phi \leftrightarrow \psi \rightarrow T(\langle\phi\rangle) \leftrightarrow T(\langle\psi\rangle) \\
\text{(MPT)} & (T(\langle\phi_1\rangle) \wedge \ldots \wedge T(\langle\phi_n\rangle) \rightarrow T(\langle\psi\rangle)) \rightarrow (\phi_1 \wedge \ldots \wedge \phi_n \rightarrow \psi) \\
\text{(SPT)} & (T(\langle\phi\rangle) \rightarrow T(\langle\psi\rangle)) \rightarrow (\phi \rightarrow \psi) \\
\text{(Sub-Out)} & T(\langle\phi\rangle) \leftrightarrow T(\langle\psi\rangle) \rightarrow (\phi \rightarrow \psi)
\end{array}
$$

It is reasonable to expect that our theory of the replacement concept(s) should include as many replacement principles—those like the above but formulated with the replacement concepts—as possible. With a single replacement for truth, one will end up with very few of these replacement principles. Consider the study by Harvey Friedman and Michael Sheard on just twelve principles that truth seems to obey. They document all the possible consistent subsets of these twelve principles.[6] One lesson from their analy-

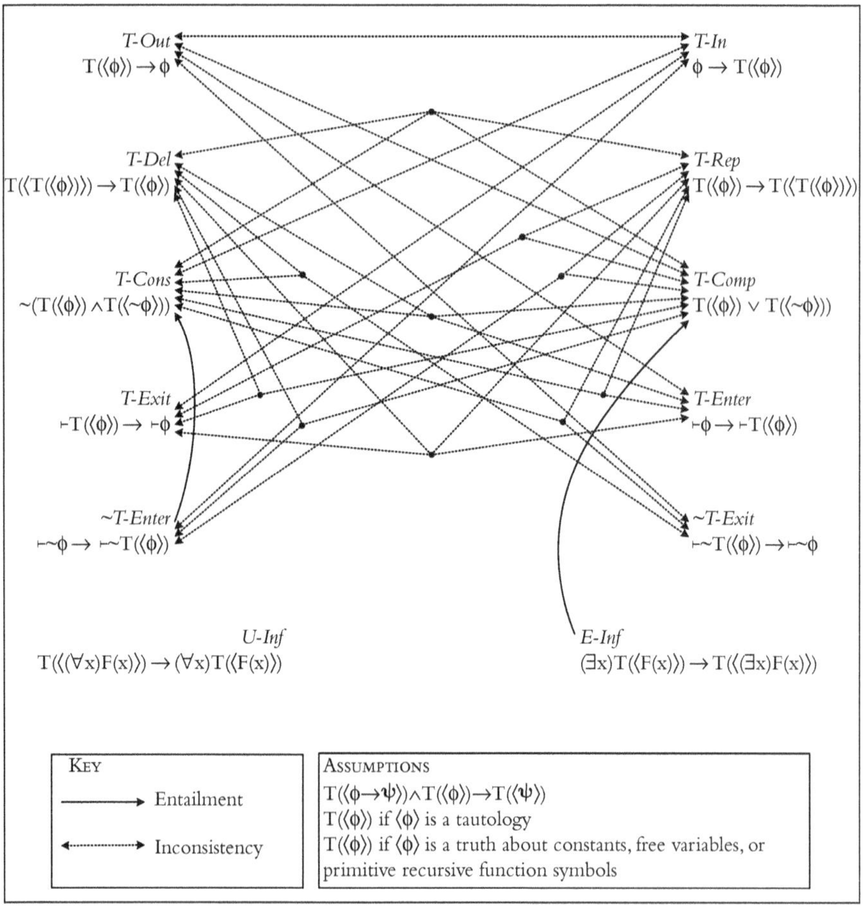

Figure 5 Aletheic Principles from Friedman and Sheard

[6] Friedman and Sheard (1987). See also Friedman and Sheard (1988) and Leigh and Rathjen (2010).

sis is that trying to find a consistent subset of even the most basic principles we unreflectively take truth to obey is like navigating a minefield—there are a ton of hidden inconsistencies in seemingly innocuous combinations of just these twelve principles; Figure 5 displays their results (any combination not labeled as inconsistent is consistent).[7]

And it only gets worse when one includes more truth-functional principles, quantification principles, and implication principles. Anyone who advocates replacing truth with a single concept would have to pick the best combination of replacement principles and give up anything like the rest of them. Even the best combination is a small subset of these principles, so most of them would be given up. However, as I indicate below, when we replace truth with *two* concepts, we have the option of accepting some replacement principles that are formulated with one concept and some replacement principles that are formulated with the other. In addition, this strategy allows for *hybrid* principles, which are formulated with both concepts. The theory of the replacement concepts I offer includes a replacement principle for every one of the principles listed above for truth. Such a thing is only possible when we replace truth with a team of concepts.

Having argued that we should not replace truth with a single concept, we still need to decide on a team of replacement concepts. There are many options here, but one obvious way to go is: pick the smallest inconsistent collection of the most obvious of truth's principles and divide them up between replacement concepts. The most obvious candidate collection is: (T-In) and (T-Out).[8] So we should have one replacement concept that obeys an analog of (T-In) but not the analog of (T-Out) and another replacement concept that obeys an analog of (T-Out) but not the analog of (T-In). Inspired by Quine's comment that (T-In) encapsulates truth's function of semantic ascent, I call the concept that obeys (T-In) *ascending truth*. The other I call *descending truth*.

6.2 Montague's theorem

The goal is to have ascending truth and descending truth be as close as possible to truth without engendering paradoxes of any kind or requiring a weakening of logic. Moreover, in sentences that do not pose any kind of threat (e.g., sentences not containing semantic predicates), ascending and descending truth should obey all the above principles. It turns out that there are several serious obstacles to satisfying these demands, and some tough choices have to be made.

[7] Remember, (T-Enter), (T-Exit), (~T-Enter), and (~T-Exit) are to be read as derivability principles rather than inference rules; e.g., (T-Enter) says that if p is derivable, then 'p is true' is derivable. To foreshadow a bit, neither of the replacement concepts I recommend obeys the first listed assumption, so they are not subject to these results.

[8] I am excluding the substitution principle from the collection since it seems integral to being a predicate at all.

The most difficult problem facing our inchoate theory of ascending and descending truth is a theorem Richard Montague proved in 1963 that has had much more impact on the philosophical discussion of necessity than the discussion of truth. Montague proved that a theory of some predicate H(x) with the following features is inconsistent:

(i) All instances of '$H(\langle\phi\rangle) \rightarrow \phi$' are theorems.
(ii) All instances of '$H(\langle H(\langle\phi\rangle) \rightarrow \phi\rangle)$' are theorems.
(iii) All instances of '$H(\langle\phi\rangle)$' where $\langle\phi\rangle$ is a logical axiom are theorems.
(iv) All instances of '$H(\langle\phi \rightarrow \psi\rangle) \rightarrow (H(\langle\phi\rangle) \rightarrow H(\langle\psi\rangle))$ are theorems.
(v) Q (i.e., Robinson arithmetic) is a subtheory.[9]

Condition (v) is present to ensure that the language in which the theory is expressed has the ability to refer to its own sentences. The other four conditions are highly desirable for *descending* truth. On this reading, note that (i) is just the replacement for (T-Out), (ii) says that all instances of the replacement for (T-Out) are descending true, (iii) says that all tautologies are descending true, and (iv) says that descending truth is closed under *modus ponens* (i.e., if a conditional is descending true and its antecedent is descending true, then its consequent is descending true). Montague's theorem shows that if descending truth is a consistent concept, then it does not obey all four of these principles. Since I am taking the replacement for (T-Out) to be constitutive of descending truth, my options are to deny (ii), deny (iii), or deny (iv). Denying (ii) results in a theory of descending truth that is not descending true, which is a version of a revenge paradox (self-refutation problem). That leaves (iii) or (iv).

A recent result by Field helps make this decision easier. He argues that the standard definition of validity is untenable in light of the aletheic paradoxes because it is incompatible with every logical approach to the paradoxes. Recall the seven categories of logical approaches: (i) classical glut, (ii) classical gap, (iii) classical symmetric, (iv) weakly classical, (v) paracomplete, (vi) paraconsistent, and (vii) substructural. Field considers only five of these (he leaves out (iii) and (vii)). Let T be the theory composed of the logic in question plus the principle(s) of truth in question (e.g., in case (i), T is classical logic plus (T-In)).

Case (i): T proves that some principles of classical logic are not truth-preserving.[10]

Case (ii): T proves that some principles of truth are not truth-preserving.[11]

Case (vi): Either T proves that some principles of truth are not truth-preserving or T proves that some principles of (weakly) classical logic are not truth-preserving.[12]

[9] Montague (1963).

[10] For a liar sentence λ (i.e., λ = 'λ is not true'), T proves that λ is true, T proves that $\ulcorner\lambda \rightarrow (\sim\lambda \rightarrow \bot)\urcorner$ is true, and T proves that $\ulcorner\sim\lambda \rightarrow \bot\urcorner$ is not true. Thus, T proves that an instance of *modus ponens* is not truth-preserving. See Field (2006a).

[11] T proves that' $\ulcorner\lambda$ is true $\rightarrow \lambda\urcorner$ is not true, but $\ulcorner\lambda$ is true $\rightarrow \lambda\urcorner$ is an instance of (T-Out). Thus, T proves that an instance of (T-Out) is not truth-preserving. See Field (2006a).

[12] See Friedman and Sheard (1987) for the argument; see also Field (2006a).

Case (v): T is inconsistent with the claim that all principles of paracomplete logic are truth-preserving.[13]

Case (vi): Either T proves that some principles of paraconsistent logic are not truth-preserving or T trivializes when conjoined with the claim that all principles of paraconsistent logic are truth-preserving.[14]

Here I am including under the heading of 'truth-preserving' the condition that the theory implies that all its axioms are true—the instance of an axiom is like a trivial inference rule. Although option (iii), classical symmetric theories, are left out of Field's treatment, there is good reason to think that they cannot treat validity as truth-preservation since they do not even allow the move from p to 'p is true' or vice versa in hypothetical contexts. The upshot is that, no matter which of the first six options one chooses, one should not accept that valid arguments are necessarily truth-preserving. Proponents of substructural views claim that they are not subject to Field's result.[15]

In general, we have two prominent ways of thinking about validity: as the property of canons of good reasoning and as necessary truth-preservation. The lesson of Field's argument can be put as: given any combination of a theory of truth and a logic, it is unacceptable that the canons of good reasoning preserve truth.[16] This argument of Field's is relatively new, and it is buried in a much more complex discussion of Gödel's Second Incompleteness Theorem and formal theories of truth, so it has yet to generate much literature. However, I find it convincing, and this conclusion has an effect on my response to the problem posed by Montague's theorem.

Field's considerations also sink any attempt to define validity in terms of descending truth-preservation. So, any theory of descending truth will have to admit that descending truth is not closed under some deducibilities. However, it is open to say that all logical truths are descending true. Thus, it makes the most sense to reject (iv) and accept (iii). As such, I stipulate that all classical tautologies are descending true; it follows by Montague's theorem that descending truth is not closed under *modus ponens*.

We know several things about ascending and descending truth already. First, we are using classical logic and we are not restricting the expressive resources of the languages we consider. So we know that we will have to deal with sentences like the following:

(a) ~A(a) [i.e., a is not ascending true]
(d) ~D(d) [i.e., d is not descending true]

From (d) and the fact that D(x) obeys (T-Out) we can prove ~D(d) and ~D(⌜~d⌝); from (a) and the fact that A(x) obeys (T-In), we can prove A(a) and A(⌜~a⌝). So we know that

[13] See Field (2006a) for the argument.

[14] See Field (2006a) for the argument.

[15] See Ripley (2012, forthcoming) and Beall and Murzi (forthcoming).

[16] The effects of this split can be seen all over the literature on logical approaches to the paradoxes. For example, Maudlin (2004) defines validity in terms of truth-preservation, and that leads him to claim that (T-In) and (T-Out) are valid on his theory. Well, they are truth-preserving according to his theory, but they are not canons of good reasoning according to his theory. See Field (2006c) for discussion.

there are some sentences such that they and their negations are ascending true and there are some sentences such that they and their negations are not descending true.

One rather tricky issue is the relation between ascending truth and descending truth (if any). Consider the relation between a sentence p, 'p is ascending true' and 'p is descending true'. p follows from 'p is descending true' but not vice versa; hence, 'p is descending true' is stronger than p. On the other hand, 'p is ascending true' follows from p, but not vice versa; hence p is stronger than 'p is ascending true'. Given these claims, 'it is not the case that p is descending true' is weaker than ⌜~p⌝ and 'it is not the case that p is ascending true' is stronger than ⌜~p⌝. So, what is the relation between 'p is ascending true' and 'it is not the case that ⌜~p⌝ is descending true'? Further, what is the relation between 'p is descending true' and 'it is not the case that ⌜~p⌝ is ascending true'? I stipulate that, in both cases, they are equivalent.[17] That is, $A(\langle\phi\rangle) \leftrightarrow {\sim}D(\langle{\sim}\phi\rangle)$ and $D(\langle\phi\rangle) \leftrightarrow {\sim}A(\langle{\sim}\phi\rangle)$. Thus, ascending truth and descending truth are *dual* predicates.[18] They have the same relation that obtains between possibility and necessity, between permission and obligation, between consistency and provability, etc. We will see below how this assumption plays out in formal treatments of ascending and descending truth.

Above, I chose to have tautologies be descending true over having descending truth be closed under *modus ponens*. So we know that tautologies are descending true. Likewise, by duality, contradictions are not ascending true.

It is pretty straightforward to add principles for negation to each concept. We can say that descending truth obeys (~-Exc) and ascending truth obeys (~-Imb), but not vice versa. Given what has been said already, we know that ascending truth does not obey (∧-Imb) and that descending truth does not obey (∨-Exc). However, we can have both descending truth and ascending truth obey (∧-Exc) and (∨-Imb).

Since we do not want to block the resources for generating self-reference in any way, it makes sense to require that the theories that ensure the kinds of expressive resources needed to construct potentially paradoxical sentences are descending true. That is, the axioms of a theory of syntax are descending true. Also, since the most important way to achieve self-reference in mathematical theories is via arithmetization (i.e., Gödel numbering), we need at least the axioms of PA to be descending true.

Finally, given the choice made above in light of Montague's theorem, we want all the axioms of the theory of ascending and descending truth to be descending true.

6.3 Safety

We have already said that descending truth obeys the principle '$D(\langle\phi\rangle) \rightarrow \phi$' and ascending truth obeys the principle '$\phi \rightarrow A(\langle\phi\rangle)$'. However, neither can obey the

[17] There are alternative ways of defining descending truth and ascending truth, but I do not consider them in this work.

[18] Many thanks to Dana Scott who impressed upon me the importance of duality in the theory of ascending and descending truth.

inverse principle on pain of contradiction. However, the potential problems raised by the inverse principles arise only for a few sentences like (α) and (δ). It does no harm (and a lot of good) to let descending truth obey a restricted version of (T-In) and let ascending truth obey a restricted version of (T-Out). We can formulate them in the following way:

(M3) $S(\langle\phi\rangle) \land \phi \rightarrow D(\langle\phi\rangle)$
(M4) $A(\langle\phi\rangle) \land S(\langle\phi\rangle) \rightarrow \phi$

where 'S(x)' is a predicate that stands for 'safety'. Intuitively, a safe sentence is one for which both directions of the principles for ascending truth and for descending truth hold. Unsafe sentences are those for which they do not.

Using the defining principles for safety and for ascending truth and descending truth we can derive the following principle of safety:

(M2) $S(\langle\phi\rangle) \leftrightarrow D(\langle\phi\rangle) \lor {\sim}A(\langle\phi\rangle)$

That is, a safe sentence is either descending true or not ascending true. Conversely, an unsafe sentence is both ascending true and not descending true. A consequence of this result is a clearer picture of the relation between descending truth and ascending truth. We know that any sentence that is descending true is ascending true. From this it also follows that any sentence that is not ascending true is not descending true. Moreover, some sentences are ascending true and not descending true and no sentence is both descending true and not ascending true.

Given the guiding analogy between the concept of truth and the concept of mass, and the fact that I want to be able to explain when one can use 'true' without running into problems, it makes sense to have several additional constraints on safety. It is acceptable to use 'mass' iff one is dealing with a situation in which the difference between relativistic mass and proper mass is negligible. Likewise, it is acceptable to use 'true' iff one is dealing with a situation in which the difference between ascending truth and descending truth is negligible. These are exactly the situations in which one is dealing with safe sentences. Thus, one should expect that if we restrict our attention to them, then ascending truth and descending truth obey all the principles we take truth to obey (i.e., all the aletheic principles from section 6.1).

6.4 A formal theory: ADT

Given what has been said above, we can summarize the principles that any theory of ascending truth and descending truth should include. I do not require such a theory to be axiomatizable, so the following is not meant to be *the* theory of ascending truth and descending truth; rather any theory of ascending truth and descending truth should have the following as a subtheory. I call the following theory ADT:

D1 $D(\langle\phi\rangle) \rightarrow \phi$
D2 $D(\langle\sim\phi\rangle) \rightarrow \sim D(\langle\phi\rangle)$
D3 $D(\langle\phi\wedge\psi\rangle) \rightarrow D(\langle\phi\rangle) \wedge D(\langle\psi\rangle)$
D4 $D(\langle\phi\rangle) \vee D(\langle\psi\rangle) \rightarrow D(\langle\phi\vee\psi\rangle)$
D5 $D(\langle\phi\rangle)$ if ϕ is a logical truth (i.e., a tautology of first-order predicate calculus)
D6 $D(\langle\phi\rangle)$ if ϕ is a theorem of PA
D7 $D(\langle\phi\rangle)$ if ϕ is an axiom of ADT (i.e., if ϕ is an instance of D1–D6, A1–A6, M1–M4, or E1–E3)

A1 $\phi \rightarrow A(\langle\phi\rangle)$
A2 $\sim A(\langle\phi\rangle) \rightarrow A(\langle\sim\phi\rangle)$
A3 $A(\langle\phi\rangle) \vee A(\langle\psi\rangle) \rightarrow A(\langle\phi\vee\psi\rangle)$
A4 $A(\langle\phi\wedge\psi\rangle) \rightarrow A(\langle\phi\rangle) \wedge A(\langle\psi\rangle)$
A5 $\sim A(\langle\phi\rangle)$ if ϕ is a logical falsity (i.e., a contradiction of first-order predicate calculus)
A6 $\sim A(\langle\phi\rangle)$ if ϕ is the negation of an axiom of PA[19]

M1 $D(\langle\phi\rangle) \leftrightarrow \sim A(\langle\sim\phi\rangle)$
M2 $S(\langle\phi\rangle) \leftrightarrow (D(\langle\phi\rangle) \vee \sim A(\langle\phi\rangle))$
M3 $\phi \wedge S(\langle\phi\rangle) \rightarrow D(\langle\phi\rangle)$
M4 $A(\langle\phi\rangle) \wedge S(\langle\phi\rangle) \rightarrow \phi$

E1 If s = t and q results from replacing some occurrences of s with t in p, then $D(p) \leftrightarrow D(q)$.
E2 If s = t and q results from replacing some occurrences of s with t in p, then $A(p) \leftrightarrow A(q)$.
E3 If s = t and q results from replacing some occurrences of s with t in p, then $S(p) \leftrightarrow S(q)$.

There are obvious redundancies in this list of axioms but I prefer this formulation of ADT over a more elegant axiomatization because once one gives up the idea that descending truth and ascending truth are preserved under derivability, there emerges a significant difference between axioms of a theory and its theorems. I want all the axioms of ADT to be descending true, but we know that not all the theorems of ADT will be descending true. I have set up ADT so that all the axioms in the above list turn out to be descending true. Actually, it is even stronger: they are all descending true, that they are descending true is descending true, that that they are descending true is descending true is descending true, and so on. Therefore, there is a good reason for leaving the redundancies in the list of axioms for ADT.[20]

[19] Axioms D5, D6, A5, and A6 hold for sentences that contain 'ascending true' and 'descending true'.

[20] My appreciation goes to Stewart Shapiro for numerous conversations about how best to formulate ADT.

6.5 Other replacements

Now that the reader has an initial grasp of ADT, I want to compare it to other teams of replacement concepts that have been proposed. Tarski offered us a consistent concept of truth that can be defined only for certain artificial languages and does not apply to sentences that contain truth predicates. Although some have tried to use Tarskian truth predicates as theories of natural-language truth predicates, Kripke demolished this program in the mid-1970s with a series of objections that convinced an entire generation to seek alternative approaches to the aletheic paradoxes.[21]

Vann McGee thinks that our "conception" of truth is inconsistent and he suggests a pair of replacement concepts.[22] He offers a vague truth predicate and uses a supervaluation-based theory of vagueness to arrive at a theory of truth. His truth predicate violates both (T-In) and (T-Out), but it does obey these principles in categorical reasoning (i.e., outside of hypothetical contexts like conditional proof, *reductio*, and the like). Like many who work on vagueness, McGee introduces a definiteness operator to distinguish unproblematic from problematic cases of application. Accordingly, McGee distinguishes between truth and definite truth. On McGee's theory, (T-In) and (T-Out) preserve definite truth, not truth. That is, the following principles hold:

(i) If p is definitely true, then 'p is true' is definitely true.
(ii) If p is definitely not true, then 'p is true' is definitely not true.
(iii) If p is unsettled, then 'p is true' is unsettled.

For his theory of definite truth, McGee uses the Strong Kleene version of Kripke's fixed-point theory. By appealing to the notion of a partially interpreted language, McGee proves that both his supervaluation semantic theory for truth and his fixed-point semantic theory for definite truth apply to the language in which they are formulated. One of the keys to this result is that the formal language in which his theories are formulated does not contain sentences that pose revenge paradoxes. That is, the sentence:

(1) (1) is false or unsettled.

is unsettled, and so not definitely true, but it is not *definitely* unsettled, thus no paradox results from it.[23] Furthermore, because (1) is not a consequence of either theory, neither theory implies that it is not true.

In addition, McGee proves that both the theory of truth and the theory of definite truth are expressible in the formal language in which they are formulated. He achieves this result by setting up his theories so that 'if p is definitely true, then p is true' is not definitely true. This is a counterintuitive result, but he needs it to ensure that (1) does not pose a revenge paradox. He also has to deny that the vague concept of truth he

[21] Kripke (1975); see discussion in Chapter 3.
[22] McGee (1991: vii).
[23] McGee (1991: Ch. 9).

presents can be made more precise because attempts at precisification result in revenge paradoxes.[24]

There are two major reasons to prefer my replacements to McGee's. First, ascending truth and descending truth, together, can perform truth's expressive role. That is, they can serve as devices of endorsement and rejection. McGee's vague notion of truth does not obey (T-In) or (T-Out), which renders it incapable of being used for this purpose. Field, especially, has made this point abundantly clear.[25] Second, ADT does not give rise to any revenge paradoxes, and the languages to which it applies have no expressive restrictions whatsoever. McGee's theory of truth and definite truth avoid revenge paradoxes only because the languages to which they apply lack certain expressive resources, like an intuitive definiteness operator (i.e., one for which 'if p is definitely true, then p is true' holds). Moreover, his theory of definite truth entails that some axioms of his theory of definite truth are not definitely true. However, all the axioms of ADT are descending true (and so ascending true). Given the significance of truth's expressive role and revenge paradoxes in debates about the aletheic paradoxes, one should prefer ascending truth and descending truth to McGee's replacements.

Consider another potential team of replacements, based on one of Solomon Feferman's axiomatic theories of truth, DT. This theory has a truth predicate and falsity predicate, where both are primitive. Instead, I introduce two truth predicates. In my framework, one can, of course, define an ascending falsity predicate and a descending falsity predicate in the usual way, but I do not see any benefit from this. However, one might compare Feferman's truth predicate to 'descending true', his falsity predicate to 'not ascending true', and his determinateness predicate to 'safe'. Then my definition of safety is analogous to his definition of determinateness. Also, Feferman's falsity predicate is related to his truth predicate in the same way that 'not ascending true' is related to 'descending true'. That is, for Feferman, p is false iff ⌜~p⌝ is true. One point of difference is that Feferman's theory does not take all logical truths to be true (e.g., the disjunction of the liar and its negation is not true on his theory), but for me, all logical truths are descending true. A major difference between the two theories is that, for Feferman's theory, determinateness is closed under logical operations, whereas safety is not. A related point is that all the axioms of the theory of ascending and descending truth are descending true, whereas not all the axioms of Feferman's DT are determinate. From my perspective, that is a deal-breaker since it is an instance of a revenge paradox (self-refutation). Moreover, Feferman takes his determinacy predicate to be inspired by the idea that each predicate meaningfully applies only to a particular range of entities—applications of the predicate outside that range are category mistakes. I think that, in the case of truth, the existence of contingent paradoxical sentences casts doubt on this idea. For sure, my notion of safety carries no such connotation. Finally, from my perspective, he overemphasizes compositionality for his determinateness predicate and does not appreciate the importance of having logic and

[24] See Yablo (1989), Simmons (1993), Priest (1994a), Tappenden (1994), and Mills (1995) for discussion of this aspect of McGee's theory.

[25] Field (2008a: Ch. 17).

his own axioms turn out definitely true. I do not put much weight on compositionality for either ascending truth or descending truth because I can appeal to hybrid principles (e.g., '$D(\langle\phi\rangle) \wedge D(\langle\psi\rangle) \rightarrow A(\langle\phi\wedge\psi\rangle)$' as a replacement principle for '$T(\langle\phi\rangle) \wedge T(\langle\psi\rangle) \rightarrow T(\langle\phi\wedge\psi\rangle)$'), which have occurrences of 'ascending true' and 'descending true'.

6.6 Semantics for ADT

One question about ADT naturally arises: is this theory consistent or are there new paradoxes hiding in here? Given Gödel's second incompleteness theorem, all we can hope for is a proof of relative consistency (i.e., if some uncontroversial theory is consistent, then ADT is consistent), but given the extreme difficulty with saying anything at all consistent about the liar paradox, a relative consistency proof seems in order, which is given in the appendix to this chapter and is based on the semantics presented in this section.[26]

Because of M1, D(x) and A(x) are *dual* predicates. For this reason, it makes sense to model their behavior using modal logic. This insight is the basis for the semantics given in this section.

Throughout this discussion it is essential to keep in mind the distinction between the theory ADT and its semantics. The theory is the set of theorems, where a theorem is either an axiom or a sentence that is deducible from the axioms by some combination of rules and classical logic. The list above contains the axioms. The semantics is a mathematical structure that we can use to prove certain things about the theory. In every case, the semantics uses a structure that is definable in set theory. A crucial part of the semantics is the definition of a valid sentence. Once we have the definition of a theorem (for the theory) and a definition of a validity (for the semantics), we can prove results about how they relate. For example, one might want to prove that the theory is sound with respect to the semantics, which requires showing that every theorem of the theory is a validity of the semantics. Or, more generally, if a formula ϕ is provable from a set of formulas Γ, then the argument from Γ to ϕ is valid. Once one has a soundness result, one can be sure that anything that is provable from the axioms will be valid in the semantics. In particular, one has a relative consistency proof for the theory in question.

6.6.1 *Normal modal logic and relational semantics*

A *normal* modal logic has the following form. Let L be a classical sentential language with the usual connectives and a 1–place operator '$\Box$' on sentences (i.e., if ϕ is a sentence then $\Box\,\phi$ is a sentence). All normal modal logics have axioms and rules. The axioms include the K axiom, which is:

(K) $\Box(\phi \rightarrow \psi) \rightarrow (\Box\,\phi \rightarrow \Box\,\psi)$

Many normal modal logics include other axioms as well. All normal modal logics include the Necessitation rule:

[26] My appreciation goes again to Dana Scott for his help in formulating and defending ADT.

(Nec) If $\vdash \phi$, then $\vdash \Box\phi$

In a normal modal logic, we can define the '$\Diamond$' operator in terms of the '$\Box$' operator in the following way:

(Duality) $\Diamond\phi \leftrightarrow {\sim}\Box{\sim}\,\phi$[27]

Every normal modal logic has Duality as a theorem. Notice that Duality is similar to M1 of ADT and this similarity is the inspiration for appealing to modal logic to model ADT.

Let us turn to the semantics for normal modal logics. Let W be a set of worlds and let R be a relation on W (called the *accessibility relation*). Together, W and R are called a *relational frame*, $\mathfrak{F} = <W, R>$. I call any semantics based on a frame of this kind a *relational semantics*. A valuation function, V, assigns to each sentential variable of L a truth value at each world in W. Together, F and V are called a *relational model*, $\mathfrak{M} = <\mathfrak{F}, V>$ for L. Each world in W is classical in that a classical scheme determines the value of each truth-functionally compound sentence. That gives us the following clauses for defining truth at a world in a model (i.e., $<\mathfrak{M}, w> \models \phi$):

(ϕ) $<\mathfrak{M}, w> \models \phi$ iff $w \in V(\phi)$ for ϕ atomic

(${\sim}$) $<\mathfrak{M}, w> \models {\sim}\phi$ iff it is not the case that $<\mathfrak{M}, w> \models \phi$

($\wedge$) $<\mathfrak{M}, w> \models \phi \wedge \psi$ iff $<\mathfrak{M}, w> \models \phi$ and $<\mathfrak{M}, w> \models \psi$

($\vee$) $<\mathfrak{M}, w> \models \phi \vee \psi$ iff $<\mathfrak{M}, w> \models \phi$ or $<\mathfrak{M}, w> \models \psi$

($\rightarrow$) $<\mathfrak{M}, w> \models \phi \rightarrow \psi$ iff if $<\mathfrak{M}, w> \models \phi$, then $<\mathfrak{M}, w> \models \psi$

($\leftrightarrow$) $<\mathfrak{M}, w> \models \phi \leftrightarrow \psi$ iff $<\mathfrak{M}, w> \models \phi$ iff $<\mathfrak{M}, w> \models \psi$

The clause for sentences of the form $\Box\phi$ is:

($\Box$) $<\mathfrak{M}, w> \models \Box\phi$ iff $\forall u \in W$ if Rwu, then $<\mathfrak{M}, u> \models \phi$

(i.e., $\Box\phi$ is true at w iff ϕ is true at all worlds accessible from w). These clauses constitute an inductive definition of truth at a world (i.e., $<\mathfrak{M}, w> \models \phi$) whatever the complexity of ϕ. A sentence ϕ is *valid in a model* $\mathfrak{M}$ (i.e., $\mathfrak{M} \models \phi$) iff $\forall w \in W$ $<\mathfrak{M}, w> \models \phi$. A sentence ϕ is *valid on a frame* $\mathfrak{F}$ (i.e., $\mathfrak{F} \models \phi$) iff for all $\mathfrak{M}$ based on $\mathfrak{F}$, $\forall w \in W$, $<\mathfrak{M}, w> \models \phi$.

If our language contains a second modal operator, $\Diamond$, then we include a separate clause, which would read:

($\Diamond$) $<\mathfrak{M}, w> \models \Diamond\phi$ iff $\exists u \in W$ s.t. Rwu and $<\mathfrak{M}, u> \models \phi$

Notice that given these clauses for $\Box$ and $\Diamond$, Duality is valid in any relational semantics.

By imposing constraints on the accessibility relation in a relational semantics, one can control which sentences are valid on the resulting frame. For example, a *reflexive* frame is any frame where the accessibility relation is reflexive (i.e., $\forall w, Rww$). Any sentence of

[27] This principle fails in intuitionistic logic, but I assume classical logic in what follows.

the form $\Box\phi \rightarrow \phi$ is valid on the class of reflexive frames. Any model that is to serve as a semantics for a theory that includes $\Box\phi \rightarrow \phi$ will be based on a reflexive frame.[28]

6.6.2 *Problems with using relational semantics for ADT*

There are several problems with using normal modal logic and its semantics for ADT.

Problem #1: every normal modal logic includes the K axiom and every relational semantics validates the K axiom. However, Richard Montague proved that the predicate version of the K axiom (i.e., $\forall\phi\forall\psi(\Box(\langle\phi \rightarrow \psi\rangle) \rightarrow (\Box(\langle\phi\rangle) \rightarrow \Box(\langle\psi\rangle)))$ is inconsistent with the combination of D1, D5, D6, and D7. Thus, no semantics that validates the K axiom can serve as a semantics for ADT.[29]

Problem #2: every normal modal logic includes the Necessitation rule and every relational semantics validates the Necessitation rule. However, Montague proved that the predicate version of the Necessitation rule (i.e., if ϕ is a theorem, then $\Box(\langle\phi\rangle)$ is a theorem) is inconsistent with the combination of D1 and D6. Thus, no semantics that validates the Necessitation rule can serve as a semantics for ADT.[30]

Problem #3: normal modal logic is a *sentential* modal logic (i.e., it deals with whole sentences and operators on whole sentences), but ADT is a theory of predicates, so I need a *first-order* modal logic that deals with parts of sentences, like predicates. First-order *normal* modal logic is well understood. We expand our language to include individual constants, individual variables, n-place predicates, and quantifiers. We expand our semantics with a domain, and treat individual constants, variables, n-place predicates, and quantifiers in the usual way. The major issue here is how to set up the domain of quantification—should every world have the same domain or should the domain differ from world to world? The former is called *constant-domain semantics* and the latter is called *variable-domain semantics*. However, given problems 1 and 2, even first-order normal modal logic is inadequate for ADT.

Problem #4: normal modal logics and relational semantics are designed for *operators* (an operator takes a sentence as input and has a sentence as output), but according to ADT, ascending truth and descending truth are *predicates* (a predicate takes a singular term as input and has a sentence as output). One major difference between operators (e.g., 'it is true that') and predicates (e.g., 'is true') is their expressive power. For example, one cannot use an operator to construct a self-referential sentence, but it is possible with a predicate; in addition, operators apply only to sentences of the same language, whereas predicates can apply to anything that can be referred to in the same language. Finally, quantification into a predicate is well-understood and uncontroversial, while quantification into an operator is contentious and complicated.

I deal with these problems in this order.

[28] See Chellas (1980), Fitting and Mendelsohn (1998), Portner (2009), and Garson (2009) for background on modal logic.

[29] Montague (1963).

[30] Montague (1963).

6.6.3 Classical modal logic and neighborhood semantics

Problem #1 and problem #2 can be remedied by using a more general semantics for modal logics—neighborhood semantics. Again, let L be a sentential language with the usual connectives and operators. Let W be a set of worlds, but let N be a function from W to the set of sets of subsets of W (N is called the *neighborhood function*); so N assigns a set of subsets of W to each world in W. Together, W and N are called a *neighborhood frame*, $\mathfrak{F} = \langle W, N\rangle$. I call any semantics based on a frame of this kind a *neighborhood semantics*. Just as in relational semantics, a valuation function, V, assigns to each sentential variable of L a truth value at each world in W. Together, $\mathfrak{F}$ and V are called a *neighborhood model*, $\mathfrak{M} = \langle\mathfrak{F}, V\rangle$ for L. Each world in W is classical in the sense that a classical scheme determines the value of truth-functionally compound sentences. Thus, we can keep all the previous clauses for defining truth at a world in a model except the (□) clause, which becomes:

$$(\Box)\quad \langle\mathfrak{M}, w\rangle \vDash \Box\phi \text{ iff } \exists X{\in}N(w) \text{ s.t. } \forall u{\in}W\ (\langle\mathfrak{M}, u\rangle \vDash \phi \leftrightarrow u{\in}X)$$

(i.e., $\Box\phi$ is true at w iff a neighborhood of w contains all the worlds at which ϕ is true). One can think of the neighborhoods assigned to a world, w, as a list of the sets of worlds that are assigned to sentences that are necessary at w. That is, if we think of the set of worlds in which a sentence ϕ is true as the proposition expressed by ϕ (symbolized as $P(\phi)$), then we can rephrase the (□) clause as:

$$(\Box)\quad \langle\mathfrak{M}, w\rangle \vDash \Box\phi \text{ iff } P(\phi){\in}N(w)$$

In neighborhood semantics, the clause for ◇ becomes:

$$(\Diamond)\quad \langle\mathfrak{M}, w\rangle \vDash \Diamond\phi \text{ iff } {\sim}(\exists X{\in}N(w) \text{ s.t. } \forall u{\in}W\ (\langle\mathfrak{M}, u\rangle \vDash {\sim}\phi \leftrightarrow u{\in}X))$$

or:

$$(\Diamond)\quad \langle\mathfrak{M}, w\rangle \vDash \Diamond\phi \text{ iff } P({\sim}\phi){\notin}N(w)$$

Validity is defined just as it was in relational semantics.

It is relatively easy to show that there are neighborhood frames on which the K axiom is invalid. For example, let $\mathfrak{M}_k$ be the neighborhood model with $W_k = \{w, x, y, z\}$, $N_k(w) = \{\{w, x\}, \{w, y, z\}\}$, $N_k(x) = \{\{x\}\}$, $N_k(y) = \{\{y\}\}$, $N_k(z) = \{\{z\}\}$, $V_k(P) = \{w, x\}$, and $V_k(Q) = \{w, y\}$. Then we have: $\langle\mathfrak{M}_k, w\rangle \vDash \Box P$, $\langle\mathfrak{M}_k, w\rangle \vDash \Box(P \rightarrow Q)$, but $\langle\mathfrak{M}_k, w\rangle \nvDash \Box Q$. So the K axiom is invalid in $\mathfrak{M}_k$. This solves problem #1. One can impose conditions on the neighborhood function to ensure that the K axiom is valid, but since we want it to be invalid, we will not consider these.

Likewise, it is relatively easy to show that there are neighborhood frames on which the Necessitation rule is invalid. For example, let $\mathfrak{M}_n$ be the neighborhood model with $W_n = \{w, x\}$, $N_n(w) = \{\{w\}\}$, $N_n(x) = \{\{x\}\}$, $V_n(P) = \{w, x\}$. Then we have: $\mathfrak{M}_n \vDash P$ but $\mathfrak{M}_n \nvDash \Box P$. So the Necessitation rule is invalid in $\mathfrak{M}_n$. This solves problem #2. One can impose conditions on the neighborhood function to ensure that the Necessitation rule is valid, but since we want it to be invalid, we will not consider these.

Even though it is not the case that the K axiom is valid in any neighborhood frame, and it is not the case that the Necessitation rule is valid in any neighborhood frame, there are axioms and rules that are valid in any neighborhood frame. Duality is an axiom that is valid on any neighborhood frame, and the following rule is valid on any neighborhood frame as well:

(E) If $\vdash \phi \leftrightarrow \psi$, then $\vdash \Box\phi \leftrightarrow \Box\psi$

Call any modal logic that includes the Duality axiom and rule E a *classical* modal logic. Notice that rule E is similar to the Necessitation rule, but it is weaker. So, the move from normal modal logics and their relational semantics to classical modal logics and their neighborhood semantics solves problem #1 and problem #2. That is, this move avoids the K axiom and the Necessitation rule, both of which would render ADT inconsistent.

6.6.4 *Yet another problem*

Although the move from normal modal logic to classical modal logic solves problem #1 and problem #2, it presents us with a new problem that is similar to problem #2:

> *Problem #5*: We want to replace our operator, $\Box$, with a predicate for descending truth, D(x). To do that, we need to move from a sentential language to a first-order language. We know that when we make the move to first-order logic and predicates, Gödel's Diagonalization Lemma guarantees that if our language can express Peano Arithmetic or its own theory of syntax (these are pretty minimal expressive constraints), then it will have a sentence d s.t. ~D(d) is provably equivalent to d. We know that $\vdash_{ADT}$ ~D(d) [assume D(d); if D(d), then d; if d, then ~D(d); so if D(d), then ~D(d); thus, ~D(d)]. We also know that $\vdash_{ADT} 0 = 0$. So we have $\vdash_{ADT}$ ~D(d) $\leftrightarrow 0 = 0$. By rule (E) we would get $\vdash_{ADT}$ D(d) $\leftrightarrow$ D('0 = 0'). We already have $\vdash_{ADT}$ D('0 = 0'); so we would have $\vdash_{ADT}$ D(d). $\bot$. Therefore, ADT cannot include rule E.[31] This argument shows that rule E is incompatible with D1 and D5; similar arguments show that rule E is also incompatible with D1 and D6, and that it is incompatible with D1 and D7. These results show that no semantics that validates rule E will work for ADT.

6.6.5 *Xeno semantics*

At this point, we have left the well-traveled paths of modal logic and are off on our own. What we need is something more general than neighborhood semantics; as far as I know, there is no such thing. So we will have to break new ground to solve problem #5.

[31] Dana Scott first noticed this problem.

In relational semantics, the extension of '$\Box$' at each world is determined by a binary accessibility relation on the set of worlds; we can think of this as a function that assigns each world a set of worlds (i.e., those accessible from it). Moreover, each sentence is assigned a proposition, which is a set of worlds (i.e., those in which it is true). In neighborhood semantics, the extension of '$\Box$' at each world is determined by a function that assigns each world a set of sets of worlds; as in relational semantics each sentence is assigned a proposition, which is a set of worlds. In the new semantics, which I call *xeno semantics*, the extension of '$\Box$' at each world is determined by both an accessibility relation *and* a neighborhood function.[32] As before, each sentence is assigned a set of worlds as its proposition. However, although the neighborhood function is unchanged, the key to xeno semantics is that the accessibility relation is relative to each type of sentence in the language. Indeed, we can think of xeno semantics as involving as many binary accessibility relations as there are syntactic types of sentences.

In *relational* semantics '$\Box\phi$' is true at a world w iff ϕ is true at all worlds accessible from w. In *neighborhood* semantics, '$\Box\phi$' is true at a world w iff the set of worlds in which ϕ is true is a neighborhood of w. In *xeno* semantics, '$\Box\phi$' is true at a world w iff the set of worlds in which ϕ is true is a neighborhood of all worlds accessible$_\phi$ from w, where 'accessible$_\phi$' is the accessibility relation assigned to ϕ's syntactic type. So one can think of xeno semantics as a blend of relational semantics and neighborhood semantics with a relativization to syntactic types. In xeno semantics, each sentence is assigned a proposition (a set of worlds) and a relation on the set of worlds. We can think of this as a sentence granting accessibility from one world to others, or we can say that the accessibility relation is relative to each sentence. Moreover, the accessibility relation alone does not determine the extension of $\Box$ at each world; rather, together the accessibility relation and the neighborhood relation determine the extension of $\Box$ *for that particular sentence* at each world. Alternatively, we can think of a proposition as a pair of a subset of W and a relation on W. But neighborhoods of a world are still just subsets of W. $\Box$'s extension at a world is then an operation on propositions, and it is determined by the whole neighborhood function, not just the neighborhoods of that world. Figure 6 illuminates the three kinds of semantics.

We need to define the syntactic type of a sentence. Let the formation rules of L be the usual ones (since it has the usual connectives and a single operator). Let any two sentences that have the same syntactic decomposition into components according to the formation rules be of the same syntactic type. So, syntactic types are equivalence classes of sentences. For example, if ϕ and ψ are distinct sentential variables then $\phi \wedge \psi \rightarrow \psi$ and $\phi \wedge \psi \rightarrow \phi$ have the same syntactic type whereas $\phi \rightarrow \psi$ differs.

Now that we have the basic idea for xeno semantics, I am going to provide a particular xeno semantics for ADT. This will be accomplished in stages. First, I provide a xeno

[32] Xeno semantics is named after our dog; thanks to Alison Duncan Kerr for the suggestion.

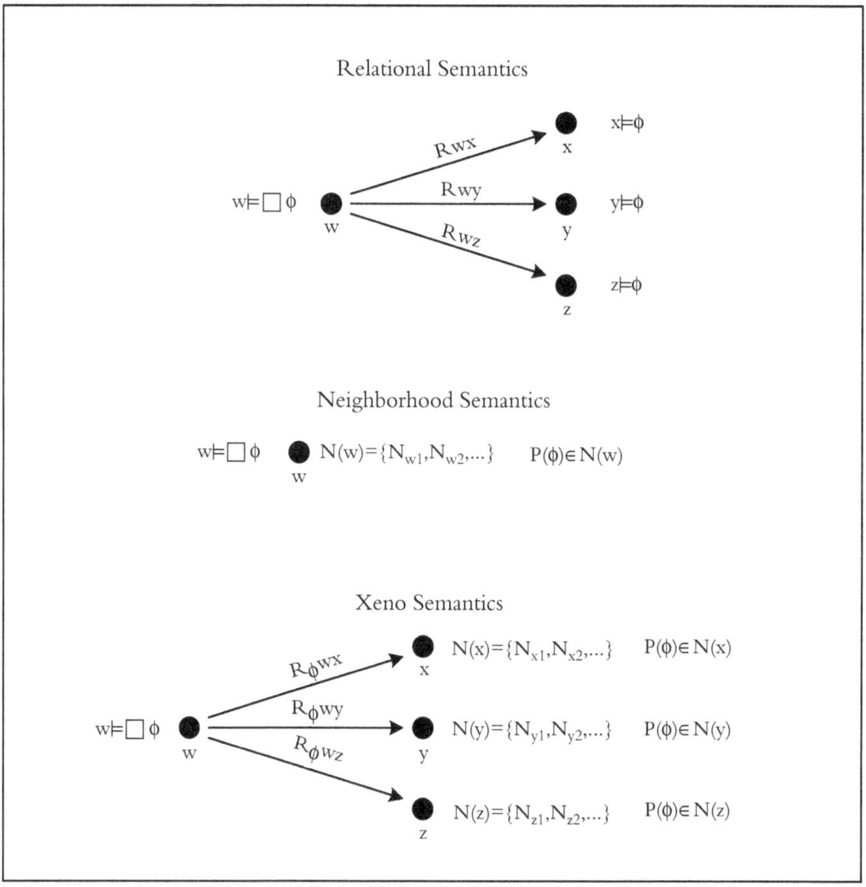

Figure 6 Three Kinds of Possible-Worlds Semantics

semantics for a classical sentential language with descending truth operator $\Box$, an ascending truth operator $\Diamond$, and a safety operator Σ; then we switch from a sentential language to a first-order language; finally, we consider a xeno semantics for a first-order language with a descending truth *predicate*, an ascending truth *predicate*, and a safety *predicate*.

Let $\mathfrak{L}$ be a sentential language with the usual connectives and three sentential operators: $\Box$, $\Diamond$, and Σ. Let L be the set of well-formed formulas of $\mathfrak{L}$. Let a *xeno frame* $\mathfrak{F}$ = <W, R, N> where W is a set of worlds, R is a denumerable set of binary relations on W, and N is a neighborhood function from W to 2^{2^W}.

Let a *xeno model* $\mathfrak{M}$ = <$\mathfrak{F}$, $\mathfrak{R}$,V> where $\mathfrak{F}$ is a xeno frame, $\mathfrak{R}$ is a function from L to R, and V is a function from the sentential variables of L to 2^W. $\mathfrak{R}$ assigns an accessibility relation to each sentence of L, and V assigns a set of worlds to each sentential variable (R_ϕ is the accessibility relation $\mathfrak{R}$ assigns to ϕ).

We can give an inductive definition of truth at a world (i.e., $<\mathfrak{M}, w> \vDash \phi$) in the following way:

(ϕ) $<\mathfrak{M}, w> \vDash \phi$ iff $w \in V(\phi)$ (for ϕ atomic)

($\sim$) $<\mathfrak{M}, w> \vDash \sim\phi$ iff it is not the case that $<\mathfrak{M}, w> \vDash \phi$

($\wedge$) $<\mathfrak{M}, w> \vDash \phi \wedge \psi$ iff $<\mathfrak{M}, w> \vDash \phi$ and $<\mathfrak{M}, w> \vDash \psi$

($\vee$) $<\mathfrak{M}, w> \vDash \phi \vee \psi$ iff $<\mathfrak{M}, w> \vDash \phi$ or $<\mathfrak{M}, w> \vDash \psi$

($\rightarrow$) $<\mathfrak{M}, w> \vDash \phi \rightarrow \psi$ iff if $<\mathfrak{M}, w> \vDash \phi$, then $<\mathfrak{M}, w> \vDash \psi$

($\leftrightarrow$) $<\mathfrak{M}, w> \vDash \phi \leftrightarrow \psi$ iff $<\mathfrak{M}, w> \vDash \phi$ iff $<\mathfrak{M}, w> \vDash \psi$

($\Box$) $<\mathfrak{M}, w> \vDash \Box\phi$ iff $\forall u \in W\ R_{\phi}wu \rightarrow \exists X \in N(u), \forall v \in W(<\mathfrak{M}, v> \vDash \phi \leftrightarrow v \in X)$

or:

($\Box$) $<\mathfrak{M}, w> \vDash \Box\phi$ iff $\forall u \in W\ R_{\phi}wu \rightarrow P(\phi) \in N(u)$

where $P(\phi)$ is the set of worlds in which ϕ is true.

We can introduce a definition for the dual operator $\Diamond$ in the following way:

($\Diamond$) $<\mathfrak{M}, w> \vDash \Diamond\phi$ iff $\sim(\forall u \in W\ R_{\sim\phi}wu \rightarrow P(\sim\phi) \in N(u))$

or:

($\Diamond$) $<\mathfrak{M}, w> \vDash \Diamond\phi$ iff $\exists u \in W\ R_{\sim\phi}wu \wedge P(\sim\phi) \notin N(u)$

It should be obvious from these definitions that $\Box$ and $\Diamond$ are dual operators in any xeno model. Finally, the clause for the safety operator Σ is:

(Σ) $<\mathfrak{M}, w> \vDash \Sigma\phi$ iff $\forall u \in W\ (R_{\phi}wu \rightarrow P(\phi) \in N(u)) \vee \exists u \in W\ (R_{\sim\phi}wu \wedge P(\sim\phi) \notin N(u))$

As I mentioned above, we eventually define Σ in terms of $\Box$ and $\Diamond$, and one advantage of working with a modal logic where duality is presupposed is that we can even define $\Box$ or $\Diamond$ in terms of the other with the help of negation.

As with all our semantics, the most important part is to define a notion of validity—in this case the obvious choice is to say that a sentence is *valid in a xeno model* iff it is true in all worlds of that model, and a sentence is *valid in a xeno frame* iff it is valid in all xeno models based on that frame. We could alter these definitions so that there is a proper subset of W on which validity is defined (the so-called "normal worlds")—we end up employing this option in the appendix.

Notice that if we stipulate that all the accessibility relations of a xeno frame are reflexive (i.e., $\forall\phi\ \forall w \in W\ R_{\phi}ww$) and co-reflexive (i.e., $\forall\phi\ \forall w \in W\ \forall u \in W\ (R_{\phi}wu \rightarrow w = u)$), then our xeno frame is equivalent to a neighborhood frame. Thus, xeno semantics is a natural generalization of neighborhood semantics. As we will see, not every xeno frame has an equivalent neighborhood frame.

For our purposes, we will need to introduce more structure on xeno frames and xeno models for them to serve as a semantics for ADT. Note first that rule E does not hold in all xeno models. For example, let S and T be logically equivalent sentences of $\mathfrak{L}$ with distinct syntactic types, and let $\mathfrak{M}$ be the following xeno model:

$W = \{a, b\}$

$N(a) = \{\{a, b\}\}$

$N(b) = \{\{b\}\}$

$R_S = \{\langle a, a\rangle, \langle b, b\rangle\}$

$R_T = \{\langle a, a\rangle, \langle b, b\rangle, \langle a, b\rangle\}$

$P(S) = \{a, b\}$

$P(T) = \{a, b\}$

It is obvious that $\forall w{\in}W\ \langle\mathfrak{M}, w\rangle \vDash S$ iff $\langle\mathfrak{M}, w\rangle \vDash T$. Thus, $S \leftrightarrow T$ is valid in $\mathfrak{M}$. Furthermore, $\forall u\ R_S au \rightarrow P(S){\in}N(u)$. Thus, $\langle\mathfrak{M}, a\rangle \vDash \Box S$. However, $\exists u\ R_T au \wedge P(s){\notin}N(u)$. Thus, $\langle\mathfrak{M}, a\rangle \vDash {\sim}\Box T$. Therefore, we have an easy violation of rule E. We have to be sure that the additional conditions we impose on our xeno frames and models preserve this feature.

Call a sentential xeno frame *acceptable* iff it has the following features:

(i) $\forall w{\in}W\ N(w){\neq}\varnothing$

(ii) $\forall w{\in}W\ \forall X{\in}N(w)\ X{\neq}\varnothing$

(iii) $\forall w{\in}W\ \forall X{\in}N(w)\ w{\in}X$

(iv) $\forall\phi{\in}L\ \forall w{\in}W\ R_\phi ww$ (i.e., R_ϕ is reflexive)

(v) if ϕ and ψ have the same syntactic type then $R_\phi = R_\psi$

Acceptable xeno frames have some nice features from our perspective. For example we can show that $\Box\phi \rightarrow \phi$ is valid on any xeno model based on an acceptable xeno frame. Assume that $\mathfrak{M}$ is such a model. Assume $\langle\mathfrak{M}, w\rangle \vDash \Box\phi$. Thus, $\forall u{\in}W\ R_\phi wu \rightarrow P(\phi){\in}N(u)$. By condition (iv) $R_\phi ww$; hence $P(\phi){\in}N(w)$. By condition (iii) $\forall X{\in}N(w)\ w{\in}X$; hence, $w{\in}P(\phi)$. Therefore, $\langle\mathfrak{M}, w\rangle \vDash \phi$.

Another nice feature is that $\Box{\sim}\phi \rightarrow {\sim}\Box\phi$ is valid on any xeno model based on an acceptable xeno frame. Assume $\langle\mathfrak{M}, w\rangle \vDash \Box{\sim}\phi$. Thus, $\forall u{\in}W\ R_\phi wu \rightarrow P({\sim}\phi){\in}N(u)$. By condition (iv), $R_\phi ww$; hence $P({\sim}\phi){\in}N(w)$. By condition (iii), $\forall X{\in}N(w)\ w{\in}X$; hence, $w{\in}P({\sim}\phi)$. Therefore, $\langle\mathfrak{M}, w\rangle \vDash {\sim}\phi$. Since all worlds are classical, it follows that $w{\notin}P(\phi)$. By condition (iv), $P(\phi){\notin}N(w)$, and by condition (iii), ${\sim}(\forall u{\in}W\ R_\phi wu \rightarrow P(\phi){\in}N(u))$. Therefore, $\langle\mathfrak{M}, w\rangle \vDash {\sim}\Box\phi$. Notice that these two principles are the operator equivalents of D1 and D2 in ADT.

Acceptable xeno frames cannot do all the work, however. We need to introduce the notion of an acceptable xeno model, but that job is made significantly more complex by the apparatus of quantifiers, individual constants, and predicates. So, let us first see how xeno semantics works for first-order languages.

6.6.6 *First-order modal logic*

So far I have addressed only problem #1 and problem #2. We saw that they are solved by moving from normal modal logic and relational semantics to classical modal logic and neighborhood semantics. However, that move brought problem #5. I have solved problem #5 by moving from classical modal logic and neighborhood semantics to xeno semantics (the kind of modal logic validated by bare xeno semantics does not have a name—we could use 'traditional modal logic' for it). That leaves us with problem #3 (how to deal with first-order languages) and problem #4 (how to use possible worlds semantics for predicates, rather than for operators) to solve still. I deal with problem #3 in this subsection and problem #4 in the next.

The next step is to define a xeno semantics for a first-order language, which will involve the whole quantifier apparatus. Luckily, the move to first-order modal logic is largely independent of the issues that forced the move to xeno semantics. It involves a change in the language, the theory, and the semantics.

Let $\mathfrak{L}$ be a first-order classical language with two modal operators, $\Box$ and $\Diamond$. $\mathfrak{L}$ has a countable set of individual variables, a countable set of n-place predicate symbols, two quantifiers, and the usual logical operators. Let L be the set of well-formed formulas of $\mathfrak{L}$.

As for the theory, let $\phi[y/x]$ denote a sentence just like ϕ except that free variable x is replaced with free variable y at all and only its free occurrences, without y thereby becoming bound at any of those occurrences. Add the following axiom and rule to the theory:

(Inst) $\forall x\phi(x) \rightarrow \phi[y/x]$

(Gen) if $\phi \rightarrow \psi$ is a theorem, then $\phi \rightarrow \forall x\psi$ is a theorem, where x is not free in ϕ

The theory that results deals with quantifiers in the usual way.[33]

The additions to the semantics require a decision about how to treat the domain—I select a constant-domain framework where each world has the same domain (variable domain frameworks are more complex and the additional complexity does not add anything). Add to the xeno frame, $\mathfrak{D}$, a non-empty set, called the *domain*; so a *constant-domain xeno frame* is $\mathfrak{F} = \langle W, N, R, \mathfrak{D}\rangle$. Instead of a valuation function, V, constant-domain xeno models will have an interpretation function, I, such that for each n-ary predicate symbol F, we have $I(F, w) \subseteq \mathfrak{D}^n$; so a *constant-domain xeno model* is $\mathfrak{M} = \langle \mathfrak{F}, \mathfrak{R}, I\rangle$. Let a *substitution* be a function from the set of individual variables to the domain. A substitution ν' is said to be an *x-variant* of ν if $\nu(y) = \nu'(y)$ for all variables y except possibly x; this will be denoted by $\nu \approx_x \nu'$. Truth in a model is defined at a world relative to a substitution.

Let $\mathfrak{M} = \langle W, N, R, \mathfrak{D}, \mathfrak{R}, I\rangle$ be any constant-domain xeno model and ν any substitution:

[33] The first-order classical modal logic and neighborhood semantics presented here is adopted from Arló Costa and Pacuit (2006).

(F) $<\mathfrak{M}, w> \models_{\nu} F(a_1,\ldots,a_n)$ (where a_i is either an individual constant or an individual variable) iff $<f(a_1),\ldots, f(a_n)>\in I(F, w)$, where if a_i is a variable x_i, then $f(a_i) = \nu(x_i)$, and if a_i is an individual constant c_i, then $f(a_i) = I(c_i)$ (for each n-place predicate F)

(~) $<\mathfrak{M}, w> \models_{\nu} {\sim}\phi$ iff it is not the case that $<\mathfrak{M}, w> \models_{\nu} \phi$

(∧) $<\mathfrak{M}, w> \models_{\nu} \phi\wedge\psi$ iff $<\mathfrak{M}, w> \models_{\nu} \phi$ and $<\mathfrak{M}, w> \models_{\nu} \psi$

(∨) $<\mathfrak{M}, w> \models_{\nu} \phi\vee\psi$ iff $<\mathfrak{M}, w> \models_{\nu} \phi$ or $<\mathfrak{M}, w> \models_{\nu} \psi$

(→) $<\mathfrak{M}, w> \models_{\nu} \phi\rightarrow\psi$ iff if $<\mathfrak{M}, w> \models_{\nu} \phi$, then $<\mathfrak{M}, w> \models_{\nu} \psi$

(↔) $<\mathfrak{M}, w> \models_{\nu} \phi\leftrightarrow\psi$ iff $<\mathfrak{M}, w> \models_{\nu} \phi$ iff $<\mathfrak{M}, w> \models_{\nu} \psi$

(∀) $<\mathfrak{M}, w> \models_{\nu} \forall x\phi(x)$ iff for each x-variant ν' $<\mathfrak{M}, w> \models_{\nu'} \phi(x)$

(∃) $<\mathfrak{M}, w> \models_{\nu} \exists x\phi(x)$ iff there is an x-variant ν' s.t. $<\mathfrak{M}, w> \models_{\nu'} \phi(x)$

The clause for sentences of the form $\Box\phi$ or $\Diamond\phi$ are:

(□) $<\mathfrak{M}, w> \models \Box\phi$ iff $\forall u\in W\ R_{\phi}wu \rightarrow \exists X\in N(u), \forall v\in W(<\mathfrak{M}, v> \models \phi \leftrightarrow v\in X)$

(◇) $<\mathfrak{M}, w> \models \Diamond\phi$ iff $\exists u\in W\ R_{\sim\phi}wu \wedge P({\sim}\phi)\notin N(u)$

Notice that the clauses for the truth functions and the modal operators do not change except that they are relativized to substitutions. In this example, we do not have individual constants, but they are easy to add once we understand how quantifiers work. This solves problem #3.

6.6.7 Revision sequences and modal logic

To summarize the discussion so far: we have seen how first-order classical modal logic with neighborhood semantics allows us to solve some of the problems we encountered with normal modal logics and relational semantics. However, classical modal logics (i.e., those for which one can give a neighborhood semantics) face a problem, which is that logically equivalent sentences have the same modal status. No logic with this feature can work for ADT since we want all instances of $D(\langle\phi\rangle) \rightarrow \phi$ to be descending true, and we want δ (i.e., the sentence such that $\delta \leftrightarrow {\sim}D(\langle\delta\rangle)$ is a theorem of syntax or arithmetic) to be not descending true. I have presented a new kind of semantics—xeno semantics—and I have shown how to do xeno semantics for sentential languages and first-order languages with modal operators. Moreover, I have presented some of the formulas that are valid in all acceptable xeno frames.

However, the biggest problem with this entire project, problem #4, has yet to be addressed. Problem #4 is that in all the modal logics considered so far, '□', '◇', and 'Σ' are operators. The fact that they are operators allows us to give an inductive (recursive) definition of truth at a world in a model (i.e., $<\mathfrak{M}, w> \models \phi$) based on the complexity of a formula (since $\Box\phi$, $\Diamond\phi$, and $\Sigma\phi$ are more complex formulas than ϕ). However, in ADT, the items to be explained are not operators, but predicates. We could try to use the xeno semantics for first-order non-classical modal logic as a semantics for ADT (altering the clauses (□), (◇), and (Σ) appropriately), so that '□' is a descending truth predicate (i.e., 'D(x)'), '◇' is an ascending truth predicate (i.e., 'A(x)'), and 'Σ' is a safety predicate (i.e., 'S(x)'). However, we can no longer define truth at a world in a model in the standard way (since D(⟨φ⟩), A(⟨φ⟩), and S(⟨φ⟩) are atomic). Thus, this strategy does not arrive at a semantics at all, much less a semantics for ADT.

Some work has been done on using modal logic for predicates instead of operators, and one way to do it involves revision sequences. Revision sequences were originally designed to handle circular definitions, in which the definiens occurs as part of the *definiendum*. They can be adapted to modal logics for predicates by thinking of the definition of truth at a world in a model as a circular definition by virtue of the modal clauses. For example, 'D(⟨φ⟩)' can occur in the definiens for $<\mathfrak{M}, w> \models_{\sigma} D(\langle\phi\rangle)$, which makes the overall definition circular. We can then use a revision sequence to arrive at particular frames and models.[34]

A revision sequence begins with a particular interpretation of the circularly defined term in question, and then one generates a sequence of interpretations through a revision rule, which is based on the circularly defined term. In our case, we start with a first-order language that contains a predicate D(x), which will serve as our descending truth predicate (we worry just about D(x) first, and then see if we can define A(x) and S(x) in terms of it). The revision sequence begins with a model of the language that is similar to the first-order xeno models discussed above, except this model will not satisfy the (D) clause. Instead, we use the (D) clause to generate a new model of the language, but it will not satisfy the (D) clause either; by repeating this process over and over, we generate a sequence of models of the language. The goal is to reach a fixed point—i.e., a point in the sequence where it stops changing. If we can reach such a point, we would then have a legitimate definition of truth at a world in a xeno model for our descending truth *predicate*—a model of the language that satisfies the (D) clause. A construction of this type solves problem #4 (providing a possible-worlds semantics for a descending truth *predicate* instead of for an *operator*).

Note that Gupta and Belnap use revision sequences to formulate a revision theory of truth, but that is not a project I endorse. Instead, I use revision sequences to define truth in a xeno model. Xeno models serve as the semantics for the theory of ascending and descending truth, which I present as replacements for our concept of truth.

One might wonder about the intuitive significance of xeno semantics. How should we interpret the accessibility relations and the neighborhood function? I take no stand on this issue in this work. With respect to this project, they should be thought of as technical devices that allow us to prove things about ADT.

[34] Stewart Shapiro suggested this strategy to me; see Gupta and Belnap (1993) and Halbach, Leitgeb, and Welch (2003) who use revision sequences to give possible-worlds semantics for predicates.

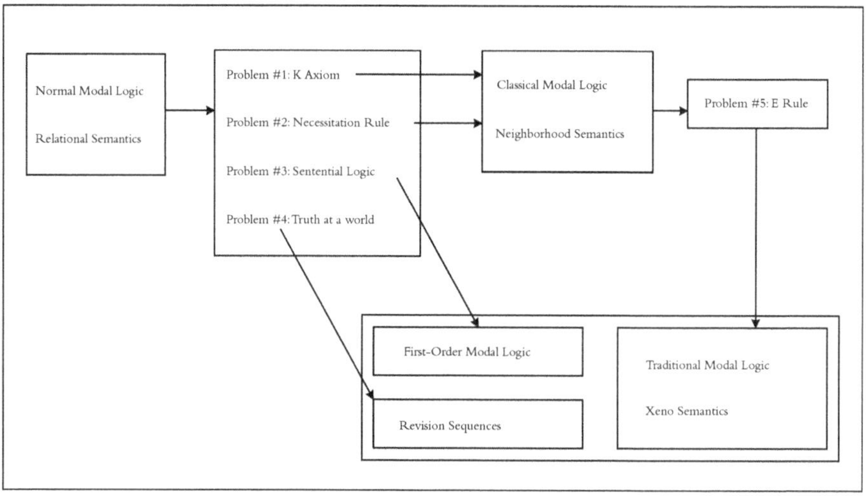

Figure 7 Problems and Solutions for Semantics for ADT

6.6.8 *Summary of problems and solutions*

Figure 7 contains a diagram depicting our starting point, normal modal logic and relational semantics, the problems it faces, and the solutions to these problems. Notice that three elements of the overall package (at the bottom) are relatively independent of one another.

All that is left to do is show that one can define truth-in-a-model for xeno semantics by proving that a revision sequence of Xeno models eventually reaches a fixed point. I present this proof in an appendix.

6.7 Features of ADT

Now that we have a rudimentary theory of ascending truth and descending truth and a semantics for it, let us explore some of its features. Remember, I do not claim that ADT is *the* theory of ascending and descending truth—it is *rudimentary* in the sense that it is a subtheory of any adequate theory of ascending and descending truth, but there is no reason to think that it contains all the important principles for ascending and descending truth. Indeed, I have given no reason to think that ADT captures all the interesting truths validated by acceptable xeno models; the theorem in the appendix is effectively a soundness proof, but I have not given a completeness proof (in fact, I think ADT is probably incomplete with respect to the class of acceptable xeno models).

6.7.1 *Interpreting ADT*

The guiding principle for interpreting ADT is that ascending truth and descending truth should be as close as possible to one another (each one thereby approximating the inconsistent concept of truth). Since the ascending truth values and descending truth values of sentences are different only for unsafe sentences, we can think of the guiding principle as saying that we should strive to minimize the set of unsafe sentences when interpreting ADT.

It is compatible with ADT that for a classical first-order language that contains no semantic vocabulary, ascending truth and descending truth coincide on all of its sentences. That is, none of its sentences are unsafe. That result holds regardless of what kinds of empirical claims or mathematical claims can be expressed in the language. So, in empirical or mathematical discourse, one can reason using either ascending truth or descending truth as if it were a truth predicate. If we add some way for the language to refer to its own sentences and add an ascending truth predicate, a descending truth predicate, and a safety predicate, then the language will contain some unsafe sentences. However, every sentence that is grounded (in something like Kripke's sense)[35] is safe. That is, ascending truth attributions and descending truth attributions that eventually ground out in sentences of the original language are safe. In addition, many ungrounded sentences, like 'every sentence is either ascending true or not ascending true' and 'no sentence is both descending true and not descending true' are safe.[36] In short, only sentences that contain 'ascending true', 'descending true', or 'safe' might turn out to be unsafe and, even among those, only sentences that would be paradoxical if 'true' were substituted in for these terms might be unsafe.

These results add quite a bit to the understanding of ascending truth and descending truth that one acquires by simply perusing the axioms in ADT. For example, if p and q are grounded, then every principle on the above list of aletheic principles is valid when either 'A' or 'D' is uniformly substituted for 'T'. Moreover, if p and q are grounded then they have the same ascending and descending truth values.

6.7.2 Principles of ascending and descending truth

So, which principles do ascending truth and descending truth obey? To begin with, ascending truth and descending truth are just normal predicates; ADT is fully compatible with classical logic, so reasoning with them does not require one to give up any of the intuitive canons of reasoning. Since they are compatible with classical logic, they are compatible with any of the weakenings of classical logic, including intuitionistic logic, relevance logic, free logic, paracomplete logic, and paraconsistent logic.[37]

[35] See Kripke (1975). I am using 'grounded' in the sense of *its ascending truth value and descending truth value are completely determined by the ascending truth values and descending truth values of sentences that have no occurrences of 'ascending true' or 'descending true'*.

[36] This is not a trivial result; see the appendix to this chapter.

[37] However, there are elements of classicality built in to ADT. If one wanted a version of ADT that does not collapse, say intuitionistic logic into classical logic, then one would need different axioms; Neil Tennant has done some work on this in Tennant (MS3).

Another point bears repeating—ascending truth and descending truth predicates are not context-dependent, or ambiguous, or vague, or typed in any way. There is nothing remarkable about them as predicates. Moreover, they are fully compatible with theories of syntax—there is no reason to think that languages that can refer to and quantify over their own terms and sentences would have any problem with ascending and descending truth. Indeed, these notions were developed with this point specifically in mind.

As for the particular principles they obey, aside from the axioms of ADT, there are other important principles for ascending and descending truth. Indeed, it would be nice to get analogs of each principle in the list of aletheic principles above—each one is a principle of either ascending truth or descending truth or both. However, that is not what we find. Instead, we do find that some of these principles hold for either ascending truth or of descending truth (or both) but, for some of them that have multiple occurrences of the truth predicate, the theorem of ADT involves both ascending truth and descending truth. For example, two of the aletheic principles are single-premise closure and single-premise tracking:

(SPC) $(\phi \rightarrow \psi) \rightarrow (T(\langle\phi\rangle) \rightarrow T(\langle\psi\rangle))$

(SPT) $(T(\langle\phi\rangle) \rightarrow T(\langle\psi\rangle)) \rightarrow (\phi \rightarrow \psi)$

If we substitute an ascending truth predicate for the truth predicate throughout, then we can find easy counterexamples to each of the principles that results; the same goes for descending truth. However, if we use both ascending truth and descending truth, then we can get analogs:

$(\phi \rightarrow \psi) \rightarrow (D(\langle\phi\rangle) \rightarrow A(\langle\psi\rangle))$

$(A(\langle\phi\rangle) \rightarrow D(\langle\psi\rangle)) \rightarrow (\phi \rightarrow \psi)$

These relate ascending truth and descending truth to the conditional in an interesting way. The upshot is that expanding our conceptual scheme with two concepts allows us an unexpected freedom in trying to accommodate the principles previously accepted for the inconsistent concept in question. We need not assign each principle to one or the other replacement concept; some principles might be *hybrid* in the sense just described. With this idea on board, we can formulate a condition of adequacy for a theory of replacements for truth: every aletheic principle should be either a principle of one of the replacement concepts or it should be hybrid. That way, every aletheic principle gets represented in the theory of the replacements. Other hybrid principles include:

$D(\langle\phi\rangle) \wedge D(\langle\psi\rangle) \rightarrow A(\langle\phi\wedge\psi\rangle)$—a hybrid version of (∧-Imb)

$D(\langle\phi\vee\psi\rangle) \rightarrow A(\langle\phi\rangle) \vee A(\langle\psi\rangle)$—a hybrid version of (∨-Exc)[38]

[38] It might be instructive to survey all the aletheic principles above, but space considerations prevent it.

Quantifiers deserve some mention. I have not gone to the trouble in this elementary exposition, but I am confident that quantifier principles could be added to ADT. In particular:

$$D(\langle(\forall x)\phi(x)\rangle) \rightarrow (\forall x)D(\langle\phi(x)\rangle)$$
$$(\forall x)A(\langle\phi(x)\rangle) \rightarrow A(\langle(\forall x)\phi(x)\rangle)$$

The first says that if a universal generalization is descending true, then every instance is descending true. The second says that if every instance of a generalization is ascending true, then that generalization is ascending true. In order to add these to ADT, one would have to alter the definition of an acceptable xeno model in the proof in the appendix.

Another matter is that ADT might seem too weak since it is hard to know how to think about ascending and descending truth values for empirical sentences (e.g., one might wonder how descending truth differs from mathematical provability).[39] However, once one takes into consideration the comments about ascending and descending truth being equivalent for empirical sentences, this worry should disappear. That is, one condition for the replacements is that empirical sentences (i.e., those without occurrences of semantic expressions like 'true', 'refers', 'ascending true', 'descending true', etc.) are all safe. That is, they are either descending true or not ascending true. Ascending truth and descending truth differ only on the unsafe sentences, all of which involve semantic notions in some way. Although this condition is not built into ADT, it is a crucial element of how ADT is applied to languages.

6.7.3 Non-principles

There are also many notable principles one might expect to find among the theorems of ADT that are absent. For example, the following are *not* principles of ascending and descending truth:

(i) p is descending true → 'p is descending true' is descending true
(ii) 'p is ascending true' is ascending true' → p is ascending true
(iii) if p is a theorem of ADT, then p is descending true
(iv) if p is ascending true, then p is a theorem of ADT

Probably the most surprising is that neither ascending truth nor descending truth is preserved under logical deduction. That is, one can have a valid argument with all ascending true premises but a conclusion that is not ascending true; the same goes for descending truth. How disturbing is this result? Not very. Recall that no logical approach (other than substructural) to the aletheic paradoxes is consistent with the claim that valid arguments necessarily preserve truth. Thus, as part of an approach to the aletheic paradoxes, one that advocates replacing truth with ascending and descending truth is no worse off than the others. One big issue is how to explain validity; I say a bit about this below. Moreover, it is not the case that valid arguments might lead one seriously astray.

[39] Thanks to Hannes Leitgeb and Neil Tennant for pushing this worry.

At worst, if the premises of a valid argument are descending true, then its conclusion might not be descending true, but it will be ascending true.[40] This kind of thing will only come up in cases of unsafe sentences.

A consequence is that although all the *axioms* of ADT are descending true (by virtue of axiom schema D7), it is not the case that all *theorems* of ADT are descending true. In fact, it is easy to find theorems that are not descending true—I present some of these in the next subsection.

Another, more far-reaching consequence is that logically interdeducible sentences might have different descending truth values or different ascending truth values. This feature can be counterintuitive to those with experience thinking about logical systems because most of us are used to equivalence classes respecting truth values but, with ADT, they do not. This is an essential feature of ADT due to the choice made back in section 6.2 for dealing with Montague's theorem. One can see the connection between the problem associated with rule E (described in the previous section) and this consequence. Recall that my diagnosis of why revenge paradoxes occur is that some instances of (T-Out) are equivalent to liar sentences. If logically interdeducible sentences have the same descending truth value, then there is no way for all instances of (T-Out) to be descending true while all ascending liars and descending liars are not descending true. This is a fundamental point that any approach to the aletheic paradoxes must grapple with.

Finally, ascending truth and descending truth iterate non-trivially. That is, one cannot infer that 'p is descending true' is descending true from the claim that p is descending true. ''p is descending true' is descending true' is stronger than 'p is descending true'. Likewise, ''p is ascending true' is ascending true' is weaker than 'p is ascending true'. I am not sure whether this is an essential feature of any theory that extends ADT.

6.7.4 The aletheic paradoxes

Now that the technical details are out of the way, we can worry about just how ascending truth and descending truth avoid the aletheic paradoxes. Recall that the theory of *truth* is presented in Chapter 9—here we only deal with *ascending truth* and *descending truth*. Since liar sentences, Curry sentences, and Yablo sentences all contain truth predicates or falsity predicates, a discussion of them is reserved for later. Here I want to consider sentences like these that contain 'ascending true' or 'descending true'. Consider the following sentences that are the analogs of liar sentences:

(d) (d) is not descending true.
(a) (a) is not ascending true.

I refer to these as the *descending liar* and the *ascending liar*. It is easy to show that (d) and (a) are both unsafe—i.e., they are ascending true and not descending true. The standard

[40] Note that we cannot derive this result *in ADT* because of Gödel's Second Incompleteness Theorem.

Table 2 Ascending and Descending Liars

Descending liar	Ascending liar
Assume (d) is descending true	Assume (a) is ascending true
'(d) is not descending true' is descending true.	'(a) is not ascending true' is ascending true.
(d) is not descending true.	*(a) is not ascending true.*
Assume (d) is not descending true.	Assume (a) is not ascending true.
'(d) is not descending true' is descending true.	'(a) is not ascending true' is ascending true.
(d) is descending true.	(a) is ascending true.

argument in the liar reasoning uses both (T-In) and (T-Out). However since neither ascending truth nor descending truth obey both these rules, the standard argument is invalid. See Table 2.

The steps leading to the italicized sentences are invalid. In the argument on the left, the inference is from '(d) is not descending true' to ' '(d) is not descending true' is descending true', which is an instance of 'if ϕ then $D(\langle\phi\rangle)$'; this inference rule is not valid in general for descending truth. In the argument on the right, the inference is from ' '(a) is not ascending true' is ascending true' to '(a) is not ascending true', which is an instance of 'if $A(\langle\phi\rangle)$ then ϕ'; this inference rule is not valid in general for ascending truth. So neither of these sentences poses a problem for ADT. Moreover, ADT implies that they are unsafe; i.e., they are ascending true and not descending true.

Since Curry paradoxes and Yablo paradoxes follow the same pattern—they depend on applications of both (T-In) and (T-Out)—the results will be the same there. Those sentences are unsafe, and those arguments do not pose a problem for ADT. The question of how ADT fares against revenge paradoxes is dealt with in section 6.7.7.

6.7.5 The expressive role

In Chapter 3, I presented truth's expressive role, which consists in its being a device of endorsement and a device of rejection. How well do ascending truth and descending truth perform these jobs? Let us consider devices of endorsement first. We know that p follows from 'p is descending true', so descending truth functions as a device of endorsement. If a person asserts 'the Flanders hypothesis is descending true', then she has thereby endorsed the Flanders hypothesis. On the other hand, ⌜~p⌝ does not necessarily follow from 'p is not descending true'; thus, if one asserts 'the Flanders hypothesis is not descending true', one need not thereby have endorsed the negation of the Flanders hypothesis. For rejections, one would want to use ascending truth; if one asserts 'the Flanders hypothesis is not ascending true' then one has committed oneself to the negation of the Flanders hypothesis. Thus, descending truth serves as a device of endorsement, and ascending truth serves as a device of rejection.

It is essential to remember that, on the proposal defended here, it is legitimate to continue using 'true' for most purposes. Only where the difference between ascending truth and descending truth is not negligible does one need to use 'descending true' or 'ascending true' instead of 'true'.

6.7.6 Contingent unsafety

The contingent paradoxes are also an important issue for ascending and descending truth because using the examples of contingent paradoxes we can construct contingently unsafe sentences. Of course, these sentences are not paradoxical since one cannot prove contradictory claims about them, but they bring out an important lesson—whether a sentence is unsafe can depend on seemingly unrelated contingent facts. For example:

(2) Every sentence of section 6.7.6 of *Replacing Truth* that begins with an 'E' is not descending true.

(2) is the only sentence of this section that begins with an 'E', so it says of itself that it is not descending true. We can prove that it is unsafe (using this fact about its location as an assumption). However if it had occurred in some other section of the book, then it would have been descending true instead of unsafe.

6.7.7 Revenge

How can I be sure that the approach I offer does not fall prey to revenge paradoxes? We know that ADT, the rudimentary theory of ascending and descending truth, is consistent if set theory (ZFC) is consistent. Moreover, ADT implies that its axioms are descending true (and ascending true). In addition, ADT requires no limitation on self-reference. Finally, ADT is compatible with classical logic, so there is no worry about purchasing the consistency at the expense of expressive limitations on the language. It is easy to have a language that: (i) obeys classical logic, (ii) contains its own semantic predicates, and (iii) expresses the theory of these semantic predicates. The language can even have a general truth predicate, as well as the theory of that truth predicate (so long as one treats the truth predicate as assessment-sensitive in the way described in Chapter 9). Moreover, the language can have any expressive resources one wants.[41] No other approach to the liar paradox has this package of benefits. If there is anything like a revenge paradox, it would most likely come in the form of some inadequacy of ascending truth and descending truth to do the work required of truth by some other philosophical theory that relies on truth.

To see how ADT avoids revenge, consider traditionally problematic revenge constructions like:

(3) (3) is either not descending true or unsafe.

(4) (4) is either not ascending true or unsafe.

The following arguments would be used to get a revenge paradox.

Assume (3) is descending true.

'(3) is either not descending true or unsafe' is descending true.

(3) is either not descending true or unsafe.

[41] If they express consistent concepts, then they are fine. If the do not, then they can still be in the language as long as they are treated in accordance with the theory in Ch. 9.

Assume (3) is either not descending true or unsafe.

'(3) is either not descending true or unsafe' is descending true.
(3) is descending true.

Assume (4) is ascending true.

'(4) is either not ascending true or unsafe' is ascending true.
(4) is either not ascending true or unsafe.

Assume (4) is either not ascending true or unsafe.

'(4) is either not ascending true or unsafe' is ascending true.
(4) is ascending true.

Just as in the cases above with (a) and (d), the arguments break down (at the italicized steps) when one tries to use a (T-In) rule with descending truth or a (T-Out) rule with ascending truth. The argument for ascending and descending liars and the argument of the revenge paradoxes break down at exactly the same point. So (3) and (4) are both unsafe. One might worry that this is a problem given what (3) and (4) say of themselves. Since ADT implies that (3) is unsafe we can conclude that (3) is ascending true, but we cannot conclude that (3) is descending true. Likewise, ADT implies that (4) is unsafe; so we can conclude that (4) is ascending true, but not that it is descending true. Neither of these results poses any problem.

Instead, one might try a different tack based on the observation that some unsafe sentences are derivable from ADT, like the descending liar, and some are not, like the ascending liar. Let U^+ (i.e., the *positive unsafe sentences*) be the class of unsafe sentences derivable from ADT and U^- (i.e., the *negative unsafe sentences*) be the class of unsafe sentences not derivable from ADT. Now consider:

(5) (5) is not descending true and (5) is not U^+.

One might think that the conjunction of descending truth and positive unsafety would act enough like truth to generate a revenge paradox. It is easy to show that (5) is unsafe. Assume (for *reductio*) it is descending true. Then '(5) is not descending true and (5) is not U^+' is descending true, which entails that (5) is not descending true and (5) is not U^+. It follows that (5) is not descending true. Thus, by *reductio*, (5) is not descending true. Assume (for *reductio*) that (5) is not ascending true. Then '(5) is not descending true and (5) is not U^+' is not ascending true, which entails the negation of (5)—i.e., (5) is descending true or (5) is U^+. Of course, if (5) is descending true or U^+, then it is ascending true. Thus, by *reductio*, (5) is ascending true. So, we have shown that (5) is unsafe. Assume for *reductio* that (5) is U^+, which means that it is an unsafe theorem of ADT. Since we can take any axiom of ADT as an assumption, and (5) follows from some set of axioms of ADT, we can conclude that (5) is not descending true and (5) is not U^+. It follows that (5) is not U^+. Thus, by *reductio*, (5) is not U^+. Therefore, we have shown that (5) is U^-. It is unsafe and it is not derivable from ADT. I leave it to the reader to try deriving something untoward from the assumption that (5) is U^-. In conclusion, (5) does not generate a revenge paradox.

I encourage the reader to play around with other examples if these are not enough to give an intuitive understanding of how ADT avoids revenge. Of course, the relative consistency proof in the appendix should convince one that there are no revenge paradoxes, but this kind of technical assurance is no substitute for an intuitive grasp of how the theory works.

It might seem that ADT faces a self-refutation revenge paradox. After all, ADT implies that some of its own theorems are not descending true. For example '(d) is not descending true' is a theorem of ADT and ADT implies that (d) is not descending true. So ADT implies that some of its theorems are unsafe.

It is correct that ADT implies that some of its own theorems are not descending true (they are, of course, ascending true), but there are two points to be made here. First, if one has only one aletheic status to work with—e.g., truth—and one's theory entails that some of its theorems do not have this status, then that is a problem. However, if one has two aletheic statuses to work with, like ascending truth and descending truth, then we can formulate a criterion of adequacy for good (i.e., trustworthy) arguments that the theory, ADT, respects: namely a valid argument will never take one from descending truths to something not ascending true. It might take you from something descending true to something unsafe, or from something unsafe to something not ascending true. For example, the descending liar is provable in ADT, the axioms of ADT are descending true, but the descending liar is unsafe. Also, the ascending liar and its negation are unsafe, but their conjunction is a contradiction and so is not ascending true. Anyone who thinks that the new aletheic statuses are not preserved by valid arguments (which is a consequence of Field's argument described in section 6.2) will be forced to distinguish between theorems of the theory that have top status, those that have middle status(es), and those that have bottom status. If valid arguments never take one from top to bottom, then the obvious condition on an acceptable theory is that all its axioms have top status. We know already that not all its *theorems* will have top status. So the best we can hope for is top-status axioms and no bottom-status theorems. That is exactly the case with ADT: all the axioms of the theory are descending true, all the theorems of ADT are ascending true, and, moreover, once one has a proper understanding of assertibility with respect to ascending and descending truth (outlined in Chapter 8), one sees that they are all assertible as well.

Appendix: A fixed-point theorem

Here we construct a revision sequence of xeno models and prove that it reaches a fixed point. Actually, our construction will be a bit more complicated—we first construct one revision sequence, Ω_0, of *neighborhood* models; we can think of this as our characterization sequence. It does not reach a fixed point, but it does classify our sentences in an illuminating way. We then use the results of this characterization sequence to construct the initial *xeno* model for a second revision sequence, Ω_1. The second revision sequence will eventually reach a fixed point. So we use a sequence of neighborhood models to construct a sequence of xeno models, and we prove that the sequence of xeno models reaches a fixed point. The fixed point for the sequence of xeno models will be a xeno model and it is our intended model for ADT.[42]

6.A.1 The characterization sequence Ω_0

Let $\mathfrak{L}^-$ be a first-order language with the usual connectives, quantifiers, individual constants, individual variables, and n-place predicates. We want $\mathfrak{L}^-$ to have the resources to express its own syntax. The usual way of ensuring this is to stipulate that PA (Peano Arithmetic) is expressible in $\mathfrak{L}^-$; however, there are some complications with this method that we explore below. We stipulate that PA is expressible in $\mathfrak{L}^-$, but we also make sure that it can directly refer to its own closed formulas by including them in the domain of any model for it. Let $\mathfrak{L}$ be the result of adding the predicate D(x) to $\mathfrak{L}^-$. Let $\mathfrak{L}^-$ be the set of well-formed formulas of $\mathfrak{L}^-$ and let L be the set of well-formed formulas of $\mathfrak{L}$.

We consider a neighborhood frame $\mathfrak{F} = <W, N, \mathfrak{D}>$, where W is a set of worlds, N is a neighborhood function from W to 2^{2^W}, and $\mathfrak{D}$ is the domain—a non-empty set. Let $\mathfrak{F}$ be a *suitable frame* iff:

(i) every neighborhood of every world in W is non-empty
(ii) every world in W has a neighborhood.

We consider a neighborhood model $\mathfrak{M} = <\mathfrak{F}, I>$, where $\mathfrak{F}$ is a suitable neighborhood frame, and I is an interpretation function.

Let $\mathfrak{M}_0 = <w_0, N_0, \mathfrak{D}_0, I_0>$ be a neighborhood model based on a suitable frame, where:

(i) $N \subset \mathfrak{D}_0$ (i.e., the domain contains the natural numbers)
(ii) $L \subset \mathfrak{D}_0$ (i.e., the domain contains the sentences of L)

[42] I am unaware of anything like this construction in the literature. However, it is based on the work of Gupta and Belnap (1993), and Halbach, Leitgeb, and Welch (2003), who show how to use revision sequences to give a *relational* possible-worlds semantics for predicates; but they do not consider neighborhood semantics, xeno semantics (obviously), classical modal logics, or traditional modal logics.

(iii) $\forall w \in W_0$, I_0 assigns the arithmetic vocabulary in L to its standard interpretation in D_0
(iv) $\forall \phi \in L\ \exists \sigma\ \sigma$ is an individual constant of $\mathfrak{L}$ and $I_0(\sigma) = \phi$
(v) $I_0(D(x), w) = \varnothing$ for all $w \in W_0$.

Let ν be a valuation (i.e., an assignment of elements from the domain to each individual variable of L).

(F) $<\mathfrak{M}, w> \models_\nu F(a_1, \ldots, a_n)$ (where a_i is either an individual constant or an individual variable) iff $<f(a_1), \ldots, f(a_n)> \in I(F, w)$, where if a_i is a variable x_i, then $f(a_i) = \nu(x_i)$, and if a_i is an individual constant c_i, then $f(a_i) = I(c_i)$ (for each n-place predicate F)

(~) $<\mathfrak{M}, w> \models_\nu \sim\phi$ iff it is not the case that $<\mathfrak{M}, w> \models_\nu \phi$

(∧) $<\mathfrak{M}, w> \models_\nu \phi \wedge \psi$ iff $<\mathfrak{M}, w> \models_\nu \phi$ and $<\mathfrak{M}, w> \models_\nu \psi$

(∨) $<\mathfrak{M}, w> \models_\nu \phi \vee \psi$ iff $<\mathfrak{M}, w> \models_\nu \phi$ or $<\mathfrak{M}, w> \models_\nu \psi$

(→) $<\mathfrak{M}, w> \models_\nu \phi \rightarrow \psi$ iff if $<\mathfrak{M}, w> \models_\nu \phi$, then $<\mathfrak{M}, w> \models_\nu \psi$

(↔) $<\mathfrak{M}, w> \models_\nu \phi \leftrightarrow \psi$ iff $<\mathfrak{M}, w> \models_\nu \phi$ iff $<\mathfrak{M}, w> \models_\nu \psi$

(∀) $<\mathfrak{M}, w> \models_\nu \forall x \phi(x)$ iff for each x-variant ν' $<\mathfrak{M}, w> \models_{\nu'} \phi(x)$

(∃) $<\mathfrak{M}, w> \models_\nu \exists x \phi(x)$ iff there is an x-variant ν' s.t. $<\mathfrak{M}, w> \models_{\nu'} \phi(x)$

We can say $<\mathfrak{M}, w> \models \phi$ iff ϕ is a closed formula and for all valuations ν, $<\mathfrak{M}, w> \models_\nu \phi$. Notice that the extension of the descending truth predicate, D(x), is stipulated to be empty in every world in $\mathfrak{M}_0$. Accordingly, $\mathfrak{M}_0$ has no clause for D(x).

$\mathfrak{M}_0$ will serve as the initial model for our first revision sequence. Before presenting the revision sequence, a few definitions are in order.

A *revision rule* ρ is an operation on the set of functions from $\{\{D(x)\} \times \mathfrak{D}\}$ to {t, f}. The members of this set of functions are ***hypotheses***. Each hypothesis interprets D(x). We focus on revision sequences Ω whose length, lh(Ω), is a limit ordinal or On, the class of all ordinals. Let Ω@α be the αth member of Ω. Let Ω|α be the restriction of Ω to ordinal α.

If $x \in \{t, f\}$ and $d \in \mathfrak{D}$, then d is *stably x in* Ω iff ∃β s.t. β<lh(Ω) and for all ordinals γ, if β≤γ<ln(Ω) then [Ω@γ](d) = x; the least such β is the *stabilization point* of d in Ω. Say d is *stable in* Ω iff for some $x \in \{t, f\}$, d is stably x in Ω.

A hypothesis h *coheres with a sequence* Ω iff for all $d \in \mathfrak{D}$ and all $x \in \{t, f\}$, if d is stably x in Ω then h(d) = x.

Ω is a *revision sequence* for ρ iff for all α<lh(Ω): (i) if α = β+1, then Ω@α = ρ(Ω@β), and (ii) if α is a limit ordinal then Ω@α coheres with Ω|α (i.e., for all $d \in \mathfrak{D}$ and all $x \in \{t, f\}$ if d is stably x in Ω|α, then Ω@α(d) = x).[43]

[43] Gupta and Belnap (1993: Ch. 5).

These definitions are based on those in Gupta and Belnap (1993), which is the standard reference for revision sequences.

Our revision rule, which will generate the revision sequence, is based on the clause (D) that we would have wanted in our first-order neighborhood semantics. Let Ω_0 be the revision sequence of length On with initial model $\mathfrak{M}_0$ generated by the following revision rule ρ_0:

(ρ_0-1) If α is not a limit ordinal, then $\forall w \in W$, if $\exists X \in N(w)$, s.t. $\forall x \in X$, $<\Omega_0@\alpha, x> \models \phi$, then $\phi \in I(D, w)$ for $\Omega_0@\alpha+1$; otherwise, $\phi \notin I(D, w)$ for $\Omega_0@\alpha+1$.

(ρ_0-2) If α is a limit ordinal and $D(\langle\phi\rangle)$ is stably true in $\Omega_0|\alpha$, then $\forall w \in W$, $\phi \in I(D, w)$ for $\Omega_0@\alpha$.

(ρ_0-3) If α is a limit ordinal and $D(\langle\phi\rangle)$ is stably false in $\Omega_0|\alpha$, then $\forall w \in W$, $\phi \notin I(D, w)$ for $\Omega_0@\alpha$.

(ρ_0-4) If α is a limit ordinal and $D(\langle\phi\rangle)$ is unstable in $\Omega_0|\alpha$, then $\forall w \in W$, $\phi \notin I(D, w)$ for $\Omega_0@\alpha$.

The revision sequence based on this rule will have a fixed set of worlds and a fixed neighborhood function on that set. Obviously, the interpretation, I, changes from step to step, but the only difference between steps will be the interpretation of D(x). The interpretation of all other expressions in L does not change. One can think of this as a set of revision sequences, one for the extension of D(x) at each world. Of course, at $\mathfrak{M}_0$, and indeed at each step throughout Ω_0, every world satisfies the same formulas.

6.A.2 The sequence Ω_1

Remember, Ω_0 is not the sequence we ultimately care about—its role is to help us assign accessibility relations to the sentences of L in a xeno semantics. That is, we use the results of Ω_0 to construct a new revision sequence of xeno models that *does* eventually reach a fixed point.

Not just any xeno frame and xeno model will do for these purposes. We need to define 'acceptable xeno frame' and 'acceptable xeno model'. There is one additional complication in the construction—we distinguish between traditional worlds (the set $C \subseteq W$) and non-traditional worlds (the set C'); the clause for D(x) is defined only on traditional worlds and validity is defined as truth at all traditional worlds. The extension of D(x) at non-traditional worlds is stipulated below.[44]

We will consider a constant-domain xeno frame $\mathfrak{F} = <W, C, N, R, \mathfrak{D}>$, where W is a set of worlds, $C \subseteq W$, N is a neighborhood function from W to 2^{2^W}, R is a denumerable set of binary relations on W, and $\mathfrak{D}$ is a non-empty set. Let $\mathfrak{F}$ be an *acceptable constant-domain xeno frame* iff:

[44] There is a sense in which the logic determined by the particular xeno semantics I provide could be called a *non-traditional* modal logic in the spirit of non-normal modal logics and non-classical modal logics. I do not know if it is possible to avoid this aspect of the construction.

1. $C \subset W$ [non-traditional worlds]
2. $\forall w \in W, N(w) \neq \varnothing$ [all worlds have neighborhoods]
3. $\forall w \in W\ \forall X \in N(w), X \neq \varnothing$ [non-empty neighborhoods]
4. $\forall w \in W\ \forall X \in N(w), w \in X$ [inclusive neighborhoods]
5. $\forall v \in C'\ \forall X \in N(v)\ \forall x \in X, x \in C'$ [non-traditional neighborhoods]
6. $\forall u \in C, C \in N(u)$ [C is a traditional neighborhood]
7. $\forall w \in C, X \in N(w) \vee Y \in N(w) \rightarrow X \cup Y \in N(w)$ [supplemented neighborhoods]
8. If $X \subset C$ then $\forall u \in C, X \notin N(u)$ [no proper subset of C is a traditional neighborhood].

It should be obvious that acceptable constant-domain xeno frames exist.

We consider a xeno model $\mathfrak{M} = <\mathfrak{F}, \mathfrak{R}, I>$ where $\mathfrak{F}$ is a xeno frame, $\mathfrak{R}$ is an accessibility function ($\mathfrak{R}$ is a function from L to R, so it assigns each sentence ϕ of L a binary relation on W, designated R_ϕ), and I is an interpretation function (I assigns each individual constant a member of the domain at each world and each n-place predicate a set of ordered n-tuples from the domain at each world). We use the following definitions for accessibility relations:

R_ϕ is *reflexive* iff $\forall w \in W\ R_\phi ww$.
R_ϕ is *coreflexive* iff $\forall u \in W\ \forall w \in W, R_\phi wu \rightarrow w = u$.
R_ϕ is *closed* iff $\forall u \in C\ \forall w \in W, R_\phi uw \rightarrow w \in C$.
R_ϕ is *open* iff $\forall u \in C\ \exists v \in C', R_\phi uv$.

Note that if an accessibility relation is coreflexive, then it is closed (but the converse fails). All accessibility relations in the xeno models we consider are reflexive. Intuitively, the accessibility relations assigned to the instances of axioms of ADT are coreflexive, as are those assigned to sentences of $\mathfrak{L}^-$.

Let $\mathfrak{M}$ be an *acceptable xeno model* iff:

1. $\mathfrak{F}$ is an acceptable constant-domain xeno frame.
2. $\forall \phi \in L\ R_\phi$ is reflexive.
3. If $I(\sigma) = I(\tau) \in L$, and ψ results from replacing occurrences of σ with τ in ϕ, then $R_\phi = R_\psi$.
4. $R_{\phi\wedge\psi} = R_{\psi\wedge\phi}$
5. $R_{\phi\vee\psi} = R_{\psi\vee\phi}$
6. $R_{\sim\sim\phi} = R_\phi$
7. R_ϕ is coreflexive for $\phi \in L^-$.
8. If R_ϕ is coreflexive then $R_{D\langle\phi\rangle}$ is coreflexive.
9. $R_{D\langle\phi\rangle\rightarrow\phi}$ is coreflexive.
10. $R_{D\langle\sim\phi\rangle\ \rightarrow\ \sim D\langle\phi\rangle}$ is coreflexive.
11. $R_{D\langle\phi\wedge\psi\rangle\ \rightarrow\ D\langle\phi\rangle\wedge D\langle\psi\rangle}$ is coreflexive.
12. $R_{D\langle\phi\rangle\ \vee\ D\langle\psi\rangle\ \rightarrow\ D\langle\phi\vee\psi\rangle}$ is coreflexive.
13. R_ϕ is coreflexive for ϕ a first-order classical logical truth.
14. R_ϕ is coreflexive for $PA \vdash \phi$.

15. If R_ϕ is coreflexive and R_ψ is coreflexive then $R_{\phi\rightarrow\psi}$, $R_{\phi\wedge\psi}$, $R_{\phi\vee\psi}$ are coreflexive.
16. R_ϕ is coreflexive iff $R_{\sim\phi}$ is coreflexive.
17. If $R_{\phi\wedge\psi}$ is closed and $C\subseteq P_\nu(\phi\wedge\psi)$, then R_ϕ is closed and R_ψ is closed.[45]
18. If R_ϕ is closed and R_ψ is closed then $R_{\phi\vee\psi}$ is closed.
19. $L\subset\mathfrak{D}$ (i.e., the domain contains all closed sentences of L)
20. $\mathbb{N}\subset\mathfrak{D}$ (i.e., the domain contains the natural numbers)
21. $\forall w\in W$, I assigns the arithmetic vocabulary in $\mathfrak{L}$ to their standard interpretation in $\mathfrak{D}$.
22. All individual constants have the same denotation in every world.
23. All predicates (except possibly D) have the same extension in every world.
24. All predicates have the same extension in all non-traditional worlds.
25. $\forall\phi\in L$, $\exists\sigma$ σ is an individual constant of $\mathfrak{L}$ and $I(\sigma) = \phi$.
26. If R_ϕ is coreflexive then $C\subseteq P_\nu(\phi)$ or $C\subseteq P_\nu(\sim\phi)$.

Let Δ_M be the set of sentences of $\mathfrak{L}$ closed under the following rules:

($\Delta_{\mathfrak{M}}$-1) $\forall\phi\in L$ if $\phi = D\langle\psi\rangle \rightarrow \psi$ then $\phi\in\Delta_{\mathfrak{M}}$.

($\Delta_{\mathfrak{M}}$-2) $\forall\phi\in L$ if $\phi\in\Delta_{\mathfrak{M}}$ and σ is an individual constant and $I(\sigma) = \phi$, then $D\sigma\in\Delta_{\mathfrak{M}}$.

That is, $\Delta_{\mathfrak{M}}$ is the set of instances of axiom schema D1 closed under applications of D.

Let $\mathfrak{M}_1 = <W_1, C_1, N_1, R_1, \mathfrak{D}_1, \mathfrak{R}_1, I_1>$ be an acceptable constant-domain xeno model, where:

(i) $I_1(D(x), w) = \varnothing$ for all $w\in W_1$.
(ii) if ϕ is stably true in Ω_0, then $R_{1\phi}$ is closed in $\mathfrak{M}_1$.
(iii) if ϕ is stably false in Ω_0, then $R_{1\phi}$ is closed in $\mathfrak{M}_1$.
(iv) if ϕ is unstable in Ω_0 and $\phi\notin\Delta_{M1}$, then $R_{1\phi}$ is open in $\mathfrak{M}_1$.

There are several issues to be settled before we can be sure that $\mathfrak{M}_1$ exists.

First, we need to show that there are acceptable constant-domain xeno models. That is easy—let $\mathfrak{M}$ be a constant-domain xeno model based on an acceptable xeno frame such that the natural numbers and the closed formulas of $\mathfrak{L}$ are members of its domain, the arithmetic vocabulary of $\mathfrak{L}$ receives its standard interpretation in every world, there is a name in $\mathfrak{L}$ for every member of the domain, the interpretation is the same at every world, and every relation in R is the identity relation. Then $\mathfrak{M}$ is an acceptable constant-domain xeno model.

Second, we need to show that $\mathfrak{R}_1$ is well-defined. Given the interpretation function I_1, we define $\Delta_{\mathfrak{M}1}$ as above. There are eighteen conditions under the definition of an acceptable xeno model that pertain to $\mathfrak{R}_1$. None of them conflict with the above specification that defines $\mathfrak{M}_1$. For example, condition 4 is: $R_{1\phi\wedge\psi} = R_{1\psi\wedge\phi}$. It is obvious that

[45] For each ϕ in L, $P_\nu(\phi) = \{w\in W: <\mathfrak{M}, w> \vDash_\nu \phi\}$

$\phi\wedge\psi$ is stable in Ω_0 iff $\psi\wedge\phi$ is stable in Ω_0; thus the specification of $\mathfrak{R}_1$ does not conflict with this condition. The same holds for all the others. One might worry about condition 9, but all instances of D1 are in $\Delta_{\mathfrak{M}1}$, so that does not pose a problem. Thus, the above specification of the accessibility relations in $\mathfrak{M}_1$ does not conflict with the definition of an acceptable xeno model. Therefore, $\mathfrak{R}_1$ is well-defined.

Let ν be a valuation (i.e., an assignment of elements from the domain to each individual variable of $\mathfrak{L}$).

(F) $<\mathfrak{M}, w> \vDash_\nu F(a_1,\ldots, a_n)$ (where a_i is either an individual constant or an individual variable) iff $<f(a_1),\ldots, f(a_n)>\in I(F, w)$, where if a_i is a variable x_i, then $f(a_i) = \nu(x_i)$, and if a_i is an individual constant c_i, then $f(a_i) = I(c_i)$ (for each n-place predicate F)

(~) $<\mathfrak{M}, w> \vDash_\nu \sim\phi$ iff it is not the case that $<\mathfrak{M}, w> \vDash_\nu \phi$

($\wedge$) $<\mathfrak{M}, w> \vDash_\nu \phi\wedge\psi$ iff $<\mathfrak{M}, w> \vDash_\nu \phi$ and $<\mathfrak{M}, w> \vDash_\nu \psi$

($\vee$) $<\mathfrak{M}, w> \vDash_\nu \phi\vee\psi$ iff $<\mathfrak{M}, w> \vDash_\nu \phi$ or $<\mathfrak{M}, w> \vDash_\nu \psi$

($\rightarrow$) $<\mathfrak{M}, w> \vDash_\nu \phi\rightarrow\psi$ iff if $<\mathfrak{M}, w> \vDash_\nu \phi$, then $<\mathfrak{M}, w> \vDash_\nu \psi$

($\leftrightarrow$) $<\mathfrak{M}, w> \vDash_\nu \phi\leftrightarrow\psi$ iff $<\mathfrak{M}, w> \vDash_\nu \phi$ iff $<\mathfrak{M}, w> \vDash_\nu \psi$

($\forall$) $<\mathfrak{M}, w> \vDash_\nu \forall x\phi(x)$ iff for each x-variant ν' $<\mathfrak{M}, w> \vDash_{\nu'} \phi(x)$

($\exists$) $<\mathfrak{M}, w> \vDash_\nu \exists x\phi(x)$ iff there is an x-variant ν' s.t. $<\mathfrak{M}, w> \vDash_{\nu'} \phi(x)$

We can say $<\mathfrak{M}, w> \vDash \phi$ iff ϕ is a closed formula and for all valuations ν, $<\mathfrak{M}, w> \vDash_\nu \phi$.

Notice that the extension of the descending truth predicate, D(x), is empty in every world in $\mathfrak{M}_1$. Accordingly, $\mathfrak{M}_1$ has no clause for D(x). Let Ω_1 be the revision sequence of length On with initial model $\mathfrak{M}_1$ generated by the following revision rule ρ_1:

($\rho_{1\_}1$) α is not a limit ordinal: if $\forall u\in C, \forall w\in W, R_\phi uw \rightarrow P_{\alpha-1}(\phi)\in N(w)$, then $\forall w\in W, \phi\in I(D, w)$ for $\Omega_1@\alpha$; otherwise, $\forall w\in W, \phi\notin I(D, w)$ for $\Omega_1@\alpha$.

($\rho_{1\_}2$) α is a limit ordinal: if $D\langle\phi\rangle$ is stably true in $\Omega_1|\alpha$, then $\forall w\in C, \phi\in I(D, w)$ for $\Omega_1@\alpha+1$.

($\rho_{1\_}3$) α is a limit ordinal: if $D\langle\phi\rangle$ is stably false in $\Omega_1|\alpha$, then $\forall w\in C, \phi\notin I(D, w)$ for $\Omega_1@\alpha+1$.

($\rho_{1\_}4$) α is a limit ordinal: if $D\langle\phi\rangle$ is unstable in $\Omega_1|\alpha$, then $\forall w\in C, \phi\notin I(D, w)$ for $\Omega_1@\alpha+1$.

The revision sequence based on this rule will have a fixed set of worlds and a fixed neighborhood function on that set. As before, the interpretation, I, changes from step to step, but the only difference between steps will be the interpretation of D(x). The interpretation of all other expressions in $\mathfrak{L}$ does not change. The assignment of accessibility relations to sentences of $\mathfrak{L}$ does not change.

6.A.3 A fixed point for Ω_1

Now we prove that Ω_1 reaches a fixed point. Before we do that, we need several more definitions and results pertaining to revision sequences.

A hypothesis h is ***cofinal in a sequence*** Ω iff for all ordinals $\alpha<\ln(\Omega)$ there is a β s.t. $\alpha\leq\beta<\ln(\Omega)$ and $\Omega@\beta = h$.

Theorem: Ω is a sequence of length On. Then:

(i) there is a hypothesis $h\in\{t, f\}^{\mathfrak{D}}$ that is cofinal in Ω
(ii) there is an ordinal α s.t. for all $\beta\geq\alpha$, $\Omega@\beta$ is cofinal in Ω; the least such ordinal is the ***initial ordinal*** for Ω
(iii) for all ordinals α there is an ordinal $\beta>\alpha$ satisfying the condition that for all hypotheses h cofinal in Ω there is an ordinal γ s.t. $\alpha\leq\gamma<\beta$ and $\Omega@\gamma = h$; such an ordinal is a ***completion ordinal*** for Ω above α.

Theorem: for all $d\in\mathfrak{D}$ and $x\in\{t,f\}$:

(i) if d is stably x in Ω then the value of d is x in all hypotheses cofinal in Ω
(ii) if $lh(\Omega)$ = On, then the converse of (i) is true.

An ordinal α is a ***reflection ordinal*** for Ω iff α is a limit ordinal $< lh(\Omega)$ s.t.

(i) $\alpha \geq$ the initial ordinal for Ω and
(ii) for all $d\in\mathfrak{D}$ and $x\in\{t, f\}$, d is stably x in $\Omega|\alpha$ iff d is stably x in Ω.

Theorem: Let Ω be a revision sequence for ρ and $\alpha<lh(\Omega)$. If $\Omega@\alpha$ is a fixed point of ρ then for all β s.t. $\alpha+\beta < lh(\Omega)$ we have $\Omega@\alpha+\beta = \Omega@\alpha$; furthermore, an object $d\in\mathfrak{D}$ is stably x in Ω iff $\Omega@\alpha(d) = x$.

A hypothesis h is ***recurring*** for ρ iff h is cofinal in some revision sequence Ω of length On for ρ.

Theorem: all and only recurring hypotheses are reflexive.[46]

So if α is a reflection ordinal, then $\Omega|\alpha$ reflects all the stabilities and instabilities in Ω.

With these definitions and results in hand, we are ready to show that Ω_1 reaches a fixed point. I use the convention '$P_\alpha(\phi)$' for $\{w\in W : <\Omega_1@\alpha, w> \models \phi\}$.

Let ζ be the initial ordinal for Ω_1, and let ξ be a reflection ordinal for Ω_1 s.t. $\xi>\zeta$, and let $\mathfrak{M}_2 = \Omega_1@\xi$. Thus, $\mathfrak{M}_2$ is a reflexive hypothesis for Ω_1; it follows that ξ is a limit ordinal.

I rely on the following lemmas:

(1) ϕ is stable in $\Omega_1|\xi$ iff ϕ is stable in Ω_1. [ξ is a reflection ordinal for Ω, so by definition, ϕ is stable in $\Omega|\xi$ iff ϕ is stable in Ω.]

[46] For proofs, see Gupta and Belnap (1993: Ch. 5).

(2) For any ordinal α, if $\exists w \in C$ s.t. $<\Omega_1@\alpha, w> \vDash \phi$, then $\forall w \in C$, $<\Omega_1@\alpha, w> \vDash \phi$. [By induction—the extension of D(x) is the same at all classical worlds in $\mathfrak{M}_1$, and if the extension of D(x) is the same at all classical worlds in $\Omega@\alpha$, then the extension of D(x) is the same at all classical worlds in $\Omega@\alpha+1$.]

To show that $\mathfrak{M}_2$ is a fixed point for ρ_1, we prove that the extension of D(x) does not change from $\mathfrak{M}_2$ to $\rho_1(\mathfrak{M}_2)$ on traditional worlds.

Let $u \in C$. Let $Q \in L$. Assume that $<\mathfrak{M}_2, u> \vDash D\langle Q\rangle$. Assume for *reductio* that $<\rho_1(\mathfrak{M}_2), u> \vDash \sim D\langle Q\rangle$. $D\langle Q\rangle$ is stably true at u in $\Omega_1|\xi$ [else $<\mathfrak{M}_2, u> \vDash \sim D\langle Q\rangle$, since ξ is a limit ordinal]. $D\langle Q\rangle$ is stably true at u in Ω_1 [by Lemma 1]. $<\rho_1(\mathfrak{M}_2), u> \vDash D\langle Q\rangle$. $\bot$. This result shows that the extension of D(x) does not decrease from $\mathfrak{M}_2$ to $\rho_1(\mathfrak{M}_2)$. Now for the other direction.

Assume that $<\mathfrak{M}_2, u> \vDash \sim D\langle Q\rangle$. Assume for *reductio* 1 that $<\rho_1(\mathfrak{M}_2), u> \vDash D\langle Q\rangle$. $\forall w \in C$, $R_Q uw \rightarrow P_\xi(Q) \in N(w)$. It follows that $R_Q uu$. Hence, $P_\xi(Q) \in N(u)$. Thus, $\forall X \in N(u), u \in X$. Therefore, $u \in P_\xi(Q)$, and it follows that $<\mathfrak{M}_2, u> \vDash Q$. Either $D\langle Q\rangle$ is stably false at u in $\Omega_1|\xi$ or $D\langle Q\rangle$ is unstable at u in $\Omega_1|\xi$ [else $<\mathfrak{M}_2, u> \vDash D\langle Q\rangle$]. Assume for *reductio* 2 that $D\langle Q\rangle$ is stably false at u in $\Omega_1|\xi$. It follows that $D\langle Q\rangle$ is stably false at u in Ω_1 [by Lemma 1]. Hence, $<\rho_1(\mathfrak{M}_2), w> \vDash \sim D\langle Q\rangle$. $\bot$ (for *reductio* 2). Now for the other disjunct. Assume for *reductio* 3 that $D\langle Q\rangle$ is unstable at u in $\Omega_1|\xi$. $D\langle Q\rangle$ is unstable at u in Ω_1 [by Lemma 1]. Assume for conditional proof that Q is stable at u in Ω_1. Hence, $\forall w \in C$, Q is stable at w in Ω_1 [by Lemma 2]. Let β be the stabilization point for Q at u in Ω_1. Then, $\forall\gamma>\beta\ u \in P_\gamma(Q)$ or $\forall\gamma>\beta\ u \notin P_\gamma(Q)$. Hence, $\forall w \in C$ ($\forall\gamma>\beta\ w \in P_\gamma(Q)$ or $\forall\gamma>\beta\ w \notin P_\gamma(Q)$). Thus, $\forall w \in W$ ($\forall\gamma>\beta\ w \in P_\gamma(Q)$ or $\forall\gamma>\beta\ w \notin P_\gamma(Q)$). Hence, $\forall\gamma>\beta\ P_\gamma(Q) \in N(u)$ or $\forall\gamma>\beta\ P_\gamma(Q) \notin N(u)$. R_Q is either open or closed; if R_Q is open, then $\sim D\langle Q\rangle$ is stably false at u in Ω_1. Thus, R_Q is closed. Either $\forall\gamma>\beta <\Omega_1@\gamma, u> \vDash D\langle Q\rangle$ or $\forall\gamma>\beta <\Omega_1@\gamma, u> \vDash \sim D\langle Q\rangle$. Hence, $D\langle Q\rangle$ is stable at u in Ω_1. By conditional proof, if Q is stable at u in Ω_1 then $D\langle Q\rangle$ is stable at u in Ω_1. So, by contraposition, if $D\langle Q\rangle$ is unstable at u in Ω_1 then Q is unstable at u in Ω_1. Thus, Q is unstable at u in Ω_1. Hence, Q is unstable at u in $\Omega_1|\xi$. Therefore, $<\mathfrak{M}_2, u> \vDash \sim Q$. We have $\bot$ for *reductio* 3. And we have $\bot$ for *reductio* 1. Consequently, we have a fixed point, and $\mathfrak{M}_2$ is the intended model for L.

Since $\mathfrak{M}_2$ is a fixed point for ρ_1, we know that for $u \in C$:

(D) $<\mathfrak{M}_2, u> \vDash D(\langle\phi\rangle)$ iff $\forall w \in W\ R_\phi uw \rightarrow P(\phi) \in N(w)$

So we have a constant-domain xeno semantics for $\mathfrak{L}$, and it satisfies the intended clause for D(x). We have not said anything about the non-traditional worlds (we have not needed to say anything about them), but to finish the interpretation of $\mathfrak{L}$, we can say that if for all $w \in C\ w \vDash \phi$, then for all $v \in C'\ v \vDash \phi$.

Recall that we have been concentrating on D(x) and ignoring A(x) and S(x). If we can define them in terms of D(x), then that would do the trick. We could use the following definitions:

(M1) $A(\langle\phi\rangle) \leftrightarrow \sim D(\langle\sim\phi\rangle)$

(M2) $S(\langle\phi\rangle) \leftrightarrow D(\langle\phi\rangle) \vee \sim A(\langle\phi\rangle)$

Let $\mathfrak{L}^+$ be the result of adding A(x) and S(x) to $\mathfrak{L}$ and let L^+ be the set of formulas of $\mathfrak{L}^+$. Here is how to interpret the new predicates. Let $\phi \in L^+/L$. Let ψ result from replacing all occurrences of $A\langle\theta\rangle$ in ϕ with $\sim D\langle\sim\theta\rangle$ and replacing all occurrences of $S\langle\theta\rangle$ in ϕ with $D\langle\theta\rangle \vee D\langle\sim\theta\rangle$. Then $R_\phi = R_\psi$ and $\forall w \in W$ $w \vDash \phi$ iff $w \vDash \psi$.

To summarize the constant-domain xeno semantics for the descending truth predicate, 'D(x)', the ascending truth predicate, 'A(x)', and the safety predicate, 'S(x)':

(F) $<\mathfrak{M}, w> \vDash_\nu F(a_1,\ldots,a_n)$ (where a_i is either an individual constant or an individual variable) iff $<f(a_1),\ldots,f(a_n)> \in I(F, w)$, where if a_i is a variable x_i, then $f(a_i) = \nu(x_i)$, and if a_i is an individual constant c_i, then $f(a_i) = I(c_i)$ (for each n-place predicate F)

(~) $<\mathfrak{M}, w> \vDash_\nu \sim\phi$ iff it is not the case that $<\mathfrak{M}, w> \vDash_\nu \phi$

(∧) $<\mathfrak{M}, w> \vDash_\nu \phi\wedge\psi$ iff $<\mathfrak{M}, w> \vDash_\nu \phi$ and $<\mathfrak{M}, w> \vDash_\nu \psi$

(∨) $<\mathfrak{M}, w> \vDash_\nu \phi\vee\psi$ iff $<\mathfrak{M}, w> \vDash_\nu \phi$ or $<\mathfrak{M}, w> \vDash_\nu \psi$

(→) $<\mathfrak{M}, w> \vDash_\nu \phi\rightarrow\psi$ iff if $<\mathfrak{M}, w> \vDash_\nu \phi$, then $<\mathfrak{M}, w> \vDash_\nu \psi$

(↔) $<\mathfrak{M}, w> \vDash_\nu \phi\leftrightarrow\psi$ iff $<\mathfrak{M}, w> \vDash_\nu \phi$ iff $<\mathfrak{M}, w> \vDash_\nu \psi$

(∀) $<\mathfrak{M}, w> \vDash_\nu \forall x\phi(x)$ iff for each x-variant ν' $<\mathfrak{M}, w> \vDash_{\nu'} \phi(x)$

(∃) $<\mathfrak{M}, w> \vDash_\nu \exists x\phi(x)$ iff there is an x-variant ν' s.t. $<\mathfrak{M}, w> \vDash_{\nu'} \phi(x)$

For all $u \in C$:

(D) $<\mathfrak{M}, u> \vDash_\nu D\langle\phi\rangle$ iff $\forall w \in W$ $R_\phi uw \rightarrow P_\nu(\phi) \in N(w)$

(A) $<\mathfrak{M}, u> \vDash_\nu A\langle\phi\rangle$ iff $\exists w \in W$ $R_{\sim\phi} uw \wedge P_\nu(\sim\phi) \notin N(w)$

(S) $<\mathfrak{M}, u> \vDash_\nu S\langle\phi\rangle$ iff $\forall w \in W$ $(R_\phi uw \rightarrow P_\nu(\phi) \in N(w)) \vee \exists u \in W$ $(R_{\sim\phi} uw \wedge P_\nu(\sim\phi) \notin N(w))$

For all $v \in C'$:

(D) $<\mathfrak{M}, v> \vDash_\nu D\langle\phi\rangle$ iff $\forall u \in C$ $<\mathfrak{M}, u> \vDash_\nu D\langle\phi\rangle$

(A) $<\mathfrak{M}, v> \vDash_\nu A\langle\phi\rangle$ iff $\forall u \in C$ $<\mathfrak{M}, u> \vDash_\nu A\langle\phi\rangle$

(S) $<\mathfrak{M}, v> \vDash_\nu S\langle\phi\rangle$ iff $\forall u \in C$ $<\mathfrak{M}, u> \vDash_\nu S\langle\phi\rangle$

We can say $<\mathfrak{M}, w> \vDash \phi$ iff ϕ is a closed formula and for all valuations ν, $<\mathfrak{M}, w> \vDash_\nu \phi$. A sentence ϕ is *valid* in a xeno model $\mathfrak{M}$ iff $\forall u \in C$ $<\mathfrak{M}, u> \vDash \phi$.

6.A.4 A soundness theorem

The fixed-point theorem from the previous section shows that we have a well-defined notion of truth at a world for an acceptable constant-domain xeno model. It follows that we have a well-defined notion of validity for constant-domain xeno models. Now, all that is left is to show that ADT is sound with respect to acceptable constant-domain xeno semantics. It follows from this result that ADT is consistent (relative to our background set theory).

In order to prove soundness, we need to go through each of the axioms of ADT and prove that they are valid in any acceptable xeno model. It is a tedious but trivial exercise to demonstrate this, and I do not give the details here.[47] The result is, if ϕ is an axiom of ADT, then ϕ is valid in any acceptable constant-domain xeno model.

ADT is sound with respect to constant-domain xeno semantics iff for all acceptable constant-domain xeno models μ, any set of sentences Γ and any sentence ϕ, if ϕ is provable from Γ, then the argument from Γ to ϕ is valid in μ. Argument validity is defined in the usual way: for all acceptable constant-domain xeno models μ if all the members of Γ are true in μ, then ϕ is true in μ. We know that all the classical logical truths are valid and all classical inference rules are valid. So our proof that all axioms of ADT are valid in any acceptable constant-domain xeno model completes our soundness proof. ADT is sound with respect to acceptable constant-domain xeno semantics.

[47] For example, to show that all instances of axiom schema D1 are valid, assume for an acceptable constant-domain xeno model that $u \in C$ $u \models D\langle\phi\rangle$. It follows that $\forall w \in W\ R_{\phi}uw \rightarrow P(\phi) \in N(w)$. By clause 2 of the definition of an acceptable xeno model, R_{ϕ} is reflexive. Thus, Ruu. Hence, $P(\phi) \in N(u)$. By clause 4 of the definition of an acceptable xeno frame, N is inclusive. Thus, $u \in P(\phi)$. Hence, $u \models \phi$. Therefore, $\models D\langle\phi\rangle \rightarrow \phi$. The proofs for the other axioms are similar.

7

Metrological Naturalism and ADT

In the previous chapter, I suggested a team of replacement concepts and some principles they obey in the form of a mathematical theory (i.e., ADT plus xeno semantics) together with its interpretation (i.e., 'ascending true' and 'descending true' are compatible with classical logic and they are univocal invariant one-place predicates). One might worry that simply familiarizing oneself with the formal theory ADT is not enough to really grasp the concept of ascending truth and the concept of descending truth. It is, after all, just a collection of axioms. In this chapter and the next, I aim to provide more grounding for the formal theory by doing two things: (i) sketching the way ADT should be physically interpreted, and (ii) describing the relations between ascending truth and descending truth and other concepts. This chapter focuses on whether ascending truth and descending truth have a nature or can be given an analysis (e.g., in terms of correspondence). In response, I outline a non-reductive account of ascending and descending truth using measurement theory and some ideas from Donald Davidson.

7.1 Davidson's theory of truth

Davidson argues that although we cannot give an analysis or reductive explanation of truth, we can trace the relationship between truth and other important concepts, like meaning, belief, and rationality in a certain way.

Instead of using a universally quantified biconditional, Davidson, inspired by Tarski's writings on truth, uses an axiomatic theory of truth. An axiomatic theory of truth is just a set of sentences that contain truth predicates and is closed under logical consequence (i.e., any sentence that is a logical consequence of some sentences in the set is also in the set). The sentences in the theory are taken to be the principles that truth predicates obey. Davidson uses an axiomatic theory that has different principles for sentences of different forms; for example, a subject-predicate sentence is true iff the thing referred to by the subject term is in the extension of the predicate, a negation is true iff the sentence negated is not true, and a conjunction is true iff both conjuncts are true. From the axiomatic theory of truth (for a certain language), one can derive a T-sentence for each sentence of the language in question: b is true-in-L iff ϕ (where $\langle\phi\rangle$ is a translation of b into the metalanguage).

This axiomatic theory of truth is quite different from the other theories of the nature of truth surveyed in Chapter 1. It does not give a conceptual analysis or reductive explanation of truth in terms of some other (perhaps more basic) concepts. One might be (justifiably) unimpressed if that was all a Davidsonian could say about truth. However, Davidson's view is that the axiomatic theory should be given empirical content, and this tells us much about the concept of truth. Although the details are subtle and complex, the basic idea is that a theory of truth plays an important role in an overall theory of a rational agent's beliefs, desires, and language.

The first step in providing empirical content to the axiomatic theory is realizing that an axiomatic theory of truth (for some language) serves as a meaning theory for that language, where a meaning theory specifies the meanings of each of the sentences of the language.[1] If enough external constraints are placed on the application of the axiomatic theory, then the T-sentences (e.g., ''snow is white' is true iff snow is white') that are derivable from it specify the meanings of the sentences of that language. That is, the sentence on the right hand side specifies the meaning of the sentence called true on the left hand side.

Davidson also has an account of the external constraints on the axiomatic theory that ensure the T-sentences specify meanings of the language in question; this can be thought of as a general method for applying the axiomatic theory to a particular language or language user. He uses the thought experiment of the radical interpreter to satisfy this demand.

The *radical interpreter* is supposed to be a person in the situation of trying to understand another person (who I call the *target*). The radical interpreter has to figure out what the target's sentences mean even though she does not understand the target's language and does not have recourse to a translator or dictionary or any other similar tool. The radical interpreter can use only publically available evidence to figure out what the target's sentences mean. She begins with observable evidence about the target (i.e., the rational entity that speaks the language in question), which includes certain attitudes the target takes toward the sentences of the language (e.g., holding-true). The interpreter also has access to which events in the target's environment cause the target to hold-true certain sentences of the language (the distal stimuli). From this basis, the radical interpreter has to construct an axiomatic theory (which includes specifying the referents of singular terms and the extensions of predicates) for the target's language and a set of beliefs held by the target. Davidson describes a complex sequence of steps the radical interpreter performs to arrive at this goal. One crucial aspect of the construction is that the radical interpreter uses a principle of charity: in the vast majority of cases, when the target holds-true a sentence in a given circumstance, the sentence is true in that circumstance. The radical interpreter is able to go from relatively thin evidence (sentences held-true) to a relatively rich explanatory structure (beliefs and meanings) by assuming that that structure has certain features characterized by the theory of truth.

[1] This claim is controversial; see Foster (1976), Davidson (1976b, 1990), and Lepore and Ludwig (2005: Chs. 4, 8, 9; 2007) for discussion.

For each pair <Tarskian axiomatic theory of truth, set of beliefs> the radical interpreter could attribute to the target, there is another pair that would be just as empirically satisfactory. Thus, to this extent, the meanings of our sentences and the contents of our beliefs are indeterminate. However, Davidson is quick to point out that (contra Quine) it does not follow there is no such thing as meaning or belief.[2] Rather, there is a hitherto unnoticed interdependence between taking a person to have certain beliefs and taking a person's sentences to have certain meanings.

Although Davidson does not formulate it in these terms, he does draw attention to a problem that is analogous to the one faced by the radical interpreter: how to attribute beliefs and desires to a rational agent on the basis of that agent's (non-verbal) behavior. The latter is a problem addressed by Bayesian decision theory as developed by Frank Ramsey, who lays out a procedure by which a person (whom we might call the *radical rationalizer*) begins with a target's preferences and arrives at a set of degrees of belief and a set of degrees of desire for the target. The formal theory in this case is the theory of probability (for degrees of belief) and the theory of utility (for degrees of desire). One crucial aspect of the construction is that the radical rationalizer assumes that the target maximizes expected utility. The radical rationalizer is able to go from relatively thin evidence (ordinal preferences) to a relatively rich explanatory structure (degrees of belief and degrees of desire) by assuming that that structure has certain features characterized by the theory of probability and the theory of utility.[3]

Davidson argues that Bayesian decision theory and the theory of interpretation need to be combined into a single unified theory of rationality. The theory of interpretation takes the agent's desires for granted in assigning meanings and beliefs, and the Bayesian decision theory takes the meanings of the agent's sentences for granted when assigning degrees of belief and degrees of desire. Moreover, the three concepts (belief, desire, and meaning) are equally unavailable to someone in the position of the radical interpreter and they are all on equal footing in terms of explanation.

To construct a unified theory for a target, a theorist begins with a particular relational attitude, preferring-true, that obtains between the target and pairs of sentences. From this basis, Davidson shows how to arrive at a meaning theory for the target's language (in the form of a Tarskian axiomatic theory of truth), a theory of the target's degrees of belief (in the form of a theory of subjective probability), and a theory of the target's degrees of desire (in the form of a theory of utility). The theorist uses both principles from above (i.e., charity and expected utility maximization) in addition to another, the *requirement of total evidence for inductive reasoning* which recommends that one give credence to the hypothesis supported by all available relevant evidence. The procedure for constructing the unified theory is a combination of the radical interpreter's procedure and the radical rationalizer's procedure.[4]

[2] Davidson (1997b).

[3] See Ramsey (1926) and Davidson (1974b, 1976a, 1990).

[4] Davidson (1974b, 1980b, 1990, 1995).

Davidson's unified theory is really a unification of formal semantics (used to explain meaning) and formal epistemology (used to explain beliefs and desires). His fundamental question is: what do rational entities have to be like in order for them to be able to interpret one another? His answer is that the unified theory—which uses the axioms of probability as constraints on degrees of belief, the axioms of utility theory as constraints on degrees of desire, and the axioms of a Tarskian theory of truth as constraints on meaning—describes what a rational agent's attitudes and linguistic competence have to be like so that her mental states and utterances are interpretable by another. The indeterminacy of interpretation still holds for the unified theory of rationality: there are multiple, equally good ways of assigning a package of degrees of belief to an agent, degrees of desire to an agent, and meanings to an agent's sentences. In sum, the axiomatic theory of truth with which we began is given empirical interpretation by being embedded in a unified theory of rationality.

For Davidson, truth cannot be analyzed or reduced to something more primitive—he is not engaged in conceptual analysis or reductive explanation.

> Here I would like to insert a remark about the methodology of my proposal. In philosophy we are used to definitions, analyses, reductions. Typically these are intended to carry us from concepts better understood, or clear, or more basic epistemologically or ontologically, to others we want to understand. The method I have suggested fits none of these categories. I have proposed a looser relation between concepts to be illuminated and the relatively more basic. At the centre stands a formal theory, a theory of truth, which imposes a complex structure on sentences containing the primitive notions of truth and satisfaction. These notions are given application by the form of the theory and the nature of the evidence. The result is a partially interpreted theory. The advantage of the method lies not in its free-style appeal to the notion of evidential support but in the idea of a powerful theory interpreted at the most advantageous point. This allows us to reconcile the need for a semantically articulated structure with a theory testable only at the sentential level. The more subtle gain is that very thin evidence in support of each of a potential infinity of points can yield rich results, even with respect to the points. By knowing only the conditions under which speakers hold sentences true, we can come out, given a satisfactory theory, with an interpretation of each sentence.[5]

A Davidsonian theory of truth describes certain essential features of rationality; it is an integral part of a unified theory of meaning, belief, desire, and action. In addition, the unified theory provides a way of giving an empirical interpretation to the axiomatic theory of truth at its heart.

It seems to me that an analogy Davidson draws between the unified theory and measurement theory illuminates many of his other philosophical views. He never gives this idea an extended treatment, but he expresses his commitment to it from his earliest work in empirical psychology through his last writings. I return to it after the next section.

[5] Davidson (1973: 137).

7.2 Measurement theory

One of Galileo Galilei's most famous sayings is:

> Philosophy is written in this grand book—I mean the universe—which stands continually open to our gaze, but it cannot be understood unless one first learns to comprehend the language in which it is written. It is written in the language of mathematics, and its characters are triangles, circles, and other geometric figures, without which it is humanly impossible to understand a single word of it; without these, one is wandering about in a dark labyrinth.[6]

The idea that the book of the world is written in the language of mathematics is arguably the driving force behind the Scientific Revolution and all its developments up to the present. For centuries, scientists have followed the strategy of using mathematical theories to explain, predict, and control the world around us. But only recently, in the late nineteenth century, did they reflect on this strategy enough to formulate an explicit theory of *it*. Today, this body of work is known as *measurement theory*.

Measurement theory is the study of how formal systems apply to the physical world; as I said, I like to think of it as somewhat analogous to set theory—it serves as an all-purpose background theory for science in the way that set theory serves as an all-purpose background theory for mathematics. Patrick Suppes, who has probably done more than anyone to develop measurement theory, writes:

> A procedure of measurement is needed in any area of science when we desire to pass from simple qualitative observations to the quantitative observations necessary for the precise prediction or control of phenomena. To justify this transition we need an algebra of empirically realizable operations and relations which can be shown to be isomorphic to an appropriately chosen numerical algebra. Satisfying this requirement is the fundamental problem of measurement representation.[7]

Any time we use mathematics to describe, explain, predict, or control the physical world, we are implicitly using measurement theory. It gives a single coherent method of applying mathematics and formal theories to empirical phenomena.

According to measurement theory, the process of measurement involves three structures:

(i) a *physical structure*, which consists of physical entities, their properties, and relations
(ii) a *relational structure*, which consists of a set of (idealized) objects defined by principles specifying their properties and relations
(iii) a *mathematical structure*, which consists of a set of mathematical entities with mathematical properties and relations.

[6] Galilei (1623) as translated in Popkin (1966: 65).
[7] Suppes (1998: 244).

In addition to these three structures, there is a connection between the physical structure and the relational structure, and there is a connection between the relational structure and the mathematical structure. I use the term 'measurement system' for something consisting of these three structures and the connections between them. *Measurement* is a two-step process: (i) specifying the connection between the physical objects and physical relations in the *physical structure* to the idealized objects and relations defined by the axioms of the idealizing *relational structure*, and (ii) constructing mathematical functions to connect the relations of the idealizing *relational structure* to relations of the *mathematical structure* so that the mathematical entities can represent the properties of the physical objects via the properties of the idealized objects.

Consider, as an example, the measurement system for length. In this case, the physical structure might be a group of straight rigid rods. People can manipulate those rods in various ways, including: (i) putting two rods next to each other with their ends flush to see which one extends beyond the other, and (ii) laying two rods end to end. The relational structure is a set of ideal rods whose members represent the rods in the physical structure together with the relations 'x is longer than y', which represents the physical relation of extending beyond, and 'z is the concatenation of x and y' which represents the physical operation of laying end to end. The axioms defining the relational structure include ' 'longer than' is transitive', 'concatenation is associative', and 'if A is longer than B, then the concatenation of A and C is longer than B'. The mathematical structure is the set of real numbers with the addition function and the greater-than relation.

The connection between the physical structure of rods and the relational structure of idealized rods is as follows. Each real rod is assigned an ideal rod. One lines up real rods A and B and determines whether A extends beyond B or B extends beyond A to determine whether the relation 'A is longer than B' holds in the relational structure between the ideal rods assigned to A and to B. One arranges real rods A and B end to end and the result is assigned a new ideal rod that is the concatenation of the ideal rods assigned to A and B. One lines up real rod A with the result of arranging B and C end to end to determine whether the relation 'A is longer than the concatenation of B and C' holds in the relational structure between the ideal rod assigned to A and to the concatenation of the ideal rods assigned to B and C.[8]

The connection between the relational structure and the mathematical structure consists of mathematical functions. For example, a function f assigns real numbers to the ideal rods in such a way that if A is longer than B then f(A) > f(B), and f(the concatenation of A and B) = f(A) + f(B). The function f assigns numbers to the ideal rods of the relational structure so that 'greater than' can represent 'longer than' and 'the concatenation of' can be represented by addition.

[8] Note that there are more ideal rods than physical rods—there is an ideal rod for the concatenation of any number of physical rods.

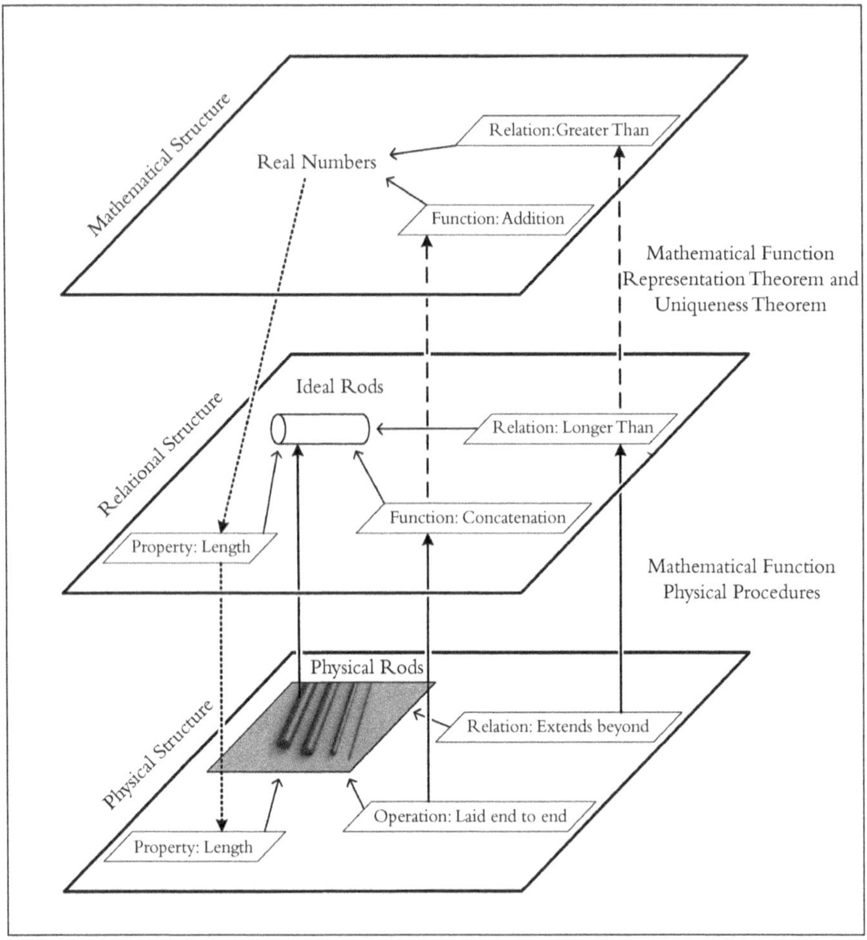

Figure 8 Measurement System for Length

In the case of length, numbers are assigned to the physical rods as their lengths by combining the connection between the physical rods and the ideal rods with the connection between the ideal rods and the real numbers. The real number assigned to an ideal rod represents the length of whatever the ideal rod models—either a physical rod or some concatenation of physical rods. Figure 8 has a diagram of the entire measurement system for length.

There are two crucial results for any measurement system: a representation theorem and a uniqueness theorem. A *representation theorem* says that there is a function from the relational structure to the mathematical structure that preserves the relations between the elements of the relational structure; e.g., a function f from the relational structure of rods, 'longer than', and concatenation to the real numbers so that rod x is longer than rod y iff $f(x) > f(y)$, and rod z is the concatenation of rods x and y iff $f(z) = f(x) + f(y)$. A *uniqueness theorem* specifies the class of relation-preserving functions from the relational structure to the mathematical structure; e.g., if f is one such function, then $f' = nf$ is another ($n>0$).

A major focus of measurement theory is in formulating conditions on relational structures that are necessary or sufficient to prove a representation theorem. The most basic kind of relational structure is an extensive structure. Let X be a set, $\succsim$ be a binary relation on X, and $^\circ$ be a closed binary operation on X. Then $\mathfrak{X} = \langle X, \succsim, ^\circ \rangle$, is an *extensive structure* iff for all $x, y, z \in X$:

(i) $\langle X, \succsim \rangle$ is a weak order [i.e., $\succsim$ is transitive and connected].
(ii) $^\circ$ is associative [i.e., $x \,^\circ\, (y \,^\circ\, z) = (x \,^\circ\, y) \,^\circ\, z)$].
(iii) $\succsim$ is monotonic with respect to $^\circ$ [i.e., $x \succsim y$ iff $x \,^\circ\, z \succsim y \,^\circ\, z$].
(iv) $\succsim$ is Archimedean with respect to $^\circ$ [i.e., if $x \succnsim y$, then there is an integer $n>0$ s.t. $y \,^\circ \ldots ^\circ\, y$ (n times) $\succsim x$].
(v) $\succsim$ is positive [i.e., $x \,^\circ\, y \succnsim x$].

With this definition in mind, we can state two important results about extensive structures (I omit the proofs).

Theorem 1: if X is an extensive structure, then there exists function ϕ from X to the real numbers such that for all $x, y \in X$:

(i) $x \succsim y$ iff $\phi(x) \geq \phi(y)$, and
(ii) $\phi(x \circ y) = \phi(x) + \phi(y)$.

Theorem 2: for any function ϕ that satisfies the conditions in Theorem 1, there is another, ψ, s.t. $\psi = n\phi$, where $n>0$.

Much of the work in measurement theory is spent generalizing these results. The generalizations take one of two forms: (i) formulating new conditions on relational structures (e.g., difference structures, conjoint structures, non-additive structures, non-Archimedean structures, non-transitive structures, non-commutative structures, partial structures), and (ii) considering new mathematical structures (e.g., non-standard reals, Euclidean spaces, vector spaces, metric spaces, topological spaces).

Symmetry is a central notion of measurement theory. A symmetry in the technical sense as it is used in science is an invariance under a collection of transformations—that is, something that is unchanged by the transformations. In our case, if $\mathfrak{X} = \langle X, R_1, \ldots, R_n \rangle$ is a relational structure and $\mathfrak{N} = \langle N, M_1, \ldots, M_n \rangle$ is a mathematical structure, then there are several kinds of transformations one might consider: (i) transformations that take members of Φ, the class of all structure-preserving functions (homomorphisms) from $\mathfrak{X}$ to $\mathfrak{N}$, to other members of Φ, (ii) structure preserving 1–1 transformations from $\mathfrak{N}$ onto $\mathfrak{N}$ (i.e., automorphisms of $\mathfrak{N}$), and (iii) structure preserving 1–1 transformations from $\mathfrak{X}$ onto $\mathfrak{X}$ (i.e., the automorphisms of $\mathfrak{X}$).

Recall that Φ is the class specified in a uniqueness theorem for the measurement system that includes $\mathfrak{X}$ and $\mathfrak{N}$, also known as the scale of measurement. It turns out that option (iii), the automorphisms of the relational structure, have special significance. First, no matter what the relational structure, its collection of automorphisms constitute a special kind of mathematical entity: a *group* with respect to the operation of functional composition.[9] One can prove many representation theorems by using considerations about the group of automorphisms of a relational structure.

In addition, one can use properties of the groups of automorphisms of relational structures to classify all the possible scale types (the classification scheme uses the properties of n-point homogeneity and n-point uniqueness). Below are some common scales:

(i) *Nominal* (simple labeling of items); e.g., Football jerseys, social security numbers.
(ii) *Ordinal* (simple ordering of items); e.g., Moh hardness, ordinal highway exits.
(iii) *Interval* (equal numerical intervals represent equal magnitudes of quantity; arbitrary zero); e.g., Celsius, Gregorian calendar, distance highway exits, utility.
(iv) *Ratio* (equal numerical intervals represent equal magnitudes of quantity; non-arbitrary zero); e.g., Kelvin, grams, meters, seconds.
(v) *Absolute* (equal numerical intervals represent equal magnitudes of quantity; non-arbitrary zero, non-arbitrary unit); e.g., counting, probability.

There is much more to be said about measurement theory and symmetry considerations, but we have enough background at this point.[10]

7.3 Davidson and measurement theory

Davidson's fundamental question is: what do rational entities have to be like in order for them to be able to interpret one another? In measurement theory, the fundamental question is: what does an physical structure have to be like in order for there to be a relational structure that has a structure-preserving mapping into the relevant mathematical structure? Davidson uses the analogy between interpretation (i.e., attributing beliefs, desires, and meanings to a rational entity) and measurement (i.e., assigning mathematical entities to physical entities) to give an answer to his fundamental question that is analogous to an answer to the fundamental question of measurement theory. Davidson's answer is that the

[9] A set G with a two-place operation $\circ$ is a *group* iff:

(i) G is closed under $\circ$
(ii) $\circ$ is associative
(iii) there is an element (identity) $e \in G$ s.t. for all $a \in G$, $a \circ e = e \circ a = a$ and
(iv) for all $a \in G$, there is an $a' \in G$ s.t. $a \circ a' = e$ [a' is the inverse of a, denoted 'a^{-1}'].

[10] For more information on measurement theory, see Suppes (1998) and Narens (2007) for an introduction and see Suppes et al (1971, 1989, 1990), and Narens (1986, 2002) for more advanced topics. See also Suppes (2002), which applies the framework of measurement theory to many scientific topics.

unified theory, which uses the axioms of probability to constrain degree of belief, the axioms of utility theory to constrain degree of desire, and the axioms of a Tarskian theory of truth to constrain meaning, describes what a rational agent's attitudes and linguistic competence have to be like in order for it to be interpretable by another.

Davidson appeals to this analogy throughout his career. Here is a representative passage:

I suggest that we think of formal semantic theories in analogy with theories of fundamental measurement. In a theory of fundamental measurement, there are one or more primitive concepts; in the case of the measurement of weight, for example, these may be the relation of one thing being at least as heavy as another and the operation of adding one thing to another (this is a function that maps two things on to their sum). These concepts are not defined, but before the theory can be applied to, or tested against, some collection of objects, a method for giving empirical content to the primitives must be indicated. (Thus *a* is at least as heavy as *b* if *a* does not go up in the pan of an equal-arm balance which holds *b* in the other pan.) A set of *axioms* then specifies the logical properties of the primitives and the entities to be measured. (So the axioms for weight will specify that the relation of being at least as heavy as is transitive, and that the sum of *a* and *b* is at least as heavy as the sum of *b* and *a*.)

The aim of the theory is to describe in precise terms the sort of structure a set of entities must have if we are to assign weights to them. If weights are to have the properties we intuitively expect, the axioms must be proven sufficient to account for these properties. One of the things we want to prove (*about* the theory, not *in* the theory) is a representation theorem, which states that numbers can be assigned to the objects covered by the theory in a way that keeps track of the relations in weight among the different objects. The second thing to be proven is a uniqueness theorem, which states that if one set of numbers represents the weights of objects, then any other set of numbers that is related to the first set by a certain kind of transformation will represent the weights just as well. In the case of weight, multiplication by any positive constant will transform one measure into another; weights in pounds are as good as weights in kilos.

Now let me compare a semantic theory for some speaker or group of speakers. Tarski's truth definitions, when modified to apply to natural languages, may be viewed as such theories. Like a theory for the measurement of weight, a semantic theory will place restrictions on one or more of primitive concepts. The most important primitive is that of truth.... The theory imposes a certain structure on any language it can describe; in giving the truth conditions of all the sentences of a language, it necessarily defines the logical relations among sentences.

We can think of such a theory as saying what is needed in order to understand a language; it describes what a speaker intuitively knows about his own language, and it can serve to interpret what such a speaker says. The adequacy of the theory for these purposes can be shown by demonstrating that one can represent the properties of the object language in some language one understands. Thus the theory serves to validate a translation manual. Just as we use numbers as a convenient way of keeping track of the weights of objects, we keep track of the semantic features of a language by using sentences we understand. What makes the numbers so suited to this job is that we know exactly what structure they have. In much the same way, the sentences of a language we understand have a known structure which we can use to understand other speakers.[11]

[11] Davidson (1997a: 130–2)

Here Davidson spells out the analogy between a measurement system for weight and the role of an axiomatic theory of truth in his unified theory. He is clear that what functions as the mathematical theory for the measurement system for rationality (i.e., the unified theory) is not a mathematical structure, but rather the structure provided by the interpreter's own language. The process the radical interpreter goes through is analogous to the proof of a representation theorem for this measurement system. That is, it proves that there is a certain kind of mapping from the relational structure that represents the rational agent's beliefs, desires, and meanings into the structure defined by the interpreter's sentences and their logical and empirical relations to one another. The mapping assigns a sentence of the interpreter's language to each of the rational agent's beliefs, the rational agent's desires, and the sentences of the rational agent's language. In other words, it shows that the beliefs, desires, and meanings of a rational agent can be represented by an interpreter's sentences.[12] The argument for the indeterminacy of interpretation is analogous to the proof of a uniqueness theorem for this measurement system. That is, it proves that for each mapping from the relational structure that represents the rational agent's beliefs, desires, and meanings into the structure defined by the interpreter's sentences, there are others that preserve all the relevant features of the relational system that represents the rational agent's beliefs, desires, and meanings. In other words, it shows that there are many equally good ways of assigning beliefs, desires, and meanings to a rational agent.

One might wonder: in what way does this provide us with a theory of the nature of truth?

Consider the following passage from Davidson:

The measurement of length, weight, temperature, or time depends (among many other things, of course) on the existence in each case of a two-place relation that is transitive and asymmetric: warmer than, later than, heavier than, and so forth. Let us take the relation *longer than* as our example. The law or postulate of transitivity is this:

(L) L(x, y) and L(y, z) $\rightarrow$ L(x, z)

[12] Davidson expands on this idea in the following passage from Davidson (1999a: 330–1):

My unified theory of belief, preferences, and meaning is a crude attempt at saying how these basic propositional attitudes are related. If this much is more or less right, then it should be possible to demonstrate that someone with normal human capacities might, in theory, worm his way into the pattern of attitudes of another thinking creature.

The "logical order of progression" I outlined that an interpreter could follow in the attempt to discover the attitudes of an agent was meant to constitute, as I said, a sort of informal proof that the pattern I had postulated had the desired properties. My model here was Ramsey's treatment of subjective probability and degree of belief. Ramsey defined a pattern he thought a rational agent's beliefs and preferences would reveal in the pattern of his or her choices. He then described a series of steps, that is, choices, which would prove that the patterns had the desired properties; in effect, he was proving an adequacy and representation theorem. It was not his idea that anyone should use this story as an experimental design, though much later various people, including me, tried (with indifferent success) to test the theory experimentally. No one supposes that in our ordinary dealings with people we undertake this series of steps to determine their subjective probabilities and relatives values.

Unless this law (or some sophisticated variant) holds, we cannot easily make sense of the concept of length. There will be no way of assigning numbers to register even so much as ranking in length, let alone the more powerful demands of measurement on a ratio scale. And this remark goes not only for any three items directly involved in an intransitivity: it is easy to show (given a few more assumptions essential to measurement of length) that there is no consistent assignment of a ranking to any item unless (L) holds in full generality.

Clearly (L) alone cannot exhaust the import of 'longer than'—otherwise it would not differ from 'warmer than' or 'later than'. We must suppose there is some empirical content, however difficult to formulate in the available vocabulary, that distinguishes 'longer than' from the other two-place transitive predicates of measurement and on the basis of which we may assert that one thing is longer than another. Imagine this empirical content to be partly given by the predicate '$O(x, y)$'. So we have this 'meaning postulate':

(M) $\quad O(x, y) \rightarrow L(x, y)$

that partly interprets (L). But now (L) and (M) together yield an empirical theory of great strength, for together they entail that there do not exist three objects *a*, *b*, and *c* such that $O(a, b)$, $O(b, c)$, and $O(c, a)$. Yet what is to prevent this happening if '$O(x, y)$' is a predicate we can ever, with confidence, apply? Suppose we *think* we observe an intransitive triad; what do we say? We could count (L) false, but then we would have no application for the concept of length. We could say (M) gives a wrong test for length; but then it is unclear what we thought was the *content* of the idea of one thing being longer than another. Or we could say that the objects under observation are not, as the theory requires, *rigid* objects. It is a mistake to think we are forced to accept some one of these answers. Concepts such as that of length are sustained in equilibrium by a number of conceptual pressures, and theories of fundamental measurement are distorted if we force the decision, among such principles as (L) and (M): analytic or synthetic. It is better to say the whole set of axioms, laws, or postulates for the measurement of length is partly constitutive of the idea of a system of macroscopic, rigid, physical objects.

Just as we cannot intelligibly assign a length to any object unless a comprehensive theory holds of objects of that sort, we cannot intelligibly attribute any propositional attitude to an agent except within the framework of a viable theory of his beliefs, desires, intentions, and decisions.[13]

For Davidson, the entire measurement system consisting of the three structures and the links between them is *constitutive* of the concepts involved. He uses the modifier 'partly', but that just leaves it open whether there are other constitutive principles as well. Just as it makes sense to think of the entire measurement system for length as constitutive of the concepts involved, the entire measurement system that comprises the unified theory of meaning, belief, and desire is constitutive of these concepts. For example, each of these aspects of the measurement system for length is constitutive of the concepts of length, longer than, concatenation, and rigid physical object. Attributing a single length to a single rigid object presupposes a measurement system for length whose elements are constitutive of the concepts of length and rigid object. Each of these aspects of the

[13] Davidson (1970: 220–1).

unified theory along with other principles involved in the whole measurement system for rationality (e.g., the principle of charity, the principle of continence, the principle of total evidence) are constitutive of the concepts of belief, desire, meaning, action, and rationality.

Others have picked up on Davidson's analogy between interpretation, rationalization, and the unified theory of meaning, belief, and desire on one hand and measurement systems on the other, including Robert Matthews' recent treatment, which focuses on propositional attitudes and semantics for propositional attitude attributions.[14] Much more can be said about the analogy, but this will do for my purposes.

7.4 The nature of ascending truth and descending truth

From the discussion in Chapter 1, it should be clear that most of those who offer views on the nature of truth take themselves to be offering conceptual analyses; of course, not all of them do—deflationists argue that no analysis is possible—but even deflationists often assume that their view is the only alternative to the philosophical analyses offered (e.g., correspondence theories, coherence theories, epistemic theories, and pragmatic theories). I think that it is outdated to expect that a proper philosophical theory of some concept ought to be an analysis. In the Introduction of this book I mentioned metrological naturalism as an alternative to conceptual analysis and other kinds of reductive explanations. That will be the kind of theory of ascending and descending truth I offer since I do not think that these concepts can be analyzed or reductively explained. It would be nice to have a detailed account of metrological naturalism beyond the basic dictum (i.e., cast a theory of some philosophical notion X in terms of a measurement system for X), and a comparison with other kinds of methodological naturalist views, but length considerations prevent it. Instead, this section is an exercise in this philosophical methodology, which will have to wait for future work for a full development.

Consider first the mathematical theories that constitute logical approaches to the aletheic paradoxes and their empirical interpretations that constitute philosophical approaches to the paradoxes (from Chapter 1). Philosophical approaches to the aletheic paradoxes do two things: they tell us something about the truth predicate that is relevant to solving the aletheic paradoxes (i.e., to pursuing one or more of the projects and solving one or more of the problems) and they tell us something about the paradoxical truth-bearers and the paradoxical reasoning. Logical approaches specify principles truth predicates obey and logics that are compatible with these principles. The theories of truth offered by logical approaches apply to certain artificial languages and these theorists use techniques from mathematical logic to investigate the properties of

[14] Matthews (2007, 2009); see also Green (1999), Dresner (2004, 2006, 2010a, 2010b), and Sassoon (2010).

these theories and prove things about them (e.g., consistency relative to a background mathematical theory).

In measurement-theoretic terms, the sections of Chapter 1 on philosophical and logical approaches are dedicated to investigating: (i) a physical structure—our practice of using the concept of truth, which includes how we use truth predicates of natural languages, (ii) relational structures—various precise principles truth predicates obey and other relevant principles (e.g., logical principles), which are studied for artificial languages, and (iii) mathematical structures—the mathematical models for artificial languages, truth predicates, principles of truth, and logics. Once we have this structure in view, it becomes clear that *philosophical approaches* to the paradoxes state conditions on relations between the physical structure and the relational structure; occasionally, they contain full-on specifications of the connection, other times we are left to guess. Either way, they tell us something about items in the physical structure (e.g., the syntactic, semantic, and pragmatic features of the truth predicate and the sentences that contain it) and its connection to the relational structure (e.g., how idealized truth predicates work in artificial languages that are meant to model natural languages). It also becomes clear that *logical approaches* specify (at least partial) relational structures, mathematical structures, and connections between them. Thus, the link between philosophical approaches and logical approaches *is* the link between the Physical–Relational connection and the Relational–Mathematical connection. Furthermore, a fully articulated combination approach to the aletheic paradoxes is a full-on measurement system for truth.

Finally, recall the distinction between the descriptive project (i.e., a theory of our aletheic practice as it is) and the prescriptive project (i.e., a theory of what our aletheic practice should be). Depending on one's diagnosis of the paradoxes, one might need two theories—a complete measurement theory for truth as we currently use it (i.e., a descriptive project) and a complete measurement theory for truth (or related notions) as we should use it (i.e., a prescriptive project).

According to metrological naturalism, a theory of ascending and descending truth ought to be a measurement theory for ascending truth and descending truth. Note that these two concepts are to be explained together given the connection between them (i.e., p is descending true iff p's negation is not ascending true). The physical structure is a natural language practice—that is, a group of rational entities that use a system of spoken and written symbols for communication, calculation, reasoning, record-keeping, and various other activities. The goal of the measurement system is to assign ascending truth values and descending truth values to the utterances in the practice.

The relational structure consists of ADT—the formal theory of ascending and descending truth, and a first-order artificial language of the type that is familiar in formal semantics and formal logic—it has an exactly specified syntax (e.g., it is decidable whether a given string is a well-formed formula of the language), logical vocabulary, and an ascending truth predicate and a descending truth predicate. This artificial language also has the ability to refer to its own syntax so it can construct sentences like ascending liars and descending liars.

The mathematical structure is the model theory of xeno semantics, which was described in the previous section. It consists of a domain of entities, a set of nodes (or worlds), and mathematical constructions on the set of nodes (e.g., the division between traditional and non-traditional, accessibility relations, and a neighborhood function).

The connection between the physical structure (the natural language) and the relational structure (ADT and the artificial language) is the usual one that linguists, logicians, and philosophers of language have studied for decades. Sentences of the natural language uttered in the linguistic practice are matched with sentences of the artificial language in such a way that the sentences of the artificial language are said to give the *logical form* of the sentences of the natural language. For example, the natural-language sentence 'all ravens are black' might be matched to the artificial language sentence '$(\forall x)(Rx \rightarrow Bx)$'.[15] This matching procedure is ridiculously complex and there are still many unresolved issues; nevertheless, it is the basis for all work in formal semantics.[16] Note that since most natural languages do not (yet!) have ascending and descending truth predicates, chances are that no sentences of the natural language will be matched to the sentences of the artificial language that contain an ascending truth predicate or a descending truth predicate.

The connection between the relational structure and the mathematical structure can be described in these terms. The linguistic expressions are represented by elements of the mathematical structure in the usual way; e.g., singular terms are assigned elements of the domain, predicates are assigned subsets of the domain, term functions are assigned functions from the domain to the domain, and so on. The focus of the last chapter was on how to represent the descending truth predicate, the ascending truth predicate, and the safety predicate. These are given an especially complex interpretation in the mathematical structure, which involves the nodes and the various constructions on the nodes in xeno semantics. The key to the representation of the relational structure is a definition of truth-in-a-model, which is used to show that a sentence of the artificial language is a theorem of the formal theory (in our case, ADT) only if every model that makes the axioms of ADT true also makes the sentence in question true. Notice that the soundness theorem in the appendix to Chapter 6 is a representation theorem for this measurement system—it says that the relational structure can be represented in the mathematical structure such that any derivation in the relational structure is valid in the mathematical structure. I have not provided a completeness proof, which would be somewhat akin to a uniqueness theorem; so, to that extent, the measurement system for ADT is incomplete and will have to await further work.[17]

[15] One might use some other formalism instead (e.g., interpreted logical forms); see Larson and Ludlow (1993).

[16] In Predelli (2005) there is a distinction between sentences uttered in the linguistic practice and clause/index pairs that are input for an interpretive system (more on this in the next chapter).

[17] Again, I am not confident that ADT is complete with respect to the class of acceptable xeno models. If it is not, then two questions arise: (i) what needs to be added to ADT to make it complete and (ii) what is ADT complete with respect to?

The assignment of ascending truth values and descending truth values goes as follows—'descending true' ends up being represented by a subset of the domain, which consists entirely of sentences of the artificial language. If a sentence of the natural language has one of these sentences as its logical form, then it is descending true. If not, then it is not descending true. Likewise for ascending truth.[18]

I want to make several points about this measurement system for ADT. First, let us say that our natural language does have words for ascending truth and descending truth. We know that we can assign descending truth values and ascending truth values to the sentences of that language without any inconsistencies since we can do that for the artificial language in the relational structure and our artificial language has no expressive limitations.

Second, one should think of the whole measurement system as an explanatory superstructure that fits over the natural linguistic practice in order to make sense of it. The entire measurement system should be fit according to some of the guiding principles already discussed. For example, ascending truth and descending truth should be as close as possible to truth—that is, the class of unsafe sentences should be made as small as possible. A result is that any sentence that contains no semantic vocabulary is safe. These principles guide the application of ADT to particular natural languages rather than appearing as specific axioms of ADT. As such, they function like the principle of charity in Davidson's unified theory.

Third, the entire measurement system for ascending and descending truth should be thought of as constitutive of these concepts (along with safety). This attitude fits perfectly with the claims made by Davidson about the elements of a measurement system being constitutive of the concepts in question. The account of constitutive principles given in Chapter 2 dovetails well with Davidson's talk of constitutivity in this context.

Fourth, Davidson thinks that a Tarskian axiomatic theory of truth serves as a meaning theory for a particular language. In Chapter 4, I argued that the choice of a Tarskian axiomatic theory is a poor one. Instead, ADT should occupy that slot in a Davidsonian unified theory. That is, the theory of ascending and descending truth serves as a meaning theory for a language. I provide the details in the next chapter.

[18] Note that although the ascending truth predicate and the descending truth predicate have normal semantics (i.e., extensions), the xeno semantics gives us a nice way of calculating what is in these sets.

8

Minimal Mutilation

When we replace a concept we have to reevaluate its connections to other concepts. For example, replacing the concept of mass had implications for how to understand force, momentum, energy, etc. Our concept of truth is a popular explanans—predication, reference, validity, meaning, knowledge, and assertion are all closely related to truth, and popular theories of these concepts explain them by appeal to truth. What is an inconsistency theorist to say about these theories?

For any given concept X that is customarily explained in terms of truth by a theory T, we have several options for a new theory T′ of X:

(i) X is conceptually tied to one of the replacements (but not the other). *Strategy*: replace 'true' in T by just one of the replacement predicates to get theory T′. *Example*: proof.

(ii) X is conceptually tied to each of the replacements. *Strategy*: replace 'true' in T by one of the replacement predicates to get one theory, T′, and replace 'true' in T by the other to get another theory, T′′. *Example*: inquiry.

(iii) X is conceptually tied to both of the replacements. *Strategy*: reformulate T in terms of some combination of the replacement predicates to get theory T′. *Examples*: objectivity, belief, and meaning.

(iv) X is not conceptually tied to either of the replacements. *Strategy*: explain X in some other way. *Examples*: assertion, knowledge, and validity.

(v) X is inconsistent as well. *Strategy*: if X is useful, then it too should be replaced, and one should search for theories T′, T′′,... linking X's replacements with truth's replacements. *Examples*: predication and reference.

Perhaps there are other options as well, but these seem to be the primary ones. In this section, there are examples of each of these five options. The discussion in this chapter should answer many questions about what happens to our conceptual scheme after the aletheic revolution. Note that each of these topics is complex, subtle, and has a vast literature; this discussion should be treated as a first step rather than the final word.

8.1 Proof

As our first example, consider the concept of proof. There is a remarkably complex mathematical theory of proof that I am not going to consider.[1] However, there is also the intuitive principle that if a proposition or sentence is proven, then it is true. The converse is obviously incorrect since there are many truths yet to be proven. Moreover, even the weaker 'if a proposition or sentence is true, then it is provable' has to be rejected because of Gödel's incompleteness theorem.[2] Nevertheless, we should consider what happens to our intuitive principle of proof:

(Proof) If a sentence or proposition is proven, it is true.

We might consider replacing 'true' in (Proof) by 'descending true'. However, we have ready-made counterexamples to the resulting principle. For example, ADT proves that descending liars (i.e., sentences that say of themselves that they are not descending true) are ascending true and not descending true. However, that the descending liar is not descending true is the content of the descending liar itself. Thus, ADT proves the descending liar (and proves that it is not descending true). Therefore, proven items need not be descending true.

Instead, we might try ascending truth. The resulting principle would be:

(Proof-A) If a sentence or proposition is proven, it is ascending true.

This principle is fine, and it follows from the definition of ascending truth. That is, if some theory T proves p, then given the definition of ascending truth, it also proves that p is ascending true. Therefore, we should use (Proof-A) as our conceptual connection between proof and the replacement concepts.

8.2 Inquiry

Many people take truth to be a goal of inquiry. I say 'a goal' instead of 'the goal' because there are many other goals as well, and truth, by itself, is never thought to be sufficient to justify inquiry. For example, one could inquire into whether there will be a prime number of Homo sapiens alive at the beginning of the next leap second, but that hardly seems like a worthwhile inquiry, even if it did produce something true.

Michael Lynch formulates the connection between truth and inquiry as:

(Inquiry) Other things being equal, true beliefs are a worthy goal of inquiry.[3]

[1] See Troelstra and Schwichtenberg (2000), Hendricks (2000), and Restall (MS) for more on proof theory.

[2] It is actually a much more technical version of this claim that is ruled out by Gödel's theorem, but the details do not matter for my purposes here. See Boolos, Burgess, and Jeffrey (2002) and Smith (2007) and for discussion.

[3] Lynch (2009: Ch. 1).

Instead of having to choose between an ascending reading of this principle and a descending reading, we can endorse both of them. That is, each of the following principles is acceptable:

(Inquiry-A) Other things being equal, ascending true beliefs are a worthy goal of inquiry.

(Inquiry-D) Other things being equal, descending true beliefs are a worthy goal of inquiry.

Of course, if a belief is descending true, then it is ascending true. However, neither is sufficient to justify an inquiry (for reasons given above). Moreover, some unsafe sentences are a worthy goal of inquiry, so it is wrong to say that any worthy inquiry results in descending true beliefs. I suppose that means I am reading a lot into the *ceteris paribus* clauses of these principles. Either way, from my perspective, the concept of inquiry is a good example of one for which option (ii) is appropriate.

8.3 Objectivity

The third option is that we might be able to reformulate the philosophical theory in question in terms of ascending truth *and* descending truth. There are several examples of this: objectivity, belief, and meaning.

The case of objectivity is extremely complex and I would like to discuss the relation between ascending and descending truth and Crispin Wright's views on objectivity, but I do not have the space.[4] Instead, consider the principle Michael Lynch presents:

(Objectivity) The belief that ϕ is true iff with respect to the belief that ϕ, things are as they are believed to be.[5]

Here we cannot just keep the same principle but substitute 'ascending true' or 'descending true' for 'true'. The problem is that 'the belief that ϕ is ascending true iff, with respect to the belief that ϕ, things are as they are believed to be' is unacceptable since the left-to-right direction fails, while 'the belief that ϕ is descending true iff, with respect to the belief that ϕ, things are as they are believed to be' is unacceptable because the right-to-left direction fails. Instead, we can have:

(Objectivity-A) The belief that ϕ is ascending true *if* with respect to the belief that ϕ, things are as they are believed to be.

(Objectivity-D) The belief that ϕ is descending true *only if*, with respect to the belief that ϕ, things are as they are believed to be.

Note that these are merely reformulations of the constitutive principles for ascending truth and descending truth, respectively. Once we split the original biconditional into its

[4] Wright (1992, 2003). [5] Lynch (2009: Ch. 1).

two component conditionals, we can reformulate each one as a legitimate principle connecting objectivity to a replacement concept.

8.4 Belief

Another principle Lynch emphasizes is:

(Norm of Belief) It is prima facie correct to believe that ϕ iff the proposition that ϕ is true.[6]

Again, substituting in 'ascending true' or 'descending true' does not work. There are ascending true propositions that it is not prima facie correct to believe (e.g., the ascending liar and the negation of the descending liar), and there are propositions it is prima facie correct to believe that are not descending true (e.g., the descending liar and the negation of the ascending liar). Instead, try:

(Norm of Belief-A) It is prima facie correct to believe that ϕ *only if* the proposition that ϕ is ascending true.

(Norm of Belief) It is prima facie correct to believe that ϕ *if* the proposition that ϕ is descending true.

Again, once we split the biconditional into its component conditionals, we can formulate acceptable principles linking the original concept to the replacement concepts.

8.5 Meaning

The connection between meaning and truth is our third example of option (iii). This topic has come up throughout the book, and encapsulates perhaps the most important explanatory function of truth. There is a huge debate in linguistics and philosophy of language about the extent to which sentences have invariant meanings and the extent to which truth conditions constitute these meanings (if anything does).[7] It is my view that there is a coming revolution in philosophy of language caused by the realization—which is already a dominant view in linguistics—that dynamic semantic theories have tremendous explanatory advantages over their static brethren, and once one makes the transition to dynamic semantics, it is not clear what place truth conditions have in explaining meaning any more.[8] Despite the potentially revolutionary consequences this change will bring for issues in philosophy of language, few, if any philosophers of

[6] Lynch (2009: Ch. 1).

[7] See Davidson (1967, 1973, 1982, 1986, 1992, 1997b), Carston (1988, 2002, 2008, 2009), Bar-On, Horisk, and Lycan (2000), Recanati (2002, 2004, 2007, 2008, 2010), King (2003), Cappelen and Lepore (2003), Stanley (2005), Predelli (2005), Lepore and Ludwig (2007), Travis (2008), and Cappelen and Hawthorne (2009) for discussion.

[8] For discussion of dynamic semantic theories, see Kamp (1981), Heim (1983), Groenendijk and Stakhof (1991), Beaver (2001), and Dekker (2010).

language seem to have paid it much attention. Nevertheless, in this section I will consider only the traditional and relatively uncontroversial (in philosophy) claim:

(Meaning) The proffered content of a sentence uttered (plus perhaps other contextually determined parameters) determines its truth conditions.[9]

Again, it does not seem that simply substituting 'ascending truth' or 'descending truth' would result in a satisfying theory, since each of those would leave something out (namely, the other). Instead, we need something more complex like:

(Meaning-AD) The proffered content of a sentence uttered (plus perhaps other contextually determined parameters) determines its ascending truth conditions and its descending truth conditions.

The main idea is that instead of a single set of conditions (i.e., truth conditions), meaning is explained in terms of dual conditions (i.e., the conditions under which the sentence is ascending true and the conditions under which the sentence is descending true). Of course, for the vast majority of sentences (i.e., all the safe ones), their ascending truth conditions and their descending truth conditions will be the same, so the new principle will not have much effect on them. However, the change makes a huge difference when it comes to sentences like liars. It is impossible for standard truth-conditional theories of meaning to assign truth conditions to liar sentences—trying to do so results in an inconsistent theory. However, together with the claim that 'true' is assessment-sensitive (coming up in Chapter 9) and the theory of the replacement concepts (ADT), (Meaning-AD) can easily account for the meanings of liar sentences, even contingently paradoxical ones. Moreover, (Meaning-AD) works for ascending liars and descending liars as well. In the rest of this section, I consider two related issues—how to use ascending and descending truth to give an account of classical expressibility delimiters (CEDs) and how to use ascending and descending truth in formal semantics.

Recall that in Chapter 4 I mentioned Lionel Shapiro's idea of a CED and its role in revenge objections. The notion of *being* G is a *classical expressibility-delimiter* for the language L just in case we get all instances (for 'H') of the following:

If a formula f(x) expresses the notion of being H, then for all names n in L:

(ia) If f(n) is G, then the referent of n is H.
(ib) If the referent of n is H, then f(n) is G.
(iia) If ¬f(n) is G, then the referent of n is not H.
(iib) If the referent of n is not H, then ¬f(n) is G.

Despite the fact that neither ascending truth nor descending truth serve as a CED by itself, one can show that, together, they can serve as an expressibility delimiter for a language L, since we get all instances of the following:

[9] The parenthetical addition is meant to accommodate non-indexical contextualism and assessment-sensitivity views (see below).

If a formula f(x) expresses the notion of being H, then for all names n in L:

(ia) If f(n) is descending true, then the referent of n is H.
(ib) If the referent of n is H, then f(n) is ascending true.
(iia) If ¬f(n) is descending true, then the referent of n is not H.
(iib) If the referent of n is not H, then ¬f(n) is ascending true.

Although I am not convinced that CEDs are of much use in dealing with natural languages, they are helpful in dealing with artificial languages, and we do not have to give this up when we replace truth.

In the rest of this subsection, I describe in detail another aspect of the connection between meaning and ascending and descending truth by showing how to do semantics with these replacements for truth. *Please note well*: this is not just an illuminating exercise—I use this framework in Chapter 9 when I offer an assessment-sensitive semantic theory for our inconsistent concept of truth.

I am going to assume that the reader has some familiarity with formal semantics in the Montogovian and Kaplanian traditions. Because there is little agreement on the terminology, especially when it comes to more contentious views like non-indexical contextualism and assessment-sensitivity, this presentation follows the recent and influential treatment of formal semantics for natural language by Stefano Predelli.[10] Although any presentation of this topic is bound to generate controversy, I do not think that the details matter—I could have used any recent account.

Predelli is careful to distinguish between a *linguistic practice*, which consists of rational entities making noises and inscriptions in the course of their interactions with other rational entities, and an *interpretive system*, which is used as a tool by natural-language semanticists to explain the semantic properties of those noises and inscriptions. On Predelli's view, there is a layer of processing that occurs between the linguistic practice and the interpretive system. For this reason, interpretive systems do not take natural-language sentences as input; instead, their inputs are complex structures that result from disambiguating sentences. I use Predelli's neutral term 'clause' for these items.[11] In addition, the interpretive system needs information about the context of utterance (for context-dependent expressions). Again, following Predelli, I use the term 'index' for the information that gets fed into the interpretive system, and 'context' for the concrete environment in which the utterance is performed.[12] Just as interpretive systems accept only specific inputs, they produce special outputs. The goal is assigning truth conditions to sentences uttered in the linguistic practice, but there is an additional level of complexity between the output of the interpretive system and the assignment of truth conditions. Instead, the interpretive system outputs *t-distributions*, which are assignments of

[10] Predelli (2005).

[11] Some theorists deny that there is a distinction between clauses (i.e., inputs to a formal semantic theory) and natural-language expressions—nothing in my treatment hangs on it.

[12] Note that contexts in this sense can be modeled using standard pragmatic theories discussed earlier in Chapters 1 and 3; see Stalnaker (1970, 1974, 1978, 1998), Lewis (1979), and Roberts (1996, 2004, 2010).

truth values to clause/index pairs (or propositions) relative to points of evaluation. The points of evaluation contain information like a possible world and a time.

In order to accommodate the assessment-sensitivity view of 'true' proposed in Chapter 9, we need to distinguish between a presemantic theory, a semantic theory and a postsemantic theory.[13] Interpretive systems are semantic theories—they take clause/index pairs as input and produce t-distributions as output. *Presemantic* theories take natural-language utterances as input and produce clause/index pairs are output. Thus presemantic theories relate natural-language utterances to semantic theory inputs. *Postsemantic* theories take t-distributions as input and produce truth values and truth conditions for natural-language utterances. Hence, postsemantic theories relate semantic theory outputs to natural-language utterances. In sum, we begin with a natural-language utterance, run it through a presemantic theory to arrive at a clause/index pair, then use a semantic theory to compute a t-distribution for that clause/index pair, and finally use a postsemantic theory on that t-distribution to generate truth conditions and a truth value for the natural-language utterance with which we began. See Figure 9 for a handy diagram.

Again, the terminology here is controversial. The distinction between semantic theory and postsemantic theory is *not* the distinction between a theory of linguistic content and a theory of pragmatic phenomena like implicature. Rather, the distinction between semantic theory and postsemantic theory is within the realm of linguistic content. It is required by any theory that distinguishes the proposition expressed by a sentence (or the content of a linguistic expression) and the truth conditions of a sentence (or the extension of a linguistic expression). As I use the terms, propositions and contents are assigned by a semantic theory, and truth conditions and extensions are assigned by a postsemantic theory, which takes as input propositions and contents together with information from the context of utterance (e.g., world) and possibly the context of assessment. Many people use 'semantic theory' to cover the totality of what I am calling presemantic theory, semantic theory, and postsemantic theory. However, nothing of substance turns on this terminological difference.

Let us now look at intensional semantic theories, which assign truth values to propositions. Following Kaplan, we distinguish between two levels in the semantic theory.[14] At the first level, expressions are assigned a character, while, at the second level, the character/index pair is assigned a content. The output of the intensional semantic theory is an assignment of an extension to this content at every point of evaluation (in the case of sentences, their contents are propositions and their extensions are truth values). As such we can think of characters as functions from indexes to contents, and we can think of contents as functions from points of evaluation to extensions. See Figure 10 for a diagram.

The output of an intensional semantics (a t-distribution) is an assignment of truth values to contents at points of evaluation. To get from this to a truth value and a truth condition for the utterance in question, we need a postsemantic theory. It is standard to use something like:

13 I get the term 'presemantic' from Perry (2001) and 'postsemantic' from MacFarlane (2003).

14 See Kaplan (1989).

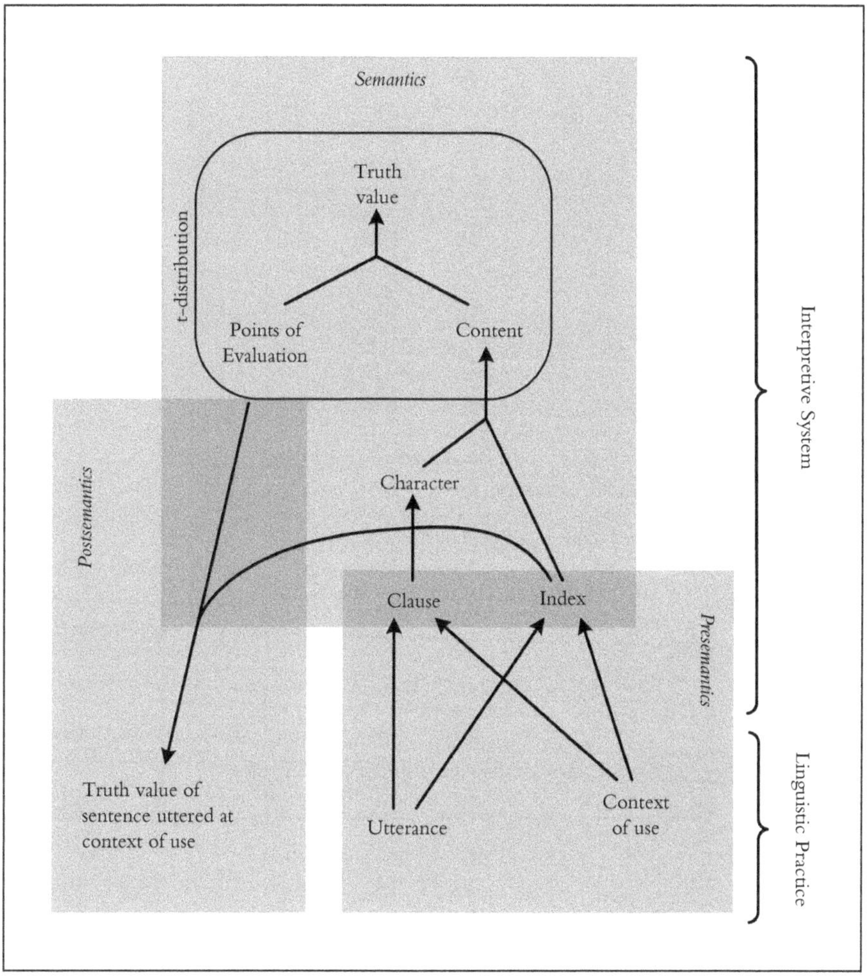

Figure 9 Presemantic, Semantic, and Postsemantic Theories

(1) A sentence p is true at a context c iff the content assigned to the clause that represents p with respect to the index that represents c is true at the point of evaluation that represents the world and time of c.

Note that we have defined clause truth at an index in terms of the output of the semantic theory—in this case, it is content truth at a point of evaluation (more on this below).

After that brief introduction, we are ready to consider how to replace truth with ascending truth and descending truth in this framework. The concept of truth plays

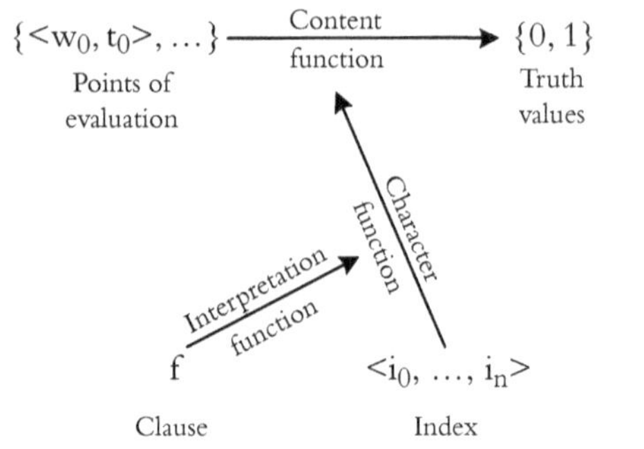

Clause: a formula of some logical calculus

Index: n-tuple of information from the context of utterance

Point of evaluation: world/time pair

Interpretation: function from clauses to characters

Character: function from indices to contents

Content: function from points to truth values

Figure 10 Intensional Semantics

no role in the presemantics, so it is fine. The semantics assigns truth values to contents as points of evaluation and the postsemantics provides a recursive definition of 'sentence x is true in a context of use' or 'sentence x is true in a context of use from a context of assessment' (depending on whether one admits assessment-sensitive expressions). I claim that truth is not really playing a role in the semantics, but it is in the postsemantics.

Begin with the postsemantics. Although the notions of truth at a context of use or truth at a context of use from a context of assessment are distinct from the concept of truth (i.e., the latter is monadic, while the former two are polyadic), they are still susceptible to paradox. In particular consider the following sentences:

(2) For all contexts of use u, (2) is not true in u.

(3) For all contexts of use u and for all contexts of assessment a, (3) is not true in u from a.

These are both paradoxical (indeed, (2) is routinely used in revenge paradoxes for context dependence approaches to the paradoxes).[15] This is good evidence that these concepts are inconsistent (I am not going to argue this point further).

In order to avoid using a postsemantic theory that appeals to inconsistent concepts, we need a new postsemantic theory. There are two obvious ways to do this:

(i) a postsemantic theory that takes as input the t-distribution from a semantic theory (whatever that turns out to be) and outputs sentence ascending truth in a context of use and descending truth in a context of use.

(ii) a postsemantic theory that takes as input the t-distribution from a semantic theory (whatever that turns out to be) and outputs sentence ascending truth in a context of use from a context of assessment and sentence descending truth in a context of use from a context of assessment.

If a language contains no assessment-sensitive terms at all, then (i) will be fine; otherwise, (ii) is appropriate.

Note that these theories make use of predicates that we have not seen yet: 'x is ascending true in context u', 'x is descending true in context u', 'x is ascending true in context u from context a', and 'x is descending true in context u from context a'. ADT, the theory of ascending and descending truth, is a theory of the 1–place predicates, 'x is ascending true', and 'x is descending true'; thus, ADT does not serve as a theory of these new polyadic predicates. Although it might be helpful to develop a formal theory of them, I am not going to do so here. Note that one need not adopt a formal theory of 'x is true in context u' to be able to use it in semantics for natural language. For example, John MacFarlane appeals to theories of assertion to help readers understand 'x is true in context u from context a', but he does not give even an intuitive theory of it, much less a formal theory.[16] From what has been said so far about ascending truth and descending truth, these new predicates should not pose any real problems in understanding. At worst, one would have to say that they are implicitly defined by the postsemantic theory in question.

So much for replacing truth in the postsemantics; what about the semantic theory? A semantic theory outputs a t-distribution, which is an assignment of a truth value to a proposition at each point of evaluation. Does this use of truth need to be replaced as well? I do not think so. If we look at the way the semantic theory works, we can see that it is powered by truth-in-a-model, not truth. Truth-in-a-model is a mathematical concept, and it is not the same as truth. For discussion, fix a model $\mathfrak{M}$. The claim that some clause is true-in-$\mathfrak{M}$ is fully representable in set theory as a mathematical function from one set-theoretic entity to another. As long as the relevant mathematical theory (e.g., ZFC) is consistent (and we have no reason to think it is not), there is no problem whatsoever with truth-in-$\mathfrak{M}$. It is not an inconsistent concept.

[15] See Juhl (1997). In addition, (3) can be used to generate a revenge paradox for someone like Billon (2011).

[16] MacFarlane (2005a).

Still, one might ask, what about paradoxes with truth-in-$\mathfrak{M}$? As long as our language has the relevant mathematical locutions, we can formulate a sentence like:

(4) (4) is not true-in-$\mathfrak{M}$.[17]

However, there is no reason to think that (4) is paradoxical. For one, (T-In) and (T-Out) fail for 'true-in-$\mathfrak{M}$'. That is, there is no reason to think that 'p is true-in-$\mathfrak{M}$' follows from p since there is no reason to think that p is even representable in the language for which $\mathfrak{M}$ is a model, and, even if it is representable, there is no reason to think that p would be true-in-$\mathfrak{M}$. For example, $\mathfrak{M}$ might assign some bizarre meaning to p. In addition, 'p is true-in-$\mathfrak{M}$' does not entail p since there is no reason to think that $\mathfrak{M}$ represents the way the world is. Obviously, representing the world is the notion that would be needed to get (T-Out), but the semantics does not appeal to it. What about sentences like:

(5) For all $\mathfrak{M}$, (5) is not true-in-$\mathfrak{M}$?

Does (5) pose a problem? No. Quantifying over set-theoretic entities is complicated business, and explaining why (5) is benign would take us too far afield into the technical details of mathematical logic. It should be sufficient to note that (5) is a mathematical claim, pure and simple. As long as set theory (ZFC will do) is consistent, we know that (5) does not pose a problem.

Still, a question remains: how do we get from a t-distribution (as the output of the semantic theory) to an assignment of ascending truth conditions and descending truth conditions? There are a couple of ways to accomplish this: (i) add an extra slot to the points of evaluation that selects whether we are evaluating the proposition in question for ascending truth or descending truth, or (ii) define ascending-truth-in-a-model and descending-truth-in-a-model and assign values for each independently to each proposition (e.g., assign either 0 or 1 for the ascending-truth-in-a-model value and either 2 or 3 for the descending-truth-in-a-model value). Although (ii) is more elegant and probably the correct way to proceed, it would require a lengthy detour through the semantics for ADT (from the Appendix to Chapter 6); it would also treat a proposition as a *relation* between the set of points of evaluation *and* $\{0, 1, 2, 3\}$ instead of as a *function* from the set of points of evaluation *to* $\{0, 1\}$, which would need some discussion. So, in this treatment, I follow the vulgar but accessible option (i), and leave (ii) for future work.

The extra parameter to be added to the points of evaluation has only two possible values: A or D. At the point of evaluation $<w_0, t_0, A>$, where w_0 and t_0 are some world and some time, the proposition in question is assigned 0 if it is not ascending true at w_0 and t_0, and it is assigned 1 if it is ascending true at w_0 and t_0. At the point of evaluation $<w_0, t_0, D>$, the proposition in question is assigned 0 if it is not descending true at w_0

[17] Actually, this is harder than it seems. It is difficult to construct a model for a language that makes one of the singular terms in that language refer to that model. The problem comes in letting the model be a member of the domain that is an element in that very model.

and t_0, and it is assigned 1 if it is descending true at w_0 and t_0. I call this parameter the *aletheic value parameter*. The aletheic value parameter is used by the postsemantic theory. To arrive at the ascending truth value for the sentence uttered, one uses the point of evaluation with the relevant world, relevant time, and the ascending aletheic value. To arrive at the descending truth value for the sentence uttered, one uses the point of evaluation with the relevant world, relevant time, and the descending aletheic value.[18]

In sum, I have shown how to replace truth with ascending truth and descending truth in (one strand of) contemporary semantics. I have suggested that truth should be replaced in the postsemantic theory with ascending truth and descending truth; that is, the postsemantic theory outputs the ascending truth value of the sentence uttered in the context of use and the descending truth value of the sentence uttered in the context of use. Accordingly, the points of evaluation have an extra parameter—the aletheic value parameter—which controls whether the proposition in question is being evaluated for ascending truth or descending truth.

8.6 Assertion

Option (iv) is to deny that the concept in question is linked to either of the replacements. As our first example of this option, consider assertion. Option (iv) works well in cases where the deflationist response to explanatory challenges works well. However, in the rest, it does not. Moreover, one can use option (iv) even in cases where the deflationist response fails, like the case of assertion. One of the principles taken to be a platitude by Crispin Wright is:

(Assertion) To assert something is to present it as true.[19]

We cannot simply insert 'ascending' or 'descending' into this principle and arrive at an acceptable result. Ascending truth is too lax since it would permit the assertion of the ascending liar and the negation of the ascending liar since both of these are ascending true (only the negation of the ascending liar should count as assertible since only it is a consequence of ADT). On the other hand, descending truth is too strong since it would not permit the assertion of the descending liar even though the descending liar is provable from ADT. The problem is that the descending liar is assertible but not descending true. Moreover, it is not clear that one could define assertibility in terms of the two replacement concepts together.

[18] One might wonder about the relation between this Kaplanian theory of meaning that invokes possible worlds, and the Davidsonian approach to meaning described in the previous chapter; especially since these theories are usually taken to be rivals. The short answer is that I see Davidson's views on the role of a theory of meaning in a theory of rationality as the fundamental structure and his choice of a Tarskian theory as the basis for a theory of meaning can be rejected in favor of a Kaplanian theory without giving up the overall structure.

[19] Wright (1992: 24). See Williamson (1996, 2000a), DeRose (2002), Engel (2002), Pagin (2007), and the papers in Brown and Cappelen (2011) for discussion.

It seems to me that the right way to define assertibility is in two stages. First, for safe sentences—remember, all sentences that do not contain 'ascending true', 'descending true', or similar vocabulary are safe—either ascending truth or descending truth is fine since they are coextensive over these sentences. However, for unsafe sentences (notice that these caused the problems in the previous paragraph), assertibility should be defined in terms of consequences of ADT. In particular, if ADT proves p, then p is assertible (or, perhaps: if for any acceptable xeno model $\mathfrak{M}$, $\mathfrak{M} \models$ p, then p is assertible). From these principles, it follows that the ascending liar is not assertible (though its negation is) and the descending liar is assertible (though its negation is not), just as it should be.

One might think that there are revenge paradoxes formulated in terms of assertibility lurking here. However, given my definition of assertibility for claims involving ascending or descending truth, the assertible sentences are a subset of those that are either descending true or positive unsafe. And in Chapter 6, I argued that the attempt to find a revenge paradox using 'x is not descending true or positive unsafe' fails. There are a host of other issues in this neighborhood, but I cannot address them here.

8.7 Knowledge

As another instance of option (iv), consider knowledge.[20] Much ink has been spilled on the topic of whether Plato was right that knowledge is justified true belief;[21] moreover, there has been a considerable amount of recent interest in the so-called *knowledge first* movement, which takes knowledge to be a primitive concept incapable of being defined or analyzed.[22] However, in this subsection, I restrict my attention to the Justified True Belief (JTB) analysis of knowledge:

(JTB) S knows that $\phi =_{df}$ S believes that ϕ, S's belief that ϕ is justified, and $\langle\phi\rangle$ is true.

It would not work to replace 'true' with 'descending true'. The problem is that I know that ascending liars and descending liars are ascending true and not descending true. However, 'ascending liars and descending liars are ascending true and not descending true' is not descending true—it is ascending true. So replacing 'true' in (JTB) with 'descending true' results in a theory that is too strong. On the other hand, it does not work to replace 'true' with 'ascending true'. The problem in this case is that the analysis no longer implies that knowledge is factive; that is, it could be that S believes that ϕ, S's

[20] Some have suggested that knowledge is also an inconsistent concept, and it might well be. The paradox of the knower (see Kaplan and Montague (1960)), Fitch's paradox (see Fitch (1963)), and epistemological skepticism (see Schiffer (1996) and Weiner (2009)) might be considered independent evidence that knowledge is an inconsistent concept. However, I ignore this view for the purposes of this subsection.

[21] Plato (1961); see Gettier (1963) for criticism.

[22] See Williamson (2000a).

belief that ϕ is justified, and $\langle\phi\rangle$ is ascending true, but $\sim\phi$ (e.g., if $\langle\phi\rangle$ = the ascending liar).[23] So the result is too weak.

Instead, I claim that we can easily update (JTB) so that it is compatible with our new conceptual scheme. Consider:

(JFB) S knows that $\phi =_{df}$ S believes that ϕ, S's belief that ϕ is justified, and ϕ.

The 'F' in 'JFB' stands for 'factive'. Here we just replaced '$\langle\phi\rangle$ is true' with 'ϕ'. The resulting theory works just as well as the JTB theory, but does not rely on the inconsistent concept of truth.

This kind of move is familiar in the face of explanatory inadequacy objections to deflationism, which say that a deflationist about truth cannot account for truth's explanatory role in theories of other concepts. Deflationists often respond to these objections by saying that 'true' does not play an explanatory role in these theories—it is merely serving its expressive role.[24] That is roughly my point, but caution is in order when making this sort of move. Substituting p for 'p is true' in JTB is unobjectionable, but it would be wrong to substitute 'p' for 'the belief that p is true' in (Objectivity) above since the left-to-right reading of the resulting principle would imply that we believe everything that is the case. The lesson is that deciding what happens to a concept's connections to other concepts post-revolution is to be decided largely on a case-by-case basis.

8.8 Validity

The following is a commonly held principle connecting truth and validity:

(Valid) An argument is valid iff, necessarily, it is truth-preserving.

We have seen that this principle is incompatible with every logical approach to the aletheic paradoxes except for, perhaps, the substructural ones, so we should not worry if we cannot make room for some variant of it in our new conceptual scheme. Of course, we would still want a theory of validity, but that is another issue.

In Chapter 6, I claimed that validity cannot be defined in terms of either ascending truth or descending truth alone. That is, the class of valid arguments is not identical to the class of those that are necessarily ascending truth-preserving, nor is it identical to the class of arguments that are necessarily descending truth-preserving. Therefore, neither option (i) nor option (ii) will work in this case. Moreover, I have been unable to find a way of defining validity in terms of a combination of ascending truth and descending truth, so I have been unable to implement option (iii). Nevertheless, in the previous section, I argued that we have a perfectly acceptable notion of truth-in-a-model, which is a

[23] I am not convinced that an analysis of knowledge should imply that the proffered content of 'S knows that p' is factive since factivity projects in these cases and that indicates that it might be a presupposition. However, this is not the place to fight this battle.

[24] See M. Williams (1999) for an example.

mathematical concept not subject to aletheic paradoxes. Using it, we can define validity in the standard way using Kreisel's squeezing argument. Thus, we already have a definition of validity that does not depend on truth, ascending truth, or descending truth.[25]

Before moving on, I should mention the possibility of option (v) for validity. That is, one might think that validity is an inconsistent concept and so should be replaced if it is deemed useful and its inconsistency impedes its utility. The reason one might think the concept of validity is inconsistent concerns a paradox about validity that stems from the following innocuous-looking principle (where 'Valid' is a two-place predicate and '$\vdash$' is the derivability operator):

(Schema V) $\vdash \text{Valid}(\langle\phi\rangle, \langle\psi\rangle)$ iff $\phi \vdash \psi$.

This principle says that the argument with premise $\langle\phi\rangle$ and conclusion $\langle\psi\rangle$ is valid iff $\langle\psi\rangle$ is derivable from $\langle\phi\rangle$.[26] To deny this principle would be to hold that some single-premise argument is valid even though its conclusion is not derivable from its premise or that one sentence is derivable from another even though the argument with the latter as premise and the former as conclusion is not valid. It should not come as a surprise that neither of these options is remotely plausible in my view. The problem with (Schema V) is that one can derive a contradiction from it by reflecting on the following sentence:

(6) The argument whose only premise is (6) and whose conclusion is $\perp$ is valid.[27]

On the one hand, I find this paradox to be compelling evidence that the concept of validity is inconsistent, but I also find the squeezing argument compelling as well, and the latter indicates that there is a close relationship between our informal notion of validity and a mathematical notion of validity. I do not, however, think that the mathematical notion of validity is inconsistent. Moreover, even if the concept of validity that has (Schema V) as a constitutive principle is inconsistent, it is not obvious that its replacements would have any connection to ascending truth and descending truth—they might, but they might not. Unfortunately, I cannot pursue this issue here, and I leave it for future work.

8.9 Predication

We have seen examples of the first four options; in this subsection, I suggest that we should pursue option (v) for the case of predication—that is, it seems to me that predication is an inconsistent concept that should be replaced.

[25] Kreisel (1972); see also Smith (2007, 2011) and Field (2008a: Ch. 2) for discussion.

[26] It is actually a bit difficult to put into English because the single turnstile is an operator—my gloss treats it as a predicate. I suppose we could say instead that an argument with premise $\langle\phi\rangle$ and conclusion $\langle\psi\rangle$ is valid iff ϕ proof theoretically entails ψ. However, that does not seem all that perspicuous either.

[27] See Beall and Murzi (forthcoming) for a clear presentation of this paradox.

Here is a common principle tying predication (or truth-of) to truth:

(Predication) A subject-predicate sentence 'Ga' is true iff 'G' is true of a.

We cannot just substitute 'ascending true' for 'true', since the negation of the ascending liar is ascending true, but we do not think that 'not ascending true' is true of the ascending liar—indeed, ADT implies that the negation of the ascending liar is ascending true. Substituting 'descending true' for 'true' will not work either since 'ascending true' is true of the descending liar, but the descending liar is not descending true. I do not see much hope in trying to explain predication in terms of ascending truth and descending truth together. Instead, one might try option (iv) with the following principle:

(Predication-F) Ga iff 'G' is true of a.

This principle seems fine at first, but there is a problem with it. Indeed, this problem is a well-known paradox associated with predication. Consider the predicate, 'heterological', defined in the following way:

(Heterological) a predicate G is heterological $=_{df}$ 'G' is not true of 'G'.

The problem is that we can derive a paradox (often called Grelling's paradox or the heterological paradox). Assume that 'heterological' is true of 'heterological'. It follows from (Predication-F) that 'heterological' is heterological. Then from (Heterological) it follows that 'heterological' is not true of 'heterological'. Thus, if 'heterological' is true of 'heterological', then 'heterological' is not true of 'heterological'. On the other hand, assume that 'heterological' is not true of 'heterological'. It follows from (Heterological) that 'heterological' is heterological. And by (Predication-F) it follows that 'heterological' is true of 'heterological'. Thus, if 'heterological' is not true of 'heterological', then 'heterological' is true of 'heterological'. Therefore, 'heterological' is true of 'heterological' iff 'heterological' is not true of 'heterological'. So it seems option (iv) does not get us an acceptable principle for predication.[28]

Note that option (v) only makes sense if there is some independent reason to think that the concept in question is inconsistent—it engenders its own paradoxes. Since it is common knowledge that predication does give rise to the paradox just presented, there is a good case to be made that predication is an inconsistent concept. It is also a useful concept, and so should be replaced.

We can, and should, replace truth-of with two concepts, ascending truth-of and descending truth-of, which are analogous to ascending truth and descending truth:

(Ascending true-of) If Ga then 'G' is ascending true-of a.
(Descending true-of) If 'G' is descending true-of a, then Ga.

[28] For more on Grelling's paradox, see Grelling and Nelson (1908), Ryle (1951), Martin (1968), Jacquette (2004), Ketland (2005a), Newhard (2005), and Field (2008a).

There are many questions this move brings up, and I can only begin to scratch the surface in this section. First, let us see how this solves the paradox. We get two Grellings with our replacement concepts:

Ascending Grelling: a predicate 'G' is Aheterological $=_{df}$ 'G' is not ascending true-of 'G'.

Descending Grelling: a predicate 'G' is Dheterological $=_{df}$ 'G' is not descending true-of 'G'.

We can prove the following results:

(i) 'Aheterological' is ascending true-of 'Aheterological'.
(ii) 'Aheterological' is not descending true-of 'Aheterological'.
(iii) 'Dheterological' is ascending true-of 'Dheterological'.
(iv) 'Dheterological' is not descending true-of 'Dheterological'.

The arguments (using the abbreviations 'Dhet', 'Ahet', 'DTrue-of', and 'ATrue-of') are as follows. Assume (for *reductio*) that 'Ahet' is not ATrue-of 'Ahet'. By the definition of ATrue-of, it follows that 'Ahet' is not Ahet. By the definition of AGrelling, it follows from the initial assumption that 'Ahet' is Ahet. Contradiction. *Therefore* (by *reductio*), 'Ahet' is ATrue-of 'Ahet'. Assume (for *reductio*) that 'Ahet' is DTrue-of 'Ahet'. From the definition of DTrue-of, it follows that 'Ahet' is Ahet. From this it follows by the definition of ATrue-of that 'Ahet' is ATrue-of 'Ahet'. Thus, by the definition of AGrelling, 'Ahet' is not Ahet. From this it follows by the definition of DTrue-of that 'Ahet' is not DTrue-of 'Ahet'. Contradiction. *Therefore* (by *reductio*), 'Ahet' is not DTrue-of 'Ahet'. Assume (for *reductio*) that 'Dhet' is not ATrue-of 'Dhet'. It follows from the definition of ATrue-of that 'Dhet' is not Dhet. Hence, by the definition of DTrue-of, 'Dhet' is not DTrue-of 'Dhet'. From this, by the definition of DGrelling, we get that 'Dhet' is Dhet. Thus, by the definition of ATrue-of, 'Dhet' is ATrue-of 'Dhet'. Contradiction. *Therefore* (by *reductio*), 'Dhet' is ATrue-of 'Dhet'. Assume (for *reductio*) that 'Dhet' is DTrue-of 'Dhet'. From the definition of DTrue-of, it follows that 'Dhet' is Dhet. From the initial assumption, it also follows by the definition of DGrelling that 'Dhet' is not Dhet. Contradiction. *Therefore* (by *reductio*), 'Dhet' is not DTrue-of 'Dhet'.

We can characterize 'Ahet' and 'Dhet' by saying that they are unsafe where:

(Predicate Safety) A predicate 'G' is safe iff 'G' is DTrue-of 'G' or 'G' is not ATrue-of 'G'.

Note that the notion of safety associated with ascending truth and descending truth applies to sentences, whereas this notion of safety applies to predicates.

One might object that the above arguments are unconvincing since I have not shown that the principles defining ATrue-of and DTrue-of are consistent. However, it is easy to define them in terms of ascending truth and descending truth (which we already know to be consistent) in the following way:

(Ascending) <Ga> is ascending true iff <G> is ascending true-of a.

(Descending) <Ga> is descending true iff <G> is descending true-of a.

In addition, one can link the notion of safety for sentences (which is defined in terms of ascending truth and descending truth) to the notion of predicate safety defined above:

(Safety) 'G' is a safe predicate iff "'G' is G' is a safe sentence.

Again, this is a major change in our conceptual scheme and I can only give the barest outline of it here.[29, 30]

8.10 Reference

Our tour through truth's conceptual connections ends with reference. A traditional link between truth and reference is:

(Reference) 'b' refers to a iff 'a = b' is true.

Again, substituting 'ascending true' or 'descending true' in for 'true' is unacceptable. We might try option (iv), which results in the following principle:

(Reference-F) 'b' refers to a iff a = b.

The problem is that this principle is inconsistent. Consider the following situation:

(√) π
(√) 6
(√) the sum of the numbers referred to by ticked expressions in Scharp's *Replacing Truth*

Assume that 'π' refers to π and that '6' refers to 6. Assume as well that 'the sum of the numbers referred to by ticked sentences in Scharp's *Replacing Truth*' (which I abbreviate as 'the Sum') refers to some number; call it k. Now we reason as follows. 'The Sum' refers to k. By (Reference-F), the Sum = k. Therefore, k = π+6+k, which is impossible. Therefore, we should reject the assumption that 'the Sum' refers to some number. However, if we assume that 'the Sum' does not refer, then 'π' and '6' are the only referring ticked expressions in this book. Thus, the sum of the numbers referred to by ticked sentences in Scharp's *Replacing Truth* = π+6. But now, by (Reference-F), we get that 'the Sum' refers to π+6. Therefore, 'the Sum' does refer to some number, which contradicts our assumption.[31]

[29] There is another kind of Grelling that deals with extensions: Let $\{\phi(x)\}$ be the extension of $\phi(x)$. We then get '$a \in \{\phi(x)\}$ iff $\phi(a)$'. The connection to 'true of' should be obvious: $a \in \{\phi(x)\} \leftrightarrow$ '$\phi(x)$' is true of $a \leftrightarrow$ '$\phi(a)$' is true $\leftrightarrow \phi(a)$. Now, let $H(x)$ be such that: $H(\langle\phi(x)\rangle) \leftrightarrow \langle\phi(x)\rangle \notin \{H(x)\}$. Using analogous reasoning to that above, we get a contradiction. So, let us define $\{\phi(x)\}_D$ and $\{\phi(x)\}_A$ in the following way:

$a \in \{\phi(x)\}_D \rightarrow \phi(a)$
$\phi(a) \rightarrow a \in \{\phi(x)\}_A$

That gives us:

$A(\phi(a)) \leftrightarrow$ '$\phi(x)$' is Atrue-of $a \leftrightarrow a \in \{\phi(x)\}_A$.
$D(\phi(a)) \leftrightarrow$ '$\phi(x)$' is Dtrue-of $a \leftrightarrow a \in \{\phi(x)\}_D$.

[30] As for the semantics of 'true of', one can treat it as assessment-sensitive along the lines of the proposal for 'true' in the next chapter.

[31] This paradox was first formulated by Keith Simmons in Simmons (2003); see also Beall (2003b). There are other famous paradoxes of reference, which include Berry's paradox, Konig's paradox, and Richard's paradox; see Simmons (1994, 2000), Chaitin (1995), Uzquiano (2004), and Field (2008a: 291–3) for discussion.

Note that option (v) makes sense in this case since reference engenders its own paradoxes, and there is a good case to be made that it is an inconsistent concept. It is also a useful concept, and so should be replaced.

We can, and should, replace reference with two concepts, ascending reference and descending reference, which are analogous to ascending truth and descending truth (and ascending truth-of and descending truth-of). We arrive at the following replacement concepts:

(Dreference) If 'b' Descending refers to a, then a = b.

(Areference) If a = b, then 'b' Ascending refers to a.

Notice the connection between the other replacement concepts for predication and truth:

(A) 'a = b' is ascending true iff 'x = b' is uniquely Atrue of a iff 'b' Arefers to a.

(D) 'a = b' is descending true iff 'x = b' is uniquely Dtrue of a iff 'b' Drefers to a.

These replacement concepts handle the paradoxes of reference in the obvious way. Consider the paradox above. There will be two versions of it, which are listed below:

(√′) π
(√′) 6
(√′) the sum of the numbers Areferred to by ticked and primed expressions in Scharp's *Replacing Truth*
(√″) π
(√″) 6
(√″) the sum of the numbers Dreferred to by ticked and double-primed expressions in Scharp's *Replacing Truth*

Begin with the first group of three. Assume that 'the sum of the numbers Areferred to by ticked and primed expressions in Scharp's *Replacing Truth*' does not Arefer to any number. Thus the sum of the numbers Areferred to by ticked and primed expressions in Scharp's *Replacing Truth* = π+6. So, by (Areference), 'the sum of the numbers Areferred to by ticked and primed expressions in Scharp's *Replacing Truth*' Arefers to π+6, which contradicts our assumption. Assume, instead, that 'the sum of the numbers Areferred to by ticked and primed expressions in Scharp's *Replacing Truth*' Arefers to π+6. We cannot infer from this claim that the sum of the numbers Areferred to by ticked and primed expressions in Scharp's *Replacing Truth* = π+6. Therefore, we cannot derive a contradiction from the assumption by the argument above. On the other hand, assume that 'the sum of the numbers Areferred to by ticked and primed expressions in Scharp's *Replacing Truth*' Drefers to some number, k. By (Dreference), it follows that the sum of the numbers Areferred to by ticked and primed expressions in Scharp's *Replacing Truth* = k. Thus, k = π+6+k, which is impossible, and we have refuted our assumption. Assume, instead, that 'the sum of the numbers Areferred to by ticked and primed expressions in Scharp's *Replacing Truth*' does not Drefer to any number. We infer that the sum of the numbers

Areferred to by ticked and primed expressions in Scharp's *Replacing Truth* = π+6. However, we cannot infer from this claim that 'the sum of the numbers Areferred to by ticked and primed expressions in Scharp's *Replacing Truth*' Drefers to π+6. Therefore, we cannot derive a contradiction from the assumption by the argument above. Putting these results together we have:

(i) 'the sum of the numbers Areferred to by ticked and primed expressions in Scharp's *Replacing Truth*' Arefers to π+6.
(ii) 'the sum of the numbers Areferred to by ticked and primed expressions in Scharp's *Replacing Truth*' does not Drefer to anything.
(iii) It is not the case that the sum of the numbers Areferred to by ticked and primed expressions in Scharp's *Replacing Truth* = π+6.

Turning now to the second group of three, we assume that 'the sum of the numbers Dreferred to by ticked and double-primed expressions in Scharp's *Replacing Truth*' does not Arefer to any number. Thus the sum of the numbers Areferred to by ticked and double-primed expressions in Scharp's *Replacing Truth* = π+6. So, by (Areference), 'the sum of the numbers Areferred to by ticked and double-primed expressions in Scharp's *Replacing Truth*' Arefers to π+6, which contradicts our assumption. Assume, instead, that 'the sum of the numbers Dreferred to by ticked and double-primed expressions in Scharp's *Replacing Truth*' Arefers to π+6. However, we cannot infer from this claim that the sum of the numbers Areferred to by ticked and double-primed expressions in Scharp's *Replacing Truth* = π+6. Therefore, we cannot derive a contradiction from the assumption by the argument above. On the other hand, assume that 'the sum of the numbers Dreferred to by ticked and double-primed expressions in Scharp's *Replacing Truth*' Drefers to some number, k. By (Dreference), it follows that the sum of the numbers Dreferred to by ticked and double-primed expressions in Scharp's *Replacing Truth* = k. Thus, k = π+6+k, which is impossible, and we have refuted our assumption. Assume, instead, that 'the sum of the numbers Dreferred to by ticked and double-primed expressions in Scharp's *Replacing Truth*' does not Drefer to any number. We infer that the sum of the numbers Dreferred to by ticked and double-primed expressions in Scharp's *Replacing Truth* = π+6. However, we cannot infer from this claim that 'the sum of the numbers Dreferred to by ticked and double-primed expressions in Scharp's *Replacing Truth*' Drefers to π+6. Therefore, we cannot derive a contradiction from the assumption by the argument above. Putting these results together we have:

(i) 'the sum of the numbers Dreferred to by ticked and double-primed expressions in Scharp's *Replacing Truth*' Arefers to π+6.
(ii) 'the sum of the numbers Dreferred to by ticked and double-primed expressions in Scharp's *Replacing Truth*' does not Drefer to anything.
(iii) The sum of the numbers Dreferred to by ticked and double-primed expressions in Scharp's *Replacing Truth* = π+6.

Again, once we distinguish between Areference and Dreference, there is no way to formulate a paradox using them in the above way. The treatment of the other paradoxes of reference is similar.[32]

One can think of the replacements for truth, predication, and reference as the basis for a new semantics. Call it *AD semantics*. In AD semantics, sentences have ascending truth values and descending truth values, for each predicate there are the items it is ascending true-of and the items it is descending true-of, and each singular term has an ascending reference and a descending reference. There is much more to be said about AD semantics, but it will have to wait for another occasion.[33]

[32] As for the semantics of 'refers', one can treat it as assessment-sensitive in the same way as the account given in the next chapter for 'true'.

[33] I gave a hint on how to implement it with the double-model option in section 8.5 of this chapter.

9

The Descriptive Theory

This is the second of the two chapters that lay out the central theories defended in this book. In Chapter 6, I introduced two concepts, ascending truth and descending truth, to replace the concept of truth. In this chapter I offer a theory that takes truth to be an inconsistent concept. The theory of truth appeals to ascending truth and descending truth, but not to truth itself.

9.1 Theories of inconsistent concepts

In order to decide on a descriptive theory for our inconsistent concept of truth, we need to decide on a theory of inconsistent concepts and apply it to truth. Let me begin by saying that in a previous publication I endorsed Joseph Camp's theory, but I am no longer confident that it is the best option.[1] I first propose some criteria for a theory and then endorse one promising option.

9.1.1 Conditions of adequacy

I present three conditions that any acceptable theory of inconsistent concepts should meet. They are:

(i) The theory should imply that the concepts in question are genuinely inconsistent (e.g., it should not reinterpret the concepts so that they have some other semantic features).

(ii) The theory should be inferentially charitable (i.e., the theory should not imply that those who employ inconsistent concepts are poor reasoners).

(iii) The theory should admit that inconsistent concepts have intelligible uses even by those who know they are inconsistent.

I discuss the conditions in order.

[1] Scharp (2008).

The first condition is that a theory of inconsistent concepts should be a theory of *inconsistent concepts*—it should not imply that there are no such things or that what we take to be an inconsistent concept is really some type of consistent concept. The strategy of reinterpreting a linguistic practice to avoid attributing an inconsistent concept might work in certain cases, but it fails as a general policy for handling inconsistent concepts.

A theory of inconsistent concepts should include at least: (i) an account of the distinction between consistent and inconsistent concepts, (ii) conditions on the logic that should be used to classify arguments that display inconsistent concepts as valid or invalid, (iii) conditions on the semantic theory that applies to sentences that express inconsistent concepts, (iv) conditions on a pragmatic theory that applies to speech acts involving inconsistent concepts, and (v) a policy for handling inconsistent concepts (i.e., a strategy to follow for those who discover that one of their concepts is inconsistent). Some of the theories of inconsistent concepts I discuss below do not include all five parts, but I do not fault them on these grounds. However, if it seems that a particular theory cannot be amended to include one of these parts, then that is a serious problem.

The second condition is that a theory of inconsistent concepts should be charitable. In particular, a theory of inconsistent concepts is unacceptable if it implies that those who employ inconsistent concepts are irrational. There are plenty of types of rationality and I do not discuss them all here. Instead, I focus on inferential rationality. A theory of inconsistent concepts has implications for the inferential rationality of those who employ inconsistent concepts. Given that an account of inconsistent concepts should include a logic for inconsistent concepts, when one adopts a certain theory of inconsistent concepts, one decides how to treat the reasoning practice of people who employ inconsistent concepts. Thus, when one adopts a theory of inconsistent concepts, one undertakes a commitment to evaluate arguments in which such concepts are expressed according to a certain standard and to treat people who employ such concepts as if they should reason according to that standard.[2]

Although I do not claim to have an exhaustive list, some of the aspects of inferential rationality include being able to determine when arguments are valid or invalid, being able to determine when inductive arguments are strong or weak, being able to weigh evidence for and against a claim, having the capacity and motivation to follow inference rules in one's reasoning, and having the capacity and the motivation to alter one's beliefs effectively in light of conflicting evidence. One can employ an inconsistent concept and still be inferentially rational in all these ways. A theory of inconsistent concepts should respect this fact.

In particular, a theory of inconsistent concepts should imply that a person who employs an inconsistent concept is: (i) capable of following the formal inference rules he accepts, (ii) capable of following the formal inference rules of the logic used to evaluate his arguments, (iii) motivated to follow the formal inference rules of the logic used to evaluate his arguments, (iv) capable of following the material inference rules he accepts

[2] See Camp (2002) and Scharp (2005) for discussion.

(i.e., capable of following his accepted strategies for weighing evidence), (v) capable of following the material inference rules of the semantic theory used to interpret his utterances and beliefs, and (vi) motivated to follow the material inference rules of the semantic theory used to interpret his utterances and beliefs.

Two features of inconsistent concepts make the inferential rationality condition on theories of inconsistent concepts especially urgent. The potential for paradoxical reasoning accompanies the employment of an inconsistent concept. Recall, for example, the arguments from Chapter 2. Let *R* be a red table. R is a table; hence, R is a rable. R is red; hence, it is not the case that R is a rable. Thus, R is a rable and it is not case that R is a rable. We have arrived at a contradiction via intuitively constitutive principles from intuitively plausible assumptions. Consider the other example. Assume for *reductio* that some red tables exist. Let R be a red table. The reasoning above shows that R is a rable and R is not a rable. Contradiction. Therefore, no red tables exist. We have proven an obviously false sentence using only logic and constitutive principles. If one accepts classical logic and treats 'rable' as univocal and invariant, then one will have a hard time avoiding these unacceptable conclusions. Hence, there is considerable pressure to endorse non-classical logics for evaluating arguments that involve inconsistent concepts.

In addition, a person can possess an inconsistent concept without knowing that it is inconsistent. Indeed, a theory of inconsistent concepts will be used primarily to interpret people who are using an inconsistent concept without knowing that it is inconsistent. Given that many employers of inconsistent concepts are ignorant of their inconsistency and that many theories of inconsistent concepts include non-standard logics for inconsistent concepts, the potential for treating those who employ inconsistent concepts as inferentially irrational is high.

The third condition is that a theory of inconsistent concepts should allow that inconsistent concepts have intelligible uses. Thus, a theory of inconsistent concepts should not imply that possessing an inconsistent concept is incompatible with rationally using it. In particular, it should not imply that possessing or using an inconsistent concept requires that one have inconsistent beliefs or some other kind of irrationality. One difficulty that theories of inconsistent concepts face is explaining what happens when one discovers that one's concept is inconsistent. Presumably, this transition will involve a change in beliefs—beliefs in the concept's constitutive principles. It will also probably involve a change in usage—the person will be reluctant to use the concept without some sense of when it gets them into trouble and when it does not. We can think of this condition as requiring a pragmatics for inconsistent concepts even when the users know that they are inconsistent. There has to be such a thing as a legitimate or felicitous use of an inconsistent concept by someone who knows it is inconsistent. Obviously, a theory of inconsistent concepts should explain why users of inconsistent concepts (both informed and ignorant) do not actually accept contradictions involving the concept (this is called the problem of *discipline*—I discuss it in sections 9.7 and 9.9 below).[3]

[3] See Eklund (2002a).

9.1.2 Theories

With those conditions under our belt, we can turn to some theories of inconsistent concepts. Below are some of the theories of inconsistent concepts that one finds in the literature.[4]

1. *Error theory*: all (perhaps atomic) claims employing the inconsistent concept are false (or indeterminate).[5]
2. *Ambiguity*: inconsistent expressions are ambiguous; whatever semantics is appropriate for ambiguous expressions should be used for inconsistent expressions. A theorist who advocates this position needs a principle of disambiguation that assigns a meaning to the inconsistent expression in each context of use.[6]
3. *Context-dependence*: inconsistent expressions are context-dependent; whatever semantics is appropriate for context-dependent expressions should be used for inconsistent expression. A theorist who advocates this position needs a *character* for the inconsistent expression—a principle that assigns a *content* to the inconsistent expression in each context of use.[7]
4. *Dialetheism*: some sentences containing inconsistent expressions are both true and false; a paraconsistent semantics, which uses a non-classical logic, is appropriate for discourse involving inconsistent expressions.[8]
5. *Fictionalism*: inconsistent expressions are part of fictional discourse; whatever semantics is appropriate for fictional discourse should be used for inconsistent expressions.[9]
6. *Supervaluation*: inconsistent expressions are referentially indeterminate—they partially denote several distinct items; one should use a supervaluation semantics for inconsistent expressions (i.e., one should calculate the truth value of sentences containing the inconsistent expression based on the truth value of the sentences that result from replacing the inconsistent expression with expressions for the items it partially denotes; if all resulting sentences have the same truth value, then the original has that truth value, and if the resulting sentences differ in truth value, then the original is a truth-value gap).[10]
7. *Weighted majority*: an inconsistent expression has semantic features that make true a weighted majority of the expression's constitutive principles.[11]

[4] This list is not meant to be exhaustive and the entries might not be exclusive.

[5] Boghossian (2006) endorses this option.

[6] This option is considered and rejected by Joseph Camp (2002: Ch. 5).

[7] This option is considered and rejected by Anil Gupta (1999: 24–9).

[8] This option has been offered by Graham Priest (1979, 2006a, 2006b) and adopted by Jc Beall (2009).

[9] This option is suggested but not evaluated by Joseph Camp (2002: Ch. 5) and it has been developed by A. Burgess (2006); see Yablo (2001), Eklund (2007), Sainsbury (2009), and the papers in Kalderon (2005a, 2005b) for background on fictionalism.

[10] This option is proposed by Hartry Field (1973, 1974); note that Field (2001d) rejects it.

[11] This option is proposed by Matti Eklund (2002a); for discussion see Chs. 2 and 5.

8. *Relevance*: sentences containing an inconsistent expression have no truth value but arguments containing such sentences should be evaluated by an epistemically interpreted relevance logic.[12]
9. *Revision*: an inconsistent expression has semantic features determined by a rule of revision; some sentences containing an inconsistent expression will not have traditional truth values.[13]
10. *Indeterminate translation*: an inconsistent expression has semantic features that are relative to translation into a set of consistent expressions; there will often be multiple equally good translations (e.g., sometimes it makes sense to translate 'mass' as 'relativistic mass', sometimes as 'proper mass'—since translation is highly context-dependent and interest-relative, the semantic features of an inconsistent expression will be too).[14]
11. *Frames*: an inconsistent expression has semantic features only relative to a frame, which is a way of privileging some of its constitutive principles over others. Frame identity and which frame is in play for a given utterance are determined by ways the expression is used, but need not be available to the users of the expression.[15]
12. *Assessment-sensitivity*: an inconsistent expression is assessment-sensitive, which means the truth values of sentences that contain it are relative to a context of utterance *and* a context of assessment.[16]

Instead of presenting each of these theories in detail and trying to assess each one (which would be tedious), I want to mention briefly what I take to be the prospects for some of them.

First, many of them (2, 3, 6, 8, 10, 12) work best with some replacement concepts for the theory to work at all. Thus, many of these views implicitly accept my replacement strategy of basing a descriptive theory on a prescriptive theory.

Second, many of these approaches (1, 4, 6, 7, 8, 12) appeal to a notion of truth. That should not be a surprise since many of the most popular semantic theories appeal to truth and most of these theories of inconsistent concepts were not designed to deal with truth itself as an inconsistent concept. It might seem that this fact disqualifies these theories from serving as descriptive theories of truth since I have taken on a commitment to *not* using truth in a descriptive theory of truth. However, this conclusion is premature. Some of these theories can be reformulated in terms of ascending truth and descending truth (I offer a suggestion for how to do this with the assessment-sensitivity theory later in the chapter).

[12] This option is proposed by Joseph Camp (2002: Chs. 11–16; 2007), endorsed by Scharp (2005, 2008), and rejected in this chapter; see also Wilson (2007) and MacFarlane (2007b).

[13] The revision theory is introduced by Gupta (1982); see also Gupta and Belnap (1993). Note that Gupta and Belnap do *not* advocate the revision theory for inconsistent concepts—they think that it is appropriate for circularly defined concepts and that circularly defined concepts are not inconsistent. This option is proposed for inconsistent concepts by Stephen Yablo (1993a, 1993b).

[14] This option is proposed by Hartry Field (1994b, 2001a, 2008a).

[15] This option is proposed by Gupta (1999) and adopted by Weiner (2009); see also Pinillos (2010).

[16] This option is proposed by John MacFarlane (2007b).

Third, a couple of these theories (2, 3) are non-starters—they treat would-be inconsistent expressions as if they merely have some hidden semantic feature that has gone unnoticed by those users who run into trouble with the concept in question; that is, they violate the first condition on theories of inconsistent concepts. I consider them in detail below.

Finally, some of these theories (4, 6, 8, 9) require non-classical logics, which limits their significance since they imply that inconsistent concepts are not usable in classical contexts; other things being equal, an approach that is compatible with classical logic is preferable.[17] My goal is a (classically) consistent theory of an inconsistent concept.

This survey is just supposed to give the reader a sense of what has been said on this topic. In this chapter I defend the assessment-sensitivity view (12). However, I do discuss many of the others in detail (1, 2, 3, 6, 11) after giving a bit of background on confusion and the assessment-sensitivity view.

9.2 Confusion and relative truth

Confusion occurs when a person thinks there is one thing (or one kind of thing), but there are really two (or more). To return to an earlier example, after the late 1600s, but prior to the advent of relativistic mechanics, we thought that there is one physical quantity, mass, which physical objects have. However, in the early twentieth century, we realized that there is no one physical quantity that satisfies all of the principles constitutive of mass; instead, there are two physical quantities that are somewhat similar to mass: relativistic mass and proper mass. A person who lived in the 1800s and accepted Newtonian mechanics was confused—he or she thought that there is one quantity, mass, but instead there are two. Throughout the rest of this work, I use 'confusion' in this technical sense, which is considerably more specific than the ordinary sense of the word.

Once one accepts that truth is an inconsistent concept *and* that it should be replaced by ascending truth and descending truth, it is natural to think that the concept of truth is confused. It turns out that there is no property of truth, at least, if by 'truth' we mean to designate a property that satisfies all what I have claimed to be the constitutive principles of the concept of truth. Instead, there are two properties, ascending truth and descending truth.

I mention confusion here because John MacFarlane has suggested that words expressing confused concepts are assessment-sensitive, which is a complex semantic feature associated with relativism. Here is the relevant passage from MacFarlane:

> Early in his discussion of the logic of confusion, Camp says:
>
> > When one first thinks about ontological confusion, it is natural and intuitively plausible to talk in terms of perspectival truth. One wants to say: "what the confused person thinks may

[17] The supervaluation option is a bit tricky because although what are probably the most familiar supervaluation consequence relations are weakly classical, some are fully classical. I return to this issue below in section 9.5.

> be true from one perspective but false from another perspective; or it may be true from both perspectives, or false from both." Perspectival truth must replace truth simpliciter when one evaluates a confused belief.[18] (125)

Camp quickly drops the talk of perspectival truth: his four epistemic values, as he notes, aren't truth values at all. But perhaps some kind of perspectival truth is just what is needed here. Think of Camp's "authorities" as occupying different perspectives: from one perspective, Fred is referring to Ant A, from another, he is referring to Ant B. Neither perspective captures the full story about Fred's confused thinking, but that is because there is no way to capture the full story and still think of Fred's thoughts as having truth values. Given that there are no "absolute" truth values for confused claims, only relativized, perspectival truth values, it seems natural to define validity in terms of these, as truth preservation in every perspective.

It seems to me that such an approach might meet Camp's desiderata even better than his own multivalued semantics:

1. Because validity is defined in terms of preservation of truth-at-a-perspective, and there is no uniquely appropriate perspective for assessing a confused reasoner, the validity criterion is compatible with Camp's idea that confused thoughts and claims are not true or false simpliciter.
2. The semantic clauses for the logical connectives can be simple and straightforward, no matter how many perspectives are in play. For example, a conjunction is true at a perspective just in case both conjuncts are true at that perspective. There are no anomalies.
3. We achieve complete inferential charity, without embarrassing exceptions like disjunctive syllogism. Since every perspective corresponds to a classical interpretation, all classically valid inferences will be valid on the perspectival-truth semantics as well.

The crucial question is whether the perspectival-truth explication of validity is authoritative for the confused reasoner. Does the confused reasoner have reason to care whether her inferences are valid in this sense? That depends, I think, on what it means to say that a claim is "true at a perspective," and in virtue of what a person "occupies" or "takes up" a particular perspective on a confused reasoner's thought and talk. Unless these questions can be answered, the proposed semantics is of merely technical interest and cannot be authoritative. But I am less pessimistic than most about the prospects for answering them.

In recent work, I have suggested giving significance to perspectival truth by embedding it in a larger theory of language, specifically in a normative account of what it is to make an assertion. I would like to propose, very tentatively, that this kind of framework might be a better home for a "semantics of confusion" than the multivalued, epistemic semantics Camp advocates.[19]

That is the entirety of MacFarlane's proposal, and to my knowledge no one else has advocated anything like this.[20] In the remainder of this chapter, I present a variety of semantic

[18] Camp (2002: 125).

[19] MacFarlane (2007b).

[20] Billon (2011) suggests that 'true' might be assessment-sensitive, but his view is not motivated by an inconsistency approach or the thought that truth is confused, and it is felled by the obvious revenge paradoxes. Pinillos (2010) suggests a non-indexical contextualist view for duration, and his theory is motivated by something like inconsistency considerations.

theories, including the assessment-sensitivity view MacFarlane advocates, and I evaluate which of them works best for confused concepts in general, and truth in particular.

9.3 Relative truth and formal semantics

In an effort to illustrate assessment-sensitivity, consider the ways theorists have tried to accommodate various linguistic phenomena using intensional semantics. Let us focus on a particular word, 'fun', and try to give a semantics for it. Imagine we have two conversations, one in which Luke utters 'Whacking Day is fun' and a second in which Mel utters 'Whacking Day is fun'. In what follows, I rely on the distinction between presemantics, semantics, and postsemantics presented in section 8.5 of Chapter 8. Here are the options I consider:

(i) 'fun' is univocal and invariant.

(ii) 'fun' is ambiguous.[21]

(iii) 'fun' has an unarticulated constituent.[22]

(iv) 'fun' is use-indexical.[23]

(v) 'fun' is use-sensitive but not use-indexical (i.e., non-indexical contextualism).[24]

(vi) 'fun' is assessment-sensitive, but not assessment-indexical (i.e., non-indexical relativism).[25]

(vii) 'fun' is assessment-indexical (i.e., indexical relativism).[26]

In the case (i), the presemantics treats 'fun' as univocal (i.e., not ambiguous) and invariant, which means that since 'fun' is a one-place predicate in the language spoken by Mel and Luke, it is represented by a one-place predicate as its clause and in the semantics, 'fun' is assigned a constant character that delivers the same content for every index. The content of Mel's sentence is the same as the content of Luke's sentence, and their contents get the same t-distribution. The postsemantics is the same for each—the sentence they utter is true in their respective contexts iff Whacking Day is fun. Nothing new here.

[21] See Cruse (1986), Atlas (1989), Gillon (2004), Wasow, Perfors, and Beaver (2005), and Kennedy (2010) for discussion of ambiguity.

[22] See Perry (1998), Recanati (2002), Clapp (2002), Borg (2005), Marti (2006), Stanley (2007), Cappelen and Lepore (2007), Hall (2008), and Sennet (2011) for discussion of unarticulated constituents.

[23] See Perry (1979, 2001), Kaplan (1989), Predelli (2005), Stanley (2007), and Cappelen and Hawthorne (2009) for discussion of indexicals.

[24] See Kölbel (2002, 2003, 2004, 2007), Richard (2004, 2008, 2011), Recanati (2007, 2008), Brogaard (2007, 2010), MacFarlane (2008, 2009, 2011a, 2011b), Cappelen and Hawthorne (2009, 2011a, 2011b), Lasersohn (2011), Glanzberg (2011), Soames (2011), and Weatherson (2011) on non-indexical contextualism.

[25] See MacFarlane (2003, 2005a, 2005b, 2007a, 2008, 2011a, 2011b, forthcoming), Lasersohn (2005, 2008, 2009, 2011), Egan, Hawthorne, and Weatherson (2005), Egan (2006, 2007, 2010), Zimmerman (2007), Glanzberg (2007, 2011), Stojanovic (2007), von Fintel and Gilles (2008), Stephenson (2008, 2009), Weatherson (2009, 2011), Cappelen and Hawthorne (2009, 2011a, 2011b), Saebo (2009), Montminy (2009b), Moltmann (2010), Schaffer (2011), Bach (2011), Greenough (2011b), Richard (2011), Glanzberg (2011), and Soames (2011), on assessment-sensitivity.

[26] See Egan (2009) and Weatherson (2009) on assessment-indexicality.

In case (ii), 'fun' is ambiguous, so the presemantics uses elements of the context in each case to disambiguate. It might be that the clause representing Mel's sentence has one one-place predicate, 'fun_1', while the clause for Luke's has a different one-place predicate, 'fun_2'. Since their clauses are different, the characters, contents, and t-distributions for these clauses might be different as well. In the postsemantics, Mel's sentence is true in his context iff Whacking Day is fun_1, while Luke's sentence is true in his context iff Whacking Day is fun_2. So, even though they uttered tokens of the same sentence type, the presemantics assigns them different clauses; consequently, the semantics and postsemantics might be very different. In sum, ambiguity is a *presemantic* phenomenon because the analyses of the two utterances diverge in the presemantics.

In case (iii), we have the unarticulated constituent view for 'fun'.[27] That is, the presemantics assigns the same clause to each sentence, but the clause differs from the surface grammar of the sentences uttered. In this case, the presemantics might assign a clause with a two-place predicate 'x is fun for y' instead of the one-place predicate 'x is fun'. So, the presemantics treats the logical form of the sentence Mel and Luke utter as different from its surface form. Since they are assigned a clause that has an extra slot, the presemantics uses the context to fill it in. In Mel's case, the presemantics uses the clause 'Whacking Day is fun for Mel', while for Luke, it uses 'Whacking Day is fun for Luke'.[28] Note that this is very different from treating 'fun' as ambiguous. In the case of unarticulated constituents, 'fun' is univocal, but its surface grammar is misleading. Since the presemantics assigns the two sentences different clauses, the semantics might assign them different characters, contents, and t-distributions. The postsemantics yields: Mel's sentence is true in his context iff Whacking Day is fun for Mel, and Luke's sentence is true in his context iff Whacking Day is fun for Luke. In sum: unarticulated constituents are a *presemantic* phenomenon since the analyses of the two utterances diverge in the presemantics.

In case (iv), 'fun' is an indexical. Here we use the term 'use-indexical' to distinguish it from more complex cases below. There are several variants on the use-indexical view, but either way the presemantics assigns their sentences the same clause. It might be 'Whacking Day is fun' or 'Whacking Day is fun-for-me'; the former treats 'fun' as something like a gradable adjective, while the later treats it like a pure indexical (note, the hyphenation indicates that 'fun-for-me' is a one-place predicate, not two-place).

[27] Note that the phrase 'unarticulated constituent' is used in different ways (sometimes by the same author). For example, Jason Stanley's definition at Stanley (2007: 47) differs from his definition at Stanley (2007: 183, n. 2). I follow the latter, which reads, "an entity (object, property, or function) e is an unarticulated constituent relative to an utterance u iff (i) e is a constituent of the proposition that a competent, reflective speaker under normal circumstances would intuitively believe to be what is expressed by u, and (ii) e is not the value of any constituent in the expression uttered in u, and (iii) e is not introduced by context-independent composition rules corresponding to the structural relations between elements in the expression uttered." The primary difference between this definition and the one that occurs earlier in his book is that the earlier one has the additional requirement that e is not the semantic value of any constituent of the logical form of the sentence uttered. On my reading, an unarticulated constituent is not the value of any constituent of the sentence uttered, but it can be the value of a constituent of the logical form (i.e., clause).

[28] These are not the only options, but they are the most natural.

Although the clause is the same, the character assigned to it by the semantics will not be. If 'fun' is like a gradable adjective, then the semantics assigns a character to it that has a slot for the standards of the index. On the other hand, if 'fun' is like a pure indexical, then the semantics assigns it a character that has a slot for the speaker. The character assigned to the clause is the same for both utterances. However, since the contexts of utterance are different, the content assigned to the clause might be different. On the pure indexical view, for Mel's case, the clause gets assigned the content that Whacking Day is fun-for-Mel, while in Luke's case it gets the content that Whacking Day is fun-for-Luke. On the gradable adjective view, for Mel's case, the clause gets assigned the content that Whacking Day is fun given the standards in Mel's conversation, while in Luke's case it gets the content that Whacking Day is fun given the standards in Luke's conversation. Since these contents might differ, they might have different t-distributions as well. The post-semantics might differ since, either way, the semantics might treat them as asserting different propositions. In sum, use-indexicality is a *semantic* phenomenon because the analyses of the two utterances diverge at the semantic level.

Case (v) is where things get interesting. It has come to be known as *non-indexical contextualism*, and it treats 'fun' as use-sensitive (i.e., its extension varies from context to context), but not use-indexical (i.e., its content is the same in every context). The presemantics is the same as in case (i)—both sentences are represented by the same clause; moreover, that clause is given a constant character, so the index has no effect (in the semantics). Thus, the clause expresses the same proposition in each index. However, the non-indexical contextualist adds an extra slot to the points of evaluation. In the case of 'fun' it would most likely be an enjoyment scale for all the objects in the domain. Thus, the clause representing the sentence uttered by Mel and Luke expresses the same content relative to the respective indexes that represent their contexts, and these contents have the same t-distribution. So the semantics treats the two cases in exactly the same way (once the change has been made to the points of evaluation). However, the post-semantics treats the t-distribution differently. Luke's sentence is true in his context iff the content expressed by the clause assigned to the sentence he uttered is true at the point of evaluation corresponding to Luke's context of utterance. The relevant point of evaluation is the one that uses the enjoyment scale operative in Luke's context. If the proposition in question is true at this point of evaluation, then the sentence he uttered is true in his context; otherwise it is false in his context. The same process is used to determine whether the proposition Mel uttered (which is the same as the one Luke uttered) is true or false. Since their contexts of utterance might employ different enjoyment scales, it might be that the sentence Mel uttered is true in his context, but the sentence Luke uttered is false in his context, despite the fact that these sentences express the same proposition in both contexts. In sum, once the change is made to the semantic theory to allow an extra slot in the points of evaluation, non-indexical use-sensitivity is a *post-semantic* phenomenon because that is where the analyses diverge.

Case (vi) is often called *assessment-sensitivity*, but a better name would be *non-indexical relativism* (for compatibility with case (v)). Again, the presemantics is the same as in case (i)—both sentences are represented by the same clause; moreover, that clause is given a constant character, so the index has no semantic effect. Thus, the clause expresses the same proposition in each index. However, the non-indexical relativist also adds an extra slot to the points of evaluation. In the case of 'fun' it would again most likely be an enjoyment scale for all the objects in the domain. The clause representing the sentence uttered by Mel and Luke expresses the same content relative to the respective indexes that represent their contexts, and so they share a single t-distribution. Thus, the semantics treats the two cases in exactly the same way (once the change has been made to the points of evaluation). However, the relativist suggests a new kind of postsemantics. Instead of defining truth for sentences in contexts (as the standard postsemantic theory does), the relativist defines truth for sentences in contexts of use from contexts of assessment, which is a three-place predicate. If we let u be a context of use, i_u be the index that represents it, a be the context of assessment, and i_a be the index that represents it, then the standard relativist postsemantics is something like:

(1) A sentence p is true in u from a iff the content assigned to the clause that represents p with respect to i_u is true at the point of evaluation <w, t, s>, where w is the world of i_u, t is the world of i_u, and s is the enjoyment scale from i_a.

Notice that the world and time of the point of evaluation encode information about the context of use, whereas the standard of the point of evaluation encodes information about the context of assessment. Thus, even though Luke and Mel assert the same proposition, that proposition might be true at the relevant point of evaluation for Mel's case and false at the relevant point of evaluation for Luke's case. It is hard to say since the scenarios as described do not include information about the context of assessment. Imagine we add this information—say Mel's utterance is assessed by Barbara, who is a participant in the same conversation, and Luke's utterance is assessed by Raghib, who overhears Luke, but is not a member of his conversation. Mel's sentence is true in his context of use from Barbara's context of assessment iff the proposition it expresses is true at the point of evaluation consisting of the world from Mel's context of use, the time from Mel's context of use, and the standard from Barbara's context of assessment. Luke's sentence is true in his context of use from Raghib's context of assessment iff the proposition it expresses is true at the point of evaluation consisting of the world from Luke's context of use, the time from Luke's context of use, and the standard from Raghib's context of assessment. Since Barbara's context of assessment and Raghib's context of assessment might differ, Luke's sentence and Mel's sentence might have different truth values relative to these contexts of assessment even though they express the same proposition. In sum, once the extra slot is added to the points of evaluation, assessment-sensitivity is a *postsemantic* phenomenon.

Finally, in case (vii), we have assessment-indexicalism or indexical relativism. It is like non-indexical relativism except that the context of assessment plays a content-determining role in the semantics instead of a truth value determining role in the post-semantics; thus, it requires changes to the presemantic theory and the semantic theory.

The presemantics requires an extra context—the context of assessment. Thus, when Mel and Luke make their utterances, there are two contexts: the context of use and the context of assessment. These might be the same, but they might not. Just as before, the presemantics posits a clause to represent the sentence uttered, and it is the same clause in both cases. However, for indexical relativism, the presemantics needs two indexes—one to represent the context of utterance, the other for the context of assessment. So the semantic theory takes as input a clause/index_u/index_a triple. In Mel's case, index_u represents Mel's context and index_a represents Barbara's context, while in Luke's case, index_u represents Luke's context and index_a represents Raghib's context. In the semantics, a single clause represents both sentences, and the clause gets a character, but the character has two slots, one for each index. The two indexes, together with the character, determine a content. That is, the clause expresses a proposition in an index of use from an index of assessment. Different indexes of assessment might take the proposition expressed in a single index of use to be different. Thus, there is no reason to think that the proposition expressed by the clause representing Mel's sentence, as used in his index and assessed from Barbara's index, is the same as the proposition expressed by the clause representing Luke's sentence as used in his index and assessed from Raghib's index. According to this option, the proposition expressed by the sentence that Mel and Luke each assert might be different in each case, since it depends on both the context of use and the context of assessment. Even if Mel and Luke occupied the same context of use and uttered the same sentence, they might express different propositions as assessed from distinct contexts. According to assessment-indexicalism, there is no such thing as *the* proposition expressed by a sentence in a context of use—instead, there is the proposition expressed by a sentence in a context of use from different contexts of assessment. Moreover, there is no reason to think that an assessment indexicalist should also be a non-indexical relativist (i.e., option (vi)). In sum, once the changes are made to the presemantics and the semantics, assessment-indexicality is a *semantic* phenomenon.[29]

See Figure 11 for a diagram of these seven options.

9.4 An assessment-sensitivity theory of truth

There are several things one might mean by 'semantic relativism about truth'. Some use the term 'semantic relativism' for two separate views, non-indexical contextualism and assessment-sensitivity.[30] The latter is more radical than the former. Both require an extra parameter in each point of evaluation, but assessment-sensitivity views also require a new postsemantic theory that outputs the truth value of the sentence in a context of utterance

[29] Perhaps Robert Brandom's idea that content specification is intrinsically perspectival should be thought of as global assessment-indexicality; see Brandom (1994) and Scharp (2012) for discussion.

[30] Recanati (2007) and Richard (2008) endorse non-indexical contextualism for certain discourses and think of it as a species of semantic relativism; MacFarlane (2005a, 2009, forthcoming), on the other hand, thinks that non-indexical contextualism is not a kind of relativism—only assessment-sensitivity fits that description.

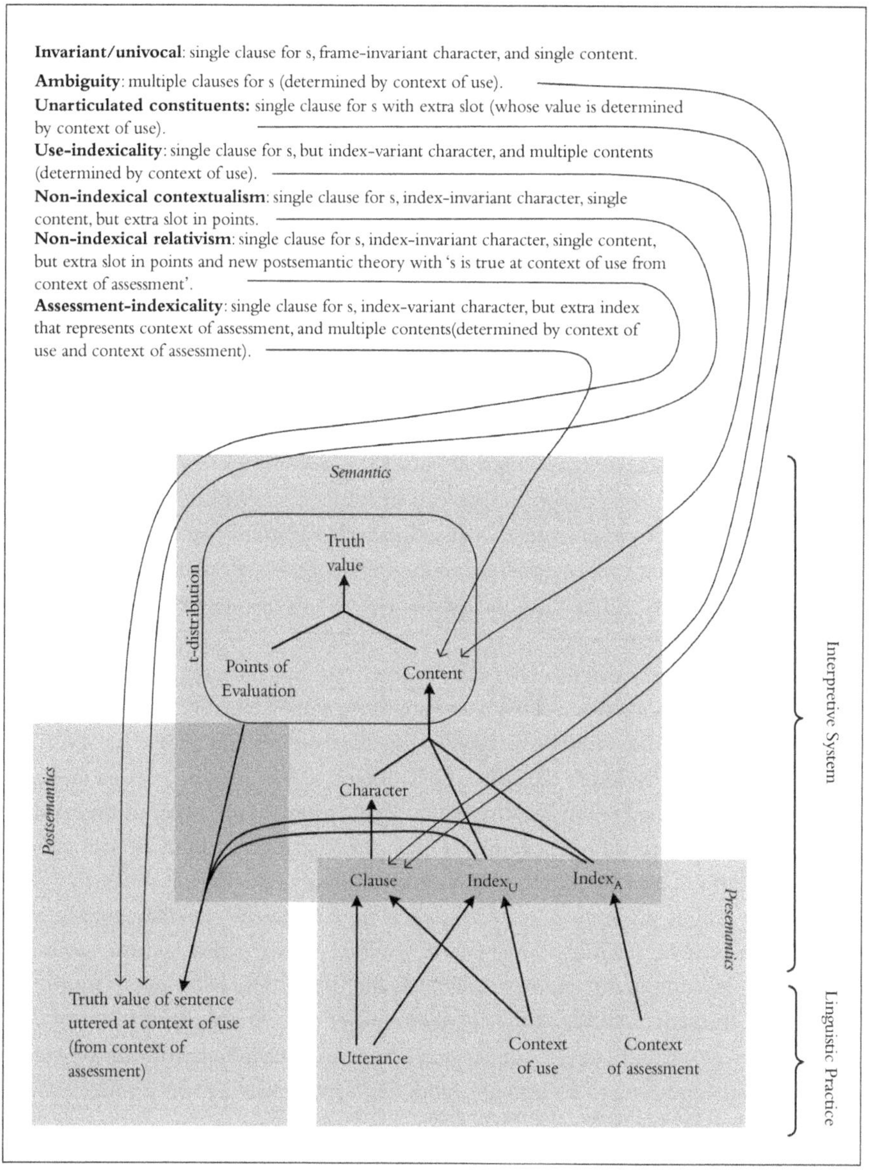

Figure 11 Presemantic, Semantic, and Postsemantic Phenomena

from a context of assessment, instead of outputting the truth value of the sentence in a context of utterance. That is, postsemantics for an assessment-sensitivity view requires a three-place predicate 'x is true at u from a', whereas the postsemantics for non-indexical contextualist views needs only the more familiar 'x is true at u'. In this section, I present my preferred semantics for the truth predicate, which is an assessment-sensitivity view. Later, I contrast it with several other options, including a non-indexical contextualist view.

Before we begin, it is worth a reminder that the presemantic theory, semantic theory, and postsemantic theory proposed do not use truth at all. Instead, in accordance with the policy of *not* using the inconsistent concept of truth in a descriptive theory of truth, the semantic theory uses truth-in-a-model (a mathematical concept) and the postsemantics uses ascending truth and descending truth. In what follows, I rely on the modified semantics from section 8.5 of Chapter 8 that provides ascending truth conditions and descending truth conditions for sentences uttered.

Consider a linguistic practice in which rational agents utter sentences that contain truth predicates; for ease of exposition, we can take them to speak English. For each one of their utterances, the presemantic theory assigns a clause/index pair. The clause represents the sentence and carries information about the sentence's syntactic structure or logical form—it treats 'x is true' as a univocal 1–place predicate; the index represents the context of the utterance.

The semantic theory assigns a character to 'true', but this character ignores the index since 'true' is not an indexical.[31] That is, the content assigned to 'true' is invariant across indexes. From the index and the character of the expressions in the clause, the semantic theory assigns a proposition to the clause. The content of 'true', of course, contributes to the proposition assigned to the entire sentence. The last step for the semantic theory is to generate a t-distribution for the proposition. Recall that a t-distribution is an assignment of a truth value to the proposition for each point of evaluation; however, the term 'truth value' might promote misunderstanding here since the semantic theory uses truth-in-a-model. So, from here on, I use 't$\mathfrak{M}$-value'. Note too that because our postsemantic theory outputs ascending truth value and descending truth value (instead of truth value), our semantic theory already needs an aletheic value parameter in its points of evaluation. That feature stems from replacing truth with ascending truth and descending truth—it has nothing to do with any kind of semantic relativism or specific view on the semantics for the truth predicate (see section 8.5 of Chapter 8).

The specifically relativist feature of the semantics is that the points of evaluation have an additional parameter, which I call the *aletheic standard*. Thus, the points of evaluation are <world, time, aletheic value, aletheic standard> quadruples. The aletheic standard provides a "reading" of the occurrences of the truth predicate in the sentence in question. There are two possibilities for the aletheic standard parameter: the ascending standard (S_A) and the descending standard (S_D). The ascending standard interprets the truth

[31] Throughout, I use 'indexical' in the general sense that includes any expression whose content depends on the context of utterance.

predicate as an ascending truth predicate, while the descending standard treats the truth predicate as a descending truth predicate. For example, a sentence 'p is true' is assigned t$\mathfrak{M}$-value 1 at points of evaluation <world, time, aletheic value, S_A> iff 'p is ascending true' would be assigned t$\mathfrak{M}$-value 1 at that world, time, and aletheic value; it is assigned t$\mathfrak{M}$-value 1 at points of evaluation <world, time, aletheic value, S_D> iff 'p is descending true' would be assigned t$\mathfrak{M}$-value 1 at that world, time, and aletheic value.[32]

It is crucial to keep the *aletheic value* parameter and the *aletheic standard* parameter distinct—the former determines whether the semantics is assigning an ascending truth value or a descending truth value to the sentence in question, while the latter determines whether the sentence in question is being read as having an ascending truth predicate or a descending truth predicate. If we return to the example just given and take w_0 to be a world and t_0 to be a time, then the semantics behaves in the following way:

(i) 'p is true' gets t$\mathfrak{M}$-value 1 at $\langle w_0, t_0, A, S_A \rangle$ iff 'p is ascending true' is ascending true at w_0 and t_0.

(ii) 'p is true' gets t$\mathfrak{M}$-value 1 at $\langle w_0, t_0, A, S_D \rangle$ iff 'p is descending true' is ascending true at w_0 and t_0.

(iii) 'p is true' gets t$\mathfrak{M}$-value 1 at $\langle w_0, t_0, D, S_A \rangle$ iff 'p is ascending true' is descending true at w_0 and t_0.

(iv) 'p is true' gets t$\mathfrak{M}$-value 1 at $\langle w_0, t_0, D, S_D \rangle$ iff 'p is descending true' is descending true at w_0 and t_0.

The *third* slot is the *aletheic value* parameter; it has nothing to do with semantic relativism and is present because we have replaced the concept of truth with the concepts of ascending truth and descending truth in the semantics and postsemantics (in section 8.5 of Chapter 8): 'A' means that the semantics is specifying the ascending truth value of the proposition in question, and 'D' means that the semantics is specifying the descending truth value of the proposition in question. The *fourth* slot is the *aletheic standard* parameter; it is present because 'true' is assessment-sensitive: 'S_A' means that the semantics treats 'true' in the sentence, 'p is true', as if it were 'ascending true', and 'S_D' means that the semantics treats 'true' in the sentence, 'p is true', as if it were 'descending true'. The biconditionals (i)–(iv) display the part of the t-distribution for 'p is true' at the particular world and time in question. In what follows, I use 'v' as an aletheic value variable and 's' as an aletheic standard variable.

An assessment-sensitive theory of truth also needs a postsemantics that takes t-distributions as input and outputs both ascending truth value in a context of use from a context of assessment and descending truth value in a context of use from a context of

[32] One might try a version of this theory with mixed standards—e.g., a standard that reads 'true' in positive positions as 'ascending true' and reads 'true' in negative positions as 'descending true'. However, I do not consider anything like this in what follows.

assessment. Here is a suggestion for that kind of postsemantic theory (letting u be a context of use, a be a context of assessment, i_u be the index representing u, and i_a be the index representing a):

(3a) A sentence p containing 'true' is *ascending true* at u from a iff the content assigned to the clause representing p with respect to i_u gets t𝔐-value 1 at the point of evaluation <w, t, v, s> where w and t are the world and time of i_u, v is the *ascending* aletheic value parameter, and s is the aletheic standard from i_a.

(3b) A sentence p containing 'true' is *descending true* at u from a iff the content assigned to the clause representing p with respect to i_u gets t𝔐-value1 at the point of evaluation <w, t, v, s> where w and t are the world and time of i_u, v is the *descending* aletheic value parameter, and s is the aletheic standard from i_a.

Notice that even though there are aletheic value slots and aletheic standards slots in the points of evaluation, they do not contribute to the content of the sentence in the context of utterance. Instead, the aletheic value slot determines which kind of truth conditions are being given (ascending or descending) for the sentence in question and the aletheic standard slot determines the reading of the truth predicate in p and is picked up from the context of assessment. In short, the postsemantics has a single input—the t-distribution from the semantics—and two outputs—the ascending truth value of the sentence at the context of use from the context of assessment and the descending truth value of the sentence at the context of use from the context of assessment. The postsemantics focuses on two points of evaluation from the t-distribution: (i) the world of the context of use, the time of the context of use, the *ascending* aletheic value, and the aletheic standard from the context of assessment; and (ii) the world of the context of use, the time of the context of use, the *descending* aletheic value, and the aletheic standard from the context of assessment. The former determines the *ascending* truth value of the sentence at the context of use from the context of assessment, and the latter determines the *descending* truth value of the sentence at the context of use from the context of assessment.

Arguments whose sentences contain 'true' are assessed for validity in a natural way—an argument whose premises are the members of the set G and whose conclusion is p is valid iff for every point of evaluation e, if all members of G are assigned t𝔐-value 1 at e, then p is assigned t𝔐-value 1 at e. Because all the points of evaluation are classical, the resulting logic of the truth predicate is classical as well.

To sum up: the semantics and postsemantics for 'true' given here differ from those for a familiar, univocal, invariant predicate in two ways. First, rather than giving us the *truth* values for sentences containing 'true', the theory gives us the *ascending truth* values and the *descending truth* values for sentences containing 'true'. It does this because we do not want the theory to use the inconsistent concept of truth, so it uses the replacement concepts instead. This feature has nothing to do with semantic relativism, and it is implemented by the aletheic *value* parameter in the points of evaluation (it could have been implemented differently). Second, rather than giving us the ascending truth value of a sentence containing 'true' at a context of use and the descending truth value of a sentence containing 'true' at a context of use, the theory gives us the ascending truth value of a sentence containing 'true' at a context of use *from a context of assessment* and the descending truth value of a sentence containing 'true' at a context of use *from a context of assessment*. It does this because it treats 'true' as assessment-sensitive. This feature is the semantic relativist aspect of the theory, and is implemented by the aletheic *standard* parameter in the points of evaluation.

9.5 Other options

This subsection is devoted to comparing and contrasting the descriptive theory that takes 'true' to be assessment-sensitive from the previous subsection with some other options, and to giving reasons in favor of the assessment-sensitivity view. I consider the following five options: (i) 'true' is univocal, invariant, and determinate, (ii) 'true' is referentially indeterminate, (iii) 'true' is ambiguous, (iv) 'true' is an indexical, and (v) 'true' is a non-indexical context-dependent expression.

Option (i): truth is univocal, invariant, and has a determinate extension. Given the central claim of an inconsistency approach to the aletheic paradoxes—that truth is an inconsistent concept—it is rather difficult to see how the predicate of English, 'true', that expresses it could be univocal, invariant, and have a determinate extension. What would its extension be? Any answer to this question is bound to be problematic since the reasoning for, say, the liar paradox can be cast as an argument that a liar sentence is in the extension of 'true' iff it is not. One could sidestep this problem by arguing that the truth predicate obeys (T-In) but not (T-Out) and so is like what has come to be known as a classical glutty truth predicate, or one could say that it obeys (T-Out) but not (T-In) and so is like what is called a classical gappy truth predicate.[33] However, it is difficult to see how one would argue for either one of these views over the other. If both (T-In) and (T-Out) are constitutive of truth, which is a central claim of the inconsistency approach, why would one of them hold and the other not? I do not see much promise for answering this question or for an inconsistency view that takes truth to be univocal, invariant, and have a determinate extension.[34]

Instead, it seems like a predicate that expresses an inconsistent concept is bound to display some kind of semantic pathology or have some surprising semantic features. In

[33] These terms are from Field (2008a); see Ch. 1 for details. Alternatively, one could argue that either the property of being ascending true or the property of being descending true (but not both) is a reference magnet; see Lewis (1983), R. Williams (2007), Hawthorne (2007), Sider (2009), and Chalmers (2012) for discussion of reference magnets.

[34] An error theory of truth would also fall into this category—it implies that all atomic sentences with an occurrence of 'true' are false. Aside from being exceedingly implausible, the implications of this theory for the validity of arguments whose sentences contain 'true' are hard to live with. For example, it implies that any argument whose conclusion is an atomic sentence with 'true' is unsound. Moreover, it implies that any argument consisting entirely of atomic sentences with 'true' is valid (it is impossible that its premises are true and its conclusion is false). We can do much better than that. See Boghossian (2006) for discussion of error theories for (what I am calling) inconsistent concepts.

addition, it seems like the replacement concepts, ascending truth and descending truth, should play some role in our understanding of the truth predicate.

Option (ii): 'true' is univocal and invariant, but it has a divided (indeterminate) reference. Before Hartry Field's conversion to deflationism, he defended a particular kind of correspondence theory of truth and introduced a phenomenon he dubbed referential indeterminacy.[35] In fact, the mass example that has guided my discussion of inconsistent concepts is adapted from Field's treatment. He suggests that 'mass' partially denotes relativistic mass and partially denotes proper mass. The semantics he suggests for 'mass' relies on two distinct interpretations of the language to which 'mass' belongs. One interpretation assigns 'mass' to the quantity of relativistic mass, and the other assigns it to the quantity of proper mass. It is straightforward to assign truth values to sentences containing 'mass' relative to each interpretation. That is, if we replace 'mass' in a sentence with 'relativistic mass' and the resulting sentence is true, then the original is true relative to the first interpretation; likewise for 'proper mass' and the second interpretation. Field claims that a sentence containing 'mass' is determinately true if it is true on both interpretations, determinately false if it is false on both interpretations, and neither determinately true nor determinately false if the interpretations differ.[36]

Field does not say how to define validity for arguments whose sentences contain an expression that is referentially indeterminate, but his method for assigning determinate truth and determinate falsity is known as *supervaluation*, and the most familiar supervaluation consequence relation takes it that an argument whose premises constitute a set G and whose conclusion is a sentence p is valid iff all the members of G are true in each interpretation, then p is true on each interpretation. Unfortunately, it is well-known that if the language in question has a predicate expressing determinate truth (i.e., truth in both interpretations in our case), then the logic of this language is not entirely classical—it is weakly classical. In particular, reasoning by cases, conditional proof, and *reductio ad absurdum* fail.[37] I stated earlier that I take it as a methodological assumption that an inconsistency approach should be compatible with classical logic. Thus, when paired with this version of supervaluationism, the indeterminacy option is unacceptable.

Instead, one might define validity differently (the above definition is often called *global*, and the following is called *local*): the argument with premises G and conclusion p is valid iff for each interpretation I, if all the members of G are true in I, then p is true in I. This version of supervaluationism has the benefit of being compatible with classical logic. It is also strikingly similar to the assessment-sensitivity theory that is the main focus of this chapter. Notice that the liar reasoning is diagnosed as breaking down at the same point on both theories—if (2) is a liar sentence (i.e., '(2) is not true'), then the instance of (T-In), 'if (2) is not true, then (2) is true', is not valid on either the local supervaluation view or the assessment-sensitivity view. Likewise, the instance of (T-Out), 'if

[35] Field (1972, 1973), respectively.

[36] Field (1973: 477–8).

[37] This is a well-known, although not uncontested, result. See Asher, Dever, and Pappas (2009) for details, and see R. Williams (2008) for an alternative view.

(2) is true, then (2) is not true', is also not valid on either account. Moreover, on both views, the truth predicate has no determinate extension. However, the local supervaluation view by itself says nothing about the content of the truth predicate in the sense of content given by an intensional semantic theory. Indeed, the local supervaluation view, conceived of as a logic for the truth predicate, is identical to the logic for the truth predicate specified by the assessment-sensitivity view. I am not going to prove this formally since it would require stating both views in considerable formal precision, which would not be worth the effort. Instead, once one recognizes that the aletheic standards in the points of evaluation of the assessment-sensitivity view function in exactly the same way as the interpretations in the local supervaluation view and that the definitions of validity are identical, it should be obvious that the theories are essentially the same. What the assessment-sensitivity view offers *in addition* to the logic of the truth predicate is an intensional semantics for the truth predicate. The interpretations used by the local supervaluation view are given empirical significance by the assessment-sensitivity theory as aletheic standards that function in contexts of assessment. Thus, the local supervaluation view and the assessment-sensitivity view are not competitors. One can think of the local supervaluationism as the logical core of the assessment-sensitivity theory of truth.[38]

Option (iii): 'true' is ambiguous. 'True' sometimes means *ascending true* and sometimes means *descending true*. There are many ambiguous expressions in English ('bank' is a common example), and they are usually treated as having two or more distinct meanings. When an ambiguous word is used in a conversation, the participants must disambiguate it—determine which meaning the speaker intended it to have. The intended meaning is usually obvious and we disambiguate words frequently without even noticing it by using contextual cues. In more technical terms, the semantics has two predicates that we might label 'true_1' and 'true_2', which are treated as totally distinct. They are assigned different characters, they have different contents, and they make different contributions to the propositions expressed by sentences in which they occur. The presemantic theory has to disambiguate 'true' based on the context of utterance so as to select either 'true_1' or 'true_2' as the clause that represents it. One of these is assigned the same character as 'ascending true' and the other is assigned the same character as 'descending true'.

There are several serious problems with the ambiguity option. First, linguists have compiled several tests for ambiguity and 'true' fails all of them.[39] For example, I cannot imagine a situation in which it would be felicitous to utter 'p is true, but p is not true', which is evidence against 'true' being ambiguous.[40] I am not going to go through all these tests—interested readers can investigate for themselves—mostly because there are,

[38] There is much more that could be said about the relation between the two theories, but space does not permit a detailed discussion. See Kremer and Kremer (2003), Varzi (2007), R. Williams (2008), Cobreros (2011a, 2011b), and Fara (2011).

[39] See Zwicky and Sadock (1975), Cruse (1986), Atlas (1989), Gillon (2004), and Kennedy (2010) on ambiguity and ambiguity tests.

[40] Obviously this test presupposes that dialetheism is unacceptable.

to my mind, more serious problems with this kind of theory. Second, many users of 'true' have no idea that it expresses an inconsistent concept and the vast majority of them have never heard of ascending truth or descending truth, so it is pretty implausible to suggest that a speaker using 'true' has to intend that it means either *ascending true* or *descending true*. Remember, the theory we select for 'true' should work for people who are totally unfamiliar with the liar paradox and any other reason for thinking that there is a problem with truth.

A defender of the ambiguity view might suggest that something other than speaker's intuitions determines which meaning gets attached to 'true'. Because some sentences are contingently unsafe, the resulting theory would violate the Content Determination Condition (CDC) defended in Chapter 3. Consider the CDC in light of a by now familiar example:

(E) Every complete sentence in section 9.5 of Scharp's *Replacing Truth* whose first letter is an 'E' is not true.

Imagine that Cletus asserts (E) in a conversational context with Brandine as his audience because he has it on good authority that all the sentences in question are indeed not true. Assume as well that neither Cletus nor Brandine have access to the relevant section of this book. It is easy to imagine that Cletus's utterance is felicitous (indeed, we frequently use 'true' and 'false' in situations like this). If option (iii), on which 'true' is ambiguous is correct, then (E) as uttered by Cletus expresses either the proposition that every complete sentence in section 9.5 of Scharp's *Replacing Truth* whose first letter is an 'E' is not descending true *or* the proposition that every complete sentence in section 9.5 of Scharp's *Replacing Truth* whose first letter is an 'E' is not ascending true. Which is it? Since (E) uniquely satisfies the definite description occurring in it, it turns out each reading of (E) is ascending true and not descending true (i.e., unsafe). However, this information is not in the context of utterance. To use Stalnaker's terminology, the common ground does not include the information about whether the sentences in question are unsafe, nor could this information be ascertained by querying the participants in the conversation. Thus, the conversational context does not determine which proposition (E) expresses; that result would indicate that Cletus's utterance is infelicitous.

Given the CDC and empirical unsafety, option (iii) gives us the false prediction that Cletus's utterance is infelicitous. We should not pick a theory of truth where content-determining information outruns what is available in a context of use. In other words, an adequate theory of truth ought to treat the conceptual inconsistency as a *postsemantic* phenomenon.

Option (iv): contextualism about 'true'. The idea here is that 'true' is univocal, the presemantics assigns a single clause to represent 'true', and the semantics assigns a single character to this clause. However, the character takes input from the index that represents the context of the conversation in question. The content of 'true' as used in a particular context is either *ascending true* or *descending true*. The important feature of this view is that the context of use determines whether 'true' has the content of 'ascending true' or the content of 'descending true'.

One problem with the contextualist option is that users of 'true' might not be familiar with ascending truth or descending truth and so might not do what is required for the context of utterance to determine that 'true' ends up with one of these contents. It is not even clear how the context of utterance would determine which content 'true' would get. Even if there is some intuitive way of letting the context determine its content, there is another problem with this view: it too violates the CDC defended in Chapter 3. The argument is analogous to the one just given for option (iii).

Option (v): non-indexical contextualism about 'true'. This is a more contentious view and some theorists doubt that it is even coherent because it requires denying that the content of an expression determines its extension. In the case of truth, the view treats 'true' as univocal and invariant—'true' gets assigned a single clause by the presemantics, and this clause disregards the index; so 'true' gets the same content regardless of the context of use. A non-indexical contextualist view requires an extra parameter in the points of evaluation for a judge or for standards. This sort of parameter makes sense in cases like predicates of personal taste (e.g., 'fun') or epistemic modals (e.g., 'might'). Usually, the judge or standard in addition to any other relevant parameters (e.g., worlds or times) together with the proposition expressed by the sentence in a context of use determine the truth value of the sentence uttered in the context of use. The idea is that an object satisfies the predicate only if it meets the standard or the judge would say that it does.[41]

Because we have replaced truth with ascending truth and descending truth for the purpose of doing semantics, we altered the semantic theory to have an aletheic value parameter and we altered the postsemantics to output the ascending truth value and the descending truth value of the sentence uttered in a context of use. Because of this change, we have two choices for the non-indexical contextualist theory. The first version adds an aletheic standard parameter to the points of evaluation and has the context of utterance determine the aletheic standard (either ascending or descending), which gives a reading to the sentence in question just as it does in the assessment-sensitivity option. The postsemantics is still conventional (i.e., it outputs ascending truth value in a context of use and descending truth value in a context of use) and would look something like (again, letting u be a context of use, a be a context of assessment, i_u be the index representing u, and i_a be the index representing a):

(4a) A sentence p is *ascending true* at u iff the content assigned to the clause representing p with respect to i_u gets t$\mathfrak{M}$-value 1 at the point of evaluation <w, t, v, s> where w, t, and s are the world, the time, and the aletheic standard of i_u, and v is the *ascending* aletheic value parameter.

(4b) A sentence p is *descending true* at u iff the content assigned to the clause representing p with respect to i_u gets t$\mathfrak{M}$-value 1 at the point of evaluation <w, t, v, s>

[41] I think that it makes the most sense to treat Gupta's theory (1999)—developed in Weiner (2009)—as a non-indexical contextualist view. Gupta's frames act like standards in points of evaluation. They facilitate assignment of an extension to the expression in question at a possible world.

where w, t, and s are the world, the time, and the aletheic standard of i_u, and v is the *descending* aletheic value parameter.

This version of non-indexical contextualism about truth seems to me to fall prey to a simple objection: those using 'true' might not know that it expresses an inconsistent concept and so might not have any idea that the context of utterance is supposed to determine an aletheic standard. Moreover, they might not have even heard of ascending truth or descending truth and so would have no idea what an aletheic standard is. So it is hard to see how a context of utterance could contribute an aletheic standard that would be used by the postsemantic theory.

Instead of this version of non-indexical contextualism, there is another that does not have the same problem. It does not rely on the context of utterance to supply an aletheic standard, and it is only possible because we have replaced truth in our theory with ascending truth and descending truth. The key is to let the aletheic *value* parameter (which is already present in the points of evaluation because we have replaced truth with ascending truth and descending truth) do its duty as an aletheic *standard* parameter. The points of evaluation have worlds, times, and aletheic values—so we have only three slots. The postsemantic theory looks like this:

(5a) A sentence p is *ascending true* at u iff the content assigned to the clause representing p with respect to i_u gets $t\mathfrak{M}$-value 1 at the point of evaluation $\langle w, t, v \rangle$ where w and t are the world and the time of i_u, v is the *ascending* aletheic value parameter.

(5b) A sentence p is *descending true* at u iff the content assigned to the clause representing p with respect to i_u gets $t\mathfrak{M}$-value 1 at the point of evaluation $\langle w, t, v \rangle$ where w and t are the world and the time of i_u, v is the *descending* aletheic value parameter.

The $t\mathfrak{M}$-value assignments are determined in the following way:

(i) 'p is true' gets $t\mathfrak{M}$-value 1 at $\langle w_0, t_0, A \rangle$ iff 'p is ascending true' is ascending true at w_0 and t_0.

(ii) 'p is true' gets $t\mathfrak{M}$-value 1 at $\langle w_0, t_0, D \rangle$ iff 'p is descending true' is descending true at w_0 and t_0.

Notice that this postsemantics does *not* take the aletheic standard to be given by the context of use. Instead, the ascending truth conditions are given by considering a point of evaluation that has the ascending value where the sentence in question is read by the ascending standard, while the descending truth conditions are given by considering the point of evaluation that has the descending value where the sentence is read by the descending standard. That is a big difference between this version of non-indexical contextualism and the previous one. Note that this would not work in general for other inconsistent concepts since the postsemantic theory would not be formulated in terms of them. Nevertheless, it offers a very pretty theory of our inconsistent concept of truth without resorting to a radical kind of relativism (i.e., assessment-sensitivity). Below, I explain why I prefer the assessment-sensitivity theory to this one; roughly, this theory classifies liar sentences and truth-teller sentences alike, but the assessment-sensitivity view distinguishes between them.

9.6 An example

To illustrate the two options still on the table, I present a toy language with a presemantic theory, the two semantic theories (i.e., one with <w, t, v> points of evaluation and one with <w, t, v, s> points of evaluation), and the two postsemantic theories (i.e., one with 'x is ascending true in context c' and 'x is descending true in context c', and one with 'x is ascending true in context of use u from context of assessment a' and 'x is descending true in context of use u from context of assessment a').

9.6.1 Syntax for L

Our language, L, has several kinds of basic expressions:

(i) *Individual constants*: 'I', 'Clancy', 'insanity pepper', 'space coyote', 'the sentence'
(ii) *One-place predicates*: 'cook', 'true'
(iii) *Logical connectives*: '~', '∧', '∨', '→'
(iv) *Operators*: 'now', 'possibly'.

The following are the formation rules for L's syntax:

(i) If α is an individual constant and γ is a one-place predicate, then '$\gamma(\alpha)$' is a sentence.
(ii) If ϕ and ψ are sentences, then '$\sim\phi$', '$\phi\wedge\psi$', '$\phi\vee\psi$', and '$\phi \rightarrow \psi$' are sentences.
(iii) If ϕ is a sentence, then 'nowϕ' and 'possiblyϕ' are sentences.

9.6.2 Semantics for L

A *frame* of L is a 7-tuple $\mathfrak{F} = \langle I, D, W, T, S, V, \mathfrak{I} \rangle$ such that:

(i) I is a non-empty set of indexes where for all $i \in I$, $i = \langle w, t, d, s, o \rangle$ where $w \in W$, $t \in T$, $d \in D$, $s \in S$, and $o \in D$ (i.e., i is a world/time/speaker/aletheic standard/object 5-tuple).[42]
(ii) D is a non-empty set (i.e., the domain), which includes every sentence of L.
(iii) W is a non-empty set (i.e., the worlds).
(iv) T is the set of real numbers (i.e., the times).
(v) $S = \{S_A, S_D\}$, where S_A is the ascending aletheic standard and S_D is the descending aletheic standard.
(vi) $V = \{A, D\}$, where A is the ascending aletheic value and D is the descending aletheic value.
(vii) $\mathfrak{I}$ is a function that assigns an intension to each individual constant and predicate other than 'I' and 'the sentence' (defined below).

Define the following functions on indexes:

[42] Remember, an index has information about a context of utterance and a context of assessment; it is distinct from the points of evaluation.

(i) W(<w, t, d, s, o>) = w (i.e., the world of the index)
(ii) T(<w, t, d, s, o>) = t (i.e., the time of the index)
(iii) A(<w, t, d, s, o>) = d (i.e., the agent of the index)
(iv) S(<w, t, d, s, o>) = s (i.e., the aletheic standard of the index)
(v) O(<w, t, d, s, o>) = o (i.e., the salient object of the index)

If α is an individual constant of L other than 'I', or 'the sentence', or a predicate of L, then $\mathfrak{I}$ assigns to α an intension $\mathfrak{I}_\alpha$ in the following way:

(i) If α is an individual constant other than 'I' or 'the sentence', then $\mathfrak{I}_\alpha$ is a function from W×T×V×S to D such that for all v, v′∈V and s, s′∈S, $\mathfrak{I}_\alpha$(w, t, v, s) = $\mathfrak{I}_\alpha$(w, t, v′, s′); i.e., the individual constants other than 'I' and 'the sentence' are assigned a member of the domain for each <world, time, aletheic value, aletheic standard> quadruple, and the function is invariant across aletheic standards and aletheic values.

(ii) If α = 'cook', then $\mathfrak{I}_\alpha$ is a function from W×T×V×S to a 2^D such that for all v, v′∈V and s, s′∈S, $\mathfrak{I}_\alpha$(w, t, v, s) = $\mathfrak{I}_\alpha$(w, t, v′, s′); i.e., 'cook' is assigned a subset of the domain for each <world, time, aletheic value, aletheic standard> quadruple that is invariant across aletheic standards and aletheic values.

(iii) If α = 'true', then $\mathfrak{I}_\alpha$ is a function from W×T×V×S to a 2^D; i.e., 'true' is assigned a subset of the domain for each <world, time, aletheic value, aletheic standard> quadruple.

If α is an individual constant or predicate, then the extension of α for frame $\mathfrak{F}$, index i, world w, time t, aletheic value v, and aletheic standard s (written as '$[[\alpha]]_{\mathfrak{F}, i, w, t, v, s}$') is defined in the following way:

(i) If α is a predicate or an individual constant other than 'I' or 'the sentence', then $[[\alpha]]_{\mathfrak{F}, i, w, t, v, s} = \mathfrak{I}_\alpha$ (w, t, v, s)
(ii) $[[I]]_{\mathfrak{F}, i, w, t, v, s}$ = A(i)
(iii) $[[\text{the sentence}]]_{\mathfrak{F}, i, w, t, v, s}$ = O(i)

Define the following extensions for sentences (for frame $\mathfrak{F}$, index i, world w, time t, aletheic value v, and aletheic standard s), where α is a constant, γ is a 1–place predicate, and ϕ and ψ are sentences:

(i) $[[\gamma(\alpha)]]_{\mathfrak{F}, i, w, t, v, s} = 1$ iff $[[\alpha]]_{\mathfrak{F}, i, w, t, v, s} \in [[\gamma]]_{\mathfrak{F}, i, w, t, v, s\ s}$
(iii) $[[\sim\phi]]_{\mathfrak{F}, i, w, t, v, s} = 1$ iff $[[\phi]]_{\mathfrak{F}, i, w, t, v, s} = 0$
(iv) $[[\phi \wedge \psi]]_{\mathfrak{F}, i, w, t, v, s} = 1$ iff $[[\phi]]_{\mathfrak{F}, i, w, t, v, s} = 1$ and $[[\psi]]_{\mathfrak{F}, i, w, t, v, s} = 1$
(v) $[[\phi \vee \psi]]_{\mathfrak{F}, i, w, t, v, s} = 1$ iff $[[\phi]]_{\mathfrak{F}, i, w, t, v, s} = 1$ or $[[\psi]]_{\mathfrak{F}, i, w, t, v, s} = 1$
(vi) $[[\phi \rightarrow \psi]]_{\mathfrak{F}, i, w, t, v, s} = 1$ iff if $[[\phi]]_{\mathfrak{F}, i, w, t, v, s} = 1$ then $[[\psi]]_{\mathfrak{F}, i, w, t, v, s} = 1$
(vii) $[[\text{Now}\phi]]_{\mathfrak{F}, i, w, t, v, s} = 1$ iff $[[\phi]]_{\mathfrak{F}, i, w, t, v, s} = 1$
(iv) $[[\text{Possibly}\phi]]_{\mathfrak{F}, i, w, t, v, s} = 1$ iff for some w′ $[[\phi]]_{\mathfrak{F}, i, w, t, v, s} = 1$

Now to define the contents for each sentence, constant, or predicate ζ:

(i) $\{\zeta\}_{\mathfrak{F}, i}$ = the function from <w, t, v, s> to $[[\zeta]]_{\mathfrak{F}, i, w, t, v, s}$

Contents are functions from points of evaluation to extensions; in the case of sentences, extensions are t$\mathfrak{M}$-values.

The above definition of a frame says little about how 'true' works other than that its t$\mathfrak{M}$-value might depend on the aletheic value parameter and the aletheic standard parameter—it says nothing about how these parameters function. It will be instructive to consider a particular class of frames that model an example conversation and a particular world and range of times in which the conversation takes place. In this class of frames, the domain includes an insanity pepper, a space coyote, Clancy, and of course all the sentences of L. Every frame in the class has an intension function that assigns (for the world and times in question) the following extensions: Clancy to 'Clancy', the insanity pepper to 'insanity pepper', the space coyote to 'space coyote', and all and only the cooks in the domain to 'cook'.

In this class of frames, at the world and times in question, the intension of 'true' is a function that behaves in the following way. For sentences that do not contain 'true', the aletheic standard parameter and aletheic value parameter have no effect. For sentences of L that contain 'true', the ascending aletheic standard treats 'true' as an ascending truth predicate and the descending standard treats 'true' as a descending truth predicate. So it seems like a simple substitution would do the trick. However, because some sentences attribute truth to other sentences that themselves contain truth predicates, we need to be a bit more global in our approach. Let L′ be the language that results from substituting 'ascending true' for 'true' in each sentence of L, and let L′′ be the language that results from substituting 'descending true' for 'true' in each sentence of L. For each sentence ϕ of L, there is a corresponding sentence ϕ′ of L′ and a sentence ϕ′′ of L′′. If ϕ does not contain a truth predicate, then ϕ = ϕ′ = ϕ′′. Now, the ascending standard treats the proposition in question, $\{\phi\}_{\mathfrak{F},i}$ as if it were $\{\phi'\}_{\mathfrak{F},i}$, the proposition expressed by the corresponding sentence of L′, and the descending standard treats $\{\phi\}_{\mathfrak{F},i}$ as if it were $\{\phi''\}_{\mathfrak{F},i}$, the proposition expressed by the corresponding sentence of L′′. In addition, the intension function for 'true' in the class of frames in question might assign different t$\mathfrak{M}$-values to a sentence at points of evaluation with different aletheic value parameters. At points with the ascending aletheic value, a sentence ϕ of L is assigned t$\mathfrak{M}$-value 1 iff the corresponding sentence (i.e., ϕ, ϕ′, or ϕ′′) is ascending true at the world and time in question, and at points with the descending aletheic value, ϕ is assigned t$\mathfrak{M}$-value 1 iff the corresponding sentence is descending true at the world and time in question. In sum, the intension function for 'true' in the class of frames in question obeys the following constraints:

(i) ϕ gets t$\mathfrak{M}$-value 1 at world w, time t, aletheic value A, and aletheic standard S_A iff ϕ′ is ascending true at w and t.

(ii) ϕ gets t$\mathfrak{M}$-value 1 at world w, time t, aletheic value A, and aletheic standard S_D iff ϕ′′ is ascending true at w and t.

(iii) ϕ gets t$\mathfrak{M}$-value 1 at world w, time t, aletheic value D, and aletheic standard S_A iff ϕ' is descending true at w and t.

(iv) ϕ gets t$\mathfrak{M}$-value 1 at world w, time t, aletheic value D, and aletheic standard S_D iff ϕ'' is descending true at w and t.

Thus, even though 'ascending true' and 'descending true' are not part of L, they show up in the semantics to handle the aletheic standards and the aletheic values.

9.6.3 Presemantics and postsemantics for L

Now that we have our semantic theory, imagine that Ned and Clancy are having a conversation using L; in their immediate vicinity is a blackboard they can write on. Assume that Clancy is a cook and that Ned is not a cook throughout their conversation.

9.6.3.1 The assessment-sensitivity option At a certain point in their conversation Clancy asserts 'I am a cook'. The presemantic theory selects a clause, 'cook(I)' to represent Clancy's sentence and an index <w, t, d, s, o> to represent the context of Clancy's utterance (w is the world, t is the time, d is the agent, s is the aletheic standard, and o is the salient object—which will be handy when they start talking about the sentence on the blackboard). Note that the aletheic standard is picked up from the context of assessment, not the context of utterance, but for ease of exposition, there is just one index that has information from the context of utterance and the context of assessment. Since Clancy's sentence does not have a truth predicate, the aletheic standard plays no role at all, and since his sentence is safe, its ascending truth value and descending truth value are the same. Thus, the semantic theory above assigns 1 to the clause relative to the index and all the world/time/aletheic value/aletheic standard quadruples where Clancy is a cook, and 0 otherwise.

The following is our postsemantic theory:

(3a) A sentence p containing 'true' is *ascending true* at u from a iff the content assigned to the clause representing p with respect to i_u gets t$\mathfrak{M}$-value 1 at the point of evaluation <w, t, v, s> where w and t are the world and time of i_u, v is the *ascending* aletheic value parameter, and s is the aletheic standard from i_a.

(3b) A sentence p containing 'true' is *descending true* at u from a iff the content assigned to the clause representing p with respect to i_u gets t$\mathfrak{M}$-value 1 at the point of evaluation <w, t, v, s> where w and t are the world and time of i_u, v is the *descending* aletheic value parameter, and s is the aletheic standard from i_a.

Our postsemantics implies that Clancy's sentence, 'I am a cook' is ascending true in the context of use iff Clancy is a cook; it implies that Clancy's sentence 'I am a cook' is descending true in the context of use iff Clancy is a cook.[43]

[43] Since 'Clancy is a cook' has no assessment-sensitive vocabulary, the postsemantics does not need to consider contexts of assessment at all. Alternatively, we could say that 'I am a cook' is ascending true in the context of use from any context of assessment iff Clancy is a cook, and that 'I am a cook' is descending true in the context of use from any context of assessment iff Clancy is a cook.

At another point in their conversation, Clancy writes 'Clancy is a cook' on the blackboard and utters 'the sentence is true'. The presemantic theory selects 'true(the sentence)' to represent Clancy's sentence and an index to represent the context of use. The index, however, picks up the aletheic standard from the context of assessment, so let us stipulate that the context of assessment is the same as the context of utterance and that Clancy decides on the ascending standard. In L, 'the sentence' acts like an indexical and it picks out whatever object is salient in the context—here, it is the sentence written on the blackboard.[44] I stipulated that every sentence of L is in the domain, so there is no problem picking out 'Clancy is a cook'. The clause representing Clancy's sentence, 'true(the sentence)', is assigned a proposition, which is then assigned t$\mathfrak{M}$-values at each point of evaluation. The t$\mathfrak{M}$-value assigned to it at a point $<w, t, v, s>$ where $s = S_D$ is the t$\mathfrak{M}$-value that would be assigned to the proposition expressed by the corresponding sentence of L′ at w, t, and v: ascending true(the sentence). That is, the points of evaluation with the ascending aletheic standard treat the proposition in question as if Clancy had uttered a sentence containing 'ascending true' instead of 'true'. (Likewise, the points of evaluation with the descending truth standard treat the proposition in question as if Clancy had uttered a sentence containing 'descending true' in place of 'true'. The t$\mathfrak{M}$-value assigned to it at a point $<w, t, v, s>$ where $s = S_D$ is the t$\mathfrak{M}$-value that would be assigned to the proposition expressed by the corresponding sentence of L′′ at w, t, and v. This would be relevant if Clancy had decided on the descending aletheic standard instead.) Since ''Clancy is a cook' is ascending true' is descending true (and thus ascending true) at the world and time in question, the semantic theory assigns 1 to the proposition at $<w_0, t_0, A, S_A>$ and at $<w_0, t_0, D, S_A>$ where w_0 and t_0 are the world and time of the index representing Clancy's context of use. Thus, the postsemantic theory implies that 'the sentence is true' is ascending true in the context of use from the context of assessment and that 'the sentence is true' is descending true in the context of use from the context of assessment. Had Clancy chosen the descending standard instead, the results would have been the same. (The reader will no doubt wonder what motivates this choice—I discuss the issue below).

Later, Ned writes 'the sentence is not true' on the blackboard. Although we have been considering utterances as verbal performances, let us be a bit more liberal and treat his inscription as an utterance. The presemantic theory selects '~true(the sentence)' to represent Ned's sentence, and the o slot in the index that represents his context picks out '~true(the sentence)' (i.e., the clause of the sentence written on the blackboard). In other words, Ned uttered a liar sentence. The proposition assigned to the clause is $\{\sim\text{true(the sentence)}\}_{\mathfrak{F},i}$; I abbreviate it as '$\{\phi\}_{\mathfrak{F},i}$'. Imagine it is being assessed by Clancy, who decides to use the descending aletheic standard in his context of assessment.

For points $<w, t, A, S_A>$ it assigns a t$\mathfrak{M}$-value based on whether the corresponding proposition $\{\phi'\}_{\mathfrak{F},i}$ is ascending true at w and t, and at points $<w, t, D, S_A>$ it assigns a t$\mathfrak{M}$-

[44] Again, this feature is an easy way to generate self-reference, but it is not a realistic take on the semantics for locutions like 'the sentence'.

value based on whether the corresponding proposition $\{\phi'\}_{\mathfrak{F},i}$ is descending true at w and t. For points $<w, t, A, S_D>$ it assigns a $t\mathfrak{M}$-value based on whether the corresponding proposition $\{\phi''\}_{\mathfrak{F},i}$ is ascending true at w and t, and at points $<w, t, D, S_D>$ it assigns a $t\mathfrak{M}$-value based on whether the corresponding proposition $\{\phi''\}_{\mathfrak{F},i}$ is descending true at w and t. Since Clancy chose the descending standard in the context of assessment, we look at L´´, where 'the sentence' refers to '~descending true(the sentence)', which is ascending true and not descending true at w and t. Hence, $[[\text{the sentence}]]_{\mathfrak{F}, i, w, t, A, SD} \in [[\text{ascending true}]]_{\mathfrak{F}, i, w, t, A, SD}$, so $[[\sim\text{descending true(the sentence)}]]_{\mathfrak{F}, i, w, t, A, SD} = 1$.[45] Therefore, $\{\phi\}_{\mathfrak{F},i}$ gets $t\mathfrak{M}$-value 1 at $<w, t, A, S_D>$. Moreover, $[[\text{the sentence}]]_{\mathfrak{F}, i, w, t, D, SD} \notin [[\text{descending true}]]_{\mathfrak{F}, i, w, t, D, SD}$, so $[[\sim\text{descending true(the sentence)}]]_{\mathfrak{F}, i, w, t, D, SD} = 0$. Therefore, $\{\phi\}_{\mathfrak{F},i}$ gets $t\mathfrak{M}$-value 0 at $<w, t, D, S_D>$. Remember, the third slot in the points of evaluation contains the aletheic value parameter, which determines whether the semantics is assessing the reading of the sentence for ascending truth or descending truth, while the fourth slot contains the aletheic standard parameter, which produces a reading of the sentence (it treats 'true' in the sentence as either 'ascending true' or 'descending true').

The postsemantics produces an ascending truth value for the sentence in a context of use from a context of assessment by considering the points of evaluation with the ascending aletheic value parameter, and it produces a descending truth value for the sentence in a context of use from a context of assessment by considering the points of evaluation with the descending aletheic value parameter. In particular, it yields the following results: Ned's sentence, 'the sentence is not true' is ascending true in Ned's context of use from Clancy's context of assessment, and the sentence is not descending true in Ned's context of use from Clancy's context of assessment. Since Ned uttered a liar sentence and Clancy's context of assessment invokes the descending standard, the semantics reads Ned's sentence as the descending liar. The ascending aletheic value assesses the descending liar for ascending truth—it is ascending true. Then the descending aletheic value assesses the descending liar for descending truth—it is not descending true. Had Clancy invoked the ascending standard instead, the results would have been the same.

9.6.3.2 The non-indexical contextualist option The major difference in the non-indexical contextualist theory is that there is no aletheic standard slot in the points of evaluation, so they are triples: $<w, t, v>$. The aletheic value parameter controls the reading of the sentence *and* whether it is being evaluated for ascending truth or descending truth. The

[45] Here I am writing as if 'ascending true' and 'descending true' have their own clauses in the semantic theory, which would be required for languages L´ and L´´. Although I have not specified these clauses explicitly, it should be obvious how it would be done.

postsemantics outputs the ascending truth value of the sentence in the context of use and the descending truth value of the sentence in the context of use.

The first sentence uttered by Clancy, 'I am a cook', is ascending true in the context of use and is descending true in the context of use. The second sentence uttered by Clancy, 'the sentence is true' referring to 'Clancy is a cook', has the same results. It is the third sentence, 'the sentence is not true', that Ned writes on the board, which refers to itself, that we want to investigate. Just as before, the presemantics selects '~true(the sentence)' to represent Ned's sentence and the o slot in the index that represents his context of utterance picks out '~true(the sentence)'. The semantic theory assigns a character to the clause for Ned's sentence, which together with the index, picks out the proposition that '~true(the sentence)' is not true; call this $\{\phi\}_{\mathfrak{F},i}$. This proposition is assigned a t$\mathfrak{M}$-value at every point. For points <w, t, A> it assigns a t$\mathfrak{M}$-value based on whether the corresponding proposition $\{\phi'\}_{\mathfrak{F},i}$ is ascending true at w and t, and at points <w, t, D> it assigns a t$\mathfrak{M}$-value based on whether the corresponding proposition $\{\phi''\}_{\mathfrak{F},i}$ is descending true at w and t. In L′, 'the sentence' refers to '~ascending true(the sentence)', which is ascending true and not descending true at w and t. Hence, $[[\text{the sentence}]]_{\mathfrak{F},i,w,t,v} \in [[\text{ascending true}]]_{\mathfrak{F},i,w,t,v}$, so $[[\sim\text{ascending true(the sentence)}]]_{\mathfrak{F},i,w,t,v} = 1$. Therefore, $\{\phi\}_{\mathfrak{F},i}$ gets t$\mathfrak{M}$-value 1 at <w, t, A>. On the other hand, in L″, 'the sentence' refers to '~descending true(the sentence)', which is ascending true and not descending true at w and t. Hence, $[[\text{the sentence}]]_{\mathfrak{F},i,w,t,v} \notin [[\text{descending true}]]_{\mathfrak{F},i,w,t,v}$, so $[[\sim\text{descending true(the sentence)}]]_{\mathfrak{F},i,w,t,v} = 0$. Therefore, $\{\phi\}_{\mathfrak{F},i}$ gets t$\mathfrak{M}$-value 0 at <w, t, D>. The postsemantics yields the following results: Ned's sentence, 'the sentence is not true' is ascending true in his context, and his sentence is not descending true in his context. Since the ascending value parameter reads his sentence as the ascending liar, it treats Ned's sentence as ascending true in his context. Since the descending value parameter reads his sentence as the descending liar, it treats Ned's sentence as not descending true in his context. Notice that there are no contexts of assessment and the reading of the sentence has nothing to do with the context of utterance.

On the non-indexical contextualist option, the reading of Ned's sentence and the evaluation of that reading are controlled by a single slot, so there are only two options—assessing the ascending liar for ascending truth or assessing the descending liar for descending truth. However, on the assessment-sensitivity option, there are two slots, and hence four options—assessing the ascending liar for ascending truth and for descending truth, and assessing the descending liar for ascending truth and for descending truth.

9.7 Resolving the paradoxes

There are pros and cons of each option that is still on the table (i.e., non-indexical contextualism and assessment-sensitivity). The former is surely simpler (i.e., one degree of variability in the aletheic standard), and I would prefer it if the latter were not more versatile (i.e., two degrees of variability). It is not yet clear whether that additional versatility might come in handy. So, I have presented the two postsemantic approaches to truth and the aletheic paradoxes without choosing between them so far.

Note that the two approaches say the same thing about the liar reasoning—it is invalid because it uses (T-In) and (T-Out), both of which have exceptions on these approaches. To justify this claim, we need to take a look at validity.

9.7.1 Validity

In Chapter 6, I mentioned that every logical approach to the paradoxes (except the substructural ones) is inconsistent with the claim that an argument is valid iff necessarily, it is truth-preserving. That might seem to leave us without an account of validity at all. I think this impression is mistaken. The reason has to do with the point made in section 8.5 of Chapter 8 that truth-in-a-model is a mathematical concept, not affected by the paradoxes associated with truth. The definition of validity is:

(Valid) $<\Gamma, \phi>$ is valid iff for every model $\mathfrak{M}$, if all the members of Γ are true-in-$\mathfrak{M}$, then ϕ is true-in-$\mathfrak{M}$.

For our purposes, a model is a point of evaluation in the structure described in the last couple of sections. Thus, an argument $<\Gamma, \phi>$ (where ϕ and all the members of Γ are sentences of L) is valid iff for every point of evaluation e in $\mathfrak{F}$, if for all $\gamma \in \Gamma$, γ is true at e, then ϕ is true at e.

Notice that all the inference rules of classical logic are valid according to (Valid) since every point of evaluation is classical. Notice also that instances of:

(T-In) If ϕ, then $\langle \phi \rangle$ is true, and

(T-Out) If $\langle \phi \rangle$ is true, then ϕ

where ϕ is a liar sentence, get t$\mathfrak{M}$-value 0 at some points of evaluation. For example, the instances of (T-In) get t$\mathfrak{M}$-value 0 at points of evaluation with the descending standard and the instances of (T-Out) get t$\mathfrak{M}$-value 0 at points of evaluation with the ascending standard. Thus, according to the categorization of logical approaches to the aletheic paradoxes given in Chapter 1, both postsemantic approaches are classical symmetric—they are fully compatible with classical logic and deny both (T-In) and (T-Out). The associated inference rules:

(T-Intro) $\phi \vdash \langle \phi \rangle$ is true, and

(T-Elim) $\langle \phi \rangle$ is true $\vdash \phi$

are invalid according to the postsemantic approaches. That is consistent with a classical symmetric logical approach.

In addition, note that on this inconsistency approach, (T-In) and (T-Out) are constitutive of truth, but they are not true in general. That is a crucial feature of any inconsistency approach that avoids dialetheism—since the constitutive principles of an inconsistent concept are inconsistent (possibly with respect to some additional assumptions), they cannot all be true.

9.7.2 The liar

One point to notice is how this theory deals with paradoxical sentences. For example:

(2) (2) is not true.

The liar argument is below:

1. (2) is true	[assumption for *reductio*]
2. '(2) is not true' is true	[(Sub) from 1]
3. (2) is not true	[(T-Out) from 2]
4. ⊥	[conjunction introduction from 1, 3]
5. (2) is not true	[*reductio* from 1–4]
6. '(2) is not true' is true	[(T-In) from 5]
7. (2) is true	[(Sub) from 6]
8. ⊥	[conjunction introduction from 5, 7]

Our language from the last section, L, cannot express this argument since the only way to refer to its sentences is 'the sentence'. Still, it would be easy to add '(2)' as a constant so we could formulate and evaluate this argument (I omit the details).

It is easy to see that the argument is invalid—it fails at two steps. It fails at step 3 because it is not the case that the inference from ''(2) is not true' is true' to '(2) is not true' is valid—it fails at points of evaluation with the ascending standard. Likewise, the argument fails at step 6 as well, since this move is invalid due to points of evaluation with the descending standard.

9.7.3 Other paradoxes

The other aletheic paradoxes are blocked as well for the same reason—neither (T-In) nor (T-Out) is true at every point of evaluation. Since the other two major aletheic paradoxes, Curry's paradox and Yablo's paradox, both require (T-In) and (T-Out), none of the arguments in them is valid according to the postsemantic approaches outlined here. We know that the other aletheic paradoxes that do not involve (T-In) and (T-Out) (e.g., Montague's paradox) are avoided because ADT is consistent (relative to a background set theory).

9.7.4 Truth-tellers

Although the truth-teller is not paradoxical, thinking about how it is handled by the non-indexical contextualist and assessment-sensitivity approaches provides us with additional data that might be relevant in deciding between them. The truth-teller is:

(6) (6) is true.

Again, L cannot express this sentence but it is easy to add '(6)' to L so that it can (I omit the details).

Non-indexical contextualism has only one slot for the aletheic standard, which serves two purposes: a reading of (6) and the entry in the aletheic conditions for (6). As I mentioned in Chapter 6, both truth-tellers are safe; the descending truth-teller is not ascending true and the ascending truth-teller is descending true.[46] Thus, the non-indexical contextualist approach has the following consequences for context u: (6) is ascending true in u and (6) is not descending true in u. That is, it has the same aletheic conditions as the liar.

The assessment-sensitivity view differs on the truth-teller. Assessment-sensitivity semantics has two slots for aletheic standards; one controls the reading of (6) and the other dictates which aletheic condition is relevant. The assessment-sensitivity approach implies that (as used in context u) (6) is descending true in u from contexts with the ascending standard and (6) is not ascending true in u from contexts with the descending standard. That is significantly different from the status the liar has. Therefore, non-indexical contextualism cannot distinguish between paradoxical sentences like the liar and merely odd sentences like the truth-teller, but the assessment-sensitivity approach can. That is a big point in favor of assessment-sensitivity, and for this reason I endorse the assessment-sensitivity approach (also known as non-indexical relativism) to the aletheic paradoxes. Nevertheless, it could turn out that the non-indexical contextualist approach is superior after more data come in.

9.8 Problems for semantic relativism

The literature on non-indexical contextualism and assessment-sensitivity is large and growing every week it seems. A brief summary is in order. Below is a list of the views that appeal to assessment-sensitivity or non-indexical contextualism:

(i) *general*: applies language-wide or at least for a large number of linguistic expressions[47]
(ii) *predicates of personal taste*: for example, 'tasty', 'disgusting', and 'fun'[48]
(iii) *epistemic modals*: for example, 'might' and 'could'[49]
(iv) *knowledge*: the word 'knows' and its cognates[50]
(v) *future*: all physically possible claims about the future[51]
(vi) *morality*: for example, 'good' and 'right'[52]

[46] Again, these claims are based on the intended xeno model for ADT; I do not know whether they are consequences of ADT.

[47] See Kölbel (2002, 2003, 2004, 2007), Predelli (2005), Recanati (2007, 2008), Predelli and Stojanovic (2008), Einheuser (2008), Egan (2009), Parsons (2011) and MacFarlane (forthcoming).

[48] See Kölbel (2002, 2003), MacFarlane (2005a, 2007a, 2011b, forthcoming), Egan (2006, 2010), Lasersohn (2005, 2008, 2009), and Einheuser (2008).

[49] See Kölbel (2002), Egan, Hawthorne, and Weatherson (2005), Egan (2007), Stephenson (2008, 2009), MacFarlane (2011a) and Einheuser (2008).

[50] See MacFarlane (2005b) and Brogaard (2008).

[51] See MacFarlane (2003, 2008) and Brogaard (2010).

[52] See Kölbel (2002, 2004, 2007) and MacFarlane and Kolodny (2010).

(vii) *color*: for example, 'red'[53]
(vii) *vagueness*: for example, 'bald' and 'heap'[54]
(viii) *confusion*: for example, 'mass' and 'boche'[55]
(ix) *relativistic*: for example, 'duration'.[56]

Those seem to be the major ones, but there might be others as well.

Most of these theorists argue that their theories capture the linguistic data better than the alternatives. The linguistic data include the surface grammar of the expressions in question, the ways in which speakers take one another to agree on certain points in certain situations and disagree on certain points in other situations, the circumstances under which agents treat one another as having said the same thing, the ways in which speakers treat themselves and one another as authoritative on certain issues, and the ways in which speakers retract claims in light of certain challenges. For example, one might think that if one person asserts that stewed rhubarb is tasty and another asserts that it is not, then they disagree, but neither of them is guilty of some cognitive fault or shortcoming. Instead, this might be a case of faultless disagreement. Some non-indexical contextualists and non-indexical relativists have argued that their views offer the best explanation of faultless disagreement.[57] In addition, some non-indexical relativists argue that their view explains speakers' tendency to retract previous claims better than non-indexical contextualism; for example, if Milhouse at age ten asserts that Squishees are tasty, but then at age twenty denies that they are tasty, he might say that his age ten utterance was mistaken. It is difficult for non-indexical contextualism to explain this behavior since it entails that the sentence Milhouse uttered at age ten is true in that context of use. However, the non-indexical relativist can say that the sentence Milhouse uttered at age ten is true in the age ten context of use from the age ten context of assessment, but the sentence he uttered at age ten is false in the age ten context of use from the age twenty context of assessment.[58]

Non-indexical contextualism and non-indexical relativism have come in for plenty of criticism as well. Below are some of the more prominent objections:

(i) *Self-refutation*: traditional forms of relativism are thought to be self-refuting—some argue that the new forms are as well.[59]

(ii) *Extra parameters*: some argue that it is unclear how to understand the extra parameters in the points of evaluation that are required by non-indexical contextualism and non-indexical relativism.[60]

53 See Egan (2006, 2010) and Brogaard (2010).
54 See Richard (2004, 2008) and Kölbel (2009).
55 See MacFarlane (2007b).
56 See Pinillos (2010).
57 See Kölbel (2002, 2003), Lasersohn (2005), Recanati (2007), and MacFarlane (2005a, 2007a, forthcoming).
58 See MacFarlane (2005a, 2007a, forthcoming) for discussion.
59 See Moruzzi (2008), Wright (2008), and Moruzzi and Wright (2009).
60 See Glanzberg (2007, 2009) and Cappelen and Hawthorne (2009).

(iii) *Faultless disagreement*: some argue that the phenomenon of faultless disagreement has been mischaracterized or does not exist.[61]

(iv) *Retraction*: some argue that the retraction data have been mischaracterized or do not exist.[62]

(v) *Representation*: some argue that non-indexical contextualism and non-indexical relativism are incompatible with the claim that the propositions in question are representational.[63]

(vi) *Indexicalism*: some argue that indexicalism offers a better explanation of the phenomena in question.[64]

(vii) *Utterance*: some argue that non-indexical contextualism has counterintuitive consequences for utterance truth.[65]

(viii) *Specific*: some present criticisms that are specific to particular applications—for example, Jason Stanley argues that non-indexical relativism with respect to knowledge entails that 'knows' is not factive.[66]

For those well-versed in the literature on semantic relativism, probably very little of the discussion of the descriptive theory of truth has been familiar. The way aletheic standards work in the theory described above differs from the way most standards work in semantic relativist theories, and the arguments given for the theories above differ from the kind of evidence usually marshaled in favor of semantic relativist treatments. Moreover, since all the non-indexical contextualists and assessment-sensitivity theorists (*postsemantic theorists* hereafter) currently advocate one of these views as descriptive theories of what they take to be *consistent* concepts (except in the case of confusion), most of the objections are irrelevant for my purposes.

In the case of truth, almost all speakers are ignorant of the fact that truth is an inconsistent concept. Thus, speakers use it as if it were consistent; hence, the above kinds of linguistic data with respect to truth are not decisive. Since speakers are ignorant of truth's inconsistency, they are bound to make mistakes with it. We already know that we do not see faultless disagreement or retraction data in the case of truth because speakers are unaware that truth is inconsistent and, hence, they are unaware that 'true' is assessment-sensitive. Remember: it need not be the case that simply possessing an inconsistent concept is enough for its possessor to come to know that it is inconsistent.

[61] See Glanzberg (2007), Zimmerman (2007), Stojanovic (2007), Iacona (2008), von Fintel and Gillies (2008), Wright (2008), Cappelen and Hawthorne (2009, 2011a, 2011b), Moltmann (2010), Greenough (2011b), and Schaffer (2011).

[62] See Dietz (2008), von Fintel and Gillies (2008), Wright (2008), Cappelen and Hawthorne (2009), Moltmann (2010), and Schaffer (2011).

[63] See Wright (2008). See also Boghossian (2006) and Zimmerman (2007).

[64] See Lopez de Sa (2007), Glanzberg (2007, forthcoming a), Cappelen (2008), Cappelen and Hawthorne (2009), von Fintel and Gillies (2008), and Schaffer (2011).

[65] Cappelen and Hawthorne (2009).

[66] Stanley (2005); see also von Fintel and Gillies (2008) on epistemic modals, and Glanzberg (2007) and Stojanovic (2007) on predicates of personal taste.

Notice, however, that I have not argued for an assessment-sensitive view in the familiar way. Instead, once one accepts an inconsistency approach to the aletheic paradoxes, one must choose presemantic, semantic, and postsemantic theories for truth on the basis of more general principles about language use, like the CDC defended above. Indeed, this condition gives us good reason to think that if truth is an inconsistent concept, then only a postsemantic approach to the aletheic paradoxes is acceptable. The reason is that truth is empirically inconsistent—it is inconsistent by virtue of the empirical context in which it is used—that is, rational agents that reason more or less classically[67] and speak natural languages that have the capacity to represent their own syntax. In this environment, any concept that has (T-In) and (T-Out) as constitutive principles is inconsistent. Had things been different, truth might not have been inconsistent. Therefore, 'true' is assessment-sensitive not entirely because of the ways in which speakers use it. It is assessment-sensitive because of the ways in which speakers use it together with the logical and syntactic environment in which it is used. Speakers can be, and often are, ignorant of the fact that this environment is hostile to a concept with (T-In) and (T-Out) as constitutive principles. Thus, speakers are ignorant of the fact that 'true' is assessment-sensitive. Moreover, a view that introduces contexts of assessment is much more suited to a situation where one group of people with a more advanced conceptual repertoire (e.g., theorists interested in the semantics for natural language who possess the concepts of ascending and descending truth) are trying to explain the behavior of another group of people with a less advanced conceptual repertoire (e.g., everyday speakers of English who use truth but have never heard of ascending truth or descending truth) because the more advanced concepts play a role only in the contexts of assessment. With an assessment-sensitivity theory, there is no expectation that users of the concept of truth have any familiarity with the replacement concepts.

Because of the CDC, it is unacceptable for us to use a presemantic approach (e.g., 'true' is ambiguous) or a semantic approach (e.g., 'true' is an indexical) because these would imply that speakers and hearers are ignorant of the propositions expressed by sentences containing 'true'. In other words, it cannot be that linguistic expressions are ambiguous or indexical by virtue of the environment in which they are used. However, a linguistic expression can be assessment-sensitive by virtue of the environment in which it is used if the concept expressed by that expression is inconsistent in that environment. That, I claim, is exactly the case with truth.

Another major difference between my use of semantic relativism and the use to which it is more often put is the standards that serve as the extra parameter in points of evaluation. The difference is that standards are usually ways of modifying or narrowing the content of the expression in question, whereas, in the case of truth, they provide an alternative reading of the truth predicate. For example, if one takes 'fun' to be assessment-sensitive or non-indexical contextual, then the points of evaluation have an extra slot for

[67] That is, deviations from classical logic are minor (e.g., I or R) compared to what is required to avoid the paradoxes (e.g., LP, BX, or K_3).

an enjoyment standard. A standard of enjoyment often just specifies that in which a particular person finds enjoyment. The standard of enjoyment does not reinterpret the word 'fun'; rather, since what is fun seems to be subjective, it provides the extra bit of information that allows one to assign an extension to 'fun'. On the other hand, in the case of truth, the aletheic standards do *not* encode what a particular person takes to be true, and the motivation for semantic relativist treatment is *not* some antecedent intuition that truth is somehow subjective. Instead, there are only two possible aletheic standards and they reinterpret the word 'true' so that the semantic theory can assign it an extension without falling into contradiction—one reads 'true' as 'ascending true' and the other reads it as 'descending true'.[68] There is no reason to think that a person will adopt one of these aletheic standards but not the other—the aletheic standards are not personal. Instead, someone who knows that truth predicates are assessment-sensitive can switch back and forth between the two in order to get a better grip on the semantic features of some sentence with an occurrence of 'true'. Unlike standards of enjoyment, which are often thrust upon us by our responses to external stimuli, an aletheic standard is chosen by an interpreter based on whether it makes more sense to consider the truth claim in question as an ascending truth claim or a descending truth claim at that moment.

By treating 'true' as assessment-sensitive, those of us who both recognize that it expresses an inconsistent concept and possess the proper replacement concepts can interpret people—in a consistent way—who use 'true'. We can understand their assertions, assess their claims, and evaluate their arguments, all without contradicting ourselves, giving up any cherished logical principles, or treating them as if they do not understand the content of 'true'. In short, the assessment-sensitive theory of truth uses the semantic relativist's formal machinery, but interprets it in a new way that satisfies one demand of an inconsistency approach to the aletheic paradoxes.

Some common objections to semantic relativism are relevant to the theories of truth presented here. For example, Herman Cappelen and John Hawthorne claim that non-indexical contextualism has horribly counterintuitive consequences for the contrast between the truth of utterances and the truth of propositions. Take non-indexical contextualism with respect to 'fun' as an example and assume that Luke asserts 'Whacking Day is not fun', while Mel asserts 'Whacking Day is fun'. Cappelen and Hawthorne claim that the non-indexical contextualist should recommend that Luke respond by asserting 'your assertion is true but the proposition that you are expressing by your assertion is not true'.[69] On the basis of this counterintuitive consequence, Cappelen and Hawthorne conclude: "when the smoke has cleared, we find it hard to see any significant avenues opened up by non-indexical contextualism."[70]

The problem with this objection is nicely diagnosed by Berit Brogaard who writes: "Two different notions of truth are in play here. One is monadic utterance truth, the

[68] This feature is not unprecedented—the supervaluation semantics considered in section 9.5 is similar.
[69] Cappelen and Hawthorne (2009: 22).
[70] Cappelen and Hawthorne (2009: 24).

other relative propositional truth. A better-tasting and more easily digestible version ... would be: your [assertion] is true simpliciter but the proposition you are expressing by your [assertion] is not true relative to me as the speaker, though it is true relative to you as the speaker."[71] Their "objection" is based on a simple equivocation.

A standard criticism of semantic relativism is that indexicalism does a better job of explaining the data.[72] However, this sort of objection has no bite in the case of truth. Very few possessors of the concept of truth are aware that it is an inconsistent concept, and very few users of truth predicates are aware that they are assessment-sensitive. As such, very few users of truth predicates treat them as one would treat an assessment-sensitive expression or as one would treat an indexical. Once one accepts an inconsistency approach to the paradoxes, one has to decide between indexicalism and semantic relativism on other considerations. I have argued that indexicalism is not a good candidate for 'true' because of the combination of empirical unsafety and the CDC. Semantic relativism, however, does not run afoul of the CDC.

One might, however, worry that the assessment-sensitivity theory does have a similar problem. After all, if truth is assessment-sensitive but very few people know that it is, then very few people will know to adopt aletheic standards in contexts of assessment. How can the assessment-sensitivity theory accurately describe and explain the facts about how truth predicates function in our natural languages when almost no one ever adopts an aletheic standard? Wouldn't we need to educate all English speakers about truth's inconsistency and the replacement concepts before the assessment-sensitivity theory could be expected to deliver the right results?

The answers to these questions and the key to replying to this objection come by answering another question: who are the consumers of approaches to the aletheic paradoxes? They are for people who are bothered by the problems posed by the aletheic paradoxes—problems like: (i) we can derive intuitively absurd conclusions from intuitively obvious assumptions via intuitively obvious inferences, and (ii) one arrives at inconsistent results when one tries to use a standard semantic theory to explain semantic features of truth predicates. These are the people to whom I am recommending the assessment-sensitivity theory of truth, and these are the people who, if they want solutions to their problems, will need to get up to speed on the concepts of ascending truth and descending truth so that they can adopt aletheic standards in contexts of assessment. People who are ignorant of the aletheic paradoxes have no need for or interest in possessing these concepts or adopting these standards. The theory is for the theorists—those who want to make sense of those who use our inconsistent concept of truth. It is only those who use the theory that adopt aletheic standards and so need to possess the concepts of ascending truth and descending truth. That is exactly the major benefit of the assessment-sensitivity view. On the ambiguity view or the indexical view, speakers

[71] Brogaard (2010: 3).

[72] See Glanzberg (2007, forthcoming a), Cappelen (2008), Cappelen and Hawthorne (2009, 2011a, 2011b), von Fintel and Gillies (2008), and Schaffer (2011).

choose between *ascending true* and *descending true* as the content of 'true', which is exceedingly implausible since most speakers do not possess these concepts. On the assessment-sensitivity view, speakers just utter sentences containing 'true', and 'true' has an invariant content. Hearers attribute contents to the claims made by speakers in the same intuitive way. The contexts of assessment and the aletheic standards are for theorists who want to attribute ascending truth conditions and descending truth conditions to sentences containing 'true'. There is no reason to think that ordinary speakers or hearers would have any interest in such a thing. The only people who should care about ascending truth conditions and descending truth conditions are those of us who want to solve the problems posed by the aletheic paradoxes.

In addition, one might wonder why the CDC (i.e., information needed to determine the contents of sentences felicitously uttered in a conversation is available to its participants) is correct but a similar Truth-Conditions Determination Condition (TCDC) (i.e., information needed to determine the truth conditions of sentences felicitously uttered in a conversation is available to its participants) is not; especially because the CDC rules out all but the assessment-sensitivity theory and a version of the non-indexical contextualist theory, and a TCDC would rule out even these two options.[73]

The CDC makes sense because participants in a conversation have to keep track of the common ground and many other elements of the conversational score (as described in Chapters 2 and 3). The primary vehicles for changing the score are uttering new sentences, challenging utterances already made, and giving reasons in response to challenges. Participants keep track of all these moves by grasping the contents of the sentences uttered. Unless the participants can grasp the contents of the sentences uttered in a conversation, they cannot effectively keep score. If participants cannot keep score properly, then they cannot determine which moves are permissible at any given point, which means they cannot effectively participate. Thus, the CDC is a natural principle to have for linguistic expressions that have an established history of usage in conversations. I think one could define a linguistic expression that violates it, but such an expression would not survive in the wild.

On the other hand, a TCDC would be much less plausible. It seems to me that a TCDC would go hand in hand with the view that a person's linguistic competence consists, at least in part, in believing or accepting a truth-conditional semantic theory for that person's language. Even Davidson, who championed truth-conditional semantic theories, does not accept this claim, and I find it rather implausible as well.[74]

A truth-conditions determination principle might seem plausible because it is plausible to think that linguistically competent speakers know whether a sentence would be true or false under a wide range of conditions. For example, consider the sentence 'Snowball is a cat'. A competent speaker should be able to say whether this sentence would be true if Snowball were a Dalmatian, if Snowball had three legs but was otherwise the same, if Snowball were suspended in the air, if Snowball had no whiskers,

[73] Thanks to Matti Eklund for pushing this objection.

[74] Davidson (1973).

etc. However, it is unrealistic to expect competent speakers to grasp all the truth conditions of every sentence. For example, consider the sentence 'the largest tree in my yard is a beech'. A competent speaker should be able to say whether this sentence would be true if this tree were ten feet taller than it actually is, if this tree lost all its leaves, if this tree had a swing hanging from it, etc. However, we should not expect such a speaker to be able to say whether the sentence would be true if this tree had samara instead of nuts, if this tree had leaves that were acuminate at the apex, etc. Thus, a Truth Conditions Determination Condition (at least in this sense) would be implausible.

Still, one might think that this is a rather weak case against participants grasping truth conditions. Perhaps it is. However, I do not really need to make this case. I use the CDC in this chapter only to help decide between semantics/postsemantics for 'true' that appeal to ascending truth and descending truth. Thus, the contrast is not between a CDC and a Truth Conditions Determination Condition; rather, it is between a CDC and an Ascending Truth-Conditions and Descending Truth-Conditions Determination Condition. It seems to me exceedingly implausible to credit speakers with a grasp of ascending truth conditions or descending truth conditions.

Consider another objection: Crispin Wright argues that semantic relativist theories are appropriate only for propositions that are non-representational because these theories allow for faultless disagreement. For example, an assessment-sensitivity theory of knowledge would be acceptable, according to Wright, only if there is nothing for knowledge attributions to represent. Presumably, many of us have the intuition that at least some knowledge attributions represent certain mental states of certain people. Thus, Wright's point, if correct, would pose a problem for these accounts of knowledge.[75] Wright's point, if it is correct, does not affect the assessment-sensitivity theory of truth since I do not think there is any property of truth to be represented by our word 'true' and our concept of truth. Instead, there are two properties, being ascending true and being descending true, and anyone who thinks there is a property of being true is confused. Thus, the claim that 'true' does not represent something (i.e., the property of being true) is one I endorse. The assessment-sensitivity view of truth does allow for limited faultless disagreement (in certain cases where the difference between ascending truth and descending truth is not negligible). Moreover, I have argued that, together, ascending truth and descending truth can give an adequate account of the representational aspect of content insofar as they play an explanatory role in the revised semantic and postsemantic theories offered above. Thus, Wright's worry is not a problem for my proposal.

9.9 Pragmatics and 'true'

Under what conditions, on an assessment-sensitivity approach, do speakers make mistakes with 'true'? Here is one obvious proposal. If the difference between ascending truth and descending truth is negligible, then it is legitimate to use 'true'. If it is not, then

[75] Wright (2008). See MacFarlane (2005b) for an assessment-sensitivity theory of knowledge.

'ascending true' and 'descending true' should be used instead. When is the difference negligible? Recall Craige Roberts' pragmatic theory (from Chapter 1). One of her innovations is the idea of a question under discussion (QUD), which guides the conversation, has a role in determining conversational implicatures and presuppositions (because it affects whether participants are following the conversational maxims—quality, quantity, relevance, and manner), and helps explain other phenomena including anaphora, deixis, ellipsis, focus, and prosody. One suggestion is that if it is in the common ground that the common ground entails that an answer to the question under discussion requires a distinction between ascending truth and descending truth, then the distinction is not negligible. Otherwise it is. Notice the two roles of the common ground here: it determines whether the distinction is needed in order to answer the question under discussion, and it determines whether people know that it makes this determination.[76]

The QUD proposal is not specific enough because questions under discussion can be given more or less detailed answers. Where am I? I am in the dining room of my house as I type this sentence, but that might not be a good answer to this question. Instead, the person asking it might want to know whether I am back in the United States after a trip to Scotland. Or whether I am on campus versus at home. I am in the United States, and I am at home, and I am in the dining room. Which one answers the question? All of them do in more or less detail. So it seems like we need to say that the common goals of the conversation in question have an impact on whether it makes sense to use 'true'. If the goals of the conversation can be met whether or not the participants distinguish between ascending truth and descending truth, then the distinction between them is negligible. In these cases, it makes sense to use the replacement concepts. We can alter the above account in the following way: if it is in the common ground that the common ground entails that an answer to the question under discussion to a degree required to meet the common goals of the conversation requires a distinction between ascending truth and descending truth, then the distinction is not negligible for that conversation.

Note that some care must be taken in applying this pragmatic theory for 'true'. Consider *ancient Monty*, who lives in 1500 BCE. If ancient Monty asserts that the Earth stands still and the Sun revolves around it, then we can hardly fault him for asserting something false since, given his level of intelligence, education, and the state of technology and common knowledge at the time, he is incapable of knowing any better. A proper pragmatic theory ought to reflect these facts. However, if we think about a person alive today, *contemporary Monty*, who asserts that the Earth stands still and the Sun revolves around it, then we should almost certainly say that his assertion is inappropriate because it is not true—and he should know better. I am suggesting that the correctness of assertion should be thought of as dependent on various aspects of context; however, I am not

[76] This suggestion requires a non-standard notion of common ground since it presupposes that not all logically true propositions are in the common ground. However, it is obvious that we need something like this anyway, otherwise it would be infelicitous to assert, say, the Modularity Theorem, even for the first time after proving it!

going to delve more deeply into this issue. It should be sufficient to say that, whatever turns out to be the right view of correct assertion, it should handle cases like these; so it should also be able to handle the distinction between cases where people inadvertently use 'true' in situations where the distinction between ascending truth and descending truth is relevant (unbeknownst to them) and in cases where they should know better. The double use of common ground and the appeal to common goals in the suggestion above is meant to be a step in this direction.

We can distinguish three important types of conversations involving 'true': (i) *ignorance cases*, where everyone involved in the conversation is ignorant of truth's inconsistency; (ii) *mixed cases*, where someone who knows that truth is inconsistent is conversing with interlocutors who do not know that it is inconsistent; and (iii) *informed cases*, where all participants know of truth's inconsistency. Given that inconsistency approaches to the aletheic paradoxes are so obscure, it makes sense to treat ignorance cases like we would treat ancient Monty. Even if (when?) the inconsistency approach I present in this book catches on and becomes the received view in linguistics, philosophy of language, and philosophical logic, it still will not make sense to treat non-specialists as if they should know better. Given the insignificance of research on the aletheic paradoxes for most people's lives, we can hardly fault those in ignorance cases for using 'true' even when the distinction between ascending truth and descending truth is non-negligible.

For informed cases, if the common goals of the conversation can be met without distinguishing between ascending truth and descending truth, then there is no reason for the participants to use the replacement concepts. If, however, the goals of the conversation cannot be met without making the distinction, and all the interlocutors realize this, then they should use the replacements. We can offer a slightly weaker formulation: if it is reasonable to think that an interlocutor should be held responsible for knowing that the goals of a particular conversation cannot be met without distinguishing between ascending truth and descending truth, then that interlocutor should not use 'true' in that conversation.

Finally, consider mixed cases. It seems to me that the informed interlocutor should not use the replacement concepts at all in a mixed case unless the goals of the conversation demand that the participants in the conversation distinguish between ascending truth and descending truth and the ignorant interlocutors are willing to let the informed interlocutor introduce them to the replacement concepts. That is, if there is no other way for them to accomplish their common goals without having the informed interlocutor explain the distinction between ascending truth and descending truth, then it makes sense for the informed interlocutor to introduce and use the replacements. However, that sort of situation is probably going to be very rare. Notice, however, that this book is being put forth in a mixed-case conversation. Very few of my interlocutors (i.e., those with an interest in what analytic philosophers have to say about the concept of truth) are informed. So although mixed cases where it makes sense to avoid 'true' are rare, they do occur.

To go back to our paradigm example of 'mass', in a conversation about how best to economically design a house so that it is most likely to survive an earthquake of 7.0 or less, the distinction between relativistic mass and proper mass is negligible, since this distinction is not needed in order to answer this question to a degree required by the goals of the conversation. However, in a conversation about the source of dark flow (i.e., the observed but currently unexplained motion of hundreds of galaxy clusters in the same direction relative to the cosmic background radiation),[77] the distinction is relevant because a failure to distinguish between proper mass and relativistic mass would most certainly prevent the participants from finding the right answer (indeed, it would probably be impossible to even frame the question since the distinction is presupposed by ΛCDM—the standard model of cosmology, which serves as a background for evidence supporting dark flow). Likewise, in a conversation about how best to give a semantics for the fragment of language that linguists use in order to do semantics for natural languages, one had better distinguish between ascending truth and descending truth, since a failure to do so would result in an inconsistent theory, which would also fail to answer the question under discussion. However, in a conversation about whether a friend, Jessica, should be trusted, the participants can almost certainly use 'true' without any trouble. Even if they end up uttering or assessing what turn out to be paradoxical sentences, these are "close enough" to non-paradoxical ones for the purposes at hand. That is, even if they had distinguished between ascending truth and descending truth, they would have arrived at the same conclusions, but with considerably more effort.

9.10 The nature of truth

The vast majority of work on the nature of truth is engaged in trying to find a conceptual analysis of truth. This would be something like a definition of truth in terms that are more primitive or more fundamental or better understood or less controversial. Many have criticized this kind of project before, mostly on the grounds that there is nothing more primitive, fundamental, better understood, or less controversial.[78] I too see no hope for such a project, and I want to say a bit about my reasons.

All the purported analyses agree that the primary aletheic principles:

(T-In) If ϕ, then $\langle\phi\rangle$ is true, and

(T-Out) If $\langle\phi\rangle$ is true, then ϕ

hold. However, as I argued in Chapter 3, when we look at logical approaches to the aletheic paradoxes that validate (T-In) and (T-Out), they all require a rejection of classical logic and with it some constitutive principles for our logical expressions.

Unless one is going to treat something as an inconsistent concept, it does not seem as though there is any way out of this mess. Since the aletheic paradoxes (including the problems canvassed pertaining to contingent paradoxes and revenge paradoxes) give us good reason to think that truth is an inconsistent concept, and we have no independent

[77] See Kashlinsky et al. (2008, 2009) for details.

[78] Davidson (1996) summarizes his reasons, which seem like good ones to me.

reason to suspect that our logical concepts are inconsistent, it seems best to avoid giving anything like an analysis of truth as part of a unified theory. No analysis of truth is going to do justice both to the primary aletheic principles and to the principles constitutive of our logical concepts. Any analysis of truth will have to, at the very least, respect the constitutive principles. I have made a case for thinking that (T-In) and (T-Out) are constitutive, based on the fact that, without them, 'true' could not play its stereotypical expressive role. An analysis that does not entail the primary aletheic principles is inadequate, while one that does is either inconsistent or incompatible with the constitutive principles of logical connectives.

That leaves us without much in the way of a view on the nature of truth. In this section, I suggest that the metrological naturalist perspective adumbrated in Chapter 7 works well as a theory of the nature of truth. As I mentioned in the Introduction, this strategy is in accord with my views on philosophical methodology; I advocate metrological naturalism (i.e., measurement-theoretic methodological naturalism) as a philosophical methodology, according to which a philosophical theory of X should have the form of a measurement system for X. It should come as no surprise that I follow the same strategy here. A theory of truth should have the form of a measurement system for truth. Although I am not alone in this view, there are not many of us. The most obvious and famous example is Donald Davidson's theory of truth. His most extended discussion occurs in his 1990 John Dewey lectures "The Structure and Content of Truth." Although Davidson does not explain his views in detail, when one follows up on his hints, one arrives at metrological naturalism with respect to truth. As far as I can tell, this kind of theory of truth has not received the attention it deserves in the debates about the nature of truth.[79]

A measurement system for truth based on the assessment-sensitivity view given in the last section has as its physical structure a natural language containing a truth predicate; as its relational structure an artificial language with an assessment-sensitive truth predicate and the theory of that assessment-sensitive truth predicate from the previous section; and as its mathematical structure the model theory for the artificial language. Let us go through these in a little more detail.

The physical structure is just as it was in Chapter 7—a natural linguistic practice with a truth predicate that has a finite lexicon and a recursive syntax. For simplicity, we can assume that it does not contain ascending truth or descending truth predicates (although we can drop this assumption once we see how the truth predicate works). The people in the linguistic practice use 'true' in their linguistic utterances. The pragmatic theory given in section 9.9 describes this practice. They also reason using the concept of truth and have tons of propositional attitudes with the concept of truth as a constituent.[80]

[79] However, see Patterson (2010) for a presentation and defense of a Davidsonian view.

[80] I have not said anything about how people arrive at their judgments pertaining to truth (i.e., what Yablo calls a psychological theory), but Patrick Suppes has taken a step in this direction; see Suppes and Béziau (2004) and Suppes (2008, 2009).

The relational structure contains a classical first-order artificial language with the usual syntax and a truth predicate. As before, the artificial language can contain anything for which we have canonical semantic theories (e.g., names, definite descriptions, mass nouns, adverbs, indexicals, demonstratives, pronouns, and gradable adjectives). The theory of truth for this language takes its truth predicate to be assessment-sensitive, as described above.

The mathematical structure consists of the standard set-theoretic structure for modeling assessment-sensitivity, which consists in the standard intensional semantics with possible worlds. However, just as in most model theory, one defines truth-in-a-model, which is a technical, mathematical concept. All of this was described above and illustrated with the example of language L.

As in the measurement system for ascending and descending truth described in Chapter 7, the connection between the physical structure and the relational structure is very complex—it consists of translating the natural language into the artificial language (as clauses) in order to arrive at the logical form of the natural-language sentences, and representing the contexts of use with indexes. There are many fascinating issues here, but none of them is specific to my project—they all bear on formal semantics in general. I have touched on many of these in this chapter and in Chapter 8 (e.g., Predelli on interpretive systems and linguistic practices, and the distinction between presemantics, semantics proper, and postsemantics).

The connection between the relational theory and the mathematical theory is accomplished in the usual way by defining truth-in-a-model. I outlined the way this works above and illustrated it with the example language L, but there are many technical details omitted in the interest of space. The definition of truth-in-a-model requires an account of ascending truth and descending truth, which is provided by ADT in Chapter 6.

Again, this measurement system for truth is an alternative to an analysis of truth or a reductive explanation of truth. Note that no consistent analysis of truth can have (T-In) and (T-Out) as consequences and be compatible with classical logic. When it comes to inconsistent concepts, both conceptual analysis and reductive explanation are non-starters unless one is happy embracing a non-classical logic. Metrological naturalism allows us to have a consistent theory of our inconsistent concept of truth. One important difference between this application of metrological naturalism and the one in Chapter 7 is that the theory of truth plays no role in a Davidsonian unified theory of belief, desire, and meaning. Instead, this role is played by ADT. 'True' is just one of the predicates in the natural language to be explained.

9.11 A unified theory of truth: CAM

Recall that a unified theory of truth consists of a theory of the nature of truth (which often consists of a conceptual analysis of truth or some other theory specifying what truth is and what kinds of things are true), a philosophical approach to the aletheic paradoxes (which specifies syntactic, semantic, or pragmatic features of natural-language truth predicates that are relevant to the aletheic paradoxes), and a logical approach to the aletheic paradoxes (which specifies which aletheic principles truth predicates obey and the strongest logic compatible with those principles). In this chapter, I have presented all the elements of a unified theory of truth.

The measurement system given in the last section is the theory of the nature of truth (together with the claims that truth is an inconsistent concept and words expressing inconsistent concepts are assessment-sensitive). This theory of the nature of truth dovetails with both a logical approach to the aletheic paradoxes and a philosophical approach to the aletheic paradoxes.

The logical approach is given by the theory of an assessment-sensitive truth predicate—it is a classical symmetric theory. That is, it is compatible with classical logic, and it takes (T-In) and (T-Out) to hold for most sentences, but they have exceptions. The exceptions are specified by the assessment-sensitive semantics. The philosophical approach is given by the claims that truth is an inconsistent concept and that words expressing inconsistent concepts are assessment-sensitive. The philosophical approach is an inconsistency view, based on the theory of inconsistent concepts from Chapter 2 and argued for in Chapters 3 and 4.

Two aspects of the unified theory of truth deserve mention: since truth is a useful inconsistent concept, it needs to be replaced with one or more consistent concepts (for me, ascending truth and descending truth), and those consistent concepts play an important role in the unified theory of truth—they serve crucial explanatory roles in the assessment-sensitivity semantics for the truth predicate. So, the theory of ascending truth and descending truth (ADT) and its formal semantics (xeno semantics) are incorporated into the unified theory of truth. We can call this a **C**lassical, **A**ssessment-sensitive, **M**etrological unified theory of truth (CAM theory). I repeat a diagram from Chapter 1 showing the other unified theories of truth that have been proposed and how the one I have presented fits into the picture (see Figure 12).

Note that not only is CAM a unified theory, but it is also an integrated theory in the sense that all the parts fit together naturally in the measurement system for truth. The other unified theories just take a view on the nature of truth (e.g., disquotationalism), a compatible logical approach (e.g., paracomplete), and a compatible philosophical approach (e.g., indeterminacy), and stick them together (often not even explicitly). By contrast, the three components of CAM theory all fall out of the measurement system for truth, which is an integrated whole.

9.12 Expressive role

Truth predicates play distinctive expressive roles—they serve as devices of endorsement and as devices of rejection (explained in Chapter 3). How does CAM do in explaining these?

First, according to CAM, (T-In) and (T-Out) are constitutive of the concept of truth, which is the reason why it is an inconsistent concept. Since (T-In) and (T-Out) explain these expressive roles, CAM can make sense of why those who use truth predicates *take them* to serve these expressive roles. Participants in linguistic practices take (T-In) and (T-Out) to be constitutive of truth, which leads them to think these principles are true,

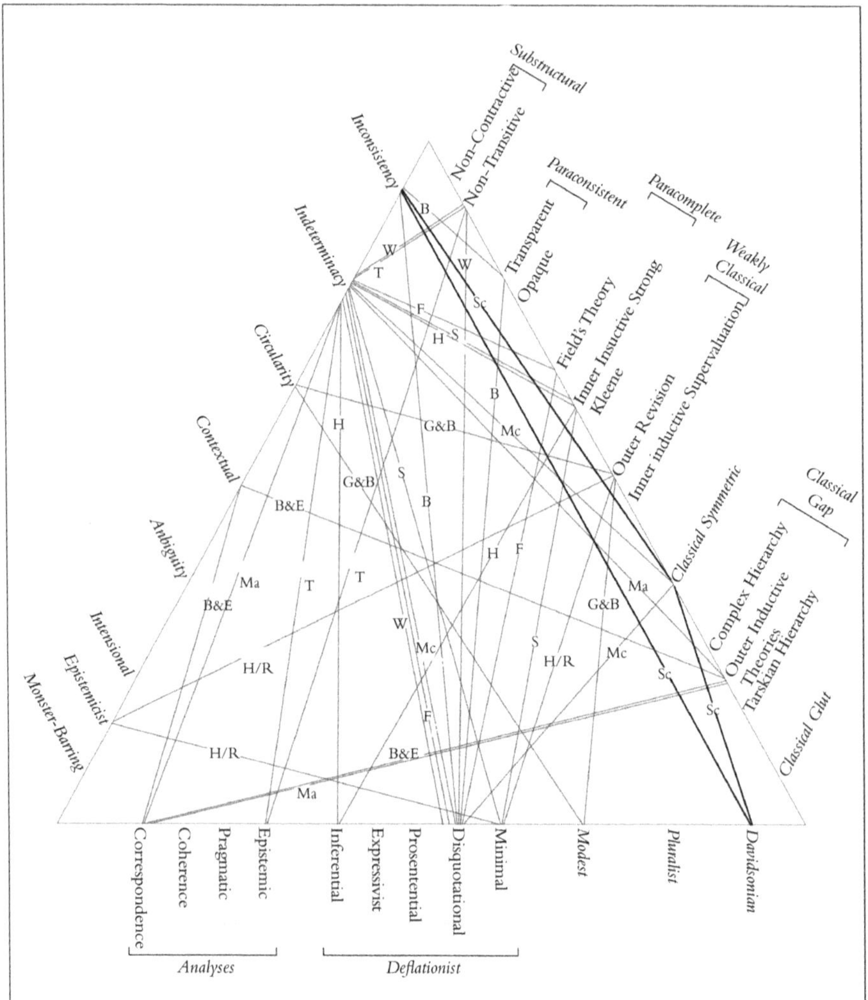

B&E	Barwise & Etchemendy	Ma	Maudlin
B	Beall	Mc	McGee
F	Field	S	Soames
G&B	Gupta & Belnap	T	Tennant
H	Horsten	W	Weir
H/R	Horwich / Restall	Sc	Scharp

Figure 12 CAM Theory

which leads them to use truth predicates as devices of endorsement and as devices of rejection. For example, in a conversation between Sherri and Terri, Sherri asserts 'Frink's theory is true'. Both Sherri and Terri take (T-In) and (T-Out) to be constitutive of 'true', so they both take Sherri to have committed herself to the claims that constitute Frink's theory, regardless of the content of those claims, or their levels, or whether Sherri or Terri knows what Frink's theory says, or the language in which Frink's theory is formulated. That is an example of 'true' being used as a device of endorsement, and CAM explains why people use it that way.

However, according to CAM, (T-In) and (T-Out) have exceptions—there are sentences p such that 'p is true' does not follow from p, and there are sentences q that do not follow from 'q is true' (it turns out that exceptions to one will also be exceptions to the other). Thus, if one calls one of these sentences true, then one has not thereby endorsed that sentence. For example, assume that one of the sentences that make up Frink's theory is an exception. Call it p. When Sherri asserts that Frink's theory is true, she commits herself to all the sentences of Frink's theory that are not exceptions, but she does not commit herself to p since p does not follow from 'p is true'. Even though Sherri and Terri both assume that she has committed herself to p, they are wrong. Thus, CAM predicts that people will use truth predicates as devices of endorsement because of its constitutive principles, but it also predicts that there will be some mistakes about these uses since users do not realize that these constitutive principles are inconsistent (given facts about syntax).

9.13 Revenge

How does CAM avoid revenge paradoxes? Consider a sentence that might seem to give rise to a revenge paradox:

(7) (7) is either false or paradoxical.

I have not shown how to introduce 'paradoxical' into our example language, but here is an intuitive way to do it:

A sentence p containing 'true' is *paradoxical* iff (T-In) and (T-Out) fail for p.

In the example language, 'paradoxical' would have as its extension all the sentences that the semantic theory treats as expressing unsafe propositions.

One might try to argue that (7) causes a problem for CAM in the following way:

1. Assume (7) is true.
2. '(7) is either false or paradoxical' is true.
3. (7) is either false or paradoxical.
4. Assume (7) is either false or paradoxical.
5. '(7) is either false or paradoxical' is true.
6. (7) is true.

If this argument were valid, it would be a problem, but it is not. CAM is fully classical, so the logical inferences in this argument are all fine. However, since (7) is paradoxical, the move from 2 to 3 is invalid and the move from 4 to 5 is invalid. The upshot is: CAM implies that (7) is paradoxical, but it does not imply that '(7) is paradoxical' is true.[81] So, of course, CAM has consequences that it deems untrue. Is this a problem? It would be a problem if CAM implied that truth is a consistent concept, but it does not. Instead, CAM implies that truth is an inconsistent concept that cannot be legitimately applied in every circumstance. Indeed, the theory of ascending truth and descending truth specifies exactly where truth can be used without running into problems (i.e., when the difference between ascending truth and descending truth is negligible). Accordingly, CAM is outside the legitimate scope of truth—according to the pragmatic theory for 'true', one should not use it here. Consider the analogy. Even though the concept of mass is inconsistent, it is fine to use it in certain situations (i.e., when the difference between relativistic mass and proper mass is negligible). However, if one tries to use mass outside these situations, say, in calibrating the atomic clocks in GPS satellites, it will not provide accurate predictions. Instead, in these circumstances, one needs to use the replacements.

In the case of truth, one can reasonably ask whether CAM is ascending true and whether it is descending true. All the central principles of CAM are descending true. Recall, however, that descending truth is not preserved under logical consequence. So it could turn out that CAM has some consequences that are not descending true. They would, of course, be ascending true. I have been unable to identify any consequences of CAM that have this feature, but I have not been able to rule it out either. If it does have these kinds of consequences, then it would be in the same boat as ADT. Either way, there are no revenge paradoxes here.

Instead, the would-be revenger might focus on the special three-place predicates introduced in Chapter 8 and utilized by the postsemantics for 'true' in this chapter. I am thinking in particular about sentences like:

(8) For all u, for all a, (8) is not ascending true in u from a,

(9) For all u, for all a, (9) is not descending true in u from a.

'u' ranges over contexts of utterance and 'a' ranges over contexts of assessment. Assume for *reductio* that for some a and u, (8) is descending true in u from a. Thus, 'for all u and for all a, (8) is descending true in u from a' is descending true in u_0 from a_0 (where 'u_0' and 'a_0' are individual constants). But since (8) does not contain any indexicals or assessment-sensitive terms, we can conclude that it is descending true. It follows that for all u, for all a, (8) is not ascending true in u from a. Again, since (8) has no indexicals or assessment-sensitive terms, we can conclude that (8) is not ascending true, and so not

[81] CAM treats 'paradoxical' defined in this way just as it would treat 'unsafe' when applied to propositions with ascending truth or descending truth as constituents. As such CAM treats '(7) is paradoxical' as an unsafety attribution, and unsafety attributions to unsafe sentences are unsafe. Thus, it is improper to infer from '(7) is paradoxical' to ' '(7) is paradoxical' is true'.

descending true. Contradiction. Therefore, (8) is not descending true. Assume for *reductio* that for some u and a, (8) is not ascending true in u from a. Thus, 'for all u, for all a, (8) is not ascending true in u from a' is ascending true in u_0 from a_0. But since (8) does not contain any indexicals or assessment-sensitive terms, we can conclude that it is not ascending true. It follows that it is not the case that for all u, for all a, (8) is not ascending true in u from a. So there is some u and a such that (8) is ascending true in u from a. Again, since (8) has no indexicals or assessment-sensitive terms, we can conclude that (8) is ascending true. Contradiction. Therefore, (8) is ascending true. In sum, (8) is ascending true and not descending true (i.e., unsafe). Similar reasoning shows that (9) is unsafe too. We could say that for all u and for all a, they are ascending true in u from a and not descending true in u from a, but that does not add anything since they do not contain any indexicals or assessment-sensitive terms. The main point is that they do not give rise to revenge paradoxes.

10

The Aletheic Revolution

In this final chapter, I take a step back and consider some of the broader ramifications of the central point of the book; i.e., that we should replace our inconsistent concept of truth with ascending truth and descending truth. I use 'aletheic revolution' as a convenient term for the conceptual revolution pertaining to truth.

Because my positive proposal for how to understand truth is complex and multifaceted, a brief summary is in order. I have endorsed the following theories:

(i) a descriptive unified theory of truth consisting of: (a) a semantic theory for 'true' on which it is assessment-sensitive, (b) a theory of inconsistent concepts on which they are expressed by assessment-sensitive expressions, (c) a pragmatic theory for 'true', (d) a metrological theory of the nature of truth, (e) a classical symmetric logical approach to the aletheic paradoxes, and (f) an inconsistency philosophical approach to the aletheic paradoxes

(ii) a prescriptive unified theory of truth consisting of: (a) an axiomatic theory of ascending and descending truth (ADT), (b) xeno semantics for ADT, (c) a metrological theory of ascending and descending truth, and (d) theories of relations between ascending and descending truth and other concepts (the most important of these is the theory of meaning, which introduces new terms: 'x is ascending true in u', 'x is descending true in u', 'x is ascending true in u from a', and 'x is descending true in u from a')

(iii) a number of additional views including: (a) metrological naturalism, (b) a theory of constitutive principles as scorekeeping commitments to which possessors are quasi-entitled, (b) Roberts' scorekeeping theory, (c) (T-In) and (T-Out) as constitutive of truth, (d) the Content Determination Condition (CDC), (e) methodological classicism (theories of inconsistent concepts should be compatible with classical logic), (f) the generality of natural-language truth predicates, and (g) Davidson's views on rational phenomena in general.

10.1 Post-revolutionary practice

In Chapters 6 and 7, I presented ADT and the measurement system for ascending truth and descending truth. In Chapter 9, I offered CAM, the classical, assessment-sensitive, measurement-theoretic, unified theory of truth. The point of this overall strategy is threefold: (i) recognize that truth is an inconsistent concept and that this feature causes the aletheic paradoxes and the revenge paradoxes that plague attempted solutions to them, (ii) offer a team of consistent concepts that can do the work we require of truth without giving rise to the paradoxes, and (iii) use the replacement concepts as the explanans in a theory of truth. The descriptive theory of truth, CAM, depends on the replacement concepts, ascending truth and descending truth, explained by the prescriptive theory, ADT.

Consider a natural language, like English, with a truth predicate that is used in accord with its constitutive principles. Now imagine what this language would be like if my advice were heeded. It would still contain a truth predicate; remember, I am NOT suggesting that we stop using truth predicates or the concept of truth—truth is a useful inconsistent concept, much like mass. The truth predicate would be treated as assessment-sensitive, as CAM describes it. The language would also contain an ascending truth predicate and a descending truth predicate. These are not assessment-sensitive, context-dependent, ambiguous, or semantically noteworthy in any way. They are just regular predicates (if there is such a thing). In addition, the language would contain the special terms used in the postsemantic theory proposed in Chapter 8 and used in Chapter 9—'ascending true in u from a' and 'descending true in u from a'. Call this a post-revolutionary linguistic practice.

One might wonder how an assessment-sensitive truth predicate, the ascending truth predicate, and the descending truth predicate interact with one another. First, ascending truth and descending truth are not going to be widely used. In any casual conversation, people will use the truth predicate instead, even when it comes to claims like 'you shouldn't say that if it isn't true'. Just as in casual conversation, people use 'mass' with the understanding that what they are saying might not be, strictly speaking, correct, but it is good enough for the purposes at hand. That is, those involved would have reached the same conclusions even if they had used the more complicated replacement concepts instead (with more effort). If a conversational participant wants to insist that the questions under consideration warrant a more precise conceptual framework, then those in the conversation can switch to the more precise terminology of relativistic mass and proper mass. Likewise, if necessary, conversational participants can switch from talk of truth to talk of ascending truth and descending truth.

In cases where the distinction between ascending truth and descending truth matters, people use these terms and stay away from the truth predicate. An example discussed below concerns semantic theories for expressively rich languages. A traditional semantic theory assigns truth values to sentences of the language across a range of conditions, and these are interpreted as truth-conditions. Of course, if the target language is classical, contains a truth predicate (i.e., one that obeys the primary aletheic principles), and the semantic theory treats this truth predicate as consistent, univocal, and invariant, then the semantic theory will be inconsistent. This is a clear case where the replacement concepts play an important role. Instead of attributing truth conditions to sentences, a semantic theory should attribute ascending truth conditions and descending truth conditions to sentences. For the vast majority of sentences, these will be the same, but there will be some for which these differ, and accounting for this difference allows for a consistent semantic theory even for expressively rich languages. Doing semantics for expressively rich languages is like doing the physics of dark flow in this respect—in both cases, one has to use the replacement concepts in order to avoid problems.

One might find oneself attributing truth to sentences that contain ascending truth predicates or descending truth predicates. In these cases, the two theories, ADT and CAM, work together to specify the results. For example:

(1) Grass is green.
(2) (1) is descending true.
(3) (1) is ascending true.
(4) (2) is true.
(5) (3) is true.

Here we have a sentence, (4), that attributes truth to a sentence with a descending truth predicate in it, (2). Since (2) is safe, (T-In) and (T-Out) hold for (4), so it follows from (4) that (1) is descending true. Since (1) is safe as well, it also follows from (4) that grass is green. All the same results hold for (3) and (5), respectively.

Here is another example:

(6) (6) is not true.
(7) (6) is ascending true.
(8) (6) is descending true.

In this example, (6) is paradoxical. (7) says of (6) that it is ascending true, while (8) says of it that it is descending true. So far, I have not discussed how ascending truth and descending truth apply to sentences containing 'true'. There are at least two options: (i) 'ascending true' and 'descending true' are invariant across the board, and (ii) 'ascending true' and 'descending true' are invariant except when they are applied to assessment-sensitive sentences, in which case they are assessment-sensitive as well. Note that many who endorse semantic relativism assume that 'true' is assessment-sensitive when applied to sentences that are assessment-sensitive.[1] If they are right and ascending truth and descending truth have the same feature, then we should pick option (ii). However, option (ii) makes the semantic theory considerably more complex; so, in the interest of simplicity, I provisionally adopt option (i) for the purposes of this chapter.

[1] For example, see MacFarlane (forthcoming).

Moreover, according to ADT as implemented in Chapter 6, only sentences containing 'ascending true' or 'descending true' are unsafe. So it seems as though (6) should be safe. Notice that (6) is ascending true relative to the ascending standard and ascending true relative to the descending standard and (6) is not descending true relative to the ascending standard and not descending true relative to the descending standard. Is (6) ascending true or descending true? Well, (6) is assessment-sensitive, so it has an ascending truth value only relative to a standard. So, is (7) ascending true? If we follow option (i), then the answer should be no.[2] So, since it is not the case that (6) is ascending true, full stop, (7) is not ascending true. Likewise, (6) is not descending true, so (8) is not ascending true.

Let us look at a converse example.

(9) (9) is not descending true.
(10) (9) is true.
(11) (9) is not true.

(9) is unsafe, so it is ascending true and not descending true. How do we evaluate (10) and (11)? CAM says that 'true' is assessment-sensitive, so (10) and (11) are assessment-sensitive. (10) is ascending true relative to the ascending standard, and not descending true relative to the descending standard. (11) is not ascending true relative to the ascending standard and descending true relative to the descending standard. But is (10) true? Recall that 'true' can only be used in situations where the difference between ascending truth and descending truth is negligible. In this case it is not, so we cannot answer whether (10) or (11) are true. Of course we can consider the further sentence:

(12) (10) is true.

CAM implies that this sentence is assessment-sensitive—(12) has exactly the same status as (10) itself: ascending true relative to the ascending standard, and not descending true relative to the descending standard.

With these in mind, compare the first example to the following one:

(13) Grass is green.
(14) (13) is true.
(15) (14) is descending true.
(16) (15) is ascending true.

Given what we said above, (14) is assessment-sensitive, so it is not descending true and it is not ascending true. Thus, (15) is not ascending true and not descending true. Nevertheless, 'grass is green' follows from (14) since it follows from (15), and 'grass is green' follows from (16) as well since (15) is safe.

[2] Notice that our guiding analogy between truth and mass is no help here since 'mass' (the type) does not have relativistic mass or proper mass.

10.2 Objections and replies

I have dealt with numerous objections all the way through the book. However, in this final section, I consider some objections that might still seem pressing and offer some replies.

10.2.1 Guide to objections

Here is a guide to the most important objections that I have raised and addressed already in the book, along with their locations:

- There are no inconsistent concepts (section 2.2).
- There is no way to possess an inconsistent concept (section 2.3).
- Inconsistency views require an analytic/synthetic distinction (section 2.3).
- Epistemic relations between concept possessors and constitutive principles are subject to Williamson's objection (section 2.3).
- Epistemic relations between concept possessors and constitutive principles do not explain the phenomenology of coming to find out that one's concept is inconsistent (section 2.6).
- My criticism of ambiguity and contextual philosophical approaches to the aletheic paradoxes is no better than the semantic blindness objection to epistemic contextualism (section 3.2.5).
- Paraconsistent approaches are justified in part by the fact that people do not take *ex falso* to be valid (section 3.3).
- Other views explain the aletheic paradoxes better (section 4.3).
- The modest attitude of the relation between philosophy and the sciences renders philosophical objections to the science moot (section 4.4).
- The argument concerning the impact of the paradoxes on truth-conditional theories of meaning can be defused by a proper understanding of the relation between theories of truth and meaning theories (section 5.1.3).
- There is no need to replace the concept of truth (section 5.3).
- A descriptive theory of truth should come before the prescriptive theory (section 5.6).
- Ascending truth and descending truth do not serve truth's expressive role (section 6.7.4).
- Ascending truth and descending truth give rise to revenge paradoxes (section 6.7.6).
- ADT is self-refuting because some of its consequences are not descending true (section 6.7.6).
- Ascending truth and descending truth cannot do the explanatory work of truth (Chapter 8).

- The standard objections to assessment-sensitivity views of epistemic modals, knowledge attributions, predicates of personal taste, etc. undermine CAM (section 9.8).
- The CDC is no more plausible than a TCDC (section 9.8).
- CAM does not respect truth's expressive role (section 9.12).
- CAM gives rise to revenge paradoxes (section 9.13).
- CAM is self-refuting because some of its consequences are not true (section 9.13).

The rest of this section considers a host of other objections that have not been raised yet.

10.2.2 *My uses of 'true'*

I use 'true' all the way through the book, so is that inconsistent? No. I have argued over and again that inconsistent concepts can be useful. Truth is one such concept. In order for an objection of this sort to be plausible, one would have to show that I use 'true' in a situation where the distinction between ascending truth and descending truth is relevant. Of course, I use 'true' in describing the views of others as well, but it hardly makes sense to use 'ascending true' or 'descending true' in these cases. The perspective from which the book is written takes these sorts of self-referential worries seriously, and all the theories contained herein are formulated explicitly to avoid these kinds of objections.

10.2.3 *Indispensability*

Truth is indispensable. Consider the following passage from Stephen Leeds:

> I think that if we were somehow to become persuaded to use the word 'true' in ways that conflicted with the T-sentences, we would immediately—so important are the disquotational uses of truth in our own language—invent an additional notion of truth—say truth*—that conformed to them; under such circumstances, I think one might as well say that we had never abandoned the T-sentences after all: we had merely decided to rename truth 'truth*' and use the word 'true' to mean something else.[3]

I do not disagree with Leeds on this point. In fact, I think this quote does a good job of explaining why theories of truth that do not treat (T-In) and (T-Out) as constitutive are non-starters. Of course, since we are using a truth predicate that has these as constitutive principles in a linguistic practice that is capable of referring to its own syntax and in which we reason according to certain logical principles, this truth predicate expresses an inconsistent concept. If that makes truth an indispensable inconsistent concept, then so be it. However, that claim has nothing to do with whether truth should be replaced. Being indispensable and being replaceable are compatible. Indeed, we should replace truth exactly because it is inconsistent and indispensible.

10.2.4 *Primary aletheic principles*

In Chapter 3, I criticize approaches to the aletheic paradoxes that do not validate the primary aletheic principles since these views cannot accommodate truth's expressive

[3] Leeds (1995: 8).

role. However, since (T-In) and (T-Out) are not true in general for my approach, I cannot accommodate truth's expressive role.

I take this to be one of the biggest problems with CAM. To be sure, I can explain why people treat 'true' as if it serves this expressive role—the reason is that (T-In) and (T-Out) are constitutive of truth. Moreover, I can show, according to a general theory of inconsistent concepts, why these constitutive principles fail in certain cases; so my rejection of them is not ad hoc. Finally, I have a semantics that specifies exactly when they hold and which sentences are exceptions to them. Nevertheless, it is a consequence of CAM that natural-language users are sometimes mistaken in treating certain speakers as committed to certain propositions. Since CAM is a descriptive theory of truth, that is a mark against it. It is no real consolation to note that everyone has this problem—no consistent (or even inconsistent) descriptive theory of truth can accommodate all our intuitions, since our intuitions trivialize in any logical system.

I think the best thing to say in response to this objection is that the case that I make for the idea that truth is an inconsistent concept is a fortiori a case for the claim that natural-language speakers are sometimes mistaken when they use truth predicates. By analogy, the (indirect) case that Einstein makes for the idea that mass is an inconsistent concept is also a case for the claim that natural-language speakers are sometimes mistaken when they use the term 'mass'; e.g., when they use it in situations where the difference between proper mass and relativistic mass is not negligible. I claim that CAM offers the best fit for our intuitions regarding truth predicates, but that does not mean that it is a perfect fit.

Compare my view on 'true' with one that has full intersubstitutability of p and 'p is true', like Field's theory. He does get more expressive power for 'true'. In particular, for Field, one can call a paradoxical sentence true and commit oneself to that paradoxical sentence; so he does justice to truth's role as a device of endorsement. However, it is inappropriate, on Field's theory, for someone to say of a paradoxical sentence that it is not true; so he does not get truth's role as a device of rejection (I argued this in Chapter 3). The question is: is that little bit of extra expressive power in the form of a device of endorsement worth giving up an intuitive negation and an intuitive conditional? I think the obvious answer is: No.

10.2.5 Endorsement

Descending truth is what is needed for a device of endorsement, since if one calls an unsafe sentence ascending true, that unsafe sentence does not follow from one's claim. Nevertheless, if one calls an unsafe sentence descending true, then the sentence one has uttered is not descending true and it is also not a theorem of ADT; thus, by the standard of assertibility advocated in Chapter 8, the sentence one has uttered is not properly assertible. Therefore, there is no way to use 'ascending true' or 'descending true' to properly endorse an unsafe sentence. For example, the descending liar, (d), which is the sentence '(d) is not descending true', is not descending true, and one can derive this result from ADT. If one asserts '(d) is ascending true', then one has failed to endorse (d) because (d) does not follow from the sentence asserted. If one asserts '(d) is descending true', then (d) does follow from the sentence asserted, but the sentence asserted is unsafe and not a theorem of ADT (its negation is a theorem of ADT), so it is not properly assertible. Therefore, neither ascending truth nor descending truth can serve as a *genuine* device of endorsement.

The objection is correct, but the problem is that there is no such thing as a consistent genuine device of endorsement. Descending truth is as close as one can get without having an inconsistent concept. Let us be more careful about devices of endorsement to see why.

A necessary condition on a predicate, F(x), that serves as a device of endorsement is that it obey (T-Out): $F(\langle\phi\rangle) \rightarrow \phi$. Otherwise, one could call a sentence F without being committed to that very sentence. In addition, the objector wants that if $\langle\phi\rangle$ is correctly assertible, then $F(\langle\phi\rangle)$ is correctly assertible. It is these two features that are required for what is called a *genuine* device of endorsement in the objection. The problem is that, together, these conditions are inconsistent, as shown by Montague.[4] Thus, there is no such thing as a genuine device of endorsement that expresses a consistent concept. Similar remarks hold of genuine devices of rejection.

10.2.6 Deflationism

The replacement strategy depends on truth's explanatory role—otherwise there is no reason to replace truth. So deflationists have no reason to accept this view.

Anyone who thinks that truth predicates perform a useful expressive role has difficulty with an approach to the aletheic paradoxes, and the deflationist is no different. Deflationists accept (T-In) and (T-Out) and there does not seem to be much hope in restricting them in a satisfiable way because of contingent paradoxes. That is, the considerations that sink monster-barring approaches sink this strategy too. Thus, deflationists are stuck with non-classical approaches. Moreover, the non-classical approaches to the paradoxes have come in for harsh criticism here—they violate constitutive principles for logical notions, they engender revenge paradoxes, they are susceptible to importation arguments, and they work only for LS truth predicates. Even once one goes non-classical, one need not retain truth's expressive role (e.g., I argued in Chapter 3 that Field does not do justice to truth's role as a device of rejection). Thus, the deflationist, who not only accepts but also emphasizes truth's expressive role, has good reason to think that truth is an inconsistent concept.

But, why accept my replacements? One important goal of linguistics is to provide semantic theories for natural languages. There are several kinds of semantic theories popular amongst linguists, but one of the most popular is truth-conditional semantics. Truth-conditional semantics uses our inconsistent concept of truth, but when we try to provide a truth-conditional semantics for a natural language, we end up with an

[4] Montague (1963). The technical result is that (T-Out) together with what we might call (T-Enter), if $\vdash \phi$, then $\vdash \langle\phi\rangle$ is true, are inconsistent (given the expressive resources needed to construct the relevant sentences).

inconsistent theory because of the aletheic paradoxes. To reject truth-conditional semantics, one of the most important tools of linguistics, out of hand on the basis of some philosophical commitment (e.g., deflationism) is to violate the modest attitude defended in Chapter 4. By adopting the replacements offered here, one can improve truth-conditional semantics in the form of AD semantics. I know of no other way to fix this important tool of linguistics and philosophy of language.

10.2.7 Retention

One might wonder whether, given the view of inconsistent concepts developed in Chapter 2, we really need to replace the concept of truth. On the view of constitutive principles and inconsistent concepts I advocate, one can explicitly reject a constitutive principle of the concept of truth and still possess it. Can we just use the concept of truth but explicitly reject one of its constitutive principles in cases where we are likely to get into trouble?

The answer is, no. Doing semantics with truth while rejecting one of its constitutive principles is effectively the same as doing semantics with a classical gappy truth predicate or a classical glutty truth predicate.[5] The former results from rejecting (T-In) and the latter results from rejecting (T-Out). There are no philosophically significant classical glut theories; so, let us consider a classical gap view. This concept (I'll use the predicate G(x) to express it) obeys (T-Out) (i.e., if $G(\langle\phi\rangle)$, then ϕ), but *not* (T-In) (i.e., if ϕ, then $G(\langle\phi\rangle)$). G(x) will, no doubt, obey other principles as well, but we need not concern ourselves with them.

Let L be the language for which we are providing a presemantics, a semantics, and a postsemantics. Since L is to model a natural language, we do not want to impose any expressive limitations on it. So it contains empirical predicates, a truth predicate, a G predicate, and some way of referring to its own syntactic features. Truth plays no role in the presemantics or in the semantics proper (instead, it is the mathematical concept of truth-in-a-model that does the work in the semantics). However, in the postsemantics, truth does play a role.

A standard postsemantic theory with truth looks something like this (u is the context of utterance and i_u is the index that represents u):

(17) A sentence p is true in u iff the content assigned to the clause representing p with respect to i_u gets $t\mathfrak{M}$-value 1 at the point of evaluation $<w>$ where w is the world of i_u.

Notice that, for simplicity, I am taking circumstances of evaluation to have only a parameter for worlds. Since we are doing postsemantics with our inconsistent concept of truth while rejecting (T-In), what we get is:

[5] And so the following argument serves also to justify replacing truth with a team of concepts over a single concept.

(18) A sentence p is G in u iff the content assigned to the clause representing p with respect to i_u gets t$\mathfrak{M}$-value 1 at the point of evaluation <w> where w is the world of i_u.

It will be helpful to break this biconditional into its conditional components and simplify them (where p is a sentence and w is the world of u):

(18a) If p is G in u, then the content of p gets t$\mathfrak{M}$-value 1 at w.

(18b) If the content of p gets t$\mathfrak{M}$-value 1 at w, then p is G in u.

As should be familiar by now, we really have two predicates here: '__ is G' and '__ is G in __'. The latter does the work in the postsemantic theory. I assume both are in L. The claim that G can serve in postsemantic theory like (18) will serve as an assumption for a *reductio*, which follows.

Consider again a standard semantic theory. It uses the following principles (where w is a possible world):

(19a) If ϕ at w, then the content of $\langle\phi\rangle$ gets t$\mathfrak{M}$-value 1 at w.

(19b) If the content of $\langle\phi\rangle$ gets t$\mathfrak{M}$-value 1 at w, then ϕ at w.

In these principles, 'ϕ' serves as a sentential variable. For example, if there is a possible world w at which snow is white, then the content of 'snow is white' gets t$\mathfrak{M}$-value 1 at w. Moreover, if 'snow is white' gets t$\mathfrak{M}$-value 1 at w, then snow is white at w. These principles are utterly uncontroversial because they involve neither truth nor G—just the mathematical concept of truth-in-a-model.

Our language L might contain a sentence like:

(g) ~G(g)

which would be similar to a liar sentence. I am going to consider a slightly different sentence that contains an occurrence of the two place G predicate:

(q) ~G(q, u_0)

where 'u_0' is the name of a particular context of utterance. q says that it is not G in context of utterance u_0. Which context of utterance is it? It is a context in which a person in the actual world utters q. That is, assume that a person utters q in context u_0 in the actual world @.

The presemantics for q are obvious, and I will not bother with it. The semantic theory provides the following t-distribution for q:

(20a) At worlds w where q is not G in u_0, the content of 'q is not G in u_0' gets t$\mathfrak{M}$-value 1 at w.

(20b) At worlds w where q is G in u_0, the content of 'q is not G in u_0' gets t$\mathfrak{M}$-value 0 at w.

It should be obvious that (20a) is an instance of (19a) and (20b) is an instance of the contrapositive of (19b).

Now for the argument that (18) is inconsistent.

1.	q is G in u_o	[assumption for *reductio*]
2.	'q is not G in u_o' is G in u_o	[from 1 by definition of q]
3.	'q is not G in u_o' gets $t\mathfrak{M}$-value 1 at @	[from 2 by (18a)]
4.	q is not G in u_o at @	[from 3 by (19b)]
5.	q is not G in u_o	[from 4 by @ rule]
6.	$\bot$	[from 1 and 5 by conjunction intro]
7.	q is not G in u_o	[from 1–6 by *reductio*]
8.	q is not G in u_o at @	[from 7 by @ rule]
9.	'q is not G in u_o' gets $t\mathfrak{M}$-value 1 at @	[from 8 by (19a)]
10.	'q is not G in u_o' is G in u_o	[from 9 by (18b)]
11.	q is G in u_o	[from 10 by definition of q]
12.	$\bot$	[from 7 and 11 by conjunction intro]

The @ rule is just that ⟨ϕ⟩ and ⟨ϕ at @⟩ are interchangeable. For example, 'snow is white' is interderivable with 'snow is white at the actual world'. There might be some metaphysical worries about it that rest on contentious claims about the nature of possible worlds, but from the point of view of linguistics and philosophy of language, this principle should not be controversial.

The argument so far shows that the proponent of using the concept of truth while rejecting (T-In) cannot endorse the standard semantics (expressed in (19a) and (19b)) together with the most obvious postsemantics (expressed in (18a) and (18b)). I claim that (19a) and (19b) should be left alone by such a proponent. Instead, it makes the most sense to reject (18b). Here is why. The classical gap view takes G to obey (T-Out), but not (T-In). So, whichever one of (18a) or (18b) is analogous to (T-In) should be rejected. It should be clear that (18b) is similar to (T-In). In fact, if we use hypothetical syllogism on (19a) and (18b) we arrive at the following principle: if ϕ at w, then ⟨ϕ⟩ is G in u. If we use hypothetical syllogism on (19b) and (18a) we arrive at: if ⟨ϕ⟩ is G in u, then ϕ at w. The former is very similar to (T-In) and the latter is very similar to (T-Out). Rejecting (18b) allows one to reject the former principle.

The advocate of the view in question would then be left with (18a) as the postsemantic theory: if ⟨ϕ⟩ is G in u, then the content of ⟨ϕ⟩ gets $t\mathfrak{M}$-value 1 at w. Or, in the more helpful contrapositive form: if the content of ⟨ϕ⟩ gets $t\mathfrak{M}$-value 0 at w, then ⟨ϕ⟩ is not G at u. One could, of course, add some instances of (18b) to the postsemantic theory, but not all of them. In particular, one can add all the instances for sentences of L that do not contain 'G', but that is a lame consolation prize. A proponent of using 'true' while rejecting (T-In) might even be able to figure out a way to add instances for all grounded sentences of L. But even that is empirically inadequate. The ungrounded sentences of L are perfectly meaningful and if the postsemantic theory cannot interpret the $t\mathfrak{M}$-values assigned to them, then it is obviously empirically inadequate.

On the other hand, replacing the standard postsemantic theory, (17), with a theory that appeals to ascending truth and descending truth is consistent and it provides ascending truth conditions and descending truth conditions to every sentence of a language like L (even when L contains 'ascending true' and 'descending true').[6]

10.2.8 Retraction

It is standard to use retraction as a test to distinguish between non-indexical use sensitivity and assessment-sensitivity. On a non-indexical contextualist view of 'fun', when Milhouse asserts at ten years old that Whacking Day is fun, the sentence in question is assigned a $t\mathfrak{M}$-value and a truth value using the enjoyment standard from the context of utterance. When Milhouse asserts at twenty years old that Whacking Day is not fun, that sentence is assigned a $t\mathfrak{M}$-value and a truth value using the enjoyment standard from that context of utterance. If the standard for enjoyment changes between the two utterances, then it might be that the first sentence is true in its context of use and the second sentence is true in its context of use, even though they are contradictory. Even if Milhouse recalls his earlier claim, he has no reason to retract it. What he said at ten years old is true relative to the only enjoyment standard that is relevant—the one in place in that context of utterance. It is impossible on the non-indexical contextualist view to evaluate the early utterance with respect to the later enjoyment standard. On the other hand, the assessment-sensitivity theorist says that the sentence Milhouse uttered early is assigned a $t\mathfrak{M}$-value and truth value relative to an enjoyment standard from a context of assessment; and there might be many contexts of assessment from which to choose. One need not use the enjoyment standard from Milhouse's early context of utterance. Thus, when Milhouse at twenty reflects on his early utterance using his twenty-year-old enjoyment standard, he should say that the sentence he uttered at ten is false in the context of use from his current context of assessment. As such, he should retract it. Of course, if Milhouse uses a context of assessment for his early utterance in which his ten-year-old enjoyment standard is operative, then he would not retract it because that sentence is true in the context of use from this context of assessment. Still, on the non-indexical contextualist view, retraction is never forced, but on the assessment-sensitivity view, it sometimes is forced.

I have endorsed the assessment-sensitivity view with respect to 'true'. As such, we should see some retraction data. If there is no situation in which a user of 'true' would retract based on differences in aletheic standard, then it seems like 'true' is not assessment-sensitive.

A first point to make in reply is that, as of the date I am writing this sentence, I am one of the only people in the world (I know of) who thinks that 'true' is assessment-sensitive. So there will be no retraction data for us to find by looking at how people use 'true'. Nevertheless, we can imagine how people who know that 'true' is assessment-sensitive should use it, and see whether there would be situations in which they would retract. For this to work, we need a case where a sentence is assigned different ascending truth values or descending truth values by different aletheic standards. A good example is the truth-teller:

[6] Thanks to Matti Eklund for discussion of this point.

(21) (21) is true.

The ascending standard reads this as the ascending truth-teller:

(22) (22) is ascending true

while the descending standard reads it as the descending truth-teller:

(23) (23) is descending true.

By the xeno semantics provided in the Appendix to Chapter 6, both (22) and (23) are safe, but (22) is descending true and (23) is not ascending true. Thus, (21) is ascending true in its context of use from the context of assessment involving the ascending standard, but (21) is not ascending true in its context of use from the context of assessment involving the descending standard.

Imagine Bort overhears Lester utter sentence (21) and uses the ascending standard in his context of assessment. As such, Bort judges that (21) is ascending true in its context of use from his context of assessment. If, later on, Bort decides to use the descending standard to figure out whether (21) is ascending true, he will judge that (21) is not ascending true in its context of use from his new context of assessment. If he reflects on his earlier judgment, would Bort retract it? He would if for some reason he thought that the descending standard (in his later context of assessment) is somehow superior to the ascending standard (in his earlier context of assessment) given the goals and purposes of the conversation in question. I think the same holds of Milhouse as well. If he has some reason to think that his older standard is somehow inferior, then he retracts. Therefore, the retraction phenomenon is the same in the two cases.

10.2.9 Generalization

Throughout the book, I have emphasized the expressive role played by truth predicates, but I have focused exclusively on their use as devices of endorsement and as devices of rejection. I have not mentioned their use as devices of generalization, which is just as important. Moreover, it is not clear that either ascending truth or descending truth serve this purpose. For example, imagine that Roy claims that a rational agent should believe that grass is green only if grass is green, and he claims that a rational agent should believe that snow is white only if snow is white. Further, he is not concerned only with 'grass is green' and 'snow is white'—he is interested in the general principle: for all ϕ, a rational agent should believe that ϕ only if ϕ. Here, I have used a (bindable) sentential variable to formulate the general principle, but that is not the most common way of formulating it, and it is not obvious that natural languages have such devices. Instead, one would probably say something like: a rational agent should believe a proposition only if that proposition is true. In this formulation, we use the truth predicate to generalize over all the instances. Notice that this is not an endorsement or a rejection. Roy is not using the truth predicate to endorse or reject any particular proposition. Because (T-Out) is constitutive of 'true', we can derive that a rational agent should believe the proposition that grass is green only if grass is green from the general principle.[7] A different example, say, 'a rational agent may believe a proposition if that proposition is true', would require (T-In) to recover the relevant instance. How can ascending truth and descending truth perform this generalizing role?

At first blush, it seems obvious that one would just substitute 'descending true' in a generalization that requires (T-Out) but not (T-In) to recover the relevant instances, and substitute 'ascending true' in a generalization that requires (T-In) but not (T-Out) to recover the relevant instances. However, there is a wrinkle here. Consider our example again. Imagine that Roy asserts 'a rational agent should believe a proposition only if that proposition is descending true'. By asserting this general principle, Roy has committed himself to 'a rational agent should believe the proposition that grass is green only if grass is green', but the general principle now seems to be mistaken. If what I have said in this book is right, then a rational agent should believe that the descending liar is not descending true (because that is a theorem of ADT). However, the proposition that the descending liar is not descending true is not descending true. Thus, there is a counterexample to the general principle formulated with 'descending true'. Similar counterexamples apply to generalizing uses of 'ascending true'.

Instead of following the above advice, one should do the opposite. That is, substitute 'ascending true' in a generalization that requires (T-Out) but not (T-In) to recover the relevant instances, and substitute 'descending true' in a generalization that requires (T-In) but not (T-Out) to recover the relevant instances. Imagine instead that Roy asserts 'a rational agent should believe a proposition only if that proposition is ascending true'. By asserting this general principle, Roy has committed himself to 'a rational agent should believe the proposition that grass is green only if grass is green', because 'grass is green' is safe. Roy has, however, not committed himself to any instances involving unsafe sentences like 'the descending liar is not descending true'. The upshot is that, when used properly, ascending truth and descending truth can play limited generalizing roles and the limitations are exactly the same as the limitations on their roles as devices of endorsement and rejection. Thus, there is no new problem here with generalizations.

10.2.10 The principle of uniform solution

CAM and ADT do not solve the other paradoxes that have often been discussed in conjunction with truth. For example, there is the sorites paradox, which affects vague expressions, Russell's paradox and the Burali-Forti paradox, which affect set theory, and Paradoxes of Generality, which affect the concept of a domain or subject matter of discourse. Some philosophers have claimed that an approach to the liar that cannot be parlayed into an approach to one or more of these other paradoxes is unacceptable. In particular, Jamie Tappenden, Matti Eklund, and Hartry Field have argued that the

[7] That is, 'for all x, for all y, if x is a rational agent and y is a proposition and x should believe y, then y is true' and 'if the proposition that grass is green is true, then grass is green' entail 'for all x, if x is a rational agent and x should believe the proposition that grass is green, then grass is green'. This argument uses the propositional version of (T-Out), but that is hardly objectionable.

paradoxes of truth and the paradoxes of vagueness ought to stand or fall together.[8] In addition, Graham Priest has defended a principle of uniform solution, which states that the aletheic paradoxes and the set-theoretic paradoxes all have the same form and should be solved together.[9]

From my point of view, paradoxes that affect a single concept should be solved together. Notice that I give a uniform solution to the liar paradox, Curry's paradox, Yablo's paradox, Montague's paradox, McGee's paradox, and all the revenge paradoxes, but there is good reason to think that these are all symptoms of truth's underlying inconsistency. I also show how to solve the paradoxes of predication and reference by applying what amounts to the same strategy, even though the approach to truth, on its own, does nothing to solve these paradoxes. I feel the same way about the other paradoxes mentioned above. There is no way I would subject the reader to a long and tedious discussion of vagueness, set theory, or absolute generality at this point. So let me say that if there is good reason to think that the concepts involved are inconsistent, useful, and their inconsistency impedes their utility, then a replacement strategy is in order. Otherwise, it is not. However, whether the concepts involved in those phenomena are inconsistent is irrelevant to assessing the merits of CAM and ADT.

[8] See Tappenden (1993, 1994), Eklund (2002a), and Field (2003b).
[9] Priest (1994b). See Smith (2000) and Priest (2000) for discussion.

Conclusion

I am not one for long conclusions—if you have read this far, then you should know what the book accomplishes. In case you are still a bit unclear, I will try to summarize it here. I began by offering, for the first time, a single framework for thinking about work on the nature of truth and work on the aletheic paradoxes. It classifies a wide range of theories, distinguishes between philosophical and logical approaches to the paradoxes, and introduces the idea of a unified theory of truth, which includes all three parts. I introduced the idea that some concepts are inconsistent, and argued that truth is an inconsistent concept. My own inconsistency approach is distinct from others in this tradition because I think that an inconsistency theorist should be in the business of replacing truth for certain purposes. The prescriptive theory—the suggestion for how we should change our conceptual scheme and linguistic practice by adding ascending truth and descending truth—is based on the formal theory, ADT, and requires a novel semantics in terms of xeno models. Instead of an analysis or reductive explanation, I prefer a measurement-theoretic account of philosophical notions and provide one for ascending and descending truth. In addition, ascending and descending truth are linked up in various ways to other philosophical concepts. Finally, I proposed a theory of truth on which 'true' is assessment-sensitive and is explained by appeal to ascending truth and descending truth.

I would like to close by mentioning a few areas for further research. The most obvious place to develop the ideas contained here is to apply them to other paradoxes, especially the set-theoretic paradoxes. It seems to me that Russell's paradox shows that the naïve concept of a set is inconsistent. It would be interesting to see how to replace it with a team of concepts in much the same way that truth is replaced by ascending truth and descending truth (focusing on the axiom of comprehension). The other set-theoretic paradoxes might be susceptible to similar treatment. In addition, there might be other philosophical problems that are caused by inconsistent concepts (some have suggested that epistemological skepticism is a symptom of an inconsistency in our concept of knowledge).[1]

[1] See Schiffer (1996) and Weiner (2009).

The approach to inconsistent concepts offered here might shed light on what to do about these philosophical problems.

Metrological naturalism as a philosophical methodology needs considerable development before one could expect it to entice others. In particular, the prospects for using measurement-theoretic tools on philosophical problems needs investigation. In addition, it would be nice to make good on my claim that Davidson's philosophical system is most perspicuously understood as applying the methods of measurement theory to the concept of rationality.

The properties of ADT and its extensions have been neglected here, mostly because I lack the technical sophistication to investigate them. I am curious about their proof-theoretic properties and their mathematio-logical relations to various kinds of xeno models. In addition, it seems to me that iterated ascending truth and descending truth attributions (e.g., ''snow is white' is ascending true' is descending true') could have interesting properties that deserve some attention.

The kind of replacement I have offered in this work is only one kind of conceptual change. There are many others, and it would be helpful to arrive at a general theory of conceptual change as an aid to getting straight on conceptual inconsistencies at the root of philosophical problems and producing replacement concepts.

Finally, the idea that most philosophical problems are caused by conceptual inconsistency—and so, philosophy is, for the most part, the study of inconsistent concepts—seems obvious to me, and I think it has the potential to make sense of deeply entrenched philosophical disagreements. Figuring out the principles responsible for these disputes and configuring replacement concepts would be a huge undertaking, but one that is badly needed. This sort of massive conceptual engineering effort is the only way, in my opinion, that philosophy will be able to move past its intractable disputes and continue the progress made over the past few centuries.

Bibliography

Alexander, Joshua (2012). *Experimental Philosophy*. Cambridge: Polity.

Almeder, Robert (2010). *Truth and Skepticism*. New York: Rowman and Littlefield.

Alston, William P. (1996). *A Realist Conception of Truth*. Ithaca: Cornell University Press.

Anderson, Hanne, Peter Barker, and Xiang Chen (2006). *The Cognitive Structure of Scientific Revolutions*. Cambridge: Cambridge University Press.

Anscombe, G. E. M. (1957). *Intention*. London: Blackwell.

Arló Costa, Horacio and Eric Pacuit (2006). "First Order Classical Modal Logic," *Studia Logica* 84: 171–210.

Armour-Garb, Bradley (2001). "Deflationism and the Meaningless Strategy," *Analysis* 61: 280–9.

Armour-Garb, Bradley, and Jc Beall (2005). "Minimalism, Epistemicism, and Paradox," in Beall and Armour-Garb (2005).

Armour-Garb, Bradley, and James Woodbridge (2010). "Why Deflationists Should Be Pretense Theorists (and Perhaps Already Are)," in Wright and Pedersen (2010).

—— (forthcoming). "Semantic Defectiveness and the Liar," *Philosophical Studies*.

Armstrong, David (1973). *Belief, Truth and Knowledge*. Cambridge: Cambridge University Press.

—— (1997). *A World of States of Affairs*. Cambridge: Cambridge University Press.

—— (2004). *Truth and Truthmakers*. Cambridge: Cambridge University Press.

Asenjo, F. G. (1966). "A Calculus of Antinomies," *Notre Dame Journal of Formal Logic* 16: 103–5.

Asher, Nicholas, Josh Dever, and Chris Pappas (2009). "Supervaluations Debugged," *Mind* 118: 901–33.

Atlas, Jay David (1989). *Philosophy without Ambiguity: A Logico-Linguistic Essay*. Oxford: Oxford University Press.

Austin, J. L. (1950). "Truth," *Proceedings of the Aristotelian Society, Supplementary Volumes* 24: 111–72.

—— (1959). "A Plea for Excuses," in J. O. Urmson and G. J. Warnock (eds.), *Philosophical Papers*. Oxford: Oxford University Press, 1979.

Ayer, A. J. (1936). *Language, Truth, and Logic*. London: Gollancz.

Bach, Kent (2011). "Perspectives on Possibilities: Contextualism, Relativism, or What?" in Egan and Weatherson (2011).

Bacon, Andrew (forthcoming a). "Non-Classical Metatheory for Non-Classical Logics," *Journal of Philosophical Logic*.

—— (forthcoming b). "A New Conditional for Naïve Truth Theory," *Notre Dame Journal of Formal Logic*.

Badici, Emil, and Kirk Ludwig (2007). "The Concept of Truth and the Semantics of the Truth Predicate," *Inquiry* 50: 622–38.

Balog, Katalin (2001). "Commentary on Frank Jackson's *From Metaphysics to Ethics*," *Philosophy and Phenomenological Research* 62: 645–52.

Bar-On, Dorit, Claire Horisk, and William Lycan (2000). "Deflationism, Meaning, and Truth-Conditions," *Philosophical Studies* 101: 1–28.

Barber, Alex (ed.) (2003). *Epistemology of Language*. Oxford: Oxford University Press.

Barwise, Jon, and John Etchemendy (1987). *The Liar: An Essay on Truth and Circularity*. Oxford: Oxford University Press.

Båve, Arvid. (2012). "On Using Inconsistent Expressions," *Erkenntnis* 77: 133–48.

Baz, Auner (2012). *When Words Are Called For*. Cambridge, MA: Harvard University Press.

Beall, Jc (1999). "Completing Sorensen's Menu: A Non-Modal Yabloesque Curry," *Mind* 108: 737–9.

—— (2001a). "Is Yablo's Paradox Non-Circular?" *Analysis* 61: 176–87.

—— (2001b). "A Neglected Deflationist Approach to the Liar," *Analysis* 61: 126–9.

—— (ed.) (2003a). *Liars and Heaps*. Oxford: Oxford University Press.

—— (2003b). "On the Singularity Theory of Denotation," in Beall (2003a).

—— (2006). "Truth and Paradox: A Philosophical Sketch," in D. Jacquette (ed.), *Philosophy of Logic*. Elsevier: Dordrecht.

—— (2008a). *Revenge of the Liar*. Oxford: Oxford University Press.

—— (2008b). "Prolegomenon to Future Revenge," in Beall (2008a).

—— (2009). *Spandrels of Truth*. Oxford: Oxford University Press.

Beall, Jc, and Bradley Armour-Garb (eds.) (2005). *Deflationism and Paradox*. Oxford: Oxford University Press.

Beall, Jc, and Michael Glanzberg (2008). "Where the Paths Meet: Remarks on Truth and Paradox," *Midwest Studies in Philosophy* 32: 169–98.

Beall, Jc, and Julien Murzi (forthcoming). "Two Flavors of Curry's Paradox," *Journal of Philosophy*.

Beall Jc, and David Ripley (forthcoming). "Non-Classical Truth Theories," in Glanzberg (forthcoming b).

Beaver, David (2001). *Presupposition and Assertion in Dynamic Semantics*. Stanford: CSLI.

Bell, John (2008). *A Primer on Infinitesimal Analysis*. 2nd ed. Cambridge: Cambridge University Press.

Benthem, J. F. A. K. van (1978). "Four Paradoxes," *Journal of Philosophical Logic* 7: 49–72.

Berk, Lon (2004). "The Liar, Context and Logical Form," *Journal of Logic, Language and Information* 13: 267–86.

Billon, Alexandre (2011). "My Own Truth: Pathologies of Self-Reference and Relative Truth," in R. Shahid, P. Giuseppe, and M. Mathieu (eds.), *Logic, Epistemology, and the Unity of Science*. New York: Springer.

Blackburn, Simon (1984). *Spreading the Word*. Oxford: Oxford University Press.

—— (1998). "Wittgenstein, Wright, Rorty, and Minimalism," *Mind* 107: 157–81.

—— (2001). *Think*. Oxford: Oxford University Press.

—— (2005). *Truth: A Guide for the Perplexed*. Oxford: Oxford University Press.

Blanshard, Brand (1939). *The Nature of Thought*. London: Allen & Unwin.

Block, Ned, and Robert Stalnaker (1999). "Conceptual Analysis, Dualism, and the Explanatory Gap," *Philosophical Review* 108: 1–46.

Boghossian, Paul (1996). "Analyticity Reconsidered," *Noûs* 30: 360–91.

—— (1997). "Analyticity," in B. Hale and C. Wright (eds.), *A Companion to the Philosophy of Language*. Oxford: Blackwell.

—— (2000). "Knowledge of Logic," in P. Boghossian and C. Peacocke (eds.), *New Essays on the A Priori*. Oxford: Oxford University Press.

—— (2001). "How Are Objective Epistemic Reasons Possible?" *Philosophical Studies* 106: 340–80.

—— (2003a). "Blind Reasoning," *Proceedings of the Aristotelian Society, Supplementary Volume* 77: 225–48.

—— (2003b). "Epistemic Analyticity: A Defense," *Grazer Philosophische Studien* 66: 15–35.

—— (2006). "What Is Relativism?" in Greenough and Lynch (2006).

Boolos, George, John Burgess, and Richard Jeffrey (2002). *Computability and Logic.* 4th ed. Cambridge: Cambridge University Press.

Borg, Emma (2005). "Saying What You Mean," in R. Elugardo and R. J. Stainton (eds.), *Ellipsis and Nonsentential Speech.* Dordrecht: Kluwer.

Braddon-Mitchell, David, and Robert Robert (eds.) (2009). *Conceptual Analysis and Philosophical Naturalism.* Cambridge, MA: MIT Press.

Bradley, F. H. (1914). *Essays on Truth and Reality.* Oxford: Clarendon Press.

Brady, Ross (1996). "Relevant Implication and the Case for a Weaker Logic," *Journal of Philosophical Logic* 25: 155–83.

—— (2006). *Universal Logic.* Stanford, CA: CSLI.

Brandom, Robert (1994). *Making It Explicit.* Cambridge, MA: Harvard University Press.

—— (2001). *Articulating Reasons.* Cambridge, MA: Harvard University Press.

—— (2002). "Explanatory vs. Expressive Deflationism about Truth," in Schantz (2002).

—— (2008). *Between Saying and Doing.* Oxford: Oxford University Press.

—— (2009a). *Reason in Philosophy.* Cambridge, MA: Harvard University Press.

—— (2009b). "Reply to Kevin Scharp," in B. Weiss and J. Wanderer (eds.), *Reading Brandom.* New York: Routledge.

—— (2011). *Perspectives on Pragmatism.* Cambridge, MA: Harvard University Press.

Brendel, Elke (2000). "Circularity and the Debate between Deflationist and Substantive Theories of Truth," in A. Chapuis and A. Gupta (eds.), *Circularity, Definition, and Truth.* New Delhi: Munshiram Manoharlal, 2000.

Brogaard, Berit (2007). "Sea Battle Semantics," *The Philosophical Quarterly* 58: 326–35.

—— (2008). "In Defense of a Perspectival Semantics for 'Know', " *Australasian Journal of Philosophy* 86: 439–59.

—— (2010). "Perspectival Truth and Color Primitivism," in Wright and Pedersen (2010).

Brown, Jessica, and Herman Cappelen (eds.) (2011). *Assertion: New Philosophical Essays.* Oxford: Oxford University Press.

Burge, Tyler (1979). "Semantical Paradox," *The Journal of Philosophy*, 76: 169–98.

—— (1982a). "Postscript to 'Semantical Paradox'," in Martin (1984).

—— (1982b). "The Liar Paradox: Tangles and Chains," *Philosophical Studies* 41: 353–66.

—— (1993). "Content Preservation," *Philosophical Review* 103: 457–88.

Burgess, Alexis (2006). *Identifying Fact and Fiction.* PhD Thesis, Princeton University.

Burgess, Alexis, and John Burgess (2011). *Truth.* Princeton: Princeton University Press.

Burgess, John (1997). "What Is Minimalism about Truth?" *Analysis* 57: 259–67.

—— (2002). "Is There a Problem about Deflationary Theories of Truth?" in Halbach and Horsten (2002).

Burgis, Ben (forthcoming). "Paracompleteness and Revenge," *Analysis.*

Caie, Michael (2012). "Belief and Indeterminacy," *Philosophical Review* 121: 1–54.

Camp Jr., Joseph L. (2002). *Confusion: A Study in the Theory of Knowledge.* Cambridge, MA: Harvard University Press.

Candlish, Stewart, and Nic Damnjanovic (2007). "A Brief History of Truth," in D. Jacquette (ed.), *Philosophy of Logic*. Elsevier: Dordrecht.

Cantini, Andrea (1990). "A Theory of Formal Truth Arithmetically Equivalent to ID," *Journal of Symbolic Logic* 55: 244–59.

—— (2009). "Paradoxes, Self-Reference, and Truth in the 20th Century," in D. M. Gabbay and J. Woods (eds.), *Handbook of the History of Logic*. Vol. 5. Amsterdam: Elsevier.

Cappelen, Herman (2008). "Content Relativism and Semantic Blindness," in García-Carpintero and Kölbel (2008).

—— (2012). *Philosophy without Intuitions*. Oxford: Oxford University Press.

Cappelen, Herman, and John Hawthorne (2009). *Relativism and Monadic Truth*. Oxford: Oxford University Press.

—— (2011a). "Reply to Lasersohn, MacFarlane, and Richard," *Philosophical Studies* 156: 449–66.

—— (2011b). "Reply to Glanzberg, Soames, and Weatherson," *Analysis* 71: 143–56.

Cappelen, Herman, and Ernie Lepore (2003). "Context Shifting Arguments," *Philosophical Perspectives* 17: 25–50.

—— (2005). *Insensitive Semantics*. Malden, MA: Wiley-Blackwell.

—— (2007). "The Myth of Unarticulated Constituents," in M. O'Rourke and C. Washington (eds.), *Situating Semantics: Essays on the Philosophy of John Perry*. Cambridge, MA: MIT Press.

Capria, Marco (ed.) (2005). *Physics Before and After Einstein*. Amsterdam: IOS Press.

Carey, Susan (2009). *The Origin of Concepts*. Oxford: Oxford University Press.

Carnap, Rudolph (1928). *The Logical Structure of the World*. Tr. Rolf A. George. University of California Press.

—— (1942). *Introduction to Semantics*. Cambridge, MA: Harvard University Press.

—— (1950). *Logical Foundations of Probability*. University of Chicago Press.

Caro, Mario de, and David Macarthur (eds.) (2004). *Naturalism in Question*. Cambridge, MA: Harvard University Press.

Carruthers, Peter (1996). *Language, Thought and Consciousness*. Cambridge: Cambridge University Press.

—— (2000). *Phenomenal Consciousness: A Naturalistic Theory*. Cambridge: Cambridge University Press.

Carston, Robyn (1988). "Implicature, Explicature and Truth-Theoretic Semantics," in R. Kempson (ed.), *Mental Representations: The Interface between Language and Reality*. Cambridge: Cambridge University Press.

—— (2002). *Thoughts and Utterances: The Pragmatics of Explicit Communication*. Oxford: Blackwell.

—— (2008). "Linguistic Communication and the Semantics-Pragmatics Distinction," *Synthese* 165: 321–45.

—— (2009). "The Explicit/Implicit Distinction in Pragmatics and the Limits of Explicit Communication," *International Review of Pragmatics* 1: 35–62.

Cartwright, Richard (1987). "A Neglected Theory of Truth," in *Philosophical Essays*. Cambridge, MA: MIT Press.

Chaitin, Gregory (1995). "The Berry Paradox," *Complexity* 1: 26–30.

Chalmers, David (2011). "Verbal Disputes," *Philosophical Review* 120: 515–66.

—— (2012). *Constructing the World*. Oxford: Oxford University Press.

Chalmers, David, and Frank Jackson (2001). "Conceptual Analysis and Reductive Explanation," *Philosophical Review* 110: 315–61.

Chang, Hasok (2004). *Inventing Temperature*. Oxford: Oxford University Press.

Chellas, Brian (1980). *Modal Logic*. Cambridge: Cambridge University Press.

Chierchia, Gennaro, and Sally McConnell-Ginet (2000). *Meaning and Grammar*. 2nd ed. Cambridge MA: MIT Press.

Chihara, Charles S. (1973). "A Diagnosis of the Liar and Other Semantical Vicious-Circle Paradoxes," in C. Roberts (ed.), *The Work of Bertrand Russell*. London: Allen and Unwin.

—— (1976). "Truth, Meaning, and Paradox," *Noûs* 10: 305–11.

—— (1979). "The Semantic Paradoxes: A Diagnostic Investigation," *The Philosophical Review* 88: 590–618.

—— (1984). "The Semantic Paradoxes: Some Second Thoughts," *Philosophical Studies* 45: 223–9.

Child, William (1994). *Causality, Interpretation, and the Mind*. Oxford: Oxford University Press.

Chomsky, Noam (1986). *Knowledge of Language*. Westport, CT: Praeger.

—— (1995). "Language and Nature," *Mind* 104: 1–61.

Clapp, Lenny (2002). "What Unarticulated Constituents Could Not Be," in J. K. Campbell, M. O'Rourke, and D. Shier (eds.), *Meaning and Truth*. New York: Seven Bridges.

Cobreros, Pablo (2011a). "Varzi on Supervaluationism and Logical Consequence," *Mind* 120: 833–43.

—— (2011b). "Supervaluationism and Fara's Argument Concerning Higher-Order Vagueness," in P. Égre and N. Klinedinst (eds.), *Vagueness and Language Use*. New York: Palgrave Macmillan.

Cook, Roy (2002). "Counterintuitive Consequences of the Revision Theory of Truth," *Analysis* 62: 16–22.

—— (2006). "There are Noncircular Paradoxes (but Yablo's Isn't One of Them)," *The Monist* 89: 118–49.

—— (2008). "Embracing Revenge: On the Indefinite Extensibility of Language," in Beall (2008a).

—— (2009). "Curry, Yablo, and Duality," *Analysis* 69: 412–20.

Costa, Newton da, Otavio Bueno, and Steven French (2005). "A Coherence Theory of Truth," Manuscrito 28: 263–90.

Cruse, D. A. (1986). *Lexical Semantics*. Cambridge: Cambridge University Press.

Culbertson, Jennifer, and Steven Gross (2009). "Are Linguists Better Subjects?" *British Journal for the Philosophy of Science* 60: 721–36.

Curry, H. (1942). "The Inconsistency of Certain Formal Logics," *Journal of Symbolic Logic* 7: 115–17.

Dauer, Francis (1974). "In Defense of the Coherence Theory of Truth," *Journal of Philosophy* 71: 791–811.

David, Marian (1989). "Truth, Eliminativism, and Disquotationalism," *Noûs* 23: 599–614.

—— (1994). *Correspondence and Disquotation: An Essay on the Nature of Truth*. Oxford: Oxford University Press.

Davidson, Donald (1967). "Truth and Meaning," in Davidson (1984).

—— (1969). "True to the Facts," in Davidson (1984).

—— (1970). "Mental Events," in Davidson (1980a).

Davidson, Donald (1973). "Radical Interpretation," in Davidson (1984).
—— (1974a). "On the Very Idea of a Conceptual Scheme," in Davidson (1984).
—— (1974b). "Belief and the Basis of Meaning," in Davidson (1984).
—— (1976a). "Hempel on Explaining Action," in Davidson (1980a).
—— (1976b). "Reply to Foster," in Davidson (1984).
—— (1980a). *Essays on Actions and Events*. Oxford University Press.
—— (1980b). "Toward a Unified Theory of Meaning and Action," *Grazer Philosophische Studien* 11: 1–12.
—— (1982). "Communication and Convention," in Davidson (1984).
—— (1984). *Inquiries into Truth and Interpretation*. Oxford: Oxford University Press.
—— (1986). "A Nice Derangement of Epitaphs," in E. LePore (ed.), *Truth and Interpretation: Perspectives on the Philosophy of Donald Davidson*. Oxford: Blackwell.
—— (1990). "The Structure and Content of Truth," in Davidson (2005).
—— (1992). "The Second Person," in Davidson (2001).
—— (1995). "Could There Be a Science of Rationality?" *International Journal of Philosophical Studies* 3: 1–16.
—— (1996). "The Folly of Trying to Define Truth," *The Journal of Philosophy* 94: 263–278.
—— (1997a). "The Emergence of Thought," in Davidson (2001).
—— (1997b). "Indeterminism and Antirealism," in Davidson (2001).
—— (1999a). "General Remarks," in U. M. Zeglen (ed.), *Donald Davidson: Truth, Meaning and Knowledge*. London: Routledge.
—— (1999b). "Reply to John McDowell," in L. E. Hahn (ed.), *The Philosophy of Donald Davidson*. Chicago: Open Court.
—— (2001). *Subjective, Intersubjective, Objective*. Oxford: Oxford University Press.
—— (2005). *Truth and Predication*. Cambridge, MA: Harvard University Press.
Dekker, Paul (2010). "Dynamic Semantics," in C. Maienborn, K. von Heusinger, and P. Portner (eds.), *Semantics: An International Handbook of Natural Language Meaning*. Vol 1. Berlin: de Gruyter.
DeRose, Keith (2002). "Assertion, Knowledge, and Context," *Philosophical Review* 111: 167–203.
—— (2006). " 'Bamboozled by Our Own Words': Semantic Blindness and Some Objections to Contextualism," *Philosophy and Phenomenological Research* 73: 316–38.
Devitt, Michael (1984). *Realism and Truth*. 2nd ed. Princeton: Princeton University Press.
—— (2006a). *Ignorance of Language*. Oxford: Oxford University Press.
—— (2006b). "Intuitions in Linguistics," *British Journal for the Philosophy of Science* 57: 481–513.
—— (2009). "Methodology in the Philosophy of Linguistics," *Australasian Journal of Philosophy* 86: 671–84.
—— (2010). "What Intuitions are Linguistic Evidence?" *Erkenntnis* 73: 251–64.
Devitt, Michael, and Georges Rey (1991). "Transcending Transcendentalism: A Response to Boghossian," *Pacific Philosophical Quarterly* 72: 87–100.
Dietz, Richard (2008). "Epistemic Modals and Correct Disagreement," in García-Carpintero and Kölbel (2008).
Dietz, Richard and Sebastiano Moruzzi (eds.) (2010). *Cuts and Clouds*. Oxford: Oxford University Press.

Dodd, Julian (1995). "McDowell and Identity Theories of Truth," *Analysis* 55: 160–5.

—— (1996). "Resurrecting the Identity Theory of Truth: A Reply to Candlish," *Bradley Studies* 2: 42–50.

—— (1999b). "Hornsby on the Identity Theory of Truth," *Proceedings of the Aristotelian Society*, 49: 225–32.

—— (2000). *An Identity Theory of Truth*. New York: St. Martin's Press.

—— (2008). "McDowell's Identity Conception of Truth: A Reply to Fish and Macdonald," *Analysis* 68: 76–85.

Dogramaci, Sinan (2010). "Knowledge of Validity," *Noûs* 44: 403–32.

Dorsey, Dale (2006). "A Coherence Theory of Truth in Ethics," *Philosophical Studies* 127: 493–523.

Dowty, David, Robert Wall, and Stanley Peters (1981). *An Introduction to Montague Semantics*. Dordrecht: D. Reidel.

Dresner, Eli (2002). "Measurement Theoretic Semantics and the Semantics of Necessity," *Synthese* 130: 413–40.

—— (2004). "Over-Assignment of Structure," *Journal of Philosophical Logic* 33: 467–80.

—— (2006). "A Measurement Theoretic Account of Propositions," *Synthese* 153: 1–22.

—— (2010a). "Language and the Measure of Mind," *Mind and Language* 25: 418–39.

—— (2010b). "Measurement-Theoretic Representation and Computation-Theoretic Realization," *Journal of Philosophy* 107: 275–92.

Dummett, Michael (1959). "Truth," *Truth and Other Enigmas*. Cambridge, MA: Harvard University Press: 1–24.

—— (1973). *Frege: Philosophy of Language*. Cambridge, MA: Harvard University Press.

—— (1978). *Truth and Other Enigmas*. Cambridge, MA: Harvard University Press.

—— (1991). *The Logical Basis of Metaphysics*. Cambridge, MA: Harvard University Press.

—— (1993). *The Seas of Language*. Cambridge, MA: Harvard University Press.

—— (1999). "Of What Kind of Thing is Truth a Property?" in S. Blackburn and K. Simmons (eds.), *Truth*. Oxford: Oxford University Press.

—— (2002). "The Two Faces of the Concept of Truth," in Schantz (2002).

Earman, John, and Arthur Fine (1977). "Against Indeterminacy," *Journal of Philosophy* 74: 535–8.

Ebbs, Gary (2009). *Truth and Words*. Oxford: Oxford University Press.

Egan, Andy (2006). "Secondary Qualities and Self-Location," *Philosophy and Phenomenological Research* 72: 97–119.

—— (2007). "Epistemic Modals, Relativism and Assertion," *Philosophical Studies* 133: 1–22.

—— (2009). "Billboards, Bombs, and Shotgun Weddings," *Synthese* 166: 251–79.

—— (2010). "Disputing about Taste," in R. Feldman and T. A. Warfield (eds.), *Disagreement*. Oxford: Oxford University Press.

Egan, Andy, and Brian Weatherson (eds.) (2011). *Epistemic Modality*. Oxford: Oxford University Press.

Egan, Andy, John Hawthorne, and Brian Weatherson, Brian. (2005). "Epistemic Modals in Context," in G. Preyer and G. Peter (eds.), *Contextualism in Philosophy*. Oxford: Oxford University Press.

Eijck, Eric van, and Albert Visser (2010). "Dynamic Semantics," *Stanford Encyclopedia of Philosophy*. Ed. Edward N. Zalta.

Einheuser, Iris (2008). "Three Forms of Truth Relativism," in García-Carpintero and Kölbel (2008).

Einstein, Albert (1916). "Ernst Mach," *Physikalische Zeitschrift* 17: 101–4.

Eklund, Matti (2002a). "Inconsistent Languages," *Philosophy and Phenomenological Research* 64: 251–75.

—— (2002b). "Deep Inconsistency," *Australasian Journal of Philosophy* 80: 321–31.

—— (2005). "What Vagueness Consists In," *Philosophical Studies* 125: 27–60.

—— (2007). "Meaning-Constitutivity," *Inquiry* 50: 559–74.

—— (2008a). "The Liar Paradox, Expressibility, Possible Languages," in Beall (2008a).

—— (2008b). "Reply to Beall and Priest," *Australasian Journal of Logic* 6: 94–106.

—— (2011). "Fictionalism," in E. N. Zalta (ed.), *Stanford Encyclopedia of Philosophy*. July 2011 edition. Ed. Edward N. Zalta. <http://plato.stanford.edu/entries/fictionalism/>.

Engel, Pascal (2002). *Truth*. Montreal: McGill-Queen's University Press.

Englebretsen, George (2006). *Bare Facts and Naked Truths*. Surrey: Ashgate.

Evans, Gareth (1982). *The Varieties of Reference*. Ed. J. McDowell. Oxford: Oxford University Press.

Everaert, Martin et al. (eds.) (2010). *The Linguistics Enterprise*. Amsterdam: John Benjamins.

Fara, Delia Graff (2011). "Truth in a Region," in P. Égre and N. Klinedinst (eds.), *Vagueness and Language Use*. Palgrave Macmillan.

Feferman, Solomon (1982). "Toward Useful Type-Free Theories, I," *The Journal of Symbolic Logic* 49: 75–111.

—— (1991). "Reflecting on Incompleteness," *The Journal of Symbolic Logic* 56: 1–49.

—— (1999). "Logic, Logics, and Logicism," *Notre Dame Journal of Formal Logic* 40: 31–54.

—— (2008). "Axioms for Determinateness and Truth," *Review of Symbolic Logic* 1: 204–17.

Field, Hartry (1972). "Tarski's Theory of Truth," in Field (2001a).

—— (1973). "Theory Change and the Indeterminacy of Reference," in Field (2001a).

—— (1974). "Quine and the Correspondence Theory," in Field (2001a).

—— (1986). "The Deflationary Conception of Truth," in G. McDonald (ed.), *Fact, Science and Morality*. Oxford: Blackwell Publishers.

—— (1994a). "Deflationist Views of Meaning and Content," in Field (2001a).

—— (1994b). "Disquotional Truth and Factually Defective Discourse," in Field (2001a).

—— (1998). "Some Thoughts on Radical Indeterminacy," in Field (2001a).

—— (2000). "Indeterminacy, Degree of Belief, and Excluded Middle," in Field (2001a).

—— (2001a). *Truth and the Absence of Fact*. Oxford: Oxford.

—— (2001b). "Attributions of Meaning and Content," in Field (2001a).

—— (2001c). Postscript to Field (1972), in Field (2001a).

—— (2001d). Postscript to Field (1973), in Field (2001a).

—— (2001e). Postscript to Field (1974), in Field (2001a).

—— (2001f). Postscript to Field (1994a), in Field (2001a).

—— (2001g). Postscript to Field (1998), in Field (2001a).

—— (2001h). Postscript to Field (2000), in Field (2001a).

—— (2002). "Saving the Truth Schema From Paradox," *Journal of Philosophical Logic* 31: 1–27.

—— (2003a). "A Revenge-Immune Solution to the Semantic Paradoxes," *Journal of Philosophical Logic* 32: 139–77.

—— (2003b). "The Semantic Paradoxes and the Paradoxes of Vagueness," in Beall (2003a).

—— (2003c). "No Fact of the Matter," *Australasian Journal of Philosophy* 81: 457–80.

—— (2004). "The Consistency of the Naïve Theory of Properties," *The Philosophical Quarterly* 54: 78–104.

—— (2005a). "Is the Liar Sentence Both True and False?" in Beall and Armour-Garb (2005).

—— (2005b). "Variations on a Theme by Yablo," in Beall and Armour-Garb (2005).

—— (2005c). "Precis of *Truth and the Absence of Fact*," *Philosophical Studies* 124: 41–4.

—— (2005d). "Replies," *Philosophical Studies* 124: 105–28.

—— (2006a). "Truth and the Unprovability of Consistency," *Mind*: 567–605.

—— (2006b). "Compositional Principles versus Schematic Reasoning," *The Monist*: 9–27.

—— (2006c). "Maudlin's Truth and Paradox," *Philosophy and Phenomenological Research*: 713–20.

—— (2008a). *Saving Truth From Paradox*. Oxford: Oxford University Press.

—— (2008b). *Logic, Normativity, and Rational Revisability*. The John Locke Lectures. Oxford University, 2008.

—— (2008c). "Solving the Paradoxes, Escaping Revenge," in Beall (2008a).

—— (2009). "What is the Normative Role of Logic?" *Proceedings of the Aristotelian Society, Supplementary Volume* 83: 251–68.

—— (2010a). "Précis of *Saving Truth from Paradox*," *Philosophical Studies* 147: 415–20.

—— (2010b). "Replies to Commentators on *Saving Truth from Paradox*," *Philosophical Studies* 147: 457–70.

—— (forthcoming). "Mathematical Undecidables, Metaphysical Realism, and Equivalent Descriptions," in *The Philosophy of Hilary Putnam, Library of Living Philosophers*.

Fintel, Kai von, and Anthony Gillies (2008). "CIA Leaks," *Philosophical Review* 117: 77–98.

Fitch, Frederic B. (1963). "A Logical Analysis of Some Value Concepts," *Journal of Symbolic Logic* 28: 135–42.

Fitting, Melvin (1986). "Notes on the Mathematical Aspects of Kripke's Theory of Truth," *Notre Dame Journal of Formal Logic* 27: 75–88.

Fitting, Melvin, and R. L. Mendelsohn (1998). *First-Order Modal Logic*. Berlin: Springer.

Fitzgerald, Gareth (2009). "Linguistic Intuitions," *British Journal for the Philosophy of Science* 61: 123–60.

Fodor, Jerry (1975). *The Language of Thought*. Cambridge, MA: Harvard University Press.

—— (1987). *Psychosemantics: The Problem of Meaning in the Philosophy of Mind*. Cambridge, MA: MIT Press.

—— (1990). *A Theory of Content and Other Essays*. Cambridge, MA: MIT Press.

—— (1998). *Concepts: Where Cognitive Science Went Wrong*. Oxford: Oxford University Press.

—— (2004). "Having Concepts: A Brief Refutation of the Twentieth Century," *Mind and Language* 19: 29–47.

—— (2008). *LOT 2: The Language of Thought Revisited*. Oxford: Oxford University Press.

Foster, John (1976). "Meaning and Truth Theory," in G. Evans and J. H. McDowell (eds.), *Truth and Meaning*. Oxford: Oxford University Press.

Fraassen, Bas C. van (1968). "Presupposition, Implication, and Self-Reference," *The Journal of Philosophy* 65: 136–52.

—— (1970a). "Inference and Self-Reference," *Synthese* 21: 425–38.

Fraassen, Bas C. van (1970b). "Truth and Paradoxical Consequences," in Martin (1970).

—— (2008). *Scientific Representation*. Oxford: Oxford University Press.

Frege, Gottlob (1918). "Thoughts: A Logical Enquiry," in *Translations from the Philosophical Writings of Gottlob Frege*. Ed. and tr. P. Geach and M. Black. Oxford: Blackwell, 1980.

Friedman, Harvey, and Michael Sheard (1987). "An Axiomatic Approach to Self-Referential Truth," *Annals of Pure and Applied Logic* 33: 1–21.

—— (1988). "The Disjunction and Existence Properties for Axiomatic Systems of Truth," *Annals of Pure and Applied Logic* 40: 1–10.

Fumerton, Richard (2002). *Realism and The Correspondence Theory of Truth*. Boston: Rowman and Littlefield.

Gaifman, Haim (1992). "Pointers to Truth," *The Journal of Philosophy* 89: 223–61.

Galilei, Galileo (1623). *The Assayer, in which are weighed with a fine and accurate balance the contents of the 'Astronomical and Philosophical Weighing Scales' of Lothario Sarsi of Siguenza, written in the form of a letter to the Illustrious and Very Reverend Monsignor Don Virginio Cesarini, Lincean Academician, and Chamberlain to his Holiness, by Signor Galileo Galilei, Lincean Academician, Gentleman of Florence, and Chief Philosopher and Mathematician to the Most Serene Grand Duke of Tuscany*. Rome: Giacomo Mascardi.

García-Carpintero, Manuel, and Max Kölbel (eds.) (2008). *Relative Truth*. Oxford: Oxford University Press.

Garson, James (2009). "Modal Logic," *The Stanford Encyclopedia of Philosophy*. Winter 2009 edn. Ed. Edward N. Zalta. <http://plato.stanford.edu/archives/win2009/entries/logic-modal/>.

Gauker, Christopher (2006). "Against Stepping Back: A Critique of Contextualist Approaches to the Semantic Paradoxes," *Journal of Philosophical Logic* 35: 393–422.

Gertler, Brie (2002). "Explanatory Reduction, Conceptual Analysis, and Conceivability Arguments about the Mind," *Noûs* 36: 22–49.

Gettier, Edumund (1963). "Is Justified True Belief Knowledge?" *Analysis* 23: 121–3.

Gillon, Brendan (2004). "Ambiguity, Indeterminacy, Deixis, and Vagueness, Evidence and Theory," in S. Davis and B. S. Gillon (eds.), *Semantics*. Oxford: Oxford University Press.

Girard, Jean-Yves, Yves Lafont, and Laurent Regnier (eds.) (1995). *Advances in Linear Logic*. Cambridge: Cambridge University Press.

Givón, Talmy (2001). *Syntax: An Introduction*. Amsterdam: John Benjamins.

Glanzberg, Michael (2001). "The Liar in Context," *Philosophical Studies* 103: 217–51.

—— (2003). "Against Truth-Value Gaps," in Beall (2003a).

—— (2004). "A Contextual-Hierarchical Approach to Truth and the Liar Paradox," *Journal of Philosophical Logic* 33: 27–88.

—— (2005). "Truth, Reflection, and Hierarchies," *Synthese* 142: 289–315.

—— (2007). "Context, Content, and Relativism," *Philosophical Studies* 136: 1–29.

—— (2009). "Semantics and Truth Relative to a World," *Synthese* 166: 281–307.

—— (2011). "More on Operators and Tense," *Analysis* 71: 112–25.

—— (forthcoming a). "Not All Contextual Parameters are Alike."

—— (forthcoming b). *The Oxford Handbook of Truth*. Oxford: Oxford University Press.

Goddard, Leonard, and Mark Johnston (1983). "The Nature of Reflexive Paradoxes Part I," *Notre Dame Journal of Formal Logic* 24: 491–508.

Gödel, Kurt (1931). "On Formally Undecidable Propositions of Principia Mathematica and Related Systems I," in J. van Heijenoort (ed.), *From Frege to Gödel*. Cambridge, MA: Harvard University Press.

Goldstein, Laurence (1985). "The Paradox of the Liar: A Case of Mistaken Identity," *Analysis* 45: 9–13.
—— (1986a). "Epimenides and Curry," *Analysis* 46: 117–21.
—— (1986b). "False Stipulation and Semantical Paradox," *Analysis* 49: 192–95.
—— (1992). "'This Statement is not True' is not True," *Analysis* 52: 1–5.
—— (1999). "A Unified Solution to Some Paradoxes," *Proceedings of the Aristotelian Society* 100: 53–74.
—— (2001). "Truth-Bearers and the Liar: A Reply to Alan Weir," *Analysis* 61: 115–26.
—— (2009). "A Consistent Way with Paradox," *Philosophical Studies* 144: 377–89.
Goldstein, Laurence, and Leonard Goddard (1980). "Strengthened Paradoxes," *Australasian Journal of Philosophy* 58: 211–21.
Green, Mitchell (1999). "Attitude Ascription's Affinity to Measurement," *International Journal of Philosophical Studies* 7: 323–48.
Greenough, Patrick (2001). "Free Assumptions and the Liar Paradox," *American Philosophical Quarterly* 38: 115–35.
—— (2011a). "Truthmaker Gaps and the No-No Paradox," *Philosophy and Phenomenological Research* 82: 547–63.
—— (2011b). "Truth-Relativism, Norm-Relativism, and Assertion," in Brown and Cappelen (2011).
Greenough, Patrick, and Lynch, Michael (eds.) (2006). *Realism and Truth*. Oxford: Oxford University Press.
Grelling, K. and L. Nelson (1908). *Bemerkungen zu den Paradoxien von Russell und Burali-Forti*. In: Abhandlungen der Fries'schen Schule II, Göttingen.
Grice, Paul (1975/1989). *Studies in the Way of Words*. Harvard University Press.
Groenendijk, Jeroen, and Martin Stakhof (1991). "Dynamic Predicate Logic," *Linguistics and Philosophy* 14: 39–100.
Gross, Steven (2005). "Linguistic Understanding and Belief," *Mind* 114: 61–6.
—— (2006). "Can Empirical Theories of Semantic Competence Really Help Limn the Structure of Reality?" *Noûs* 40: 43–81.
Grover, Dorothy (1976). "'This Is False' on the Prosentential Theory," *Analysis* 36: 80–3.
—— (1977). "Inheritors and Paradox," *The Journal of Philosophy* 74: 500–604.
Grover, Dorothy, Joseph Camp, and Nuel Belnap (1975). "A Prosentential Theory of Truth," *Philosophical Studies* 27: 73–125.
Gupta, Anil (1982). "Truth and Paradox," *Journal of Philosophical Logic* 11: 1–60.
—— (1999). "Meaning and Misconceptions," in R. Jackendoff, P. Bloom, and K. Wynn (eds.), *Language, Logic, and Concepts*. Cambridge, MA: MIT Press.
—— (2005). "Do the Paradoxes Pose a Special Problem for Deflationism?" in Jc Beall and B. Armour-Garb (eds.), *Deflationary Truth*. Chicago: Open Court.
Gupta, Anil, and Nuel Belnap (1993). *The Revision Theory of Truth*. Cambridge, MA: MIT Press.
Habermas, Jürgen (1973). "Wahrheitstheorien," in H. Fahrenbach (ed.), *Wirklichkeit und Reflexion*. Pfüllingen: Neske.
—— (2003). *Truth and Justification*. Tr. B. Fultner. Cambridge, MA: MIT Press.
Halbach, Volker (1999). "Disquotationalism and Infinite Conjunctions," *Mind* 108: 1–22.
—— (2002). "Modalized Disquotationalism," in Halbach and Horsten (2002).
—— (2011). *Axiomatic Theories of Truth*. Cambridge: Cambridge University Press.
Halbach, Volker, and Leon Horsten (eds.) (2002). *Principles of Truth*. Munich: Frankfurt am Main.

Halbach, Volker, Hannes Leitgeb, and Philip Welch (2003). "Possible-Worlds Semantics for Modal Notions Conceived as Predicates," *Journal of Philosophical Logic* 32: 179–223.

Hall, Alison (2008). "Free Enrichment or Hidden Indexicals?" *Mind and Language* 23: 426–56.

Harman, Gilbert (1986). *Change in View: Principles of Reasoning.* Cambridge, MA: MIT Press.

—— (2009). "Field on the Normative Role of Logic," *Proceedings of the Aristotelian Society* 83: 251–68.

Hawthorne, John (2004). *Knowledge and Lotteries.* Oxford: Oxford University Press.

—— (2007). "Craziness and Metasemantics," *Philosophical Review* 116: 427–40.

Heck, Richard (2005). "Truth and Disquotation," *Synthese* 142: 317–52.

Heim, Irene (1983). "File Change Semantics and the Familiarity Theory of Definiteness," in R. Bäuerle and C. Schwarze (eds.), *Meaning, Use, and the Interpretation of Language.* Berlin: de Gruyter.

Hellman, Geoffrey (2006). "Mathematical Pluralism: The case of Smooth Infinetesimal Analysis," *Journal of Philosophical Logic* 35: 621–51.

Hendricks, Vincent (ed.) (2000). *Proof Theory: History and Philosophical Significance*, Berlin: Springer.

Herzberger, Hans G. (1982). "Naïve Semantics and the Liar Paradox," *The Journal of Philosophy* 79: 479–97.

Hill, Christopher (2002). *Thought and World: An Austere Portrayal of Truth, Reference, and Semantic Correspondence.* Cambridge: Cambridge University Press.

Hodges, Wilfred (2009). "Logic and Games," *Stanford Encyclopedia of Philosophy.* Ed. E. N. Zalta. <http://plato.stanford.edu/archives/spr2009/entries/logic-games/>.

Hofweber, Thomas (1999). "Contextualism and the Meaning-Intention Problem," in K. Korta, E. Sosa, and J. Arrozola (eds.), *Cognition, Agency and Rationality.* Dordrecht: Kluwer.

—— (2008). "Validity, Paradox, and the Ideal of Deductive Logic," in Beall (2008a).

—— (2009). "Ambitious, Yet Modest, Metaphysics," in D. Chalmers, D. Manley, and R. Wasserman (eds.), *Metametaphysics.* Oxford: Oxford University Press.

—— (2010). "Inferential Role and the Ideal of Deductive Logic," in D. Patterson (ed.), *Meaning, Understanding, and Knowledge.* Manhattan, KS: New Prairie Press.

Hohwy, Jakob, and Jesper Kallestrup (eds.) (2008). *Being Reduced: New Essays on Reduction, Explanation, and Causation.* Oxford: Oxford University Press.

Hom, Christopher (2008). "The Semantics of Racial Epithets," *Journal of Philosophy* 105: 416–40.

Horn, Lawrence (2001). *A Natural History of Negation.* 2nd ed. Stanford: CSLI Publications.

Hornsby, Jennifer (1997). "Truth: The Identity Theory," *Proceedings of the Aristotelian Society* 97: 1–24.

—— (2005). "Truth without Truthmaking Entities," in H. Beebee and J. Dodd (eds.), *Truthmakers: The Contemporary Debate.* Oxford: Oxford University Press.

Horsten, Leon (1995). "The Semantical Paradoxes, the Neutrality of Truth and the Neutrality of the Minimalist Theory of Truth," in P. Cortois (ed.), *The Many Problems of Realism.* Tilburg: Tilburg University Press.

—— (2009). "Levity," *Mind* 118: 555–81.

—— (2011). *The Tarskian Turn.* Cambridge, MA: MIT Press.

Horwich, Paul (1998). *Truth.* 2nd ed. Oxford: Clarendon Press.

—— (1999). "The Minimalist Conception of Truth," in S. Blackburn and K. Simmons (eds.), *Truth: Oxford Readings in Philosophy.* Oxford: Oxford University Press.

—— (2001). "A Defense of Minimalism," *Synthese* 126: 149–65.

—— (2005). *Reflections on Meaning*. Oxford: Oxford University Press.

—— (2011). *Truth-Meaning-Reality*. Oxford: Oxford University Press.

Iacona, Andrea (2008). "Faultless or Disagreement," in García-Carpintero and Kölbel (2008).

Jackson, Frank (1997). *From Metaphysics to Ethics: A Defense of Conceptual Analysis*. Oxford: Oxford University Press.

—— (2001a). "Précis of *From Metaphysics to Ethics*," *Philosophy and Phenomenological Research* 62: 617–24.

—— (2001b). "Responses," *Philosophy and Phenomenological Research* 62: 653–64.

Jacquette, Dale (2004). "Grelling's Revenge," *Analysis* 64: 251–6.

James, William (1907). *Pragmatism*. Cambridge, MA: Harvard University Press.

—— (1909). *The Meaning of Truth*. Cambridge, MA: Harvard University Press.

Jammer, Max (2000). *Concepts of Mass in Contemporary Physics and Philosophy*. Princeton: Princeton University Press.

Jocahim, Harold (1906). *The Nature of Truth*. Oxford: Clarendon Press.

Johnston, Mark (1993). "Objectivity Refigured: Pragmatism without Verificationism," in J. Haldane and C. Wright (eds.), *Reality, Representation, and Projection*. Oxford: Oxford University Press.

Jorgensen, Jorgen (1953). "Some Reflections on Reflexivity," *Mind* 62: 289–300.

—— (1955). "On Kattsoff's Reflections on Jorgensen's Reflections in Reflexivity," *Mind* 64: 542.

Juhl, Cory F. (1997). "A Context-Sensitive Liar," *Analysis* 57: 202–4.

Kalderon, Mark (ed.) (2005a). *Moral Fictionalism*. Oxford: Clarendon Press.

—— (ed.) (2005b). *Fictionalism in Metaphysics*. Oxford: Clarenden Press.

Kamp, Hans (1981). "A Theory of Truth and Semantic Representation," in J. Groenendijk, T. Janssen, and M. Stokhof (eds.), *Formal Methods in the Study of Language*. Amsterdam: Mathematical Centre Tracts 135.

Kaplan, David (1989). "Demonstratives: An Essay on the Semantics, Logic, Metaphysics, and Epistemology of Demonstratives and Other Indexicals," in J. Almog, J. Perry, and H. K. Wettstein (eds.), *Themes From Kaplan*. Oxford: Oxford University Press.

Kaplan, David, and Richard Montague (1960). "A Paradox Regained," *Notre Dame Journal of Formal Logic* 1: 79–90.

Kashlinsky et. al. (2008). "A Measurement of Large-Scale Peculiar Velocities of Clusters of Galaxies: Results and Cosmological Implications," *The Astrophysical Journal Letters* 686. doi: 10.1086/592947

—— (2009). "A Measurement of Large-Scale Peculiar Velocities of Clusters of Galaxies: Technical Details," *The Astrophysical Journal Letters* 691. doi: 10.1088/0004–637X/691/2/1479

Kattsoff, L. O. (1955). "Some Reflections on Jorgensen's Reflections in Reflexivity," *Mind* 64: 96–8.

Katz, Jerrold (ed.) (1985). *The Philosophy of Linguistics*. Oxford: Oxford University Press.

Kearns, John (2007). "An Illocutionary Logical Explanation of the Liar Paradox," *History and Philosophy of Logic*, 28: 31–66.

Keene, G. B. (1983). "Self-Referent Inference and the Liar Paradox," *Mind* 92: 430–2.

Kempson, Ruth, Tim Fernando, and Nicholas Asher (eds.) (2012). *Philosophy of Linguistics*. Oxford: Elsevier.

Kennedy, Chris (1999). *Projecting the Adjective: The Syntax and Semantics of Gradability and Comparison*. PhD Dissertation, University of California, Santa Cruz.

—— (2010). "Ambiguity and Vagueness: An Overview," in C. Maienborn, K. von Heusinger, and P. Portner (eds.), *Semantics: An International Handbook of Natural Language Meaning*. Vol. 1. Berlin: de Gruyter.

Kerr, Alison Duncan (MS). "Relevant Disjunctive Syllogism."

Ketland, Jeffrey (2003). "Can a Many-Valued Language Functionally Represent Its Own Semantics?" *Analysis* 63: 292–7.

—— (2005a). "Jacquette on Grelling's Paradox," *Analysis* 65: 258–60.

—— (2005b). "Yablo's Paradox and Ω-Inconsistency," *Synthese* 145: 295–302.

King, Jeffrey (2003). "Tense, Modality and Semantic Values," *Philosophical Perspectives* 17: 195–246.

—— (forthcoming). "Speaker Intentions in Context," *Noûs*.

Kirkham, Richard (1995). *Theories of Truth*. Cambridge, MA: MIT Press.

Kitcher, Philip (2002). "On the Explanatory Role of Correspondence Truth," *Philosophy and Phenomenological Research* 6: 346–64.

Kneale, William C. (1972). "Propositions and Truth in Natural Languages," *Mind* 81: 225–43.

Knobe, Joshua, and Shawn Nichols (eds.) (2008). *Experimental Philosophy*. Oxford: Oxford University Press.

Kölbel, Max (2002). *Truth without Objectivity*. London: Routledge.

—— (2003). "Faultless Disagreement," *Proceedings of the Aristotelian Society* 104: 53–73.

—— (2004). "Indexical Relativism versus Genuine Relativism," *International Journal of Philosophical Studies* 12: 297–313.

—— (2007). "How to Spell Out Genuine Relativism and How to Defend Indexical Relativism," *International Journal of Philosophical Studies* 15: 281–8.

—— (2008). " 'True' as Ambiguous," *Philosophy and Phenomenological Research* 77: 359–84.

—— (2009). "The Evidence for Relativism," *Synthese* 166: 375–95.

Kraut, Robert (1993). "Robust Deflationism," *Philosophical Review* 102: 247–63.

Kreisel, Georg (1972). "Informal Rigor and Completeness Proofs," in I. Lakatos (ed.), *Problems in Philosophy of Mathematics*. Amsterdam: North Holland.

Kremer, Michael (2002). "Intuitive Consequences of the Revision Theory of Truth," *Analysis* 62: 330–6.

Kremer, Philip (2000). "On the 'Semantics' for Languages with Their Own Truth Predicates," in Chapuis and Gupta (2000).

Kremer, Philip, and Michael Kremer (2003). "Some Supervaluation Based Consequence Relations," *Journal of Philosophical Logic* 32: 225–44.

Kripke, Saul (1972). *Naming and Necessity*. Cambridge, MA: Harvard University Press. 1980.

—— (1975). "Outline of a Theory of Truth," *The Journal of Philosophy* 72: 690–716.

—— (1977). "Speaker's Reference and Semantic Reference," *Midwest Studies in Philosophy* 2: 255–76.

—— (1982). *Wittgenstein on Rules and Private Language*. Cambridge, MA: Harvard University Press.

Kroedel, Thomas (2012). "Implicit Definition and the Application of Logic," *Philosophical Studies* 158: 131–48.

Kuhn, Thomas (1962). *The Structure of Scientific Revolutions*. Chicago: University of Chicago Press.

Kukla, Rebecca and Mark Lance (2009). *'Yo!' and 'Lo!': The Pragmatic Topography of the Space of Reasons*. Cambridge, MA: Harvard University Press.

Künne, Wolfgang (2002). "Disquotationalist Conceptions of Truth," in Schantz (2002).

—— (2003). *Conceptions of Truth*. Oxford: Clarendon Press.

Kuusela, Oskari (2008). *The Struggle Against Dogmatism: Wittgenstein and the Concept of Philosophy*. Cambridge, MA: Harvard University Press.

Lakatos, Imre (1976). *Proofs and Refutations*. Cambridge: Cambridge University Press.

Lance, Mark (1996). "Quantification, Substitution, and Conceptual Content," *Noûs* 30: 481–507.

—— (1997). "The Significance of Anaphoric Theories of Truth and Reference," *Philosophical Issues* 8: 181–98.

—— (1998). "Some Reflections on the Sport of Language," *Philosophical Perspectives* 12: 219–40.

—— (2001). "The Logical Structure of Linguistic Commitment III: Brandomian Scorekeeping and Incompatibility," *Journal of Philosophical Logic* 30: 439–64.

Lance, Mark, and Philip Kremer (1994). "The Logical Structure of Linguistic Commitment I," *Journal of Philosophical Logic* 23: 369–400.

—— (1996). "The Logical Structure of Linguistic Commitment II: Systems of Relevant Commitment Entailment," *Journal of Philosophical Logic* 25: 425–49.

Larson, Richard, and Peter Ludlow (1993). "Interpreted Logical Forms," *Synthese* 95: 305–55.

Lasersohn, Peter (2005). "Context Dependence, Disagreement, and Predicates of Personal Taste," *Linguistics and Philosophy* 28: 643–86.

—— (2008). "Quantification and Perspective in Relativist Semantics," *Philosophical Perspectives* 22: 305–37.

—— (2009). "Relative Truth, Speaker Commitment, and Control of Implicit Arguments," *Synthese* 166: 359–74.

—— (2011). "Context, Relevant Parts, and (Lack of) Disagreement Over Taste," *Philosophical Studies* 156: 433–9.

Leeds, Stephen (1978). "Theories of Reference and Truth," *Erkenntnis* 13: 111–29.

—— (1995). "Truth, Correspondence, and Success," *Philosophical Studies* 79: 1–36.

—— (2000). "A Disquotationalist Looks at Vagueness," *Philosophical Topics* 28: 107–28.

—— (2007). "Correspondence Truth and Scientific Realism," *Synthese* 159: 1–21.

Leigh, Graham and Michael Rathjen (2010). "An Ordinal Analysis for Theories of Self-Referential Truth," *Archive for Mathematical Logic* 49: 213–47.

Leitgeb, Hannes (2002). "What is a Self-Referential Sentence?" *Logique et Analyse* 117: 3–14.

—— (2007). "What Theories of Truth Should Be Like (but Cannot Be)," *Philosophical Compass* 2: 276–90.

—— (2008). "On the Metatheory of Field's 'Solving the Paradoxes, Escaping Revenge'," in Beall (2008a).

Lepore, Ernie, and Kirk Ludwig (2005). *Donald Davidson: Meaning, Truth, Language, and Reality*. Oxford: Oxford University Press.

—— (2007). *Donald Davidson's Truth Theoretic Semantics*. Oxford: Oxford University Press.

Lewis, David (1970). "How to Define Theoretical Terms," *Journal of Philosophy* 67: 427–46.

Lewis, David (1974). "Radical Interpretation," *Synthese* 27: 331–44.

—— (1979). "Scorekeeping in a Language Game," in *Philosophical Papers*. Vol. 1. Oxford: Oxford University Press. 1983.

—— (1983). "New Work for a Theory of Universals," *Australasian Journal of Philosophy* 61: 343–77.

—— (1994). "Reduction of Mind," in S. Guttenplan (ed.), *A Companion to Philosophy of Mind*, Oxford: Blackwell.

Longworth, Guy (2008a). "Linguistic Understanding and Knowledge," *Noûs* 42: 50–79.

—— (2008b). "Comprehending Speech," *Philosophical Perspectives* 22: 339–73.

—— (2009). "A Plea for Understanding," in S. Sawyer (ed.), *New Waves in the Philosophy of Language*. New York: Palgrave.

Lopez de Sa, Dan (2007). "The Many Relativisms and the Question of Disagreement," *International Journal of Philosophical Studies* 15: 269–79.

Ludlow, Peter (2011). *The Philosophy of Generative Linguistics*. Oxford: Oxford University Press.

Ludwig, Kirk (2001). "What is the Role of a Truth Theory in a Meaning Theory?" in *Truth and Meaning: Topics in Contemporary Philosophy*. New York: Seven Bridges Press.

Lycan, William (2012). "A Truth Predicate in the Object Language," in G. Preyer (ed.), *Davidson's Philosophy*. Oxford: Oxford University Press.

Lynch, Michael (2009). *Truth as One and Many*. Oxford: Oxford University Press.

McDonald, Brian Edison (2000). "On Meaningfulness and Truth," *Journal of Philosophical Logic* 29: 433–82.

McDowell, John (1994). *Mind and World*. Cambridge, MA: Harvard University Press.

—— (1999). "Scheme-Content Dualism and Empiricism," in L. E. Hahn (ed.), *The Philosophy of Donald Davidson*. Chicago: Open Court.

—— (2009). "Wittgensteinian Quietism," *Common Knowledge* 15: 365–72.

MacFarlane, John (2003). "Future Contingents and Relative Truth," *The Philosophical Quarterly* 53: 321–36.

—— (2005a). "Making Sense of Relative Truth," *Proceedings of the Aristotelian Society* 105: 321–39.

—— (2005b). "The Assessment Sensitivity of Knowledge Attributions," *Oxford Studies in Epistemology* 1: 197–233.

—— (2007a). "Relativism and Disagreement," *Philosophical Studies* 132: 17–31.

—— (2007b). "The Logic of Confusion," *Philosophy and Phenomenological Research* 74: 700–8.

—— (2008). "Truth in the Garden of Forking Paths," in García-Carpintero and Kölbel (2008).

—— (2009). "Nonindexical Contextualism," *Synthese* 166: 231–50.

—— (2011a). "Epistemic Modals Are Assessment-Sensitive," in Egan and Weatherson (2011).

—— (2011b). "Simplicity Made Difficult," *Philosophical Studies* 156: 441–8.

—— (forthcoming). *Assessment Sensitivity: Relative Truth and its Applications*.

MacFarlane, John and Nico Kolodny (2010). "Ifs and Oughts," *Journal of Philosophy* 107: 115–43.

McGee, Vann (1985a). "A Counterexample to *Modus Ponens*," *Journal of Philosophy* 82: 462–71.

—— (1985b). "How Truthlike Can a Predicate Be? A Negative Result," *Journal of Philosophical Logic* 14: 399–410.

—— (1991). *Truth, Vagueness, and Paradox: An Essay on the Logic of Truth*. Cambridge: Hackett Publishing Company.

—— (1993). "A Semantic Conception of Truth?" *Philosophical Topics* 21: 83–111.

—— (2010). "Field's Logic of Truth," *Philosophical Studies* 147: 421–32.

McGinn, Colin (2011). *Truth by Analysis*. Oxford: Oxford University Press.

McGrath, Matthew (2000). *Between Deflationism and the Correspondence Theory*. New York: Garland.

Machery, Eduard (2009). *Doing without Concepts*. Oxford: Oxford University Press.

Mackie, J. L. (1973). *Truth Probability and Paradox: Studies in Philosophical Logic*. Oxford: Clarendon Press.

Mackie, J. L., and J. J. C. Smart (1953). "A Variant of the 'Heterological' Paradox," *Analysis* 13: 61–5.

—— (1954). "A Variant of the 'Heterological' Paradox: A Further Note," *Analysis* 14: 146–9.

Maddy, Penelope (2007). *Second Philosophy: A Naturalistic Method*. Oxford: Oxford University Press.

Malcolm, Norman (1959). *Dreaming*. New York: Routledge and Kegan Paul.

Margolis, Eric, and Stephen Lawrence (1999). *Concepts: Core Readings*. Cambridge, MA: MIT Press.

Marino, Patricia (2006). "What Should a Correspondence Theory Be and Do?" *Philosophical Studies* 127: 415–57.

—— (2008). "Toward a Modest Correspondence Theory of Truth," *Dialogue* 47: 81–102.

—— (2010). "Representation-Friendly Deflationism versus Modest Correspondence," in Wright and Pedersen (2010).

Martí, Luisa (2006). "Unarticulated Constituents Revisited," *Linguistics and Philosophy* 29: 135–66.

Martin, Robert L. (1968). "On Grelling's Paradox," *The Philosophical Review* 77: 321–31.

Martinich, A. P. (1983). "A Pragmatic Solution to the Liar Paradox," *Philosophical Studies* 43: 63–7.

Mates, Benson (1981). "Two Antinomies," in *Skeptical Essays*. Chicago: Chicago University Press.

Matthews, Robert (2007). *The Measure of Mind*. Oxford: Oxford University Press.

—— (2009). "A Measurement-Theoretic Account of Propositional Attitudes," in B. McLaughlin and A. Beckermann (eds.), *Oxford Handbook of Philosophy of Mind*. Oxford: Oxford University Press.

Maudlin, Tim (2004). *Truth and Paradox: Solving the Riddles*. Oxford: Oxford University Press.

—— (2006a). Précis of Maudlin (2004). *Philosophy and Phenomenological Research* 73: 696–704.

—— (2006b). "Replies," *Philosophy and Phenomenological Research* 73: 728–39.

—— (2008). "Reducing Revenge to Discomfort," in Beall (2008a).

Millikan, Ruth (1986). "The Price of Correspondence Truth," *Noûs* 20: 453–68.

—— (2000). *On Clear and Confused Ideas: An Essay about Substance Concepts*. Cambridge: Cambridge University Press.

Mills, Andrew P. (1995). "Unsettled Problems with Vague Truth," *Canadian Journal of Philosophy* 25: 103–17.

Misak, Cheryl (2004). *Truth and the End of Inquiry*. Cambridge: Cambridge University Press.

Moltmann, Friederike (2010). "Relative Truth and the First Person," *Philosophical Studies* 150: 187–220.

Montague, Richard (1963). "Syntactical Treatments of Modality, with Corollaries on Reflection Principles and Finite Axiomatizability," *Acta Philosophica Fennica* 16: 153–67.

Montminy, Martin (2009a). "Contextualism, Invariantism and Semantic Blindness," *Australasian Journal of Philosophy* 87: 639–57.

—— (2009b). "Contextualism, Relativism, and Ordinary Speakers," *Philosophical Studies* 143: 341–56.

Moore, G. E. (1899). "The Nature of Judgment," *Mind* 8: 176–93.

Moruzzi, Sebastiano (2008). "Assertion, Belief, and Disagreement: A Problem for Truth-Relativism," in García-Carpintero and Kölbel (2008).

Moruzzi, Sebastiano, and Crispin Wright (2009). "Trumping Assessments and the Aristotelian Future," *Synthese* 166: 301–39.

Murphy, Gregory (2002). *The Big Book of Concepts*. Cambridge, MA: MIT Press.

Naess, A. (1938). *'Truth' as Conceived by those who are not Professional Philosophers*. Oslo: I Komisjon Hos Jacob Dybwad.

Narens, Louis (1986). *Abstract Measurement Theory*. Cambridge, MA: MIT Press.

—— (2002). *Theories of Meaningfulness*. Mahwah, NJ: Lawrence Erlbaum Associates.

—— (2007). *Introduction to the Theories of Measurement and Meaningfulness and the Use of Invariance in Science*. Mahwah, NJ: Lawrence Erlbaum Associates.

Neale, Stephen (1992). "Paul Grice and the Philosophy of Language," *Linguistics & Philosophy* 15: 509–59.

Nersessian, Nancy (2008). *Creating Scientific Concepts*. Cambridge, MA: MIT Press.

Newhard, Jay (2005). "Grelling's Paradox," *Philosophical Studies* 126: 1–21.

Newman, Andrew (2002). *The Correspondence Theory of Truth*. Cambridge: Cambridge University Press.

Pagin, Peter (2007). "Assertion," *Stanford Encyclopedia of Philosophy*. Jan. 2007 edition. Ed. Edward N. Zalta. <http://plato.stanford.edu/archives/win2003/entries/assertion/>.

Papineau, David (2007). "Naturalism," *Stanford Encyclopedia of Philosophy*. Feb. 2007 edition. Ed. Edward N. Zalta. <http://plato.stanford.edu/entries/naturalism/>.

Parsons, Charles (1974). "The Liar Paradox," *Journal of Philosophical Logic* 3: 381–412.

—— (1983). Postscript to Parsons (1974), in *Mathematics in Philosophy*, Ithaca, NY: Cornell University Press.

Parsons, Josh (2011). "Assessment-Contextual Indexicals," *Australasian Journal of Philosophy* 89: 1–17.

Patterson, Douglas (2006). "Tarski, the Liar and Inconsistent Languages," *The Monist* 89: 150–78.

—— (2007). "Inconsistency Theories: The Significance of Semantic Ascent," *Inquiry* 50: 575–589.

—— (2008). "Understanding the Liar," in Beall (2008a).

—— (2009). "Inconsistency Theories of Semantic Paradox," *Philosophy and Phenomenological Research* 79: 387–422.

—— (2010). "Truth as Conceptually Primitive," in Wright and Pedersen (2010).

Peacocke, Christopher (1992). *A Study of Concepts*. Cambridge, MA: MIT Press.

Pederson, Nikolaj, and Cory Wright (forthcoming). *Truth and Pluralism*. Oxford: Oxford University Press.

Peirce, Charles Sanders (1877). "The Fixation of Belief," *Popular Science Monthly* 12: 1–15.

—— (1878). "How to Make Our Ideas Clear," *Popular Science Monthly* 12: 286–302.

Peregrin, Jaroslav (2008). "An Inferentialist Approach to Semantics: Time for a New Kind of Structuralism?" *Philosophy Compass* 3: 1208–23.

Perry, John (1979). "The Problem of the Essential Indexical." *Noûs* 13: 3–21.

—— (1998). "Indexicals, Contexts and Unarticulated Constituents," in *Proceedings of the 1995 CSLI-Amsterdam Logic, Language and Computation Conference*. Stanford: CSLI Publications.

—— (2001). *Reference and Reflexivity*. Stanford: CSLI Publications.

Petkov, Vesselin (2009). *Relativity and the Nature of Spacetime*. Berlin: Springer.

Pettit, Dean (2002). "Why Knowledge is Unnecessary for Understanding Language," *Mind* 111: 519–50.

—— (2005). "Belief and Understanding: A Rejoinder to Gross," *Mind* 114: 67–74.

Pettit, Philip (2004). 'Existentialism, Quietism and the Role of Philosophy', in B. Leiter (ed.), *The Future for Philosophy*. Oxford: Oxford University Press.

Pinillos, N. Angel (2010). "Time-Dilation, Context, and Relative Truth," *Philosophy and Phenomenological Research* 81: 65–92.

Plato (1961). "Theaetetus," in *Plato: Collected Dialogues*. Tr. F. Cornford. Princeton: Princeton University Press.

Popkin, Richard (1966). *The Philosophy of the Sixteenth and Seventeenth Centuries*. New York: Free Press.

Popper, Karl R. (1954). "Self-Reference and Meaning in Ordinary Language," *Mind* 63: 162–69.

Portner, Paul (2009). *Modality*. Oxford: Oxford University Press.

Portner, Paul and Barbara Partee (eds.) (2002). *Formal Semantics: The Essential Readings*. New York: Blackwell.

Predelli, Stefano (2005). *Contexts: Meaning, Truth, and the Use of Language*. Oxford: Oxford University Press.

Predelli, Stefano, and Stojanovic, Isidora (2008). "Semantic Relativism and the Logic of Indexicals," in García-Carpintero and Kölbel (2008).

Preyer, Gerhard, and Georg Peter (eds.) (2005). *Contextualism in Philosophy: Knowledge, Meaning, and Truth*. Oxford: Oxford University Press.

Price, Huw (2003). "Truth as Convenient Friction. *Journal of Philosophy* 100: 167–90.

—— (2010). *Naturalism without Mirrors*. Oxford: Oxford University Press.

Priest, Graham (1979). "The Logic of Paradox," *Journal of Philosophical Logic* 8: 219–41.

—— (1990). "Boolean Negation and All That," *Journal of Philosophical Logic* 19: 201–15.

—— (1994a). Review of McGee (1991). *Mind* 103: 387–91.

—— (1994b). "The Structure of the Paradoxes of Self-Reference," *Mind* 103: 25–34.

—— (1997). "Yablo's Paradox," *Analysis* 57: 236–42.

—— (2000). "On the Principle of Uniform Solution," *Mind* 109: 123–6.

—— (2005). "Spiking the Field-Artillery," in Beall and Armour-Garb (2005).

—— (2006a). *In Contradiction: A Study of the Transconsistent*. 2nd ed. Oxford: Oxford University Press.

—— (2006b). *Doubt Truth to Be a Liar*. Oxford University Press.

—— (2008). "Revenge, Field, and ZF," in Beall (2008a).

—— (2010). "Hopes Fade for Saving Truth," *Philosophy* 85: 109–40.

Priest, Graham, Jc Beall, and Bradley Armour-Garb (2004). *The Law of Non-Contradiction*. Oxford: Oxford University Press.

Prinz, Jesse (2002). *Furnishing the Mind*. Cambridge, MA: MIT Press.

Prior, A. N. (1958). "Epimenides the Cretan," *The Journal of Symbolic Logic* 23: 261–6.

—— (1960). "The Runabout Inference Ticket," *Analysis* 21: 38–9.

—— (1961). "On a Family of Paradoxes," *Notre Dame Journal of Formal Logic* 2: 16–32.

Putnam, Hilary (1962). "It Ain't Necessarily So," *Journal of Philosophy* 59: 658–71.

—— (1971). *Philosophy of Logic*. New York: Harper and Row.

—— (1975). "On the Meaning of 'Meaning'," in *Mind, Language and Reality*, Cambridge: Cambridge University Press.

—— (1981). *Reason, Truth, and History*. Cambridge: Cambridge University Press.

—— (1985). "A Comparison of Something with Something Else," *New Literary History* 17: 61–79.

Quine, W.V. (1951). "Two Dogmas of Empiricism," in *From a Logical Point of View*. Harvard University Press. 1953.

—— (1960). *Word and Object*. Cambridge, MA: MIT Press.

—— (1970). *The Philosophy of Logic*. Cambridge, MA: Harvard University Press.

—— (1992). *The Pursuit of Truth*. Cambridge, MA: Harvard University Press.

Ramsey, F. P. (1926). "Truth and Probability," in R. B. Braithwaite (ed.), *Foundations of Mathematics and Other Logical Essays*. London: Routledge and Kegan Paul, 1931.

—— (1929). "Theories," in R. B. Braithwaite (ed.), *Foundations of Mathematics*. London: Routledge and Kegan Paul, 1931.

Ray, Greg (2002). "Tarski, the Liar, and Truth Definitions," in D. Jacquette (ed.), *Blackwell Companion to Philosophical Logic*. Malden, MA: Blackwell.

—— (2003). "Tarski and the Metalinguistic Liar," *Philosophical Studies* 115: 55–80.

Rayo, Agustin, and Philip Welch (2008). "Field on Revenge," in Beall (2008a).

Recanati, François (2002). "Unarticulated Constituents," *Linguistics and Philosophy* 25: 299–345.

—— (2004). *Literal Meaning*. Cambridge: Cambridge University Press.

—— (2007). *Perspectival Thought*. Oxford: Oxford University Press.

—— (2008). "Contextualism and Relativism," in García-Carpintero and Kölbel (2008).

—— (2010). *Truth-Conditional Pragmatics*. Oxford: Oxford University Press.

Reinhardt, William N. (1986). "Some Remarks on Extending and Interpreting Theories with a Partial Predicate for Truth," *Journal of Philosophical Logic* 15: 219–51.

Resnik, Michael (1990). "Immanent Truth," *Mind* 99: 405–24.

Restall, Greg (1994). *On Logics without Contraction*. PhD. Thesis, The University of Queensland.

—— (2000). *An Introduction to Substructural Logics*. New York: Routledge.

—— (2005). "Minimalists about Truth Can (and Should) Be Epistemicists, and It Helps if They Are Revision Theorists Too," in Beall and Armour-Garb (2005).

—— (2007). "Curry's Revenge: the Costs of Non-classical Solutions to the Paradoxes of Self-Reference," in Beall (2008a).

—— (2008). "Assertion and Denial, Commitment and Entitlement, and Incompatibility (and Some Consequence)," *Studies in Logic* 1: 26–36.

—— (2009). Appendix to Kukla and Lance (2009).

—— (2010). "What Are We to Accept, and What Are We to Reject, when Saving Truth from Paradox?" *Philosophical Studies* 147: 433–43.

—— (MS). *Proof Theory and Philosophy*.

Richard, Mark (1997). "Deflating Truth," *Philosophical Issues* 8: 57–78.

—— (2004). "Contextualism and Relativism," *Philosophical Studies* 119: 215–42.

—— (2008). *When Truth Gives Out*. Oxford: Oxford University Press.

—— (2011). "Relativistic Content and Disagreement," *Philosophical Studies* 156: 421–31.

Richards, Thomas J. (1967). "Self-Referential Paradoxes," *Mind* 76: 387–403.

Ripley, David (2012). "Conservatively Extending Classical Logic with Transparent Truth," *Review of Symbolic Logic* 5: 354–78.

—— (forthcoming). "Paradoxes and Failures of Cut," *Australasian Journal of Philosophy*.

Roberts, Craige (1996/2012). "Information Structure: Towards an Integrated Formal Theory of Pragmatics," *Semantics and Pragmatics* 5, article 6: 1–69.

—— (1998). "Focus, the Flow of Information, and Universal Grammar," in P. Culicover and L. McNally (eds.), *The Limits of Syntax*. Bingley: Emerald Group Publishing.

—— (2002). "Demonstratives as Definites," in K. van Deemter and R. Kibble (eds.), *Information Sharing: Reference and Presupposition in Language Generation and Interpretation*. Stanford: CSLI.

—— (2003). "Uniqueness in Definite Noun Phrases," *Linguistics and Philosophy* 26: 287–350.

—— (2004). "Context in Dynamic Interpretation," in Horn and Ward (2004).

—— (2005). Pronouns as Definites," in M. Reimer and A. Bezuidenhout (eds.), *Descriptions and Beyond*. Oxford: Oxford University Press.

—— (2010). "*Retrievability and Definite Noun Phrases,*" talk given at the philosophy department of The Ohio State University, 5 Feb. 2010.

Roeper, Peter (2010). "Reasoning with Truth," *Journal of Philosophical Logic* 39: 275–306.

Rorty, Richard (2007). "Naturalism and Quietism," in *Philosophy as Cultural Politics*. Cambridge: Cambridge University Press.

Rosenberg, Jay (1974). *Linguistic Representation*. D. Reidel: Dordrecht, Holland.

Ross, Alf (1969). "On Self-Reference and a Puzzle in Constitutional Law," *Mind* 78: 1–24.

Russell, Bertrand (1910). "Knowledge by Acquaintance and Knowledge by Description," *Proceedings of the Aristotelian Society*, 11, 108–28.

Ryle, Gilbert (1931). "Systematically Misleading Expressions," *Proceedings of the Aristotelian Society* 32: 139–70.

—— (1949). *The Concept of Mind*. London: Hutchinson.

—— (1951). "Heterologicality," *Analysis* 11: 61–9.

Saebo, Kjell (2009). "Judgment Ascriptions," *Linguistics and Philosophy* 32: 327–52.

Sainsbury, R. M. (2009). *Fiction and Fictionalism*. New York: Routledge.

Sassoon, Galit (2010). "Measurement Theory in Linguistics," *Synthese* 174: 151–80.

Schaffer, Jonathan (2011). "Contextualism for Taste Claims and Epistemic Modals," in Egan and Weatherson (2011).

Schantz, Richard (ed.) (2002). *What Is Truth?* Berlin: Walter de Gruyter.

Scharp, Kevin (2005). "Scorekeeping in a Defective Language Game," *Pragmatics and Cognition* 13: 203–26.

—— (2007). "Replacing Truth," *Inquiry* 50: 606–21.

—— (2008). "Aletheic Vengeance," in Beall (2008a).

—— (2009a). "Truth's Savior? Critical Study of Field's *Saving Truth From Paradox*," *The Philosophical Quarterly* 60: 183–8.

—— (2009b). "Truth and Expressive Completeness," in B. Weiss and J. Wanderer (eds.), *Reading Brandom*. New York: Routledge.

Scharp, Kevin (2012). "Robert Brandom: Inference and Meaning," in J. Hannon and R. Rutland (eds.), *Philosophical Profiles in the Theory of Communication*. McGill-Queen's University Press.
—— (forthcoming a). "Truth, the Liar, and Relativism," *The Philosophical Review*.
—— (forthcoming b). "Truth, Revenge, and Internalizability," *Erkenntnis*.
Schiffer, Stephen (1996). "Contextualist Solutions to Skepticism," *Proceedings of the Aristotelian Society*, 96: 317–33.
—— (2003). *The Things We Mean*. Oxford: Oxford University Press.
Schlenker, Philipe (2007). "The Elimination of Self-Reference (Generalized Yablo-Series and the Theory of Truth)," *Journal of Philosophical Logic* 36: 251–307.
—— (2011). "Super Liars," *Review of Symbolic Logic* 3: 374–414.
Scholz, Barbara, Francis Pelletier, and Geoffrey Pullman (2011). "Philosophy and Linguistics," *Dialogue* 39: 605–7.
Schroeder, Mark (2010). "How to Be an Expressivist about Truth," in Wright and Pedersen (2010).
Sellars, Wilfrid (1963). *Science, Perception and Reality*. London: Routledge and Kegan Paul.
Sennet, Adam (2011). "Unarticulated Constituents and Propositional Structure," *Mind and Language* 26: 412–35.
Shapiro, Lionel (2006). "The Rationale Behind Revision-Rule Semantics," *Philosophical Studies* 129: 477–515.
—— (2011). "Expressibility and the Liar's Revenge," *Australasian Journal of Philosophy* 89: 297–314.
Shapiro, Stewart (2000). "The Status of Logic," in P. Boghossian and C. Peacocke (eds.), *New Essays on the Apriori*. Oxford: Oxford University Press.
—— (2002a). *Vagueness in Context*. Oxford: Oxford University Press.
—— (2002b). "Incompleteness and Inconsistency," *Mind* 111: 817–32.
—— (2003). "The Guru, the Logician, and the Deflationist: Truth and Logical Consequence," *Noûs* 37: 113–32.
—— (2004). "Simple Truth, Contradiction, and Consistency," in Priest, Beall, and Armour-Garb (2004).
—— (2005). "Gurus, Logical Consequence, and Truth-bearers: What is that is True?" in Jc Beall and B. Armour-Garb (eds.), *Deflationary Truth*. Peru, IL: Open Court.
—— (2010). "So Truth is Safe From Paradox: Now What?" *Philosophical Studies* 147: 445–55.
—— (forthcoming). "Truth, Function, and Paradox," *Analysis*.
Sheard, Michael (1994). "A Guide to Truth Predicates in the Modern Era," *The Journal of Symbolic Logic* 59: 1032–54.
Sider, Ted (2009). "Ontological Realism," in D. Chalmers, D. Manley, and R. Wasserman (eds.), *Metametaphysics: New Essays on the Foundations of Ontology*. Oxford: Oxford University Press.
Simmons, Keith (1993). *Universality and the Liar: An Essay on Truth and the Diagonal Argument*. Cambridge: Cambridge University Press.
—— (1994). "Paradoxes and Denotation," *Philosophical Studies* 76: 71–106.
—— (1999). "Deflationary Truth and the Liar," *Journal of Philosophical Logic* 28: 455–88.
—— (2000). "Three Paradoxes: Circles and Singularities," in Chapuis and Gupta (2000).
—— (2003). "Reference and Paradox," in Beall (2003).
—— (2008). "Revenge and Context," in Beall (2008a).
Skinner, R. C. (1959). "The Paradox of the Liar," *Mind* 68: 322–35.
Skyrms, Brian (1970a). "Return of the Liar: Three-Valued Logic and the Concept of Truth," *American Philosophical Quarterly* 7: 153– 61.

—— (1970b). "Notes on Quantification and Self-Reference," in R. Martin (ed.), *The Paradox of the Liar.* New Haven, CT: Yale University Press.
—— (1984). "Intensional Aspects of Semantical Self-Reference," in R. Martin (ed.), *Recent Essays on Truth and Paradox.* Oxford: Oxford University Press.
Smith, Nicholas J. J. (2000). "The Principle of Uniform Solution (of the Paradoxes of Self-Reference)," *Mind* 109: 117–22.
Smith, Peter (2007). *An Introduction to Gödel's Theorems.* Cambridge: Cambridge University Press.
—— (2011). "Squeezing Arguments," *Analysis* 71: 27–30.
Soames, Scott (1997). "The Truth about Deflationism," in *Philosophical Issues.* Vol. 8. Ed. E. Villanueva. Atascadero, CA: Ridgeview Press.
—— (1999). *Understanding Truth.* Oxford: Oxford University Press.
—— (2011). "True At," *Analysis* 71: 124–33.
Sorensen, Roy (1998). "Yablo's Paradox and Kindred Infinite Liars," *Mind* 107:137–55.
—— (2001). *Vagueness and Contradiction.* Oxford: Clarendon Press.
—— (2005). "Reply to Critics," *Philosophy and Phenomenological Research* 71: 695–703.
Spade, Paul Vincent (1988). *Lies, Language and Logic in the Later Middle Ages.* London: Variorum Reprints.
Stalnaker, Robert (1970). "Pragmatics," in Stalnaker (1999).
—— (1973). "Presuppositions," *Journal of Philosophical Logic* 2: 447–57.
—— (1974). "Pragmatic Presuppositions," in Stalnaker (1999).
—— (1978). "Assertion," in Stalnaker (1999).
—— (1998). "On the Representation of Context," in Stalnaker (1999).
—— (1999). *Context and Content.* Oxford: Oxford University Press.
—— (2001). "Metaphysics without Conceptual Analysis," *Philosophy and Phenomenological Research*, 62: 631–36.
—— (2002). "Common Ground," *Linguistics and Philosophy* 25: 701–21.
—— (2004). "Assertion Revisited: On the Interpretation of Two-Dimensional Modal Semantics," *Philosophical Studies* 118: 299–322.
—— (2009). "A Response to Abbott on Presupposition and Common Ground," *Linguistics and Philosophy* 31: 539–44.
Stanley, Jason (2005). *Knowledge and Practical Interests.* Oxford: Oxford University Press.
—— (2007). *Language in Context.* Oxford: Oxford University Press.
Stebbins, Sarah (1992). "A Minimal Theory of Truth," *Philosophical Studies* 66: 109–37.
Stenius, Erik (1972). *Critical Essays.* Amsterdam: North-Holland Publishing Company.
Stephenson, Tamina (2008). "Judge Dependence, Epistemic Modals, and Predicates of Personal Taste," *Linguistics and Philosophy* 30: 487–525.
—— (2009). "Relativism and the *De Se* Interpretation of PRO," in A. Schardl, M. Walkow, and M. Abdurrahman (eds.), *Proceedings of the 38th Annual Meeting of the North East Linguistic Society.* Amherst, MA: GLSA.
Stich, Stephen and Jonathan Weinberg (2001). "Jackson's Empirical Assumptions," *Philosophy and Phenomenological Research* 62: 637–43.
Stojanovic, Isidora (2007). "Talking about Taste: Disagreement, Implicit Arguments, and Relative Truth," *Linguistics and Philosophy* 30: 691–706.
Strawson, P. F. (1950). "Truth," *Proceedings of the Aristotelian Society, Supplementary Volumes* 24: 111–72.

Strawson, P. F. (1959). *Individuals: An Essay in Descriptive Metaphysics*. London: Methuen.

Suppes, Patrick (1998). "Theory of Measurement," in E. Craig (ed.), *Routledge Encyclopedia of Philosophy*. London: Routledge.

—— (2002). *Representation and Invariance of Scientific Structures*. Stanford: CSLI.

—— (2008). "A Revised Agenda for Philosophy of Mind (and Brain)," in M. Frauchiger and W. K. Essler (eds.), *Representation, Evidence, and Justification: Themes from Suppes*. Frankfurt: Ontos-Verlag.

—— (2009). "Neurophysiological Foundations of Philosophy," in A. Heike and H. Leitgeb (eds.), *Reduction*. Frankfurt: Onto-Verlag.

Suppes, Patrick, and Jean-Yves Beziau (2004). "Semantic Computations of Truth, Based on Associations Already Learned," in C. Delrieux and J. Legris (eds.), *Computer Modeling of Scientific Reasoning*. Argentina: Ediuns.

Suppes, Patrick et al. (1971). *Foundations of Measurement. Vol. 1: Additive and Polynomial Representations*. New York: Academic Press.

—— (1989). *Foundations of Measurement. Vol. 2: Geometrical, Threshold, and Probabilistic Representations*. New York: Academic Press.

—— (1990). *Foundations of Measurement. Vol. 3: Representation, Axiomatization, and Invariance*. New York: Academic Press.

Szabo, Zoltan Gendler (2006). "Sensitivity Training," *Mind and Language* 21: 31–8.

Tappenden, Jamie (1993). "The Liar and Sorites Paradoxes: Toward a Unified Treatment," *The Journal of Philosophy* 90: 551–77.

—— (1994). Review of McGee (1991), *The Philosophical Review* 103: 142–4.

Tarski, Alfred (1933). "The Concept of Truth in Formalized Languages," in *Logic, Semantics, Meta-Mathematics*. Tr. J. H. Woodger. Ed. J. Corcoran. Indianapolis: Hackett Publishing Company, 1983.

—— (1944). "The Semantic Conception of Truth," *Philosophy and Phenomenological Research* 4: 341–76.

Tennant, Neil (1982). "Proof and Paradox," *Dialectica* 36: 265–96.

—— (1995). "On Paradox without Self-Reference," *Analysis* 55: 199–207.

—— (1997). *The Taming of the True*. Oxford: Oxford University Press.

—— (2005). "Rule-Circularity and the Justification of Deduction," *Philosophical Quarterly* 55: 625–48.

—— (MS1). "Truth, Provability and Paradox: On Some Theorems of Lob, Montague and McGee, and a Conjecture about Constructivizability."

—— (MS2). "A New Unified Account of Truth and Paradox."

—— (MS3). "On Scharpening the Rules of Truth."

Textor, Mark (2009). "Devitt on the Epistemic Authority of Linguistic Intuitions," *Erkenntnis* 71: 395–405.

Thagard, Paul (1992). *Conceptual Revolutions*. Princeton: Princeton University Press.

—— (2007). "Coherence, Truth, and the Development of Scientific Knowledge," *Philosophy of Science* 74: 28–47.

—— (2012). *The Cognitive Science of Science*. Cambridge, MA: MIT Press.

Thomason, Richmond H. (1976). "Necessity, Quotation, and Truth: An Indexical Theory," in A. Kasher (ed.), *Language in Focus*. Holland: D. Reidel.

—— (1986). "Paradoxes and Semantic Representation," in J. Y. Halpern (ed.), *Proceedings of Theoretical Aspects of Rationality and Knowledge 1986*. San Francisco: Morgan Kaufmann.

Toms, Eric (1956). "The Liar-Paradox," *The Philosophical Review* 65: 542–7.
Travis, Charles (2008). *Occasion-Sensitivity: Selected Essays*. Oxford: Oxford University Press.
Troelstra, A., and H. Schwichtenberg (2000), *Basic Proof Theory*. 2nd ed. Cambridge: Cambridge University Press.
Ushenko, A. P. (1955). "A Note on the Liar-Paradox," *Mind* 64: 543.
—— (1957). "An Addendum to the Note on the Liar-Paradox," *Mind* 66: 98.
Uzquiano, Gabriel (2004). "An Infinitary Paradox of Denotation," *Analysis* 64: 128–31.
Valin, Robert van (2001). *An Introduction to Syntax*. Cambridge: Cambridge University Press.
Varzi, Achille (2007). "Supervaluationism and Its Logics," *Mind* 116: 633–76.
Vision, Gerald (2004). *Veritas: The Correspondence Theory and its Critics*. Cambridge, MA: MIT Press.
Visser, Albert (2001). "Semantics and the Liar Paradox," in D. M. Gabbay and F. Guenthner (eds.), *Handbook of Philosophical Logic*. 2nd ed. Vol. 7. Amsterdam: D. Reidel.
Walker, Ralph (1989). *The Coherence Theory of Truth: Realism, Anti-Realism, Idealism*. New York: Routledge.
—— (1997). "Theories of Truth," in R. Hale and C. Wright (eds.), *A Companion to Philosophy of Language*. Oxford: Blackwell.
Wasow, Thomas, Amy Perfors, and David Beaver (2005). "The Puzzle of Ambiguity," in O. Orgun and P. Sells (eds.), *Morphology and the Web of Grammar: Essays in Memory of Steven G. Lapointe*. Stanford, CA: CSLI.
Weatherson, Brian (2009). "Conditionals and Indexical Relativism," *Synthese* 166: 333–57.
—— (2011). "No Royal Road to Relativism," *Analysis* 71: 133–43.
Weiner, Matt (2009). "The (Mostly Harmless) Inconsistency of Knowledge Ascriptions," *Philosophers' Imprint* 9: 1–25.
Weir, Alan (1996). "Ultramaximalist Minimalism!" *Analysis* 56: 10–22.
—— (2000). "Token Relativism and the Liar," *Analysis* 60: 156–70.
—— (2001). "Rejoinder to Laurence Goldstein on the Liar," *Analysis* 61: 26–34.
—— (2005). "Naive Truth and Sophisticated Logic," in Beall and Armour-Garb (2005).
—— (2010). *Truth and Proof: A Formalist Foundation for Mathematics*. Oxford: Oxford University Press.
Williams, C. J. F. (1969). "What does 'X is true' Say about X?" *Analysis* 29: 113–24.
Williams, Michael (1986). "Do We (Epistemologists) Need a Theory of Truth?" *Philosophical Topics* 14: 223–42.
—— (1999). "Meaning and Deflationary Truth," *The Journal of Philosophy* 96: 545–64.
—— (2002). "On Some Critics of Deflationism," in Schantz (2002).
Williams, J. Robert G. (2007). "Eligibility and Inscrutability," *Philosophical Review* 116: 361–99.
—— (2008). "Supervaluationism and Logical Revisionism," *Journal of Philosophy* 105: 192–212.
Williamson, Timothy (1994). *Vagueness*. London: Routledge.
—— (1996). "Knowing and Asserting." *Philosophical Review* 105: 489–523.
—— (2000a). *Knowledge and Its Limits*. Oxford: Oxford University Press.
—— (2000b). "Semantic Paradox and Semantic Change," in *Proceedings of the Twentieth World Congress of Philosophy*. Vol. 6. Ed. A. Kanamori. Bowling Green: Philosophy Documentation Center.
—— (2001). "Ethics, Supervenience, and Ramsey Sentences," *Philosophy and Phenomenological Research* 62: 625–30.

Williamson, Timothy (2003). "Understanding and Inference," *The Aristotelian Society, Supplement* 77: 249–93.
—— (2006). " 'Conceptual truth'," *The Aristotelian Society, Supplement* 80: 1–41.
—— (2008). *The Philosophy of Philosophy*. Oxford: Blackwell.
Wilson, Mark (2006). *Wandering Significance*. Oxford: Oxford University Press.
—— (2007). "Semantics Balkanized," *Philosophy and Phenomenological Research* 74: 709–19.
Wittgenstein, Ludwig (1923). *Tractatus Logico-Philosophicus. Tr.* C. K. Ogden. London: Routledge & Kegan Paul.
—— (1953). *Philosophical Investigations*. Tr. G. E. M. Anscombe. Oxford: Blackwell.
Woodbridge, James (2005). "Truth as Pretense," in Kalderone (2005b).
Woods, John (2002). *Paradox and Paraconsistency*. Cambridge: Cambridge University Press.
Wright, Cory and Nikolaj Pedersen (2010). *New Waves in Truth*. New York: Palgrave.
Wright, Crispin (1975). "On the Coherence of Vague Predicates," *Synthese* 30: 325–65.
—— (1992). *Truth and Objectivity.* Cambridge, MA: Harvard University Press.
—— (1998). "Comrades against Quietism: Reply to Simon Blackburn on Truth and Objectivity," *Mind* 107: 183–203.
—— (2003). *Saving the Differences: Essays on Themes from "Truth and Objectivity"*. Cambridge, MA: Harvard University Press.
—— (2004a). "Warrant for Nothing (and Foundations for Free)?" *Aristotelian Society Supplementary Volume* 78: 167–212.
—— (2004b). "Intuition, Entitlement and the Epistemology of Logical Laws," *Dialectica* 58: 155–75.
—— (2008). "Relativism about Truth Itself: Haphazard Thoughts about the Very Idea," in García-Carpintero and Kölbel (2008).
Yablo, Stephen (1985). "Truth and Reflection," *Journal of Philosophical Logic* 14: 297–349.
—— (1989). "Truth, Definite Truth, and Paradox," *The Journal of Philosophy* 86: 539–41.
—— (1993a). "Definitions, Consistent and Inconsistent," *Philosophical Studies* 72: 147–75.
—— (1993b). "Hop, Skip and Jump: The Agnostic Conception of Truth," *Philosophical Perspectives* 7: 371–96.
—— (1993c). "Paradox without Self-Reference," *Analysis* 53: 251–2.
—— (2001). "Go Figure: A Path Through Fictionalism," *Midwest Studies in Philosophy* 25: 72–102.
—— (2003). "New Grounds for Naïve Truth Theory," in Beall (2003).
—— (2004). "Circularity and Paradox," in Thomas Bolander, Vincent F. Hendricks, and Stig Andur Pedersen (eds.), *Self-Reference*. Stanford, CA: CSLI.
Yaqub, Aladdin M. (1993). *The Liar Speaks the Truth*. Oxford: Oxford University Press.
Young, J. O. (1995). *Global Anti-Realism*. Aldershot: Avebury.
—— (2001). "A Defense of the Coherence Theory of Truth," *The Journal of Philosophical Research*, 26: 89–101.
Zalta, Edward (2001). "Fregean Senses, Modes of Presentation, and Concepts," *Philosophical Perspectives*, 15: 333–59.
Zangwell, Nick (1992). "Quietism," *Midwest Studies in Philosophy* 17: 160–76.
Zardini, Elia (2011). "Truth without Contra(di)ction," *Review of Symbolic Logic* 4: 498–535.
Ziff, Paul (1960). *Semantic Analysis*. Ithaca: Cornell.
Zimmerman, Aaron (2007). "Against Relativism," *Philosophical Studies* 133: 313–48.
Zwicky, Arnold and Jerrold Sadock (1975). "Ambiguity Tests and How to Fail Them," in John Kimball (ed.), *Syntax and Semantics 4*. New York: Academic Press.

Index

(Sub) 16–18, 23, 85, 147, 149n8
(T-Elim) 23, 24, 45, 78, 147, 254
(T-Enter) 23n41, 147, 149n7, 281n4
(T-Exit) 23n41, 147, 149n7
(T-In) 16–18, 23, 24, 25, 57, 62–78, 79, 82, 85, 93, 111, 116, 134–6, 142, 146–7, 149, 151, 153, 155, 174, 176, 214, 241, 242, 254–5, 259, 266, 271, 274–5, 276, 279–80, 282–285, 287, *see also* aletheic principles
(T-Intro) 23, 24, 45, 78, 147, 254
(T-Out) 16–18, 23, 24, 25, 57, 62–78, 79, 82, 85, 100, 111, 116, 134–6, 142, 146–7, 149, 150, 151, 153, 155, 173, 174, 176, 214, 241, 242, 254–5, 259, 266, 271, 274–5, 276, 279–80, 281, 282–5, 286, *see also* aletheic principles
@-rule 284
abductive argument for the inconsistency approach, the 84, 116–21, *see also* philosophical approaches to the aletheic paradoxes, inconsistency
abilities 35
abstract entities 35
accessibility relation 158–9, 162, 163, 164, *see also* semantics, relational
  closed 181
  coreflexive 181
ADT (axiomatic theory of ascending and descending truth) 153–4, 155, 159, 161, 162, 164–5, 167–74, 178, 186–7, 188, 201–3, 208, 213, 215–16, 219, 255, 256n46, 268, 271, 272, 274–6, 278–9, 280–1, 287, 288, 289–90, *see also* ascending truth; descending truth
agreement 257
aletheic paradoxes *see* paradoxes, aletheic
aletheic principle 16–19, 100, 147–9
aletheic revolution 274–7
aletheic standard 71–4, 238–41, 243, 245–6, 247–53, 254–6, 258, 259–60, 261, *see also* ascending standard; descending standard
aletheic value 215, 238–41, 245–6, 247–53
ambiguity approach *see* approaches to the aletheic paradoxes, ambiguity
ambiguity LS theory 113–14
ambiguity 12, 68, 69–70, 71, 78, 110, 112–16, 143, 171, 228, 232, 233, 241, 243–4, 261, 275, 278
  tests 243–4
analytic pragmatism 6, 7
analyticity 47, 109, 127, 278
anaphora 264
angle brackets xv
Anscombe, Elizabeth 70
antirealism 13, 82
application set 40, *see also* disapplication set; overdetermined set
apriority 5, 47, 139
arithmetization 152
Armour-Garb, Bradley 59–61
ascending Grelling 220
ascending liar 151, 173–4, 176, 208, 253
ascending reference 222
ascending Simmons 222–4
ascending standard 238–41, 245–6, 247–53, 254, 255, 286, *see also* aletheic standard; descending standard
ascending truth conditions 208, 262, 276, 285
ascending truth-of 219–21
ascending truth 9–10, 125, 146, 149, 151–4, 156, 163, 167–77, 201–3, 205, 206, 207, 208, 211–18, 219–20, 222, 225, 230, 238–46, 249–53, 259, 261, 264–5, 267–71, 274–7, 280–1, 284, 287, 289, *see also* descending truth; ADT
assertion 9, 52, 102–4, 136–7, 138, 204, 215–6, 265–73, 280–1
assessment-indexical 232, 235–6
assessment-sensitivity 9, 143, 175, 208, 209–10, 213, 221n30, 224n32, 229, 230–2, 234–5, 237–41, 242–3, 250–2, 253–63, 267, 271, 272–3, 274–9, 285–6, 289, *see also* semantic relativism; postsemantic theory
Atlas, Jay 110
Austin, J. L. 5
axiom of comprehension 289

Badici, Amil 129–33
Barwise, Jon 32, 34, 270
Beall, Jc 24, 28, 32, 34, 80–1, 87–8, 89–94, 97–8, 104–6, 108, 122, 270
belief 43, 44, 138, 140–2, 188, 190, 197, 204, 206
Belnap, Nuel 28, 29, 88, 122, 168, 180, 270
bivalence 61
Blackburn, Simon 11
boche 36n7, 108–9
Boghossian, Paul 44, 46
Brady, Ross 24, 83n57
Brandom, Robert 6, 51n41
Brogaard, Berit 260–1

burden of proof 104–6
Burge, Tyler 28, 29, 46, 71
Burgess, Alexis 45, 136–7, 138, 143, 146

CAM *see* classical, assessment–sensitivity, metrological unified theory of truth
Camp, Joseph 225, 230–2
canonical proof procedure 131–3
Cappelen, Herman 71n34, 260
Carnap, Rudolph 4
Chang, Hasok 144
character 60, 68–9, 71, 210, 228, 232–7, 238–41, *see also* context-dependence
characterization sequence (Ω_0) 178–80
charity, principle of 42–3, 189–91, 200, 203, 225, *see also* truth, Davidsonian theory of
Churchill, Winston 57
circularity approach *see* philosophical approaches to the aletheic paradoxes, circularity
classical expressibility delimiter (CED) 95–9, 208–9
classical fragment 91–3
classical gap approach *see* logical approaches to the aletheic paradoxes, classical gap
classical glut approach *see* logical approaches to the aletheic paradoxes, classical glut
classical symmetric approach *see* logical approaches to the aletheic paradoxes, classical symmetric
classical, assessment-sensitive, metrological unified theory of truth (CAM) 270–3, 276, 288
clause 209–15, 232–7, 238–41, 268, *see also* logical form; semantics, intensional
coherence theory of truth *see* truth, coherence theory of
coherence with a sequence 179
color 257
common goals 51–3, 264–5, *see also* pragmatics; scorekeeping
common ground 52–3, 67–9, 72, 244, 262, 264–5, *see also* pragmatics; scorekeeping
completeness 202
compositionality 156
concept pragmatism 43, 48, 54
concept 35
  application-inconsistent 41
  classical 90–4
  coextensive 15
  inconsistent 3, 7, 8, 22, 35–56, 57, 94, 100–1, 103, 106, 116–17, 119, 121, 124, 126–39, 143–5, 209, 213, 217–18, 219, 222, 225, 230, 238, 240–1, 244, 246, 258, 261, 265, 271, 274–5, 278–9, 280, 282, 289–90, *see also* philosophical approaches to the aletheic paradoxes, inconsistency; replacement strategy
  Kreiselian 118
  model-dependent 90
  possession of 12, 35, 36–8, 43–9, 53–6, 63, 134–5, 144–5, 262–3, 278
  partial 40
  range-inconsistent 41
  replacement 2, 7, 137–9, 146–57, 171, 229, 240–6, 260–1, 264, 276, 282, 290, *see also* replacement strategy
  unsatisfiable 39
conceptual analysis 3, 4–5, 6, 13, 15, 97, 188–9, 200, 266–8, 289
conceptual engineering 4, 7, 11, 139, 290
conceptual problem 19
conceptual revolution 2, 137–9, 144–5, 290
conceptual scheme 4
conditional principles 23
conditional proof 79–81
conditional 78–84, 116, 120, 280
conditionalization 44
confission 4
confusion 4, 230, 257, 263
constants xv
constitutive principles 36, 37, 38, 43–56, 57, 62–83, 90–1, 93–4, 97, 101, 106, 116–17, 120, 126–7, 134–5, 142, 199–200, 203, 218, 227, 241, 254, 259, 266, 270–1, 274–5, 278–80, 281, 282, 286
constitutive propositions 55
constitutive sentences 55
constitutivity credence 55–6
constitutivity threshold 55–6
content determination condition (CDC) 66–73, 75, 78, 114–16, 143, 244, 245, 259, 261–3, 274–5
content 60, 68, 71, 208, 228, 232–7, 238–41, 249–53, 262
context 10, 209–15, 232–7, 238–41, 264
  of assessment 210, 238–41, 243, *see also* assessment-sensitivity
  set 67
  -dependence 68–9, 71–5, 78, 86, 110, 117–19, 143, 171, 228, 232, 241, 244–45, 261, 275, 278
contextual approach *see* philosophical approaches to the aletheic paradoxes, contextual
contingent level-determination 66, 70
contingent paradoxicality 59–62, 64–6, 71, 75–8, 143, 156, 208, 266, 281
contraction 79–81
contradiction 59
conversational implicature 69, 73, 110, 210, 264, *see also* pragmatics
conversational score *see* scorekeeping
conversations
  ignorance 265–6

informed 265–6
mixed 265–6
Cook, Roy 26, 28
cooperation principle 68
coordination theory 68n28
correspondence theory of truth *see* truth, correspondence theory of

dark flow 266, 276
Davidson, Donald 7, 9, 31, 32, 48, 122, 188–91, 196–200, 262, 267, 274, 290
Davidsonian theory of truth *see* truth, Davidsonian theory of
decision theory 190–1
deflationism *see* truth, deflationary theory of
deixis 264
derivability 23n40, 80, 116, 218
principles 23n41, 149n7
derivation problem 18
descending Grelling 220
descending liar 151, 173–4, 176, 208, 252, 253, 280, 287
descending reference 222
descending Simmons 222–4
descending standard 238–41, 245–6, 247–53, 254, 255, 286
descending truth conditions 208, 262, 276, 285
descending truth-of 219–21
descending truth 9–10, 125, 146, 149, 150–4, 156, 161, 163, 167–77, 201–3, 206, 207, 208, 211–18, 219–20, 222, 225, 230, 238–46, 249–53, 259, 261, 264–5, 267–71, 274–7, 280–1, 284, 287, 289, *see also* ascending truth; ADT
descriptive project 20, 31, 201
descriptive theory 9–10, 136–7, 144, 146, 225–73, 274, 278
designatedness 96–9
desire 190–1, 197–200
determinateness 26–7, 33–4, 70, 75–8, 88–9, 98, 106–10, 118–19, 120, 156–7, 190, 191, 242–3, *see also* philosophical approaches to the aletheic paradoxes, indeterminacy
device of endorsement 63–6, 78, 100, 103–4, 146–7, 174, 270–1, 280–1, 287, *see also* truth, expressive role of
device of generalization 286–287, *see also* truth, expressive role of
device of rejection 63–6, 77–8, 146–7, 174, 270–1, 280, 281, 287, *see also* truth, expressive role of
diagnostic project 19
diagonalization 95
dialetheism 22, 33, 45, 61, 83, 104, 126–7, 228, 254, *see also* logical approach to the aletheic paradoxes, paraconsistent
opaque 28n61
transparent 28n61
disagreement 257
faultless 257, 258, 263
test 71n34
disapplication set 40
disquotational theory of truth *see* truth, disquotational theory of
domain 40
DT 156–7
duality 152, 157, 158, 161, 164, *see also* modal logic
Dummett, Michael 109

Earman, John 38–9, 54
Ebbs, Gary 115n55
EE operator 93–4, 105, 106, *see also* negation
Einstein, Albert 38, 139, 280
Eklund, Matti 44–5, 111–12, 116, 134–5, 138, 287
eliminativism 1–2
ellipsis 264
enjoyment scale 234, 235, 260
entitlement 46–9, 278
quasi- 47–9, 53–4, 274–5
Epimenides 16
epistemic modals 245, 256
epistemic theory of truth *see* truth, epistemic theory of
epistemicism 21, 28, 32, 34
epistemological contextualism 73–5, 278, *see also* context-dependence; semantic blindness
epistemological skepticism 289–90
error theory 228, 241n34
Etchemendy, John 32, 34, 270
Eubulides 16
ex falso 82–3, 93, 106, 107
excluded middle 91, 93, 106, 107
exhaustive characterization project 20, 95n21
experimental philosophy 6
explication 4, *see also* conceptual revolution; replacement strategy
expressibility delimiter *see* classical expressibility delimiter
expressivism 14, 32, 62–3
extension 210
extensive structure 195, *see also* measurement theory

false by default 65–6
Feferman, Solomon 81, 156–7
felicity 68–9, 72, 244, *see also* pragmatics; scorekeeping
fictionalism 136–7, 146, 228
Field, Hartry 24, 26–7, 28, 29, 32, 33–4, 37, 75–8, 88–9, 104, 106–10, 115n54, 117, 119–21, 122, 127, 150–1, 156, 242, 270, 280, 281, 287

Fine, Arthur 38, 54
fixed point 185
  minimal 84–5, 98
focus 264
Fodor, Jerry 43
formal epistemology 191, *see also* knowledge; decision theory
fragmentary theories of truth *see* truth, fragmentary theories of
frame theory of inconsistent concepts 229
frame 247
  acceptable xeno 180–1
  neighborhood 160
  reflexive 158
  relational 158
  suitable 178
  xeno 163–8, 178, 180–7
Friedman, Harvey 23n41, 148–9
FS 24
fun 232–7, 259–60
future 256

Galilei, Galileo 192
Glanzberg, Michael 28, 72n35, 117–19, 120–1
Godel's Diagonalization Lemma 161
Godel's Second Incompleteness Theorem 151, 157
Goldstein, Laurence 58–9
gradable adjective 234
Greek letters xv
Grice, Paul 52, 68, 70
groundedness 60, 102–3, 120, 170, 284
group 196
Gupta, Anil 28, 29, 32, 34, 41, 88, 122, 168, 180, 270

Harman, Gilbert 82–3
Hawthorne, John 71n34, 74, 260
heterological 219–21, *see also* paradox, Grelling; predication
higherians 41–2, 43, *see also* up above
Hofweber, Thomas 73–4, 123–5, 139–42
Horn, Laurence 110
Horsten, Leon 28, 32, 34, 270
Horwich, Paul 21, 32, 34, 270
hybrid principles 149, 157, 171, *see also* aletheic principles
hypothesis 179
  cofinal 184
  recurring 184

illusion 45
importation problem 111–16, 120, 281, *see also* paradox, revenge
inconsistency approach *see* philosophical approaches to the aletheic paradoxes, inconsistency
inconsistency problem 100–1, 102–3, 116, 120–1, 175–7, *see also* paradox, revenge
inconsistent concept *see* concept, inconsistent
inconsistent language *see* language, inconsistent
indeterminacy approach *see* philosophical approaches to the aletheic paradoxes, indeterminacy
indeterminacy of translation 109
indeterminate translation theory of inconsistent concepts 229
index 247–53, 268
indispensability 279
inexpressibility schema 95, 99, *see also* classical expressibility delimiter
inference vs. implication 82–3
inferential principles 23, 149n7
inferential theory of truth *see* truth, inferential theory of
infinitesimals 91
inflationism 63
inner inductive theory 24n38, *see also* outer inductive theory
inquiry 204, 205–6
intelligibility 105–10, 119, 121
intension 247–50
intensional approach *see* philosophical approaches to the aletheic paradoxes, intensional
intercontextual disquotation test 71n34
interpretation problem 18–19
interpretation 38, 47–8, 49–56, 127, 260–1, *see also* radical interpreter
  indeterminacy of 190–1, 198
interpreted logical forms 202n14
interpretive red flag 53 *see also* constitutive principles
interpretive system 209–10
intersubstitutability principle 27, *see also* (T-In); (T-Out)
invariance 195
italics xv

James, William xvii

K_3 76
Kaplan, David 210
Kaplanian theory of context-dependence 72, 210–11, 215
KF 24
King, Jeffrey 68n28
knowledge 9, 73–5, 138, 204, 216–17, 256, 263, 289–90
Kreisel's squeezing argument 218
Kreiselian concept *see* concept, Kreiselian
Kripke, Saul 2, 29, 60, 64–6, 69–70, 75, 84, 103, 107–8, 118n61, 122, 155
Künne, Wolfgang 15

language
  artificial 3, 12, 26–7, 87, 89–94, 97–8, 106–7, 108–10, 202, 208–9, 267–8
  inconsistent 128n3, 134–5
  natural 3, 10, 20, 22, 26–7, 30, 64, 68, 69–70, 88, 89–94, 97–8, 108–10, 111–16, 121, 122, 143, 201–3, 208–9, 259, 266–8, 281
  target 121–2
  trivial 93–4, 98
Leeds, Stephen 279
length 193–5, 198–9, *see also* measurement theory
Lepore, Ernest 71n34
levels of sentences 66
Lewis, David 50–1, 67, 72, 140–2
liar paradox *see* paradox, liar
linguistic competence 12, 53–6, 63, 128, 134–5, 191, 262–3, *see also* concept, possession of
linguistic practice 209
  post-revolutionary 275
linguistics 110, 123–5, 127, 141, 202, 207, 243, 265, 266, 281–2, 284
logic 2, 78–83, 201–2, 226
  classical 9–10, 23, 30, 32, 34, 78–83, 90–4, 99, 102, 142, 170, 175, 227, 240, 242, 254, 259, 266, 270, 274–6
  intuitionistic 42, 79, 82, 91, 120, 170
  non-classical 30, 32, 33, 34, 78–83, 90–4, 99, 170, 227, 230, 281
  paracomplete 24, 27, 32, 34, 76, 86, 170
  paraconsistent 24, 32, 34, 86, 92, 170
  relevance 42, 79, 82, 170
  substructural 24, 25, 32, 34, 80–1
  weakly classical 24, 30, 32, 34
logical approaches to the aletheic paradoxes 8, 9, 11, 23–34, 78–83, 85n2, 99–100, 104, 135, 150–1, 200–1, 254, 266, 268–70, 289, *see also* paradoxes, aletheic
  classical gap 24, 28, 29, 32, 34, 102–4, 135, 150, 241, 282–5
  classical glut 24, 28, 32, 150, 241, 282
  classical symmetric 24, 25n54, 28, 29, 32, 34, 150, 254, 271, 274–5
  non-classical 30, 34, *see also* logic, non–classical
  orthodox 2, 28, 29, 64–6, 69–70, 71, 75, 103, *see also*, ambiguity approach; truth, Tarskian theory of
  paracomplete 24, 26–7, 28, 29, 32, 34, 75–8, 79, 86, 88–9, 93, 106–10, 127, 150–1, 270, *see also* logic, paracomplete
  paraconsistent 24, 28, 29, 32, 33, 34, 79, 82, 86, 89, 93, 104, 126–7, 150–1, 278, *see also*, logic, paraconsistent
  postsemantic 254, 258
  substructural 25, 28, 29, 32, 34, 79–81, 150–1, 217, 254
  weakly classical 24, 28, 32, 34, 136, 242–3
logical form 202–3, 233n27, 238, 268
logical truth 150–1
Ludwig, Kirk 123, 129–33, 136, 138
Lynch, Michael 14, 205, 206, 207

M-conditions 60–1
M-sentences 131–3
MacFarlane, John 213, 230–2
mammamonkey 40–1
mass 4, 37–9, 43–4, 45, 54, 57, 83, 125, 137–9, 153, 204, 230, 242, 265, 275, 277n2, 280
mathematical structure 7–8, 26, 192–6, 198, 201–2, 267–8, *see also* physical structure; relational structure; measurement theory
Matthews, Robert 200
Maudlin, Tim 28, 29, 32, 34, 102–4, 122, 151n16, 270
McDowell, John 6
McGee, Vann 24, 28, 29, 32, 34, 79, 88, 122, 146, 155–6, 270
meaning argument for the inconsistency approach, the 84, 121–5, 129–34, *see also* philosophical approaches to the aletheic paradoxes, inconsistency
meaning 9, 37, 59–62, 122–3, 127, 128, 131–3, 136–7, 138, 140–2, 188–91, 197–200, 204, 207, 274, 278
  containment 83n57
meaningless approach *see* philosophical approaches to the aletheic paradoxes, meaningless
measurement system 7, 26, 192–6, 198–203, 267–68, 270, *see also* measurement theory
measurement theory 7–8, 9, 26, 188, 191, 192–203, 267–8, 289, *see also* naturalism, metrological
mental representations 35
meta-rules 23n42, 79, 136
metrological naturalism *see* naturalism, metrological
minimal theory of truth *see* truth, minimal theory of
modal logic 157–69
  classical 160–1, 167, 169, *see also* semantics, neighborhood
  first order 159, 166–7
  for predicates 159, 162–3, 168
  non-classical 180n44
  non-normal 180n44
  non-traditional 180n44
  normal 157–9, 167, 169, *see also* semantics, relational
  sentential 159
  traditional 166–9, 180–7, 202–3, *see also* semantics, xeno

model
acceptable xeno 181–2
mathematical 26
neighborhood 160, 178–80
relational 158
scientific 26–8
xeno 163–8, 178, 180–7, 216, 256n46, 289
modest attitude toward philosophy and science 123–5, 127, 278, 282
modest theory of truth *see* truth, modest theory of
modified Occam's Razor 70
modus ponens 79–81
monoaletheism 135
monster-barring approach *see* philosophical approaches to the aletheic paradoxes, monster–barring
Montague, Richard 150, 159
Montague's theorem 149–52, 159, 173, 255, 281
morality 256
Murzi, Julien 80–1

natural deduction 23n41
naturalism 5
methodological 6–8, 200, 267
metrological 7–8, 9–10, 188–203, 267, 274–5, 290, *see also* measurement theory
necessitation 159
necessity 47, 139, 160
negation 70, 90, 120, 280
Boolean 86–7, 98, 104, 105, 108–9, 142
choice 40, 91, 108, 110
exclusion 40, 91, 98, 100, 107, 110
neighborhood function 160–1, 162, *see also* modal logic, classical; semantics, neighborhood
non-classical approach *see* logical approaches to the aletheic paradoxes, non–classical
non-indexical contextualism 232, 234, 237, 238, 241, 245–6, 252–3, 255–6, 257–63, 285, *see also* semantic relativism
non-red-table 39
non-triviality project 20

objectivity 138, 204, 206–7, 217
obvious argument for the inconsistency approach, the 8, 57–83, 103, 120, *see also* constitutive principles; philosophical approaches to the aletheic paradoxes, inconsistency
ordinal
completion 184
initial 184
reflection 184
orthodox approach *see* philosophical approaches to the aletheic paradoxes, orthodox
outer inductive theory 24n38, 28n61
overdetermined set 40, 42, 116–17

paracomplete approach *see* logical approaches to the aletheic paradoxes, paracomplete
paraconsistent approach *see* logical approaches to the aletheic paradoxes, paraconsistent
paradox
aletheic 2–3, 8–10, 16–34, 57–83, 84–125, 173–4, 175–7, 212–14, 253–6, 259, 261, 266, 275, 287–8, 289–90, *see also* paradox, liar; paradox Curry's; paradox, Yablo's
Burali-Forti 287–8
Curry's 17, 79–80, 141, 173, 255, 288
derivability 218
Grelling's 219
of implication 82
liar 1–2, 16, 57–61, 99–100, 173, 241, 242, 244, 246, 251–53, 255, 275, 288, *see also* ascending liar; descending liar
McGee's 288
of generality 287–8
permissibility 102–3
revenge 8, 22, 27, 76–7, 84–125, 126–7, 143, 150, 155–6, 157, 175–7, 213, 216, 266, 271–3, 275, 278, 281, 288, *see also* self-refutation problem; inconsistency problem
Russell's 287–8
set-theoretic 287–8, 289
Simmons' 221
sorites 287–8, *see also* vagueness
Yablo's 17–18, 173, 255, 288
Patterson, Douglas 39n12, 128–9, 138
Peacocke, Christopher 47–8
Peano Arithmetic 152, 161, 178
persons, general theory of 140–2
phenomenalism 5
philosophical approaches to the aletheic paradoxes 8, 9–10, 11, 16, 21–2, 25–34, 85n2, 99–100, 104, 135, 200–1, 268–70, 289
ambiguity 22, 28, 29, 30, 32
circularity 22, 28, 32, 34, 122, 135
contextual 22, 28, 29, 30, 32, 34, 71–5, 86, 89, 117–19, 213, 244–5
inconsistency 9, 22, 28, 29, 32, 34, 84, 126–46, 241, 259, 274–5, *see also* concept, inconsistent
indeterminacy 22, 28, 29, 30, 32, 33, 34, 270, *see also* determinateness
intensional 21, 28, 32
meaningless 59–61, 128
monster-barring 21, 28, 32, 57–62, 281
orthodox 2, 28, 29, 64–6, 69–70, 71, 75, 103, *see also*, philosophical approaches to the aletheic paradoxes, ambiguity; truth, Tarskian theory of
postsemantic 254, 258
philosophical methodology 3–5, 267, 290, *see also* naturalism, metrological
philosophy of language 3

philosophy, analytic 2, 11
physical structure 7–8, 26, 192–6, 198, 201–2, 267–8, *see also* measurement theory
Plato 216
pluralist theory of truth *see* truth, pluralist theory of
point of evaluation 210–15, 233–7, 238–41, 245–6, 247–53
possession conditions *see* concept, possession of
postsemantic approaches *see* philosophical approaches to the aletheic paradoxes, postsemantic
postsemantic theory 210–15, 232–53, 258–63, 282–5, *see also* presemantic theory; semantic theory
pragmatic theory of truth *see* truth, pragmatic theory of
pragmatics 49–56, 67–74, 210, 226, 263–6, 272, 274–5, *see also* scorekeeping
pragmatism 13
Predelli, Stefano 209, 268
predicates of personal taste 245, 256
predication 9, 204, 218–21, 288
prescriptive project 20, 31, 201
prescriptive theory 9–10, 137, 144, 146–77, 229, 274–5, 278, 289
presemantic theory 210–15, 232–53, 258–63, 282–5, *see also* semantic theory; postsemantic theory
presupposition 67, 110, 264, *see also* pragmatics
preventative project 20n28
Priest, Graham 24, 28, 32, 87, 88, 104–6, 108, 288
prime numbers 81–2
principle of uniform solution 287–8
probability 33, 190–1, 197–200
problem of discipline 227
proof 117, 172, 204, 205
properties 12, 33
proposition 210–15, 233–7
prosentential theory of truth *see* truth, prosentential theory of
prosody 264
Protagoras 1
psychological project 20, 267n80

quantifiers 172
question under discussion 52–3, 264–5, *see also* pragmatics; scorekeeping
question 52
quietism 5
Quine, W.V. 109, 149
quotes, corner xv
quotes, single xv

rable 36–7, 41, 42, 45, 57, 83, 227
radical interpreter 48, 189–91, 198–200, *see also* truth, Davidsonian theory of
radical rationalizer 190–1
Ramsey, Frank 44, 190
range of applicability 40
rationality 31, 138, 188, 191, 196–200, 290
  inferential 226–7
  unified theory of 190–1, 196–200, 203, 215n18, 268, 274–5, 290
reductive explanation 5, 15, 188–9, 268, 289
reference magnet 241n33
reference 9, 204, 221–4, 288
referential indeterminacy 241, 242–3
reflection principle 117–18
relational structure 7–8, 26, 192–6, 198, 201–2, 267–8, *see also* physical structure, mathematical structure, measurement theory
relativism 1n3
relativity 257
relevance theory of inconsistent concepts 229
replacement principles 148–9
replacement strategy 1–2, 7, 9, 126, 136, 137–45, 204, 211, 229, 238, 274–5, 278, 279, 281–2, 288, 289
representation theorem 194–5, 198, 202
request 52
requirement of expected utility maximization 190
requirement of total evidence 190–1, 200
Restall, Greg 83, 270
restricted theories of truth *see* truth, restricted theories of
retraction 257, 258, 285–6, *see also* assessment-sensitivity
retrievability 68–75, *see also* content determination condition
revenge argument for the inconsistency approach, the 84, 100–16, 126–7, *see also* paradox, revenge; philosophical approaches to the aletheic paradoxes, inconsistency
revenge objections 88–100
revenge paradox *see* paradox, revenge
revenge recipes 87–8, 89–90, 104–5, 108, *see also* paradox, revenge
revision rule 179–80, 183
revision sequences 167–9, 178–87
revision theory of inconsistent concepts 229
revision theory of truth *see* truth, revision theory of
Richard, Mark 63–4
Ripley, David 25
Roberts, Craige 50–2, 67, 72, 264, 274
Robinson Arithmetic 150
Rorty, Richard 1
rule E 161, 165, 173, *see also* modal logic
rule-circularity 105–6
Ryle, Gilbert 5

safety 152–3, 156, 170, 203, 206, 208, 244, 256, 261, 271, 276–7, 280–1, 286
  predicate 220–1
  contingent 175
  negative 176–7
  positive 176–7, 216
satisfaction 112
scale 196
schema T *see* T-Schema
Schiffer, Stephen 73, 137
Schlenker, Philipe 28
science 25–6, 110, 123–5, 127, 140–2, 192–6
scientific revolution 3, 192, *see also* conceptual revolution
scope 110
scorekeeping 50–3, 67–75, 262–3, 274–5, *see also* pragmatics
  semantic 55–6
  transparent 53, 55–6
self-refutation problem 100–1, 102–4, 116, 120–1, 150, 156, 177, 278, *see also* paradox, revenge
self-refutation 257
Sellars, Wilfrid 6
semantic ascent 149
semantic blindness 73–5, 278, *see also* content determination condition
semantic project 20
semantic relativism 237–41, 247–53, 257–63, 276–7, *see also* assessment sensitivity; non–indexical contextualism
semantic theory 210–15, 232–53, 258–63
semantics 121–3, 157–69, 191, 201–2, 208–15, 226, 232–53, 266, 281–2
  ascending and descending (AD semantics) 125, 224, 282
  dynamic 123, 207
  game theoretic 123
  intensional 210–15, 232–53
  neighborhood 160–1, 162, 163, 167, 169, *see also* modal logic, classical
  possible worlds with constant domain 159, 166–7
  possible worlds with variable domain 159, 166–7
  relational 158–9, 162, 163, 167, 169, *see also* modal logic, normal
  truth conditional 121–3, 125, 131–3, 144, *see also* truth conditions
  xeno 161–9, 178–87, 202–3, 270, 274–5, *see also* modal logic, traditional
sentential variables xv, 14n8
set theory 192
Shapiro, Lionel 28, 89, 94–9, 208
Shapiro, Stewart 26, 115n54
Sheard, Michael 23n41, 148–9
Simmons, Keith 28, 72n36
smidget 40
smooth infinitesimal analysis 91
Soames, Scott 28, 32, 34, 40, 270
soundness 186–7, 202
squircle 39
stability 179
stabilization point 179
Stalnaker, Robert 67–8, 72, 244
Stanley, Jason 233n27, 258
Strawson, P. F. 5, 58
strengthened liars 84, *see also* paradox, revenge
Strong Kleene scheme 24, 26, 91, 98, 122
strong liar reasoning 118–19
structural rules 23, 79–81
substructural approach *see* logical approaches to the aletheic paradoxes, substructural
supervaluation 155–6, 228, 242–3
supervenience 5n16
Suppes, Patrick 25–6, 192, 267n80
symmetry 195
syntactic type 162
syntax 171, 201
Szabo, Zoltan 75

t-distribution 209–15, 232–37, 238–41, 283–5
T-schema 14, 56, 93, 97; *see also* (T-In); (T-Out)
T-sentence 26–7, 30, 76, 131–3, 188
Tappenden, Jamie 287
Tarski, Alfred 2, 22, 114n52, 146, 155
Tarski's theorem 130
Tarskian hierarchy 28n61, 29, 32, 71
Tarskian theory of truth *see* truth, Tarskian theory of
temperature 144, *see also* measurement theory
Tennant, Neil 25, 28, 32, 34, 80, 170, 270
theoretical virtues 142–3
tonk 36n7, 108–9
too easy revenge 89–94, *see also* paradox, revenge
transitivity 80–1
translation 5, 15, 109, 114–16
translational LS theory 114–16, *see also* ambiguity LS theory
Travis, Charles 5
truth conditions 60–1, 121–5, 207–10, 263, 275, 278, 281
truth conditions determination condition (TCDC) 262–63, *see also* content determination condition
truth value gaps 84–6, 120
truth-teller 117n58, 246, 255–6, 285–6
truth 1–3, 7, 8–10, 11–34, 35, 54, 56, 57–143, 145, 146–9, 173, 175, 188–91, 197, 204–8, 229–32, 237–56, 258–65, 266–73, 274–88, 289–90
  -aptness 62–3
  -bearers 12
  -in-a-model (true-in-M) 202, 212–14, 217, 238–41, 249–53, 254, 268, 282–5

coherence theory of 13, 30, 32, 200
correspondence theory of 13, 30, 32, 33, 34, 200, 242
Davidsonian theory of 15, 31, 32, 188–191, 196–203, 267–8, 274–5
definite 155–6
deflationary theory of 14, 30, 32, 34, 62–3, 112–16, 122n67, 124, 200, 215, 217, 242, 281–2
disquotational theory of 14, 32, 33, 122n67, 124, 271
epistemic theory of 13, 30, 32, 34, 200
expressive role of 63–6, 69–70, 71, 75–8, 103–4, 113–16, 142–3, 156, 217, 267, 270–1, 278–9, 280–1, 286–7, *see also* device of endorsement; device of rejection; device of generalization
fragmentary theories of 30, 75–7, 117–18
inferential theory of 14, 32
language-specific 2n4, 22, 111–16, 120, 142, 143, 274–5, 281, *see also* translational LS theory; ambiguity LS theory
minimal theory of 14, 32, 34
modest theory of 14, 30, 32, 34
nature of 2–3, 9, 11–16, 30–4, 289
pluralist theory of 14, 30, 32
pragmatic theory of 13, 30, 32, 200
prosentential theory of 14, 32
restricted theories of 110–16, 121–3
revision theory of 29, 76, 86, 89, 135
Tarskian theory of 15, 28n61, 64, 71, 121–2, 155, 188, 197, 215n18
unified theory of 3, 8, 13, 30–4, 142–3, 146, 267, 268–73, 274–5, 289

unarticulated constituents 232, 233
understanding 60–1
unhappy face solutions 137n19
unified theory of rationality *see* rationality, unified theory of
unified theory of truth *see* truth, unified theory of
uniform substitution 92–3
uniqueness theorem 194–5, 198, 202
unrestricted quantification 117
unsafe *see* safety
unsettled 155–6
up above 41–2, 57, 83, *see also* higherians
utility 190–1, 197–200

vagueness 26, 33, 146, 155–6, 171, 257, 287–8
validity 9, 81–2, 138, 150–1, 157, 158, 160, 164, 172–3, 180, 186, 202, 204, 217–18, 240, 242, 254
van Fraassen, Bas 28
VF 24

weakly classical approach *see* logical approaches to the aletheic paradoxes, weakly classical
weighted majority theory of inconsistent concepts 228–9
Weir, Alan 25, 28, 29, 32, 34, 270
Williamson, Timothy 48–9, 54, 278
Wittgenstein, Ludwig 6
Woodbridge, James 59–61
worlds
non-traditional 180, 185–6
normal 164
traditional 180
Wright, Crispin 14, 46, 206, 215, 263

Yablo, Stephen 28, 29, 135–6, 138, *see also* paradox, Yablo's

Zardini, Elia 28